W9-AKV-343

myPerspectives®
ENGLISH LANGUAGE ARTS

SAVVAS
LEARNING COMPANY

ISBN-13: 978-1-41-837113-5
ISBN-10:   1-41-837113-0

4 2022

Welcome!

myPerspectives™ *English Language Arts* is a student-centered learning environment where you will analyze text, cite evidence, and respond critically about your learning. You will take ownership of your learning through goal-setting, reflection, independent text selection, and activities that allow you to collaborate with your peers.

Each unit of study includes selections of different genres—including multimedia—all related to a relevant and meaningful Essential Question. As you read, you will engage in activities that inspire thoughtful discussion and debate with your peers allowing you to formulate, and defend, your own perspectives.

myPerspectives ELA offers a variety of ways to interact directly with the text. You can annotate by writing in your print consumable, or you can annotate in your digital Student Edition. In addition, exciting technology allows you to access multimedia directly from your mobile device and communicate using an online discussion board!

We hope you enjoy using *myPerspectives ELA* as you develop the skills required to be successful throughout college and career.

Authors' Perspectives

myPerspectives is informed by a team of respected experts whose experiences working with students and study of instructional best practices have positively impacted education. From the evolving role of the teacher to how students learn in a digital age, our authors bring new ideas, innovations, and strategies that transform teaching and learning in today's competitive and interconnected world.

> " The teaching of English needs to focus on engaging a new generation of learners. How do we get them excited about reading and writing? How do we help them to envision themselves as readers and writers? And, how can we make the teaching of English more culturally, socially, and technologically relevant? Throughout the curriculum, we've created spaces that enhance youth voice and participation and that connect the teaching of literature and writing to technological transformations of the digital age."

Ernest Morrell, Ph.D.

is the Macy professor of English Education at Teachers College, Columbia University, a class of 2014 Fellow of the American Educational Research Association, and the Past-President of the National Council of Teachers of English (NCTE). He is also the Director of Teachers College's Institute for Urban and Minority Education (IUME). He is an award-winning author and in his spare time he coaches youth sports and writes poems and plays. Dr. Morrell has influenced the development of *my*Perspectives in Assessment, Writing & Research, Student Engagement, and Collaborative Learning.

Elfrieda Hiebert, Ph.D.

is President and CEO of TextProject, a nonprofit that provides resources to support higher reading levels. She is also a research associate at the University of California, Santa Cruz. Dr. Hiebert has worked in the field of early reading acquisition for 45 years, first as a teacher's aide and teacher of primary-level students in California and, subsequently, as a teacher and researcher. Her research addresses how fluency, vocabulary, and knowledge can be fostered through appropriate texts. Dr. Hiebert has influenced the development of *my*Perspectives in Vocabulary, Text Complexity, and Assessment.

" The signature of complex text is challenging vocabulary. In the systems of vocabulary, it's important to provide ways to show how concepts can be made more transparent to students. We provide lessons and activities that develop a strong vocabulary and concept foundation—a foundation that permits students to comprehend increasingly more complex text."

Kelly Gallagher, M.Ed.

teaches at Magnolia High School in Anaheim, California, where he is in his thirty-first year. He is the former co-director of the South Basin Writing Project at California State University, Long Beach. Mr. Gallagher has influenced the development of *my*Perspectives in Writing, Close Reading, and the Role of Teachers.

" The *my*Perspectives classroom is dynamic. The teacher inspires, models, instructs, facilitates, and advises students as they evolve and grow. When teachers guide students through meaningful learning tasks and then pass them ownership of their own learning, students become engaged and work harder. This is how we make a difference in student achievement—by putting students at the center of their learning and giving them the opportunities to choose, explore, collaborate, and work independently."

" It's critical to give students the opportunity to read a wide range of highly engaging texts and to immerse themselves in exploring powerful ideas and how these ideas are expressed. In *my*Perspectives, we focus on building up students' awareness of how academic language works, which is especially important for English language learners."

Jim Cummins, Ph.D.

is a Professor Emeritus in the Department of Curriculum, Teaching and Learning of the University of Toronto. His research focuses on literacy development in multilingual school contexts as well as on the potential roles of technology in promoting language and literacy development. In recent years, he has been working actively with teachers to identify ways of increasing the literacy engagement of learners in multilingual school contexts. Dr. Cummins has influenced the development of *my*Perspectives in English Language Learner and English Language Development support.

UNIT 1 Inside the Nightmare

INDEPENDENT LEARNING

These selections can be accessed via the Interactive Student Edition.

PERFORMANCE-BASED
ASSESSMENT PREP

PERFORMANCE-BASED ASSESSMENT

UNIT REFLECTION

DIGITAL PERSPECTIVES

- Unit Introduction Videos
- Media Selections
- Modeling Videos
- Selection Audio Recordings

Additional digital resources can be found in:

- Interactive Student Edition
- *my*Perspectives+

INDEPENDENT LEARNING

These selections can be accessed via the Interactive Student Edition.

PERFORMANCE-BASED ASSESSMENT PREP

PERFORMANCE-BASED ASSESSMENT

UNIT REFLECTION

DIGITAL PERSPECTIVES

- Unit Introduction Videos
- Media Selections
- Modeling Videos
- Selection Audio Recordings

Additional digital resources can be found in:

- Interactive Student Edition
- *my*Perspectives+

INDEPENDENT LEARNING

These selections can be accessed via the Interactive Student Edition.

PERFORMANCE-BASED ASSESSMENT PREP

PERFORMANCE-BASED ASSESSMENT

UNIT REFLECTION

DIGITAL PERSPECTIVES

- Unit Introduction Videos
- Media Selections
- Modeling Videos
- Selection Audio Recordings

Additional digital resources can be found in:

- Interactive Student Edition
- *my*Perspectives+

UNIT (4) All That Glitters

(icon) INDEPENDENT LEARNING

MEDIA: INFORMATIONAL GRAPHIC
The Gold Series: A History of Gold
Visual Capitalist

NEWS ARTICLE
Ads May Spur Unhappy Kids to Embrace Materialism
Amy Norton

SHORT STORY
A Dose of What the Doctor Never Orders
*Ihara Saikaku,
translated by G. W. Sargent*

MAGAZINE ARTICLE
My Possessions, Myself
Russell W. Belk

NEWS ARTICLE
Heirlooms' Value Shifts from Sentiment to Cash
Rosa Salter Rodriguez

These selections can be accessed via the Interactive Student Edition.

(icon) PERFORMANCE-BASED ASSESSMENT PREP

(icon) PERFORMANCE-BASED ASSESSMENT

UNIT REFLECTION

DIGITAL PERSPECTIVES

- Unit Introduction Videos
- Media Selections
- Modeling Videos
- Selection Audio Recordings

Additional digital resources can be found in:

- Interactive Student Edition
- *my*Perspectives+

INDEPENDENT LEARNING

These selections can be accessed via the Interactive Student Edition.

PERFORMANCE-BASED ASSESSMENT PREP

PERFORMANCE-BASED ASSESSMENT

UNIT REFLECTION

DIGITAL PERSPECTIVES

- Unit Introduction Videos
- Media Selections
- Modeling Videos
- Selection Audio Recordings

Additional digital resources can be found in:
- Interactive Student Edition
- *my*Perspectives+

UNIT (6) Blindness and Sight

✓ PERFORMANCE TASK

WRITING FOCUS

✓ PERFORMANCE TASK

SPEAKING AND LISTENING FOCUS

INDEPENDENT LEARNING

These selections can be accessed via the Interactive Student Edition.

✓ PERFORMANCE-BASED ASSESSMENT PREP

✓ PERFORMANCE-BASED ASSESSMENT

UNIT REFLECTION

DIGITAL PERSPECTIVES

- Unit Introduction Videos
- Media Selections
- Modeling Videos
- Selection Audio Recordings

Additional digital resources can be found in:

- Interactive Student Edition
- *my*Perspectives+

Standards Overview

The following English Language Arts standards will prepare you to succeed in college and your future career. The College and Career Readiness Anchor Standards define what you need to achieve by the end of high school, and the grade-specific Standards define what you need to know by the end of your current grade level.

The following provides an overview of the Standards.

Standards for Reading

College and Career Readiness Anchor Standards for Reading
Key Ideas and Details
1. Read closely to determine what the text says explicitly and to make logical inferences from it; cite specific textual evidence when writing or speaking to support conclusions drawn from the text.
2. Determine central ideas or themes of a text and analyze their development; summarize the key supporting details and ideas.
3. Analyze how and why individuals, events, and ideas develop and interact over the course of a text.
Craft and Structure
4. Interpret words and phrases as they are used in a text, including determining technical, connotative, and figurative meanings, and analyze how specific word choices shape meaning or tone.
5. Analyze the structure of texts, including how specific sentences, paragraphs, and larger portions of the text (e.g., a section, chapter, scene, or stanza) relate to each other and the whole.
6. Assess how point of view or purpose shapes the content and style of a text.
Integration of Knowledge and Ideas
7. Integrate and evaluate content presented in diverse formats and media, including visually and quantitatively, as well as in words.
8. Delineate and evaluate the argument and specific claims in a text, including the validity of the reasoning as well as the relevance and sufficiency of the evidence.
9. Analyze how two or more texts address similar themes or topics in order to build knowledge or to compare the approaches the authors take.
Range of Reading and Level of Text Complexity
10. Read and comprehend complex literary and informational texts independently and proficiently.

Grade 10 Reading Standards for Literature

Standard

Key Ideas and Details

Cite strong and thorough textual evidence to support analysis of what the text says explicitly as well as inferences drawn from the text.

Determine a theme or central idea of a text and analyze in detail its development over the course of the text, including how it emerges and is shaped and refined by specific details; provide an objective summary of the text.

Analyze how complex characters (e.g., those with multiple or conflicting motivations) develop over the course of a text, interact with other characters, and advance the plot or develop the theme.

Craft and Structure

Determine the meaning of words and phrases as they are used in the text, including figurative and connotative meanings; analyze the cumulative impact of specific word choices on meaning and tone (e.g., how the language evokes a sense of time and place; how it sets a formal or informal tone).

Analyze how an author's choices concerning how to structure a text, order events within it (e.g., parallel plots), and manipulate time (e.g., pacing, flashbacks) create such effects as mystery, tension, or surprise.

Analyze a particular point of view or cultural experience reflected in a work of literature from outside the United States, drawing on a wide reading of world literature.

Integration of Knowledge and Ideas

Analyze the representation of a subject or a key scene in two different artistic mediums, including what is emphasized or absent in each treatment (e.g., Auden's "Musée des Beaux Arts" and Breughel's *Landscape with the Fall of Icarus*).

Analyze how an author draws on and transforms source material in a specific work (e.g., how Shakespeare treats a theme or topic from Ovid or the Bible or how a later author draws on a play by Shakespeare).

Range of Reading and Level of Text Complexity

By the end of Grade 10, read and comprehend literature, including stories, dramas, and poems, at the high end of the grades 9–10 text complexity band independently and proficiently.

Standards Overview

Grade 10 Reading Standards for Informational Text

Standard

Key Ideas and Details

Cite strong and thorough textual evidence to support analysis of what the text says explicitly as well as inferences drawn from the text.

Determine a central idea of a text and analyze its development over the course of the text, including how it emerges and is shaped and refined by specific details; provide an objective summary of the text.

Analyze how the author unfolds an analysis or series of ideas or events, including the order in which the points are made, how they are introduced and developed, and the connections that are drawn between them.

Craft and Structure

Determine the meaning of words and phrases as they are used in a text, including figurative, connotative, and technical meanings; analyze the cumulative impact of specific word choices on meaning and tone (e.g., how the language of a court opinion differs from that of a newspaper).

Analyze in detail how an author's ideas or claims are developed and refined by particular sentences, paragraphs, or larger portions of a text (e.g., a section or chapter).

Determine an author's point of view or purpose in a text and analyze how an author uses rhetoric to advance that point of view or purpose.

Integration of Knowledge and Ideas

Analyze various accounts of a subject told in different mediums (e.g., a person's life story in both print and multimedia), determining which details are emphasized in each account.

Delineate and evaluate the argument and specific claims in a text, assessing whether the reasoning is valid and the evidence is relevant and sufficient; identify false statements and fallacious reasoning.

Analyze seminal U.S. documents of historical and literary significance (e.g., Washington's Farewell Address, the Gettysburg Address, Roosevelt's Four Freedoms speech, King's "Letter from Birmingham Jail"), including how they address related themes and concepts.

Range of Reading and Level of Text Complexity

By the end of Grade 10, read and comprehend literary nonfiction at the high end of the grades 9–10 text complexity band independently and proficiently.

Standards for Writing

Standards Overview

Grade 10 Writing Standards

Standard

Text Types and Purposes (continued)

Develop claim(s) and counterclaims fairly, supplying evidence for each while pointing out the strengths and limitations of both in a manner that anticipates the audience's knowledge level and concerns.

Use words, phrases, and clauses to link the major sections of the text, create cohesion, and clarify the relationships between claim(s) and reasons, between reasons and evidence, and between claim(s) and counterclaims.

Establish and maintain a formal style and objective tone while attending to the norms and conventions of the discipline in which they are writing.

Provide a concluding statement or section that follows from and supports the argument presented.

Write informative/explanatory texts to examine and convey complex ideas, concepts, and information clearly and accurately through the effective selection, organization, and analysis of content.

Introduce a topic; organize complex ideas, concepts, and information to make important connections and distinctions; include formatting (e.g., headings), graphics (e.g., figures, tables), and multimedia when useful to aiding comprehension.

Develop the topic with well-chosen, relevant, and sufficient facts, extended definitions, concrete details, quotations, or other information and examples appropriate to the audience's knowledge of the topic.

Use appropriate and varied transitions to link the major sections of the text, create cohesion, and clarify the relationships among complex ideas and concepts.

Use precise language and domain-specific vocabulary to manage the complexity of the topic.

Establish and maintain a formal style and objective tone while attending to the norms and conventions of the discipline in which they are writing.

Provide a concluding statement or section that follows from and supports the information or explanation presented (e.g., articulating implications or the significance of the topic).

Write narratives to develop real or imagined experiences or events using effective technique, well-chosen details, and well-structured event sequences.

Engage and orient the reader by setting out a problem, situation, or observation, establishing one or multiple point(s) of view, and introducing a narrator and/or characters; create a smooth progression of experiences or events.

Use narrative techniques, such as dialogue, pacing, description, reflection, and multiple plot lines, to develop experiences, events, and/or characters.

Use a variety of techniques to sequence events so that they build on one another to create a coherent whole.

Grade 10 Writing Standards

Standard

Text Types and Purposes (continued)

Use precise words and phrases, telling details, and sensory language to convey a vivid picture of the experiences, events, setting, and/or characters.

Provide a conclusion that follows from and reflects on what is experienced, observed, or resolved over the course of the narrative.

Production and Distribution of Writing

Produce clear and coherent writing in which the development, organization, and style are appropriate to task, purpose, and audience.

Develop and strengthen writing as needed by planning, revising, editing, rewriting, or trying a new approach, focusing on addressing what is most significant for a specific purpose and audience.

Use technology, including the Internet, to produce, publish, and update individual or shared writing products, taking advantage of technology's capacity to link to other information and to display information flexibly and dynamically.

Research to Build and Present Knowledge

Conduct short as well as more sustained research projects to answer a question (including a self-generated question) or solve a problem; narrow or broaden the inquiry when appropriate; synthesize multiple sources on the subject, demonstrating understanding of the subject under investigation.

Gather relevant information from multiple authoritative print and digital sources, using advanced searches effectively; assess the usefulness of each source in answering the research question; integrate information into the text selectively to maintain the flow of ideas, avoiding plagiarism and following a standard format for citation.

Draw evidence from literary or informational texts to support analysis, reflection, and research.

Apply *grades 9–10 Reading standards* to literature (e.g., "Analyze how an author draws on and transforms source material in a specific work [e.g., how Shakespeare treats a theme or topic from Ovid or the Bible or how a later author draws on a play by Shakespeare]").

Apply *grades 9–10 Reading standards* to literary nonfiction (e.g., "Delineate and evaluate the argument and specific claims in a text, assessing whether the reasoning is valid and the evidence is relevant and sufficient; identify false statements and fallacious reasoning").

Range of Writing

Write routinely over extended time frames (time for research, reflection, and revision) and shorter time frames (a single sitting or a day or two) for a range of tasks, purposes, and audiences.

Standards Overview

Standards for Speaking and Listening

College and Career Readiness
Anchor Standards for Speaking and Listening

Comprehension and Collaboration

1. Prepare for and participate effectively in a range of conversations and collaborations with diverse partners, building on others' ideas and expressing their own clearly and persuasively.

2. Integrate and evaluate information presented in diverse media and formats, including visually, quantitatively, and orally.

3. Evaluate a speaker's point of view, reasoning, and use of evidence and rhetoric.

Presentation of Knowledge and Ideas

4. Present information, findings, and supporting evidence such that listeners can follow the line of reasoning and the organization, development, and style are appropriate to task, purpose, and audience.

5. Make strategic use of digital media and visual displays of data to express information and enhance understanding of presentations.

6. Adapt speech to a variety of contexts and communicative tasks, demonstrating command of formal English when indicated or appropriate.

Grade 10 Standards for Speaking and Listening

Standard

Comprehension and Collaboration

Initiate and participate effectively in a range of collaborative discussions (one-on-one, in groups, and teacher-led) with diverse partners on grades 9–10 topics, texts, and issues, building on others' ideas and expressing their own clearly and persuasively.

Come to discussions prepared, having read and researched material under study; explicitly draw on that preparation by referring to evidence from texts and other research on the topic or issue to stimulate a thoughtful, well-reasoned exchange of ideas.

Work with peers to set rules for collegial discussions and decision-making (e.g., informal consensus, taking votes on key issues, presentation of alternate views), clear goals and deadlines, and individual roles as needed.

Propel conversations by posing and responding to questions that relate the current discussion to broader themes or larger ideas; actively incorporate others into the discussion; and clarify, verify, or challenge ideas and conclusions.

Respond thoughtfully to diverse perspectives, summarize points of agreement and disagreement, and, when warranted, qualify or justify their own views and understanding and make new connections in light of the evidence and reasoning presented.

Integrate multiple sources of information presented in diverse media or formats (e.g., visually, quantitatively, orally) evaluating the credibility and accuracy of each source.

Evaluate a speaker's point of view, reasoning, and use of evidence and rhetoric, identifying any fallacious reasoning or exaggerated or distorted evidence.

Presentation of Knowledge and Ideas

Present information, findings, and supporting evidence clearly, concisely, and logically such that listeners can follow the line of reasoning and the organization, development, substance, and style are appropriate to purpose, audience, and task.

Make strategic use of digital media (e.g., textual, graphical, audio, visual, and interactive elements) in presentations to enhance understanding of findings, reasoning, and evidence and to add interest.

Adapt speech to a variety of contexts and tasks, demonstrating command of formal English when indicated or appropriate. (See grades 9–10 Language Standards 1 and 3 for specific expectations.)

Standards Overview

Standards for Language

College and Career Readiness Anchor Standards for Language
Conventions of Standard English 1. Demonstrate command of the conventions of standard English grammar and usage when writing or speaking. 2. Demonstrate command of the conventions of standard English capitalization, punctuation, and spelling when writing.
Knowledge of Language 3. Apply knowledge of language to understand how language functions in different contexts, to make effective choices for meaning or style, and to comprehend more fully when reading or listening.
Vocabulary Acquisition and Use 4. Determine or clarify the meaning of unknown and multiple-meaning words and phrases by using context clues, analyzing meaningful word parts, and consulting general and specialized reference materials, as appropriate. 5. Demonstrate understanding of figurative language, word relationships, and nuances in word meanings. 6. Acquire and use accurately a range of general academic and domain-specific words and phrases sufficient for reading, writing, speaking, and listening at the college and career readiness level; demonstrate independence in gathering vocabulary knowledge when considering a word or phrase important to comprehension or expression.

Grade 10 Standards for Language
Standard
Conventions of Standard English
Demonstrate command of the conventions of standard English grammar and usage when writing or speaking.
Use parallel structure.
Use various types of phrases (noun, verb, adjectival, adverbial, participial, prepositional, absolute) and clauses (independent, dependent; noun, relative, adverbial) to convey specific meanings and add variety and interest to writing or presentations.
Demonstrate command of the conventions of standard English capitalization, punctuation, and spelling when writing.
Use a semicolon (and perhaps a conjunctive adverb) to link two or more closely related independent clauses.

Grade 10 Standards for Language

Standard

Conventions of Standard English (continued)

Use a semicolon (and perhaps a conjunctive adverb) to link two or more closely related independent clauses.

Use a colon to introduce a list or quotation.

Spell correctly.

Knowledge of Language

Apply knowledge of language to understand how language functions in different contexts, to make effective choices for meaning or style, and to comprehend more fully when reading or listening.

Write and edit work so that it conforms to the guidelines in a style manual (e.g., *MLA Handbook*, Turabian's *Manual for Writers*) appropriate for the discipline and writing type.

Vocabulary Acquisition and Use

Determine or clarify the meaning of unknown and multiple-meaning words and phrases based on *grades 9–10 reading and content*, choosing flexibly from a range of strategies.

Use context (e.g., the overall meaning of a sentence, paragraph, or text; a word's position or function in a sentence) as a clue to the meaning of a word or phrase.

Identify and correctly use patterns of word changes that indicate different meanings or parts of speech (e.g., *analyze, analysis, analytical; advocate, advocacy*).

Consult general and specialized reference materials (e.g., dictionaries, glossaries, thesauruses), both print and digital, to find the pronunciation of a word or determine or clarify its precise meaning, its part of speech, or its etymology.

Verify the preliminary determination of the meaning of a word or phrase (e.g., by checking the inferred meaning in context or in a dictionary).

Demonstrate understanding of figurative language, word relationships, and nuances in word meanings.

Interpret figures of speech (e.g., euphemism, oxymoron) in context and analyze their role in the text.

Analyze nuances in the meaning of words with similar denotations.

Acquire and use accurately general academic and domain-specific words and phrases, sufficient for reading, writing, speaking, and listening at the college and career readiness level; demonstrate independence in gathering vocabulary knowledge when considering a word or phrase important to comprehension or expression.

Inside the Nightmare

Spine-tingling movies, books, and experiences are everywhere. What draws us to explore—and to enjoy—frightening themes?

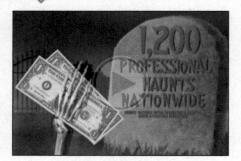

Spooky Business: American Economy

💬 **Discuss It** Why is Halloween big business?

Write your response before sharing your ideas.

UNIT INTRODUCTION

ESSENTIAL QUESTION:

What is the allure of fear?

LAUNCH TEXT
EXPLANATORY MODEL
My Introduction to
Gothic Literature

WHOLE-CLASS LEARNING

ANCHOR TEXT: SHORT STORY

The Fall of the
House of Usher
Edgar Allan Poe

ANCHOR TEXT: SHORT STORY

House Taken Over
Julio Cortázar

COMPARE

MEDIA: INFORMATIONAL GRAPHIC

from How to Tell
You're Reading a
Gothic Novel—In
Pictures
Adam Frost and
Zhenia Vasiliev

SMALL-GROUP LEARNING

SHORT STORY

Where Is Here?
Joyce Carol Oates

MEDIA: PHOTO GALLERY

from The Dream
Collector
Arthur Tress

INTERVIEW

Why Do Some Brains
Enjoy Fear?
Allegra Ringo

POETRY COLLECTION

beware: do not read
this poem
Ishmael Reed

The Raven
Edgar Allan Poe

Windigo
Louise Erdrich

INDEPENDENT LEARNING

CRITICISM

How Maurice
Sendak's "Wild
Things" Moved
Children's Books
Toward Realism
Gloria Goodale

EXPLANATORY NONFICTION

Sleep Paralysis: A
Waking Nightmare

SHORT STORY

The Feather Pillow
Horacio Quiroga, translated
by Margaret Sayers Peden

NEWSPAPER ARTICLE

Stone Age Man's
Terrors Still Stalk
Modern Nightmares
Robin McKie

PERFORMANCE TASK

WRITING FOCUS:
Write an Explanatory Essay

PERFORMANCE TASK

SPEAKING AND LISTENING FOCUS:
Deliver an Explanatory Presentation

PERFORMANCE-BASED ASSESSMENT PREP

Review Evidence for an
Explanatory Essay

PERFORMANCE-BASED ASSESSMENT

Explanatory Text: Essay and Informal Talk

PROMPT:

In what ways does transformation play a role in stories meant to scare us?

Unit Goals

Throughout this unit, you will deepen your understanding of scary literature by reading, writing, speaking, presenting, and listening. These goals will help you succeed on the Unit Performance-Based Assessment.

Rate how well you meet these goals right now. You will revisit your ratings later when you reflect on your growth during this unit.

SCALE	1 NOT AT ALL WELL	2 NOT VERY WELL	3 SOMEWHAT WELL	4 VERY WELL	5 EXTREMELY WELL

READING GOALS	1	2	3	4	5
• Evaluate written narratives by analyzing how authors introduce and develop the events in their writing.	○	○	○	○	○
• Expand your knowledge and use of academic and concept vocabulary.	○	○	○	○	○

WRITING AND RESEARCH GOALS	1	2	3	4	5
• Write an explanatory essay in which you use a narrative as evidence for your main idea. Apply your knowledge of texts in the unit.	○	○	○	○	○
• Conduct research projects of various lengths to explore a topic and clarify meaning.	○	○	○	○	○

LANGUAGE GOAL	1	2	3	4	5
• Use figurative language, connotation, and denotation to convey meaning and add variety and interest to your writing and presentations.	○	○	○	○	○

SPEAKING AND LISTENING GOALS	1	2	3	4	5
• Collaborate with your team to build on the ideas of others, develop consensus, and communicate.	○	○	○	○	○
• Integrate audio, visuals, and text in presentations.	○	○	○	○	○

≣ STANDARDS

Language
Acquire and use accurately general academic and domain-specific words and phrases, sufficient for reading, writing, speaking, and listening at the college and career readiness level; demonstrate independence in gathering vocabulary knowledge when considering a word or phrase important to comprehension or expression.

Academic Vocabulary: Explanatory Text

Academic terms appear in all subjects and can help you read, write, and discuss with more precision. Here are five academic words that will be useful to you in this unit as you analyze and write explanatory texts.

Complete the chart.

1. Review each word, its root, and the mentor sentences.

2. Use the information and your own knowledge to predict the meaning of each word.

3. For each word, list at least two related words.

4. Refer to a dictionary or other resources if needed.

TIP

FOLLOW THROUGH
Study the words in this chart and mark them or their forms wherever they appear in the unit.

WORD	MENTOR SENTENCES	PREDICT MEANING	RELATED WORDS
motivate ROOT: **-mot-** "move"	**1.** A mentor should try to *motivate* a student to perform well. **2.** What might *motivate* a character to do something so deceitful?		motivation; unmotivated
dimension ROOT: **-mens-** "measure"	**1.** We have to consider every *dimension* of the problem before we can solve it. **2.** That classic TV show told stories that explored another *dimension* of time, space, and imagination.		
manipulate ROOT: **-man-** "hand"	**1.** We watch as the sculptors *manipulate* the clay with great skill and speed. **2.** People often become defensive when they believe others are trying to *manipulate* them.		
psychological ROOT: **-psych-** "mind"; "spirit"	**1.** The director's new film is a *psychological* thriller, and I found it extremely suspenseful. **2.** The *psychological* effects of fear can last a long time.		
perspective ROOT: **-spec-** "look"; "see"	**1.** The narrator's *perspective* was limited and left readers wondering what other characters thought. **2.** Living in another part of the country helped to broaden my *perspective* on the world.		

LAUNCH TEXT | EXPLANATORY MODEL

This selection is an example of an **explanatory essay**. In this example, the writer includes narrative, or storytelling, elements to help explain a topic. This is the type of writing you will develop in the Performance-Based Assessment at the end of the unit.

As you read, look at the way the writer includes both explanatory and narrative elements to convey ideas. What important details does the writer include to convey information in a vivid way?

My Introduction to Gothic Literature

1   How does someone fall in love with a particular kind of writing or an author who has long departed this life? What draws us to find in words the echoes of our own fears or longings? For those of us lucky enough to have a literary passion, the story of how we met our first love is probably just like tales of other first meetings—funny or quirky, full of accident and coincidence. My literary passion is Edgar Allan Poe, and I met him—in print—when I was fourteen years old.

2   It was just after a huge storm that had featured an alarmingly beautiful display of lightning and wind. The power had been knocked out, and I was sitting at a window, watching the wet night grow darker. I had been living with my grandmother for a few weeks while my parents "figured things out." I loved my grandmother, but I couldn't shake the sadness and anxiety I was feeling. The storm had been a welcome diversion. As the clouds cleared, a fog rose and filtered the moonlight, casting a bluish hue over the yard. The scene was moody and solemn, but beautiful. My grandmother broke my reverie by bustling into the room, carrying two lit candles and a book. "It'll take hours for the electric company to get all the way out here to fix the power," she said. "Why don't you read? I'll go find some batteries for the flashlights."

3   She set the book and a candle on the floor, and rushed out as though she had to catch the batteries before they fled. I picked up the book she had left on the floor. It was a collection of old stories—just a paperback and not much to look at. I turned to one by

Poe—"The Cask of Amontillado." Set during the carnival season in an unnamed European city, the story features an unhinged narrator named Montresor who plots revenge on an acquaintance. I liked the gruesome setting of a mysterious burial vault. In Poe's descriptions, I could practically smell the dust and mold. And I was stunned by the horrible ending. But what struck me most was how Montresor spoke directly to the reader—to me. He expected my sympathy as he brought his terrible revenge. Up to that point, all the stories I had ever read had set the criminal or lunatic at a distance. They didn't draw me into a mind that was a truly scary place to be. This one did.

4   I finished Poe's story and turned to another. My grandmother came back with a flashlight, and I kept reading. There were more stories by Poe and others by authors whom I had never heard of but who came to feel like friends—Amelia B. Edwards, Horace Walpole, Ann Radcliffe. I later learned that these stories were part of the Gothic tradition, but I didn't care about that. I fell into them and was carried away, like someone swimming in a river. In all of them, characters were driven by intense emotions of love or hate or jealousy. Some featured ghosts or monsters, but others featured regular people whose sorrow made them ghostly or monstrous. They were tales full of darkness and light, just like the storm I had enjoyed with its thunder and lightning. They were stories that made all I felt and feared seem less of a burden.

5   That evening spent in darkness both real and imaginary never left me. The stories helped me understand that life is not easy and people are complex—simultaneously strong and weak, wonderful and terrible. Though I could not articulate it then, I can now: The stories helped me see that life can be a mansion full of secrets and dark passages, but also of beauty and light. They helped me choose to embrace it all. After another week at my grandmother's, I went home, armed with stories to see me through whatever might come.

WORD NETWORK FOR THE LITERATURE OF FEAR

Vocabulary A Word Network is a collection of words related to a topic. As you read the selections in this unit, identify interesting words related to the idea of fear, and add them to your Word Network. For example, you might begin by adding words from the Launch Text, such as *unhinged, vault,* and *revenge*. Continue to add words as you complete the unit.

🔧 **Tool Kit** Word Network Model

unhinged

vault

revenge

FEAR

Summary

Write a summary of "My Introduction to Gothic Literature." A **summary** is a concise, complete, and accurate overview of a text. It should not include a statement of your opinion or an analysis.

Launch Activity

Conduct a Horror-Story Election Consider this question: **Which character is the best horror-story hero?**

- Form two "parties" to gather and choose candidates for an election. You will be voting on the best horror-story "hero." In this case, the heroes are the monsters and other villains.

- With your party, discuss the main characters from horror stories with which you are familiar. Include characters from movies and television, as well as books. When you feel you have discussed the characters thoroughly, nominate a candidate who will represent your party in a whole-class election.

- Choose a party member to deliver the campaign speech telling why your candidate is the best horror-story "hero."

- After both campaign speeches have been delivered, hold a class election. Then, tally the votes for each candidate. If you vote against your own party, be ready to explain why.

QuickWrite

Consider class discussions, presentations, the video, and the Launch Text as you think about the prompt. Record your first thoughts here.

PROMPT: **In what ways does transformation play a role in stories meant to scare us?**

EVIDENCE LOG FOR INSIDE THE NIGHTMARE

Review your QuickWrite. Summarize your initial position in one sentence to record in your Evidence Log. Then, record evidence from "My Introduction to Gothic Literature" that supports your position.

Prepare for the Performance-Based Assessment at the end of the unit by completing the Evidence Log after each selection.

🔧 Tool Kit
Evidence Log Model

Title of Text: _____ Date: _____

CONNECTION TO PROMPT	TEXT EVIDENCE/DETAILS	ADDITIONAL NOTES/IDEAS

How does this text change or add to my thinking? Date: _____

ESSENTIAL QUESTION:

What is the allure of fear?

What is it that draws us to visit haunted houses on Halloween and read stories that keep us up all night startled by every strange noise we hear? The allure of fear is a powerful attraction. Similarly, the concept of "scary but fun" appeals to many of us. The selections you will read offer insight into why people enjoy stories that put them on the edges of their seats.

Whole-Class Learning Strategies

Throughout your life, in school, in your community, and in your career, you will continue to learn and work in large-group environments.

Review these strategies and the actions you can take to practice them as you work with your whole class. Add ideas of your own for each step. Get ready to use these strategies during Whole-Class Learning.

STRATEGY	ACTION PLAN
Listen actively	• Eliminate distractions. For example, put your cellphone away. • Keep your eyes on the speaker. •
Clarify by asking questions	• If you're confused, other people probably are, too. Ask a question to help your whole class. • If you see that you are guessing, ask a question instead. •
Monitor understanding	• Notice what information you already know, and be ready to build on it. • Ask for help if you are struggling. •
Interact and share ideas	• Share your ideas and answer questions, even if you are unsure. • Build on the ideas of others by adding details or making a connection. •

CONTENTS

PERFORMANCE TASK

WRITING FOCUS

Write an Explanatory Text

Both Whole-Class readings involve dark, ominous settings that are full of mysterious, unexplained forces. The informational graphic describes the elements of Gothic literature. After reading, you will write an explanatory essay about portrayals of fear and reason in these selections.

THE FALL OF THE HOUSE OF USHER

HOUSE TAKEN OVER

Comparing Texts

In this lesson, you will read and compare two stories: "The Fall of the House of Usher," by Edgar Allan Poe, and "House Taken Over," by Julio Cortázar. First, you will complete the first-read and close-read activities for Poe's story. Then, you will compare that story to the story Cortázar wrote a little more than a century later.

About the Author

Edgar Allan Poe (1809–1849) is regarded as the first American literary critic and the inventor of the detective story. Despite his literary success, Poe's life was almost as dark and dismal as the fiction he wrote. Shortly after his birth, his father deserted the family, and his mother died. He was raised by a wealthy yet miserly merchant and lived most of his adult life in extreme poverty. Poe died at the age of 40. The circumstances of his death remain a mystery.

🔧 **Tool Kit**
First-Read Guide and Model Annotation

STANDARDS

Reading Literature
By the end of grade 10, read and comprehend literature, including stories, dramas, and poems, at the high end of the grades 9–10 text complexity band independently and proficiently.

The Fall of the House of Usher

Concept Vocabulary

You will encounter the following words as you read "The Fall of the House of Usher." Before reading, note how familiar you are with each word. Rank the words in order from most familiar (1) to least familiar (6).

WORD	YOUR RANKING
annihilate	
antiquity	
fissure	
dissolution	
rending	
tumultuous	

After completing the first read, come back to the concept vocabulary and review your rankings. Mark changes to your original rankings as needed.

First Read FICTION

Apply these strategies as you conduct your first read. You will have an opportunity to complete the close-read notes after your first read.

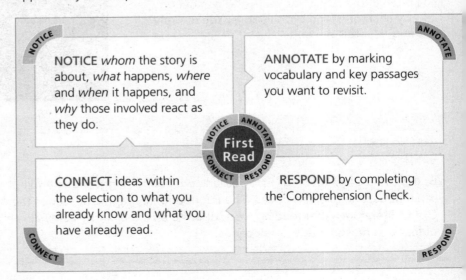

NOTICE whom the story is about, what happens, where and when it happens, and why those involved react as they do.

ANNOTATE by marking vocabulary and key passages you want to revisit.

CONNECT ideas within the selection to what you already know and what you have already read.

RESPOND by completing the Comprehension Check.

First Read

The Fall of the House of Usher

Edgar Allan Poe

BACKGROUND

In this story, Edgar Allan Poe shows his sympathy for the Romantic movement, which was at its height in Europe when he was writing, in the early nineteenth century. The Romantics explored themes of love and death, often with an intense interest in human psychology. For Poe, the darkest aspects of the mind and heart were most revealing of what it means to be human.

1   During the whole of a dull, dark, and soundless day in the autumn of the year, when the clouds hung oppressively low in the heavens, I had been passing alone, on horseback, through a singularly dreary tract of country; and at length found myself, as the shades of the evening drew on, within view of the melancholy House of Usher. I know not how it was—but, with the first glimpse of the building, a sense of insufferable gloom pervaded my spirit. I say insufferable; for the feeling was unrelieved by any of that half-pleasurable, because poetic, sentiment, with which the mind usually receives even the sternest natural images of the desolate

NOTES

ANNOTATE: Mark words and phrases in paragraph 1 that refer to the imagination or altered reality, and others that refer to falling or sinking.

QUESTION: What is happening to the narrator as he looks at the house?

CONCLUDE: What is the effect of these strong descriptive details?

annihilate (uh NY uh layt) *v.* destroy completely

or terrible. I looked upon the scene before me—upon the mere house, and the simple landscape features of the domain—upon the bleak walls—upon the vacant eyelike windows—upon a few rank sedges[1]—and upon a few white trunks of decayed trees—with an utter depression of soul, which I can compare to no earthly sensation more properly than to the after-dream of the reveler upon opium—the bitter lapse into everyday life—the hideous dropping off of the veil. There was an iciness, a sinking, a sickening of the heart—an unredeemed dreariness of thought which no goading of the imagination could torture into aught[2] of the sublime. What was it—I paused to think—what was it that so unnerved me in the contemplation of the House of Usher? It was a mystery all insoluble; nor could I grapple with the shadowy fancies that crowded upon me as I pondered. I was forced to fall back upon the unsatisfactory conclusion, that while, beyond doubt, there are combinations of very simple natural objects which have the power of thus affecting us, still the analysis of this power lies among considerations beyond our depth. It was possible, I reflected, that a mere different arrangement of the particulars of the scene, of the details of the picture, would be sufficient to modify, or perhaps to **annihilate** its capacity for sorrowful impression; and, acting upon this idea, I reined my horse to the precipitous brink of a black and lurid tarn[3] that lay in unruffled luster by the dwelling, and gazed down—but with a shudder even more thrilling than before—upon the remodeled and inverted images of the gray sedge, and the ghastly tree-stems, and the vacant and eyelike windows.

2   Nevertheless, in this mansion of gloom I now proposed to myself a sojourn of some weeks. Its proprietor, Roderick Usher, had been one of my boon companions in boyhood; but many years had elapsed since our last meeting. A letter, however, had lately reached me in a distant part of the country—a letter from him—which, in its wildly importunate nature, had admitted of no other than a personal reply. The MS[4] gave evidence of nervous agitation. The writer spoke of acute bodily illness—of a mental disorder which oppressed him—and of an earnest desire to see me, as his best and indeed his only personal friend, with a view of attempting, by the cheerfulness of my society, some alleviation of his malady. It was the manner in which all this, and much more, was said—it was the apparent *heart* that went with his request—which allowed me no room for hesitation; and I accordingly obeyed forthwith what I still considered a very singular summons.

3   Although, as boys, we had been even intimate associates, yet I really knew little of my friend. His reserve had been always excessive and habitual. I was aware, however, that his very ancient family had been noted, time out of mind, for a peculiar sensibility

---

1. **sedges** *n.* grasslike plants.
2. **aught** (awt) *n.* anything.
3. **tarn** *n.* small lake.
4. **MS** *abbr.* manuscript; document written by hand.

of temperament, displaying itself, through long ages, in many works of exalted art, and manifested, of late, in repeated deeds of munificent yet unobtrusive charity, as well as in a passionate devotion to the intricacies, perhaps even more than to the orthodox and easily recognizable beauties, of musical science. I had learned, too, the very remarkable fact, that the stem of the Usher race, all time-honored as it was, had put forth, at no period, any enduring branch: in other words, that the entire family lay in the direct line of descent, and had always, with very trifling and very temporary variation, so lain. It was this deficiency, I considered, while running over in thought the perfect keeping of the character of the premises with the accredited character of the people, and while speculating upon the possible influence which the one, in the long lapse of centuries, might have exercised upon the other—it was this deficiency, perhaps of collateral issue,[5] and the consequent undeviating transmission, from sire to son, of the patrimony[6] with the name, which had, at length, so identified the two as to merge the original title of the estate in the quaint and equivocal appellation of the "House of Usher"—an appellation which seemed to include, in the minds of the peasantry who used it, both the family and the family mansion.

4   I have said that the sole effect of my somewhat childish experiment—that of looking down within the tarn—had been to deepen the first singular impression. There can be no doubt that the consciousness of the rapid increase of my superstition—for why should I not so term it?—served mainly to accelerate the increase itself. Such, I have long known, is the paradoxical law of all sentiments having terror as a basis. And it might have been for this reason only, that, when I again uplifted my eyes to the house itself, from its image in the pool, there grew in my mind a strange fancy—a fancy so ridiculous, indeed, that I but mention it to show the vivid force of the sensations which oppressed me. I had so worked upon my imagination as really to believe that about the whole mansion and domain there hung an atmosphere peculiar to themselves and their immediate vicinity—an atmosphere which had no affinity with the air of heaven, but which had reeked up from the decayed trees, and the gray wall, and the silent tarn—a pestilent and mystic vapor, dull, sluggish, faintly discernible, and leaden-hued.

5   Shaking off from my spirit what *must* have been a dream, I scanned more narrowly the real aspect of the building. Its principal feature seemed to be that of an excessive **antiquity**. The discoloration of ages had been great. Minute fungi overspread the whole exterior, hanging in a fine tangled web-work from the eaves. Yet all this was apart from any extraordinary dilapidation. No portion of the masonry had fallen; and there appeared to be

antiquity (an TIHK wuh tee) *n.* very great age

---

5. **of collateral issue** descended from the same ancestors but in a different line.
6. **patrimony** (PA truh moh nee) *n.* property inherited from one's father.

fissure (FIHSH uhr) *n.* long, narrow crack or opening

a wild inconsistency between its still perfect adaptation of parts, and the crumbling condition of the individual stones. In this there was much that reminded me of the specious totality of old woodwork which has rotted for long years in some neglected vault, with no disturbance from the breath of the external air. Beyond this indication of extensive decay, however, the fabric gave little token of instability. Perhaps the eye of a scrutinizing observer might have discovered a barely perceptible **fissure**, which, extending from the roof of the building in front, made its way down the wall in a zigzag direction, until it became lost in the sullen waters of the tarn.

6   Noticing these things, I rode over a short causeway to the house. A servant in waiting took my horse, and I entered the Gothic[7] archway of the hall. A valet, of stealthy step, thence conducted me, in silence, through many dark and intricate passages in my progress to the studio of his master. Much that I encountered on the way contributed, I know not how, to heighten the vague sentiments of which I have already spoken. While the objects around me—while the carvings of the ceilings, the somber tapestries of the walls, the ebon blackness of the floors, and the phantasmagoric[8] armorial trophies which rattled as I strode, were but matters to which, or to such as which, I had been accustomed from my infancy—while I hesitated not to acknowledge how familiar was all this—I still wondered to find how unfamiliar were the fancies which ordinary images were stirring up. On one of the staircases, I met the physician of the family. His countenance, I thought, wore a mingled expression of low cunning and perplexity. He accosted me with trepidation and passed on. The valet now threw open a door and ushered me into the presence of his master.

7   The room in which I found myself was very large and lofty. The windows were long, narrow, and pointed, and at so vast a distance from the black oaken floor as to be altogether inaccessible from within. Feeble gleams of encrimsoned light made their way through the trellised panes, and served to render sufficiently distinct the more prominent objects around; the eye, however, struggled in vain to reach the remoter angles of the chamber, or the recesses of the vaulted and fretted[9] ceiling. Dark draperies hung upon the walls. The general furniture was profuse, comfortless, antique, and tattered. Many books and musical instruments lay scattered about, but failed to give any vitality to the scene. I felt that I breathed an atmosphere of sorrow. An air of stern, deep, and irredeemable gloom hung over and pervaded all.

8   Upon my entrance, Usher arose from a sofa on which he had been lying at full length, and greeted me with a vivacious warmth which had much in it, I at first thought, of an overdone

---

7. **Gothic** *adj.* high and ornate.
8. **phantasmagoric** (fan taz muh GAWR ihk) *adj.* fantastic or dreamlike.
9. **fretted** *adj.* ornamented with a pattern of small, straight, intersecting bars.

cordiality—of the constrained effort of the *ennuyé*[10] man of the world. A glance, however, at his countenance convinced me of his perfect sincerity. We sat down; and for some moments, while he spoke not, I gazed upon him with a feeling half of pity, half of awe. Surely, man had never before so terribly altered, in so brief a period, as had Roderick Usher! It was with difficulty that I could bring myself to admit the identity of the wan being before me with the companion of my early boyhood. Yet the character of his face had been at all times remarkable. A cadaverousness[11] of complexion; an eye large, liquid, and luminous beyond comparison; lips somewhat thin and very pallid, but of a surpassingly beautiful curve; a nose of a delicate Hebrew model, but with a breadth of nostril unusual in similar formations; a finely molded chin, speaking, in its want of prominence, of a want of moral energy; hair of a more than weblike softness and tenuity— these features, with an inordinate expansion above the regions of the temple, made up altogether a countenance not easily to be forgotten. And now in the mere exaggeration of the prevailing character of these features, and of the expression they were wont to convey, lay so much of change that I doubted to whom I spoke. The now ghastly pallor of the skin, and the now miraculous luster of the eye, above all things startled and even awed me. The silken hair, too, had been suffered to grow all unheeded, and as, in its wild gossamer[12] texture, it floated rather than fell about the face, I could not, even with effort, connect its Arabesque[13] expression with any idea of simple humanity.

9   In the manner of my friend I was at once struck with an incoherence—an inconsistency; and I soon found this to arise from a series of feeble and futile struggles to overcome an habitual trepidancy—an excessive nervous agitation. For something of this nature I had indeed been prepared, no less by his letter, than by reminiscences of certain boyish traits, and by conclusions deduced from his peculiar physical conformation and temperament. His action was alternately vivacious and sullen. His voice varied rapidly from a tremulous indecision (when the animal spirits seemed utterly in abeyance) to that species of energetic concision—that abrupt, weighty, unhurried, and hollow-sounding enunciation—that leaden, self-balanced, and perfectly modulated guttural utterance, which may be observed in the lost drunkard, or the irreclaimable eater of opium, during the periods of his most intense excitement.

10   It was thus that he spoke of the object of my visit, of his earnest desire to see me, and of the solace he expected me to afford him. He entered, at some length, into what he conceived to be the nature of his malady. It was, he said, a constitutional and a family evil, and one

NOTES

CLOSE READ
ANNOTATE: Mark details in paragraph 8 that relate to the absence of color and force.

QUESTION: What portrait of Usher do these details create?

CONCLUDE: What does this portrayal of Usher help the reader understand?

10. *ennuyé* (on wee AY) *adj.* French for "bored."
11. **cadaverousness** (kuh DAV uhr uhs nihs) *n.* quality of being like a dead body.
12. **gossamer** (GOS uh muhr) *adj.* very delicate and light, like a cobweb.
13. **Arabesque** (ar uh BEHSK) *adj.* of complex and elaborate design.

for which he despaired to find a remedy—a mere nervous affection,[14] he immediately added, which would undoubtedly soon pass off. It displayed itself in a host of unnatural sensations. Some of these, as he detailed them, interested and bewildered me; although, perhaps, the terms and the general manner of the narration had their weight. He suffered much from a morbid acuteness of the senses; the most insipid food was alone endurable; he could wear only garments of certain texture; the odors of all flowers were oppressive; his eyes were tortured by even a faint light; and there were but peculiar sounds, and these from stringed instruments, which did not inspire him with horror.

11   To an anomalous species of terror I found him a bounden slave. "I shall perish:" said he, "I *must* perish in this deplorable folly. Thus, thus, and not otherwise, shall I be lost. I dread the events of the future, not in themselves, but in their results. I shudder at the thought of any, even the most trivial, incident, which may operate upon this intolerable agitation of soul. I have, indeed, no abhorrence of danger, except in its absolute effect—in terror. In this unnerved, in this pitiable, condition I feel that the period will sooner or later arrive when I must abandon life and reason together, in some struggle with the grim phantasm, FEAR."

---

14. **affection** *n.* affliction; illness.

12   I learned, moreover, at intervals, and through broken and equivocal hints, another singular feature of his mental condition. He was enchained by certain superstitious impressions in regard to the dwelling which he tenanted, and whence, for many years, he had never ventured forth—in regard to an influence whose supposititious[15] force was conveyed in terms too shadowy here to be restated—an influence which some peculiarities in the mere form and substance of his family mansion, had, by dint of long sufferance, he said, obtained over his spirit—an effect which the physique of the gray walls and turrets, and of the dim tarn into which they all looked down, had at length, brought about upon the morale of his existence.

13   He admitted, however, although with hesitation, that much of the peculiar gloom which thus afflicted him could be traced to a more natural and far more palpable origin—to the severe and long-continued illness—indeed to the evidently approaching dissolution—of a tenderly beloved sister—his sole companion for long years, his last and only relative on earth. "Her decease," he said, with a bitterness which I can never forget, "would leave him (him, the hopeless and the frail) the last of the ancient race of the Ushers." While he spoke, the lady Madeline (for so was she called) passed slowly through a remote portion of the apartment, and, without having noticed my presence, disappeared. I regarded her with an utter astonishment not unmingled with dread; and yet I found it impossible to account for such feelings. A sensation of stupor oppressed me, as my eyes followed her retreating steps. When a door, at length, closed upon her, my glance sought instinctively and eagerly the countenance of the brother; but he had buried his face in his hands, and I could only perceive that a far more than ordinary wanness had overspread the emaciated fingers through which trickled many passionate tears.

14   The disease of the lady Madeline had long baffled the skill of her physicians. A settled apathy, a gradual wasting away of the person, and frequent although transient affections of a partially cataleptical[16] character were the unusual diagnosis. Hitherto she had steadily borne up against the pressure of her malady, and had not betaken herself finally to bed; but on the closing in of the evening of my arrival at the house, she succumbed (as her brother told me at night with inexpressible agitation) to the prostrating power of the destroyer; and I learned that the glimpse I had obtained of her person would thus probably be the last I should obtain—that the lady, at least while living, would be seen by me no more.

15   For several days ensuing, her name was unmentioned by either Usher or myself; and during this period I was busied in earnest endeavors to alleviate the melancholy of my friend. We painted

---

NOTES

dissolution (dihs uh LOO shuhn) *n.* ending or downfall

CLOSE READ
ANNOTATE: In the first two sentences of paragraph 13, mark the sections that are set off by dashes or parentheses.

QUESTION: Why does the author structure these sentences in this way?

CONCLUDE: What do these fragmented sentences suggest about the way Usher speaks and behaves?

---

15. **supposititious** (suh poz uh TIHSH uhs) *adj.* supposed.
16. **cataleptical** (kat uh LEHP tihk uhl) *adj.* in a state in which consciousness and feeling are suddenly and temporarily lost and the muscles become rigid.

and read together, or I listened, as if in a dream, to the wild improvisations of his speaking guitar. And thus, as a closer and still closer intimacy admitted me more unreservedly into the recesses of his spirit, the more bitterly did I perceive the futility of all attempt at cheering a mind from which darkness, as if an inherent positive quality, poured forth upon all objects of the moral and physical universe, in one unceasing radiation of gloom.

16   I shall ever bear about me a memory of the many solemn hours I thus spent alone with the master of the House of Usher. Yet I should fail in any attempt to convey an idea of the exact character of the studies, or of the occupations, in which he involved me, or led me the way. An excited and highly distempered ideality[17] threw a sulfureous luster over all. His long improvised dirges will ring forever in my ears. Among other things, I hold painfully in mind a certain singular perversion and amplification of the wild air of the last waltz of von Weber.[18] From the paintings over which his elaborate fancy brooded, and which grew, touch by touch, into vaguenesses at which I shuddered the more thrillingly, because I shuddered knowing not why—from these paintings (vivid as their images now are before me) I would in vain endeavor to educe more than a small portion which should lie within the compass of merely written words. By the utter simplicity, by the nakedness of his designs, he arrested and overawed attention. If ever mortal painted an idea, that mortal was Roderick Usher. For me at least, in the circumstances then surrounding me, there arose out of the pure abstractions which the hypochondriac contrived to throw upon his canvas, an intensity of intolerable awe, no shadow of which felt I ever yet in the contemplation of the certainly glowing yet too concrete reveries of Fuseli.[19]

17   One of the phantasmagoric conceptions of my friend, partaking not so rigidly of the spirit of abstraction, may be shadowed forth, although feebly, in words. A small picture presented the interior of an immensely long and rectangular vault or tunnel, with low walls, smooth, white and without interruption or device. Certain accessory points of the design served well to convey the idea that this excavation lay at an exceeding depth below the surface of the earth. No outlet was observed in any portion of its vast extent, and no torch, or other artificial source of light was discernible; yet a flood of intense rays rolled throughout, and bathed the whole in a ghastly and inappropriate splendor.

18   I have just spoken of that morbid condition of the auditory nerve which rendered all music intolerable to the sufferer, with the exception of certain effects of stringed instruments. It was, perhaps,

---

17. **ideality** (y dee AL uh tee) *n.* something that is ideal or has no reality.
18. **von Weber** (fon VAY buhr) Carl Maria von Weber (1786–1826), German Romantic composer whose music was highly emotional and dramatic.
19. **Fuseli** (FYOO zuh lee) Johann Heinrich Füssli (1741–1825), also known as Henry Fuseli, Swiss-born painter who lived in England and was noted for his depictions of dreamlike and sometimes nightmarish images.

the narrow limits to which he thus confined himself upon the guitar, which gave birth, in great measure, to the fantastic character of his performances. But the fervid facility of his impromptus could not be so accounted for. They must have been, and were, in the notes, as well as in the words of his wild fantasias (for he not unfrequently accompanied himself with rhymed verbal improvisations), the result of that intense mental collectedness and concentration to which I have previously alluded as observable only in particular moments of the highest artificial excitement. The words of one of these rhapsodies I have easily remembered. I was, perhaps, the more forcibly impressed with it, as he gave it because, in the under or mystic current of its meaning, I fancied that I perceived, and for the first time, a full consciousness on the part of Usher of the tottering of his lofty reason upon her throne. The verses, which were entitled "The Haunted Palace," ran very nearly, if not accurately, thus:

NOTES

I

19

In the greenest of our valleys,
    By good angels tenanted,
Once a fair and stately palace—
    Radiant palace—reared its head.
In the monarch Thought's dominion—
    It stood there!
Never seraph[20] spread a pinion[21]
    Over fabric half so fair.

II

20

Banners yellow, glorious, golden,
    On its roof did float and flow
(This—all this—was in the olden
    Time long ago)
And every gentle air that dallied,
    In that sweet day,
Along the ramparts plumed and pallid,
    A winged odor went away.

III

21

Wanderers in that happy valley
    Through two luminous windows saw
Spirits moving musically
    To a lute's well-tuned law;
Round about a throne, where sitting
    (Porphyrogene!)[22]
In state his glory well befitting,
    The ruler of the realm was seen.

---

20. **seraph** (SEHR uhf) *n.* angel.
21. **pinion** (PIHN yuhn) *n.* wing.
22. **Porphyrogene** (pawr fehr oh JEEN) *adj.* born to royalty or "the purple."

IV

22

And all with pearl and ruby glowing
Was the fair palace door,
Through which came flowing, flowing, flowing
And sparkling evermore.
A troop of Echoes whose sweet duty
Was but to sing,
In voices of surpassing beauty,
The wit and wisdom of their king.

V

23

But evil things, in robes of sorrow,
Assailed the monarch's high estate;
(Ah, let us mourn, for never morrow
Shall dawn upon him, desolate!)
And, round about his home, the glory
That blushed and bloomed
Is but a dim-remembered story
Of the old time entombed.

VI

24

And travelers now within that valley,
Through the red-litten[23] *windows, see*
Vast forms that move fantastically
To a discordant melody;
While, like a rapid ghastly river,
Through the pale door,
A hideous throng rush out forever,
And laugh—but smile no more.

25   I well remember that suggestions arising from this ballad led us into a train of thought wherein there became manifest an opinion of Usher's which I mention not so much on account of its novelty (for other men have thought thus), as on account of the pertinacity[24] with which he maintained it. This opinion, in its general form, was that of the sentience of all vegetable things. But, in his disordered fancy the idea had assumed a more daring character, and trespassed, under certain conditions, upon the kingdom of inorganization.[25] I lack words to express the full extent, or the earnest abandon of his persuasion. The belief, however, was connected (as I have previously hinted) with the gray stones of the home of his forefathers. The conditions of the sentience had been here, he imagined, fulfilled in the method of collocation of these stones—in the order of their arrangement, as well as in that of the many fungi which overspread them, and of the decayed trees which stood around—above all, in the long undisturbed endurance of

---

23. *litten* *adj.* lighted.
24. **pertinacity** (purt uhn AS uh tee) *n.* determined stubbornness.
25. **inorganization** *n.* inanimate objects.

this arrangement, and in its reduplication in the still waters of the tarn. Its evidence—the evidence of the sentience—was to be seen, he said (and I here started as he spoke), in the gradual yet certain condensation of an atmosphere of their own about the waters and the walls. The result was discoverable, he added, in that silent, yet importunate and terrible influence which for centuries had molded the destinies of his family, and which made him what I now saw him—what he was. Such opinions need no comment, and I will make none.

26　　Our books—the books which, for years, had formed no small portion of the mental existence of the invalid—were, as might be supposed, in strict keeping with this character of phantasm. We pored together over such works as the *Ververt et Chartreuse* of Gresset; the *Belphegor* of Machiavelli; the *Heaven and Hell* of Swedenborg; the *Subterranean Voyage of Nicholas Klimm* by Holberg; the *Chiromancy* of Robert Flud, of Jean D'Indaginé, and of De la Chambre; the *Journey into the Blue Distance* of Tieck; and the *City of the Sun* of Campanella.[26] One favorite volume was a small octavo edition of the *Directorium Inquisitorium*, by the Dominican Eymeric de Gironne; and there were passages in Pomponius Mela, about the old African Satyrs and Œgipans, over which Usher would sit dreaming for hours. His chief delight, however, was found in the perusal of an exceedingly rare and curious book in quarto Gothic— the manual of a forgotten church—the *Vigiliae Mortuorum secundum Chorum Ecclesiae Maguntinae*.

27　　I could not help thinking of the wild ritual of this work, and of its probable influence upon the hypochondriac, when, one evening, having informed me abruptly that the lady Madeline was no more, he stated his intention of preserving her corpse for a fortnight (previously to its final interment), in one of the numerous vaults within the main walls of the building. The worldly reason, however, assigned for this singular proceeding, was one which I did not feel at liberty to dispute. The brother had been led to his resolution (so he told me) by consideration of the unusual character of the malady of the deceased, of certain obtrusive and eager inquiries on the part of her medical men, and of the remote and exposed situation of the burial ground of the family. I will not deny that when I called to mind the sinister countenance of the person whom I met upon the staircase, on the day of my arrival at the house, I had no desire to oppose what I regarded as at best but a harmless, and by no means an unnatural precaution.

28　　At the request of Usher, I personally aided him in the arrangements for the temporary entombment. The body having been encoffined, we two alone bore it to its rest. The vault in which we placed it (and which had been so long unopened that our torches, half smothered in its oppressive atmosphere, gave us little

---

26. *Ververt et Chartreuse* of Gresset . . . *City of the Sun* of Campanella All the books listed deal with magic or mysticism.

opportunity for investigation) was small, damp, and entirely without means of admission for light; lying, at great depth, immediately beneath that portion of the building in which was my own sleeping apartment. It had been used, apparently, in remote feudal times, for the worst purposes of a donjon-keep,[27] and, in later days, as a place of deposit for powder, or some other highly combustible substance, as a portion of its floor, and the whole interior of a long archway through which we reached it, were carefully sheathed with copper. The door, of massive iron, had been, also, similarly protected. Its immense weight caused an unusually sharp, grating sound, as it moved upon its hinges.

29　Having deposited our mournful burden upon trestles within this region of horror, we partially turned aside the yet unscrewed lid of the coffin, and looked upon the face of the tenant. A striking similitude between the brother and sister now first arrested my attention; and Usher, divining, perhaps, my thoughts, murmured out some few words from which I learned that the deceased and himself had been twins, and that sympathies of a scarcely intelligible nature had always existed between them. Our glances, however, rested not long upon the dead—for we could not regard her unawed. The disease which had thus entombed the lady in the maturity of youth, had left, as usual in all maladies of a strictly cataleptical character, the mockery of a faint blush upon the bosom and the face, and that suspiciously lingering smile upon the lip which is so terrible in death. We replaced and screwed down the lid, and, having secured the door of iron, made our way, with toil, into the scarcely less gloomy apartments of the upper portion of the house.

CLOSE READ

ANNOTATE: In paragraph 30, mark words that relate to physical actions and behavior.

QUESTION: What do these physical details show about Usher's mental state and emotions?

CONCLUDE: What is the effect of these descriptive details?

30　And now, some days of bitter grief having elapsed, an observable change came over the features of the mental disorder of my friend. His ordinary manner had vanished. His ordinary occupations were neglected or forgotten. He roamed from chamber to chamber with hurried, unequal, and object-less step. The pallor of his countenance had assumed, if possible, a more ghastly hue—but the luminousness of his eye had utterly gone out. The once occasional huskiness of his tone was heard no more; and a tremulous quaver, as if of extreme terror, habitually characterized his utterance. There were times, indeed, when I thought his unceasingly agitated mind was laboring with some oppressive secret, to divulge which he struggled for the necessary courage. At times, again, I was obliged to resolve all into the mere inexplicable vagaries[28] of madness, for I beheld him gazing upon vacancy for long hours, in an attitude of the profoundest attention, as if listening to some imaginary sound. It was no wonder that his condition terrified—that it infected me. I felt creeping upon me, by

---

27. **donjon-keep** (DUHN juhn keep) *n.* inner storage room of a castle; dungeon.
28. **vagaries** (VAY guhr eez) *n.* odd, unexpected actions or notions.

slow yet certain degrees, the wild influences of his own fantastic yet impressive superstitions.

31   It was, especially, upon retiring to bed late in the night of the seventh or eighth day after the placing of the lady Madeline within the donjon, that I experienced the full power of such feelings. Sleep came not near my couch—while the hours waned and waned away. I struggled to reason off the nervousness which had dominion over me. I endeavored to believe that much, if not all of what I felt, was due to the bewildering influence of the gloomy furniture of the room—of the dark and tattered draperies, which, tortured into motion by the breath of a rising tempest, swayed fitfully to and fro upon the walls, and rustled uneasily about the decorations of the bed. But my efforts were fruitless. An irrepressible tremor gradually pervaded my frame; and, at length, there sat upon my very heart an incubus[29] of utterly causeless alarm. Shaking this off with a gasp and a struggle, I uplifted myself upon the pillows, and, peering earnestly

29. **incubus** (IHN kyuh buhs) *n.* something nightmarishly burdensome.

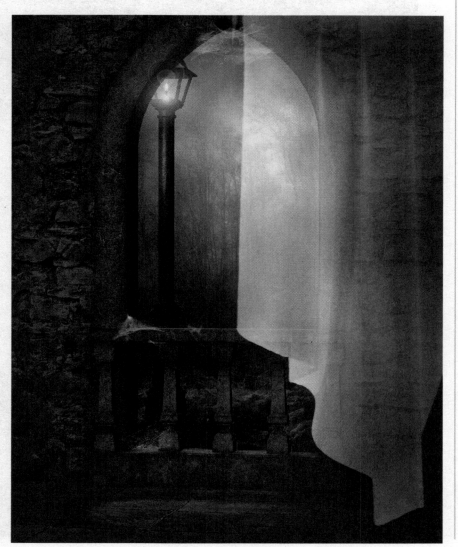

within the intense darkness of the chamber, hearkened—I know not why, except that an instinctive spirit prompted me—to certain low and indefinite sounds which came, through the pauses of the storm, at long intervals, I knew not whence. Overpowered by an intense sentiment of horror, unaccountable yet unendurable, I threw on my clothes with haste (for I felt that I should sleep no more during the night), and endeavored to arouse myself from the pitiable condition into which I had fallen, by pacing rapidly to and fro through the apartment.

32   I had taken but few turns in this manner, when a light step on an adjoining staircase arrested my attention. I presently recognized it as that of Usher. In an instant afterward he rapped, with a gentle touch, at my door, and entered, bearing a lamp. His countenance was, as usual, cadaverously wan—but, moreover, there was a species of mad hilarity in his eyes—an evidently restrained hysteria in his whole demeanor. His air appalled me—but anything was preferable to

the solitude which I had so long endured, and I even welcomed his presence as a relief.

33   "And you have not seen it?" he said abruptly, after having stared about him for some moments in silence—"you have not then seen it?—but, stay! you shall." Thus speaking, and having carefully shaded his lamp, he hurried to one of the casements, and threw it freely open to the storm.

34   The impetuous fury of the entering gust nearly lifted us from our feet. It was, indeed, a tempestuous yet sternly beautiful night, and one wildly singular in its terror and its beauty. A whirlwind had apparently collected its force in our vicinity; for there were frequent and violent alterations in the direction of the wind; and the exceeding density of the clouds (which hung so low as to press upon the turrets of the house) did not prevent our perceiving the lifelike velocity with which they flew careering from all points against each other, without passing away into the distance. I say that even their exceeding density did not prevent our perceiving this—yet we had no glimpse of the moon or stars, nor was there any flashing forth of the lightning. But the under surfaces of the huge masses of agitated vapor, as well as all terrestrial objects immediately around us, were glowing in the unnatural light of a faintly luminous and distinctly visible gaseous exhalation which hung about and enshrouded the mansion.

35   "You must not—you shall not behold this!" said I, shudderingly, to Usher, as I led him, with a gentle violence, from the window to a seat. "These appearances, which bewilder you, are merely electrical phenomena not uncommon—or it may be that they have their ghastly origin in the rank miasma[30] of the tarn. Let us close this casement:—the air is chilling and dangerous to your frame. Here is one of your favorite romances. I will read, and you shall listen:—and so we will pass away this terrible night together."

36   The antique volume which I had taken up was the *Mad Trist* of Sir Launcelot Canning;[31] but I had called it a favorite of Usher's more in sad jest than in earnest; for, in truth, there is little in its uncouth and unimaginative prolixity which could have had interest for the lofty and spiritual ideality of my friend. It was, however, the only book immediately at hand; and I indulged a vague hope that the excitement which now agitated the hypochondriac, might find relief (for the history of mental disorder is full of similar anomalies) even in the extremeness of the folly which I should read. Could I have judged, indeed, by the wild overstrained air of vivacity with which he harkened, or apparently harkened, to the words of the tale, I might well have congratulated myself upon the success of my design.

37   I had arrived at that well-known portion of the story where Ethelred, the hero of the Trist, having sought in vain for peaceable admission into the dwelling of the hermit, proceeds to make good

NOTES

CLOSE READ
ANNOTATE: In paragraph 34, mark words and phrases that suggest extremes, whether of emotion, action, or size.

QUESTION: What is noteworthy about this storm?

CONCLUDE: What greater meaning do these details give to the storm?

30. **miasma** (my AZ muh) *n.* unwholesome atmosphere.
31. **Mad Trist of Sir Launcelot Canning** fictional book and author.

an entrance by force. Here, it will be remembered, the words of the narrative run thus:

38   "And Ethelred, who was by nature of a doughty[32] heart, and who was now mighty withal, on account of the powerfulness of the wine which he had drunken, waited no longer to hold parley[33] with the hermit, who, in sooth, was of an obstinate and maliceful turn, but, feeling the rain upon his shoulders, and fearing the rising of the tempest, uplifted his mace outright, and, with blows, made quickly room in the plankings of the door for his gauntleted hand; and now pulling therewith sturdily, he so cracked, and ripped, and tore all asunder, that the noise of the dry and hollow-sounding wood alarumed and reverberated throughout the forest."

39   At the termination of this sentence I started and, for a moment, paused; for it appeared to me (although I at once concluded that my excited fancy had deceived me)—it appeared to me that, from some very remote portion of the mansion, there came, indistinctly, to my ears, what might have been, in its exact similarity of character, the echo (but a stifled and dull one certainly) of the very cracking and ripping sound which Sir Launcelot had so particularly described. It was, beyond doubt, the coincidence alone which had arrested my attention; for, amid the rattling of the sashes of the casements, and the ordinary commingled noises of the still increasing storm, the sound, itself, had nothing, surely, which should have interested or disturbed me. I continued the story:

40   "But the good champion Ethelred, now entering within the door, was sore enraged and amazed to perceive no signal of the maliceful hermit; but, in the stead thereof, a dragon of a scaly and prodigious demeanor, and of a fiery tongue, which sate in guard before a palace of gold, with a floor of silver; and upon the wall there hung a shield of shining brass with this legend enwritten—

Who entereth herein, a conqueror hath bin;

Who slayeth the dragon, the shield he shall win.

41   And Ethelred uplifted his mace, and struck upon the head of the dragon, which fell before him, and gave up his pesty breath, with a shriek so horrid and harsh, and withal so piercing, that Ethelred had fain to close his ears with his hands against the dreadful noise of it, the like whereof was never before heard."

42   Here again I paused abruptly, and now with a feeling of wild amazement—for there could be no doubt whatever that, in this instance, I did actually hear (although from what direction it proceeded I found it impossible to say) a low and apparently distant, but harsh, protracted, and most unusual screaming or grating sound—the exact counterpart of what my fancy had already conjured up for the dragon's unnatural shriek as described by the romancer.

43   Oppressed, as I certainly was, upon the occurrence of this second and most extraordinary coincidence, by a thousand conflicting

32. **doughty** (DOWT ee) *adj.* brave.
33. **parley** (pahr LEE) *n.* conference; discussion.

sensations, in which wonder and extreme terror were predominant, I still retained sufficient presence of mind to avoid exciting, by any observation, the sensitive nervousness of my companion. I was by no means certain that he had noticed the sounds in question; although, assuredly, a strange alteration had, during the last few minutes, taken place in his demeanor. From a position fronting my own, he had gradually brought round his chair, so as to sit with his face to the door of the chamber; and thus I could but partially perceive his features, although I saw that his lips trembled as if he were murmuring inaudibly. His head had dropped upon his breast—yet I knew that he was not asleep, from the wide and rigid opening of the eye as I caught a glance of it in profile. The motion of his body, too, was at variance with this idea—for he rocked from side to side with a gentle yet constant and uniform sway. Having rapidly taken notice of all this, I resumed the narrative of Sir Launcelot, which thus proceeded:

44 "And now, the champion, having escaped from the terrible fury of the dragon, bethinking himself of the brazen shield, and of the breaking up of the enchantment which was upon it, removed the carcass from out of the way before him, and approached valorously over the silver pavement of the castle to where the shield was upon the wall; which in sooth tarried not for his full coming, but fell down at his feet upon the silver floor, with a mighty great and terrible ringing sound."

45 No sooner had these syllables passed my lips, than—as if a shield of brass had indeed, at the moment, fallen heavily upon a floor of silver—I became aware of a distinct, hollow, metallic, and clangorous, yet apparently muffled, reverberation. Completely unnerved, I leaped to my feet; but the measured rocking movement of Usher was undisturbed. I rushed to the chair in which he sat. His eyes were bent fixedly before him, and throughout his whole countenance there reigned a stony rigidity. But, as I placed my hand upon his shoulder, there came a strong shudder over his whole person; a sickly smile quivered about his lips; and I saw that he spoke in a low, hurried, and gibbering murmur, as if unconscious of my presence. Bending closely over him I at length drank in the hideous import of his words.

46 "Not hear it?—yes, I hear it, and have heard it. Long—long— long—many minutes, many hours, many days, have I heard it— yet I dared not—oh, pity me, miserable wretch that I am!—I *dared* not—I dared not speak! *We have put her living in the tomb!* Said I not that my senses were acute? I *now* tell you that I heard her first feeble movements in the hollow coffin. I heard them—many, many days ago—yet I dared not—*I dared not speak!* and now—tonight— Ethelred—ha! ha!—the breaking of the hermit's door, and the death cry of the dragon, and the clangor of the shield—say, rather, the **rending** of her coffin, and the grating of the iron hinges of her prison, and her struggles within the coppered archway of the vault! Oh! wither shall I fly? Will she not be here anon? Is she not hurrying to

NOTES

CLOSE READ
ANNOTATE: Mark examples of repeated words in paragraph 46.

QUESTION: Why do these words merit being repeated?

CONCLUDE: What is the effect of these repeated words?

rending (REHN dihng) *n.* violent or forceful pulling apart of something upbraid me for my haste? Have I not heard her footstep on the stair? Do I not distinguish that heavy and horrible beating of her heart? Madman!"—here he sprang furiously to his feet, and shrieked out his syllables, as if in the effort he were giving up his soul—"*Madman! I tell you that she now stands without the door!*"

47   As if in the superhuman energy of his utterance there had been found the potency of a spell, the huge antique panels to which the speaker pointed, threw slowly back, upon the instant, their ponderous and ebony jaws. It was the work of the rushing gust—but then without those doors there *did* stand the lofty and enshrouded figure of the lady Madeline of Usher. There was blood upon her white robes, and the evidence of some bitter struggle upon every portion of her emaciated frame. For a moment she remained trembling and reeling to and fro upon the threshold—then, with a low moaning cry, fell heavily inward upon the person of her brother, and in her violent and now final death agonies, bore him to the floor a corpse, and a victim to the terrors he had anticipated.

48   From that chamber, and from that mansion, I fled aghast. The storm was still abroad in all its wrath as I found myself crossing the old causeway. Suddenly there shot along the path a wild light, and I turned to see whence a gleam so unusual could have issued; for the vast house and its shadows were alone behind me. The radiance was that of the full, setting, and bloodred moon, which now shone vividly through that once barely discernible fissure, of which I have before spoken as extending from the roof of the building, in a zigzag direction, to the base. While I gazed, this fissure rapidly widened—there came a fierce breath of the whirlwind—the entire orb of the satellite burst at once upon my sight—my brain reeled as I saw the mighty walls rushing asunder—there was a long **tumultuous** shouting sound like the voice of a thousand waters—and the deep and dank tarn at my feet closed sullenly and silently over the fragments of the *"House of Usher."* ❧

tumultuous (too MUHL choo uhs) *adj.* loud, excited, and emotional

Comprehension Check

Complete the following items after you finish your first read.

1. Why does the narrator go to visit Usher?

2. Early in the story, what flaw in the front of the house does the narrator observe?

3. What forms of artistic expression does Usher share with the narrator?

4. What does the narrator learn about the relationship between Usher and Madeline after her death?

5. What confession does Usher make to the narrator during the final storm?

6. 🖥 **Notebook** Draw a storyboard that summarizes the events of "The Fall of the House of Usher" to confirm your understanding of the story.

- -

RESEARCH

Research to Clarify Choose at least one unfamiliar detail from the text. Briefly research that detail. In what way does the information you learned shed light on an aspect of the story?

Research to Explore Choose a detail or reference in the text that interests you, and formulate a research question.

Close Read the Text

This model, from paragraph 11 of the text, shows two sample annotations, along with questions and conclusions. Close read the passage, and find another detail to annotate. Then, write a question and your conclusion.

Close Read — ANNOTATE · QUESTION · CONCLUDE

> **ANNOTATE:** Poe begins this passage with two long, complex sentences.
>
> **QUESTION:** Why does Poe pack so many ideas into these sentences?
>
> **CONCLUDE:** These complex sentences suggest that Usher's thoughts are racing, that he is being swept away with fear.

ANNOTATE: Poe ends two sentences with the synonyms *terror* and *FEAR*.

QUESTION: Why does Poe emphasize these words—one with a dash, one with capitals?

CONCLUDE: Poe is conveying the idea that Usher is not afraid of danger; rather, he is afraid of fear itself.

> I shudder at the thought of any, even the most trivial, incident, which may operate upon this intolerable agitation of soul. I have, indeed, no abhorrence of danger, except in its absolute effect—in terror. In this unnerved, in this pitiable condition, I feel that the period will sooner or later arrive when I must abandon life and reason together, in some struggle with the grim phantasm, FEAR.

🔧 Tool Kit
Close-Read Guide and
Model Annotation

Analyze the Text

CITE TEXTUAL EVIDENCE to support your answers.

📓 **Notebook** Respond to these questions.

1. **(a) Interpret** Which descriptive details of the interior of the house suggest that the narrator has entered a realm that is very different from the ordinary world? **(b) Make Inferences** In what ways is the appearance of the interior of the house related to Usher's appearance and the condition of his mind?

2. **(a) Connect** How do the works of art described in the story reflect the story's events? **(b) Interpret** What idea about the relationship between art and life is supported by these elements of the story? Explain.

3. **(a) Analyze** In what ways is the narrator affected by Usher's condition? **(b) Evaluate** Do you think the narrator is a reliable witness to the events he describes? Explain.

4. **Make a Judgment** Is Usher responsible for the death of his sister and the collapse of his home? Explain.

5. **Essential Question:** *What is the allure of fear?* What have you learned from this story about portrayals of fear in literature?

☷ STANDARDS
Reading Literature
• Cite strong and thorough textual evidence to support analysis of what the text says explicitly as well as inferences drawn from the text.
• Analyze how an author's choices concerning how to structure a text, order events within it, and manipulate time create such effects as mystery, tension, or surprise.

Analyze Craft and Structure

Literary Style "The Fall of the House of Usher" is an example of **Gothic literature**, a literary genre that began in England in the late 1700s. The term *Gothic* was originally used as an architectural term. It refers to medieval buildings, such as castles and cathedrals, that were seen as dark and gloomy by later generations. When writers began to set their stories in those buildings of the past, the term for the architecture was applied to the literature. The Gothic style, which has the following elements, appealed to Edgar Allan Poe's dark view of the world:

- Bleak or remote settings
- Characters in psychological and/or physical torment
- Plots that involve weird or violent incidents and supernatural or otherworldly occurrences
- Strongly dramatic and intensely descriptive language
- A gloomy, melancholy, or eerie mood
- Symbolism that evokes ideas and feelings through repeated images

Practice

CITE TEXTUAL EVIDENCE to support your answers.

Use the chart to record passages from the story that exemplify elements of the Gothic literary tradition. Explain each choice.

GOTHIC ELEMENT	PASSAGE	EXPLANATION
bleak setting		
tortured characters		
strange or violent plot		
dramatic description		
gloomy mood		
recurring symbolism		

THE FALL OF THE HOUSE
OF USHER

Concept Vocabulary

| annihilate | fissure | rending |
| antiquity | dissolution | tumultuous |

Why These Words? These concept vocabulary words convey decay and destruction. For example, the narrator talks about a *fissure* in the wall, a long crack from the roof down, as evidence of the house's decay.

1. How does the concept vocabulary contribute to the sense of finality suggested by the title of the story?

2. What other words in the selection connect to the concepts of decay and destruction?

Practice

📓 **Notebook** The concept vocabulary words appear in "The Fall of the House of Usher."

1. Use the concept words to complete the paragraph.

   The black and suffocating night air hung close as _____ winds threatened to snap tree trunks and toss them aloft. Seeking shelter from the raging storm, I approached the gloomy mansion. The _____ of the home was obvious from the style, which had not been popular for a century. When my initial knocking produced no result, I began to bang harder and harder. A thin _____ in the wooden panel shuddered with each blow of my hand. Would my pounding lead to _____ this ancient slab in two? In my desperation to enter, I cared little that I might _____ the door. I had arrived to prevent the _____ of the family Usher.

2. Explain the context clues that help you determine the correct words.

Word Study

Denotation and Connotation A word's **denotation** is its literal definition that you would find in a dictionary. The associations or feelings that a word suggests are its **connotations**. Words can have connotations that express the extreme nature of an act or a quality. *Annihilate* means "to destroy completely." Its connotations suggest an extreme form of destruction in which something is not merely destroyed but utterly wiped out or obliterated. Complete these activities, using a thesaurus or college-level dictionary as needed.

1. Provide the denotation and connotations of *dissolution, antiquity,* and *tumultuous*.

2. Name a synonym for each concept vocabulary word, and tell how its connotations differ.

Conventions

Sentence Structure Sentences can be classified by the number of independent and dependent clauses they contain. An **independent clause** has a subject and a verb and can stand alone as a complete thought. A **dependent**, or **subordinate**, **clause** also has a subject and a verb, but it cannot stand alone as a complete thought.

This chart shows examples from "The Fall of the House of Usher" of the four basic sentence structures.

CLARIFICATION
Refer to the Grammar Handbook to learn more about these terms.

SENTENCE STRUCTURE	ELEMENTS	EXAMPLE
simple	a single <u>independent</u> clause	<u>The general furniture was profuse, comfortless, antique, and tattered.</u> (paragraph 7)
compound	two or more <u>independent</u> clauses, joined either by a comma and a coordinating conjunction or by a semicolon	<u>A servant in waiting took my horse</u>, and <u>I entered the Gothic archway of the hall.</u> (paragraph 6)
complex	one <u>independent</u> clause and one or more <u>dependent</u> clauses	<u>Although, as boys, we had been even intimate associates</u>, . . . <u>I really knew little of my friend</u>. (paragraph 3)
compound-complex	two or more <u>independent</u> clauses and one or more <u>dependent</u> clauses	<u>We sat down[,] and . . .</u> , <u>while he spoke not</u>, <u>I gazed upon him with a feeling half of pity, half of awe</u>. (paragraph 8)

Read It

1. Reread paragraph 2 of "The Fall of the House of Usher." Mark independent and dependent clauses. Then, classify each sentence as simple, compound, complex, or compound-complex.

2. Reread the final paragraph of the story. Identify the structure of each sentence.

Write It

📓 **Notebook** In the example, a simple sentence has been expanded to create other types of sentences. Expand the simple sentences below by adding details to create compound, complex, and compound-complex sentences.

> Example
> **Simple:** The house collapses.
> **Compound:** The house collapses, and the lake seems to swallow it whole.
> **Complex:** The house collapses as I flee in terror.
> **Compound-Complex:** The house collapses, and the lake seems to swallow it whole, as I flee in terror.

1. Madeline wanders in a distant hallway.

2. Usher sings a melancholy song.

📝 EVIDENCE LOG

Before moving on to a new selection, go to your Evidence Log and record what you learned from "The Fall of the House of Usher."

Comparing Texts

You will now read "House Taken Over." First, complete the first-read and close-read activities. Then, compare the literary styles of "The Fall of the House of Usher" and "House Taken Over."

THE FALL OF THE HOUSE OF USHER

HOUSE TAKEN OVER

About the Author

Julio Cortázar (1914–1984) grew up in a suburb of Buenos Aires, in Argentina. Because he had health problems as a child, he spent much of his time in bed, reading, but he grew to be an impressive man, about six feet six inches tall. His talents were impressive, too. After teaching for several years in Argentina, he moved to Paris, where he lived out his days writing and translating distinguished English-language literature, particularly that of Edgar Allan Poe, into Spanish. Cortázar remained connected to his Argentinian roots throughout his life.

🔧 Tool Kit
First-Read Guide and Model Annotation

☰ STANDARDS

Reading Literature
By the end of grade 10, read and comprehend literature, including stories, dramas, and poems, at the high end of the grades 9–10 text complexity band independently and proficiently.

House Taken Over

Concept Vocabulary

You will encounter the following words as you read "House Taken Over." Before reading, note how familiar you are with each word. Then, rank the words in order from most familiar (1) to least familiar (6).

WORD	YOUR RANKING
spacious	
unvoiced	
obscure	
recessed	
vestibule	
muffled	

After completing the first read, come back to the concept vocabulary and review your rankings. Mark changes to your original rankings as needed.

First Read FICTION

Apply these strategies as you conduct your first read. You will have an opportunity to complete the close-read notes after your first read.

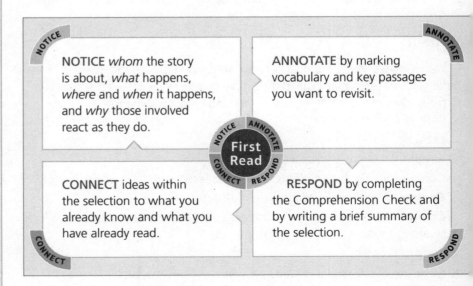

NOTICE *whom* the story is about, *what* happens, *where* and *when* it happens, and *why* those involved react as they do.

ANNOTATE by marking vocabulary and key passages you want to revisit.

CONNECT ideas within the selection to what you already know and what you have already read.

RESPOND by completing the Comprehension Check and by writing a brief summary of the selection.

First Read

House Taken Over

Julio Cortázar

BACKGROUND

In 1946, when this story was written, Julio Cortázar lived in Buenos Aires, Argentina. World War II had only recently ended, and Argentina was in a state of political turmoil. Young people, including Cortázar, were critical of a conservative element in the government that had refused to join the Allied cause against Adolf Hitler until late in the war, by which time communication with Europe had all but stopped. The young author left Buenos Aires five years after writing this story, in protest against the policies of Juan Peron, who was increasingly dominating Argentinian politics.

1   We liked the house because, apart from its being old and **spacious** (in a day when old houses go down for a profitable auction of their construction materials), it kept the memories of great-grandparents, our paternal grandfather, our parents and the whole of childhood.

> NOTES
>
> **spacious** (SPAY shuhs) *adj.*
> large; roomy

unvoiced (uhn VOYST) *adj.*
not spoken out loud or
expressed

obscure (uhb SKYAWR) *adj.*
not well-known

CLOSE READ

ANNOTATE: Mark details
in paragraphs 3 and 4 that
relate to the idea of being
necessary or unnecessary,
useful or useless.

QUESTION: Why might
concepts of necessity and
uselessness be important?

CONCLUDE: What do these
details show about the
characters and their lives?

2   Irene and I got used to staying in the house by ourselves, which
was crazy, eight people could have lived in that place and not have
gotten in each other's way. We rose at seven in the morning and got
the cleaning done, and about eleven I left Irene to finish off whatever
rooms and went to the kitchen. We lunched at noon precisely; then
there was nothing left to do but a few dirty plates. It was pleasant to
take lunch and commune with the great hollow, silent house, and it
was enough for us just to keep it clean. We ended up thinking, at times,
that that was what had kept us from marrying. Irene turned down
two suitors for no particular reason, and María Esther went and died
on me before we could manage to get engaged. We were easing into
our forties with the **unvoiced** concept that the quiet, simple marriage
of sister and brother was the indispensable end to a line established in
this house by our grandparents. We would die here someday, **obscure**
and distant cousins would inherit the place, have it torn down, sell the
bricks and get rich on the building plot; or more justly and better yet,
we would topple it ourselves before it was too late.

3   Irene never bothered anyone. Once the morning housework was
finished, she spent the rest of the day on the sofa in her bedroom,
knitting. I couldn't tell you why she knitted so much; I think women
knit when they discover that it's a fat excuse to do nothing at all. But
Irene was not like that, she always knitted necessities, sweaters for
winter, socks for me, handy morning robes and bedjackets for herself.
Sometimes she would do a jacket, then unravel it the next moment
because there was something that didn't please her; it was pleasant
to see a pile of tangled wool in her knitting basket fighting a losing
battle for a few hours to retain its shape. Saturdays I went downtown
to buy wool; Irene had faith in my good taste, was pleased with the
colors and never a skein[1] had to be returned. I took advantage of
these trips to make the rounds of the bookstores, uselessly asking if
they had anything new in French literature. Nothing worthwhile had
arrived in Argentina since 1939.

4   But it's the house I want to talk about, the house and Irene, I'm not
very important. I wonder what Irene would have done without her
knitting. One can reread a book, but once a pullover is finished you
can't do it over again, it's some kind of disgrace. One day I found that
the drawer at the bottom of the chiffonier, replete with mothballs, was
filled with shawls, white, green, lilac. Stacked amid a great smell of
camphor—it was like a shop; I didn't have the nerve to ask her what
she planned to do with them. We didn't have to earn our living, there
was plenty coming in from the farms each month, even piling up. But

---

1. **skein** (skayn) *n.* quantity of thread or yarn wound in a coil.

Irene was only interested in the knitting and showed a wonderful dexterity, and for me the hours slipped away watching her, her hands like silver sea urchins, needles flashing, and one or two knitting baskets on the floor, the balls of yarn jumping about. It was lovely.

5   How not to remember the layout of that house. The dining room, a living room with tapestries, the library and three large bedrooms in the section most **recessed**, the one that faced toward Rodríguez Peña.[2] Only a corridor with its massive oak door separated that part from the front wing, where there was a bath, the kitchen, our bedrooms and the hall. One entered the house through a **vestibule** with enameled tiles, and a wrought-iron grated door opened onto the living room. You had to come in through the vestibule and open the gate to go into the living room; the doors to our bedrooms were on either side of this, and opposite it was the corridor leading to the back section; going down the passage, one swung open the oak door beyond which was the other part of the house; or just before the door, one could turn to the left and go down a narrower passageway which led to the kitchen and the bath. When the door was open, you became aware of the size of the house; when it was closed, you had the impression of an apartment, like the ones they build today, with barely enough room to move around in. Irene and I always lived in this part of the house and hardly ever went beyond the oak door except to do the cleaning. Incredible how much dust collected on the furniture. It may be Buenos Aires[3] is a clean city, but she owes it to her population and nothing else. There's too much dust in the air, the slightest breeze and it's back on the marble console tops and in the diamond patterns of the tooled-leather desk set. It's a lot of work to get it off with a feather duster; the motes[4] rise and hang in the air, and settle again a minute later on the pianos and the furniture.

6   I'll always have a clear memory of it because it happened so simply and without fuss. Irene was knitting in her bedroom, it was eight at night, and I suddenly decided to put the water up for *mate*.[5] I went down the corridor as far as the oak door, which was ajar, then turned into the hall toward the kitchen, when I heard something in the library or the dining room. The sound came through muted and indistinct, a chair being knocked over onto the carpet or the **muffled** buzzing of a conversation. At the same time or a second later, I heard it at the end of the passage which led from those two rooms toward the door. I hurled myself against the door before it was too late and

2. **Rodríguez Peña** fashionable street in Buenos Aires.
3. **Buenos Aires** capital of Argentina.
4. **motes** *n.* specks of dust or other tiny particles.
5. *mate* (MAH tay) *n.* beverage made from the dried leaves of a South American evergreen tree.

NOTES

recessed (rih SEHST) *adj.* remote; set back

vestibule (VEHS tuh byool) *n.* entrance room

muffled (MUH fuhld) *adj.* difficult to hear because something is covering and softening the sound

CLOSE READ

ANNOTATE: In paragraphs 8–13, mark the short sentences.

QUESTION: Why does the author use so many shorter sentences?

CONCLUDE: How do these short sentences add to the portrayal of the characters' reactions?

shut it, leaned on it with the weight of my body; luckily, the key was on our side; moreover, I ran the great bolt into place, just to be safe.

7   I went down to the kitchen, heated the kettle, and when I got back with the tray of *mate,* I told Irene:

8   "I had to shut the door to the passage. They've taken over the back part."

9   She let her knitting fall and looked at me with her tired, serious eyes.

10   "You're sure?"

11   I nodded.

12   "In that case," she said, picking up her needles again, "we'll have to live on this side."

13   I sipped at the *mate* very carefully, but she took her time starting her work again. I remember it was a gray vest she was knitting. I liked that vest.

14   The first few days were painful, since we'd both left so many things in the part that had been taken over. My collection of French literature, for example, was still in the library. Irene had left several folios of stationery and a pair of slippers that she used a lot in the winter. I missed my briar pipe, and Irene, I think, regretted the loss of an ancient bottle of Hesperidin.[6] It happened repeatedly (but only in the first few days) that we would close some drawer or cabinet and look at one another sadly.

15   "It's not here."

16   One thing more among the many lost on the other side of the house.

17   But there were advantages, too. The cleaning was so much simplified that, even when we got up late, nine thirty for instance, by eleven we were sitting around with our arms folded. Irene got into the habit of coming to the kitchen with me to help get lunch. We thought about it and decided on this: while I prepared the lunch, Irene would cook up dishes that could be eaten cold in the evening. We were happy with the arrangement because it was always such a bother to have to leave our bedrooms in the evening and start to cook. Now we made do with the table in Irene's room and platters of cold supper.

18   Since it left her more time for knitting, Irene was content. I was a little lost without my books, but so as not to inflict myself on my sister, I set about reordering papa's stamp collection; that killed some time. We amused ourselves sufficiently, each with his own thing, almost always getting together in Irene's bedroom, which was the more comfortable. Every once in a while, Irene might say:

19   "Look at this pattern I just figured out, doesn't it look like clover?"

6. **Hesperidin** substance that comes from the rind of certain citrus fruits and is used for various medicinal purposes.

20   After a bit it was I, pushing a small square of paper in front of her so that she could see the excellence of some stamp or another from Eupen-et-Malmédy.[7] We were fine, and little by little we stopped thinking. You can live without thinking.

21   (Whenever Irene talked in her sleep, I woke up immediately and stayed awake. I never could get used to this voice from a statue or a parrot, a voice that came out of the dreams, not from a throat. Irene said that in my sleep I flailed about enormously and shook the blankets off. We had the living room between us, but at night you could hear everything in the house. We heard each other breathing, coughing, could even feel each other reaching for the light switch when, as happened frequently, neither of us could fall asleep.

22   Aside from our nocturnal rumblings, everything was quiet in the house. During the day there were the household sounds, the metallic click of knitting needles, the rustle of stamp-album pages turning. The oak door was massive, I think I said that. In the kitchen or the bath, which adjoined the part that was taken over, we managed to talk loudly, or Irene sang lullabies. In a kitchen there's always too much noise, the plates and glasses, for there to be interruptions from other sounds. We seldom allowed ourselves silence there, but when we went back to our rooms or to the living room, then the house grew quiet, half-lit, we ended by stepping around more slowly so as not to disturb one another. I think it was because of this that I woke up irremediably[8] and at once when Irene began to talk in her sleep.)

23   Except for the consequences, it's nearly a matter of repeating the same scene over again. I was thirsty that night, and before we went to sleep, I told Irene that I was going to the kitchen for a glass of water. From the door of the bedroom (she was knitting) I heard the noise in the kitchen; if not the kitchen, then the bath, the passage off at that angle dulled the sound. Irene noticed how brusquely I had paused, and came up beside me without a word. We stood listening to the noises, growing more and more sure that they were on our side of the oak door, if not the kitchen then the bath, or in the hall itself at the turn, almost next to us.

24   We didn't wait to look at one another. I took Irene's arm and forced her to run with me to the wrought-iron door, not waiting to look back. You could hear the noises, still muffled but louder, just behind us. I slammed the grating and we stopped in the vestibule. Now there was nothing to be heard.

25   "They've taken over our section," Irene said. The knitting had reeled off from her hands and the yarn ran back toward the door and

---

7. **Eupen-et-Malmédy** (yoo PEHN ay mahl may DEE) districts in eastern Belgium.
8. **irremediably** (ihr ih MEE dee uh blee) *adv.* in a way that cannot be helped or corrected.

disappeared under it. When she saw that the balls of yarn were on the other side, she dropped the knitting without looking at it.

26   "Did you have time to bring anything?" I asked hopelessly.

27   "No, nothing."

28   We had what we had on. I remembered fifteen thousand pesos[9] in the wardrobe in my bedroom. Too late now.

29   I still had my wrist watch on and saw that it was 11 P.M. I took Irene around the waist (I think she was crying) and that was how we went into the street. Before we left, I felt terrible; I locked the front door up tight and tossed the key down the sewer. It wouldn't do to have some poor devil decide to go in and rob the house, at that hour and with the house taken over. ❧

---

9. **fifteen thousand pesos** large sum of money at the time of the story.

Comprehension Check

Complete the following items after you finish your first read.

1. Briefly describe the house in which the narrator and his sister live.

2. What is the source of the siblings' income?

3. How do Irene and the narrator occupy their time?

4. What decision do Irene and the narrator make when they realize the back part of the house has been taken over?

5. What happens to the brother and sister at the end of the story?

6. **⬗ Notebook** Write a summary of "House Taken Over" to confirm your understanding of the story.

- -

RESEARCH

Research to Clarify Choose at least one unfamiliar detail from the text. Briefly research that detail. In what way does the information you learned shed light on an aspect of the story.

Research to Explore Research the origin of the story. Discover information about the home in Buenos Aires Province that inspired it.

Close Read the Text

1. This model, from paragraph 6 of the text, shows two sample annotations, along with questions and conclusions. Close read the passage, and find another detail to annotate. Then, write a question and your conclusion.

> **ANNOTATE:** The words describing the sounds the intruders make seem intentionally vague.
>
> **QUESTION:** Why does the writer give so little detail about the intruders?
>
> **CONCLUDE:** By providing only vague hints, the writer makes the invaders seem more frightening and mysterious.

Close Read
ANNOTATE · QUESTION · CONCLUDE

> **ANNOTATE:** The writer includes a series of action verbs in one sentence.
>
> **QUESTION:** Why does the writer pack all of these actions into a single sentence?
>
> **CONCLUDE:** Packed into one sentence, this series of urgent actions shows the narrator's intense fear.

> . . . I heard something in the library or the dining room. The sound came through muted and indistinct, a chair being knocked over onto the carpet or the muffled buzzing of a conversation. . . . I hurled myself against the door before it was too late and shut it, leaned on it with the weight of my body; luckily, the key was on our side; moreover, I ran the great bolt into place, just to be safe.

2. For more practice, go back into the text and complete the close-read notes.

3. Revisit a section of the text you found important during your first read. Read this section closely, and **annotate** what you notice. Ask yourself **questions** such as "Why did the author make this choice?" What can you **conclude**?

🔧 **Tool Kit**
Close-Read Guide and
Model Annotation

Analyze the Text

CITE TEXTUAL EVIDENCE
to support your answers.

📖 **Notebook** Respond to these questions.

1. **(a) Interpret** To what social class do the brother and sister belong? How do you know? **(b) Connect** How are the characters' hobbies evidence of their social class?

2. **(a) Compare and Contrast** How is the behavior the siblings exhibit during sleep different from their behavior while awake?
(b) Analyze What does this difference suggest about their true reactions to the invasion of the house?

3. **Extend** Cortázar wrote this story after having a nightmare. In what ways does this story resemble a nightmare? Explain.

4. **Essential Question:** *What is the allure of fear?* What have you learned from this story about portrayals of fear in literature?

▤ **STANDARDS**
Reading Literature
• Analyze how an author's choices concerning how to structure a text, order events within it, and manipulate time create such effects as mystery, tension, or surprise.
• Analyze a particular point of view or cultural experience reflected in a work of literature from outside the United States, drawing on a wide reading of world literature.

Analyze Craft and Structure

Literary Style "House Taken Over" is an example of **Magical Realism**, a literary genre closely associated with some Latin American twentieth-century authors. Magical Realism combines two seemingly contrasting elements: reality and fantasy. By introducing supernatural or unreal elements into carefully observed depictions of real life, writers in this genre shock and surprise readers while also providing insightful commentary on human nature and perceptions. Elements of magical realism include:

- Recognizable characters who feel, act, and react in customary ways
- Realistic settings that include ordinary details of everyday life
- Fantastic events that coexist with realistic characters and actions
- An accepting or unimpressed narrative **tone,** or attitude, that presents fantastic events as logical parts of life

Cortázar balances these elements carefully, creating a unique representation of a realistic world where dreamlike events can still happen.

Practice

CITE TEXTUAL EVIDENCE to support your answers.

Use the chart to record passages from the story that exemplify elements of Magical Realism. Explain each choice.

MAGICAL REALIST ELEMENT	PASSAGE(S)	EXPLANATION
Recognizable Characters		
Realistic Setting and Details		
Fantastic Events		
Unimpressed Tone		

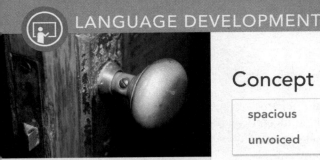

HOUSE TAKEN OVER

Concept Vocabulary

spacious	obscure	vestibule
unvoiced	recessed	muffled

Why These Words? These concept vocabulary words express different types of emptiness, including those of emotion, sound, and space. For example, the narrator describes one part of his home as being "the most recessed." Something *recessed* is set back or remote.

1. How does the author use the concept vocabulary to describe the house vividly and precisely?

2. What other words in the selection connect to the idea of emptiness?

Practice

 Notebook The concept vocabulary words appear in "House Taken Over." Tell whether each sentence is true or false, and explain why.

1. A *spacious* home would probably be cheaper than a cramped one.

2. People's loud, persistent complaints are usually *unvoiced*.

3. You should consider visiting *obscure* places if you want to avoid crowds.

4. A *recessed* set of shelves sticks out into a room.

5. A *vestibule* is a small building that stands at a distance from a house.

6. It is easy to understand a *muffled* announcement over a PA system.

Word Study

Patterns of Word Changes Suffixes and prefixes can be added to base words to change their meanings. Often, suffixes change a word's part of speech. The base word *space*, a noun—from the Latin *spatium*—becomes *spacious*, an adjective, when the suffix *-ious* is added.

1. The word *voice*, when it is used as a verb, means "to speak out loud." Explain how this word is changed by the addition of the prefix *un-* and the suffix *-ed*.

2. Find two other examples in the story of words that contain either a prefix or a suffix. Explain how the meaning of the base word is changed by the addition of the prefix or suffix.

WORD NETWORK

Add words related to fear from the text to your Word Network.

STANDARDS

Language
• Demonstrate command of the conventions of standard English grammar and usage when writing or speaking.
• Use various types of phrases and clauses to convey specific meanings and add variety and interest to writing or presentations.
• Identify and correctly use patterns of word changes that indicate different meanings or parts of speech.
• Demonstrate understanding of figurative language, word relationships, and nuances in word meanings.

Conventions

Types of Phrases A **preposition** connects a noun or a pronoun to another word in the sentence. A **prepositional phrase** is made up of a preposition, the object of the preposition, and any modifiers of the object. Prepositional phrases modify other words by functioning either as adjectives or as adverbs. In these examples from "House Taken Over," the prepositions are underlined once, and the objects of the prepositions are underlined twice.

TIP

CLARIFICATION
Refer to the Grammar Handbook to learn more about these terms.

in the house	*by ourselves*	*at seven*
of the day	*from the front wing*	*through a vestibule*
into the living room	*before the door*	*with a feather duster*
on the sofa	*down the corridor*	*against the door*

Read It

1. Mark all of the prepositional phrases in each sentence. Then, label each preposition and its object.

   a. I lived in this part of the house and rarely went beyond the oak door.

   b. A chair was knocked onto the carpet and dragged along the floor.

   c. I hurried toward the door and pushed the heavy bolt into place.

2. Reread paragraph 24 of the story. Mark the prepositional phrases, and tell how these phrases help to clarify the action.

Write It

📖 **Notebook** In the example, the second sentence in each pair contains prepositional phrases that help clarify, describe, or explain. Revise the paragraph below. Add prepositional phrases to make the paragraph more interesting and detailed.

> **EXAMPLE**
> I tossed the key. I tossed the key *down the drain* *in the gutter*.
> I heard a noise. *At midnight*, I heard a noise *behind the door*.

We heard a noise that was impossible to describe. When the noise grew louder, we decided to run. We didn't have time to grab anything. We found ourselves outside. We looked but could see nothing.

THE FALL OF THE HOUSE
OF USHER

HOUSE TAKEN OVER

Writing to Compare

You have read "The Fall of the House of Usher" and "House Taken Over," two short stories that have similarities but represent two different literary styles, or genres. Now, deepen your understanding of both stories by comparing and writing about them.

Assignment

Write an **explanatory essay** in which you compare and contrast Gothic style and Magical Realism as seen in the stories by Poe and Cortázar. Include the following elements in your essay:

- definitions of the two genres

- a discussion of how each story is a good example of its genre

- effective use of evidence from the stories

- an evaluation of the effect each story has on the reader

Make sure you are clear about the qualities that define the Gothic style and Magical Realism. If necessary, do a little research or reread the instruction about the genres.

Planning and Prewriting

Analyze the Texts When you are analyzing complex works, a smaller focus can help you see the bigger picture more clearly. For example, instead of analyzing all the elements of both stories, you might focus on the siblings, the supernatural elements, or another specific aspect of each story. For this assignment, compare and contrast the settings—the two houses and the worlds they occupy. Use the chart to gather story details that relate to that focus.

| FOCUS: DETAILS RELATED TO SETTING ||
THE FALL OF THE HOUSE OF USHER	HOUSE TAKEN OVER

Notebook Respond to these questions.

1. How are the settings of the two stories similar? How are they different?

2. In each story, how does the setting affect the characters and the choices they make?

STANDARDS

Reading Literature
Analyze how an author's choices concerning how to structure a text, order events within it, and manipulate time create such effects as mystery, tension, or surprise.

Writing
• Write informative/explanatory texts to examine and convey complex ideas, concepts, and information clearly and accurately through the effective selection, organization, and analysis of content.
• Draw evidence from literary or informational texts to support analysis, reflection, and research.
• Apply *grades 9–10 Reading standards* to literature.

Drafting

Synthesize Ideas Review your Prewriting notes. Decide how setting reveals Gothic sensibilities in Poe's story and Magical Realist ideas in Cortázar's story, and how those styles are both similar and different. Record your ideas using these sentence frames:

In both stories, the setting _____

_____

_____.

However, in Poe's story "The Fall of the House of Usher," the setting: _____

_____

_____.

Similarly/By contrast, in Cortázar's story "House Taken Over," the setting ____

_____

_____.

Identify Supporting Details Identify passages to use as examples for your ideas. Make sure each passage presents a clear similarity or difference, and demonstrates either a Gothic or a Magical Realist approach. Note the passages you will use and the ideas each one will support.

PASSAGE	IDEA

Organize Ideas Make some organizational decisions before you begin to write. Consider using one of these two structures:

Grouping Ideas: discuss all the similarities between the settings and genres of the two stories and then all the differences

Grouping Texts: discuss the setting and genre of one story and then the setting and genre of the other story

Review, Revise, and Edit

Once you are done drafting, review your essay. Because your essay is about multiple subjects—two different settings and two different genres—clarity and balance are critical. Reread your draft, and mark the points at which you discuss Poe's story and the Gothic. Use a different mark to identify the points at which you discuss Cortázar's story and Magical Realism. Check your draft to see if you have addressed the two stories in a balanced way. Add more analysis or examples as needed. Then, proofread and edit your essay for grammatical and spelling errors.

📝 EVIDENCE LOG

Before moving on to a new selection, go to your Evidence Log and record what you learned from "House Taken Over."

About the Designers

Adam Frost is a designer of websites, games, books, and exhibitions. His children's books include such titles as *Stop, There's a Snake in Your Suitcase!* Frost currently works as the Data Visualization Manager at the *Guardian* newspaper and specializes in creating infographic articles such as this one.

Zhenia Vasiliev is a London-based designer and graphic artist. His clients include Sony, Google, the *Guardian*, NBC Universal, and others. He has been featured in several art shows and is a recipient of the Macmillan Children's Books Prize.

STANDARDS
Reading Informational Text
• By the end of grade 10, read and comprehend literary nonfiction at the high end of the grades 9–10 text complexity band independently and proficiently.

from How to Tell You're Reading a Gothic Novel—In Pictures

Concept Vocabulary

You will encounter the following words as you read and view these informational graphics.

WORD	PRONUNCIATION AND MEANING
reclusive	(rih KLOO sihv) *adj.* solitary; avoiding the company of others
sinister	(SIHN uh stuhr) *adj.* giving the impression that something harmful or evil is happening or will happen
ethereal	(ih THIHR ee uhl) *adj.* extremely delicate and light in a way that seems too perfect for this world

First Read MEDIA: INFORMATIONAL GRAPHIC

Apply these strategies as you conduct your first read. You will have an opportunity to complete a close read after your first read.

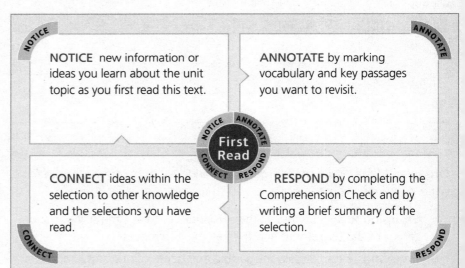

NOTICE new information or ideas you learn about the unit topic as you first read this text.

ANNOTATE by marking vocabulary and key passages you want to revisit.

First Read

CONNECT ideas within the selection to other knowledge and the selections you have read.

RESPOND by completing the Comprehension Check and by writing a brief summary of the selection.

Reading Strategy: Text and Graphics

As you encounter each screen of the informational graphic, read all of the text, and note how the different visuals support the text.

from How to Tell You're Reading a Gothic Novel—In Pictures

Adam Frost and Zhenia Vasiliev

BACKGROUND

The Gothic literary genre began in 1764 with Horace Walpole's novel *The Castle of Otranto*. The term *Gothic* came from the Visigoths, a Germanic people who once ruled land that includes what is now Spain, parts of Portugal, and France. The Visigoths contributed to the fall of the Roman Empire and were regarded as barbaric and wild. To this day, Gothic ideas, such as madness, horror, and the supernatural, remain popular in literature, movies, and television.

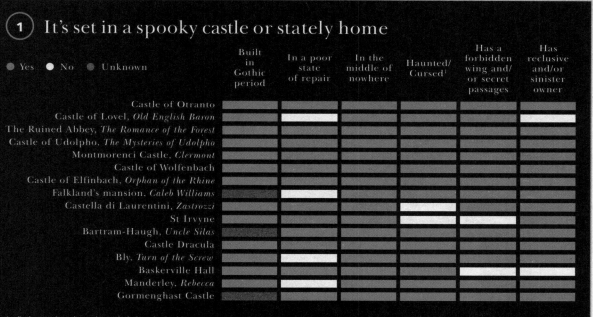

① It's set in a spooky castle or stately home

● Yes ● No ● Unknown

	Built in Gothic period	In a poor state of repair	In the middle of nowhere	Haunted/Cursed[1]	Has a forbidden wing and/or secret passages	Has a reclusive and/or sinister owner
Castle of Otranto						
Castle of Lovel, *Old English Baron*		No				No
The Ruined Abbey, *The Romance of the Forest*						
Castle of Udolpho, *The Mysteries of Udolpho*						
Montmorenci Castle, *Clermont*						
Castle of Wolfenbach						
Castle of Elfinbach, *Orphan of the Rhine*						
Falkland's mansion, *Caleb Williams*	Unknown	No				
Castella di Laurentini, *Zastrozzi*				No		
St Irvyne				No	No	
Bartram-Haugh, *Uncle Silas*						
Castle Dracula						
Bly, *Turn of the Screw*		No				
Baskerville Hall					No	No
Manderley, *Rebecca*		No				
Gormenghast Castle	Unknown					

1 By haunted, we have also included castles/buildings that are mistakenly believed to be haunted (e.g. Udolpho, Wolfenbach). Note that the haunting should ideally be linked to a terrible crime, usually the murder of the castle's legitimate owner or the current owner's wife, father or brother.

NOTES

② There is (probably) a ghost or monster[1]

GHOST	MONSTER	WITCH/ SORCERESS	VAMPIRE	THE DEVIL	NOT REALLY A GHOST AT ALL[2]
The Old English Baron	Frankenstein	Vathek	The Vampyre	The Monk	The Mysteries of Udolpho
A Christmas Carol	Wagner the Wehr-Wolf	The Lancashire Witches	Varney the Vampire	Zofloya	Wieland
The Uninhabited House	Dr Jekyll and Mr Hyde	She	'Carmilla'	Confessions of a Justified Sinner	The Castle of Wolfenbach
The Turn of the Screw	Lair of the White Worm	'The Withered Arm'	Dracula	Melmoth the Wanderer	The Italian

1   We focussed on eighteenth and nineteenth century Gothic here. After that, Gothic splits into innumerable sub-categories, 'weird fiction', 'horror', 'Southern Gothic', 'Southern Ontario Gothic' etc. Also, after 1900, it is film rather than prose that produces the most notable Gothic monsters. In addition, we focussed on English-language Gothic (so no Hoffman, Gogol etc) and 'serious' Gothic only – so no satires (e.g. Northanger Abbey). We had to impose some limits as Gothic is such a potentially gigantic subject – sorry if we missed any of your favourites.

2   In these stories, the groans, clankings and/or strange ethereal music end up being caused by dastardly humans. Think *Scooby Doo*.

NOTES

③ It's set in the olden days[1]

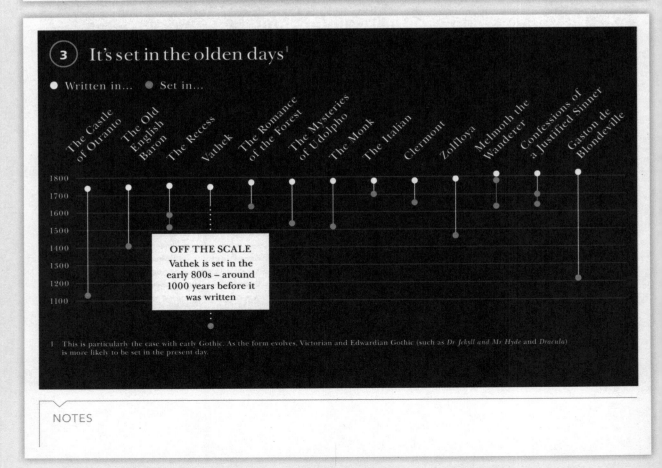

● Written in...   ● Set in...

OFF THE SCALE
Vathek is set in the early 800s – around 1000 years before it was written

1   This is particularly the case with early Gothic. As the form evolves, Victorian and Edwardian Gothic (such as *Dr Jekyll and Mr Hyde* and *Dracula*) is more likely to be set in the present day.

NOTES

4 The weather is always awful

Mentions of weather in key Gothic novels[1]

Wind · Storm · Thunder · Rain · Fog · Snow · Lightning · Mist · Sunshine/Sunny

1 We used 15 novels here: *Dracula, Frankenstein, Dr Jekyll and Mr Hyde, Melmoth the Wanderer, The Monk, The Castle of Otranto, The Mysteries of Udolpho, Caleb Williams, Confessions of a Justified Sinner, The Hound of the Baskervilles, The Picture of Dorian Gray, The Old English Baron, The Turn of the Screw, Vathek* and *Uncle Silas*.

Note: we only counted the terms/descriptions above when they were used to describe weather. So where a character exclaims 'By thunder!' or if they 'move like lightning', these occurrences are excluded.

NOTES

5 People talk funny

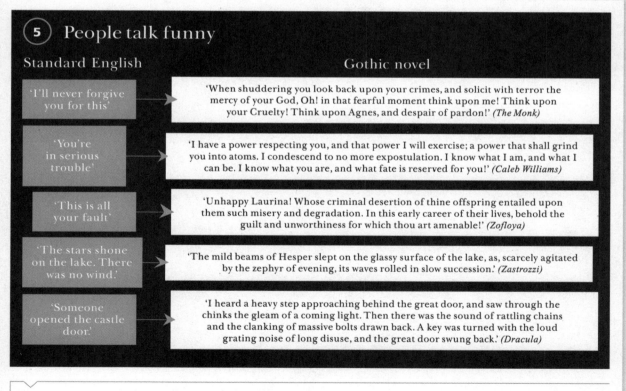

Standard English	Gothic novel
'I'll never forgive you for this'	'When shuddering you look back upon your crimes, and solicit with terror the mercy of your God, Oh! in that fearful moment think upon me! Think upon your Cruelty! Think upon Agnes, and despair of pardon!' *(The Monk)*
'You're in serious trouble'	'I have a power respecting you, and that power I will exercise; a power that shall grind you into atoms. I condescend to no more expostulation. I know what I am, and what I can be. I know what you are, and what fate is reserved for you!' *(Caleb Williams)*
'This is all your fault'	'Unhappy Laurina! Whose criminal desertion of thine offspring entailed upon them such misery and degradation. In this early career of their lives, behold the guilt and unworthiness for which thou art amenable!' *(Zofloya)*
'The stars shone on the lake. There was no wind.'	'The mild beams of Hesper slept on the glassy surface of the lake, as, scarcely agitated by the zephyr of evening, its waves rolled in slow succession.' *(Zastrozzi)*
'Someone opened the castle door.'	'I heard a heavy step approaching behind the great door, and saw through the chinks the gleam of a coming light. Then there was the sound of rattling chains and the clanking of massive bolts drawn back. A key was turned with the loud grating noise of long disuse, and the great door swung back.' *(Dracula)*

NOTES

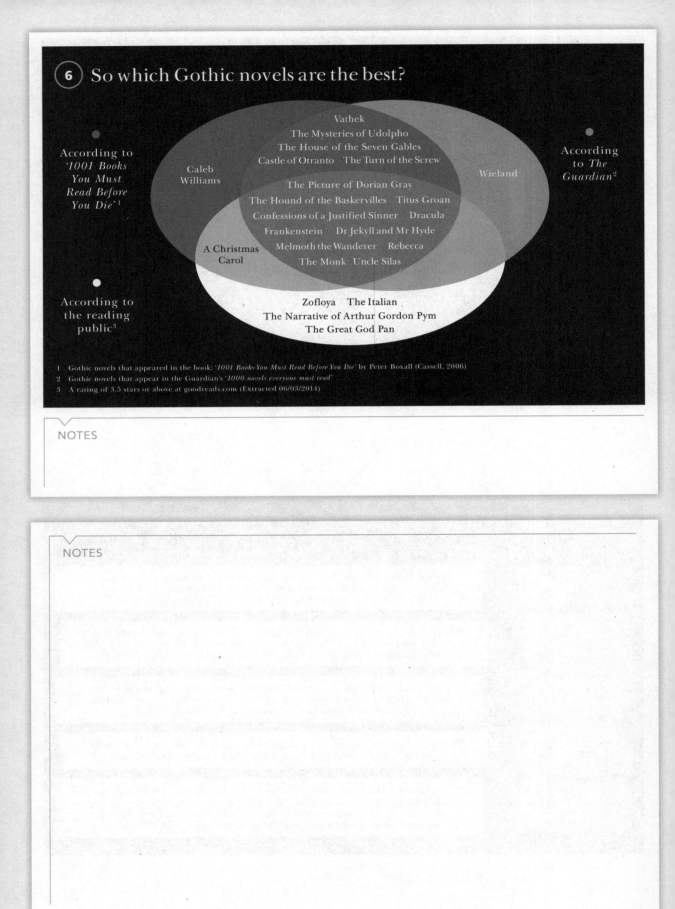

6 So which Gothic novels are the best?

According to '1001 Books You Must Read Before You Die'[1]

According to the reading public[3]

According to *The Guardian*[2]

Caleb Williams

Vathek
The Mysteries of Udolpho
The House of the Seven Gables
Castle of Otranto   The Turn of the Screw

Wieland

The Picture of Dorian Gray
The Hound of the Baskervilles   Titus Groan
Confessions of a Justified Sinner   Dracula
Frankenstein   Dr Jekyll and Mr Hyde
Melmoth the Wanderer   Rebecca
The Monk   Uncle Silas

A Christmas Carol

Zofloya   The Italian
The Narrative of Arthur Gordon Pym
The Great God Pan

1   Gothic novels that appeared in the book: '*1001 Books You Must Read Before You Die*' by Peter Boxall (Cassell, 2006)
2   Gothic novels that appear in the Guardian's '*1000 novels everyone must read*'
3   A rating of 3.5 stars or above at goodreads.com (Extracted 06/03/2014)

NOTES

NOTES

Comprehension Check

Complete the following items after you finish your first read.

1. Where do many Gothic novels take place?

2. What is the weather like in many Gothic novels?

3. What are some types of characters you might encounter in a Gothic novel?

4. When do most Gothic novels take place?

5. 🗒 **Notebook** Write a three- or four-sentence summary that describes the basic elements of Gothic literature.

- -

RESEARCH

Research to Clarify Choose at least one unfamiliar detail from the informational graphics. Briefly research that detail. In what way does the information you learned add to your understanding of the topic?

Research to Explore Choose something that interests you from the text, and formulate a research question.

HOW TO TELL YOU'RE READING A
GOTHIC NOVEL—IN PICTURES

Close Read the Text

Review the informational graphics again. **Annotate** details
that you notice. What **questions** do you have? What can
you **conclude**?

Analyze the Text

Notebook Respond to these questions.

1. **Make a Judgment** Consider the types of places in which the authors
   say Gothic novels are set. Do these places support the idea, presented
   in graphic 1, that all Gothic novels are set "in the middle of nowhere"?
   Explain.

2. **Infer** What types of events and moods would you expect to find in any
   Gothic novel?

3. **(a) Describe** What **tone**, or attitude, do these writers seem to take
   toward Gothic novels? Explain. **(b) Analyze** How does the tone add to
   the impact of the informational graphics?

4. **Essential Question:** *What is the allure of fear?* What have you learned
   about portrayals of fear in literature by reading this text?

WORD NETWORK

Add words related to
portrayals of fear in literature
from the text to your Word
Network.

Concept Vocabulary

| reclusive | sinister | ethereal |

Why These Words? The three concept vocabulary words relate to
different elements of Gothic literature.

1. How does the concept vocabulary help readers understand the elements
   of Gothic literature?

2. What other words in the informational graphics capture the essence of
   Gothic literature?

STANDARDS

Reading Informational Text
Cite strong and thorough textual
evidence to support analysis of what
the text says explicitly as well as
inferences drawn from the text.

Speaking and Listening
• Integrate multiple sources of
information presented in diverse
media or formats evaluating the
credibility and accuracy of each
source.
• Present information, findings,
and supporting evidence clearly,
concisely, and logically such that
listeners can follow the line of
reasoning and the organization,
development, substance, and style
are appropriate to purpose, audience,
and task.
• Make strategic use of digital
media in presentations to enhance
understanding of findings, reasoning,
and evidence and to add interest.

Practice

Notebook Confirm your understanding of the concept vocabulary
words by using them in sentences. Be sure to include context clues that
signal the meanings of the words.

Speaking and Listening

Assignment

Informational graphics, such as those presented in "How to Tell You're Reading A Gothic Novel—In Pictures," are an effective way to communicate ideas. The use of images, symbols, graphs, and text allows writers to explain and depict the complexities of a topic in a clear, engaging, and sometimes funny way. Create and present your own **informational graphic,** in which you show how elements of "The Fall of the House of Usher" combine to create a Gothic tale.

1. **Organize Your Content**

   - Use words, images, and symbols to create an informational graphic.
   - Sketch your ideas on a sheet of paper. Plan each element of your graphic separately.
   - Use symbols or icons to represent ideas. For example, you could use a small picture of a lightning bolt and clouds to represent stormy weather.
   - Consider using the concept vocabulary words (*reclusive, sinister, ethereal*) in your informational graphic.

2. **Prepare Your Presentation** When you have completed a draft of your informational graphic, review it to make sure it is accurate and visually engaging. Revise it as necessary to make it clearer or more interesting. Present your work to the class. As you share your graphic, keep these presentation techniques in mind:

   - Speak clearly and naturally, and avoid rushing.
   - Refer to your graphic, but try not to read from it. Instead, glance at it, and then make eye contact with your listeners.
   - Do your best to avoid standing in a stiff, uncomfortable way.

3. **Evaluate Presentations** As your classmates deliver their presentations, listen attentively. Use a presentation evaluation guide to analyze their presentations.

PRESENTATION EVALUATION GUIDE

Rate each statement on a scale of 1 (not demonstrated) to 6 (demonstrated).

☐ The speaker used examples from Poe's story effectively.

☐ The speaker maintained eye contact with the audience.

☐ The speaker seemed comfortable and at ease.

☐ The information was presented logically and effectively.

EVIDENCE LOG

Before moving on to a new selection, go to your Evidence Log and record what you learned from "How to Tell You're Reading a Gothic Novel—In Pictures."

WRITING TO SOURCES

- THE FALL OF THE HOUSE OF USHER
- HOUSE TAKEN OVER
- HOW TO TELL YOU'RE READING A GOTHIC NOVEL—IN PICTURES

🔧 **Tool Kit**
Student Model of an Explanatory Essay

ACADEMIC VOCABULARY

As you craft your essay, consider using some of the academic vocabulary you learned in the beginning of the unit.

dimension
motivate
manipulate
perspective
psychological

▤ STANDARDS

Writing
- Write informative/explanatory texts to examine and convey ideas, concepts, and information clearly and accurately through the effective selection, organization, and analysis of content.
- Write narratives to develop real or imagined experiences or events using effective technique, well-chosen details, and well-structured event sequences.
- Produce clear and coherent writing in which the development, organization, and style are appropriate to task, purpose, and audience.
- Draw evidence from literary or informational texts to support analysis, reflection, and research.
- Write routinely over extended time frames and shorter time frames for a range of tasks, purposes, and audiences.

Write an Explanatory Essay

You have just read three selections having to do with the literature of fear. In "The Fall of the House of Usher," Edgar Allan Poe creates a chilling Gothic tale in which a brother and sister seem to be decaying along with their house. In "House Taken Over," another brother and sister are driven from their home when it is invaded by unwelcome visitors—or is it? The creators of "How to Tell You're Reading a Gothic Novel—In Pictures" play infographic games with some scary elements of the Gothic tradition. Now, use your knowledge of the topic to write an explanatory essay about fear in life and literature. In addition to references to the texts, you will incorporate an anecdote, or brief story, as evidence to support your central idea.

Assignment

Use your knowledge of these texts and your own experience or observations to write an **explanatory essay** that answers this question:

How and when does imagination overcome reason?

Support your ideas with references to the selections in Whole-Class Learning, as well as an anecdote—or brief narrative—from your own experience, that of someone you know, film or TV, or another literary work. Present the narrative as a specific example of a general idea.

Elements of an Explanatory Essay with Narrative Evidence

An **explanatory essay** explains a topic by presenting information and insights in a logical, well-ordered sequence. An effective explanatory essay includes the following elements:

- a central point that will increase readers' knowledge of the subject or help readers understand the subject better
- varied evidence that engages readers and clarifies ideas—An anecdote, or brief narrative, is one type of evidence; facts examples, and textual details from literary works are other types of evidence.
- the use of transitions that clarify relationships among ideas
- precise language and correct grammar
- a tone appropriate to the audience and the subject

Analyze Writing Model

LAUNCH TEXT

Explanatory Essay Model For a model of a well-crafted explanatory essay that incorporates nonfiction narrative, see the Launch Text, "My Introduction to Gothic Literature."

Challenge yourself to find all the elements of an explanatory text that uses narrative evidence in the text. You will have the opportunity to review these elements as you start to write your essay.

Prewriting / Planning

Focus Your Ideas Think about the texts you've read. Consider how imagination works in "The Fall of the House of Usher" and "House Taken Over." Consider other examples in literature, popular culture, and your own life.

- What does imagination make the characters feel?

- What does it make them do?

- What happens when people "let their imaginations run away with them"?

Now, decide on your central point. What would you like to explain? Your central point should be an insight into how and when imagination can overcome reason and create mindless fear. Write a sentence that states the idea you want to explain to your readers.

Central Idea: _____

_____ .

Gather Evidence You have now given a lot of thought to your central idea. It's time to get specific. What evidence can you use to support your point? Think about these possibilities:

- Situations and events from "The Fall of the House of Usher," "House Taken Over," and other works of fiction

- Quotations from experts in psychology or sociology—people who study fear

- A brief narrative based on your own experience or your observations of others

Including thoughts and feelings about a relevant text will help make your essay stronger. For example, in the Launch Text, the writer explains what it was like to first read Poe's "The Cask of Amontillado."

> *But what struck me most was how Montresor spoke directly to the reader—to me. He expected my sympathy as he brought his terrible revenge. Up to that point, all the stories I had ever read had set the criminal or the lunatic at a distance. They didn't draw me into a mind that was a truly scary place to be. This one did.*
> —from "My Introduction to Gothic Literature"

Connect Across Texts As you write your essay, consider how the authors of the selections in Whole-Class Learning explore the relationships among imagination, reason, and fear. Make sure that you are conveying the ideas of the original text accurately.

EVIDENCE LOG

Review your Evidence Log and identify key details you may want to cite in your essay.

STANDARDS
Writing
- Introduce a topic; organize complex ideas, concepts, and information to make important connections and distinctions; include formatting, graphics and multimedia when useful to aiding comprehension.
- Develop a topic with well-chosen, relevant, and sufficient facts, extended definitions, concrete details, quotations, or other information and examples appropriate to the audience's knowledge of the topic.

Drafting

Identify Sources of Narrative Evidence The selections in Whole-Class Learning will provide most of your supporting evidence. However, you also need to incorporate an anecdote as a specific example of a general idea. Consider these types of sources for narrative evidence.

- **Real Life** Do you have friends who imagine dangers on amusement park rides to make them scarier? Have you ever been at a sleepover where people were trying to scare themselves and one another? These sorts of experiences may provide strong narrative evidence for your essay.

- **Movies** Have you seen movies about people who were in spooky situations? How did they behave? How did their imaginations affect their decisions?

- **Books** Have you read books in which people faced similar dangers but reacted in different ways? Who approached fear with reason? Who didn't? How did their reactions affect the outcome of events?

Use the chart to gather your ideas for different types of evidence you will use in this essay.

EVIDENCE	WHAT IT SHOWS ABOUT IMAGINATION, REASON, FEAR
example from real life	
example from media	
example from literature	

Connect Ideas and Evidence Use your insights from the selections in Whole-Class Learning to connect to your other evidence. For example, you might write, "In 'House Taken Over,' the brother and sister are afraid, but the source of that fear is mysterious. The unknown can be terrifying." You might support this point with a real-life example, such as this: "Last year, raccoons nested in our attic. At night, we heard murmurs and scurrying sounds. It was terrifying, until we learned what was causing it."

Maintain a Formal Style and Tone Throughout the essay, your style and tone should be appropriately formal, even during the section (or sections) in which you relate an anecdote. Avoid the use of slang and exclamations, and follow grammatical rules. Consider these examples.

Casual Style and Tone: I figured the sounds couldn't be anything that serious, but those raccoons totally freaked me out!

Appropriate Style and Tone: Reason told me there was no real danger, but the sounds of the raccoons terrified me anyway.

Use Appropriate Structure Begin your essay with a paragraph that draws the reader in and states your central point. Then, in a few paragraphs, present your evidence, including your narrative. Finish the essay with a conclusion that briefly summarizes your ideas and evidence. You may add a clever or thought-provoking last sentence.

☰ STANDARDS

Writing
• Develop the topic with well-chosen, relevant, and sufficient facts, extended definitions, concrete details, quotations, or other information and examples appropriate to the audience's knowledge of the topic.
• Establish and maintain a formal style and objective tone while attending to the norms and conventions of the discipline in which they are writing.
• Write narratives to develop real or imagined experiences or events using effective technique, well-chosen details, and wellstructured event sequences.

LANGUAGE DEVELOPMENT: AUTHOR'S STYLE

Descriptive Details

Descriptive details give readers precise information about people, settings, events, and ideas. These details often appeal to the senses—sight, hearing, smell, touch, and taste. For example, in the Launch Text, instead of writing, "The power went out," the author writes: "The power had been knocked out, and I was sitting at a window, watching the wet night grow darker." Descriptive details in characterization help create a sense that the reader can see, hear, and even know a person or character.

Read It

In these sentences from the selections and the Launch Text, the authors use precise, descriptive details to portray characters, settings, and events.

- *The now ghastly pallor of the skin, and the now miraculous luster of the eye, above all things startled and even awed me.* ("The Fall of the House of Usher")

- *[I]t was pleasant to see a pile of tangled wool in her knitting basket fighting a losing battle for a few hours to retain its shape.* ("House Taken Over")

- *As the clouds cleared, a fog rose and filtered the moonlight, casting a bluish hue over the yard.* ("My Introduction to Gothic Literature")

- *The stories helped me see that life can be a mansion full of secrets and dark passages, but also of beauty and light.* ("My Introduction to Gothic Literature")

- *In Poe's descriptions, I could practically smell the dust and mold.* ("My Introduction to Gothic Literature")

Write It

Think about the brief story or anecdote you are going to tell in your essay. Ask yourself, "Which details will make this story come alive for readers *and* support my main point about fear and imagination?" Then, fill in the chart with details. Try to identify details that relate to senses other than sight.

DETAILS ABOUT PEOPLE	DETAILS ABOUT SETTING	DETAILS ABOUT EVENTS

> **TIP**
>
> **STYLE**
> Make your descriptions as specific as possible. For example, when writing about a car, instead of "blue car," you might write "light-blue 1960s convertible."

STANDARDS
Writing
- Use precise language and domain-specific vocabulary to manage the complexity of the topic.
- Use precise words and phrases, telling details, and sensory language to convey a vivid picture of the experiences, events, setting, and/or characters.

Revising

Evaluating Your Draft

Use the following checklist to evaluate the effectiveness of your first draft. Then, use your evaluation and the instruction on this page to guide your revision.

FOCUS AND ORGANIZATION	EVIDENCE AND ELABORATION	CONVENTIONS
☐ Provides an introduction that clearly states a central idea about how fear can overcome reason.	☐ Includes specific details and descriptions to create a vivid picture of events and characters.	☐ Attends to the norms and conventions of the discipline, especially using descriptive details and precise language.
☐ Creates a smooth progression of ideas with appropriate transitions.	☐ Includes an anecdote or brief story that supports the central idea of the essay.	
☐ Presents a strong conclusion that follows from and reflects on the ideas and insights in the essay.	☐ Establishes a clear point of view.	

WORD NETWORK

Include interesting words from your Word Network in your explanatory essay.

STANDARDS

Writing
• Use appropriate and varied transitions to link the major sections of the text, create cohesion, and clarify the relationships among complex ideas and concepts.
• Provide a concluding statement or section that follows from and supports the information or explanation presented.
• Develop and strengthen writing as needed by planning, revising, editing, rewriting, or trying a new approach, focusing on addressing what is most significant for a specific purpose and audience.

Revising for Focus and Organization

Strengthen Your Conclusion Reread your essay, making sure you have set out your central idea in the introduction, developed it thoroughly in the body of your essay, and restated it in your conclusion. If your conclusion seems disconnected from the rest of the essay, consider these revision options:

- Reflect on the insights and ideas you expressed.
- Summarize your insights and ideas.
- Explain why the topic and your insights are important.

Revising for Evidence and Elaboration

Strengthen Transitions Make sure that the transitional words and phrases you use lead your reader logically from one idea to the next, or from an idea to its supporting evidence. Consider this abbreviated list of transitional expressions:

To introduce an example: *for example; to illustrate; in this case*

To introduce a second example: *in addition; furthermore; similarly*

To indicate cause and effect: *as a result; consequently; for this reason*

To indicate emphasis: *above all; in fact; certainly*

There are numerous transitional words, phrases, and expressions in English. Consult a style handbook or other resource to make sure you have chosen the ones that best express your meaning. Add or replace transitions in your essay as needed.

Exchange essays with a classmate. Use the checklist to evaluate your classmate's essay and provide supportive feedback.

1. Does the introduction clearly present the central point of the essay?

   ☐ yes   ☐ no   If no, explain what confused you.

2. Are the ideas and evidence, including an anecdote or other narrative, sequenced logically?

   ☐ yes   ☐ no   If no, what about the sequence did not work?

3. Does the conclusion flow directly from the writer's insights and reflections about how fear can overcome reason?

   ☐ yes   ☐ no   If no, explain what you thought was missing.

4. What is the strongest part of your classmate's essay? Why?

   _____

   _____

   _____

   _____

Editing and Proofreading

Edit for Conventions Reread your draft for accuracy and consistency. Correct errors in grammar and word usage. Edit to include a variety of sentence structures so that your essay reads well.

Proofread for Accuracy Read your draft carefully, looking for errors in spelling and punctuation. Quotation marks should surround a speaker's exact words or thoughts.

Publishing and Presenting

Create a final version of your explanatory essay. Share it with a small group so that your classmates can read it and make comments. In turn, review and comment on your classmates' work. Afterward, discuss what your different essays suggest about the ways in which one's imagination may overcome reason. Take turns speaking during the discussion.

Reflecting

Think about what you learned while writing your essay. What did you learn about planning your draft that you would use when writing another essay? What would you work to improve in your next essay? Finally, how did your combining explanation with narrative evidence help you understand imagination and reason better?

≡ STANDARDS

Writing
Develop and strengthen writing as needed by planning, revising, editing, rewriting, or trying a new approach, focusing on addressing what is most significant for a specific purpose and audience.

ESSENTIAL QUESTION:
What is the allure of fear?

In real life, fear is useful because it keeps us from doing dangerous things. However, there are other dimensions to fear that seem less logical. For example, what draws us to go on scary roller coasters? Why do we enjoy literature, movies, and art that let us dabble in our fears? The selections you will read present different answers to these questions. You will work in a group to continue exploring the allure of fear.

Small-Group Learning Strategies

Throughout your life, in school, in your community, and in your career, you will continue to develop strategies when you work in teams.

Review these strategies and the actions you can take to practice them. Add ideas of your own for each step. Get ready to use these strategies during Small-Group Learning.

STRATEGY	ACTION PLAN
Prepare	• Complete your assignments so that you are prepared for group work. • Organize your thinking so you can contribute to your group's discussion. •
Participate fully	• Make eye contact to signal that you are listening and taking in what is being said. • Use text evidence. •
Support others	• Build off ideas from others in your group. • Invite others who have not yet spoken to do so. •
Clarify	• Paraphrase the ideas of others to ensure that your understanding is correct. • Ask follow-up questions. •

CONTENTS

PERFORMANCE TASK

SPEAKING AND LISTENING FOCUS
Deliver an Explanatory Presentation
The Small-Group readings deal with our fears and how we may sometimes invite fear into our lives. After reading, you will produce a presentation on why we sometimes enjoy letting our imaginations get the best of us.

Working as a Team

1. **Choose a topic** In your group, discuss the following question:

   Does the emotion of fear make us stronger or weaker?

   As you take turns sharing your responses, be sure to provide details to explain your position. After all group members have shared, discuss some of the circumstances in which fear might make us stronger or weaker.

2. **List Your Rules** As a group, decide on the rules that you will follow as you work together. Samples are provided; add two more of your own. As you work together, you may add or revise the rules based on your experience working together.

   - Everyone should participate in group discussions.
   - People should not interrupt.

   - _____

     _____

   - _____

     _____

3. **Apply the Rules** Share what you have learned about the literature of fear. Make sure each person in the group contributes. Take notes and be prepared to share with the class one thing that you heard from another member of your group.

4. **Name Your Group** Choose a name that reflects the unit topic.

   Our group's name: _____

5. **Create a Communication Plan** Decide how you want to communicate with one another. For example, you might use online collaboration tools, email, or instant messaging.

   Our group's decision: _____

   _____

Making a Schedule

First, find out the due dates for the Small-Group activities. Then, preview the texts and activities with your group, and make a schedule for completing the tasks.

SELECTION	ACTIVITIES	DUE DATE
Where Is Here?		
The Dream Collector		
Why Do Some Brains Enjoy Fear?		
beware: do not read this poem The Raven Windigo		

Working on Group Projects

As your group works together, you'll find it more effective if each person has a specific role. Different projects require different roles. Before beginning a project, discuss the necessary roles, and choose one for each group member. Here are some possible roles; add your own ideas.

Project Manager: monitors the schedule and keeps everyone on task

Researcher: organizes research activities

Recorder: takes notes during group meetings

_____

_____

_____

_____

_____

About the Author

Joyce Carol Oates
(b. 1937) began writing
novels at age fourteen when
she received a typewriter as a
gift. In 1960, she graduated
first in her class from
Syracuse University. Oates,
who teaches at Princeton
University, is famous for
having wide-ranging
interests. She has written
novels, short stories, poetry,
plays, and essays in many
different styles and genres.
Her writing often combines
the small matters of everyday
life with violence and horror.

Where Is Here?

Concept Vocabulary

As you perform your first read of "Where Is Here?" you will encounter the following words.

gregarious	amiably	stoical

Context Clues If these words are unfamiliar to you, try using **context clues**—other words and phrases that appear in the text—to help you determine their meanings. There are various types of context clues that may help you as you read. This box shows three examples.

> **Synonyms:** The recent **dearth** of milk has resulted in a <u>shortage</u> of other dairy products.
>
> **Elaborating Details:** During her campaign, the senator was positively **monomaniacal,** <u>speaking passionately about one issue and one issue only</u>.
>
> **Contrast of Ideas:** The <u>shallowness</u> of the second speech made the **profundity** of the first even more evident.

Apply your knowledge of context clues and other vocabulary strategies to determine the meanings of unfamiliar words you encounter during your first read.

First Read FICTION

Apply these strategies as you conduct your first read. You will have an opportunity to complete a close read after your first read.

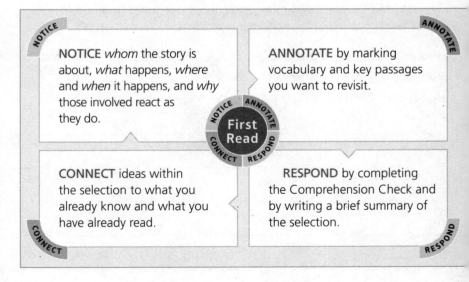

NOTICE *whom* the story is about, *what* happens, *where* and *when* it happens, and *why* those involved react as they do.

ANNOTATE by marking vocabulary and key passages you want to revisit.

CONNECT ideas within the selection to what you already know and what you have already read.

RESPOND by completing the Comprehension Check and by writing a brief summary of the selection.

▤ STANDARDS

Reading Literature
By the end of grade 10, read and
comprehend literature, including
stories, dramas, and poems at the
high end of the grades 9–10 text
complexity band independently and
proficiently.

Language
• Determine or clarify the meaning
of unknown and multiple-meaning
words and phrases based on *grades
9–10 reading and content*, choosing
flexibly from a range of strategies.

• Use context as a clue to the
meaning of a word or phrase.

Where Is Here?

Joyce Carol Oates

BACKGROUND

The novels of Ann Radcliffe, an English writer, and the short stories of Edgar Allan Poe inspired Joyce Carol Oates to write Gothic literature. "Horror is a fact of life," she has said. "As a writer I'm fascinated by all facets of life." In this story, Oates highlights the uncertainty and potential danger that lurk under the surface of everyday events.

1   For years they had lived without incident in their house in a quiet residential neighborhood when, one November evening at dusk, the doorbell rang, and the father went to answer it, and there on his doorstep stood a man he had never seen before. The stranger apologized for disturbing him at what was probably the dinner hour and explained that he'd once lived in the house—"I mean, I was a child in this house"—and since he was in the city on business he thought he would drop by. He had not seen the house since January 1949 when he'd been eleven years old and his widowed mother had sold it and moved away but, he said, he thought of it often, dreamt of it often, and never more powerfully than in recent months. The father said, "Would you like to come inside for a few minutes and look around?" The stranger hesitated, then said firmly, "I think I'll just poke around outside for a while, if you don't mind. That might be sufficient." He was in his late forties, the father's approximate age. He wore a dark suit, conservatively cut; he was hatless, with thin silver-tipped neatly combed hair; a plain, sober, intelligent face and frowning eyes. The father, reserved by nature, but genial and even gregarious when taken unaware, said amiably, "Of course we don't mind. But I'm afraid many things have changed since 1949."

2   So, in the chill, damp, deepening dusk, the stranger wandered around the property while the mother set the dining room table and the father peered covertly out the window. The children were upstairs in their rooms. "Where is he now?" the mother asked. "He just went into the garage," the father said. "The garage! What does he want in

NOTES

Mark context clues or indicate another strategy you used that helped you determine meaning.

gregarious (gruh GAIR ee uhs) *adj.*

MEANING:

amiably (AY mee uh blee) *adv.*

MEANING:

there?" the mother said uneasily. "Maybe you'd better go out there with him." "He wouldn't want anyone with him," the father said. He moved stealthily to another window, peering through the curtains. A moment passed in silence. The mother, paused in the act of setting down plates, neatly folded paper napkins, and stainless-steel cutlery, said impatiently, "And where is he now? I don't like this." The father said, "Now he's coming out of the garage," and stepped back hastily from the window. "Is he going now?" the mother asked. "I wish I'd answered the door." The father watched for a moment in silence then said, "He's headed into the backyard." "Doing what?" the mother asked. "Not *do*ing anything, just walking," the father said. "He seems to have a slight limp." "Is he an older man?" the mother asked. "I didn't notice," the father confessed. "Isn't that just like you!" the mother said.

3   She went on worriedly, "He could be anyone, after all. Any kind of thief, or mentally disturbed person, or even murderer. Ringing our doorbell like that with no warning and you don't even know what he looks like!"

4   The father had moved to another window and stood quietly watching, his cheek pressed against the glass. "He's gone down to the old swings. I hope he won't sit in one of them, for memory's sake, and try to swing—the posts are rotted almost through." The mother drew breath to speak but sighed instead, as if a powerful current of feeling had surged through her. The father was saying, "Is it possible he remembers those swings from his childhood? I can't believe they're actually that old." The mother said vaguely, "They were old when we bought the house." The father said, "But we're talking about forty years or more, and that's a long time." The mother sighed again, involuntarily. "Poor man!" she murmured. She was standing before her table but no longer seeing it. In her hand were objects—forks, knives, spoons—she could not have named. She said, "We can't bar the door against him. That would be cruel." The father said, "What? No one has barred any door against anyone." "Put yourself in his place," the mother said. "He told me he didn't *want* to come inside," the father said. "Oh—isn't that just like you!" the mother said in exasperation.

5   Without a further word she went to the back door and called out for the stranger to come inside, if he wanted, when he had finished looking around outside.

6   They introduced themselves rather shyly, giving names, and forgetting names, in the confusion of the moment. The stranger's handshake was cool and damp and tentative. He was smiling hard, blinking moisture from his eyes; it was clear that entering his childhood home was enormously exciting yet intimidating to him. Repeatedly he said, "It's so nice of you to invite me in—I truly hate to disturb you—I'm really so grateful, and so—" But the perfect word eluded him. As he spoke his eyes darted about the kitchen almost like eyes out of control. He stood in an odd stiff posture, hands gripping the lapels of his suit as if he meant to crush them. The mother,

meaning to break the awkward silence, spoke warmly of their satisfaction with the house and with the neighborhood, and the father concurred, but the stranger listened only politely, and continued to stare, and stare hard. Finally he said that the kitchen had been so changed—"so modernized"—he almost didn't recognize it. The floor tile, the size of the windows, something about the position of the cupboards—all were different. But the sink was in the same place of course; and the refrigerator and stove; and the door leading down to the basement—"That *is* the door leading down to the basement, isn't it?" He spoke strangely, staring at the door. For a moment it appeared he might ask to be shown the basement but the moment passed, fortunately—this was not a part of their house the father and mother would have been comfortable showing to a stranger.

7   Finally, making an effort to smile, the stranger said, "Your kitchen is so—pleasant." He paused. For a moment it seemed he had nothing further to say. Then, "A—controlled sort of place. My mother— When we lived here—" His words trailed off into a dreamy silence and the mother and father glanced at each other with carefully neutral expressions.

8   On the windowsill above the sink were several lushly blooming African violet plants in ceramic pots and these the stranger made a show of admiring. Impulsively he leaned over to sniff the flowers— "Lovely!"—though African violets have no smell. As if embarrassed, he said, "Mother too had plants on this windowsill but I don't recall them ever blooming."

9   The mother said tactfully, "Oh, they were probably the kind that don't bloom—like ivy."

10   In the next room, the dining room, the stranger appeared to be even more deeply moved. For some time he stood staring, wordless. With fastidious slowness he turned on his heel, blinking, and frowning, and tugging at his lower lip in a rough gesture that must have hurt. Finally, as if remembering the presence of his hosts, and the necessity for some display of civility, the stranger expressed his admiration for the attractiveness of the room, and its coziness. He'd remembered it as cavernous, with a ceiling twice as high. "And dark most of the time," he said wonderingly. "Dark by day, dark by night." The mother turned the lights of the little brass chandelier to their fullest: shadows were dispersed like ragged ghosts and the cut-glass fruit bowl at the center of the table glowed like an exquisite multifaceted jewel. The stranger exclaimed in surprise. He'd extracted a handkerchief from his pocket and was dabbing carefully at his face, where beads of perspiration shone. He said, as if thinking aloud, still wonderingly, "My father was a unique man. Everyone who knew him admired him. He sat *here*," he said, gingerly touching the chair that was in fact the father's chair, at one end of the table. "And Mother sat *there*," he said, merely pointing. "I don't recall my own place or my sister's but I suppose it doesn't matter. . . . I see you have four place settings, Mrs. . . . ? Two children, I suppose?" "A boy

eleven, and a girl thirteen," the mother said. The stranger stared not at her but at the table, smiling. "And so too *we* were—I mean, there were two of us: my sister and me."

11   The mother said, as if not knowing what else to say, "Are you—close?"

12   The stranger shrugged, distractedly rather than rudely, and moved on to the living room.

13   This room, cozily lit as well, was the most carefully furnished room in the house. Deep-piled wall-to-wall carpeting in hunter green, cheerful chintz[1] drapes, a sofa and matching chairs in nubby heather green, framed reproductions of classic works of art, a gleaming gilt-framed mirror over the fireplace: wasn't the living room impressive as a display in a furniture store? But the stranger said nothing at first. Indeed, his eyes narrowed sharply as if he were confronted with a disagreeable spectacle. He whispered, "Here too! Here too!"

14   He went to the fireplace, walking, now, with a decided limp; he drew his fingers with excruciating slowness along the mantel as if testing its materiality. For some time he merely stood, and stared, and listened. He tapped a section of wall with his knuckles—"There used to be a large water stain here, like a shadow."

15   "Was there?" murmured the father out of politeness, and "Was there!" murmured the mother. Of course, neither had ever seen a water stain there.

16   Then, noticing the window seat, the stranger uttered a soft surprised cry, and went to sit in it. He appeared delighted: hugging his knees like a child trying to make himself smaller. "This was one of my happy places! At least when Father wasn't home. I'd hide away here for hours, reading, daydreaming, staring out the window! Sometimes Mother would join me, if she was in the mood, and we'd plot together—oh, all sorts of fantastical things!" The stranger remained sitting in the window seat for so long, tears shining in his eyes, that the father and mother almost feared he'd forgotten them. He was stroking the velvet fabric of the cushioned seat, gropingly touching the leaded windowpanes. Wordlessly, the father and mother exchanged a glance: who was this man, and how could they tactfully get rid of him? The father made a face signaling impatience and the mother shook her head without seeming to move it. For they couldn't be rude to a guest in their house.

17   The stranger was saying in a slow, dazed voice, "It all comes back to me now. How could I have forgotten! Mother used to read to me, and tell me stories, and ask me riddles I couldn't answer. 'What creature walks on four legs in the morning, two legs at midday, three legs in the evening?' 'What is round, and flat, measuring mere inches in one direction, and infinity in the other?' 'Out of what does our life arise? Out of what does our consciousness arise? Why are we here? Where *is* here?'"

---

1. **chintz** *n.* printed cotton fabric used especially for curtains and upholstery.

18   The father and mother were perplexed by these strange words and hardly knew how to respond. The mother said uncertainly, "Our daughter used to like to sit there too, when she was younger. It *is* a lovely place." The father said with surprising passion, "I hate riddles—they're moronic some of the time and obscure the rest of the time." He spoke with such uncharacteristic rudeness, the mother looked at him in surprise.

19   Hurriedly she said, "Is your mother still living, Mr. . . . ?" "Oh no. Not at all," the stranger said, rising abruptly from the window seat, and looking at the mother as if she had said something mildly preposterous. "I'm sorry," the mother said. "Please don't be," the stranger said. "We've all been dead—*they've* all been dead—a long time."

20   The stranger's cheeks were deeply flushed as if with anger and his breath was quickened and audible.

21   The visit might have ended at this point but so clearly did the stranger expect to continue on upstairs, so purposefully, indeed almost defiantly, did he limp his way to the stairs, neither the father nor the mother knew how to dissuade him. It was as if a force of nature, benign at the outset, now uncontrollable, had swept its way into their house! The mother followed after him saying nervously, "I'm not sure what condition the rooms are in, upstairs. The children's rooms especially—" The stranger muttered that he did not care in the slightest about the condition of the household and continued on up without a backward glance.

22   The father, his face burning with resentment and his heart accelerating as if in preparation for combat, had no choice but to follow the stranger and the mother up the stairs. He was flexing and unflexing his fingers as if to rid them of stiffness.

23   On the landing, the stranger halted abruptly to examine a stained-glass fanlight—"My God, I haven't thought of this in years!" He spoke excitedly of how, on tiptoe, he used to stand and peek out through the diamonds of colored glass, red, blue, green, golden yellow: seeing with amazement the world outside so *altered*. "After such a lesson it's hard to take the world on its own terms, isn't it?" he asked. The father asked, annoyed, "On what terms should it be taken, then?" The stranger replied, regarding him levelly, with a just perceptible degree of disdain, "Why, none at all."

24   It was the son's room—by coincidence, the stranger's old room—the stranger most wanted to see. Other rooms on the second floor, the "master" bedroom in particular, he decidedly did not want to see. As he spoke of it, his mouth twitched as if he had been offered something repulsive to eat.

25   The mother hurried on ahead to warn the boy to straighten up his room a bit. No one had expected a visitor this evening! "So you have two children," the stranger murmured, looking at the father with a small quizzical smile. "Why?" The father stared at him as if he hadn't heard correctly. "'Why'?" he asked. "Yes. *Why*?" the stranger repeated. They looked at each other for a long strained moment, then

the stranger said quickly, "But you love them—of course." The father controlled his temper and said, biting off his words, "Of course."

26   "Of course, of course," the stranger murmured, tugging at his necktie and loosening his collar, "otherwise it would all come to an end." The two men were of approximately the same height but the father was heavier in the shoulders and torso; his hair had thinned more severely so that the scalp of the crown was exposed, flushed, damp with perspiration, sullenly alight.

27   With a stiff avuncular[2] formality the stranger shook the son's hand. "So this is your room, now! So you live here, now!" he murmured, as if the fact were an astonishment. Not used to shaking hands, the boy was stricken with shyness and cast his eyes down. The stranger limped past him, staring. "The same!—the same!—walls, ceiling, floor—window—" He drew his fingers slowly along the windowsill; around the frame; rapped the glass, as if, again, testing materiality; stooped to look outside—but it was night, and nothing but his reflection bobbed in the glass, ghostly and insubstantial. He groped against the walls, he opened the closet door before the mother could protest, he sat heavily on the boy's bed, the springs creaking beneath him. He was panting, red-faced, dazed. "And the ceiling overhead,"

---

2. **avuncular** (uh VUHN kyoo luhr) *adj.* having traits considered typical of uncles; jolly, indulgent, stodgy.

he whispered. He nodded slowly and repeatedly, smiling. "And the floor beneath. That is what *is*."

28   He took out his handkerchief again and fastidiously wiped his face. He made a visible effort to compose himself.

29   The father, in the doorway, cleared his throat and said, "I'm afraid it's getting late—it's almost six."

30   The mother said, "Oh yes I'm afraid—I'm afraid it *is* getting late. There's dinner, and the children have their homework—"

31   The stranger got to his feet. At his full height he stood for a precarious moment swaying, as if the blood had drained from his head and he was in danger of fainting. But he steadied himself with a hand against the slanted dormer ceiling. He said, "Oh yes!—I know!—I've disturbed you terribly!—you've been so *kind*." It seemed, surely, as if the stranger *must* leave now, but, as chance had it, he happened to spy, on the boy's desk, an opened mathematics textbook and several smudged sheets of paper, and impulsively offered to show the boy a mathematical riddle—"You can take it to school tomorrow and surprise your teacher!"

32   So, out of dutiful politeness, the son sat down at his desk and the stranger leaned familiarly over him, demonstrating adroitly with a ruler and a pencil how "what we call 'infinity'" can be contained within a small geometrical figure on a sheet of paper. "First you draw a square; then you draw a triangle to fit inside the square; then you draw a second triangle, and a third, and a fourth, each to fit inside the square, but without their points coinciding, and as you continue—here, son, I'll show you—give me your hand, and I'll show you—the border of the triangles' common outline gets more complex and measures larger, and larger, and larger—and soon you'll need a magnifying glass to see the details, and then you'll need a microscope, and so on and so forth, forever, laying triangles neatly down to fit inside the original square *without their points coinciding*—!" The stranger spoke with increasing fervor; spittle gleamed in the corners of his mouth. The son stared at the geometrical shapes rapidly materializing on the sheet of paper before him with no seeming comprehension but with a rapt staring fascination as if he dared not look away.

33   After several minutes of this the father came abruptly forward and dropped his hand on the stranger's shoulder. "The visit is over," he said calmly. It was the first time since they'd shaken hands that the two men had touched, and the touch had a galvanic[3] effect upon the stranger: he dropped ruler and pencil at once, froze in his stooped posture, burst into frightened tears.

34   Now the visit truly was over; the stranger, at last, *was* leaving, having wiped away his tears and made a **stoical** effort to compose himself; but on the doorstep, to the father's astonishment, he made a final, preposterous appeal—he wanted to see the basement. "Just to sit on

---

3. **galvanic** (gal VAN ihk) *adj.* startling; stimulating as if by electric current.

Mark context clues or indicate another strategy you used that helped you determine meaning.

stoical (STOH ih kuhl) *adj.*

MEANING:

the stairs? In the dark? For a few quiet minutes? And you could close the door and forget me, you and your family could have your dinner and—"

35   The stranger was begging but the father was resolute. Without raising his voice he said, "No. *The visit is over.*"

36   He shut the door, and locked it.

37   Locked it! His hands were shaking and his heart beat angrily.

38   He watched the stranger walk away—out to the sidewalk, out to the street, disappearing in the darkness. Had the streetlights gone out?

39   Behind the father the mother stood apologetic and defensive, wringing her hands in a classic stance. "Wasn't that sad! Wasn't that—*sad!* But we had no choice but to let him in, it was the only decent thing to do." The father pushed past her without comment. In the living room he saw that the lights were flickering as if on the brink of going out; the patterned wallpaper seemed drained of color; a shadow lay upon it shaped like a bulbous cloud or growth. Even the robust green of the carpeting looked faded. Or was it an optical illusion? Everywhere the father looked, a pulse beat mute with rage. "*I* wasn't the one who opened the door to that man in the first place," the mother said, coming up behind the father and touching his arm. Without seeming to know what he did the father violently jerked his arm and thrust her away.

40   "Shut up. We'll forget it," he said.

41   "But—"

42   "*We'll forget it.*"

43   The mother entered the kitchen walking slowly as if she'd been struck a blow. In fact, a bruise the size of a pear would materialize on her forearm by morning. When she reached out to steady herself she misjudged the distance of the doorframe—or did the doorframe recede an inch or two—and nearly lost her balance.

44   In the kitchen the lights were dim and an odor of sourish smoke, subtle but unmistakable, made her nostrils pinch.

45   She slammed open the oven door. Grabbed a pair of pot holders with insulated linings. "*I* wasn't the one, . . ." she cried, panting, "and you know it." ❧

Comprehension Check

Complete the following items after you finish your first read. Review and clarify
details with your group.

1. Why has the stranger come to visit the house?

2. What are the initial suspicions that the mother has about the stranger?

3. How does the stranger react when the father tells him, "The visit is over"?

4. How do the rooms of the house seem changed after the stranger's visit?

5. 🔲 **Notebook** Choose four key events that best capture the plot of the story.
Write a summary of the story based on these four events.

- -

RESEARCH

Research to Clarify Choose at least one unfamiliar detail from the text. Briefly
research that detail. In what way does the information you learned shed light on an
aspect of the story?

Research to Explore This story may spark your curiosity to learn more about the author
or the genre. Briefly research a topic that interests you. You may want to share what you
learn with your group.

WHERE IS HERE?

Close Read the Text

With your group, revisit sections of the text you marked during your first read. **Annotate** details that you notice. What **questions** do you have? What can you **conclude**?

Analyze the Text

CITE TEXTUAL EVIDENCE
to support your answers.

Complete the activities.

1. **Review and Clarify** With your group, reread paragraph 25. The stranger discovers the father has two children and asks, "Why?" Do you find that question unsettling? Explain.

2. **Present and Discuss** Now, work with your group to share other key passages from "Where Is Here?" What made you choose these particular passages? Take turns presenting your passages. Discuss what details you noticed, what questions you asked, and what conclusions you reached.

3. **Essential Question:** *What is the allure of fear?* What has this selection taught you about portrayals of fear in literature? Discuss with your group.

LANGUAGE DEVELOPMENT

Concept Vocabulary

| gregarious | amiably | stoical |

Why These Words? The three concept vocabulary words are related. With your group, determine what the words have in common. How do these word choices enhance the impact of the text?

Practice

 Notebook Confirm your understanding of each word by using it in a sentence. Be sure to use context clues that suggest the word's meaning.

Word Study

Notebook **Adverbs of Manner** An **adverb** is a word that modifies a verb, an adjective, or another adverb. Many adverbs, particularly those describing the manner in which an action verb is performed, are formed by adding the Anglo-Saxon suffix *-ly* to an adjective. Sometimes, the addition of this suffix requires a change in the ending of the adjective. For instance, the father in "Where Is Here?" states something *amiably*—or in an *amiable* manner.

Reread paragraph 2 of the story. Mark the adverbs ending in *-ly*. Then, write the adjectives from which they are formed.

WORD NETWORK
Add words related to fear from the text to your Word Network.

STANDARDS
Reading Literature
Analyze how an author's choices concerning how to structure a text, order events within it, and manipulate time (e.g., pacing, flashbacks) create such effects.

Language
• Spell correctly.

• Identify and correctly use patterns of word changes that indicate different meanings or parts of speech.

Analyze Craft and Structure

Literary Style Through the use of gloomy settings, suffering characters, supernatural events, and sudden plot twists, traditional Gothic writers such as Edgar Allan Poe constructed stories of imagination, fear, and horror. Today, **modern Gothic** writers still produce stories marked by fear and dread. However, they modify elements to suit modern tastes and ideas.

LITERARY ELEMENT	TRADITIONAL GOTHIC	MODERN GOTHIC
Setting	Remote, exotic settings, such as a gloomy mansion or castle	Ordinary places, which may make strange events more unsettling
Characters	Strange, eccentric people, often of high social standing	Ordinary people, to whom readers can easily relate
Plot Events	Unusual occurrences involving violence or supernatural elements	Situations in which normal life is interrupted in disturbing ways
Endings	Dramatic endings that fully resolve the dark, scary events	Ambiguous endings that leave questions unanswered

The effect of these shifts is to relocate the source of readers' fear. Modern Gothic literature does not allow readers a comfortable distance from dark situations. Instead, the unusual events feel as if they could happen to us.

Practice

CITE TEXTUAL EVIDENCE to support your answers.

Work individually to identify details in "Where Is Here?" that relate to each literary element. Then, discuss your choices with your group. Focus especially on your interpretations of the ambiguous ending.

LITERARY ELEMENTS	DETAILS FROM "WHERE IS HERE?"
Setting	
Characters	
Events	
Ending	

WHERE IS HERE?

Author's Style

Character Development Conversation between characters in a story, or **dialogue,** is one of the tools fiction writers use to make their characters come alive on the page. Authors use dialogue to show readers what characters are like, how they interact with others, how they feel about their situations, and what motivates them. Consider this example from "Where Is Here?":

> **Example of Dialogue:** The stranger hesitated, then said firmly, "I think I'll just poke around outside for a while, if you don't mind. That might be sufficient."
>
> **How It Develops Character:** Paired with descriptive elements, such as the idea that the stranger "hesitated" but then spoke "firmly," the dialogue reveals that the stranger is polite, well-spoken, and nervous.

Read It

Work individually. Use this chart to analyze the mother in "Where Is Here?" Explain what you learn about her character from each example of dialogue. Then, compare your responses to those of your group.

DIALOGUE	HOW IT DEVELOPS CHARACTER
"Isn't that just like you!" the mother said. *She went on worriedly, "He could be anyone, after all. Any kind of thief, or mentally disturbed person, or even murderer. Ringing our doorbell like that with no warning and you don't even know what he looks like!"*	
The mother sighed again, involuntarily. "Poor man!" she murmured. She was standing before her table but no longer seeing it. In her hand were objects—forks, knives, spoons—she could not have named. She said, "We can't bar the door against him. That would be cruel."	
"I wasn't the one who opened the door to that man in the first place," the mother said, coming up behind the father and touching his arm.	

Write It

:e: **Notebook** Write a paragraph in which you describe an interaction between two people. They may be fictional or real. Use dialogue to make the interaction come alive.

:≡: STANDARDS

Reading Literature
Analyze how complex characters develop over the course of a text, interact with other characters, and advance the plot or develop the theme.

Writing
Write narratives to develop real or imagined experiences or events using effective technique, well-chosen details, and well-structured event sequences.

Writing to Sources

Every work of fiction is set in a particular time and place. In our imaginations, though, the characters exist before and after the story.

Assignment

With your group, write a brief **narrative** that extends the scope of "Where Is Here?" Make sure that your narrative stays true to the characterizations, style, and tone of the story. Choose one of the following topics:

☐ Write a **prequel** that reveals the stranger's past. Who is he, and which details of the story he tells to the family are true? What is the stranger's goal in visiting the house—does he simply want to see his home again, or does he have another, more sinister reason for wanting to return?

☐ Write a **sequel** in which the stranger returns to the house after some time has passed. How has he changed, having seen his childhood home earlier? How is he greeted by the family this time? Are the mother and father more or less suspicious of him and his motives?

☐ Write a **police report** filed after the stranger leaves. Imagine that the mother and father call the police to report the incident. What kinds of questions are the police likely to ask about the stranger? What kinds of answers are they likely to receive?

Project Plan Use this chart to plan your narrative. In the middle column, plan the action. In the right-hand column, explain the goal of each paragraph. Follow the chart to draft the narrative, and then present your narrative to the class. Have different group members read portions of the narrative aloud.

✎ EVIDENCE LOG

Before moving on to a new selection, go to your Evidence Log and record what you learned from "Where Is Here?"

PARAGRAPH	WHAT HAPPENS	NARRATIVE GOAL
1		
2		
3		
4		

About the Photographer

As a teenager in the Coney Island section of Brooklyn, New York, **Arthur Tress** (b. 1940) liked to photograph the neighborhood's dilapidated amusement parks in various states of disrepair. His style combines improvised elements of everyday life with the theatrical and is referred to as "magical realism." Tress has worked as a photographer for more than 50 years, and he has traveled the world, often photographing people he meets along the way.

☷ STANDARDS

Reading Informational Text
By the end of grade 10, read and comprehend literary nonfiction at the high end of the grades 9–10 text complexity band independently and proficiently.

Language
Acquire and use accurately general academic and domain-specific words and phrases, sufficient for reading, writing, speaking, and listening at the college and career readiness level; demonstrate independence in gathering vocabulary knowledge when considering a word or phrase important to comprehension or expression.

from The Dream Collector

Media Vocabulary

The following words will be useful to you as you analyze, discuss, and write about photographs.

Composition: arrangement of the parts of a photograph; the *foreground* is closer to the viewer, whereas the *background* is farther away	• The composition may stress one part of an image more than another. • The composition may show what the photographer thinks is important in the subject.
Perspective or Angle: vantage point from which a photograph is taken	• The camera may be looking down, looking up, or looking head-on at the subject. • The subject may seem very far away, at a middle distance, or very close.
Lighting and Color: use of light, shadow, and color in a photograph	• Some images are full color, whereas others are black and white. • Some parts of an image may be brighter or darker than others.
Subject: primary figure(s), object(s), or other content in a photograph	• The subject may be a person or group of people, often in the foreground. • Alternatively, the subject may be an object, a set of objects, or an entire location.
Location: place or scene in which a photograph is taken	• The location may be indoors, in a particular type of building or context. • Alternatively, the location may be outdoors, and it might be obvious or subtle in its details.

First Review MEDIA: ART AND PHOTOGRAPHY

Apply these strategies as you conduct your first review. You will have an opportunity to complete a close review after your first review.

LOOK at each image and determine *who* or *what* it portrays.

NOTE elements in each image that you find interesting and want to revisit.

CONNECT details in the images to other media you've experienced, texts you've read, or images you've seen.

RESPOND by completing the Comprehension Check.

from The Dream Collector

Arthur Tress

BACKGROUND

Photographer Arthur Tress began working on his study of the unconscious mind in the late 1960s by interviewing children about their most memorable dreams. At the time, photography that documented real events was still the dominant form of the medium, and there was some prejudice against staged photography. Tress's photographs from *The Dream Collector* helped elevate the art of photography, and many photographers since have acknowledged their debt to his work.

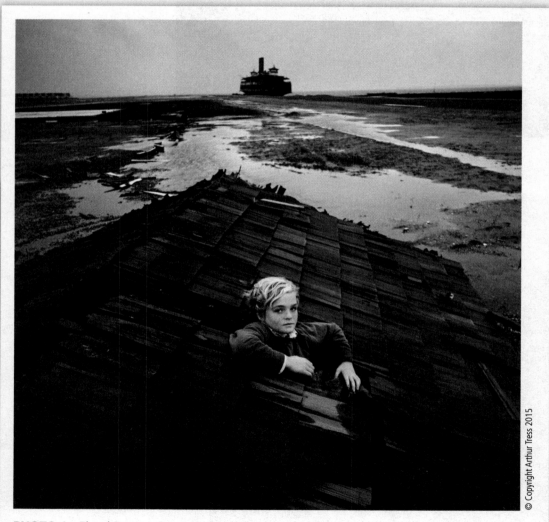

© Copyright Arthur Tress 2015

PHOTO 1: *Flood Dream, Ocean City, New Jersey, 1971*

NOTES

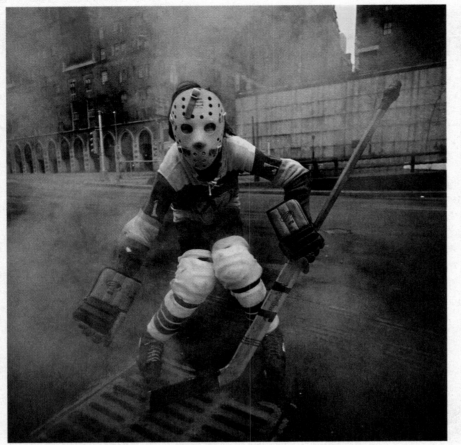

PHOTO 2: *Hockey Player, New York City, 1970*

NOTES

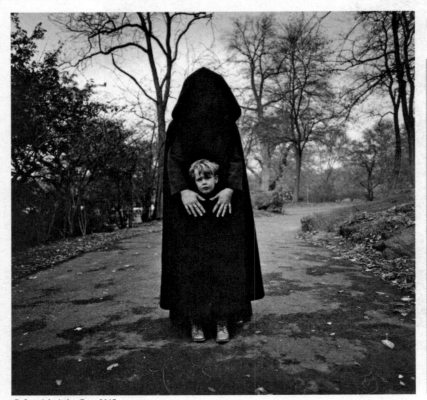

PHOTO 3: *Young Boy and Hooded Figure, New York City, 1971*

NOTES

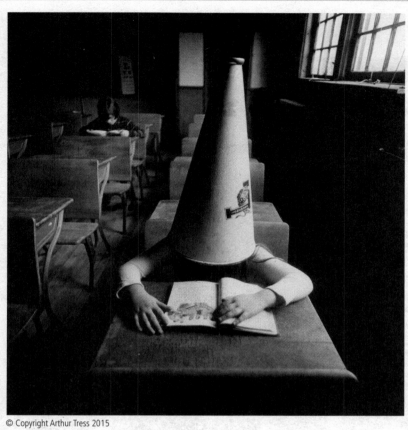

PHOTO 4: *Girl With Dunce Cap, New York City, 1972*

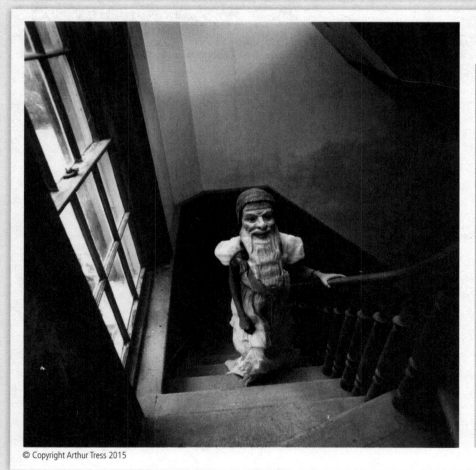

PHOTO 5: *Girl With Mask, Rhinebeck, 1972*

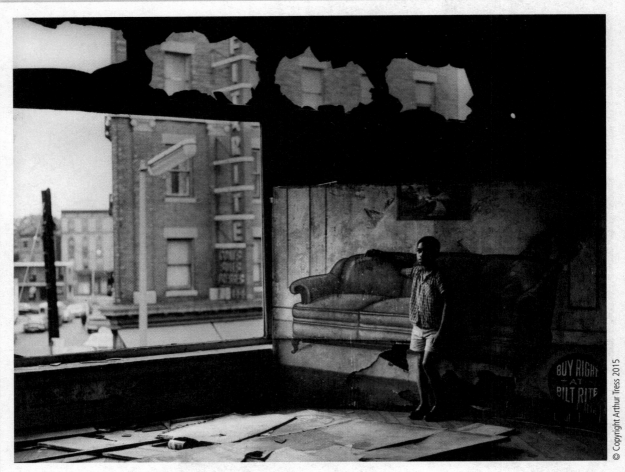

PHOTO 6: *Boy in Burnt-Out Furniture Store, Newark, 1969*

NOTES

NOTES

Comprehension Check

Use the chart to note details in each of the photographs. Identify people, objects, location, and activities. Review and clarify details with your group.

PHOTO	PEOPLE	OBJECTS	LOCATION	ACTIVITIES
PHOTO 1				
PHOTO 2				
PHOTO 3				
PHOTO 4				
PHOTO 5				
PHOTO 6				
NOTES				

from THE DREAM COLLECTOR

Close Review

With your group, revisit the photographs, your first-review notes, and the Comprehension Check chart. Record any new observations that seem important. What **questions** do you have? What can you **conclude**?

Analyze the Media

Complete the activities.

1. **Present and Discuss** Determine which photograph from the collection seems most closely related to the theme of fear. Prepare to justify your choice with specific details from the photo. Share your analysis with your group.

2. **Review and Synthesize** With your group, look over the photographs. Do they share a common style and theme? Defend or challenge the choice to group them together, citing specific details.

3. 📓 **Notebook** **Essential Question:** *What is the allure of fear?* What makes something alluring even when it is simultaneously frightening? How can images be particularly effective in getting to the root of this question? Support your responses with evidence from the photographs.

LANGUAGE DEVELOPMENT

Media Vocabulary

composition	lighting and color	location
perspective or angle	subject	

Use the vocabulary in your responses to the following questions.

1. In Photo 2, what is in the foreground? What is in the background? How does the position of the figure in the photo add to its impact?

2. In what ways do the figures shown in Photo 3 present a startling contrast? Explain.

3. In Photo 5, how does the position of the camera in relationship to the subject add to the photo's effect?

4. Which aspects of Photo 6 seem dreamlike, and which seem realistic? Explain.

STANDARDS

Speaking and Listening
• Make strategic use of digital media in presentations to enhance understanding of findings, reasoning, and evidence to add interest.
• Adapt speech to a variety of contexts and tasks, demonstrating command of formal English when indicated or appropriate.

Language
Acquire and use accurately general academic and domain-specific words and phrases, sufficient for reading, writing, speaking, and listening at the college and career readiness level; demonstrate independence in gathering vocabulary knowledge when considering a word or phrase important to comprehension or expression.

Speaking and Listening

Assignment

Create a **visual presentation** in which you incorporate both text and images. Choose from the following options.

☐ With your group, review the collection of photographs, and choose one you all prefer. Then, work independently to write a **narrative of a dream** that might accompany the photo you chose. Share your story with your group. Once your group has compiled a set of stories, present them to the class in an organized form.

☐ Working independently, write down a dream that you have had, or a fictional dream. Then, plan and take a **photograph** that you feel represents the dream. As a group, organize your dreams and images into a coherent presentation, and share it with the class.

☐ Imagine that you are responsible for convincing a museum to purchase one of these photos for its permanent collection. As a group, choose the photo you think the museum should purchase. Then, working independently, write a **letter** in which you describe the photo and explain why people should get the chance to see it. Organize your letters into a cohesive presentation, and share it with the class.

Writing From Photographs Working on your own, use the chart to identify elements of the photograph that you will reflect in your narrative, dream, or letter. Consider obvious qualities, such as the setting and large objects. Also, note subtler details—such as facial expressions, clothing, and gestures—that contribute to an effect you will capture in your writing.

IMAGE DESCRIPTION	MAIN ELEMENTS OF PHOTO	IMPORTANT DETAILS IN PHOTO

📝 EVIDENCE LOG

Before moving on to a new selection, go to your Evidence Log and record what you've learned from *The Dream Collector*.

About the Author

Allegra Ringo is a freelance writer and comedian based in Los Angeles, California. Her work includes articles, humorous essays, film reviews, and comedy sketches for the Upright Citizens Brigade Theatre. At California State University, Long Beach, where she completed her undergraduate degree in film, Ringo received the Women in Film Scholarship.

▤ STANDARDS

Reading Informational Text
By the end of grade 10, read and comprehend literary nonfiction at the high end of the grades 9–10 text complexity band independently and proficiently.

Language
• Determine or clarify the meaning of unknown and multiple-meaning words and phrases based on *grades 9–10 reading and content,* choosing flexibly from a range of strategies.
• Identify and correctly use patterns of word changes that indicate different meanings or parts of speech.

Why Do Some Brains Enjoy Fear?

Technical Vocabulary

As you perform your first read of the interview, you will encounter the following words.

stimulus	dissonance	cognitive

Familiar Word Parts When determining the meaning of an unfamiliar word, look for word parts—base words, roots, prefixes, and suffixes—that you know. Doing so may help you unlock word meanings. Here is an example of applying the strategy.

> **Unfamiliar Word:** *socialization*
>
> **Familiar Base Word:** *social,* meaning "having to do with being part of a group, community, or society."
>
> **Familiar Suffixes:** *-ize,* which forms verbs and means "to make" or "to become"; *-ation,* which forms abstract nouns
>
> **Conclusion:** Combining the meanings of these three familiar word parts, you can determine that the word *socialization* probably means "the process of becoming social, or part of a community."

Apply your knowledge of familiar word parts and other vocabulary strategies to determine the meanings of unfamiliar words you encounter during your first read.

First Read NONFICTION

Apply these strategies as you conduct your first read. You will have an opportunity to complete a close read after your first read.

NOTICE the general ideas of the text. *What* is it about? *Who* is involved?

ANNOTATE by marking vocabulary and key passages you want to revisit.

CONNECT ideas within the selection to what you already know and what you have already read.

RESPOND by completing the Comprehension Check and by writing a brief summary of the selection.

First Read

Why Do Some Brains Enjoy Fear?

Allegra Ringo

BACKGROUND

As human beings, we are equipped with a variety of different survival mechanisms. One system detects danger. If we could not recognize dangerous situations, we would not be able to avoid them. For that reason, our brains are hard-wired to feel fear when we encounter a threat. Our fear response releases "fight or flight" chemicals into our bloodstreams, and these help make us stronger, quicker, and more alert. In other words, fear makes us ready to fight or flee.

NOTES

1   This time of year, thrillseekers can enjoy horror movies, haunted houses, and prices so low it's scary. But if fear is a natural survival response to a threat, or danger, why would we seek out that feeling?

2   Dr. Margee Kerr is the staff sociologist at ScareHouse, a haunted house in Pittsburgh that takes all year to plan. She also teaches at Robert Morris University and Chatham University, and is the only person I've ever heard referred to as a "scare specialist." Dr. Kerr is an expert in the field of fear. I spoke with her about what fear is, and why some of us enjoy it so much.

Why do some people like the feeling of being scared, while others don't?

3   Not everyone enjoys being afraid, and I don't think it's a stretch to say that no one wants to experience a truly life-threatening situation. But there are those of us (well, a lot of us) who really enjoy the experience. First, the natural high from the fight-or-flight response can feel great. There is strong evidence that this isn't just about personal choice, but our brain chemistry. New research from David Zald shows that people differ in their chemical response to thrilling situations. One of the main hormones released during scary and thrilling activities is dopamine, and it turns out some individuals may get more of a kick from this dopamine response than others do.

> To really enjoy a scary situation, we have to know we're in a safe environment.

Basically, some people's brains lack what Zald describes as "brakes" on the dopamine release and re-uptake[1] in the brain. This means some people are going to really enjoy thrilling, scary, and risky situations while others, not so much.

4   Lots of people also enjoy scary situations because it leaves them with a sense of confidence after it's over. Think about the last time you made it through a scary movie, or through a haunted house. You might have thought, "Yes! I did it! I made it all the way through!" So it can be a real self-esteem boost. But again, self-scaring isn't for everyone, and there are lots of psychological and personal reasons someone may not enjoy scary situations. I've talked to more than a handful of people who will never set foot in a haunted house because they went to a haunt at a young age and were traumatized. I always recommend parents thoroughly check out the content and rating of a haunted attraction before bringing a child. The chemicals that are released during fight-or-flight can work like glue to build strong memories ("flashbulb memories") of scary experiences, and if you're too young to know the monsters are fake, it can be quite traumatic and something you'll never forget, in a bad way.

What happens in our brains when we're scared? Is it different when we're scared "in a fun way" versus being actually afraid?

5   To really enjoy a scary situation, we have to know we're in a safe environment. It's all about triggering the amazing fight-or-flight response to experience the flood of adrenaline, endorphins, and dopamine, but in a completely safe space. Haunted houses are great at this—they deliver a startle scare by triggering one of our senses with different sounds, air blasts, and even smells. These senses are directly tied to our fear response and activate the physical reaction, but our brain has time to process the fact that these are not "real" threats. Our brain is lightning-fast at processing threat. I've seen the process thousands of times from behind the walls in ScareHouse—someone screams and jumps and then immediately starts laughing and smiling. It's amazing to observe. I'm really interested to see where our boundaries are in terms of when and how we really know or feel we're safe.

What qualities do "scary things" share across cultures, or does it vary widely?

6   One of the most interesting things about studying fear is looking at the social constructions of fear, and learned fears versus those fears

---

1. **re-uptake** *n.* reabsorption of a neurotransmitter. This process regulates the levels of a neurotransmitter in the body.

that appear to be more innate, or even genetic. When we look across time and across the world, we find that people truly can become afraid of anything. Through fear conditioning (connecting a neutral **stimulus** with a negative consequence), we can link pretty much anything to a fear response. Baby Albert, of course, is the exemplar case of this. The poor child was made deathly afraid of white rabbits in the 1920's, before researchers were required to be ethical. So we know that we can learn to fear, and this means our socialization and the society in which we are raised is going to have a lot to do with what we find scary.

7   Each culture has its own superhero monsters—the Chupacabra (South America), the Loch Ness Monster, the Yōkai (supernatural monsters from Japanese folklore), Alps (German nightmare creatures)—but they all have a number of characteristics in common. Monsters are defying the general laws of nature in some way. They have either returned from the afterlife (ghosts, demons, spirits) or they are some kind of nonhuman or semihuman creature. This speaks to the fact that things that violate the laws of nature are terrifying. And really anything that doesn't make sense or causes us some sort of **dissonance**, whether it is **cognitive** or aesthetic,[2] is going to be scary (axe-wielding animals, masked faces, contorted bodies).

8   Another shared characteristic of monsters across the globe is their blurred relationship with death and the body. Humans are obsessed with death; we simply have a hard time wrapping our mind around what happens when we die. This contemplation has led to some of the most famous monsters, with each culture creating their own version of the living dead, whether it's zombies, vampires, reanimated and reconstructed corpses, or ghosts. We want to imagine a life that goes on after we die. Or better yet, figure out a way to live forever. Again, though, that would violate the laws of nature and is therefore terrifying. So while the compositions and names of the monsters are different, the motivations and inspirations behind their constructions appear across the globe.

What are some early examples of people scaring themselves on purpose?

9   Humans have been scaring themselves and each other since the birth of the species, through all kinds of methods like storytelling, jumping off cliffs, and popping out to startle each other from the recesses of some dark cave. And we've done this for lots of different reasons—to build group unity, to prepare kids for life in the scary world, and, of course, to control behavior. But it's only really in the last few centuries that scaring ourselves for fun (and profit) has become a highly sought-after experience.

2. **aesthetic** (ehs THEHT ihk) *adj.* of or relating to art or beauty.

Mark familiar word parts or indicate another strategy you used that helped you determine meaning.

stimulus (STIHM yuh luhs) *n.*

MEANING:

> Things that violate the laws of nature are terrifying.

dissonance (DIHS uh nuhns) *n.*

MEANING:

cognitive (KOG nuh tihv) *adj.*

MEANING:

10   My favorite example of one of the early discoveries of the joys of self-scaring is actually found in the history of roller coasters. The Russian Ice Slides began, not surprisingly given the name, as extended sleigh rides down a snowy mountain in the mid-17th century. Much like they do today, riders would sit in sleds and speed down the mountain, which sometimes included additional man-made bumps to make it a little more exciting. The Russian Ice Slides became more sophisticated throughout the 18th century, with wooden beams and artificial mountains of ice. Eventually, instead of ice and sleds, tracks and carriages were constructed to carry screaming riders across the "Russian Mountains." Even more exhilarating terror came when innovative creators decided to paint scary scenes on the walls that shocked and thrilled riders as they passed by. These came to be known as "Dark Rides." People were terrified, but they loved it.

11   We haven't just enjoyed physical thrills—ghost stories were told around the campfire long before we had summer camps. The Graveyard Poets of the 18th century, who wrote of spiders, bats, and skulls, paved the road for the Gothic novelists of the 19th century, like Poe and Shelley. These scary stories provided, and continue to deliver, intrigue, exhilaration, and a jolt of excitement to our lives.

12   The 19th century also brought the precursors to the haunted attraction industry. Sideshows or "freak shows," and the museums and houses of "oddities" have existed since the mid-1800s. Perhaps the most notable is Barnum's American Museum, operated by P. T. Barnum, best known for being half of the Ringling Brothers and Barnum and Bailey Circus. His museum contained things like monkey torsos with fish tails attached, and other characters meant to frighten and startle. Much like modern haunts, customers would line up to challenge themselves and their resilience and dare each other to enter the freak shows and face the scary scenes and abnormalities. The haunted attraction industry has come a long way from fish tails and plastic bats—modern haunts incorporate Hollywood-quality sets, and a crazy amount of modern technology all designed to scare us silly.

There's a common belief that if you meet somebody for the first time in a fearful situation, you'll feel more attached or more attracted to that person than you would if you'd met them in a low-stress situation. Is there any truth to that?

13   One of the reasons people love Halloween is because it produces strong emotional responses, and those responses work to build stronger relationships and memories. When we're happy, or afraid, we're releasing powerful hormones, like oxytocin, that are working to make these moments stick in our brain. So we're going to remember the people we're with. If it was a good experience, then we'll remember them fondly and feel close to them, more so than if we

were to meet them during some neutral unexciting event. Shelley Taylor discussed this in her article "Tend and Befriend: Biobehavioral Bases of Affiliation Under Stress." She shows that we do build a special closeness with those we are with when we're in an excited state, and more importantly, that it can be a really good thing. We're social and emotional beings. We need each other in times of stress, so the fact that our bodies have evolved to make sure we feel close to those we are with when afraid makes sense. So yes, take your date to a haunted house or for a ride on a roller coaster; it'll be a night you'll never forget. ❧

NOTES

Comprehension Check

Complete the following items after you finish your first read. Review and clarify details with your group.

1. According to Dr. Kerr, how are our bodies affected by things that scare us?

2. According to Dr. Kerr, what critical information do we need to have in order to enjoy a scary situation?

3. What happened to Baby Albert?

4. 🗐 **Notebook** Confirm your understanding of the text by writing a summary.

- -

RESEARCH

Research to Clarify Choose at least one unfamiliar detail from the text. Briefly research that detail. In what way does the information you learned shed light on an aspect of the interview?

Research to Explore This interview may spark your curiosity to learn more. Briefly research a topic from the text that interests you. Share what you discover with your group.

WHY DO SOME BRAINS
ENJOY FEAR?

Close Read the Text

With your group, revisit sections of the text you marked during your first read. **Annotate** details that you notice. What **questions** do you have? What can you **conclude**?

Analyze the Text

CITE TEXTUAL EVIDENCE
to support your answers.

☐ Notebook **Complete the activities.**

1. **Review and Clarify** With your group, reread paragraph 6 of the selection. How can fear be both "innate" and "learned"?

2. **Present and Discuss** Work with your group to share the passages from the selection that you found especially relevant. Take turns presenting your passages. Discuss what you noticed in the selection, what questions you asked, and what conclusions you reached.

3. **Essential Question:** *What is the allure of fear?* What has this selection taught you about portrayals of fear? Discuss with your group.

⚓ WORD NETWORK

Add words related to fear from the text to your Word Network.

LANGUAGE DEVELOPMENT

Technical Vocabulary

stimulus   dissonance   cognitive

Why These Words? The three technical vocabulary words are related. With your group, discuss the words, and determine the concept they share. How do these words contribute to your understanding of the text?

☷ STANDARDS

Reading Informational Text
Analyze how the author unfolds an analysis or series of ideas or events, including the order in which the points are made, how they are introduced and developed, and the connections that are drawn between them.

Language
• Identify and correctly use patterns of word changes that indicate different meanings or parts of speech.
• Acquire and use accurately general academic and domain-specific words and phrases, sufficient for reading, writing, speaking, and listening at the college and career readiness level; demonstrate independence in gathering vocabulary knowledge when considering a word or phrase important to comprehension or expression.

Practice

☐ Notebook **Confirm your understanding of these words by using them in sentences. Include context clues that hint at each word's meaning.**

Word Study

Patterns of Word Changes Many Latin roots can combine with both the suffix *-ion*, which forms abstract nouns, and the suffix *-ive*, which forms adjectives—creating a related pair of words. For instance, the abstract noun *cognition* and the related adjective *cognitive* are both formed from the root *-cognit-*, meaning "knowledge" or "thought."

Reread paragraph 10 of the interview. Mark the adjective ending in *-ive*, and write the abstract noun to which it is related.

Analyze Craft and Structure

Speaker's Claims and Evidence An **interview** is a structured conversation between two people that is presented either in written or in broadcast format. Usually, the interviewer is a journalist, and the interviewee is a person with special knowledge. In print, the conversational structure is reflected in the **question-and-answer format,** in which both questions and answers appear in the text.

Interviewees often express **claims,** or assertions of a position or truth. In order to be credible, those claims must be supported with evidence. In interviews that involve personal experiences, evidence may involve impressions and feelings. However, in an interview about a scientific subject, most of the evidence should involve facts rather than feelings. Fact-based evidence includes findings from research studies, data, and other documented information.

Practice

CITE TEXTUAL EVIDENCE to support your answers.

Dr. Margee Kerr is the expert whose claims are expressed in this interview. With your group, complete the chart. Identify the evidence with which Dr. Kerr supports each claim, and consider its credibility.

CLAIM	EVIDENCE	NOTES ON CREDIBILITY
Some people enjoy fear because the natural high of the fight-or-flight response feels great.		
Not everyone enjoys being afraid.		
Being scared is only fun when we recognize it's not "real."		
Much of the appeal of scaring ourselves stems from our fascination with death.		

WHY DO SOME BRAINS
ENJOY FEAR?

Author's Style

Scientific and Technical Diction A writer's **diction**, or word choice, reflects his or her purpose, audience, and topic. For example, articles about poetry may include technical literary terms—words such as *meter, scansion,* or *sonnet.* In a similar way, writings about scientific or technical subjects will include **scientific and technical terms**—words and phrases with precise scientific or technical meanings. Consider these two passages based on the interview.

> **Passage A** *It's about triggering a response we have to fear that releases chemicals in our brains.*

> **Passage B** *It's about triggering the amazing fight-or-flight response to experience the flood of adrenaline, endorphins, and dopamine.*

Passage A provides information, but it lacks specificity and leaves questions unanswered: Which response to fear? Which chemicals? In contrast, Passage B uses scientific and technical terms, such as *fight-or-flight, adrenaline,* and *endorphins,* that have exact meanings. Scientific and technical terms allow writers to present information with precision. For this reason, even general-interest articles on scientific topics may include technical language.

Read It

Record sentences containing scientific and technical terms from the interview in this chart. Use context clues to define each term, or to approximate its general meaning. Then, verify definitions using a dictionary. Discuss with your group how each term adds to the reader's understanding of the topic.

SCIENTIFIC/TECHNICAL TERM	SENTENCE	DEFINITION
adrenaline		
dopamine		
endorphins		
sociologist		
fight-or-flight response		
oxytocin		

Write It

📖 **Notebook** Write a paragraph in which you explain how reading this interview gave you insights into why some people seek out scary experiences. Use at least three scientific or technical terms in your paragraph.

Research

Assignment

Research cultural dimensions of the ways in which people experience and express fear. Then, collect your findings and present them in a **digital presentation**. Choose from these options:

☐ Design and conduct a **poll** to determine how people feel about scary but generally safe experiences, such as roller coasters, movies, and even extreme sports. Write a series of at least ten yes/no questions that you will have people answer. Calculate the results, gather visuals, and organize your findings into a presentation to share with the class.

☐ Conduct a **film study** of scary movies from the 1950s or 1960s. Watch two films, or segments of more, and analyze the sources of fear in each one. Draw conclusions about the types of things that scared mid-twentieth-century Americans. Locate images or video clips, and organize your findings and visuals into a report to share with the class. (Clear the movies you will watch with your teacher before proceeding.)

☐ Conduct a **historical study** of comets as objects of fear in ancient societies. Find out how ancient peoples explained what comets were and what they meant, and consider some of the reasons for those perceptions. Locate drawings and other visuals that will help communicate your findings. Then, organize and deliver your presentation.

Project Plan List the research, discussion, and writing tasks you will need to accomplish in order to complete your project, and make sure you attend to each one. Consult a variety of reliable research sources to gather accurate information and images. Include citations.

Evaluating Visuals Make sure the visuals you select will enhance your audience's understanding of your information. Use this chart to organize your evaluation and confirm your choices.

DESCRIPTION OF VISUAL	POINT THE VISUAL MAKES	CITATION

EVIDENCE LOG

Before moving on to the next selection, go to your Evidence Log and record what you learned from "Why Do Some Brains Enjoy Fear?"

POETRY COLLECTION

beware: do not read this poem

The Raven

Windigo

Concept Vocabulary

As you perform your first read, you will encounter these words.

entreating	implore	beguiling

Familiar Word Parts When determining the meaning of an unfamiliar word, look for word parts—roots and affixes—that you know. Doing so may help you unlock word meanings. Here is an example of applying the strategy.

Unfamiliar Word: *incredulity*

Familiar Root: *-cred-*, meaning "believe," as in *credible*

Familiar Affixes: the prefix *in-*, which means either "into" or "not"; the suffix *-ity*, which forms abstract nouns

Conclusion: You can determine that the word *incredulity* must mean something like "state of not believing."

Apply your knowledge of familiar word parts and other vocabulary strategies to determine the meanings of unfamiliar words you encounter during your first read.

First Read POETRY

Apply these strategies as you conduct your first read. You will have an opportunity to complete a close read after your first read.

▤ STANDARDS

Reading Literature
By the end of grade 10, read and comprehend literature, including stories, dramas, and poems, at the high end of the grades 9–10 text complexity band independently and proficiently.

Language
• Determine or clarify the meaning of unknown and multiple-meaning words and phrases based on *grades 9–10 reading and content*, choosing flexibly from a range of strategies.

• Identify and correctly use patterns of word changes that indicate different meanings or parts of speech.

NOTICE who or what is "speaking" the poem and whether the poem tells a story or describes a single moment.

ANNOTATE by marking vocabulary and key passages you want to revisit.

First Read

CONNECT ideas within the selection to what you already know and what you have already read.

RESPOND by completing the Comprehension Check.

About the Poets

Ishmael Reed (b. 1938) is a prolific author who has written novels, poems, plays, and essays in a variety of different styles and genres. He was born in Chattanooga, Tennessee, and raised in Buffalo, New York. Reed's works have been translated into many languages and published in a number of notable magazines and newspapers. Reed is the recipient of numerous honors for his work, including a Guggenheim Foundation fellowship, and a MacArthur Foundation "Genius" Award.

Edgar Allan Poe (1809–1849) is internationally recognized as a pioneer of the short story, as well as the horror and detective genres. Poe was born in Boston, Massachusetts, and raised in Richmond, Virginia, by tobacco farmer John Allan. During his lifetime, Poe was only mildly successful as a writer and struggled with poverty and loss. He died somewhat mysteriously at the age of forty. Many of his works, including "The Raven," remain popular today.

Louise Erdrich (b. 1954) is the author of many highly regarded novels and poetry collections. Erdrich was born in Minnesota, grew up on the plains of North Dakota, and was part of the first group of women admitted to Dartmouth College. In her work, Erdrich often explores her Native American heritage through her choices of characters and themes.

Backgrounds

beware: do not read this poem

In the first stanza of the poem, the word *thriller* appears in italic type to indicate it is a reference to a fictional television show. The poem contains abbreviations: *abt* for *about*, *yr* for *your*, and *frm* for *from*.

The Raven

When Poe wrote this poem, he drew from a long tradition that viewed the raven as a bird of ill omen. Yet, in some cultures, the raven enjoys a more positive image. For example, when the Vikings were lost at sea, they would release a raven. The raven would fly toward land, thus directing the lost ship.

Windigo

Windigos are evil, ice-coated, man-eating creatures that appear in many Native American folktales, including those from the poet's Chippewa culture. In Chippewa folklore, it is believed that a person who commits a sin is turned into a Windigo as punishment. The human spirit is said to live inside the creature, but the only escape is death. This poem presents a different perspective on the traditional tale.

beware:
do not read this poem

Ishmael Reed

tonite, *thriller* was
abt an ol woman , so vain she
surrounded her self w/
    many mirrors

5 it got so bad that finally she
locked herself indoors & her
whole life became the
    mirrors

one day the villagers broke
10 into her house, but she was too
swift for them. she disappeared
            into a mirror
each tenant who bought the house
after that, lost a loved one to
15   the ol woman in the mirror:
            first a little girl
            then a young woman
            then the young woman/s husband

the hunger of this poem is legendary
20 it has taken in many victims
back off from this poem
it has drawn in yr feet
back off from this poem
it has drawn in yr legs
25 back off from this poem
it is a greedy mirror
you are into this poem. from
      the waist down
nobody can hear you can they?
30 this poem has had you up to here
            belch
this poem aint got no manners
you cant call out frm this poem
relax now & go w/this poem
35 move & roll on to this poem

do not resist this poem
this poem has yr eyes
this poem has his head
this poem has his arms
40 this poem has his fingers
this poem has his fingertips

this poem is the reader & the
reader this poem

statistic: the us bureau of missing persons reports
45   that in 1968 over 100,000 people disappeared
            leaving no solid clues
                  nor trace   only
a space   in the lives of their friends

The **Raven**

Edgar Allan Poe

NOTES

Once upon a midnight dreary, while I pondered, weak and weary,
Over many a quaint and curious volume of forgotten lore—
While I nodded, nearly napping, suddenly there came a tapping,
As of some one gently rapping, rapping at my chamber door.
5 "'Tis some visitor," I muttered, "tapping at my chamber door—
        Only this, and nothing more."

Ah, distinctly I remember it was in the bleak December,
And each separate dying ember wrought its ghost upon the floor.
Eagerly I wished the morrow—vainly I had sought to borrow
10 From my books surcease[1] of sorrow—sorrow for the lost Lenore—
For the rare and radiant maiden whom the angels name Lenore—
        Nameless *here* for evermore.

And the silken, sad, uncertain rustling of each purple curtain
Thrilled me—filled me with fantastic terrors never felt before;
15 So that now, to still the beating of my heart, I stood repeating
"'Tis some visitor **entreating** entrance at my chamber door—
Some late visitor entreating entrance at my chamber door—
        This it is, and nothing more."

Mark familiar word parts or indicate another strategy you used that helped you determine meaning.

entreating (ehn TREET ihng) *adj.*

MEANING:

---

1. **surcease** *n*. end.

Presently my soul grew stronger; hesitating then no longer,
20 "Sir," said I, "or Madam, truly your forgiveness I **implore**;
But the fact is I was napping, and so gently you came rapping,
And so faintly you came tapping, tapping at my chamber door,
That I scarce was sure I heard you"—here I opened wide the door—
      Darkness there, and nothing more.

25 Deep into that darkness peering, long I stood there wondering, fearing,
Doubting, dreaming dreams no mortal ever dared to dream before;
But the silence was unbroken, and the darkness gave no token,
And the only word there spoken was the whispered word "Lenore?"
This I whispered, and an echo murmured back the word "Lenore!"
30   Merely this, and nothing more.

Back into the chamber turning, all my soul within me burning,
Soon again I heard a tapping somewhat louder than before.
"Surely," said I, "surely that is something at my window lattice;
Let me see, then, what thereat is, and this mystery explore—
35 Let my heart be still a moment and this mystery explore—
      'Tis the wind, and nothing more!"

Open here I flung the shutter, when, with many a flirt and flutter,
In there stepped a stately Raven of the saintly days of yore;
Not the least obeisance² made he; not a minute stopped or stayed he;
40 But, with mien of lord or lady, perched above my chamber door—
Perched upon a bust of Pallas³ just above my chamber door—
      Perched, and sat, and nothing more.

Then this ebony bird **beguiling** my sad fancy into smiling,
By the grave and stern decorum of the countenance⁴ it wore,
45 "Though thy crest be shorn and shaven, thou," I said, "art sure no
    craven,⁵
Ghastly grim and ancient Raven wandering from the Nightly shore—
Tell me what thy lordly name is on the Night's Plutonian⁶ shore!"
      Quoth the Raven, "Nevermore."

Much I marveled this ungainly fowl to hear discourse so plainly,
50 Though its answer little meaning—little relevancy bore;
For we cannot help agreeing that no living human being
Ever yet was blessed with seeing bird above his chamber door—
Bird or beast above the sculptured bust above his chamber door,
      With such name as "Nevermore."

55 But the Raven, sitting lonely on the placid bust, spoke only
That one word, as if his soul in that one word he did outpour.

---

2. **obeisance** (oh BAY suhns) *n.* gesture of respect.
3. **Pallas** *n.* Pallas Athena, Greek goddess of wisdom.
4. **countenance** *n.* facial expression.
5. **craven** *adj.* cowardly.
6. **Plutonian** *adj.* of the underworld; refers to Pluto, Greek god of the underworld.

Mark familiar word parts or indicate another strategy you used that helped you determine meaning.

implore (ihm PLAWR) *v.*

MEANING:

Mark familiar word parts or indicate another strategy you used that helped you determine meaning.

beguiling (bih GYL ihng) *adj.*

MEANING:

Nothing further then he uttered—not a feather then he fluttered—
Till I scarcely more than muttered, "Other friends have flown
    before—
On the morrow *he* will leave me, as my Hopes have flown before."
60   Quoth the Raven, "Nevermore."

Startled at the stillness broken by reply so aptly spoken,
"Doubtless," said I, "what it utters is its only stock and store,
Caught from some unhappy master whom unmerciful Disaster
Followed fast and followed faster till his songs one burden bore—
65 Till the dirges of his Hope that melancholy burden bore
           Of 'Never—nevermore.'"

But the Raven still beguiling my sad fancy into smiling,
Straight I wheeled a cushioned seat in front of bird, and bust, and
    door;
Then, upon the velvet sinking, I betook myself to linking
70 Fancy unto fancy, thinking what this ominous[7] bird of yore—
What this grim, ungainly, ghastly, gaunt, and ominous bird of yore
           Meant in croaking, "Nevermore."

This I sat engaged in guessing, but no syllable expressing
To the fowl whose fiery eyes now burned into my bosom's core;
75 This and more I sat divining, with my head at ease reclining
On the cushion's velvet lining that the lamplight gloated o'er,
But whose velvet violet lining with the lamplight gloating o'er,
           She shall press, ah, nevermore!

Then, methought, the air grew denser, perfumed from an unseen censer
80 Swung by seraphim whose footfalls tinkled on the tufted floor.
"Wretch," I cried, "thy God hath lent thee—by these angels he hath
    sent thee
Respite—respite and nepenthe[8] from thy memories of Lenore!
Quaff, oh quaff this kind nepenthe and forget this lost Lenore!"
           Quoth the Raven, "Nevermore."

85 "Prophet!" said I, "thing of evil!—prophet still, if bird or devil!—
Whether Tempter sent, or whether tempest tossed thee here ashore,
Desolate, yet all undaunted, on this desert land enchanted—
On this home by Horror haunted—tell me truly, I implore—
Is there—*is* there balm in Gilead?[9]—tell me—tell me, I implore!"
90   Quoth the Raven, "Nevermore."

"Prophet!" said I, "thing of evil!—prophet still, if bird or devil!

---

7. **ominous** *adj.* threatening or sinister.
8. **nepenthe** (nih PEHN thee) *n.* drug that the ancient Greeks believed could relieve
    sorrow.
9. **balm in Gilead** in the Bible, a healing ointment made in Gilead, a region of ancient
    Palestine.

By that Heaven that bends above us—by that God we both adore—
Tell this soul with sorrow laden if, within the distant Aidenn,[10]
It shall clasp a sainted maiden whom the angels named Lenore—
95 Clasp a rare and radiant maiden whom the angels named Lenore."
              Quoth the Raven, "Nevermore."

"Be that word our sign of parting, bird or fiend!" I shrieked,
    upstarting—
"Get thee back into the tempest and the Night's Plutonian shore!
Leave no black plume as a token of that lie thy soul hath spoken!
100 Leave my loneliness unbroken!—quit the bust above my door!
Take thy beak from out my heart, and take thy form from off my door!"
              Quoth the Raven, "Nevermore."

And the Raven, never flitting, still is sitting, *still* is sitting
On the pallid bust of Pallas just above my chamber door;
105 And his eyes have all the seeming of a demon's that is dreaming,
And the lamplight o'er him streaming throws his shadow on the floor;
And my soul from out that shadow that lies floating on the floor
              Shall be lifted—nevermore!

---

10. **Aidenn** *n.* Arabic for Eden or heaven.

Windigo

Louise Erdrich

NOTES

You knew I was coming for you, little one,
when the kettle jumped into the fire.
Towels flapped on the hooks,
and the dog crept off, groaning,
5 to the deepest part of the woods.

In the hackles[1] of dry brush a thin laughter started up.
Mother scolded the food warm and smooth in the pot
and called you to eat.
But I spoke in the cold trees:
10 *New one, I have come for you, child hide and lie still.*

The sumac[2] pushed sour red cones through the air.
Copper burned in the raw wood.
You saw me drag toward you.
Oh touch me, I murmured, and licked the soles of your feet.
15 You dug your hands into my pale, melting fur.

---

1. **hackles** *n.* usually used to mean the hairs on the neck and back of a dog that stiffen when the dog is ready to attack. In this case, the poet is using the word figuratively.
2. **sumac** *n.* bright shrub or small tree with multi-part leaves and fruit clusters.

I stole you off, a huge thing in my bristling armor.
Steam rolled from my wintry arms, each leaf shivered
from the bushes we passed
until they stood, naked, spread like the cleaned spines of fish.

10 Then your warm hands hummed over and shoveled themselves full
of the ice and the snow. I would darken and spill
all night running, until at last morning broke the cold earth
and I carried you home,
a river shaking in the sun.

Comprehension Check

Complete the following items after you finish your first read. Review and clarify
details with your group.

BEWARE: DO NOT READ THIS POEM

1. What happened to the vain old woman who surrounded herself with mirrors?

2. After that, what happened to each tenant of the old woman's house?

THE RAVEN

1. At the beginning of the poem, why is the speaker sorrowful?

2. With what word does the Raven respond to all the speaker's questions?

WINDIGO

1. Who is the speaker of the poem?

2. Where does the speaker take the child?

RESEARCH

Research to Clarify Choose at least one unfamiliar detail from one of the poems. Briefly
research that detail. In what way does the information you learned shed light on an aspect
of the poem?

POETRY COLLECTION

Close Read the Text

With your group, revisit sections of the poems you marked during your first read. **Annotate** details that you notice. What **questions** do you have? What can you **conclude**?

ANNOTATE QUESTION **Close Read** CONCLUDE

Analyze the Text

Complete the activities.

1. **Review and Clarify** With your group, reread lines 1–12 of "The Raven." Discuss the ways in which Poe establishes the setting for the poem. How do the time of day and the season match the speaker's state of mind? What overall mood or atmosphere does the poet create?

2. **Present and Discuss** Work with your group to share the passages from the selections that you found especially important. Take turns presenting your passages. Discuss what details you noticed, what questions you asked, and what conclusions you reached.

3. **Essential Question:** *What is the allure of fear?* What have these poems taught you about portrayals of fear in literature?

LANGUAGE DEVELOPMENT

Concept Vocabulary

| entreating | implore | beguiling |

Why These Words? The three concept vocabulary words are related. With your group, discuss what the words have in common. How do these word choices enhance the impact of the text?

Practice

📓 **Notebook** Confirm your understanding of these words by using them in sentences. Include context clues that hint at each word's meaning.

Word Study

Anglo-Saxon Prefix: *be-* The word *beguiling* begins with the Anglo-Saxon prefix *be-*, an ancient suffix with a variety of meanings. Sometimes, it means "to make," as in *becalm*. Other times, it acts as an intensifier meaning "thoroughly" or "completely," as in *bedazzle*.

Identify the base word in each of the following: *becloud, befriend, belittle*. Then, write the meaning of each word. Use a college-level dictionary to verify your definitions.

TIP

GROUP DISCUSSION
Keep in mind that group members will have different interpretations of the poems. These different perspectives enable group members to learn from one another and to clarify their own thoughts. Very often, there is no single interpretation or conclusion.

WORD NETWORK

Add words related to fear from the texts to your Word Network.

STANDARDS

Reading Literature
Determine a theme or central idea of a text and analyze in detail its development over the course of the text, including how it emerges and is shaped and refined by specific details; provide an objective summary of the text.

Language
• Identify and correctly use patterns of word changes that indicate different meanings or parts of speech.
• Verify the preliminary determination of the meaning of a word or phrase.

Analyze Craft and Structure

Development of Theme A **narrative poem** relates a story in verse. Like a narrator in prose fiction, the **speaker** of a poem is an imaginary voice that "tells" the story. Interpreting a poem often depends on recognizing who the speaker is, whom the speaker is addressing, and what the speaker feels about the subject—his or her **tone.**

A **theme** is a central message or insight expressed in a literary work. Some poems state a theme directly, but most convey their messages indirectly. Readers must look for clues to a poem's theme in its language and details. These details include **imagery,** or sensory language that creates word pictures in readers' minds. Imagery makes a narrative poem more vivid, and also suggests its themes.

Practice

CITE TEXTUAL EVIDENCE
to support your answers.

Use the chart to analyze each poem. Consider how the speaker's tone and the poem's imagery reveal the theme.

BEWARE: DO NOT READ THIS POEM	
speaker/speaker's tone	
possible theme	We cannot separate ourselves from the things that we read.
details that develop this theme	
THE RAVEN	
speaker/speaker's tone	
possible theme	Great sorrow may lead to madness.
details that develop this theme	
WINDIGO	
speaker/speaker's tone	
possible theme	Mystery is at the heart of life.
details that develop this theme	

1. Choose one of the poems, and identify another theme it expresses.
2. List details that suggest this theme, and explain your interpretation.

POETRY COLLECTION

Author's Style

Point of View In narrative literature, whether stories or poems, the point of view is the perspective, or vantage point, from which the story is told. The point of view is very important, since it controls what the reader learns about events and what he or she can logically infer.

In **first-person point of view,** the narrator is a character in the literary work and refers to him- or herself with the first-person pronoun *I* or *me*. Since the narrator participates directly in the action, his or her point of view is *limited*. A first-person narrator can reliably relate only those events he or she witnesses, experiences firsthand, or learns about from others.

In **omniscient third-person point of view,** the narrator is not a character in the story. He or she stands "outside" the story and is, thus, free to be omniscient, or "all-knowing." The omniscient narrator knows what all of the characters are thinking and feeling.

STANDARDS

Reading Literature
Analyze how an author's choices concerning how to structure a text, order events within it, and manipulate time create such effects as mystery, tension, or suspense.

Read It

Work individually. Use this chart to identify the point of view employed in each poem. Then, consider the effects of this choice—what does the point of view allow readers to learn, and what does it keep hidden? When you finish, reconvene as a group to discuss your responses.

BEWARE: DO NOT READ THIS POEM	
Point of view:	Effects:

THE RAVEN	
Point of view:	Effects:

WINDIGO	
Point of view:	Effects:

Write It

Notebook Write two brief versions of the same scene. In one version of the scene, describe events from the first-person point of view. In the other version, describe the same events using the omniscient third-person point of view.

Speaking and Listening

Assignment

Create and deliver a **group presentation**. As you deliver your presentation, pay close attention to such things as eye contact, body language, clear pronunciation, tone, speaking rate, and volume. Choose from the following topics.

☐ Conduct a **mock interview** with one of the poets. Prepare a list of questions you would like to ask the poet about the inspiration behind his or her poem. Each group member should write at least one question and create an answer. Then, one group member should play the poet, while the others pose questions. Present the role-play for the class.

☐ Present a **compare-and-contrast analysis** of two of the poems, focusing on the personalities and tones of the speakers. How do the speakers change over the course of the poems? Cite evidence from the text to support your ideas. Present your analysis to the class.

☐ Present a **retelling** of one of the poems. For example, you might present it as a short story, a hip-hop song, or a play. Present your retelling for the class.

Project Plan Before you begin, make a list of the tasks you will need to accomplish in order to complete the assignment you have chosen. Then, assign individual group members to each task. Use this chart to organize your ideas.

MOCK INTERVIEW	
Tasks:	Additional notes:

COMPARE-AND-CONTRAST ANALYSIS	
Tasks:	Additional notes:

RETELLING	
Tasks:	Additional notes:

EVIDENCE LOG

Before moving on to a new selection, go to your Evidence Log and record what you learned from "beware: do not read this poem," "The Raven," and "Windigo."

STANDARDS

Speaking and Listening
• Initiate and participate effectively in a range of collaborative discussions with diverse partners on *grades 9–10 topics, texts, and issues,* building on others' ideas and expressing their own clearly and persuasively.
• Adapt speech to a variety of contexts and tasks, demonstrating command of formal English, when indicated or appropriate.

Deliver an Explanatory Presentation

Assignment

You have read literature that deals with fear and some of its causes and effects. Work with your group to develop a presentation that addresses this question:

> **In literature, how does a sense of uncertainty help to create an atmosphere of fear?**

Plan With Your Group

Analyze the Text With your group, discuss the types of situations or dilemmas that different characters face in the selections you have read. Think about whether you as a reader were uncertain about what was happening, as well as whether the characters experienced uncertainty. Use the chart to list your ideas. For each selection, identify how uncertainty relates to an atmosphere of fear. If you choose, you may also draw on experiences in your own life, and discuss whether uncertainty played a role.

TITLE	KEY EXPERIENCES
Where Is Here?	
from The Dream Collector	
Why Do Some Brains Enjoy Fear?	
beware: do not read this poem	
The Raven	
Windigo	
group member's story, if desired	

Gather Evidence and Media Identify specific passages to read from the selections to support your group's ideas. Test your choices by reading the passages to each other, with appropriate inflection and emphasis, to see whether others agree that each one effectively illustrates your ideas about fear and uncertainty. Brainstorm for types of media you can use to enhance the mood and impact of your readings. Consider including images, such as photographs and illustrations. You may also include music and other sound effects.

STANDARDS

Speaking and Listening
• Initiate and participate effectively in a range of collaborative discussions with diverse partners on *grades 9–10 topics, texts, and issues*, building on others' ideas and expressing their own clearly and persuasively.

• Work with peers to set rules for collegial discussions and decision-making, clear goals and deadlines, and individual roles as needed.

• Present information, findings, and supporting evidence clearly, concisely, and logically such that listeners can follow the line of reasoning and the organization, development, substance, and style are appropriate to purpose, audience, and task.

Organize Ideas As a group, organize the script for your presentation. Make decisions about the following content and tasks:

- Who will introduce the group's main findings?
- Who will read the selection passages that illustrate the findings?
- Who will summarize findings and take questions from the audience?
- Who will display and manage visuals?
- Who will play and manage music and sound effects?

Then, plan where in your presentation you will incorporate your media.

Rehearse With Your Group

Practice With Your Group Use this checklist to evaluate the effectiveness of your group's first run-through. Then, use your evaluation and the instruction here to guide your revision.

CONTENT	USE OF MEDIA	PRESENTATION TECHNIQUES
☐ The presentation has a clear introduction and a strong conclusion.	☐ The media are consistent with the mood and tone of the passages from the texts.	☐ Media are visible and audible.
☐ Main ideas are well supported with readings from the texts.	☐ The media add interest to the passages.	☐ Transitions are smooth.
	☐ Media do not distract from the passages or the ideas of the presentation.	☐ Each speaker speaks clearly.

Fine-Tune the Content Make sure you have enough examples that illustrate your main findings about uncertainty and fear. Verify that each passage you choose to read is clear and dramatic, and rehearse the readings for maximum impact. Check with your group to identify key points in your introduction and conclusion that might not be clear to listeners. Find another way to word these ideas.

Improve Your Use of Media Review all visuals, music, and sound effects to make sure they add interest and help create a cohesive presentation. If a visual or sound cue does not capture the right mood, replace it with a more appropriate item.

Brush Up on Your Presentation Techniques Practice delivering your group presentation before you present to the whole class. Make sure that you speak clearly, avoiding slang and informal language, and use appropriate eye contact while you are speaking.

Present and Evaluate

When you present as a group, be sure that each member has taken into account each of the checklist items. As you listen to other groups, evaluate how well they adhere to the checklist.

STANDARDS
Speaking and Listening
• Make strategic use of digital media in presentations to enhance understanding of findings, reasoning, and evidence and to add interest.
• Adapt speech to a variety of contexts and tasks, demonstrating command of formal English when indicated or appropriate.

ESSENTIAL QUESTION:

What is the allure of fear?

Fear is a part of life. It both helps and hurts us, bonds and divides us. In this section, you will complete your study of the literature of fear by exploring an additional selection related to the topic. You'll then share what you learn with classmates. To choose a text, follow these steps.

Look Back Think about the selections you have already studied. What more do you want to know about the topic of fear and its appeal in literature and life?

Look Ahead Preview the selections by reading the descriptions. Which one seems most interesting and appealing to you?

Look Inside Take a few minutes to scan the text you chose. Choose a different one if this text doesn't meet your needs.

Independent Learning Strategies

Throughout your life, in school, in your community, and in your career, you will need to rely on yourself to learn and work on your own. Review these strategies and the actions you can take to practice them during Independent Learning. Add ideas of your own for each category.

STRATEGY	ACTION PLAN
Create a schedule	• Understand your goals and deadlines. • Make a plan for what to do each day. •
Practice what you have learned	• Use first-read and close-read strategies to deepen your understanding. • After reading, evaluate the usefulness of the evidence to help you understand the topic. • Consider the quality and reliability of the source. •
Take notes	• Record important ideas and information. • Review your notes before preparing to share with a group. •

Choose one selection. Selections are available online only.

CONTENTS

First-Read Guide

Use this page to record your first-read ideas.

Selection Title: _____

🔧 **Tool Kit**
First-Read Guide and
Model Annotation

NOTICE new information or ideas you learn about the unit topic as you first read this text.

ANNOTATE by marking vocabulary and key passages you want to revisit.

First Read

NOTICE · ANNOTATE · CONNECT · RESPOND

CONNECT ideas within the selection to other knowledge and the selections you have read.

RESPOND by writing a brief summary of the selection.

:≡ STANDARD

Reading Read and comprehend complex literary and informational texts independently and proficiently.

Close-Read Guide

Use this page to record your close-read ideas.

🔧 Tool Kit
Close-Read Guide and
Model Annotation

Selection Title: _____

Close Read the Text

Revisit sections of the text you marked during your first read. Read these sections closely and **annotate** what you notice. Ask yourself **questions** about the text. What can you **conclude**? Write down your ideas.

Analyze the Text

Think about the author's choices of patterns, structure, techniques, and ideas included in the text. Select one, and record your thoughts about what this choice conveys.

QuickWrite

Pick a paragraph from the text that grabbed your interest. Explain the power of this passage.

_____
_____
_____
_____
_____
_____
_____
_____

▤ STANDARD
Reading Read and comprehend complex literary and informational texts independently and proficiently.

EVIDENCE LOG

Go to your Evidence Log and record what you learned from the text you read.

Share Your Independent Learning

Prepare to Share

What is the allure of fear?

Even when you read something independently, your understanding continues to grow when you share what you have learned with others. Reflect on the text you explored independently, and write notes about its connection to the unit. In your notes, consider why this text belongs in this unit.

Learn From Your Classmates

Discuss It Share your ideas about the text you explored on your own. As you talk with others in your class, jot down a few ideas that you learned from them.

Reflect

Review your notes, and mark the most important insight you gained from these writing and discussion activities. Explain how this idea adds to your understanding of the allure of fear in literature.

STANDARDS
Speaking and Listening
• Initiate and participate effectively range of collaborative discussions with diverse partners on *grades 9–10 topics, texts, and issues,* building on others' ideas and expressing their own clearly and persuasively.
• Come to discussions prepared, having read and researched material under study; explicitly draw on that preparation by referring to evidence from texts and other research on the topic or issue to stimulate a thoughtful, well-reasoned exchange of ideas.

Review Evidence for an Explanatory Essay

At the beginning of the unit, you expressed a point about the following question:

In what ways does transformation play a role in stories meant to scare us?

Review your Evidence Log and your QuickWrite from the beginning of the unit. Did you learn anything new?

NOTES

Identify at least three pieces of evidence that interested you about the reasons people enjoy scary literature.

1. _____

2. _____

3. _____

Identify a real-life experience or an example from one of the selections that connects to your new knowledge about the literature of fear.

_____

_____

_____

Develop your thoughts into a topic sentence for an explanatory essay. Complete this sentence starter:

I learned a great deal about literary portrayals of fear when

_____

_____

_____

Evaluate Your Evidence Consider your point of view. How did the texts you read impact your point of view?

▤ STANDARDS
Writing
Introduce a topic; organize complex ideas, concepts, and information to make important connections and distinctions; include formatting, graphics, and multimedia when useful to aiding comprehension.

SOURCES

• WHOLE–CLASS SELECTIONS

• SMALL–GROUP SELECTIONS

• INDEPENDENT–LEARNING SELECTION

PART 1
Writing to Sources: Explanatory Essay

In this unit, you read about various characters whose lives are transformed in scary circumstances. In some cases, the transformations reveal something that was there the whole time but disguised or hidden.

Assignment

Write an **explanatory essay** on the following topic:

> In what ways does transformation play a role in stories meant to scare us?

Use evidence from at least three of the selections you read and researched in this unit to support your perspective. Include a narrative dimension in the form of an anecdote, or brief story from your own experience or that of someone you know. Ensure that your ideas are fully supported, that you use precise words, and that your organization is logical and easy to follow.

Reread the Assignment Review the assignment to be sure you fully understand it. The assignment may reference some of the academic words presented at the beginning of the unit. Be sure you understand each of the words given below in order to complete the assignment correctly.

Academic Vocabulary

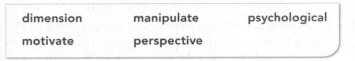

dimension	manipulate	psychological
motivate	perspective	

Review the Elements of an Effective Explanatory Text Before you begin writing, read the Explanatory Text Rubric. Once you have completed your first draft, check it against the rubric. If one or more of the elements is missing or not as strong as it could be, revise your essay to add or strengthen that component.

🔗 WORD NETWORK

As you write and revise your explanatory essay, use your Word Network to help vary your word choices.

⬛ STANDARDS

Writing
• Write informative/explanatory texts to examine and convey complex ideas, concepts, and information clearly and accurately through the effective selection, organization, and analysis of content.
• Draw evidence from literary or informational texts to support analysis, reflection, and research.
• Write routinely over extended time frames and shorter time frames for a range of tasks, purposes, and audiences.

Explanatory Text Rubric

	Focus and Organization	Evidence and Elaboration	Conventions
4	The introduction engages the reader and states a thesis in a compelling way. The essay includes a clear introduction, body, and conclusion. The essay uses facts and evidence from a variety of reliable, credited sources The conclusion summarizes ideas and offers fresh insight into the thesis.	The essay includes specific reasons, details, facts, narratives, and quotations to support the thesis. If a narrative is used, it is coherent and provides strong support for the thesis. The tone of the essay is appropriately formal and objective for the audience and topic. The language is always precise and appropriate for the audience and purpose.	The essay intentionally uses standard English conventions of usage and mechanics.
3	The introduction engages the reader and sets forth a thesis. The essay includes an introduction, a body, and a conclusion. The essay uses facts and evidence from a variety of credited sources. The conclusion summarizes ideas.	The research includes some specific reasons, details, facts, narratives, and quotations to support the thesis. If a narrative is used, it is coherent and provides some support for the thesis. The tone of the research is mostly appropriate for the audience and topic. The language is generally precise and appropriate for the audience and purpose.	The essay demonstrates general accuracy in standard English conventions of usage and mechanics.
2	The introduction sets forth a thesis. The essay includes an introduction, a body, and a conclusion, but one or more parts are weak. The essay uses facts and evidence from a few credited sources. The conclusion partially summarizes ideas.	The research includes a few reasons, details, facts, narratives, and quotations to support the thesis. If a narrative is used, it provides little support for the thesis. The tone of the research is occasionally appropriate for the audience and topic. The language is somewhat precise and appropriate for the audience and purpose.	The presentation demonstrates some accuracy in standard English conventions of usage and mechanics.
1	The introduction does not state a thesis clearly. The essay does not include an introduction, a body, and a conclusion. The essay does not use a variety of facts, and information and evidence are not credited. The conclusion does not summarize ideas.	Reliable and relevant evidence is not included. If a narrative is used, it provides no support for the thesis. The tone of the essay is not objective or formal. The language used is imprecise and not appropriate for the audience and purpose.	The essay contains mistakes in standard English conventions of usage and mechanics.

PART 2
Speaking and Listening: Informal Talk

Assignment
After completing the final draft of your explanatory essay, use it as the foundation for a three- to five-minute **informal talk.**

Do not read your explanatory essay aloud. Instead, use your knowledge to speak informally but with confidence about your topic. Take the following steps to prepare your talk.

- Go back to your essay, and annotate the most important ideas from your introduction, body paragraphs, and conclusion. Also, note any anecdote or descriptive details you used.
- Use your annotations to make a list of the key points and content you want to share in your informal talk.
- As you speak, refer to your list of ideas to keep your talk focused.

Review the Rubric The criteria by which your informal talk will be evaluated appear in the rubric below. Review these criteria before speaking to ensure that you are prepared.

STANDARDS

Speaking and Listening
Present information, findings, and supporting evidence clearly, concisely, and logically such that listeners can follow the line of reasoning and the organization, development, substance, and style are appropriate to purpose, audience, and task.

	Content	Organization	Presentation
3	The introduction engages and orients the reader by setting out a clear observation or analysis. The talk includes both descriptive details and narrative techniques. The conclusion follows from and reflects on ideas presented earlier in the talk.	The speaker uses time very effectively by spending the right amount of time on each part of the discussion. The talk includes a smooth sequence of ideas with clear transitions that listeners can follow.	The speaker maintains effective eye contact and speaks clearly. The speaker varies tone, volume, and emphasis to create an engaging presentation.
2	The introduction sets out a problem, situation, or observation. The talk includes some descriptive details and narrative techniques. The conclusion follows from ideas presented earlier in the talk.	The speaker uses time effectively by spending adequate time on each part. The talk includes a smooth sequence of ideas with transitions that listeners can mostly follow.	The speaker mostly maintains effective eye contact and usually speaks clearly. The speaker sometimes varies tone, volume, and emphasis to create an engaging presentation.
1	The introduction does not set out an observation or analysis. The talk does not include descriptive details or narrative techniques. The conclusion does not follow from ideas presented earlier in the talk.	The speaker does not use time effectively and devotes too much or too little time to each part. The talk does not include a clear sequence of ideas with transitions that listeners can follow.	The speaker does not maintain effective eye contact or speak clearly. The speaker does not vary tone, volume, and emphasis to create an engaging presentation.

Reflect on the Unit

Now that you've completed the unit, take a few moments to reflect on your learning.

Reflect on the Unit Goals

Look back at the goals at the beginning of the unit. Use a different colored pen to rate yourself again. Think about readings and activities that contributed the most to the growth of your understanding. Record your thoughts.

Reflect on the Learning Strategies

Discuss It Write a reflection on whether you were able to improve your learning based on your Action Plans. Think about what worked, what didn't, and what you might do to keep working on these strategies. Record your ideas before a class discussion.

Reflect on the Text

Choose a selection that you found challenging, and explain what made it difficult.

Explain something that surprised you about a text in the unit.

Which activity taught you the most about the literature of fear? What did you learn?

STANDARDS

Speaking and Listening
• Initiate and participate effectively in a range of collaborative discussions with diverse partners on *grades 9–10 topics, texts, and issues,* building on other's ideas and expressing their own clearly and persuasively.
• Come to discussions prepared, having read and researched material under study; explicitly draw on that preparation by referring to evidence from texts and other research on the topic or issue to stimulate a thoughtful, well-reasoned exchange of ideas.

Outsiders
and
Outcasts

The idea of social isolation is a common thread throughout literature. Is it because being alone is just a natural part of life?

Socrates

💬 **Discuss It** What can happen to great thinkers when their ideas are critical of others?

Write your response before sharing your ideas.

UNIT INTRODUCTION

ESSENTIAL QUESTION:

Do people need to belong?

LAUNCH TEXT
ARGUMENT MODEL
Isn't Everyone a Little
Bit Weird?

WHOLE-CLASS LEARNING

ANCHOR TEXT: SHORT STORY

The Metamorphosis
Franz Kafka,
translated by
Ian Johnston

MEDIA: VIDEO

Franz Kafka and Metamorphosis
BBC

SMALL-GROUP LEARNING

SHORT STORY

The Doll's House
Katherine Mansfield

POETRY COLLECTION

Sonnet, With Bird
Sherman Alexie

Elliptical
Harryette Mullen

Fences
Pat Mora

ARGUMENT

Revenge of the Geeks
Alexandra Robbins

LECTURE

Encountering the Other: The Challenge for the 21st Century
Ryszard Kapuscinski

INDEPENDENT LEARNING

MYTH

The Orphan Boy and the Elk Dog
Blackfoot,
retold by Richard Erdoes
and Alfonso Ortiz

MEMOIR

By Any Other Name
from **Gifts of Passage**
Santha Rama Rau

NEWSPAPER ARTICLE

Outsider's Art Is Saluted at Columbia, Then Lost Anew
Vivian Yee

MEDIA: RADIO BROADCAST

Fleeing to Dismal Swamp, Slaves and Outcasts Found Freedom
Sandy Hausman

PERFORMANCE TASK

WRITING FOCUS:
Write an Argument

PERFORMANCE TASK

SPEAKING AND LISTENING FOCUS:
Deliver a Multimedia Presentation

PERFORMANCE-BASED ASSESSMENT PREP

Review Evidence for
an Argument

PERFORMANCE-BASED ASSESSMENT

Argument: Essay and Oral Presentation

PROMPT:

Is the experience of being an outsider universal?

Unit Goals

Throughout this unit, you will deepen your perspective of outsiders and outcasts by reading, writing, speaking, presenting, and listening. These goals will help you succeed on the Unit Performance-Based Assessment.

Rate how well you meet these goals right now. You will revisit your ratings later when you reflect on your growth during this unit.

SCALE	1	2	3	4	5
	NOT AT ALL WELL	NOT VERY WELL	SOMEWHAT WELL	VERY WELL	EXTREMELY WELL

READING GOALS   1   2   3   4   5

- Evaluate written arguments by analyzing how authors state and support their claims.

- Expand your knowledge and use of academic and concept vocabulary.

WRITING AND RESEARCH GOALS   1   2   3   4   5

- Write an argumentative essay in which you effectively incorporate the key elements of an argument.

- Conduct research projects of various lengths to explore a topic and clarify meaning.

LANGUAGE GOAL   1   2   3   4   5

- Correctly use phrases and clauses to convey meaning and add variety and interest to your writing and presentations.

SPEAKING AND LISTENING GOALS   1   2   3   4   5

- Collaborate with your team to build on the ideas of others, develop consensus, and communicate.

- Integrate audio, visuals, and text in presentations.

Academic Vocabulary: Argument

Academic terms appear in all subjects and can help you read, write, and discuss with more precision. Here are five academic words that will be useful to you in this unit as you analyze and write arguments.

Complete the chart.

1. Review each word, its base, and the mentor sentences.

2. Use the information and your own knowledge to predict the meaning of each word.

3. For each word, list at least two related words.

4. Refer to a dictionary or other resources if needed.

TIP

FOLLOW THROUGH
Study the words in this chart, and mark them or their forms wherever they appear in the unit.

WORD	MENTOR SENTENCES	PREDICT MEANING	RELATED WORDS
contradict ROOT: **-dict-** "speak"; "talk"	1. Your sister will probably be unhappy if you continue to *contradict* her. 2. The two sources that I used for my research paper *contradict* one another on some important points.		contradiction; contradictory
negate ROOT: **-neg-** "no"; "not"	1. The one time you lie may *negate* all the times you tell the truth. 2. Getting a bad grade on the final exam will *negate* all the hard work I put into this class.		
objection ROOT: **-ject-** "throw"	1. My only *objection* to the plan is that some of the steps seem vague and should be more precise. 2. When you have an *objection* to a proposal, explain your concerns in polite terms.		
verify ROOT: **-ver-** "truth"	1. Maria will *verify* the information before we include it in the presentation. 2. I checked the band's tour schedule to *verify* that the concert is this weekend.		
advocate ROOT: **-voc-** "voice"; "call out"	1. I'm voting for her because she has always been an *advocate* for causes that are important to me. 2. I would *advocate* that we study tonight so that we can go to the movies tomorrow.		

This selection is an example of an **argumentative text**, a type of writing in which an author states and defends a position on a topic. This is the type of writing you will develop in the Performance-Based Assessment at the end of the unit.

As you read, look at the way the writer builds a case. What is the writer's position and how is it supported?

Isn't Everyone a Little Bit Weird?

NOTES

1   Everyone is a little bit weird. That's not a bad thing. It just happens to be true.

2   The common definition of the adjective *weird* is "unusual or strange." The connotation, or implied meaning, of the term is that there is something wrong with a person who is described in this way. While many people might feel the connotation is accurate, I would argue that it's wrong for two reasons. First, the most gifted, successful people are often eccentric. Second, some traits we now think of as being weird were once highly regarded and not weird at all.

3   Consider Benjamin Franklin. One of the framers of the United States Constitution, Franklin (1706–1790) was a leading author, political theorist, politician, scientist, inventor, activist, and businessperson. He invented the lightning rod, bifocal glasses, and the Franklin stove. His discoveries regarding electricity are important to the history of physics. His public push for colonial solidarity was vital to the formation of the Union. He became wealthy as the writer and publisher of *Poor Richard's Almanack*.

4   There's nothing weird in that list of accomplishments. *Brilliant* would better describe Franklin, and yet the man some call "the first American" had certain ways about him you might consider odd. He once pranked a competing publisher by astrologically predicting when the man's life would end. He created his own alphabet, dispensing with the letters *c, j, q, w, x,* and *y,* and adding others he made up to stand in for common sounds. He is said to have favored "air baths," often writing his essays and letters while sitting in a cold room with nothing on.

5   Some aspects of Franklin's life that people today might see as weird would have been viewed as unremarkable during his lifetime. Take, for example, his appearance. In famous portraits, he wears ruffled shirts, breeches, and tight stockings pulled up to the knee. He wore his hair long well into old age. Today's viewers of those portraits might think him odd, but those were common fashions of his era. Likewise, consider Franklin's education. He quit school at age ten and was apprenticed as a printer at age twelve—a career move that today would be considered both weird and illegal.

6   Perhaps Franklin's oddness actually sparked his genius. He saw things in ways that challenged what other people accepted as fact. Additionally, he had the courage to communicate his insights, act on them, and turn them into achievements. It may have been Franklin's weirdness that made him great.

7   Some might argue that weird people are just plain weird. By most people's standards, an undressed man sitting in a cold room writing with a quill pen is undoubtedly strange. But that view of human nature is too narrow. It doesn't recognize the important idea that many of those who see things differently turn out to be the most creative and ingenious among us.

8   Everyone has eccentricities—slightly odd, perhaps unique ways of thinking or behaving. These might be the first traits you notice in someone, or the last. Being a little bit weird may be one of the things that actually connects us, and makes us uniquely human.

9   Ben Franklin wrote, "Life's tragedy is that we get old too soon and wise too late." It takes wisdom to look past what seems weird in people—what makes them different—to find the offbeat humanity that unites us all.

NOTES

WORD NETWORK FOR OUTSIDERS AND OUTCASTS

Vocabulary A Word Network is a collection of words related to a topic. As you read the selections in this unit, identify interesting words related to the idea of the outsider and add them to your Word Network. For example, you might begin by adding words from the Launch Text, such as *weird*, *eccentric*, and *unusual*. Continue to add words as you complete the unit.

🔧 **Tool Kit**
Word Network Model

offbeat

eccentric

unusual

OUTSIDER

Summary

Write a summary of "Isn't Everyone a Little Bit Weird?" A **summary** is a concise, complete, and accurate overview of a text. It should not include a statement of your opinion or an analysis.

Launch Activity

Conduct a Small Group Discussion Consider this question: **Why might exceptionally talented people be considered odd?**

- Record your position on the question and explain your thinking.

  _____

  _____

- Get together with a small group of students and discuss your responses. Consider similarities in your points of view, and work to clarify differences. Support your ideas with examples from texts you have read or your own observations.

- After your discussion, have a representative from each group present a two- to three-minute summary of the group's conversation.

- After all the groups have presented, discuss as a class the similarities and differences among the views presented.

QuickWrite

Consider class discussions, presentations, the video, and the Launch Text as you think about the prompt. Record your first thoughts here.

PROMPT: **Is the experience of being an outsider universal?**

EVIDENCE LOG FOR OUTSIDERS AND OUTCASTS

Review your QuickWrite, and summarize your initial position in one sentence to record in your Evidence Log. Then, record evidence from "Isn't Everyone a Little Bit Weird?" that supports your position.

After each selection, you will continue to use your Evidence Log to record the evidence you gather and the connections you make.

🔧 **Tool Kit**
Evidence Log Model

Title of Text: _____ Date: _____

CONNECTION TO PROMPT	TEXT EVIDENCE/DETAILS	ADDITIONAL NOTES/IDEAS

How does this text change or add to my thinking? Date: _____

ESSENTIAL QUESTION:
Do people need to belong?

Do we all feel like outsiders at some point in our lives? Is being an outsider always a negative experience? Can being an outsider offer any advantages? You will work with your whole class to explore the ins and outs of being an outsider.

Whole-Class Learning Strategies

Throughout your life, in school, in your community, and in your career, you will continue to learn and work in large-group environments.

Review these strategies and the actions you can take to practice them as you work with your whole class. Add ideas of your own for each step. Get ready to use these strategies during Whole-Class Learning.

STRATEGY	ACTION PLAN
Listen actively	• Eliminate distractions. For example, put your cell phone away. • Keep your eyes on the speaker. •
Clarify by asking questions	• If you're confused, other people probably are, too. Ask a question to help your whole class. • If you see that you are guessing, ask a question instead. •
Monitor understanding	• Notice what information you already know and be ready to build on it. • Ask for help if you are struggling. •
Interact and share ideas	• Share your ideas and answer questions, even if you are unsure. • Build on the ideas of others by adding details or making a connection. •

About the Author

Franz Kafka (1883–1924) was one of the greatest German-speaking writers of the twentieth century, but he received no support from his family. His mother did not understand his passion for literature. His father, a man obsessed with materialism, would not accept "author" as a legitimate profession. Kafka was also torn between multiple social worlds. His German identity clashed constantly with his Jewish heritage. Themes of domestic pressure and social anxiety recur often in Kafka's fiction.

🔧 Tool Kit
First-Read Guide and Model Annotation

The Metamorphosis

Concept Vocabulary

You will encounter the following words as you read "The Metamorphosis." Before reading, note how familiar you are with each word. Rank the words in order from most familiar (1) to least familiar (6).

WORD	YOUR RANKING
distress	
amelioration	
aversion	
asphyxiation	
listlessly	
travail	

After completing your first read, come back to the selection vocabulary and review your rankings. Mark changes to your original rankings as needed.

First Read FICTION

Apply these strategies as you conduct your first read. You will have an opportunity to complete the close-read notes after your first read.

NOTICE *whom* the story is about, *what* happens, *where* and *when* it happens, and *why* those involved react as they do.

ANNOTATE by marking vocabulary and key passages you want to revisit.

CONNECT ideas within the selection to what you already know and what you have already read.

RESPOND by completing the Comprehension Check and by writing a brief summary of the selection.

First Read

📑 STANDARDS
Reading Literature
By the end of grade 10, read and comprehend literature, including stories, dramas, and poems, at the high end of the grades 9-10 text complexity band independently and proficiently.

The
Metamorphosis

Franz Kafka

translated by Ian Johnston

BACKGROUND

Many authors produce great writing that moves, challenges, and inspires readers. Only a few, however, make such distinctive contributions that their names become synonymous with specific literary qualities. Such is the case with Kafka. The term *Kafkaesque* describes a nightmarish mood—specifically the feeling that one is trapped in a dangerous, distorted world. This story, which many scholars consider to be one of the greatest literary works of the twentieth century, is a prime example of Kafka's work.

~I~

1 One morning, as Gregor Samsa was waking up from anxious dreams, he discovered that in bed he had been changed into a monstrous verminous bug. He lay on his armor-hard back and saw, as he lifted his head up a little, his brown, arched abdomen divided up into rigid bow-like sections. From this height the blanket, just about ready to slide off completely, could hardly stay in place. His numerous legs, pitifully thin in comparison to the rest of his circumference, flickered helplessly before his eyes.

2 "What's happened to me," he thought. It was no dream. His room, a proper room for a human being, only somewhat too small, lay quietly between the four well-known walls. Above the table, on which an unpacked collection of sample cloth goods was spread out (Samsa was a traveling salesman), hung the picture which he had cut out of an illustrated magazine a little while ago and set in a pretty gilt frame. It was a picture of a woman with a fur hat and a fur boa. She sat erect there, lifting up in the direction of the viewer a solid fur muff into which her entire forearm disappeared.

NOTES

CLOSE READ

ANNOTATE: In paragraphs 3–5, mark details that relate to Gregor's physical transformation. Mark other details that show what he is thinking.

QUESTION: Why does Kafka devote so much more space to Gregor's thoughts than to his physical change?

CONCLUDE: What is the effect of this choice?

3   Gregor's glance then turned to the window. The dreary weather (the raindrops were falling audibly down on the metal window ledge) made him quite melancholy. "Why don't I keep sleeping for a little while longer and forget all this foolishness," he thought. But this was entirely impractical, for he was used to sleeping on his right side, and in his present state he couldn't get himself into this position. No matter how hard he threw himself onto his right side, he always rolled again onto his back. He must have tried it a hundred times, closing his eyes, so that he would not have to see the wriggling legs, and gave up only when he began to feel a light, dull pain in his side which he had never felt before.

4   "O God," he thought, "what a demanding job I've chosen! Day in, day out on the road. The stresses of trade are much greater than the work going on at head office, and, in addition to that, I have to deal with the problems of traveling, the worries about train connections, irregular bad food, temporary and constantly changing human relationships, which never come from the heart. To hell with it all!" He felt a slight itching on the top of his abdomen. He slowly pushed himself on his back closer to the bedpost so that he could lift his head more easily, found the itchy part, which was entirely covered with small white spots (he did not know what to make of them), and wanted to feel the place with a leg. But he retracted it immediately, for the contact felt like a cold shower all over him.

5   He slid back again into his earlier position. "This getting up early," he thought, "makes a man quite idiotic. A man must have his sleep. Other traveling salesmen live like harem women. For instance, when I come back to the inn during the course of the morning to write up the necessary orders, these gentlemen are just sitting down to breakfast. If I were to try that with my boss, I'd be thrown out on the spot. Still, who knows whether that mightn't be really good for me. If I didn't hold back for my parents' sake, I would've quit ages ago. I would've gone to the boss and told him just what I think from the bottom of my heart. He would've fallen right off his desk! How weird it is to sit up at the desk and talk down to the employee from way up there. The boss has trouble hearing, so the employee has to step up quite close to him. Anyway, I haven't completely given up that hope yet. Once I've got together the money to pay off the parents' debt to him—that should take another five or six years—I'll do it for sure. Then I'll make the big break. In any case, right now I have to get up. My train leaves at five o'clock."

6   And he looked over at the alarm clock ticking away by the chest of drawers. "Good God," he thought. It was half past six, and the hands were going quietly on. It was past the half hour, already nearly quarter to. Could the alarm have failed to ring? One saw from the bed that it was properly set for four o'clock. Certainly it had rung. Yes, but was it possible to sleep through this noise that made the furniture shake? Now, it's true he'd not slept quietly, but evidently he'd slept all the more deeply. Still, what should he do now? The

next train left at seven o'clock. To catch that one, he would have to go in a mad rush. The sample collection wasn't packed up yet, and he really didn't feel particularly fresh and active. And even if he caught the train, there was no avoiding a blow up with the boss, because the firm's errand boy would've waited for the five o'clock train and reported the news of his absence long ago. He was the boss's minion, without backbone or intelligence. Well then, what if he reported in sick? But that would be extremely embarrassing and suspicious, because during his five years' service Gregor hadn't been sick even once. The boss would certainly come with the doctor from the health insurance company and would reproach his parents for their lazy son and cut short all objections with the insurance doctor's comments; for him everyone was completely healthy but really lazy about work. And besides, would the doctor in this case be totally wrong? Apart from a really excessive drowsiness after the long sleep, Gregor in fact felt quite well and even had a really strong appetite.

7   As he was thinking all this over in the greatest haste, without being able to make the decision to get out of bed (the alarm clock was indicating exactly quarter to seven) there was a cautious knock on the door by the head of the bed.

8   "Gregor," a voice called (it was his mother!), "it's quarter to seven. Don't you want to be on your way?" The soft voice! Gregor was startled when he heard his voice answering. It was clearly and unmistakably his earlier voice, but in it was intermingled, as if from below, an irrepressibly painful squeaking which left the words positively distinct only in the first moment and distorted them in the reverberation, so that one didn't know if one had heard correctly. Gregor wanted to answer in detail and explain everything, but in these circumstances he confined himself to saying, "Yes, yes, thank you, Mother. I'm getting up right away." Because of the wooden door the change in Gregor's voice was not really noticeable outside, so his mother calmed down with this explanation and shuffled off. However, as a result of the short conversation the other family members became aware of the fact that Gregor was unexpectedly still at home, and already his father was knocking on one side door, weakly but with his fist. "Gregor, Gregor," he called out, "what's going on?" And after a short while he urged him on again in a deeper voice. "Gregor! Gregor!" At the other side door, however, his sister knocked lightly. "Gregor? Are you all right? Do you need anything?" Gregor directed answers in both directions, "I'll be ready right away." He made an effort with the most careful articulation and by inserting long pauses between the individual words to remove everything remarkable from his voice. His father turned back to his breakfast. However, his sister whispered, "Gregor, open the door, I beg you." Gregor had no intention of opening the door, but congratulated himself on his precaution, acquired from traveling, of locking all doors during the night, even at home.

CLOSE READ

ANNOTATE: In paragraph 10, mark words and phrases that describe how Gregor is moving.

QUESTION: What do these details suggest about Gregor's ability to control his new body?

CONCLUDE: What is the effect of this word choice?

9   First he wanted to stand up quietly and undisturbed, get dressed, above all have breakfast, and only then consider further action, for (he noticed this clearly) by thinking things over in bed he would not reach a reasonable conclusion. He remembered that he had already often felt a light pain or other in bed, perhaps the result of an awkward lying position, which later turned out to be purely imaginary when he stood up, and he was eager to see how his present fantasies would gradually dissipate. That the change in his voice was nothing other than the onset of a real chill, an occupational illness of commercial travelers, of that he had not the slightest doubt.

10   It was very easy to throw aside the blanket. He needed only to push himself up a little, and it fell by itself. But to continue was difficult, particularly because he was so unusually wide. He needed arms and hands to push himself upright. Instead of these, however, he had only many small limbs which were incessantly moving with very different motions and which, in addition, he was unable to control. If he wanted to bend one of them, then it was the first to extend itself, and if he finally succeeded doing with this limb what he wanted, in the meantime all the others, as if left free, moved around in an excessively painful agitation. "But I must not stay in bed uselessly," said Gregor to himself.

11   At first he wanted to get out of bed with the lower part of his body, but this lower part (which he incidentally had not yet looked at and which he also couldn't picture clearly) proved itself too difficult to move. The attempt went so slowly. When, having become almost frantic, he finally hurled himself forward with all his force and without thinking, he chose his direction incorrectly, and he hit the lower bedpost hard. The violent pain he felt revealed to him that the lower part of his body was at the moment probably the most sensitive.

12   Thus, he tried to get his upper body out of the bed first and turned his head carefully toward the edge of the bed. He managed to do this easily, and in spite of its width and weight his body mass at last slowly followed the turning of his head. But as he finally raised his head outside the bed in the open air, he became anxious about moving forward any further in this manner, for if he allowed himself eventually to fall by this process, it would take a miracle to prevent his head from getting injured. And at all costs he must not lose consciousness right now. He preferred to remain in bed.

13   However, after a similar effort, while he lay there again sighing as before and once again saw his small limbs fighting one another, if anything worse than before, and didn't see any chance of imposing quiet and order on this arbitrary movement, he told himself again that he couldn't possibly remain in bed and that it might be the most reasonable thing to sacrifice everything if there was even the slightest hope of getting himself out of bed in the process. At the same moment, however, he didn't forget to remind himself from time to time of the fact that calm (indeed the calmest) reflection might

be better than the most confused decisions. At such moments, he directed his gaze as precisely as he could toward the window, but unfortunately there was little confident cheer to be had from a glance at the morning mist, which concealed even the other side of the narrow street. "It's already seven o'clock," he told himself at the latest striking of the alarm clock, "already seven o'clock and still such a fog." And for a little while longer he lay quietly with weak breathing, as if perhaps waiting for normal and natural conditions to reemerge out of the complete stillness.

14 But then he said to himself, "Before it strikes a quarter past seven, whatever happens I must be completely out of bed. Besides, by then someone from the office will arrive to inquire about me, because the office will open before seven o'clock." And he made an effort then to rock his entire body length out of the bed with a uniform motion. If he let himself fall out of the bed in this way, his head, which in the course of the fall he intended to lift up sharply, would probably remain uninjured. His back seemed to be hard; nothing would really happen to that as a result of the fall. His greatest reservation was a worry about the loud noise which the fall must create and which presumably would arouse, if not fright, then at least concern on the other side of all the doors. However, it had to be tried.

15 As Gregor was in the process of lifting himself half out of bed (the new method was more of a game than an effort; he needed only to rock with a constant rhythm) it struck him how easy all this would be if someone were to come to his aid. Two strong people (he thought of his father and the servant girl) would have been quite sufficient. They would have only had to push their arms under his arched back to get

distress (dihs TREHS) *n.*
unhappiness or pain

him out of the bed, to bend down with their load, and then merely to exercise patience and care that he completed the flip onto the floor, where his diminutive legs would then, he hoped, acquire a purpose. Now, quite apart from the fact that the doors were locked, should he really call out for help? In spite of all his **distress**, he was unable to suppress a smile at this idea.

16   He had already got to the point where, with a stronger rocking, he maintained his equilibrium with difficulty, and very soon he would finally have to decide, for in five minutes it would be a quarter past seven. Then there was a ring at the door of the apartment. "That's someone from the office," he told himself, and he almost froze while his small limbs only danced around all the faster. For one moment everything remained still. "They aren't opening," Gregor said to himself, caught up in some absurd hope. But of course then, as usual, the servant girl with her firm tread went to the door and opened it. Gregor needed to hear only the visitor's first word of greeting to recognize immediately who it was, the manager himself. Why was Gregor the only one condemned to work in a firm where at the slightest lapse someone immediately attracted the greatest suspicion? Were all the employees then collectively, one and all, scoundrels? Was there then among them no truly devoted person who, if he failed to use just a couple of hours in the morning for office work, would become abnormal from pangs of conscience and really be in no state to get out of bed? Was it really not enough to let an apprentice make inquiries, if such questioning was even necessary? Must the manager himself come, and in the process must it be demonstrated to the entire innocent family that the investigation of this suspicious circumstance could only be entrusted to the intelligence of the manager? And more as a consequence of the excited state in which this idea put Gregor than as a result of an actual decision, he swung himself with all his might out of the bed. There was a loud thud, but not a real crash. The fall was absorbed somewhat by the carpet and, in addition, his back was more elastic than Gregor had thought. For that reason the dull noise was not quite so conspicuous. But he had not held his head up with sufficient care and had hit it. He turned his head, irritated and in pain, and rubbed it on the carpet.

> Then there was a ring at the door of the apartment. "That's someone from the office," he told himself, and he almost froze while his small limbs only danced around all the faster.

17   "Something has fallen in there," said the manager in the next room on the left. Gregor tried to imagine to himself whether anything similar to what was happening to him today could have also happened at some point to the manager. At least one had to concede the possibility of such a thing. However, as if to give a rough answer to this question, the manager now took a few determined steps in the next room, with a squeak of his polished boots. From the neighboring room on the right

his sister was whispering to inform Gregor: "Gregor, the manager is here." "I know," said Gregor to himself. But he did not dare make his voice loud enough so that his sister could hear.

18   "Gregor," his father now said from the neighboring room on the left, "Mr. Manager has come and is asking why you have not left on the early train. We don't know what we should tell him. Besides, he also wants to speak to you personally. So please open the door. He will be good enough to forgive the mess in your room."

19   In the middle of all this, the manager called out in a friendly way, "Good morning, Mr. Samsa." "He is not well," said his mother to the manager, while his father was still talking at the door, "He is not well, believe me, Mr. Manager. Otherwise how would Gregor miss a train! The young man has nothing in his head except business. I'm almost angry that he never goes out at night. Right now he's been in the city eight days, but he's been at home every evening. He sits there with us at the table and reads the newspaper quietly or studies his travel schedules. It's quite a diversion for him if he busies himself with fretwork.[1] For instance, he cut out a small frame over the course of two or three evenings. You'd be amazed how pretty it is. It's hanging right inside the room. You'll see it immediately, as soon as Gregor opens the door. Anyway, I'm happy that you're here, Mr. Manager. By ourselves, we would never have made Gregor open the door. He's so stubborn, and he's certainly not well, although he denied that this morning."

20   "I'm coming right away," said Gregor slowly and deliberately and didn't move, so as not to lose one word of the conversation. "My dear lady, I cannot explain it to myself in any other way," said the manager; "I hope it is nothing serious. On the other hand, I must also say that we businesspeople, luckily or unluckily, however one looks at it, very often simply have to overcome a slight indisposition for business reasons."

21   "So can Mr. Manager come in to see you now?" asked his father impatiently and knocked once again on the door. "No," said Gregor. In the neighboring room on the left a painful stillness descended. In the neighboring room on the right his sister began to sob.

22   Why didn't his sister go to the others? She'd probably just gotten up out of bed now and hadn't even started to get dressed yet. Then why was she crying? Because he wasn't getting up and wasn't letting the manager in; because he was in danger of losing his position, and because then his boss would badger his parents once again with the old demands? Those were probably unnecessary worries right now. Gregor was still here and wasn't thinking at all about abandoning his family. At the moment he was lying right there on the carpet, and no one who knew about his condition would've seriously demanded that he let the manager in. But Gregor wouldn't be casually dismissed right away because of this small discourtesy, for which he would find an easy and suitable excuse later on. It

---

1. **fretwork** (FREHT wurk) *n.* decorative woodworking.

seemed to Gregor that it might be far more reasonable to leave him in peace at the moment, instead of disturbing him with crying and conversation. But it was the very uncertainty which distressed the others and excused their behavior.

23   "Mr. Samsa," the manager was now shouting, his voice raised, "what's the matter? You are barricading yourself in your room, answer with only a yes and a no, are making serious and unnecessary troubles for your parents, and neglecting (I mention this only incidentally) your commercial duties in a truly unheard-of manner. I am speaking here in the name of your parents and your employer, and I am requesting you in all seriousness for an immediate and clear explanation. I am amazed. I am amazed. I thought I knew you as a calm, reasonable person, and now you appear suddenly to want to start parading around in weird moods. The Chief indicated to me earlier this very day a possible explanation for your neglect— it concerned the collection of cash entrusted to you a short while ago—but in truth I almost gave him my word of honor that this explanation could not be correct. However, now I see here your unimaginable pigheadedness, and I am totally losing any desire to speak up for you in the slightest. And your position is not at all the most secure. Originally I intended to mention all this to you privately, but since you are letting me waste my time here uselessly, I don't know why the matter shouldn't come to the attention of your parents. Your productivity has also been very unsatisfactory recently. Of course, it's not the time of year to conduct exceptional business, we recognize that, but a time of year for conducting no business, there is no such thing at all, Mr. Samsa, and such a thing must never be."

24   "But Mr. Manager," called Gregor, beside himself and in his agitation forgetting everything else, "I'm opening the door immediately, this very moment. A slight indisposition, a dizzy spell, has prevented me from getting up. I'm still lying in bed right now. But now I'm quite refreshed once again. I'm in the midst of getting out of bed. Just have patience for a short moment! Things are not going so well as I thought. But things are all right. How suddenly this can overcome someone! Just yesterday evening everything was fine with me. My parents certainly know that. Actually just yesterday evening I had a small premonition. People must have seen that in me. Why have I not reported that to the office! But people always think that they'll get over sickness without having to stay at home. Mr. Manager! Take it easy on my parents! There is really no basis for the criticisms which you are now making against me, and really nobody has said a word to me about that. Perhaps you have not read the latest orders which I shipped. Besides, now I'm setting out on my trip on the eight o'clock train; the few hours' rest have made me stronger. Mr. Manager, do not stay. I will be at the office in person right away. Please have the goodness to say that and to convey my respects to the Chief."

25   While Gregor was quickly blurting all this out, hardly aware of what he was saying, he had moved close to the chest of drawers without effort, probably as a result of the practice he had already had in bed, and now he was trying to raise himself up on it. Actually, he wanted to open the door; he really wanted to let himself be seen by and to speak with the manager. He was keen to witness what the others now asking after him would say at the sight of him. If they were startled, then Gregor had no more responsibility and could be calm. But if they accepted everything quietly, then he would have no reason to get excited and, if he got a move on, could really be at the station around eight o'clock.

26   At first he slid down a few times from the smooth chest of drawers. But at last he gave himself a final swing and stood upright there. He was no longer at all aware of the pains in his lower body, no matter how they might still sting. Now he let himself fall against the back of a nearby chair, on the edge of which he braced himself with his thin limbs. By doing this he gained control over himself and kept quiet, for he could now hear the manager.

27   "Did you understand a single word?" the manager asked the parents. "Is he playing the fool with us?" "For God's sake," cried the mother already in tears, "perhaps he's very ill and we're upsetting him. Grete! Grete!" she yelled at that point. "Mother?" called the sister from the other side. They were making themselves understood through Gregor's room. "You must go to the doctor right away. Gregor is sick. Hurry to the doctor. Have you heard Gregor speak yet?"

28   "That was an animal's voice," said the manager, remarkably quietly in comparison to the mother's cries.

29   "Anna! Anna!" yelled the father through the hall into the kitchen, clapping his hands, "fetch a locksmith right away!" The two young women were already running through the hall with swishing skirts (how had his sister dressed herself so quickly?) and yanked open the doors of the apartment. One couldn't hear the doors closing at all. They probably had left them open, as is customary in an apartment in which a huge misfortune has taken place.

30   However, Gregor had become much calmer. All right, people did not understand his words any more, although they seemed clear enough to him, clearer than previously, perhaps because his ears had gotten used to them. But at least people now thought that things were not all right with him and were prepared to help him. The confidence and assurance with which the first arrangements had been carried out made him feel good. He felt himself included once again in the circle of humanity and was expecting from both the doctor and the locksmith, without differentiating between them with any real precision, splendid and surprising results. In order to get as clear a voice as possible for the critical conversation which was imminent, he coughed a little, and certainly took the trouble to do this in a really subdued way, since it was possible that even this noise sounded like something different from a human cough. He no longer

trusted himself to decide any more. Meanwhile in the next room it had become really quiet. Perhaps his parents were sitting with the manager at the table and were whispering; perhaps they were all leaning against the door and listening.

31   Gregor pushed himself slowly toward the door, with the help of the easy chair, let go of it there, threw himself against the door, held himself upright against it (the balls of his tiny limbs had a little sticky stuff on them), and rested there momentarily from his exertion. Then he made an effort to turn the key in the lock with his mouth. Unfortunately it seemed that he had no real teeth. How then was he to grab hold of the key? But to make up for that his jaws were naturally very strong; with their help he managed to get the key really moving, and he did not notice that he was obviously inflicting some damage on himself, for a brown fluid came out of his mouth, flowed over the key, and dripped onto the floor.

32   "Just listen for a moment," said the manager in the next room, "he's turning the key." For Gregor that was a great encouragement. But they all should've called out to him, including his father and mother, "Come on, Gregor!" They should've shouted, "Keep going, keep working on the lock!" Imagining that all his efforts were being followed with suspense, he bit down frantically on the key with all the force he could muster. As the key turned more, he danced around the lock. Now he was holding himself upright only with his mouth, and he had to hang onto the key or then press it down again with the whole weight of his body, as necessary. The quite distinct click of the lock as it finally snapped really woke Gregor up. Breathing heavily he

said to himself, "So I didn't need the locksmith," and he set his head against the door handle to open the door completely.

33   Because he had to open the door in this way, it was already open very wide without him yet being really visible. He first had to turn himself slowly around the edge of the door, very carefully, of course, if he did not want to fall awkwardly on his back right at the entrance into the room. He was still preoccupied with this difficult movement and had no time to pay attention to anything else, when he heard the manager exclaim a loud "Oh!" (it sounded like the wind whistling), and now he saw him, nearest to the door, pressing his hand against his open mouth and moving slowly back, as if an invisible constant force was pushing him away. His mother (in spite of the presence of the manager she was standing here with her hair sticking up on end, still a mess from the night) with her hands clasped was looking at his father; she then went two steps toward Gregor and collapsed right in the middle of her skirts spreading out all around her, her face sunk on her breast, completely concealed. His father clenched his fist with a hostile expression, as if he wished to push Gregor back into his room, then looked uncertainly around the living room, covered his eyes with his hands, and cried so that his mighty breast shook.

34   At this point Gregor did not take one step into the room, but leaned his body from the inside against the firmly bolted wing of the door, so that only half his body was visible, as well as his head, tilted sideways, with which he peeped over at the others. Meanwhile it had become much brighter. Standing out clearly from the other side of the street was a part of the endless gray-black house situated opposite (it was a hospital) with its severe regular windows breaking up the facade. The rain was still coming down, but only in large individual drops visibly and firmly thrown down one by one onto the ground. The breakfast dishes were standing piled around on the table, because for his father breakfast was the most important meal time in the day, which he prolonged for hours by reading various newspapers. Directly across on the opposite wall hung a photograph of Gregor from the time of his military service; it was a picture of him as a lieutenant, as he, smiling and worry-free, with his hand on his sword, demanded respect for his bearing and uniform. The door to the hall was ajar, and since the door to the apartment was also open, one saw out into the landing of the apartment and the start of the staircase going down.

35   "Now," said Gregor, well aware that he was the only one who had kept his composure. "I'll get dressed right away, pack up the collection of samples, and set off. You'll allow me to set out on my way, will you not? You see, Mr. Manager, I am not pigheaded, and I am happy to work. Traveling is exhausting, but I couldn't live without it. Where are you going, Mr. Manager? To the office? Really? Will you report everything truthfully? A person can be incapable of work momentarily, but that is precisely the best time to remember the earlier achievements and to consider that later, after

CLOSE READ

ANNOTATE: In paragraph 34, mark details that describe Gregor at a different time in his life.

QUESTION: Why does Kafka include these details?

CONCLUDE: What effect does Kafka achieve by including this description?

the obstacles have been shoved aside, the person will work all the more keenly and intensely. I am really so indebted to Mr. Chief—you know that perfectly well. On the other hand, I am concerned about my parents and my sister. I'm in a fix, but I'll work myself out of it again. Don't make things more difficult for me than they already are. Speak up on my behalf in the office! People don't like traveling salesmen. I know that. People think they earn pots of money and thus lead a fine life. People don't even have any special reason to think through this judgment more clearly. But you, Mr. Manager, you have a better perspective on the interconnections than the other people, even, I tell you in total confidence, a better perspective than Mr. Chairman himself, who in his capacity as the employer may let his judgment make casual mistakes at the expense of an employee. You also know well enough that the traveling salesman who is outside the office almost the entire year can become so easily a victim of gossip, coincidences, and groundless complaints, against which it's impossible for him to defend himself, since for the most part he doesn't hear about them at all and only then when he's exhausted after finishing a trip, and gets to feel in his own body at home the nasty consequences, which can't be thoroughly explored back to their origins. Mr. Manager, don't leave without speaking a word telling me that you'll at least concede that I'm a little in the right!"

36   But at Gregor's first words the manager had already turned away, and now he looked back at Gregor over his twitching shoulders with pursed lips. During Gregor's speech he was not still for a moment, but was moving away toward the door, without taking his eyes off Gregor, but really gradually, as if there was a secret ban on leaving the room. He was already in the hall, and after the sudden movement with which he finally pulled his foot out of the living room, one could have believed that he had just burned the sole of his foot. In the hall, however, he stretched out his right hand away from his body toward the staircase, as if some truly supernatural relief was waiting for him there.

37   Gregor realized that he must not under any circumstances allow the manager to go away in this frame of mind, especially if his position in the firm was not to be placed in the greatest danger. His parents did not understand all this very well. Over the long years, they had developed the conviction that Gregor was set up for life in his firm and, in addition, they had so much to do nowadays with their present troubles that all foresight was foreign to them. But Gregor had this foresight. The manager must be held back, calmed down, convinced, and finally won over. The future of Gregor and his family really depended on it! If only his sister had been there! She was clever. She had already cried while Gregor was still lying quietly on his back. And the manager, this friend of the ladies, would certainly let himself be guided by her. She would have closed the door to the apartment and talked him out of his fright in the hall. But his sister was not even there. Gregor must deal with it himself.

38   Without thinking that as yet he didn't know anything about his present ability to move and without thinking that his speech possibly (indeed probably) had once again not been understood, he left the wing of the door, pushed himself through the opening, and wanted to go over to the manager, who was already holding tight onto the handrail with both hands on the landing in a ridiculous way. But as he looked for something to hold onto, with a small scream Gregor immediately fell down onto his numerous little legs. Scarcely had this happened, when he felt for the first time that morning a general physical well-being. The small limbs had firm floor under them; they obeyed perfectly, as he noticed to his joy, and strove to carry him forward in the direction he wanted. Right away he believed that the final **amelioration** of all his suffering was immediately at hand. But at the very moment when he lay on the floor rocking in a restrained manner quite close and directly across from his mother (apparently totally sunk into herself) she suddenly sprang right up with her arms spread far apart and her fingers extended and cried out, "Help, for God's sake, help!" She held her head bowed down, as if she wanted to view Gregor better, but ran senselessly back, contradicting that gesture, forgetting that behind her stood the table with all the dishes on it. When she reached the table, she sat down heavily on it, as if absentmindedly, and did not appear to notice at all that next to her coffee was pouring out onto the carpet in a full stream from the large overturned container.

39   "Mother, mother," said Gregor quietly, and looked over toward her. The manager momentarily had disappeared completely from his mind; by contrast, at the sight of the flowing coffee he couldn't stop himself snapping his jaws in the air a few times. At that his mother screamed all over again, hurried from the table, and collapsed into the arms of his father, who was rushing toward her. But Gregor had no time right now for his parents: The manager was already on the staircase. His chin level with the banister, the manager looked back for the last time. Gregor took an initial movement to catch up to him if possible. But the manager must have suspected something, because he made a leap down over a few stairs and disappeared, still shouting, "Huh!" The sound echoed throughout the entire stairwell.

40   Now, unfortunately this flight of the manager also seemed completely to bewilder his father, who earlier had been relatively calm, for instead of running after the manager himself or at least not hindering Gregor from his pursuit, with his right hand he grabbed hold of the manager's cane, which he had left behind with his hat and overcoat on a chair. With his left hand, his father picked up a large newspaper from the table and, stamping his feet on the floor, he set out to drive Gregor back into his room by waving the cane and

amelioration (uh MEEL yuh RAY shuhn) *n.* act of making something better or less painful

> But as he looked for something to hold onto, with a small scream Gregor immediately fell down onto his numerous little legs.

the newspaper. No request of Gregor's was of any use; no request would even be understood. No matter how willing he was to turn his head respectfully, his father just stomped all the harder with his feet.

41   Across the room from him his mother had pulled open a window, in spite of the cool weather, and leaning out with her hands on her cheeks, she pushed her face far outside the window. Between the alley and the stairwell a strong draft came up, the curtains on the window flew around, the newspapers on the table swished, and individual sheets fluttered down over the floor. The father relentlessly pressed forward pushing out sibilants, like a wild man. Now, Gregor had no practice at all in going backwards; it was really going very slowly. If Gregor only had been allowed to turn himself around, he would have been in his room right away, but he was afraid to make his father impatient by the time-consuming process of turning around, and each moment he faced the threat of a mortal blow on his back or his head from the cane in his father's hand. Finally Gregor had no other option, for he noticed with horror that he did not understand yet how to maintain his direction going backwards. And so he began, amid constantly anxious sideways glances in his father's direction, to turn himself around as quickly as possible (although in truth this was only very slowly). Perhaps his father noticed his good intentions, for he did not disrupt Gregor

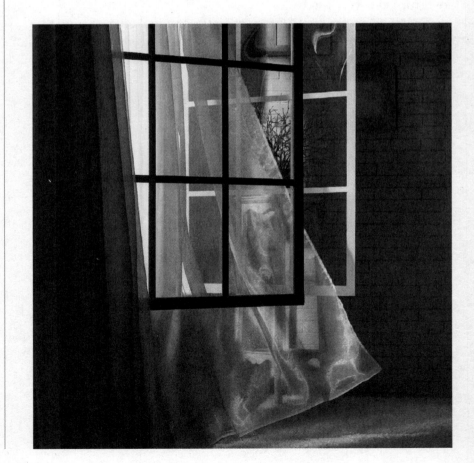

in this motion, but with the tip of the cane from a distance he even directed here and there Gregor's rotating movement.

42   If only there hadn't been his father's unbearable hissing! Because of that Gregor totally lost his head. He was already almost totally turned around, when, always with this hissing in his ear, he just made a mistake and turned himself back a little. But when he finally was successful in getting his head in front of the door opening, it became clear that his body was too wide to go through any further. Naturally his father, in his present mental state, had no idea of opening the other wing of the door a bit to create a suitable passage for Gregor to get through. His single fixed thought was that Gregor must get into his room as quickly as possible. He would never have allowed the elaborate preparations that Gregor required to orient himself and thus perhaps get through the door. On the contrary, as if there were no obstacle and with a peculiar noise, he now drove Gregor forward. Behind Gregor the sound was at this point no longer like the voice of only a single father. Now it was really no longer a joke, and Gregor forced himself, come what might, into the door. One side of his body was lifted up. He lay at an angle in the door opening. His one flank was sore with the scraping. On the white door ugly blotches were left. Soon he was stuck fast and would have not been able to move any more on his own. The tiny legs on one side hung twitching in the air above, the ones on the other side were pushed painfully into the floor. Then his father gave him one really strong liberating push from behind, and he scurried, bleeding severely, far into the interior of his room. The door was slammed shut with the cane, and finally it was quiet.

~ II ~

43 Gregor first woke up from his heavy swoon-like sleep in the evening twilight. He would certainly have woken up soon afterwards without any disturbance, for he felt himself sufficiently rested and wide awake, although it appeared to him as if a hurried step and a cautious closing of the door to the hall had aroused him. The shine of the electric streetlights lay pale here and there on the ceiling and on the higher parts of the furniture, but underneath around Gregor it was dark. He pushed himself slowly toward the door, still groping awkwardly with his feelers, which he now learned to value for the first time, to check what was happening there. His left side seemed one single long unpleasantly stretched scar, and he really had to hobble on his two rows of legs. In addition, one small leg had been seriously wounded in the course of the morning incident (it was almost a miracle that only one had been hurt) and dragged lifelessly behind.

44   By the door he first noticed what had really lured him there: It was the smell of something to eat. For there stood a bowl filled with sweetened milk, in which swam tiny pieces of white bread. He

CLOSE READ

ANNOTATE: In paragraphs 41 and 42, mark details that describe the father's voice.

QUESTION: Why does Kafka emphasize what the father sounds like?

CONCLUDE: What effect do these details have?

aversion (uh VUR zhuhn) *n.* strong dislike

ANNOTATE: In paragraph 45, mark details that relate to silence and stillness. Mark other, fewer details that relate to movement.

QUESTION: Why does Kafka include these details?

CONCLUDE: How do these details emphasize Gregor's alienation from his family?

almost laughed with joy, for he now had a much greater hunger than in the morning, and he immediately dipped his head almost up to and over his eyes down into the milk. But he soon drew it back again in disappointment, not just because it was difficult for him to eat on account of his delicate left side (he could eat only if his entire panting body worked in a coordinated way), but also because the milk, which otherwise was his favorite drink and which his sister had certainly placed there for that reason, did not appeal to him at all. He turned away from the bowl almost with **aversion** and crept back into the middle of the room.

45 In the living room, as Gregor saw through the crack in the door, the gas was lit, but where on other occasions at this time of day the father was accustomed to read the afternoon newspaper in a loud voice to his mother and sometimes also to his sister, at the moment not a sound was audible. Now, perhaps this reading aloud, about which his sister had always spoken and written to him, had recently fallen out of their general routine. But it was so still all around, in spite of the fact that the apartment was certainly not empty. "What a quiet life the family leads," said Gregor to himself and, as he stared fixedly out in front of him into the darkness, he felt a great pride that he had been able to provide such a life in a beautiful apartment like this for his parents and his sister. But how would things go if now all tranquility, all prosperity, all contentment should come to a horrible end? In order not to lose himself in such thoughts, Gregor preferred to set himself moving and crawled up and down in his room.

46 Once during the long evening one side door and then the other door was opened just a tiny crack and quickly closed again. Someone presumably needed to come in but had then thought better of it. Gregor immediately took up a position by the living room door, determined to bring in the hesitant visitor somehow or other or at least to find out who it might be. But now the door was not opened any more, and Gregor waited in vain. Earlier, when the door had been barred, they had all wanted to come in to him; now, when he had opened one door and when the others had obviously been opened during the day, no one came any more, and the keys were stuck in the locks on the outside.

47 The light in the living room was turned off only late at night, and now it was easy to establish that his parents and his sister had stayed awake all this time, for one could hear clearly as all three moved away on tiptoe. Now it was certain that no one would come into Gregor any more until the morning. Thus, he had a long time to think undisturbed about how he should reorganize his life from scratch. But the high, open room, in which he was compelled to lie flat on the floor, made him anxious, without his being able to figure out the reason, for he had lived in the room for five years. With a half-unconscious turn and not without a slight shame he scurried under the couch, where, in spite of the fact that his back was a little cramped

and he could no longer lift up his head, he felt very comfortable and was sorry only that his body was too wide to fit completely under it.

48   There he remained the entire night, which he spent partly in a state of semi-sleep, out of which his hunger constantly woke him with a start, but partly in a state of worry and murky hopes, which all led to the conclusion that for the time being he would have to keep calm and with patience and the greatest consideration for his family tolerate the troubles which in his present condition he was now forced to cause them.

49   Already early in the morning (it was still almost night) Gregor had an opportunity to test the power of the decisions he had just made, for his sister, almost fully dressed, opened the door from the hall into his room and looked eagerly inside. She did not find him immediately, but when she noticed him under the couch (God, he had to be somewhere or other; for he could hardly fly away) she got such a shock that, without being able to control herself, she slammed the door shut once again from the outside. However, as if she was sorry for her behavior, she immediately opened the door again and walked in on her tiptoes, as if she was in the presence of a serious invalid or a total stranger. Gregor had pushed his head forward just to the edge of the couch and was observing her. Would she really notice that he had left the milk standing, not indeed from any lack of hunger, and would she bring in something else to eat more suitable for him? If she did not do it on her own, he would sooner starve to death than call her attention to the fact, although he had a really powerful urge to move beyond the couch, throw himself at his sister's feet, and beg her for something or other good to eat. But his sister noticed right away with astonishment that the bowl was still full, with only a little milk spilled around it. She picked it up immediately (although not with her bare hands but with a rag), and took it out of the room. Gregor was extremely curious what she would bring as a substitute, and he pictured to himself different ideas about that. But he never could have guessed what his sister out of the goodness of her heart in fact did. She brought him, to test his taste, an entire selection, all spread out on an old newspaper. There were old half-rotten vegetables, bones from the evening meal, covered with a white sauce which had almost solidified, some raisins and almonds, cheese, which Gregor had declared inedible two days earlier, a slice of dry bread, a slice of salted bread smeared with butter. In addition to all this, she put down a bowl (probably designated once and for all as Gregor's) into which she had poured some water. And out of her delicacy of feeling, since she knew that Gregor would not eat in front of her, she went away very quickly and even turned the key in the lock, so that Gregor could now observe that he could make himself as comfortable as he wished. Gregor's small limbs buzzed as the time for eating had come. His wounds must, in any case, have already healed completely. He felt no handicap on that score. He was astonished at that and thought about it, how more than a month ago he had cut his finger slightly

Certainly they would not have wanted Gregor to starve to death, but perhaps they could not have endured finding out what he ate other than by hearsay.

asphyxiation (uhs fihk see AY shuhn) *n.* state of being unable to breathe

with a knife and how this wound had hurt enough even the day before yesterday.

50   "Am I now going to be less sensitive," he thought, already sucking greedily on the cheese, which had strongly attracted him right away, more than all the other foods. Quickly and with his eyes watering with satisfaction, he ate one after the other the cheese, the vegetables, and the sauce; the fresh food, by contrast, didn't taste good to him. He couldn't bear the smell and even carried the things he wanted to eat a little distance away. By the time his sister slowly turned the key as a sign that he should withdraw, he was long finished and now lay lazily in the same spot. The noise immediately startled him, in spite of the fact that he was already almost asleep, and he scurried back again under the couch. But it cost him great self-control to remain under the couch, even for the short time his sister was in the room, because his body had filled out somewhat on account of the rich meal and in the narrow space there he could scarcely breathe. In the midst of minor attacks of **asphyxiation**, he looked at her with somewhat protruding eyes, as his unsuspecting sister swept up with a broom, not just the remnants, but even the foods which Gregor had not touched at all, as if these were also now useless, and as she dumped everything quickly into a bucket, which she closed with a wooden lid, and then carried all of it out of the room. She had hardly turned around before Gregor had already dragged himself out from the couch, stretched out, and let his body expand.

51   In this way Gregor got his food every day, once in the morning, when his parents and the servant girl were still asleep, and a second time after the common noon meal, for his parents were, as before, asleep then for a little while, and the servant girl was sent off by his sister on some errand or other. Certainly they would not have wanted Gregor to starve to death, but perhaps they could not have endured finding out what he ate other than by hearsay. Perhaps his sister wanted to spare them what was possibly only a small grief, for they were really suffering quite enough already.

52   What sorts of excuses people had used on that first morning to get the doctor and the locksmith out of the house Gregor was completely unable to ascertain. Since he was not comprehensible, no one, not even his sister, thought that he might be able to understand others, and thus, when his sister was in her room, he had to be content with listening now and then to her sighs and invocations to the saints. Only later, when she had grown somewhat accustomed to everything (naturally there could never be any talk of her growing completely accustomed to it) Gregor sometimes caught a comment which was intended to be friendly or could be interpreted as such. "Well, today it tasted good to him," she said, if Gregor had really cleaned up what

he had to eat; whereas, in the reverse situation, which gradually repeated itself more and more frequently, she used to say sadly, "Now everything has stopped again."

53   But while Gregor could get no new information directly, he did hear a good deal from the room next door, and as soon as he heard voices, he scurried right away to the relevant door and pressed his entire body against it. In the early days especially, there was no conversation which was not concerned with him in some way or other, even if only in secret. For two days at all meal times discussions on that subject could be heard on how people should now behave; but they also talked about the same subject in the times between meals, for there were always at least two family members at home, since no one really wanted to remain in the house alone and people could not under any circumstances leave the apartment completely empty. In addition, on the very first day the servant girl (it was not completely clear what and how much she knew about what had happened) on her knees had begged his mother to let her go immediately, and when she said goodbye about fifteen minutes later, she thanked them for the dismissal with tears in her eyes, as if she was receiving the greatest favor which people had shown her there, and, without anyone demanding it from her, she swore a fearful oath not to betray anyone, not even the slightest bit.

54   Now his sister had to team up with his mother to do the cooking, although that didn't create much trouble because people were eating almost nothing. Again and again Gregor listened as one of them vainly invited another one to eat and received no answer other than "Thank you. I have enough" or something like that. And perhaps they had stopped having anything to drink, too. His sister often asked his father whether he wanted to have a beer and gladly offered to fetch it herself, and when his father was silent, she said, in order to remove any reservations he might have, that she could send the caretaker's wife to get it. But then his father finally said a resounding "No," and nothing more would be spoken about it.

55   Already during the first day his father laid out all the financial circumstances and prospects to his mother and to his sister as well. From time to time he stood up from the table and pulled out of the small lockbox salvaged from his business, which had collapsed five years previously, some document or other or some notebook. The sound was audible as he opened up the complicated lock and, after removing what he was looking for, locked it up again. These explanations by his father were, in part, the first enjoyable thing that Gregor had the chance to listen to since his imprisonment. He had thought that nothing at all was left over for his father from that business; at least his father had told him nothing to contradict that view, and Gregor in any case hadn't asked him about it. At the time Gregor's only concern had been to devote everything he had in order to allow his family to forget as quickly as possible the business misfortune which had brought them all into a state of

CLOSE READ

ANNOTATE: Mark details in paragraph 53 that show how the servant girl behaves when she quits her job.

QUESTION: Why does Kafka describe the servant girl's behavior in such detail?

CONCLUDE: What is the effect of this description?

complete hopelessness. And so at that point he'd started to work with a special intensity and from an assistant had become, almost overnight, a traveling salesman, who naturally had entirely different possibilities for earning money and whose successes at work at once were converted into the form of cash commissions, which could be set out on the table at home in front of his astonished and delighted family. Those had been beautiful days, and they had never come back afterwards, at least not with the same splendor, in spite of the fact that Gregor later earned so much money that he was in a position to bear the expenses of the entire family, expenses which he, in fact, did bear. They had become quite accustomed to it, both the family and Gregor as well. They took the money with thanks, and he happily surrendered it, but the special warmth was no longer present. Only the sister had remained still close to Gregor, and it was his secret plan to send her (in contrast to Gregor she loved music very much and knew how to play the violin charmingly) next year to the conservatory, regardless of the great expense which that must necessitate and which would be made up in other ways. Now and then during Gregor's short stays in the city the conservatory was mentioned in conversations with his sister, but always only as a beautiful dream, whose realization was unimaginable, and their parents never listened to these innocent expectations with pleasure. But Gregor thought about them with scrupulous consideration and intended to explain the matter ceremoniously on Christmas Eve.

56   In his present situation, such futile ideas went through his head, while he pushed himself right up against the door and listened. Sometimes in his general exhaustion he couldn't listen any more and let his head bang **listlessly** against the door, but he immediately pulled himself together, for even the small sound which he made by this motion was heard nearby and silenced everyone. "There he goes on again," said his father after a while, clearly turning toward the door, and only then would the interrupted conversation gradually be resumed again.

57   Gregor found out clearly enough (for his father tended to repeat himself often in his explanations, partly because he had not personally concerned himself with these matters for a long time now, and partly also because his mother did not understand everything right away the first time) that, in spite of all bad luck, a fortune, although a very small one, was available from the old times, on which the interest (which had not been touched) had in the intervening time gradually allowed to increase a little. Furthermore, in addition to this, the money which Gregor had brought home every month (he had kept only a few florins for himself) had not been completely spent and had grown into a small capital amount. Gregor, behind his door, nodded eagerly, rejoicing over this unanticipated foresight and frugality. True, with this excess money, he could have paid off more of his father's debt to his employer and the day on which he could be rid of this position would have been

listlessly (LIHST lihs lee) *adv.* without energy or interest

CLOSE READ

ANNOTATE: In paragraph 57, mark the parts of sentences that are set off in parentheses.

QUESTION: Why does the author separate out this information?

CONCLUDE: What is the effect of setting these sections apart in this way?

a lot closer, but now things were doubtless better the way his father had arranged them.

58   At the moment, however, this money was nowhere near sufficient to permit the family to live on the interest payments. Perhaps it would be enough to maintain the family for one or at most two years, that's all. Thus it came only to an amount which one should not really take out and which must be set aside for an emergency. But the money to live on must be earned. Now, his father was a healthy man, although he was old, who had not worked at all for five years now and thus could not be counted on for very much. He had in these five years, the first holidays of his trouble-filled but unsuccessful life, put on a good deal of fat and thus had become really heavy. And should his old mother now maybe work for money, a woman who suffered from asthma, for whom wandering through the apartment even now was a great strain and who spent every second day on the sofa by the open window laboring for breath? Should his sister earn money, a girl who was still a seventeen-year-old child, whose earlier life style had been so very delightful that it had consisted of dressing herself nicely, sleeping in late, helping around the house, taking part in a few modest enjoyments and, above all, playing the violin? When it came to talking about this need to earn money, at first Gregor went away from the door and threw himself on the cool leather sofa beside the door, for he was quite hot from shame and sorrow.

59   Often he lay there all night long. He didn't sleep a moment and just scratched on the leather for hours at a time. He undertook the very difficult task of shoving a chair over to the window. Then he crept up on the windowsill and, braced in the chair, leaned against the window to look out, obviously with some memory or other of the satisfaction which that used to bring him in earlier times. Actually from day to day he perceived things with less and less clarity, even those a short distance away: The hospital across the street, the all too frequent sight of which he had previously cursed, was not visible at all any more, and if he had not been precisely aware that he lived in the quiet but completely urban Charlotte Street, he could have believed that from his window he was peering out at a featureless wasteland, in which the gray heaven and the gray earth had merged and were indistinguishable. His attentive sister must have observed a couple of times that the chair stood by the window; then, after cleaning up the room, each time she pushed the chair back right against the window and from now on she even left the inner casement open.

60   If Gregor had only been able to speak to his sister and thank her for everything that she had to do for him, he would have tolerated her service more easily. As it was he suffered under it. The sister admittedly sought to cover up the awkwardness of everything as much as possible, and, as time went by, she naturally got more successful at it. But with the passing of time Gregor also came to understand everything more precisely. Even her entrance was terrible for him. As soon as she entered, she ran straight to the window,

without taking the time to shut the door (in spite of the fact that she was otherwise very considerate in sparing anyone the sight of Gregor's room), and yanked the window open with eager hands, as if she was almost suffocating, and remained for a while by the window breathing deeply, even when it was still so cold. With this running and noise she frightened Gregor twice every day. The entire time he trembled under the couch, and yet he knew very well that she would certainly have spared him gladly if it had only been possible to remain with the window closed in a room where Gregor lived.

61   On one occasion (about one month had already gone by since Gregor's transformation, and there was now no particular reason any more for his sister to be startled at Gregor's appearance) she came a little earlier than usual and came upon Gregor as he was still looking out the window, immobile and well positioned to frighten someone. It would not have come as a surprise to Gregor if she had not come in, since his position was preventing her from opening the window immediately. But she not only did not step inside; she even retreated and shut the door. A stranger really could have concluded from this that Gregor had been lying in wait for her and wanted to bite her. Of course, Gregor immediately concealed himself under the couch, but he had to wait until the noon meal before his sister returned, and she seemed much less calm than usual. From this he realized that his appearance was still constantly intolerable to her and must remain intolerable in the future, and that she really had to exert a lot of self-control not to run away from a glimpse of only the small part of his body which stuck out from under the couch. In order to spare her even this sight, one day he dragged the sheet on his back onto the

couch (this task took him four hours) and arranged it in such a way that he was now completely concealed and his sister, even if she bent down, could not see him. If this sheet was not necessary as far as she was concerned, then she could remove it, for it was clear enough that Gregor could not derive any pleasure from isolating himself away so completely. But she left the sheet just as it was, and Gregor believed he even caught a look of gratitude when on one occasion he carefully lifted up the sheet a little with his head to check as his sister took stock of the new arrangement.

62   In the first two weeks his parents could not bring themselves to visit him, and he often heard how they fully acknowledged his sister's present work; whereas, earlier they had often got annoyed at his sister because she had seemed to them a somewhat useless young woman. However, now both his father and his mother often waited in front of Gregor's door while his sister cleaned up inside, and as soon as she came out she had to explain in detail how things looked in the room, what Gregor had eaten, how he had behaved this time, and whether perhaps a slight improvement was perceptible. In any event, his mother comparatively soon wanted to visit Gregor, but his father and his sister restrained her, at first with reasons which Gregor listened to very attentively and which he completely endorsed. Later, however, they had to hold her back forcefully, and when she then cried, "Let me go to Gregor. He's my unlucky son! Don't you understand that I have to go to him?" Gregor then thought that perhaps it would be a good thing if his mother came in, not every day, of course, but maybe once a week. She understood everything much better than his sister, who in spite of all her courage was still a child and, in the last analysis, had perhaps undertaken such a difficult task only out of childish recklessness.

63   Gregor's wish to see his mother was soon realized. While during the day Gregor, out of consideration for his parents, did not want to show himself by the window, he couldn't crawl around very much on the few square meters of the floor. He found it difficult to bear lying quietly during the night, and soon eating no longer gave him the slightest pleasure. So for diversion he acquired the habit of crawling back and forth across the walls and ceiling. He was especially fond of hanging from the ceiling. The experience was quite different from lying on the floor. It was easier to breathe, a slight vibration went through his body, and in the midst of the almost happy amusement which Gregor found up there, it could happen that, to his own surprise, he let go and hit the floor. However, now he naturally controlled his body quite differently, and he did not injure himself in such a great fall. His sister noticed immediately the new amusement which Gregor had found for himself (for as he crept around he left behind here and there traces of his sticky stuff), and so she got the idea of making Gregor's creeping around as easy as possible and thus of removing the furniture which got in the way, especially the chest of drawers and the writing desk.

CLOSE READ

ANNOTATE: In paragraph 63, mark details that describe Gregor's growing comfort in and knowledge of his new body.

QUESTION: Why does the author provide these details?

CONCLUDE: What is the effect of these details?

64   But she was in no position to do this by herself. She did not dare to ask her father to help, and the servant girl would certainly not have assisted her, for although this girl, about sixteen years old, had courageously remained since the dismissal of the previous cook, she had begged for the privilege of being allowed to stay permanently confined to the kitchen and of having to open the door only in answer to a special summons. Thus, his sister had no other choice but to involve his mother while his father was absent. His mother approached Gregor's room with cries of excited joy, but she fell silent at the door. Of course, his sister first checked whether everything in the room was in order. Only then did she let his mother walk in. In great haste Gregor had drawn the sheet down even further and wrinkled it more. The whole thing really looked just like a coverlet thrown carelessly over the couch. On this occasion, Gregor held back from spying out from under the sheet. Thus, he refrained from looking at his mother this time and was just happy that she had come. "Come on; he is not visible," said his sister, and evidently led his mother by the hand. Now Gregor listened as these two weak women shifted the still heavy old chest of drawers from its position, and as his sister constantly took on herself the greatest part of the work, without listening to the warnings of his mother who was afraid that she would strain herself. The work lasted a long time. After about a quarter of an hour had already gone by his mother said that it would be better if they left the chest of drawers where it was, because, in the first place, it was too heavy: they would not be finished before his father's arrival, and with the chest of drawers in the middle of the room it would block all Gregor's pathways, but, in the second place, it might not be certain that Gregor would be pleased with the removal of the furniture. To her the reverse seemed to be true; the sight of the empty walls pierced her right to the heart, and why should Gregor not feel the same, since he had been accustomed to the room furnishings for a long time and in an empty room would thus feel himself abandoned.

65   "And is it not the case," his mother concluded very quietly, almost whispering as if she wished to prevent Gregor, whose exact location she really didn't know, from hearing even the sound of her voice (for she was convinced that he did not understand her words), "and isn't it a fact that by removing the furniture we're showing that we're giving up all hope of an improvement and are leaving him to his own resources without any consideration? I think it would be best if we tried to keep the room exactly in the condition in which it was before, so that, when Gregor returns to us, he finds everything unchanged and can forget the intervening time all the more easily."

66   As he heard his mother's words Gregor realized that the lack of all immediate human contact, together with the monotonous life surrounded by the family over the course of these two months must have confused his understanding, because otherwise he couldn't

explain to himself that he in all seriousness could've been so keen to have his room emptied. Was he really eager to let the warm room, comfortably furnished with pieces he had inherited, be turned into a cavern in which he would, of course, then be able to crawl about in all directions without disturbance, but at the same time with a quick and complete forgetting of his human past as well? Was he then at this point already on the verge of forgetting and was it only the voice of his mother, which he had not heard for a long time, that had aroused him? Nothing was to be removed; everything must remain. In his condition he couldn't function without the beneficial influences of his furniture. And if the furniture prevented him from carrying out his senseless crawling about all over the place, then there was no harm in that, but rather a great benefit.

67   But his sister unfortunately thought otherwise. She had grown accustomed, certainly not without justification, so far as the discussion of matters concerning Gregor was concerned, to act as a special expert with respect to their parents, and so now the mother's advice was for his sister sufficient reason to insist on the removal, not only of the chest of drawers and the writing desk, which were the only items she had thought about at first, but also of all the furniture, with the exception of the indispensable couch. Of course, it was not only childish defiance and her recent very unexpected and hard won self-confidence which led her to this demand. She had also actually observed that Gregor needed a great deal of room to creep about; the furniture, on the other hand, as far as one could see, was not of the slightest use.

68   But perhaps the enthusiastic sensibility of young women of her age also played a role. This feeling sought release at every opportunity, and with it Grete now felt tempted to want to make Gregor's situation even more terrifying, so that then she would be able to do even more for him than now. For surely no one except Grete would ever trust themselves to enter a room in which Gregor ruled the empty walls all by himself. And so she did not let herself be dissuaded from her decision by her mother, who in this room seemed uncertain of herself in her sheer agitation and soon kept quiet, helping his sister with all her energy to get the chest of drawers out of the room. Now, Gregor could still do without the chest of drawers if need be, but the writing desk really had to stay. And scarcely had the women left the room with the chest of drawers, groaning as they pushed it, when Gregor stuck his head out from under the sofa to take a look at how he could intervene cautiously and with as much consideration as possible. But unfortunately it was his mother who came back into the room first, while Grete had her arms wrapped around the chest of drawers in the next room and was rocking it back and forth by herself, without moving it from its position. His mother was not used to the sight of Gregor; he could have made her ill, and so, frightened, Gregor scurried backwards right to the other end of the sofa, but he could no longer prevent the sheet from moving

forward a little. That was enough to catch his mother's attention. She came to a halt, stood still for a moment, and then went back to Grete.

69   Although Gregor kept repeating to himself over and over that really nothing unusual was going on, that only a few pieces of furniture were being rearranged, he soon had to admit to himself that the movements of the women to and fro, their quiet conversations, the scratching of the furniture on the floor affected him like a great swollen commotion on all sides, and, so firmly was he pulling in his head and legs and pressing his body into the floor, he had to tell himself unequivocally that he wouldn't be able to endure all this much longer. They were cleaning out his room, taking away from him everything he cherished; they had already dragged out the chest of drawers in which the fret saw and other tools were kept, and they were now loosening the writing desk which was fixed tight to the floor, the desk on which he, as a business student, a school student, indeed even as an elementary school student, had written out his assignments. At that moment he really didn't have any more time to check the good intentions of the two women, whose existence he had in any case almost forgotten, because in their exhaustion they were working really silently, and the heavy stumbling of their feet was the only sound to be heard.

70   And so he scuttled out (the women were just propping themselves up on the writing desk in the next room in order to take a breather) changing the direction of his path four times. He really didn't know what he should rescue first. Then he saw hanging conspicuously on the wall, which was otherwise already empty, the picture of the woman dressed in nothing but fur. He quickly scurried up over it and pressed himself against the glass that held it in place and which made his hot abdomen feel good. At least this picture, which Gregor at the moment completely concealed, surely no one would now take away. He twisted his head toward the door of the living room to observe the women as they came back in.

71   They had not allowed themselves very much rest and were coming back right away. Grete had placed her arm around her mother and held her tightly. "So what shall we take now?" said Grete and looked around her. Then her glance crossed with Gregor's from the wall. She kept her composure only because her mother was there. She bent her face toward her mother in order to prevent her from looking around, and said, although in a trembling voice and too quickly, "Come, wouldn't it be better to go back to the living room for just another moment?" Grete's purpose was clear to Gregor: she wanted to bring his mother to a safe place and then chase him down from the wall. Well, let her just attempt that! He squatted on his picture and did not hand it over. He would sooner spring into Grete's face.

72   But Grete's words had immediately made the mother very uneasy. She walked to the side, caught sight of the enormous brown splotch on the flowered wallpaper, and, before she became truly aware that what she was looking at was Gregor, screamed out in a high pitched

raw voice "Oh God, oh God" and fell with outstretched arms, as if she was surrendering everything, down onto the couch and lay there motionless. "Gregor, you . . . ," cried out his sister with a raised fist and an urgent glare. Since his transformation those were the first words which she had directed right at him. She ran into the room next door to bring some spirits or other with which she could revive her mother from her fainting spell. Gregor wanted to help as well (there was time enough to save the picture), but he was stuck fast on the glass and had to tear himself loose forcefully. Then he also scurried into the next room, as if he could give his sister some advice, as in earlier times, but then he had to stand there idly behind her, while she rummaged about among various small bottles. Still, she was frightened when she turned around. A bottle fell onto the floor and shattered. A splinter of glass wounded Gregor in the face, some corrosive medicine or other dripped over him. Now, without lingering any longer, Grete took as many small bottles as she could hold and ran with them into her mother. She slammed the door shut with her foot. Gregor was now shut off from his mother, who was perhaps near death, thanks to him. He could not open the door, and he did not want to chase away his sister who had to remain with her mother. At this point he had nothing to do but wait, and overwhelmed with self-reproach and worry, he began to creep and crawl over everything: walls, furniture, and ceiling. Finally, in his despair, as the entire room started to spin around him, he fell onto the middle of the large table.

73   A short time elapsed. Gregor lay there limply. All around was still. Perhaps that was a good sign. Then there was a ring at the door. The servant girl was naturally shut up in her kitchen, and Grete must therefore go to open the door. The father had arrived. "What's happened," were his first words. Grete's appearance had told him everything. Grete replied with a dull voice; evidently she was pressing her face into her father's chest: "Mother fainted, but she's getting better now. Gregor has broken loose."

74   "Yes, I have expected that," said his father. "I always told you that, but you women don't want to listen."

75   It was clear to Gregor that his father had badly misunderstood Grete's short message and was assuming that Gregor had committed some violent crime or other. Thus, Gregor now had to find his father to calm him down, for he had neither the time nor the opportunity to clarify things for him. And so he rushed away to the door of his room and pushed himself against it, so that his father could see right away as he entered from the hall that Gregor fully intended to return at once to his room, that it was not necessary to drive him back, but that one only needed to open the door and he would disappear immediately.

76   But his father was not in the mood to observe such niceties. "Ah," he yelled as soon as he entered, with a tone as if he were all at once angry and pleased. Gregor pulled his head back from the door and

CLOSE READ

ANNOTATE: Mark the sentences in paragraph 73 that are five words long or shorter.

QUESTION: How are these sentences different from Kafka's usual sentences?

CONCLUDE: What is the effect of this sentence variation?

raised it in the direction of his father. He had not really pictured his father as he now stood there. Of course, what with his new style of creeping all around, he had in the past while neglected to pay attention to what was going on in the rest of the apartment, as he had done before, and really should have grasped the fact that he would encounter different conditions. Nevertheless, nevertheless, was that still his father? Was that the same man who had lain exhausted and buried in bed in earlier days when Gregor was setting out on a business trip, who had received him on the evenings of his return in a sleeping gown and armchair, totally incapable of standing up, who had only lifted his arm as a sign of happiness, and who in their rare strolls together a few Sundays a year and on the important holidays made his way slowly forward between Gregor and his mother (who themselves moved slowly), always a bit more slowly than them, bundled up in his old coat, all the time setting down his walking stick carefully, and who, when he had wanted to say something, almost always stood still and gathered his entourage around him?

77   But now he was standing up really straight, dressed in a tight fitting blue uniform with gold buttons, like the ones servants wear in a banking company. Above the high stiff collar of his jacket his firm double chin stuck out prominently, beneath his bushy eyebrows the glance of his black eyes was freshly penetrating and alert, his otherwise disheveled white hair was combed down into a carefully exact shining part. He threw his cap, on which a gold monogram (apparently the symbol of the bank) was affixed, in an arc across the entire room onto the sofa and moved, throwing back the edge of the long coat of his uniform, with his hands in his trouser pockets and a grim face, right up to Gregor.

78   He really didn't know what he had in mind, but he raised his foot uncommonly high anyway, and Gregor was astonished at the gigantic size of his sole of his boot. However, he did not linger on that point. For he knew from the first day of his new life that as far as he was concerned his father considered the greatest force the only appropriate response. And so he scurried away from his father, stopped when his father remained standing, and scampered forward again when his father merely stirred. In this way they made their way around the room repeatedly, without anything decisive taking place; indeed because of the slow pace it didn't look like a chase. Gregor remained on the floor for the time being, especially as he was afraid that his father could take a flight up onto the wall or the ceiling as an act of real malice. At any event Gregor had to tell himself that he couldn't keep up this running around for a long time, because whenever his father took a single step, he had to go through an enormous number of movements. Already he was starting to suffer from a shortage of breath, just as in his earlier days his lungs had been quite unreliable. As he now staggered around in this way in order to gather all his energies for running, hardly keeping his eyes open, in his listlessness he had no notion at all of any escape other

CLOSE READ

ANNOTATE: Mark the verbs in paragraph 78 that indicate Gregor's movements. When there is a "not," include that in your annotation.

QUESTION: What kind of movement do these verbs describe?

CONCLUDE: What do these movements indicate about Gregor's feelings toward his father?

than by running and had almost already forgotten that the walls were available to him, although they were obstructed by carefully carved furniture full of sharp points and spikes—at that moment something or other thrown casually flew down close by and rolled in front of him. It was an apple; immediately a second one flew after it. Gregor stood still in fright. Further flight was useless, for his father had decided to bombard him.

79 From the fruit bowl on the sideboard his father had filled his pockets, and now, without for the moment taking accurate aim, was throwing apple after apple. These small red apples rolled as if electrified around on the floor and collided with each other. A weakly thrown apple grazed Gregor's back but skidded off harmlessly. However another thrown immediately after that one drove into Gregor's back really hard. Gregor wanted to drag himself off, as if the unexpected and incredible pain would go away if he changed his position. But he felt as if he was nailed in place and lay stretched out completely confused in all his senses. Only with his final glance did he notice how the door of his room was pulled open and how, right in front of his sister (who was yelling), his mother ran out in her undergarments, for his sister had undressed her in order to give her some freedom to breathe in her fainting spell, and how his mother then ran up to his father, on the way her tied-up skirts one after the other slipped toward the floor, and how, tripping over her skirts, she hurled herself onto his father and, throwing her arms around him, in complete union with him—but at this moment Gregor's powers of sight gave way—as her hands reached to the back of his father's head and she begged him to spare Gregor's life.

80 Gregor's serious wound, from which he suffered for over a month (since no one ventured to remove the apple, it remained in his flesh as a visible reminder), seemed by itself to have reminded the father that, in spite of his present unhappy and hateful appearance, Gregor was a member of the family, something one should not treat as an enemy, and that it was, on the contrary, a requirement of family duty to suppress one's aversion and to endure—nothing else, just endure. And if through his wound Gregor had now apparently lost for good his ability to move and for the time being needed many, many minutes to crawl across his room, like an aged invalid (so far as creeping up high was concerned, that was unimaginable), nevertheless for this worsening of his condition, in his opinion, he did get completely satisfactory compensation, because every day toward evening the door to the living room, which he was in the habit of keeping a sharp eye on even one or two hours beforehand, was opened, so that he, lying down in the darkness of his room, invisible from the living room, could see the entire family at the illuminated table and listen to their conversation, to a certain extent with their common permission, a situation quite different from what happened before.

81 Of course, it was no longer the animated social interaction of former times, about which Gregor in small hotel rooms had always thought with a certain longing, when, tired out, he had to throw himself in the damp bedclothes. For the most part what went on now was very quiet. After the evening meal the father fell asleep quickly in his armchair; the mother and sister talked guardedly to each other in the stillness. Bent far over, the mother sewed fine undergarments for a fashion shop. The sister, who had taken on a job as a salesgirl, in the evening studied stenography and French, so as perhaps later to obtain a better position. Sometimes the father woke up and, as if he was quite ignorant that he had been asleep, said to the mother, "How long you have been sewing today!" and went right back to sleep, while the mother and the sister smiled tiredly to each other.

82 With a sort of stubbornness the father refused to take off his servant's uniform even at home, and while his sleeping gown hung unused on the coat hook, the father dozed completely dressed in his place, as if he was always ready for his responsibility and even here was waiting for the voice of his superior. As a result, in spite of all the care of the mother and sister, his uniform, which even at the start was not new, grew dirty, and Gregor looked, often for the entire evening, at this clothing, with stains all over it and with its gold buttons always polished, in which the old man, although very uncomfortable, slept peacefully nonetheless.

83 As soon as the clock struck ten, the mother tried encouraging the father gently to wake up and then persuading him to go to bed, on the ground that he couldn't get a proper sleep here and the father,

who had to report for service at six o'clock, really needed a good sleep. But in his stubbornness, which had gripped him since he had become a servant, he insisted always on staying even longer by the table, although he regularly fell asleep and then could only be prevailed upon with the greatest difficulty to trade his chair for the bed. No matter how much the mother and sister might at that point work on him with small admonitions, for a quarter of an hour he would remain shaking his head slowly, his eyes closed, without standing up. The mother would pull him by the sleeve and speak flattering words into his ear; the sister would leave her work to help her mother, but that would not have the desired effect on the father. He would settle himself even more deeply in his armchair. Only when the two women grabbed him under the armpits would he throw his eyes open, look back and forth at the mother and sister, and habitually say, "This is a life. This is the peace and quiet of my old age." And propped up by both women, he would heave himself up, elaborately, as if for him it was the greatest travail, allow himself to be led to the door by the women, wave them away there, and proceed on his own from there, while the mother quickly threw down her sewing implements and the sister her pen in order to run after the father and help him some more.

84   In this overworked and exhausted family who had time to worry any longer about Gregor more than was absolutely necessary? The household was constantly getting smaller. The servant girl was now let go. A huge bony cleaning woman with white hair flapping all over her head came in the morning and the evening to do the heaviest work. The mother took care of everything else in addition to her considerable sewing work. It even happened that various pieces of family jewelry, which previously the mother and sister had been overjoyed to wear on social and festive occasions, were sold, as Gregor found out in the evening from the general discussion of the prices they had fetched. But the greatest complaint was always that they could not leave this apartment, which was too big for their present means, since it was impossible to imagine how Gregor might be moved. But Gregor fully recognized that it was not just consideration for him which was preventing a move (for he could have been transported easily in a suitable box with a few air holes); the main thing holding the family back from a change in living quarters was far more their complete hopelessness and the idea that they had been struck by a misfortune like no one else in their entire circle of relatives and acquaintances.

85   What the world demands of poor people they now carried out to an extreme degree. The father bought breakfast to the petty officials at the bank, the mother sacrificed herself for the undergarments of strangers, the sister behind her desk was at the beck and call of customers, but the family's energies did not extend any further. And the wound in his back began to pain Gregor all over again, when now the mother and sister, after they had escorted the father to bed, came

NOTES

travail (truh VAYL) *n.* difficult situation or work

CLOSE READ
ANNOTATE: Mark the nouns in paragraph 86 that name people.

QUESTION: Why does Kafka include these details?

CONCLUDE: What sense of Gregor's past life do these references evoke?

back, let their work lie, moved close together, and sat cheek to cheek and when his mother would now say, pointing to Gregor's room, "Close the door, Grete," and when Gregor was again in the darkness, while close by the women mingled their tears or, quite dry-eyed, stared at the table.

86   Gregor spent his nights and days with hardly any sleep. Sometimes he thought that the next time the door opened he would take over the family arrangements just as he had earlier. In his imagination appeared again, after a long time, his employer and supervisor and the apprentices, the excessively gormless custodian, two or three friends from other businesses, a chambermaid from a hotel in the provinces, a loving fleeting memory, a female cashier from a hat shop, whom he had seriously, but too slowly courted— they all appeared mixed in with strangers or people he had already forgotten, but instead of helping him and his family, they were all unapproachable, and he was happy to see them disappear.

87   But then he was in no mood to worry about his family. He was filled with sheer anger over the wretched care he was getting, even though he couldn't imagine anything for which he might have an appetite. Still, he made plans about how he could take from the larder what he at all account deserved, even if he wasn't hungry. Without thinking any more about how one might be able to give Gregor special pleasure, the sister now kicked some food or other very quickly into his room in the morning and at noon, before she ran off to her shop, and in the evening, quite indifferent about whether the food had perhaps only been tasted or, what happened most frequently, remained entirely undisturbed, she whisked it out with one sweep of her broom. The task of cleaning his room, which she now always carried out in the evening, could not be done any more quickly. Streaks of dirt ran along the walls; here and there lay tangles of dust and garbage. At first, when his sister arrived, Gregor positioned himself in a particularly filthy corner in order with this posture to make something of a protest. But he could have well stayed there for weeks without his sister's changing her ways. Indeed, she perceived the dirt as much as he did, but she had decided just to let it stay.

88   In this business, with a touchiness which was quite new to her and which had generally taken over the entire family, she kept watch to see that the cleaning of Gregor's room remained reserved for her. Once his mother had undertaken a major cleaning of Gregor's room, which she had only completed successfully after using a few buckets of water. But the extensive dampness made Gregor sick and he lay supine, embittered and immobile on the couch. However, the mother's punishment was not delayed for long. For in the evening the sister had hardly observed the change in Gregor's room before she ran into the living room mightily offended and, in spite of her mother's hand lifted high in entreaty, broke out in a fit of crying. Her parents (the father had, of course, woken up with a start in

his armchair) at first looked at her astonished and helpless; until they started to get agitated. Turning to his right, the father heaped reproaches on the mother that she was not to take over the cleaning of Gregor's room from the sister and, turning to his left, he shouted at the sister that she would no longer be allowed to clean Gregor's room ever again, while the mother tried to pull the father, beside himself in his excitement, into the bedroom; the sister, shaken by her crying fit, pounded on the table with her tiny fists, and Gregor hissed at all this, angry that no one thought about shutting the door and sparing him the sight of this commotion.

89 But even when the sister, exhausted from her daily work, had grown tired of caring for Gregor as she had before, even then the mother did not have to come at all on her behalf. And Gregor did not have to be neglected. For now the cleaning woman was there. This old widow, who in her long life must have managed to survive the worst with the help of her bony frame, had no real horror of Gregor. Without being in the least curious, she had once by chance opened Gregor's door. At the sight of Gregor, who, totally surprised, began to scamper here and there, although no one was chasing him, she remained standing with her hands folded across her stomach staring at him. Since then she did not fail to open the door furtively a little every morning and evening to look in on Gregor. At first, she also called him to her with words which she presumably thought were friendly, like "Come here for a bit, old dung beetle!" or "Hey, look at the old dung beetle!" Addressed in such a manner, Gregor answered nothing, but remained motionless in his place, as if the door had not been opened at all. If only, instead of allowing this cleaning woman to disturb him uselessly whenever she felt like it, they had instead given her orders to clean up his room every day! One day in the early morning (a hard downpour, perhaps already a sign of the coming spring, struck the window panes) when the cleaning woman started up once again with her usual conversation, Gregor was so bitter that he turned toward her, as if for an attack, although slowly and weakly. But instead of being afraid of him, the cleaning woman merely lifted up a chair standing close by the door and, as she stood there with her mouth wide open, her intention was clear: She would close her mouth only when the chair in her hand had been thrown down on Gregor's back. "This goes no further, all right?" she asked, as Gregor turned himself around again, and she placed the chair calmly back in the corner.

90 Gregor ate hardly anything any more. Only when he chanced to move past the food which had been prepared did he, as a game, take a bit into his mouth, hold it there for hours, and generally spit it out again. At first he thought it might be his sadness over the condition of his room which kept him from eating, but he very soon became reconciled to the alterations in his room. People had grown accustomed to put into storage in his room things which they couldn't put anywhere else, and at this point there were many such

things, now that they had rented one room of the apartment to three lodgers. These solemn gentlemen (all three had full beards, as Gregor once found out through a crack in the door) were meticulously intent on tidiness, not only in their own room but (since they had now rented a room here) in the entire household, and particularly in the kitchen. They simply did not tolerate any useless or shoddy stuff. Moreover, for the most part they had brought with them their own pieces of furniture. Thus, many items had become superfluous, and these were not really things one could sell or things people wanted to throw out. All these items ended up in Gregor's room, even the box of ashes and the garbage pail from the kitchen. The cleaning woman, always in a hurry, simply flung anything that was momentarily useless into Gregor's room. Fortunately Gregor generally saw only the relevant object and the hand which held it. The cleaning woman perhaps was intending, when time and opportunity allowed, to take the stuff out again or to throw everything out all at once, but in fact the things remained lying there, wherever they had ended up at the first throw, unless Gregor squirmed his way through the accumulation of junk and moved it. At first he was forced to do this because otherwise there was no room for him to creep around, but later he did it with a growing pleasure, although after such movements, tired to death and feeling wretched, he didn't budge for hours.

91   Because the lodgers sometimes also took their evening meal at home in the common living room, the door to the living room stayed shut on many evenings. But Gregor had no trouble at all going without the open door. Already on many evenings when it was open he had not availed himself of it, but, without the family noticing, was stretched out in the darkest corner of his room. However, once the cleaning woman had left the door to the living room slightly ajar, and it remained open even when the lodgers came in in the evening and the lights were put on. They sat down at the head of the table, where

in earlier days the mother, the father, and Gregor had eaten, unfolded their serviettes, and picked up their knives and forks. The mother immediately appeared in the door with a dish of meat and right behind her the sister with a dish piled high with potatoes. The food gave off a lot of steam. The gentlemen lodgers bent over the plate set before them, as if they wanted to check it before eating, and in fact the one who sat in the middle (for the other two he seemed to serve as the authority) cut off a piece of meat still on the plate obviously to establish whether it was sufficiently tender and whether or not something should be shipped back to the kitchen. He was satisfied, and the mother and sister, who had looked on in suspense, began to breathe easily and to smile.

92   The family itself ate in the kitchen. In spite of that, before the father went into the kitchen, he came into the room and with a single bow, cap in hand, made a tour of the table. The lodgers rose up collectively and murmured something in their beards. Then, when they were alone, they ate almost in complete silence. It seemed odd to Gregor that out of all the many different sorts of sounds of eating, what was always audible was their chewing teeth, as if by that Gregor should be shown that people needed their teeth to eat and that nothing could be done even with the most handsome toothless jawbone. "I really do have an appetite," Gregor said to himself sorrowfully, "but not for these things. How these lodgers stuff themselves, and I am dying."

93   On this very evening (Gregor didn't remember hearing it all through this period) the violin sounded from the kitchen. The lodgers had already ended their night meal, the middle one had pulled out a newspaper and had given each of the other two a page, and they were now leaning back, reading and smoking. When the violin started playing, they became attentive, got up, and went on tiptoe to the hall door, at which they remained standing pressed up against one another. They must have been audible from the kitchen, because the father called out, "Perhaps the gentlemen don't like the playing? It can be stopped at once."

94   "On the contrary," stated the lodger in the middle, "might the young woman not come in to us and play in the room here, where it is really much more comfortable and cheerful?"

95   "Oh, thank you," cried out the father, as if he were the one playing the violin. The men stepped back into the room and waited. Soon the father came with the music stand, the mother with the sheet music, and the sister with the violin. The sister calmly prepared everything for the recital. The parents, who had never previously rented a room and therefore exaggerated their politeness to the lodgers, dared not sit on their own chairs. The father leaned against the door, his right hand stuck between two buttons of his buttoned up uniform. The mother, however, accepted a chair offered by one lodger. Since she left the chair where the gentleman had chanced to put it, she sat to one side in a corner.

96　　The sister began to play. The father and mother followed attentively, one on each side, the movements of her hands. Attracted by the playing, Gregor had ventured to advance a little further forward and his head was already in the living room. He scarcely wondered about the fact that recently he had had so little consideration for the others; earlier this consideration had been something he was proud of. And for that very reason he would've had at this moment more reason to hide away, because as a result of the dust which lay all over his room and flew around with the slightest movement, he was totally covered in dirt. On his back and his sides he carted around with him dust, threads, hair, and remnants of food. His indifference to everything was much too great for him to lie on his back and scour himself on the carpet, as he often had done earlier during the day. In spite of his condition he had no timidity about inching forward a bit on the spotless floor of the living room.

97　　In any case, no one paid him any attention. The family was all caught up in the violin playing. The lodgers, by contrast, who for the moment had placed themselves, their hands in their trouser pockets, behind the music stand much too close to the sister, so that they could all see the sheet music, something that must certainly bother the sister, soon drew back to the window conversing in low voices with bowed heads, where they then remained, worriedly observed by the father. It now seemed really clear that, having assumed they were to hear a beautiful or entertaining violin recital, they were disappointed, and were allowing their peace and quiet to be disturbed only out of politeness. The way in which they all blew the smoke from their cigars out of their noses and mouths in particular led one to conclude that they were very irritated. And yet his sister was playing so beautifully. Her face was turned to the side, her gaze followed the score intently and sadly. Gregor crept forward still a little further and kept his head close against the floor in order to be able to catch her gaze if possible. Was he an animal that music so seized him? For him it was as if the way to the unknown nourishment he craved was revealing itself to him. He was determined to press forward right to his sister, to tug at her dress and to indicate to her in this way that she might still come with her violin into his room, because here no one valued the recital as he wanted to value it. He did not wish to let her go from his room any more, at least not as long as he lived. His frightening appearance would for the first time become useful for him. He wanted to be at all the doors of his room simultaneously and snarl back at the attackers. However, his sister should not be compelled but would remain with him voluntarily; she would sit next to him on the sofa, bend down her ear to him, and he would then confide in her that he firmly intended to send her to the conservatory and that, if his misfortune had not arrived in the interim, he would have announced this to everyone last Christmas (had Christmas really already come and gone?) and would have accepted no objections. After this explanation his sister would break

CLOSE READ
ANNOTATE: Beginning with the sentence that starts, "His frightening appearance," mark the auxiliary, or helping, verbs in paragraph 97.

QUESTION: What do those verbs indicate about the scene Gregor describes?

CONCLUDE: How do the verbs contribute to a sense of fantasy or wishing?

out in tears of emotion, and Gregor would lift himself up to her armpit and kiss her throat, which she, from the time she started going to work, had left exposed without a band or a collar.

98 "Mr. Samsa," called out the middle lodger to the father, and pointed his index finger, without uttering a further word, at Gregor as he was moving slowly forward. The violin fell silent. The middle lodger smiled, first shaking his head once at his friends, and then looked down at Gregor once more. Rather than driving Gregor back again, the father seemed to consider it of prime importance to calm down the lodgers, although they were not at all upset and Gregor seemed to entertain them more than the violin recital. The father hurried over to them and with outstretched arms tried to push them into their own room and simultaneously to block their view of Gregor with his own body. At this point they became really somewhat irritated, although one no longer knew whether that was because of the father's behavior or because of knowledge they had just acquired that they had had, without knowing it, a neighbor like Gregor. They demanded explanations from his father, raised their arms to make their points, tugged agitatedly at their beards, and moved back toward their room quite slowly. In the meantime, the isolation which had suddenly fallen upon his sister after the sudden breaking off of the recital had overwhelmed her. She had held onto the violin and bow in her limp hands for a little while and had continued to look at the sheet music as if she was still playing. All at once she pulled herself together, placed the instrument in her mother's lap (the mother was still sitting in her chair having trouble breathing and with her lungs laboring) and ran into the next room, which the lodgers, pressured by the father, were already approaching more rapidly. One could observe how under the sister's practiced hands the sheets and pillows on the beds were thrown on high and arranged. Even before the lodgers had reached the room, she was finished fixing the beds and was slipping out. The father seemed so gripped once again with his stubbornness that he forgot about the respect which he always owed to his renters. He pressed on and on, until at the door of the room the middle gentleman stamped loudly with his foot and thus brought the father to a standstill. "I hereby declare," the middle lodger said, raising his hand and casting his glance both on the mother and the sister, "that considering the disgraceful conditions prevailing in this apartment and family," with this he spat decisively on the floor, "I immediately cancel my room. I will, of course, pay nothing at all for the days which I have lived here; on the contrary I shall think about whether or not I will initiate some sort of action against you, something which—believe me—will be very easy to establish." He fell silent and looked directly in front of him, as if he was waiting for something. In fact, his two friends immediately joined in with their opinions, "We also give immediate notice." At that he seized the door handle, banged the door shut, and locked it.

99   The father groped his way tottering to his chair and let himself fall in it. It looked as if he was stretching out for his usual evening snooze, but the heavy nodding of his head (which looked as if it was without support) showed that he was not sleeping at all. Gregor had lain motionless the entire time in the spot where the lodgers had caught him. Disappointment with the collapse of his plan and perhaps also his weakness brought on by his severe hunger made it impossible for him to move. He was certainly afraid that a general disaster would break over him at any moment, and he waited. He was not even startled when the violin fell from the mother's lap, out from under her trembling fingers, and gave off a reverberating tone.

100   "My dear parents," said the sister banging her hand on the table by way of an introduction, "things cannot go on any longer in this way. Maybe if you don't understand that, well, I do. I will not utter my brother's name in front of this monster, and thus I say only that we must try to get rid of it. We have tried what is humanly possible to take care of it and to be patient. I believe that no one can criticize us in the slightest."

101   "She is right in a thousand ways," said the father to himself. The mother, who was still incapable of breathing properly, began to cough numbly with her hand held up over her mouth and a manic expression in her eyes.

102   The sister hurried over to her mother and held her forehead. The sister's words seemed to have led the father to certain reflections. He sat upright, played with his uniform hat among the plates, which still lay on the table from the lodgers' evening meal, and looked now and then at the motionless Gregor.

103   "We must try to get rid of it," the sister now said decisively to the father, for the mother, in her coughing fit, wasn't listening to anything. "It is killing you both. I see it coming. When people have to work as hard as we all do, they cannot also tolerate this endless torment at home. I just can't go on any more." And she broke out into such a crying fit that her tears flowed out down onto her mother's face. She wiped them off her mother with mechanical motions of her hands.

104   "Child," said the father sympathetically and with obvious appreciation, "then what should we do?"

105   The sister only shrugged her shoulders as a sign of the perplexity which, in contrast to her previous confidence, had come over her while she was crying.

106   "If only he understood us," said the father in a semi-questioning tone. The sister, in the midst of her sobbing, shook her hand energetically as a sign that there was no point thinking of that.

107   "If he only understood us," repeated the father and by shutting his eyes he absorbed the sister's conviction of the impossibility of this point, "then perhaps some compromise would be possible with him. But as it is . . ."

108   "It must be gotten rid of," cried the sister. "That is the only way, Father. You must try to get rid of the idea that this is Gregor. The fact

that we have believed for so long, that is truly our real misfortune. But how can it be Gregor? If it were Gregor, he would have long ago realized that a communal life among human beings is not possible with such an animal and would have gone away voluntarily. Then we would not have a brother, but we could go on living and honor his memory. But this animal plagues us. It drives away the lodgers, will obviously take over the entire apartment, and leave us to spend the night in the alley. Just look, Father," she suddenly cried out, "he's already starting up again." With a fright which was totally incomprehensible to Gregor, the sister even left the mother, pushed herself away from her chair, as if she would sooner sacrifice her mother than remain in Gregor's vicinity, and rushed behind her father who, excited merely by her behavior, also stood up and half raised his arms in front of the sister as though to protect her.

109   But Gregor did not have any notion of wishing to create problems for anyone and certainly not for his sister. He had just started to turn himself around in order to creep back into his room, quite a startling sight, since, as a result of his suffering condition, he had to guide himself through the difficulty of turning around with his head, in this process lifting and banging it against the floor several times. He paused and looked around. His good intentions seem to have been recognized. The fright had only lasted for a moment. Now they looked at him in silence and sorrow. His mother lay in her chair, with her legs stretched out and pressed together; her eyes were almost shut from weariness. The father and sister sat next to one another. The sister had set her hands around the father's neck.

110   "Now perhaps I can actually turn myself around," thought Gregor and began the task again. He couldn't stop puffing at the effort and had to rest now and then.

111   Besides no one was urging him on. It was all left to him on his own. When he had completed turning around, he immediately began to wander straight back. He was astonished at the great distance which separated him from his room and did not understand in the least how in his weakness he had covered the same distance a short time before, almost without noticing it. Constantly intent only on creeping along quickly, he hardly paid any attention to the fact that no word or cry from his family interrupted him.

112   Only when he was already in the door did he turn his head, not completely, because he felt his neck growing stiff. At any rate he still saw that behind him nothing had changed. Only the sister was standing up. His last glimpse brushed over the mother who was now completely asleep. Hardly was he inside his room when the door was pushed shut very quickly, bolted fast, and barred. Gregor was startled by the sudden commotion behind him, so much so that his little limbs bent double under him. It was his sister who had been in such a hurry. She had stood up right away, had waited, and had then sprung forward nimbly. Gregor had not heard anything of her approach. She cried out, "Finally!" to her parents, as she turned the key in the lock.

113   "What now?" Gregor asked himself and looked around him in the darkness. He soon made the discovery that he could no longer move at all. He was not surprised at that. On the contrary, it struck him as unnatural that he had really been able up to this point to move around with these thin little legs. Besides he felt relatively content. True, he had pains throughout his entire body, but it seemed to him that they were gradually becoming weaker and weaker and would finally go away completely. The rotten apple in his back and the inflamed surrounding area, entirely covered with white dust, he hardly noticed. He remembered his family with deep feeling and love. In this business, his own thought that he had to disappear was, if possible, even more decisive than his sister's. He remained in this state of empty and peaceful reflection until the tower clock struck three o'clock in the morning. From the window he witnessed the beginning of the general dawning outside. Then without willing it, his head sank all the way down, and from his nostrils flowed out weakly his last breath.

114   Early in the morning the cleaning woman came. In her sheer energy and haste she banged all the doors (in precisely the way people had already asked her to avoid), so much so that once she arrived a quiet sleep was no longer possible anywhere in the entire apartment. In her customarily brief visit to Gregor she at first found nothing special. She thought he lay so immobile there intending to play the offended party. She gave him credit for as complete an understanding as possible. Because she happened to hold the long broom in her hand, she tried to tickle Gregor with it from the door. When that was quite unsuccessful, she became irritated and poked Gregor a little, and only when she had shoved him from his place without any resistance did she become attentive. When she quickly realized the true state of affairs, her eyes grew large, she whistled to herself, but didn't restrain herself for long. She pulled open the door of the bedroom and yelled in a loud voice into the darkness, "Come and look. It's kicked the bucket. It's lying there, totally snuffed!"

115   The Samsa married couple sat upright in their marriage bed and had to get over their fright at the cleaning woman before they managed to grasp her message. But then Mr. and Mrs. Samsa climbed very quickly out of bed, one on either side. Mr. Samsa threw the bedspread over his shoulders, Mrs. Samsa came out only in her nightshirt, and like this they stepped into Gregor's room. Meanwhile the door of the living room (in which Grete had slept since the lodgers had arrived on the scene) had also opened. She was fully clothed, as if she had not slept at all; her white face also seemed to indicate that. "Dead?" said Mrs. Samsa and looked questioningly at the cleaning woman, although she could check everything on her own and even understand without a check. "I should say so," said the cleaning woman and, by way of proof, poked Gregor's body with the broom a considerable distance more to the side. Mrs. Samsa made a movement as if she wished to restrain the broom, but didn't

CLOSE READ

ANNOTATE: At the end of paragraph 114 and in paragraph 115, mark details that show how the cleaning woman treats and speaks about Gregor.

QUESTION: Why does Kafka include these details?

CONCLUDE: What is the effect of these details, especially when combined with the family's reaction to Gregor's death?

do it. "Well," said Mr. Samsa, "now we can give thanks to God." He crossed himself, and the three women followed his example.

116   Grete, who did not take her eyes off the corpse, said, "Look how thin he was. He had eaten nothing for such a long time. The meals which came in here came out again exactly the same." In fact, Gregor's body was completely flat and dry. That was apparent really for the first time, now that he was no longer raised on his small limbs and, moreover, now that nothing else distracted one's gaze.

117   "Grete, come into us for a moment," said Mrs. Samsa with a melancholy smile, and Grete went, not without looking back at the corpse, behind her parents into the bedroom. The cleaning woman shut the door and opened the window wide. In spite of the early morning, the fresh air was partly tinged with warmth. It was already the end of March.

118   The three lodgers stepped out of their room and looked around for their breakfast, astonished that they had been forgotten. "Where is the breakfast?" asked the middle one of the gentlemen grumpily to the cleaning woman. However, she laid her finger to her lips and then quickly and silently indicated to the lodgers that they could come into Gregor's room. So they came and stood around Gregor's corpse, their hands in the pockets of their somewhat worn jackets, in the room, which was already quite bright.

119   Then the door of the bedroom opened, and Mr. Samsa appeared in his uniform, with his wife on one arm and his daughter on the other. All were a little tear-stained. Now and then Grete pressed her face onto her father's arm.

120   "Get out of my apartment immediately," said Mr. Samsa and pulled open the door, without letting go of the women. "What do you mean?" said the middle lodger, somewhat dismayed and with a sugary smile. The two others kept their hands behind them and constantly rubbed them against each other, as if in joyful anticipation of a great squabble which must end up in their favor. "I mean exactly what I say," replied Mr. Samsa and went directly with his two female companions up to the lodger. The latter at first stood there motionless and looked at the floor, as if matters were arranging themselves in a new way in his head. "All right, then we'll go," he said and looked up at Mr. Samsa as if, suddenly overcome by humility, he was asking fresh permission for this decision. Mr. Samsa merely nodded to him repeatedly with his eyes open wide.

121   Following that, the lodger actually went immediately with long strides into the hall. His two friends had already been listening for a while with their hands quite still, and now they hopped smartly after him, as if afraid that Mr. Samsa could step into the hall ahead of them and disturb their reunion with their leader. In the hall all three of them took their hats from the coat rack, pulled their canes from the cane holder, bowed silently, and left the apartment. In what turned out to be an entirely groundless mistrust, Mr. Samsa stepped with the two women out onto the landing, leaned against the railing, and

looked down as the three lodgers slowly but steadily made their way down the long staircase, disappeared on each floor in a certain turn of the stairwell and in a few seconds came out again. The deeper they proceeded, the more the Samsa family lost interest in them, and when a butcher with a tray on his head came to meet them and then with a proud bearing ascended the stairs high above them, Mr. Samsa, together with the women, left the banister, and they all returned, as if relieved, back into their apartment.

122   They decided to pass that day resting and going for a stroll. Not only had they earned this break from work, but there was no question that they really needed it. And so they sat down at the table and wrote three letters of apology: Mr. Samsa to his supervisor, Mrs. Samsa to her client, and Grete to her proprietor. During the writing the cleaning woman came in to say that she was going off, for her morning work was finished. The three people writing at first merely nodded, without glancing up. Only when the cleaning woman was still unwilling to depart, did they look up angrily. "Well?" asked Mr. Samsa. The cleaning woman stood smiling in the doorway, as if she had a great stroke of luck to report to the family but would only do it if she was asked directly. The almost upright small ostrich feather in her hat, which had irritated Mr. Samsa during her entire service, swayed lightly in all directions. "All right then, what do you really want?" asked Mrs. Samsa, whom the cleaning lady still usually respected. "Well," answered the cleaning woman (smiling so happily she couldn't go on speaking right away), "about how that rubbish from the next room should be thrown out, you mustn't worry about it. It's all taken care of." Mrs. Samsa and Grete bent down to their letters, as though they wanted to go on writing; Mr. Samsa, who noticed that the cleaning woman wanted to start describing everything in detail, decisively prevented her with an outstretched hand. But since she was not allowed to explain, she remembered the great hurry she was in, and called out, clearly insulted, "Ta ta, everyone," turned around furiously, and left the apartment with a fearful slamming of the door.

123   "This evening she'll be let go," said Mr. Samsa, but he got no answer from either his wife or from his daughter, because the cleaning woman seemed to have upset once again the tranquility they had just attained. They got up, went to the window and remained there, with their arms about each other. Mr. Samsa turned around in his chair in their direction and observed them quietly for a while. Then he called out, "All right, come here then. Let's finally get rid of old things. And have a little consideration for me." The women attended to him at once. They rushed to him, caressed him, and quickly ended their letters.

124   Then all three left the apartment together, something they had not done for months now, and took the electric tram into the open air outside the city. The car in which they were sitting by themselves was totally engulfed by the warm sun. They talked to each other, leaning

back comfortably in their seats, about future prospects, and they discovered that on closer observation these were not at all bad, for all three had employment, about which they had not really questioned each other at all, which was extremely favorable and with especially promising prospects. The greatest improvement in their situation at this moment, of course, had to come from a change of dwelling. Now they wanted to rent an apartment smaller and cheaper but better situated and generally more practical than the present one, which Gregor had found. While they amused themselves in this way, it struck Mr. and Mrs. Samsa almost at the same moment how their daughter, who was getting more animated all the time, had blossomed recently, in spite of all the troubles which had made her cheeks pale, into a beautiful and voluptuous young woman. Growing more silent and almost unconsciously understanding each other in their glances, they thought that the time was now at hand to seek out a good honest man for her. And it was something of a confirmation of their new dreams and good intentions when at the end of their journey the daughter first lifted herself up and stretched her young body. &

NOTES

CLOSE READ
ANNOTATE: In paragraph 124, mark words and phrases with positive associations of comfort and health.

QUESTION: Why does Kafka include these details that are so different from those in the rest of the story?

CONCLUDE: What effect does this final paragraph have on the reader?

Comprehension Check

Complete the following items after you finish your first read.

1. Into what kind of creature is Gregor Samsa transformed?

2. How do the family's activities change to accommodate Gregor's new condition?

3. What happens when Grete gives a violin recital for the three lodgers?

4. ⊟ Notebook Confirm your understanding of the story by writing a summary.

- -

RESEARCH

Research to Clarify Choose at least one unfamiliar detail from the text. Briefly research that detail. In what way does the information you learned shed light on an aspect of the story?

THE METAMORPHOSIS

Close Read the Text

1. This model, from paragraph 2 of the story, shows two sample annotations, along with questions and conclusions. Close read the passage, and find another detail to annotate. Then, write a question and your conclusion.

Close Read

ANNOTATE: These words suggest something delicate or precious.

QUESTION: What contrast does this description emphasize?

CONCLUDE: The delicacy of the picture emphasizes the awfulness of Gregor's transformation.

ANNOTATE: The repetition of *fur* and the use of the word *disappeared* are surprising.

QUESTION: Why does the author use these details?

CONCLUDE: These details reinforce the idea of transformation— like Gregor, the woman seems to be changing into a nonhuman creature.

> Above the table . . . hung the picture which he had cut out of an illustrated magazine a little while ago and set in a pretty gilt frame. It was a picture of a woman with a fur hat and a fur boa. She sat erect there, lifting up in the direction of the viewer a solid fur muff into which her entire forearm disappeared.

2. For more practice, go back into the text and complete the close-read notes.

3. Revisit a section of the text you found important during your first read. Read this section closely, and **annotate** what you notice. Ask yourself **questions** such as "Why did the author make this choice?" What can you **conclude**?

🔧 Tool Kit
Close-Read Guide and Model Annotation

Analyze the Text

CITE TEXTUAL EVIDENCE
to support your answers.

📓 **Notebook** Respond to these questions.

1. (a) **Compare and Contrast** Describe how Gregor's insect-like body changes from the opening of the story to the ending. (b) **Interpret** How do these physical changes reflect Gregor's evolving emotional state?

2. **Make a Judgment** In what ways, if any, are the family members responsible for Gregor's tragic outcome? Consider their actions at the end of the story before you answer.

3. **Hypothesize** Would Gregor's fate have been different if he had been transformed into a different kind of animal? Explain.

4. **Essential Question:** *Do people need to belong?* What have you learned about the condition of being an outsider by reading this story?

▦ STANDARDS
Reading Literature
Analyze how an author's choices concerning how to structure a text, order events within it, and manipulate time create such effects as mystery, tension, or surprise.

Analyze Craft and Structure

Literary Movement: Modernism "The Metamorphosis" is one of the landmark works of **Modernism**, an artistic movement that developed during the twentieth century and represented a radical break with the traditions of the past. Modernists such as Kafka responded to dramatic changes in the world, including the rapid rise of industry, the shift from rural to urban society, and the brutal horrors of World War I. Often unsettling and even disturbing, Modernist works present the world as a fractured place in which goodness is not rewarded and evil is not punished. Kafka's story is an example of **Absurdist literature**, a form of Modernist writing that includes these elements:

- **Ambiguity:** The story is open-ended, and key elements are never explained.

- **Fantastic or Dreamlike Elements:** Events blur the boundary between what is real and what is unreal.

- **Themes of Alienation:** Modernist works often feature isolated characters who experience increasing alienation or disconnection.

Practice

CITE TEXTUAL EVIDENCE to support your answers.

📓 **Notebook** Respond to these questions.

1. Use the chart to identify examples from the story that demonstrate each element of Absurdist literature.

AMBIGUITY	FANTASTIC OR DREAMLIKE ELEMENTS	ALIENATION/ISOLATION

2. Toward the end of the story, the family begins to refer to Gregor as "it" rather than "he." How does this pronoun shift relate to the Absurdist emphasis on alienation?

3. Many Modernist works draw attention to the techniques used to create them. In what way is this true of Kafka's tale? Identify passages that remind readers that they are reading a fictional tale.

4. Why do you think Kafka provides no reason for Gregor's transformation?

5. Has Gregor done anything to deserve his fate? Why or why not?

THE METAMORPHOSIS

Concept Vocabulary

| distress | aversion | listlessly |
| amelioration | asphyxiation | travail |

Why These Words? These concept words relate to the idea of discomfort, or uneasiness. For example, the narrator describes the *distress* that Gregor feels when he is unable to control his insect body and get out of bed. In response to his difficulties, Gregor shows his frustration by banging his head *listlessly* against the door.

1. How does the concept vocabulary help describe Gregor's alienation?

2. What other words in the selection connect to the concept of discomfort?

Practice

Notebook **The concept vocabulary words appear in "The Metamorphosis."**

1. Use each concept word to complete the paragraph.

The salesperson was horrified by his reassignment to the lunch counter because he had a(n) _____ to fried foods. His _____ only increased when he learned that he was to spend the entire day deep-frying batter-dipped cupcakes. Before the store opened, he stirred the batter _____. He sighed as though he were facing a day's _____ in a coal mine. Though he hoped for a poor turnout, there would be no _____ of his misery, since the new product turned out to be wildly popular. As the greasy steam rose from the hot fat into his face, he was sure _____ would be his fate.

2. Explain the context clues that help you determine the correct words.

Word Study

Notebook **Denotation and Connotation** A word's **denotation** is its literal definition, the one you would find in a dictionary. The associations or feelings that a word suggests are its **connotations**. Words with close meanings can express different degrees of an idea. For example, *distress* refers to pain. *Discomfort* and *inconvenience* describe the same idea with less intensity. *Anguish* and *agony* suggest greater intensity.

1. Name synonyms for three of the concept vocabulary words, and tell whether or not their connotations differ in degree of intensity.

2. For each of the three concept words you chose, write three sentences. In the first, use the concept word itself. In the second, use a synonym that has a lower degree of intensity. In the third, use a synonym that has a higher degree of intensity.

WORD NETWORK

Add interesting words related to outsiders from the text to your Word Network.

STANDARDS

Reading Literature
Determine the meaning of words and phrases as they are used in the text, including figurative and connotative meanings; analyze the cumulative impact of specific word choices on meaning and tone.

Language
• Demonstrate command of the conventions of standard English grammar and usage when writing or speaking.
• Use various types of phrases and clauses to convey specific meanings and add variety and interest to writing or presentations.
• Demonstrate understanding of figurative language, word relationships, and nuances in word meanings.
• Analyze nuances in the meaning of words with similar denotations.

Conventions

Types of Phrases Writers use various types of phrases to convey specific meanings. A **verb phrase** consists of a main verb and one or more auxiliary, or helping, verbs. These auxiliary verbs precede the main verb and provide additional information about the verb phrase, such as its tense, its mood, or its voice. Certain forms of the following verbs can be used as auxiliary verbs: *be, do, have, will, shall, can, may,* and *must.*

A verb phrase is often interrupted by one or more other words in a sentence, such as *not, never,* or another adverb. These interrupting words are not considered part of the verb phrase.

Observe how the underlined verb phrases in this sentence from paragraph 25 of "The Metamorphosis" help convey the time relationships of Gregor's various actions.

> While Gregor <u>was</u> quickly <u>blurting</u> all this out, hardly aware of what he <u>was saying</u>, he <u>had moved</u> close to the chest of drawers without effort, probably as a result of the practice he <u>had</u> already <u>had</u> in bed, and now he <u>was trying</u> to raise himself up on it.

CLARIFICATION
Refer to the Grammar Handbook to learn more about verb tense, verb mood, and active and passive voice.

Read It

Mark each verb phrase in these sentences from "The Metamorphosis." Remember not to mark any word or words that interrupt the verb phrase.

1. One morning, as Gregor Samsa was waking up from anxious dreams, he discovered that in bed he had been changed into a monstrous verminous bug.

2. He had already got to the point where, with a stronger rocking, he maintained his equilibrium with difficulty, and very soon he would finally have to decide, for in five minutes it would be a quarter past seven.

3. He must have tried it a hundred times, closing his eyes, so that he would not have to see the wriggling legs, and gave up only when he began to feel a light, dull pain in his side which he had never felt before.

Write It

📓 **Notebook** In the example, the sample sentences have been revised to add auxiliary verbs. Rewrite the sentences below to include auxiliary verbs.

> Example
> **Sample:** Gregor gropes awkwardly for many hours.
> **Revision:** Gregor has been groping awkwardly for many hours.
> **Sample:** His family listens at the door.
> **Revision:** His family must have been listening at the door.

1. Gregor climbs the walls and sticks to the ceiling.

2. The lodgers laugh, but soon they storm out of the room.

THE METAMORPHOSIS

Writing to Sources

A successful argument presents a careful, well-reasoned analysis of a topic, and draws logical conclusions that are supported with strong evidence. The evidence not only must clearly connect to the topic—it must also appeal to the audience.

Assignment

In a movie pitch, a writer tries to convince a movie studio to make a particular film. Write a **pitch** in which you argue that "The Metamorphosis" should be made into a major Hollywood feature film. In making your pitch, you will need to include a number of selling points.

- the reasons the movie will be entertaining and attractive to a large audience
- specific story details that will capture readers' interest, along with descriptions of how these elements can be adapted for film
- a description of the film's genre and style
- dramatic scenes that will make the film exciting

You might decide to support the visual look of your proposed film by creating a storyboard or flowchart of images to accompany your pitch.

Vocabulary and Conventions Connection Consider including several of the concept vocabulary words in your pitch, and try to use a variety of verb phrases.

distress	aversion	listlessly
amelioration	asphyxiation	travail

Reflect on Your Writing

After you have written your pitch, answer these questions.

1. Which piece of supporting evidence do you think makes your pitch effective?

2. What did you learn about Kafka's story by arguing that it should be adapted for film?

3. **Why These Words?** The words you choose make a difference in your writing. Which words did you specifically choose to add power to your pitch?

:= STANDARDS

Writing
- Write arguments to support claims in an analysis of substantive topics or texts, using valid reasoning and relevant and sufficient evidence.
- Produce clear and coherent writing in which the development, organization, and style are appropriate to task, purpose, and audience.

Speaking and Listening
- Initiate and participate effectively in a range of collaborative discussions with diverse partners on *grades 9–10 topics, texts, and issues*, building on others' ideas and expressing their own clearly and persuasively.
- Evaluate a speaker's point of view, reasoning, and use of evidence and rhetoric, identifying any fallacious reasoning or exaggerated or distorted evidence.
- Adapt speech to a variety of contexts and tasks, demonstrating command of formal English when indicated or appropriate.

Speaking and Listening

Assignment

Imagine that your school is considering whether to place Kafka's "The Metamorphosis" on its required reading list. Work with a partner to prepare for a **debate** about the question. If you take the "pro" position, you are in favor of placing the story on the list. If you take the "con" position, you are against it. After you have prepared, conduct the debate against an opposing team.

1. **Take a Position** Decide whether you will argue the pro or the con position. Note that you can effectively argue a view you don't personally support.

2. **Organize Ideas and Evidence** With your partner, discuss the arguments in favor of your position. Consider the literary merit of the story, its significance in literary history, and other qualities that you find important. Refer to the text as you work. Use the chart to gather your ideas and evidence.

POINT	SUPPORTING EVIDENCE

3. **Anticipate Counterarguments** In a debate, the opposing team is given the opportunity to present counterarguments in a rebuttal. Discuss with your partner points that the opposing team might make against your position. Prepare to defend your position with reasons and evidence.

4. **Write an Opening Statement** Write a strong opening statement of your position. Practice delivering the statement clearly and with conviction. Continue to speak clearly and forcefully throughout the debate.

✐ EVIDENCE LOG

Before moving on to a new selection, go to your Evidence Log and record what you learned from "The Metamorphosis."

Franz Kafka and Metamorphosis

Media Vocabulary

The following words or concepts will be useful to you as you analyze, discuss, and write about videos.

Stock Footage: film or video that has been shot for one purpose and is available for use in other projects	• Stock footage may be film recycled from past news programs. • It may also be footage from movies, television, or advertising.
Silhouette: dark figure that is seen as a filled-in shape against a light background	• Silhouettes may be created with bright light shining behind a figure. • Silhouettes are a kind of shadow.
Commentators: people who discuss or write about events for film, television, radio, or newspapers	• Documentary films and videos often include commentators who are experts on the topic. • A commentator may share his or her own point of view or present facts.
Background Music: music that is not the focus of a show but is added for effect	• Background music may highlight or contrast with the words and images of a show. • Music may create a mood and influence listeners' feelings about the content of a program.
Editing: taking pieces of film or video and putting them together in a new way	• Film and video editors may work with still photographs and film footage to create many different effects.

First Review MEDIA: VIDEO

Apply these strategies as you conduct your first review.

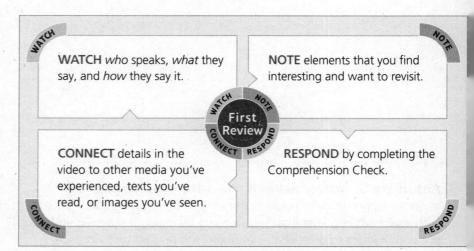

WATCH who speaks, *what* they say, and *how* they say it.

NOTE elements that you find interesting and want to revisit.

CONNECT details in the video to other media you've experienced, texts you've read, or images you've seen.

RESPOND by completing the Comprehension Check.

Notebook As you watch, write down your observations and questions, making sure to note time codes so you can easily revisit sections later.

▦ STANDARDS

Reading Informational Text
By the end of grade 10, read and comprehend literary nonfiction at the high end of the grades 9–10 text complexity band independently and proficiently.

Language
Acquire and use accurately general academic and domain-specific words and phrases, sufficient for reading, writing, speaking, and listening at the college and career readiness level; demonstrate independence in gathering vocabulary knowledge when considering a word or phrase important to comprehension or expression.

Franz Kafka and Metamorphosis

BBC

BACKGROUND

Biological transformations are a common occurrence in nature, especially among insects. Such a transformation marks the shift in an organism's development from the juvenile to the adult stage. People, however, transition more slowly from childhood to adulthood. Likewise, we have a sense of continuity in our physical senses of self because we keep most of our physical traits throughout our lives. Perhaps that is one reason the idea of transformation draws both our curiosity and our fear, as this video suggests.

NOTES

Comprehension Check

Complete the following items after you finish your first review.

1. What is this video primarily about?

2. What two works of literature are discussed in the video?

3. According to the second commentator, how do human beings feel about the possibility of change?

4. 🗒 **Notebook** Confirm your understanding of the video by listing three key ideas it presents.

- -

RESEARCH

Research to Clarify Choose an unfamiliar detail from the video. Briefly research that detail. How does the information you learned clarify an aspect of the video's content?

Close Review

Watch the video again. Write down any new observations that seem important. What **questions** do you have? What can you **conclude**?

- -

Analyze the Media

🗒 **Notebook** Respond to these questions.

1. (a) What does the first commentator say is bound up with our outer appearance? (b) **Interpret** Why do you think she talks about this with regard to Kafka's "The Metamorphosis"?

2. (a) **Contrast** In what way is Dr. Jekyll's metamorphosis different from Gregor Samsa's? (b) **Interpret** Do you think this difference is important? Explain.

3. (a) According to the video content, in what two ways do human beings transform themselves? (b) **Infer** Based on this evidence, what is the most powerful tool humans have for change?

4. **Essential Question:** *Do people need to belong?* What have you learned about the nature of being an outsider from this video?

FRANZ KAFKA AND
METAMORPHOSIS

Writing to Sources

Film and video use images to tell stories, set scenes, and create moods. Images often have symbolic meanings. The ability to interpret symbolic images is critical to understanding and writing about film and video.

Assignment

Write a **visual analysis**. Choose one image from the video, such as locusts, smokestacks, or airplanes. In a paragraph, describe the image. In your paragraph, make sure to answer these questions:

- What kind of image is it—a still photograph or a motion picture?

- Does the image include color, or is it in black-and-white?

- Is the background of the image meaningful? Does it emphasize the main subject of the image in some way?

- What emotional quality or mood does the image convey? What elements of the image contribute to that mood?

Then, draw your observations together to write another paragraph in which you answer these questions: Why did the filmmakers use this image as a symbol for metamorphosis? Is that choice effective?

Speaking and Listening

This video comments on Franz Kafka's important short story "The Metamorphosis" and explores the effect change can have on individual identity.

Assignment

With a partner, conduct a **discussion** about the following questions:

- What kinds of metamorphoses, or changes, are discussed or alluded to in the video?

- Are these metamorphoses positive, negative, or both? Explain.

- What insights into the idea of metamorphosis does the video present? Of these insights, which do you think is most surprising or illuminating? Why?

Write a paragraph summarizing your discussion. Then, share your paragraph with the class.

📝 EVIDENCE LOG

Before moving on to a new selection, go to your Evidence Log and record what you learned from "Franz Kafka and Metamorphosis."

☷ STANDARDS

Writing
Write informative/explanatory texts to examine and convey complex ideas, concepts, and information clearly and accurately through the effective selection, organization, and analysis of content.

Speaking and Listening
Present information, findings, and supporting evidence clearly, concisely, and logically such that listeners can follow the line of reasoning and the organization, development, substance, and style are appropriate to purpose, audience, and task.

WRITING TO SOURCES

- THE METAMORPHOSIS
- FRANZ KAFKA AND METAMORPHOSIS

Write an Argument

You have read a short story and viewed a video on the theme of outsiders. In "The Metamorphosis," Franz Kafka tells the story of a man who wakes up one day as some sort of bug-like vermin. The video presents additional insights about both the story and the ideas of transformation and alienation. Now, you will use your knowledge of the story and video to write an argument about people's need to belong.

Assignment

Apply your own experience, your analysis of the short story "The Metamorphosis," and your understanding of the related video to write an **argumentative essay** on this question:

> Are outsiders simply those who are misjudged or misunderstood?

Elements of an Argument

An **argument** is a logical way of presenting a belief, conclusion, or position. A well-written argumentative essay attempts to convince readers to accept what is written, change their minds, or take a certain action.

An effective argument contains these elements:

- a precise claim, or statement of a position
- consideration of counterclaims, or opposing positions, and a discussion of their strengths and weaknesses
- a logical organization that connects the claim, counterclaim, reasons, and evidence
- valid reasoning and relevant and sufficient evidence
- a concluding statement or section that logically completes the argument
- a formal style and objective tone
- correct grammar, including accurate use of transitions

Model Argument For a model of a well-crafted argumentative essay, see the Launch Text, "Isn't Everyone a Little Bit Weird?"

Challenge yourself to find all of the elements of an effective argument in the text. You will have the opportunity to review these elements as you start to write your own argument.

LAUNCH TEXT

ACADEMIC VOCABULARY

As you craft your essay, consider using some of the academic vocabulary you learned in the beginning of the unit.

contradict
negate
objection
verify
advocate

Tool Kit
Student Model of an Argument

STANDARDS

Writing
- Write arguments to support claims in an analysis of substantive topics or texts, using valid reasoning and relevant and sufficient evidence.
- Write routinely over extended time frames and shorter time frames for a range of tasks, purposes, and audiences.

Prewriting / Planning

Narrow the Topic The prompt for this assignment—are outsiders simply those who are misjudged or misunderstood?—is a large topic. You will write a more effective essay if you narrow the topic and give it a smaller focus. For example, you might discuss a particular group of people who are misunderstood or a particular cause of misunderstanding. It can help to think about issues with which you have some familiarity. Use this chart to consider ways to narrow the topic.

Broad Topic
Familiar Area
Specific Example Within That Area
Focused Topic

Use Varied Types of Evidence There are many different types of evidence you can use in an argument:

- **examples:** specific illustrations of a general idea

- **anecdotes:** brief stories that illustrate a point or insight

- **facts:** data or other information that can be proved true

- **expert opinion:** information or statements from experts

Using a variety of evidence can make your argument stronger. For example, in the Launch Text, the writer uses examples and anecdotes.

Take, for example, his appearance. In famous portraits, he wears ruffled shirts, breeches, and tight stockings pulled up to the knee. . . . Today's viewers might think him odd, but those were common fashions of his era. Likewise, consider Franklin's education. He quit school at age ten and was apprenticed as a printer at age twelve—a career move that today would be considered both weird and illegal.

—"Isn't Everyone a Little Bit Weird?"

Connect Across Texts As you write your argument, you will be using evidence from the selections to support your claims. Incorporate that evidence in different ways. If the precise words are important, use **exact quotations**. To clarify a complex idea, **paraphrase**, or restate it in your own words. Make sure that your paraphrases accurately reflect the original text. Consult an online or print style manual to confirm how to incorporate quotations or paraphrases into your essay correctly.

EVIDENCE LOG

Review your Evidence Log and identify key details you may want to cite in your argument.

STANDARDS

Writing
Develop claim(s) and counterclaims fairly, supplying evidence for each while pointing out the strengths and limitations of both in a manner that anticipates the audience's knowledge level and concerns.

Language
Write and edit work so that it conforms to the guidelines in a style manual appropriate for the discipline and writing type.

Drafting

Organize your ideas in a logical sequence that leads your reader from one part of your argument to the next.

Write an Engaging Introduction Use your introduction to engage your reader. Consider including a compelling statement that will pique readers' interest. For example, the Launch Text begins with a provocative first line: "Everyone is a little bit weird." The writer then explains that sentence just enough to lead the reader to the main claim.

Write your ideas for a compelling introduction:

_____

_____

_____

State a Clear Claim In your introduction, present your main idea, or claim, in clear, uncertain language. Your claim should be a debatable idea—one that can be argued. Your task will be to support your position with the help of strong reasons and evidence.

Order Your Ideas Logically Present supporting reasons for your claim in a logical sequence. Consider using one of these organizational structures:

ORDER OF IMPORTANCE	NESTORIAN ORDER
Present your strongest supporting reasons first, and then your less important reasons.	This is also called "reverse order of importance." It can sometimes be more effective to begin with your weakest reason and build up to your strongest reason.

Anticipate Counterarguments Identify points those who disagree with your position might raise. In this passage, the writer of the Launch Text addresses a counterargument: "Some might argue that weird people are just plain weird." The writer then goes on to state why this counterargument is not convincing.

Write a First Draft Use the organizational ideas you generated to write your first draft. As you write, keep the following points in mind:

- Use a formal, objective **tone,** or attitude.
- Use precise words. Avoid slang, contractions, and other elements of casual language that are inappropriate for academic writing.
- As you draft, new ideas may occur to you. Allow yourself to explore those ideas, but make a note to go back and work them into your logical sequence. Your goal is to carry a consistent set of ideas through from the introduction to the body to the conclusion.

STANDARDS

Writing
• Introduce precise claim(s), distinguish the claim(s) from alternate or opposing claims, and create an organization that establishes clear relationships among claim(s), counterclaims, reasons, and evidence.
• Establish and maintain a formal style and objective tone while attending to the norms and conventions of the discipline in which they are writing.
• Provide a concluding statement or section that follows from and supports the argument presented.

Create Cohesion: Transitions

Transitions and **transitional expressions** are words and phrases that hold your argument together. They show relationships among ideas, and the ways in which one concept leads to another. They help you connect, contrast, and compare ideas. Without accurate transitions, your argument can seem like a random assortment of unrelated information and observations.

Read It

These sentences from the Launch Text use accurate transitions to show how ideas are connected.

- _First,_ the most gifted, successful people are often eccentric. **(lists ideas and indicates order of importance)**
- Brilliant _would describe Ben Franklin better, and yet the man some call "the first American" had some ways about him you might consider odd._ **(shows contrast)**
- _Take, **for example**, his appearance._ **(shows or illustrates idea)**
- _Likewise, consider Franklin's education._ **(shows similarity)**
- **On top of that,** _he had the courage to communicate his insights, act on them, and turn them into achievements._ **(adds emphasis)**

Write It

As you draft your argument, choose transitions that help readers follow the flow of your ideas from sentence to sentence, paragraph to paragraph, and introduction to conclusion.

Use a chart like this to track your choices of transitions.

If you want to . . .	consider using one of these transitions:
list or add ideas	first of all, secondly, then, in addition, also
show similarity	similarity, equally, likewise
show contrast	although, however, yet, on the other hand
emphasize	in fact, most importantly, immediately
show effect	consequently, as a result, therefore
illustrate or show	for example, for instance, specifically

☰ STANDARDS

Writing
Use words, phrases, and clauses to link the major sections of the text, create cohesion, and clarify the relationships between claim(s) and reasons, between reasons and evidence, and between claim(s) and counterclaims.

REVISING

Evaluating Your Draft

Use the following checklist to evaluate the effectiveness of your first draft. Then, use your evaluation and the instruction on this page to guide your revision.

FOCUS AND ORGANIZATION	EVIDENCE AND ELABORATION	CONVENTIONS
☐ Provides an introduction that engages readers and introduces a precise claim.	☐ Develops the claims and opposing claims fairly, supplying evidence for each, while pointing out the strengths and limitations of both.	☐ Attends to the norms and conventions of the discipline, especially the correct use and punctuation of transitions.
☐ Establishes a logical order of supporting reasons and evidence.	☐ Provides adequate examples for each major idea.	
☐ Anticipates and addresses opposing claims.	☐ Uses vocabulary and word choice that is appropriate for the audience and purpose.	
☐ Develops a logical progression from the introduction, through the body, to the conclusion.	☐ Establishes and maintains a formal style and an objective tone.	

Revising for Focus and Organization

Logical Organization Reread your argument, paying special attention to the organization and progression of ideas.

- Jot down the main idea of each paragraph.
- Review these notes to determine whether your ideas flow logically.
- Reorder any paragraphs or sections that do not build in a logical way.
- Add or change transitional words or sentences to help readers understand the connections among ideas.
- Make sure that the ideas in your introduction match the ideas in the conclusion.

Revising for Evidence and Elaboration

Evidence Reread your essay, looking for any points at which the evidence seems weak. Then, find additional details from the text and video in this section to replace or strengthen your evidence.

Style Make sure that you have used an appropriately formal style that includes precise and vivid language, accurate use of academic terms, and transitions that establish clear relationships among your ideas. Reread to ensure that you have used words and phrases that communicate exactly what you mean.

⚓ WORD NETWORK

Include interesting words from your Word Network in your argument.

☰ STANDARDS

Writing
- Establish and maintain a formal style and objective tone while attending to the norms and conventions of the discipline in which they are writing.
- Provide a concluding statement or section that follows from and supports the argument presented.

Exchange essays with a classmate. Use the checklist to evaluate your classmate's argumentative essay and provide supportive feedback.

1. Is the claim clear?

☐ yes   ☐ no   If no, explain what confused you.

2. Is the counterclaim clear?

☐ yes   ☐ no   If no, point out what was unclear.

3. Does the evidence support the argument well?

☐ yes   ☐ no   If no, explain how it could be improved.

4. What is the strongest part of your classmate's essay? Why?

_____

_____

_____

_____

Editing and Proofreading

Edit for Conventions Reread your draft for accuracy and consistency. Edit to include a variety of sentence structures so that your essay reads well. If necessary, consult a style manual to clarify sentence types and improve your sentence variety.

Proofread for Accuracy Read your draft carefully, correcting errors in grammar, word usage, spelling, and punctuation.

Publishing and Presenting

Create a final version of your essay. Share it with a small group so that your classmates can read it and make comments. In turn, review and comment on your classmates' work. Afterward, discuss how your arguments answer the question of whether outsiders are simply those who are misjudged or misunderstood. Make sure that everyone takes a turn presenting his or her view, and listen carefully while others speak.

Reflecting

Think about what you learned while writing your argumentative essay. What did you learn about planning your draft that you will use when writing another argument? How did thinking about texts you read and viewed in this section inform your argument? What will you strive to improve in your next argument? For example, you might outline reasons for your claim before writing a first draft.

STANDARDS

Writing
Develop and strengthen writing as needed by planning, revising, editing, rewriting, or trying a new approach, focusing on addressing what is most significant for a specific purpose and audience.

Language
Write and edit work so that it conforms to the guidelines in a style manual appropriate for the discipline and writing type.

ESSENTIAL QUESTION:

Do people need to belong?

Why is it that people often feel like they don't belong? What makes others view certain people as outsiders or as insiders? The selections you will read address these questions and offer a range of differing perspectives. You will work in a group to continue your exploration of outsiders and outcasts.

Small-Group Learning Strategies

Throughout your life, in school, in your community, and in your career, you will continue to learn and work with others.

Review these strategies and the actions you can take to practice them. Add ideas of your own for each step. Use these strategies during Small-Group Learning.

STRATEGY	ACTION PLAN
Prepare	• Complete your assignments so that you are prepared for group work. • Organize your thinking so that you can contribute to your group's discussions. •
Participate fully	• Make eye contact to signal that you are listening and taking in what is being said. • Use text evidence. • •
Support others	• Build off ideas from others in your group. • Invite others who have not yet spoken to join the discussion. •
Clarify	• Paraphrase the ideas of others to ensure that your understanding is correct. • Ask follow-up questions. •

CONTENTS

PERFORMANCE TASK

SPEAKING AND LISTENING FOCUS

Deliver a Multimedia Presentation

The Small-Group readings raise questions about the ways in which communities define themselves or deal with those they see as outsiders. After reading, you will create a multimedia presentation in which you take a position on the question of whether difference is a weakness or a strength.

Working as a Team

1. Choose a topic In your group, discuss the following question:

> **Is the exclusion of others a problem we need to solve, or is the experience of being an outsider simply part of growing up?**

As you take turns sharing your responses, be sure to provide details to explain your position. After all group members have shared, discuss some of the pros and cons of being an outsider.

2. List Your Rules As a group, decide on the rules that you will follow as you work together. Samples are provided; add two more of your own. As you work together, you may add or revise rules based on your experience together.

- Everyone should participate in group discussions.
- Listen carefully and then contribute your own ideas.

- _____

  _____

- _____

  _____

3. Apply the Rules Share what you have learned about outsiders and outcasts. Make sure each person in the group contributes. Take notes on and be prepared to share with the class one thing that you heard from another member of your group.

4. Name Your Group Choose a name that reflects the unit topic.

Our group's name: _____

5. Create a Communication Plan Decide how you want to communicate with one another. For example, you might use online collaboration tools, email, or instant messaging.

Our group's decision: _____

_____

Making a Schedule

First, find out the due dates for the Small-Group activities. Then, preview the texts and activities with your group, and make a schedule for completing the tasks.

SELECTION	ACTIVITIES	DUE DATE
The Doll's House		
Sonnet, With Bird Elliptical Fences		
Revenge of the Geeks		
Encountering the Other: The Challenge for the 21st Century		

Working on Group Projects

As your group works together, you'll find it more effective if each person has a specific role. Different projects require different roles. Before beginning a project, discuss the necessary roles, and choose one for each group member. Some possible roles are listed here. Add your own ideas to the list.

Project Manager: monitors the schedule and keeps everyone on task

Researcher: organizes information-gathering activities

Recorder: takes notes during group meetings

_____

_____

_____

_____

_____

About the Author

Katherine Mansfield
(1888–1923) was born in
Wellington, New Zealand,
to an affluent family. She
published her first stories
at age ten and moved
to England in 1903 to
complete her education.
There she married writer
and editor John Middleton
Murry and befriended
Modernist authors Virginia
Woolf and D. H. Lawrence.
Mansfield died tragically
young of tuberculosis. She
is still counted among the
greatest short-story writers
in modern world literature.

The Doll's House

Concept Vocabulary

As you perform your first read of "The Doll's House," you will encounter
these words.

> shunned   sneered   spitefully

Context Clues If these words are unfamiliar to you, try using **context
clues**—other words and phrases that appear nearby in a text—to help you
determine their meanings. There are various types of context clues that may
help you as you read.

> **Synonyms:** The mother of the Kelvey girls is a **spry**, energetic little
> washerwoman.
>
> **Contrast of Ideas:** Normally **docile**, Kezia takes the risk of breaking
> Aunt Beryl's rules.

Apply your knowledge of context clues and other vocabulary strategies to
determine the meanings of unfamiliar words you encounter during your first
read. Use a print or online dictionary to verify your definitions.

First Read FICTION

Apply these strategies as you conduct your first read. You will have an
opportunity to complete a close read after your first read.

NOTICE *whom* the story is about, *what* happens, *where* and *when* it happens, and *why* those involved react as they do.

ANNOTATE by marking vocabulary and key passages you want to revisit.

First Read

CONNECT ideas within the selection to what you already know and what you have already read.

RESPOND by completing the Comprehension Check and by writing a brief summary of the selection.

☰ STANDARDS

Reading Literature
By the end of grade 10, read and
comprehend literature, including
stories, dramas, and poems, at the
high end of the grades 9–10 text
complexity band independently and
proficiently.

Language
• Use context as a clue to the
meaning of a word or phrase.
• Verify the preliminary
determination of the meaning of a
word or phrase.

The Doll's House   Katherine Mansfield

BACKGROUND

The plot of "The Doll's House" relies on characters' awareness of class—the arrangement of society in order of rank, where the members of each class are considered inherently different from those of other classes. Katherine Mansfield was aware of the divisions in social classes in New Zealand, where she lived as a child, and in England, where she spent her adult life.

1   When dear old Mrs. Hay went back to town after staying with the Burnells she sent the children a doll's house. It was so big that the carter and Pat carried it into the courtyard, and there it stayed, propped up on two wooden boxes beside the feed-room door. No harm could come of it; it was summer. And perhaps the smell of paint would have gone off by the time it had to be taken in. For, really, the smell of paint coming from that doll's house ("Sweet of old Mrs. Hay, of course; most sweet and generous!")—but the smell of paint was quite enough to make anyone seriously ill, in Aunt Beryl's opinion. Even before the sacking[1] was taken off. And when it was . . .

2   There stood the doll's house, a dark, oily, spinach green, picked out with bright yellow. Its two solid little chimneys, glued on to the roof, were painted red and white, and the door, gleaming with yellow varnish, was like a little slab of toffee. Four windows, real

NOTES

---

1. **sacking** *n.* coarse fabric.

windows, were divided into panes by a broad streak of green. There was actually a tiny porch, too, painted yellow, with big lumps of congealed paint hanging along the edge.

3   But perfect, perfect little house! Who could possibly mind the smell? It was part of the joy, part of the newness.

4   "Open it quickly, someone!"

5   The hook at the side was stuck fast. Pat pried it open with his penknife, and the whole house front swung back, and—there you were, gazing at one and the same moment into the drawing room and dining room, the kitchen and two bedrooms. That is the way for a house to open! Why don't all houses open like that? How much more exciting than peering through the slit of a door into a mean little hall with a hatstand and two umbrellas! That is—isn't it?—what you long to know about a house when you put your hand on the knocker. Perhaps it is the way God opens houses at the dead of night when He is taking a quiet turn with an angel . . .

6   "Oh-oh!" The Burnell children sounded as though they were in despair. It was too marvelous; it was too much for them. They had never seen anything like it in their lives. All the rooms were papered. There were pictures on the walls, painted on the paper, with gold frames complete. Red carpet covered all the floors except the kitchen; red plush chairs in the drawing room, green in the dining room; tables, beds with real bedclothes, a cradle, a stove, a dresser with tiny plates and one big jug. But what Kezia liked more than anything, what she liked frightfully, was the lamp. It stood in the middle of the dining-room table, an exquisite little amber lamp with a white globe. It was even filled all ready for lighting, though, of course, you couldn't light it. But there was something inside that looked like oil, and moved when you shook it.

7   The father and mother dolls, who sprawled very stiff as though they had fainted in the drawing room, and their two little children asleep upstairs, were really too big for the doll's house. They didn't look as though they belonged. But the lamp was perfect. It seemed to smile at Kezia, to say, "I live here." The lamp was real.

8   The Burnell children could hardly walk to school fast enough the next morning. They burned to tell everybody, to describe, to—well—to boast about their doll's house before the school bell rang.

9   "I'm to tell," said Isabel, "because I'm the eldest. And you two can join in after. But I'm to tell first."

10   There was nothing to answer. Isabel was bossy, but she was always right, and Lottie and Kezia knew too well the powers that went with being eldest. They brushed through the thick buttercups at the road edge and said nothing.

11   "And I'm to choose who's to come and see it first. Mother said I might."

12   For it had been arranged that while the doll's house stood in the courtyard they might ask the girls at school, two at a time, to come

and look. Not to stay to tea, of course, or to come traipsing through the house. But just to stand quietly in the courtyard while Isabel pointed out the beauties, and Lottie and Kezia looked pleased . . .

13   But hurry as they might, by the time they had reached the tarred palings[2] of the boys' playground the bell had begun to jangle. They only just had time to whip off their hats and fall into line before the roll was called. Never mind. Isabel tried to make up for it by looking very important and mysterious and by whispering behind her hand to the girls near her, "Got something to tell you at playtime."

14   Playtime came and Isabel was surrounded. The girls of her class nearly fought to put their arms round her, to walk away with her, to beam flatteringly, to be her special friend. She held quite a court under the huge pine trees at the side of the playground. Nudging, giggling together, the little girls pressed up close. And the only two who stayed outside the ring were the two who were always outside, the little Kelveys. They knew better than to come anywhere near the Burnells.

15   For the fact was, the school the Burnell children went to was not at all the kind of place their parents would have chosen if there had been any choice. But there was none. It was the only school for miles. And the consequence was all the children of the neighborhood, the judge's little girls, the doctor's daughters, the storekeeper's children, the milkman's, were forced to mix together. Not to speak of there being an equal number of rude, rough little boys as well. But the line had to be drawn somewhere. It was drawn at the Kelveys. Many of the children, including the Burnells, were not allowed even to speak to them. They walked past the Kelveys with their heads in the air, and as they set the fashion in all matters of behavior, the Kelveys were **shunned** by everybody. Even the teacher had a special voice for them, and a special smile for the other children when Lil Kelvey came up to her desk with a bunch of dreadfully common-looking flowers.

16   They were the daughters of a spry, hard-working little washerwoman, who went about from house to house by the day. This was awful enough. But where was Mr. Kelvey? Nobody knew for certain. But everybody said he was in prison. So they were the daughters of a washerwoman and a gaolbird.[3] Very nice company for other people's children! And they looked it. Why Mrs. Kelvey made them so conspicuous was hard to understand. The truth was they were dressed in "bits" given to her by the people for whom she worked. Lil, for instance, who was a stout, plain child, with big freckles, came to school in a dress made from a green art-serge[4] tablecloth of the Burnells', with red plush sleeves from the Logans' curtains. Her hat, perched on top of her high forehead, was a grown-up woman's hat, once the property of Miss Lecky, the

NOTES

Mark context clues or indicate another strategy you used that helped you determine meaning.

shunned (shuhnd) *v.*

MEANING:

---

2. **palings** *n.* pieces of wood that form the upright parts of a wooden fence.
3. **gaolbird** (JAYL burd) *n.* British English spelling of *jailbird*, a person who has been in prison often.
4. **serge** (surj) *n.* strong cloth with a pronounced ribbing on the back.

postmistress. It was turned up at the back and trimmed with a large scarlet quill. What a little guy[5] she looked! It was impossible not to laugh. And her little sister, our Else, wore a long white dress, rather like a nightgown, and a pair of little boy's boots. But whatever our Else wore she would have looked strange. She was a tiny wishbone of a child, with cropped hair and enormous solemn eyes—a little white owl. Nobody had ever seen her smile; she scarcely ever spoke. She went through life holding on to Lil, with a piece of Lil's skirt screwed up in her hand. Where Lil went, our Else followed. In the playground, on the road going to and from school, there was Lil marching in front and our Else holding on behind. Only when she wanted anything, or when she was out of breath, our Else gave Lil a tug, a twitch, and Lil stopped and turned round. The Kelveys never failed to understand each other.

Mark context clues or indicate another strategy you used that helped you determine meaning.

sneered (sneerd) *v.*

MEANING:

17   Now they hovered at the edge; you couldn't stop them listening. When the little girls turned round and **sneered**, Lil, as usual, gave her silly, shamefaced smile, but our Else only looked.

18   And Isabel's voice, so very proud, went on telling. The carpet made a great sensation, but so did the beds with real bedclothes, and the stove with an oven door.

19   When she finished Kezia broke in. "You've forgotten the lamp, Isabel."

20   "Oh, yes," said Isabel, "and there's a teeny little lamp, all made of yellow glass, with a white globe that stands on the dining-room table. You couldn't tell it from a real one."

21   "The lamp's best of all," cried Kezia. She thought Isabel wasn't making half enough of the little lamp. But nobody paid any attention. Isabel was choosing the two who were to come back with them that afternoon and see it. She chose Emmie Cole and Lena Logan. But when the others knew they were all to have a chance, they couldn't be nice enough to Isabel. One by one they put their arms round Isabel's waist and walked her off. They had something to whisper to her, a secret. "Isabel's *my* friend."

22   Only the little Kelveys moved away forgotten; there was nothing more for them to hear.

23   Days passed, and as more children saw the doll's house, the fame of it spread. It became the one subject, the rage. The one question was, "Have you seen Burnells' doll's house? "Oh, ain't it lovely!" "Haven't you seen it? Oh, I say!"

24   Even the dinner hour was given up to talking about it. The little girls sat under the pines eating their thick mutton sandwiches and big slabs of johnnycake[6] spread with butter. While always, as near as they could get, sat the Kelveys, our Else holding on to Lil, listening too, while they chewed their jam sandwiches out of a newspaper soaked with large red blobs.

---

5. **guy** *n.* British English slang for "person whose appearance is odd."
6. **johnnycake** *n.* bread made with cornmeal.

25   "Mother," said Kezia, "can't I ask the Kelveys just once?"

26   "Certainly not, Kezia."

27   "But why not?"

28   "Run away, Kezia; you know quite well why not."

29   At last everybody had seen it except them. On that day the subject rather flagged. It was the dinner hour. The children stood together under the pine trees, and suddenly, as they looked at the Kelveys eating out of their paper, always by themselves, always listening, they wanted to be horrid to them. Emmie Cole started the whisper.

30   "Lil Kelvey's going to be a servant when she grows up."

31   "O-oh, how awful!" said Isabel Burnell, and she made eyes at Emmie.

32   Emmie swallowed in a very meaning way and nodded to Isabel as she'd seen her mother do on those occasions.

33   "It's true—it's true—it's true," she said.

34   Then Lena Logan's little eyes snapped. "Shall I ask her?" she whispered.

35   "Bet you don't," said Jessie May.

36   "Pooh, I'm not frightened," said Lena. Suddenly she gave a little squeal and danced in front of the other girls. "Watch! Watch me! Watch me now!" said Lena. And sliding, gliding, dragging one foot, giggling behind her hand, Lena went over to the Kelveys.

37   Lil looked up from her dinner. She wrapped the rest quickly away. Our Else stopped chewing. What was coming now?

38   "Is it true you're going to be a servant when you grow up, Lil Kelvey?" shrilled Lena.

39   Dead silence. But instead of answering, Lil only gave her silly, shamefaced smile. She didn't seem to mind the question at all. What a sell for Lena! The girls began to titter.

40   Lena couldn't stand that. She put her hands on her hips; she shot forward. "Yah, yer father's in prison!" she hissed, spitefully.

41   This was such a marvelous thing to have said that the little girls rushed away in a body, deeply, deeply excited, wild with joy. Someone found a long rope, and they began skipping. And never did they skip so high, run in and out so fast, or do such daring things as on that morning.

42   In the afternoon Pat called for the Burnell children with the buggy and they drove home. There were visitors. Isabel and Lottie, who liked visitors, went upstairs to change their pinafores.[7] But Kezia thieved out at the back. Nobody was about; she began to swing on the big white gates of the courtyard. Presently, looking along the road, she saw two little dots. They grew bigger, they were coming toward her. Now she could see that one was in front and one close behind. Now she could see that they were the Kelveys. Kezia stopped swinging. She slipped off the gate as if she was going to run away.

Mark context clues or indicate another strategy you used that helped you determine meaning.

spitefully (SPYT fuhl ee) *adv.*

MEANING:

---

7. **pinafores** (PIHN uh fawrz) *n.* sleeveless garments fastened in the back and worn as an apron or dress.

Then she hesitated. The Kelveys came nearer, and beside them walked their shadows, very long, stretching right across the road with their heads in the buttercups. Kezia clambered back on the gate; she had made up her mind; she swung out.

43 "Hullo," she said to the passing Kelveys.

44 They were so astounded that they stopped. Lil gave her silly smile. Our Else stared.

45 "You can come and see our doll's house if you want to," said Kezia, and she dragged one toe on the ground. But at that Lil turned red and shook her head quickly.

46 "Why not?" asked Kezia.

47 Lil gasped, then she said, "Your ma told our ma you wasn't to speak to us."

48 "Oh, well," said Kezia. She didn't know what to reply. "It doesn't matter. You can come and see our doll's house all the same. Come on. Nobody's looking."

49 But Lil shook her head still harder.

50 "Don't you want to?" asked Kezia.

51 Suddenly there was a twitch, a tug at Lil's skirt. She turned round. Our Else was looking at her with big, imploring eyes; she was frowning; she wanted to go. For a moment Lil looked at our Else very doubtfully. But then our Else twitched her skirt again. She started forward. Kezia led the way. Like two little stray cats they followed across the courtyard to where the doll's house stood.

52 "There it is," said Kezia.

53 There was a pause. Lil breathed loudly, almost snorted; our Else was still as a stone.

54 "I'll open it for you," said Kezia kindly. She undid the hook and they looked inside.

55 "There's the drawing room and the dining room, and that's the—"

56 "Kezia!"

57 Oh, what a start they gave!

58 "Kezia!"

59 It was Aunt Beryl's voice. They turned round. At the back door stood Aunt Beryl, staring as if she couldn't believe what she saw.

60 "How dare you ask the little Kelveys into the courtyard?" said her cold, furious voice. "You know as well as I do, you're not allowed to talk to them. Run away, children, run away at once. And don't come back again," said Aunt Beryl. And she stepped into the yard and shooed them out as if they were chickens.

61 "Off you go immediately!" she called, cold and proud.

62 They did not need telling twice. Burning with shame, shrinking together, Lil huddling along like her mother, our Else dazed, somehow they crossed the big courtyard and squeezed through the white gate.

63 "Wicked, disobedient little girl!" said Aunt Beryl bitterly to Kezia, and she slammed the doll's house to.

64 The afternoon had been awful. A letter had come from Willie Brent, a terrifying, threatening letter, saying if she did not meet him that evening in Pulman's Bush, he'd come to the front door and ask the reason why! But now that she had frightened those little rats of Kelveys and given Kezia a good scolding, her heart felt lighter. That ghastly pressure was gone. She went back to the house humming.

65 When the Kelveys were well out of sight of Burnells', they sat down to rest on a big red drainpipe by the side of the road. Lil's cheeks were still burning; she took off the hat with the quill and held it on her knee. Dreamily they looked over the hay paddocks, past the creek, to the group of wattles[8] where Logan's cows stood waiting to be milked. What were their thoughts?

66 Presently our Else nudged up close to her sister. But now she had forgotten the cross lady. She put out a finger and stroked her sister's quill; she smiled her rare smile.

67 "I seen the little lamp," she said, softly.

68 Then both were silent once more. ❧

---

8. **wattles** *n.* walls or other simple structures made of woven reeds or twigs.

Comprehension Check

Complete the following items after you finish your first read. Review and clarify details with your group.

1. What object in the doll's house is Kezia's favorite?

2. How does Lena taunt Lil Kelvey?

3. What does Kezia do that makes Aunt Beryl angry?

4. 🖸 **Notebook** Confirm your understanding of the story by writing a summary.

- -

RESEARCH

Research to Clarify Choose at least one unfamiliar detail from the text. Briefly research that detail. In what way does the information you learned shed light on an aspect of the story?

THE DOLL'S HOUSE

Close Read the Text

With your group, revisit sections of the text you marked during your first read. **Annotate** details that you notice. What **questions** do you have? What can you **conclude**?

Analyze the Text

CITE TEXTUAL EVIDENCE
to support your answers.

Complete the activities.

1. **Review and Clarify** With your group, reread paragraph 16 of the selection. Discuss the author's description of Lil's and Else's appearances and mannerisms. How does the author succeed in prompting the reader's sympathy for the little girls?

2. **Present and Discuss** Now work with your group to share the passages from the selection that you found especially important. Take turns presenting your passages. Discuss what you notice in the selection, what questions you asked, and what conclusions you reached.

3. **Essential Question:** *Do people need to belong?* What has this story taught you about outsiders and outcasts? Discuss with your group.

LANGUAGE DEVELOPMENT

Concept Vocabulary

| shunned | sneered | spitefully |

Why These Words? The three concept vocabulary words are related. With your group, discuss the words, and determine what they have in common. How do these word choices enhance the impact of the text?

Practice

⊟ **Notebook** Confirm your understanding of these words by using them in sentences. Include context clues that hint at each word's meaning.

Word Study

⊟ **Notebook** **Words With Multiple Suffixes** To determine the meaning of a word that ends with multiple suffixes, such as *spitefully,* begin with the meaning of the base word. Then, working from left to right, analyze the effect each suffix has on the word's meaning and part of speech.

Write the meanings of these words: *hopelessness, luminosity, colorization.* Consult a dictionary if needed.

⊞ WORD NETWORK

Add interesting words related to outsiders from the text to your Word Network.

☰ STANDARDS

Reading Literature
Determine a theme or central idea of a text and analyze in detail its development over the course of the text, including how it emerges and is shaped and refined by specific details; provide an objective summary of the text.

Language
Identify and correctly use patterns of word changes that indicate different meanings or parts of speech.

Analyze Craft and Structure

Symbol and Theme In literature, a **symbol** is a character, setting, object, or image that stands both for itself and for something else, often an abstract idea. Traditional literary forms, such as myths or folk tales, often feature universal symbols. For example, water often symbolizes life or rebirth. In modern literature, symbols are often specific to a work rather than universal. In order to understand the deeper meaning of a literary symbol, look at the details used to describe it. Ask questions such as these: *Why is this character, setting, or object important? What do other characters think and say about it? How do they interact with it? What does it look like?*

A **theme** is a central message or insight into life revealed by a literary work. In most works of fiction and poetry, the theme is implicit, or suggested. Readers figure it out by analyzing details and looking for patterns or relationships among them. Symbols are often key elements to the development of a theme.

TIP

GROUP DISCUSSION
Members of your group may state the symbolic meanings and the story's theme in a variety of ways. You should not expect your responses to be identical.

Practice

CITE TEXTUAL EVIDENCE
to support your answers.

Work on your own to complete the chart. Then, share your responses with your group.

SYMBOL	DETAILS IN TEXT	SYMBOLIC MEANING(S)
the lamp	• Kezia is "frightfully" enchanted by it; which suggests it tempts her or challenges her in some way. •	The lamp symbolizes enlightened attitudes, kindness, and acceptance.
the doll's house		
the Kelvey's clothing		

📓 **Notebook** Answer these questions.

1. Why do you think Kezia invites the Kelveys to see the doll's house?

2. What does Else's statement at the end of the story suggest about both the lamp's symbolic meaning and the story's theme?

3. What is a possible theme of the story? Explain.

THE DOLL'S HOUSE

Author's Style

Diction and Syntax In writing and speech, **diction** refers to an author's or speaker's word choice, especially with regard to range of vocabulary, use of slang, and level of formality.

> **Informal Diction:** Are ya gonna drive to the store?
> **Formal Diction:** Who among us will drive to the store?

Syntax refers to the way in which words and phrases are joined together in sentences. A writer's syntax may include short punchy sentences, long complex ones, or a combination of both.

> **Simple Syntax:** We arrived at the theater. There were many cars in the lot.
> **Complex Syntax:** When we arrived at the theater, we saw dozens of cars in the lot and an excited crowd waiting on line.

Diction and syntax are key elements of a writer's style. They also help to reveal a writer's **tone,** or attitude toward the subject. For example, in "The Doll's House," Mansfield often combines informal words and slang with complex sentence structures. The tension between these two aspects of her style hints at the story's conflicts around class and social status.

Read It

Work individually. For each quotation write whether the diction is formal or informal and whether the syntax is simple or complex. Then, write notes about the tone these choices create and the story conflicts they suggest. Discuss your responses with your group.

STANDARDS

Reading Literature
Determine the meaning of words and phrases as they are used in the text, including figurative and connotative meanings; analyze the cumulative impact of specific word choices on meaning and tone.

Writing
Write arguments to support claims in an analysis of substantive topics or texts, using valid reasoning and relevant and sufficient evidence.

QUOTATION	DICTION	SYNTAX	NOTES
Not to stay to tea, of course, or to come traipsing through the house. (paragraph 12)			
So they were the daughters of a washerwoman and a gaolbird. Very nice company for other people's children! (paragraph 16)			
"Oh, ain't it lovely!" (paragraph 23)			
Lena couldn't stand that. She put her hands on her hips; she shot forward. "Yah, yer father's in prison!" she hissed, spitefully. (paragraph 40)			

Write It

📝 **Notebook** Write a description of a character and something he or she does. Use informal diction and simple syntax. Then, rewrite the description using elevated diction and complex syntax. Explain the effects of these stylistic choices.

Writing to Sources

Assignment

Write a **response to literature,** a type of argument in which you explain and defend your interpretation of a text. Be sure to state your claim, or main idea, and support it with details and evidence from the story. Choose one of the following topics:

☐ At the end of the story, the narrator asks about the Kelveys, "What were their thoughts?" In a brief **character analysis** of Lil and Else, use evidence from the story to explain what the Kelveys might have been thinking. Defend your analysis with story details that reveal each girl's character.

☐ In a **composition** of several paragraphs, compare and contrast social divisions in "The Doll's House" to those in American society today. Cite evidence from the story to support your account of how social divisions are presented in "The Doll's House."

☐ Write a **critical response** to this statement: In Katherine Mansfield's "The Doll's House," the world of the adults is far crueler than that of the children. Cite evidence from the story to support your response.

Project Plan Work together to discuss the story and gather ideas, but work on your own to draft and revise your response to literature.

Charting Main Ideas Use this chart to record your ideas. Remember to include appropriate citations of evidence.

📝 EVIDENCE LOG

Before moving on to a new selection, go to your Evidence Log and record what you learned from "The Doll's House."

MAIN IDEAS	SUPPORTING DETAILS	EVIDENCE

POETRY COLLECTION

Sonnet, With Bird

Elliptical

Fences

Concept Vocabulary

As you perform your first read of these poems, you will encounter these words.

| perspective | entitled | interactions |

Base Words If these words are unfamiliar to you, analyze each one to see whether it contains a base word you know. Then, use your knowledge of the "inside" word, along with context, to determine the meaning.

> **Unfamiliar Word:** *extrasensory*
>
> **Familiar Base Word:** *sensory,* which means "of or relating to the senses"
>
> **Context:** *I wrote down the address and took a taxi driven by one of those cabdrivers with* **extrasensory** *memory.*
>
> **Conclusion:** Cabdrivers are known for their exceptional memories for directions. Perhaps *extrasensory* means "beyond the ordinary perception of the senses."

Apply your knowledge of base words and other vocabulary strategies to determine the meanings of unfamiliar words you encounter during your first read.

First Read POETRY

Apply these strategies as you conduct your first read. You will have the opportunity to complete a close read after your first read.

≣ STANDARDS

Reading Literature
By the end of grade 10, read and comprehend literature, including stories, dramas, and poems, at the high end of the grades 9–10 text complexity band independently and proficiently.

Language

• Use context as a clue to the meaning of a word or phrase.

• Identify and correctly use patterns of word changes that indicate different meanings or parts of speech.

NOTICE *who* or *what* is "speaking" the poem and whether the poem tells a story or describes a single moment.

ANNOTATE by marking vocabulary and key passages you want to revisit.

First Read

CONNECT ideas within each selection to what you already know and what you have already read.

RESPOND by completing the Comprehension Check.

About the Poets

Sherman Alexie (b. 1966) grew up on the Spokane Indian Reservation in Washington State. As a child, Alexie suffered from seizures and spent much of his time in bed reading. After college, his career as a writer took off. Since then, Alexie has won numerous awards for his novels, stories, screenplays, and poems, including a PEN/Hemingway Award and the National Book Award.

Harryette Mullen (b. 1953) grew up primarily in Texas and now teaches English at the University of California, Los Angeles. Mullen's poetry has been described as "crossing lines" between the political and the personal. Mullen credits much of her success to attending poetry readings in which she realized that poetry is "not just something on the page" but instead something that has to be heard out loud to be fully appreciated.

Pat Mora (b. 1942) grew up in El Paso, Texas, and became a teacher, museum director, and university administrator before turning to writing. Mora writes poetry in both English and Spanish, often including Spanish words and phrases in her English-language poems. Her transcultural style gives a voice to her Mexican American heritage of the Southwest.

Backgrounds

Sonnet, With Bird

The sonnet form is one of the most enduring poetic forms, having survived five centuries essentially unchanged. A sonnet follows a strict fourteen-line arrangement in a specific rhyme scheme. The final two lines of a sonnet resolve or summarize the preceding lines. In this poem, Sherman Alexie reinvents the sonnet, presenting one of our most traditional forms in an entirely new way.

Elliptical

Ellipsis—often represented with punctuation marks known as ellipsis points (. . .)—is the omission, often intentional, of a word or words that would be needed for a thought to be complete. Sometimes, the missing word or words are understood from context. Other times, they are left to the reader's imagination. This poem, whose title means "involving ellipsis," plays with both of these ideas.

Fences

This poem was inspired by Puerto Vallarta, a beach resort city in Mexico. Many places, including Puerto Vallarta, rely on tourism as a major income source. This tourist economy, however, means that many locals must accommodate tourists who enjoy an affluent lifestyle that they themselves cannot afford.

Sonnet, With Bird

Sherman Alexie

NOTES

1. Seventeen months after I moved off the reservation, and on the second plane flight of my life, I traveled to London to promote my first internationally published book. 2. A Native American in England! I imagined the last Indian in England was Maria Tall Chief, the Osage[1] ballerina who was once married to Balanchine.[2] An Indian married to Balanchine! 3. My publishers put me in a quaint little hotel near the Tate Gallery. I didn't go into the Tate. Back then, I was afraid of paintings of and by white men. I think I'm still afraid of paintings of and by white men. 4. This was long before I had a cell phone, so I stopped at payphones to call my wife. I miss the intensity of a conversation measured by a dwindling stack of quarters. 5. No quarters in England, though, and I don't remember what the equivalent British coin was called. 6. As with every other country I've visited, nobody thought I was Indian. This made me lonely. 7. Lonely enough to cry in my hotel bed one night as I kept thinking, "I am the only Indian in this country right now. I'm the only Indian within a five-thousand-mile circle." 8. But I wasn't the only Indian;

---

1. **Osage** Native American tribe based in the Midwestern United States.
2. **Balanchine** George Balanchine (1904–1983), dance choreographer who founded the New York City Ballet and is considered the father of American ballet.

I wasn't even the only Spokane Indian.[3] 9. On the payphone, my mother told me that a childhood friend from the reservation was working at a London pub. So I wrote down the address and took a taxi driven by one of those cabdrivers with extrasensory memory. 10. When I entered the pub, I sat in a corner, and waited for my friend to discover me. When he saw me, he leapt over the bar and hugged me. "I thought I was the only Indian in England," he said. 11. His name was Aaron and he died of cancer last spring. I'd rushed to see him in his last moments, but he passed before I could reach him. Only minutes gone, his skin was still warm. I held his hand, kissed his forehead, and said, "England." 12. "England," in our tribal language, now means, "Aren't we a miracle?" and "Goodbye." 13. In my strange little hotel near the Tate, I had to wear my suit coat to eat breakfast in the lobby restaurant. Every morning, I ordered eggs and toast. Everywhere in the world, bread is bread, but my eggs were impossibly small. "What bird is this?" I asked the waiter. "That would be quail," he said. On the first morning, I could not eat the quail eggs. On the second morning, I only took a taste. On third day, I ate two and ordered two more. 14. A gathering of quail is called a bevy. A gathering of Indians is called a tribe. When quails speak, they call it a song. When Indians sing, the air is heavy with grief. When quails grieve, they lie down next to their dead. When Indians die, the quail speaks.

---

3. **Spokane Indian** Native American from the northeastern part of Washington State.

Elliptical

Harryette Mullen

They just can't seem to . . . They should try harder to . . . They ought to be more . . . We all wish they weren't so . . . They never . . . They always . . . Sometimes they . . . Once in a while they . . . However it is obvious that they . . . Their overall tendency has been . . . The consequences of which have been . . . They don't appear to understand that . . . If only they would make an effort to . . . But we know how difficult it is for them to . . . Many of them remain unaware of . . . Some who should know better simply refuse to . . . Of course, their **perspective** has been limited by . . . On the other hand, they obviously feel **entitled** to . . . Certainly we can't forget that they . . . Nor can it be denied that they . . . We know that this has had an enormous impact on their . . . Nevertheless their behavior strikes us as . . . Our **interactions** unfortunately have been . . .

Mark base words or indicate another strategy you used that helped you determine meaning.

perspective (puhr SPEHK tihv) *n.*

MEANING:

entitled (ehn TY tuhld) *adj.*

MEANING:

interactions (ihn tuhr AK shuhnz) *n.*

MEANING:

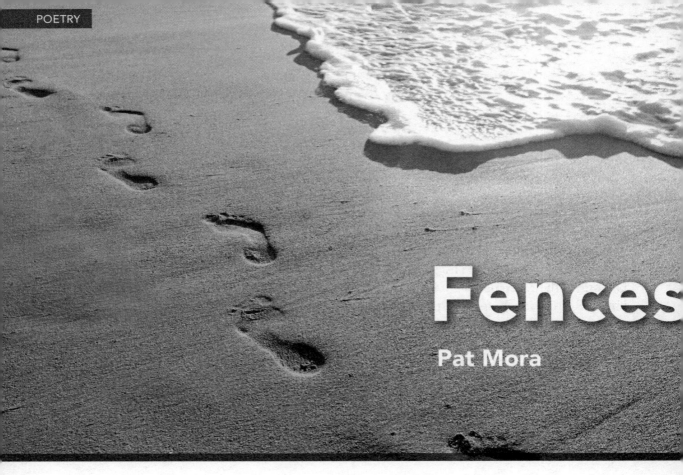

Fences

Pat Mora

Mouths full of laughter,
the *turistas* come to the tall hotel
with suitcases full of dollars.

Every morning my brother makes
5 the cool beach new for them.
With a wooden board he smooths
away all footprints.

I peek through the cactus fence
and watch the women rub oil
10 sweeter than honey into their arms and legs
while their children jump waves
or sip drinks from long straws,
coconut white, mango yellow.

Once my little sister
15 ran barefoot across the hot sand
for a taste.

My mother roared like the ocean,
"No. No. It's their beach.
It's their beach."

Comprehension Check

Complete the following items after you finish your first read. Review and clarify details with your group.

SONNET, WITH BIRD

1. Why does the speaker go to London?

2. Whom does the speaker meet in London?

ELLIPTICAL

3. How does each sentence of "Elliptical" end?

4. What pronoun appears in the first nine sentences of the poem?

FENCES

5. What does the speaker's brother do each day?

6. What does the speaker's little sister do that causes the mother to react?

RESEARCH

Research to Clarify Choose at least one unfamiliar detail from one of the poems. Briefly research that detail. In what way does the information you learned shed light on an aspect of the poem.

POETRY COLLECTION

Close Read the Text

With your group, revisit sections of the text you marked during your first read. **Annotate** details that you notice. What **questions** do you have? What can you **conclude**?

Analyze the Text

CITE TEXTUAL EVIDENCE
to support your answers.

📝 **Notebook** Complete the activities.

1. **Review and Clarify** With your group, reread the lines of "Sonnet, With Bird" numbered 11 and 12. What point does the author make by defining England in two different ways? Explain.

2. **Present and Discuss** Now, work with your group to share other key lines from the poems. What made you choose these particular passages? Take turns presenting your choices. Discuss what you notice in the poem, what questions you asked, and what conclusions you reached.

3. **Essential Question:** *Do people need to belong?* What have these poems taught you about being an outsider? Discuss with your group.

Concept Vocabulary

| perspective | entitled | interactions |

Why These Words? The three concept vocabulary words are related. With your group, identify the concept they have in common. How do these word choices enhance the text?

Practice

📝 **Notebook** Confirm your understanding of these words by using them in sentences. Include context clues that hint at their meanings.

Word Study

📝 **Notebook** **Latin Prefix: en-** The concept vocabulary word *entitled* begins with the Latin prefix *en-*, meaning "in," "into," or "on." Write the meanings of these other words beginning with the prefix *en: enamor*, *encapsulate*, *encipher*. Consult a college-level dictionary as needed.

👥 TIP

GROUP DISCUSSION
Take turns reading portions of each poem aloud. Discuss how listening to a poem read aloud helps you hear rhythm, rhyme, and other sound devices. Discuss the connection between the sound of the poem and its meaning.

🔗 WORD NETWORK

Add words related to outsiders from the texts to your Word Network.

▤ STANDARDS

Reading Literature
Analyze how an author's choices concerning how to structure a text, order events within it, and manipulate time create such effects as mystery, tension, or surprise.

Language
• Identify and correctly use patterns of word changes that indicate different meanings or parts of speech.
• Consult general and specialized reference materials, both print and digital, to find the pronunciation of a word or determine or clarify its precise meaning, its part of speech, or its etymology.

Analyze Craft and Structure

Author's Choices: Poetic Form Poems can be written in any number of different poetic forms. A **poetic form** is a set pattern of poetic elements. For example, a poetic form may call for a fixed number of lines, a particular pattern of rhyme or meter, or any combination of those elements. Some poems, however, avoid the use of fixed patterns altogether. For example, **free verse** poems do not follow any set patterns. Instead, they present carefully crafted lines that re-create the rhythms of natural speech or present unexpected combinations of language. To create these effects, free verse poets often play with line breaks, or the ways in which lines end.

- **End-stopped lines** are lines that complete a grammatical unit; they usually end with a punctuation mark, such as a comma or period.
- **Enjambed lines** do not end with a grammatical break and do not make full sense without the line that follows.

The **prose poem** is a poetic form that looks like prose, or a non-poetic work, but sounds like poetry. Prose poems lack the line breaks most often found in poetry, but they may contain other poetic techniques such as repetition or rhyme.

Practice

CITE TEXTUAL EVIDENCE to support your answers.

Work together as a group to answer the following questions.

1. In "Fences," which lines are end-stopped and which are enjambed? Explain how the different types of lines emphasize meaning or affect how a reader hears and understands the poem.

2. (a) What type of poem is "Elliptical"? Explain. (b) In what ways does the choice of form affect how the reader experiences the poem? (c) Rewrite the poem, adding line breaks that make sense to you. Compare with the original. What is lost and what is gained by the poet's choice of form?

3. (a) What poetic techniques does "Sonnet, With Bird" use that make it a poem rather than prose? (b) How does the combination of poetic and prose-like elements affect its meaning?

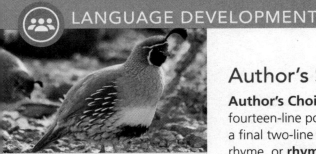

POETRY COLLECTION

Author's Style

Author's Choices: Poetic Form A traditional, Shakespearean **sonnet** is a fourteen-line poem that contains three four-line stanzas, or **quatrains**, and a final two-line stanza, or **couplet**. It has a regular meter and set pattern of rhyme, or **rhyme scheme.**

Shakespeare's "Sonnet 18" features three quatrains that develop a theme and follow an *abab*, *cdcd*, *efef* rhyme pattern. Here is the first quatrain.

> *Shall I compare thee to a summer's day? (a)*
> *Thou art more lovely and more temperate. (b)*
> *Rough winds do shake the darling buds of May, (a)*
> *And summer's lease hath all too short a* date. *(b)*

The final two lines in the sonnet form a rhyming couplet.

> *So long as men can breathe or eyes can see, (g)*
> *So long lives this and this gives life to thee. (g)*

Traditionally, the rhyming couplet that ends a sonnet dramatically redefines or twists the thematic ideas expressed in the earlier lines.

Read It

In "Sonnet, With Bird," Sherman Alexie uses the sonnet form as a starting point, then changes it drastically. Work individually to reread the poem. Chart how Alexie's poem reimagines the Shakespearean sonnet.

SONNET CHARACTERISTIC	SONNET, WITH BIRD	COMMENT
number of lines		
rhyme scheme		
three quatrains that develop a theme		
final couplet that presents a twist		

Write It

📓 **Notebook** Write a paragraph in which you explain how Alexie experiments with the Shakespearean sonnet to create a prose poem. Use the information in your chart to cite examples from the poem.

STANDARDS

Reading Literature
• Analyze how an author's choices concerning how to structure a text, order events within it, and manipulate time create such effects as mystery, tension, or surprise.
• Analyze how an author draws on and transforms source material in a specific work.

Speaking and Listening
Present information, findings, and supporting evidence clearly, concisely, and logically such that listeners can follow the line of reasoning and the organization, development, substance, and style are appropriate to purpose, audience, and task.

Speaking and Listening

Assignment

As a group, rewrite one of the poems in this collection, altering a key aspect of its form or content. Then, deliver a **poetry reading** of the revised work. Afterward, take questions from listeners about the decisions you made as you created the revised poem. Choose from the following options:

☐ Complete each sentence in the poem "Elliptical." Work together as a group. Write out the poem in its entirety.

Use questions such as the following to guide your work: *To whom does "they" refer in the original poem? How does completing the sentences change the meaning of the poem? Does the poem have greater impact with completed sentences or without them?*

☐ Change the structure of "Sonnet, With Bird" by rearranging line breaks and phrasing. Note that poets use line breaks and phrasing to group together discrete thoughts, images, and emotions.

Use questions such as the following to guide your work: *Which thoughts, feelings, images, or emotions does the restructuring affect? In what ways? How does the restructuring change the meaning of the poem?*

☐ Rewrite "Fences" as a prose poem. Include the same general information and images as the original, but change the line breaks and modify sentences so that they work as prose. Add more detail if necessary.

Use questions such as the following to guide your work: *How does the change in structure affect the meaning of the poem? Does the poem have a greater impact in its original form or as a prose poem?*

Project Plan Assign each member of the group a portion of the poem to memorize and read aloud as part of the recitation. Before you recite your poem to the class, practice it with your group several times. Provide helpful feedback on the tone, speed, and dramatic qualities of each reading.

Present and Discuss As your present your work to the class, make sure your delivery reflects the structural changes you introduced. Compare the poem your group wrote with those of the other small groups in the class.

☑ EVIDENCE LOG

Before moving on to a new selection, go to your Evidence Log and record what you learned from "Sonnet, With Bird," "Elliptical," and "Fences."

About the Author

Alexandra Robbins
(b. 1976) is a journalist
and bestselling author.
She has written for several
newspapers and magazines,
including the *Los Angeles
Times,* the *Washington Post,*
and the *Atlantic.* Robbins's
journalism is highly regarded;
she was a recipient of the
John Bartlow Martin Award.
Her most recent work, *The
Nurses: A Year of Secrets,
Drama, and Miracles With
the Heroes of the Hospital,*
has been praised for its
investigative merit and
captivating narrative of the
nursing profession.

Revenge of the Geeks

Concept Vocabulary

As you perform your first read of "Revenge of the Geeks," you will encounter these words.

marginalize	pariah	bigotry

Context Clues If these words are unfamiliar, try using **context clues**—other words and phrases that appear nearby in the text—to help you determine their meanings. There are different types of context clues.

> **Definition:** In some cases, **psychologists** and **sociologists** do related work. The former <u>study individual behavior,</u> whereas the latter <u>study group behavior.</u>
>
> **Elaborating Details:** She was once a loner, but is now a media **tycoon** and one of the <u>richest women in the world.</u>
>
> **Antonym, or Contrast of Ideas:** Some members of the group are sadly **indolent,** but others <u>work extremely hard.</u>

Apply your knowledge of context clues and other vocabulary strategies to determine the meanings of unfamiliar words you encounter during your first read. Use a resource such as a dictionary or a thesaurus to verify your definitions.

First Read NONFICTION

Apply these strategies as you conduct your first read. You will have an opportunity to complete a close read after your first read.

NOTICE the general ideas of the text. *What* is it about? *Who* is involved?

ANNOTATE by marking vocabulary and key passages you want to revisit.

CONNECT ideas within the selection to what you already know and what you have already read.

RESPOND by completing the Comprehension Check and by writing a brief summary of the selection.

First Read

⬛ STANDARDS

Reading Informational Text
By the end of grade 10, read and
comprehend literary nonfiction at
the high end of the grades 9–10 text
complexity band independently and
proficiently.

Language
• Use context as a clue to the
meaning of a word or phrase.
• Verify the preliminary
determination of the meaning of a
word or phrase.

Revenge of the Geeks

Alexandra Robbins

BACKGROUND

The word *geek* has a long history—one of its earliest appearances was as *gecke* in the works of Shakespeare, as a word for "fool." It became *geek* in the late nineteenth century, and by the middle of the twentieth century it had come to be used as a generic, all-purpose insult. In the 1970s, however, *geek* came to mean, specifically, "an overly eager student," especially one interested in computers.

1   Many popular students approach graduation day with bittersweet nostalgia: Excitement for the future is tempered by fear of lost status. But as cap-and-gown season nears, let's also stop to consider the outcasts, students for whom finishing high school feels like liberation from a state-imposed sentence.

2   In seven years of reporting from American middle and high schools, I've seen repeatedly that the differences that cause a student to be excluded in high school are often the same traits or skills that will serve him or her well after graduation.

3   Examples abound: Taylor Swift's classmates left the lunch table as soon as she sat down because they disdained her taste for country music. Last year, the Grammy winner was the nation's top-selling recording artist.

4   Students mocked Tim Gunn's love of making things; now he is a fashion icon with the recognizable catchphrase "Make it work."

5   J. K. Rowling, author of the bestselling "Harry Potter" series, has described herself as a bullied child "who lived mostly in books and daydreams." It's no wonder she went on to write books populated with kids she describes as "outcasts and comfortable with being so."

6   For many, says Sacred Heart University psychology professor Kathryn LaFontana, high school is the "first foray[1] into the adult world where [kids] have to think about their own status." And for

NOTES

---

1. **foray** *n.* attempt to do something.

teenagers, says LaFontana, who studies adolescent peer relationships and social status, "the worst thing in the world is to be different from other people; that's what makes someone unpopular."

7   In the rabidly conformist school environment, the qualities that make people different make them targets. In adulthood, however, the qualities that make people different make them compelling.

8   Some students are vaguely aware of this reality. An eighth-grade boy in Indiana told me: "I'm always single, so it's tough. Never can get a girl. The smart thing repels girls. I like being smart because I breeze through school. . . . That's the good thing, but the girl thing is killing me."

9   It's hard to know when you're in high school that "the smart thing" is likely to translate into later success, or that "the girl thing" is bound to improve. That's why it's up to adults to convey constantly to teenagers that the characteristics that **marginalize** them can pay off after graduation.

10   Geeks profit from their technological knowhow. Emos benefit from being empathetic and unafraid to display emotion. Skaters, punks, and others who pursue their arts with fervor benefit from the creativity they've honed. Gamers have learned both problem-solving skills and the ability to collaborate through collective intelligence.

11   In the adult world, being out is in. "Geek chic" and "nerd merch" are on the rise. Nerdcore hip-hop artists have penetrated mainstream consciousness. And the nerd prom known as Comic Con draws high-profile celebrities and throngs of smitten fans. They're all part of what Jerry Holkins, creator of the Penny Arcade webcomic and video game conference, calls "the social **pariah** outcast aesthetic."

12   Adults tend to be mature enough to recognize that there would be no progress—cures for diseases, ways to harness new energy sources—without people who are different. Successful scientists think distinctively.

13   So what happens to high school's popular students? Research shows that they are more likely than outsiders to conform, which can also mean they're less likely to innovate. They are more likely to be both targets and instigators of aggression—whether physical or relational, which includes rumors, gossip, and backstabbing. They are more likely to drink and engage in other risky behaviors. Students who are popular and involved in aggression are less likely to do well in school. Psychologists point out that high-status cliques teach the exclusionary behavior that may be the foundation for eventual racism, anti-Semitism, sexism, and other forms of **bigotry**.

14   That's not to say, of course, that popularity in high school necessarily leads to mediocrity or worse in adulthood. But neither is there necessarily something wrong with a student merely because he is excluded by classmates. We don't view a saxophonist as musically challenged if he can't play the violin. He's just a different kind of musician. A sprinter is still an athlete even if she can't play basketball. She's a different kind of athlete. Similarly, we might acknowledge

---

Mark context clues or indicate another strategy you used that helped you determine meaning.

marginalize (MAHR juh nuh lyz) *v.*

MEANING:

pariah (puh RY uh) *n.*

MEANING:

bigotry (BIHG uh tree) *n.*

MEANING:

that students who don't follow the popular crowd's lead aren't any less socially successful; they're just a different kind of social.

15   The education landscape would be so much more bearable if students could understand this. And if schools found better ways to nurture kids who reject the in-crowd image.

16   The worst aspect of the treatment of student outsiders isn't the name-calling. It isn't the loneliness. It isn't even the demise of attitudes and programs that are important for fostering creativity and independence. The most heartbreaking consequence of this treatment is that tens of thousands of students—imaginative, interesting, impressionable people—think that they have done or felt something wrong.

17   It's not enough to merely tell them that in the real world, "it gets better." They need to know before graduation that being different is not a problem but a strength. ❧

Comprehension Check

Complete the following items after you finish your first read. Review and clarify details with your group.

1. According to the author, why did Taylor Swift's classmates leave the lunch table as soon as Swift sat down?

2. According to psychology professor Kathryn LaFontana, what is the worst thing in the world for teenagers?

3. What does Robbins believe that adults should constantly convey to teenagers?

4. How do successful scientists think, according to Robbins?

5. 📓 **Notebook** Confirm your understanding by writing a summary of the text.

- -

RESEARCH

Research to Clarify Choose at least one unfamiliar detail from the text. Briefly research that detail. In what way does the information you learned shed light on an aspect of the argument?

REVENGE OF THE GEEKS

Close Read the Text

With your group, revisit sections of the text you marked during your first read. **Annotate** details that you notice. What **questions** do you have? What can you **conclude**?

Analyze the Text

> **CITE TEXTUAL EVIDENCE**
> to support your answers.

📓 **Notebook** Complete the activities.

1. **Review and Clarify** Reread the first five paragraphs of the selection. Where does the author state her claim, or main idea, in this argument? Restate the claim in your own words. What three examples does Robbins cite in this section of the text to support this claim?

2. **Present and Discuss** Now, work with your group to share the passages from the selection that you found especially important. Take turns presenting your passages. Discuss what you notice in the selection, what questions you asked, and what conclusions you reached.

3. **Essential Question:** *Do people need to belong?* What has this text taught you about outsiders and outcasts? Discuss with your group.

LANGUAGE DEVELOPMENT

Concept Vocabulary

| marginalize | pariah | bigotry |

Why These Words? The three concept vocabulary words are related. With your group, determine what the words have in common. How do these word choices enhance the impact of the text?

Practice

📓 **Notebook** Confirm your understanding of these words by using them in sentences. Include context clues that hint at each word's meaning.

Word Study

📓 **Notebook** **Denotation and Connotation** The **denotation** of a word is its literal definition that you would find in a dictionary. A word's **connotations** are its emotional overtones or nuances. For example, the word *pariah* literally means "outcast." Its connotations are overwhelmingly negative. This word came into English from Tamil, an Indian language, where it signified someone from the lowest social caste, or group.

Use a dictionary to research the denotations and connotations of the following words from the selection: *nostalgia, disdain, conformist, smitten, distinctively*. Then, use each word in a sentence that clearly indicates both its denotation and its connotation.

🔗 **WORD NETWORK**

Add interesting words related to outsiders from the text to your Word Network.

📋 **STANDARDS**

Reading Informational Text
• Delineate and evaluate the argument and specific claims in a text, assessing whether the reasoning is valid and the evidence is relevant and sufficient; identify false statements and fallacious reasoning.

Language
• Determine or clarify the meaning of unknown and multiple-meaning words and phrases based on *grades 9–10 reading and content,* choosing flexibly from a range of strategies.
• Demonstrate understanding of figurative language, word relationships, and nuances in word meanings.
• Analyze nuances in the meaning of words with similar denotations.

Analyze Craft and Structure

Reasoning and Evidence "Revenge of the Geeks" is an **argument,** a type of nonfiction in which a writer states a **claim,** or position on a debatable issue, and then defends that claim with sound reasoning and evidence. **Evidence** includes facts, data, information, explanations, anecdotes, quotations, examples, and any other details that support the writer's reasons or main claim.

When reading an argument, it is important to evaluate both the writer's reasoning and the quality of the evidence he or she uses to support it. Strong reasoning should have clear, logical connections. Strong evidence should have the following qualities:

- **Variety:** A writer should include different types of evidence, such as facts, data, and quotations. It should come from a range of sources.
- **Credibility:** Evidence should be drawn from reliable, authoritative sources. A credible source may present a distinct perspective, but it should not display bias, unfounded judgments, or sweeping generalizations.
- **Relevance:** Evidence should be current and connect logically to the writer's ideas.

Practice

CITE TEXTUAL EVIDENCE to support your answers.

📓 **Notebook** **Work on your own to answer the questions. Then, share and discuss your responses with your group.**

1. How does Robbins support her claim that the qualities that make students outcasts in high school are those that make them successful in adulthood?

2. How does Robbins develop her argument that being popular in high school may actually work against people when they enter the adult world?

3. Use the chart to identify the types of evidence Robbins uses and to evaluate its credibility and relevance.

CLAIM	EVIDENCE	CREDIBILITY	RELEVANCE

4. Write a paragraph in which you evaluate the validity of Robbins's argument. Cite evidence from your chart as examples.

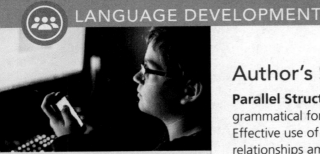

REVENGE OF THE GEEKS

Author's Style

Parallel Structure Parallelism, or **parallel structure,** is the use of similar grammatical forms or patterns to express ideas of equal significance. Effective use of parallelism creates rhythm and balance and clarifies the relationships among ideas. When writing lacks parallelism, it presents equally significant ideas in an unnecessary mix of grammatical forms. This inconsistency can be awkward, confusing, or distracting for readers.

This chart shows examples of nonparallel and parallel structure.

SENTENCE ELEMENTS	NONPARALLEL	PARALLEL
words	<u>Planning</u>, <u>drafting</u> and **revision** are three steps in the writing process.	<u>Planning</u>, <u>drafting</u>, and **revising** are three steps in the writing process.
phrases	I could not wait <u>to hop on that plane</u> <u>to leave the country</u>, and **for some world exploration**.	I could not wait <u>to hop on that plane</u>, <u>to leave the country</u>, and **to explore the world**.
clauses	Ari likes his new school: <u>The teachers are good</u>, <u>the students are nice</u>, and he **likes the new building**.	Ari likes his new school: <u>The teachers are good</u>, <u>the students are nice</u>, and **the building is new**.

Read It

Mark the parallel sentence elements in each of these passages from "Revenge of the Geeks." Parallel elements may appear in a single sentence or in mutiple sentences.

1. In the rabidly conformist school environment, the qualities that make people different make them targets. In adulthood, however, the qualities that make people different make them compelling.

2. Geeks profit from their technological knowhow. Emos benefit from being empathetic and unafraid to display emotion. Skaters, punks, and others . . . benefit from the skills and the ability to collaborate through collective intelligence.

3. Research shows that they are more likely . . . to conform, which can also mean they're less likely to innovate.

4. Psychologists point out that high-status cliques teach the exclusionary behavior that may be the foundation for eventual racism, anti-Semitism, sexism and other forms of bigotry.

STANDARDS

Language
• Use parallel structure.
• Apply knowledge of language to understand how language functions in different contexts, to make effective choices for meaning or style, and to comprehend more fully when reading or listening.

Write It

🔘 **Notebook** Write a paragraph about "Revenge of the Geeks." Include at least one example of parallel structure. Mark your examples.

Speaking and Listening

Assignment

Create a **multimedia presentation** in which you incorporate text and images to explain a subject. Choose from the following options.

☐ Prepare an **informational video** in which you share what you learned from Robbins's argument. Cite evidence from the text that proves your points and supports your opinions.

☐ Design a **social media campaign** with the goal of effecting change in how students who are "different" are treated in school. Explain why change is needed, and cite evidence from Robbins's argument to support your claim. In your presentation, show how your campaign will have a lasting impact.

☐ Choose a side, explaining why you agree or disagree with Robbins. Construct your argument or counterargument using evidence from the text. Create and present a **poster** publicizing your position visually. If members of your group disagree, split into two groups. Have each group complete a poster arguing the side it favors.

Project Plan Before you begin, make a list of the tasks you will need to complete in order to finish your project. Then, assign individual group members to each task. Finally, determine how you will make decisions about choices of images, text, and design elements.

Developing Your Argument Use this chart to collect ideas and images for your presentation. Remember to include appropriate citations for all evidence.

ARGUMENT	EVIDENCE	IMAGE

✒ EVIDENCE LOG

Before moving on to a new selection, go to your Evidence Log and record what you learned from "Revenge of the Geeks."

☰ STANDARDS

Speaking and Listening
• Work with peers to set rules for collegial discussions and decision-making, clear goals and deadlines, and individual roles as needed.
• Present information, findings, and supporting evidence clearly, concisely, and logically such that listeners can follow the line of reasoning and the organization, development, substance, and style are appropriate to purpose, audience, and task.
• Make strategic use of digital media in presentations to enhance understanding of findings, reasoning, and evidence and to add interest.

About the Author

Ryszard Kapuscinski

(1932–2007) began his career in journalism by keeping two notepads. In one, he detailed concrete facts for his investigative articles sold to Polish newspapers. The other was filled with personal notes and unique experiences. His first notebook brought him an income, yet his thoughts in the second were the basis for his highly regarded books. Kapuscinski often covered and supported African nations in the fight against colonialism.

Encountering the Other: The Challenge for the 21st Century

Concept Vocabulary

As you perform your first read of "Encountering the Other: The Challenge for the 21st Century," you will encounter the following words.

> doctrine   totalitarian   ideologies

Base Words If these words are unfamiliar to you, analyze each one to see whether it contains a base word you know. Then, use your knowledge of the "inside" word, along with context, to determine the meaning of the concept word. Here is an example of how to apply the strategy.

> **Unfamiliar Word:** *dismissively*
>
> **Familiar "Inside" Word:** *dismissive*, meaning "disinterested; scornful"
>
> **Context:** Should they throw themselves in fury on those other people? Or walk past **dismissively** and keep going?
>
> **Conclusion:** The *-ly* ending shows that the word is an adverb that tells the manner in which something is being done. *Dismissively* must mean "behaving in a way that shows disinterest or scorn."

Apply your knowledge of base words and other vocabulary strategies to determine the meanings of unfamiliar words you encounter during your first read.

First Read NONFICTION

Apply these strategies as you conduct your first read. You will have an opportunity to complete a close read after your first read.

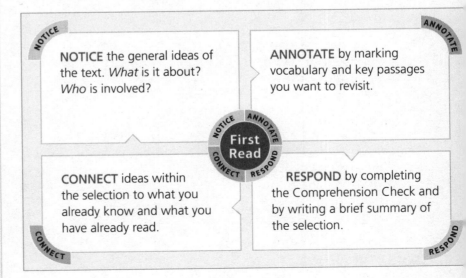

NOTICE the general ideas of the text. *What* is it about? *Who* is involved?

ANNOTATE by marking vocabulary and key passages you want to revisit.

CONNECT ideas within the selection to what you already know and what you have already read.

RESPOND by completing the Comprehension Check and by writing a brief summary of the selection.

☰ STANDARDS

Reading Informational Text
By the end of grade 10, read and comprehend literary nonfiction at the high end of the grades 9–10 text complexity band independently and proficiently.

Language
• Determine or clarify the meaning of unknown and multiple-meaning words and phrases based on *grades 9–10 reading and content,* choosing flexibly from a range of strategies
• Identify and correctly use patterns of word change that indicate different meanings or parts of speech.

Encountering the Other:

The Challenge for the 21st Century

Ryszard Kapuscinski

BACKGROUND

Globalization is the interaction and integration of people, companies, and governments of different countries. It is one of the most visible trends in modern culture. With increasingly common and efficient intercontinental travel, communication, and trade, regional life has become tied to cultures around the world. The globe is, metaphorically, getting smaller.

NOTES

1   The encounter with the Other, with other people, has always been a universal and fundamental experience for our species.

2   Archaeologists tell us that the very earliest human groups were small family-tribes numbering 30 to 50 individuals. Had such a community been larger, it would have had trouble moving around quickly and efficiently. Had it been smaller, it would have found it harder to defend itself effectively and to fight for survival.

3   So here is our little family-tribe going along searching for nourishment, when it suddenly comes across another family-tribe. What a significant movement in the history of the world, what a momentous discovery! The discovery that there are other people in the world! Until then, the members of these primal groups could live in the conviction, as they moved around in the company of 30 to 50 of their kinfolk, that they knew all the people in the world. Then it turned out that they didn't—that other similar beings, other people, also inhabited the world! But how to behave in the face of such a revelation? What to do? What decision to make?

4   Should they throw themselves in fury on those other people? Or walk past dismissively and keep going? Or rather try to get to know and understand them?

5   That same choice that our ancestors faced thousands of years ago faces us today as well, with undiminished intensity—a choice as fundamental and categorical as it was back then. How should we act toward Others? What kind of attitude should we have toward them? It might end up in a duel, a conflict, or a war. Every archive contains evidence of such events, which are also marked by countless battlefields and ruins scattered around the world.

6   All this is proof of man's failure—that he did not know how, or did not want, to reach an understanding with Others. The literature of all countries in all epochs[1] has taken up this situation, this tragedy and weakness, as subject matter of infinite variety and moods.

7   But it might also be the case that, instead of attacking and fighting, this family-tribe that we are watching decides to fence itself off from others, to isolate and separate itself. This attitude leads, over time, to objects like the Great Wall of China, the towers and gates of Babylon, the Roman limes[2] and or the stone walls of the Inca.

8   Fortunately, there is evidence of a different human experience scattered abundantly across our planet. These are the proofs of cooperation—the remains of marketplaces, of ports, of places where there were agoras[3] and sanctuaries, of where the seats of old universities and academies are still visible, and of where there remain vestiges of such trade routes as the Silk Road, the Amber Route, and the Trans-Saharan caravan route.

9   All of these were places where people met to exchange thoughts, ideas, and merchandise, and where they traded and did business, concluded covenants and alliances, and discovered shared goals and values. "The Other" stopped being a synonym of foreignness and hostility, danger and mortal evil. People discovered within themselves a fragment of the Other, and they believed in this and lived confidently.

10   People thus had three choices when they encountered the Other: They could choose war, they could build a wall around themselves, or they could enter into dialogue.

11   Over the expanse of history, mankind has never stopped wavering among these options, and, depending on changing times and cultures, has chosen one or the other; we can see that mankind is fickle here and does not always feel certain, does not always stand on firm ground. War is hard to justify. I think that everyone always loses because war is a disaster for human beings. It exposes their incapacity for understanding, for putting themselves in the shoes of others, for goodness and sense. The encounter with the Other usually ends tragically in such cases, in a catastrophe of blood and death.

12   The idea that led people to build great walls and gaping moats, to surround themselves with them and fence themselves off from

---

1. **epochs** (EHP uks) *n.* periods of historical time.
2. **limes** *n.* walls mortared with quicklime plaster.
3. **agoras** (uh GAWR uhz) *n.* open gathering places.

others, has been given the contemporary name of apartheid.[4] This concept has been erroneously confined to the policies of the now-defunct white regime in South Africa. However, apartheid was already being practiced in the earliest mists of time. In simple terms, proponents of this view proclaim that everyone is free to live as he chooses, as long as it's as far away from me as possible, if he isn't part of my race, religion, or culture. If that were all!

NOTES

Mark base words or indicate another strategy you used that helped you determine meaning.

doctrine (DOK truhn) *n.*

MEANING:

13   In reality, we are looking at a **doctrine** of the structural inequality of the human race. The myths of many tribes and peoples include the conviction that only we are human—the members of our clan, our community—while others, all others, are subhuman or aren't human at all. An ancient Chinese belief expressed it best: A non-Chinese was regarded as the devil's spawn, or at best as a victim of fate who did not manage to be born Chinese. The Other, according to this belief, was presented as a dog, as a rat, as a creeping reptile. Apartheid was and still is a doctrine of hatred, contempt, and revulsion for the Other, the foreigner.

14   How different was the image of the Other in the epoch of anthropomorphic[5] beliefs, the belief that the gods could assume human form and act like people. Back then you could never tell whether the approaching wanderer, traveler, or newcomer was a person or a god in human guise. That uncertainty, that fascinating ambivalence, was one of the roots of the culture of hospitality that mandated showing all kindness to the newcomer, that ultimately unknowable being.

15   Cyprian Norwid writes about this when he ponders, in his introduction to the *Odyssey*, the sources of the hospitality that Odysseus encounters on his journey back to Ithaca. "There, with every beggar and foreign wanderer," Norwid remarks, "the first suspicion was that he might have been sent by God. . . . No one could have been received as a guest if the first question were: 'Who is this newcomer?' But only when the divinity in him was respected did the human questions follow, and that was called hospitality, and for that very reason it was numbered among the pious practices and virtues. There was no 'last among men!' with Homer's Greeks—he was always the first, which means divine."

16   In this Greek understanding of culture, cited by Norwid, things reveal a new significance that is favorable to people. Doors and gates are not only for closing against the Other—they can also open for him and welcome him inside. The road need not serve hostile columns; it can also be a highway along which one of the gods, in pilgrim's garb, comes to us. Thanks to such an interpretation, the world we inhabit

---

4. **apartheid** (uh PAHR tyd) *n.* South African policy of extreme racial segregation under which the native African majority was not allowed to vote and suffered intense repression. Apartheid ended in 1994 with the first free elections. The word is often used to refer to other systems of repressive ethnic segregation.
5. **anthropomorphic** (an thruh poh MAWR fihk) *adj.* described or thought of as having human behaviors or characteristics.

Mark base words or indicate another strategy you used that helped you determine meaning.

totalitarian (toh tal uh TAIR ee uhn) *adj.*

MEANING:

ideologies (y dee OL uh jeez) *n.*

MEANING:

starts being not only richer and more diverse, but also kinder to us, a world in which we ourselves will want to encounter the Other.

17   Emmanuel Levinas calls the encounter with the Other an "event," or even a "fundamental event," the most important experience, reaching to the farthest horizons. Levinas, as we know, was one of the philosophers of dialogue, along with Martin Buber, Ferdinand Ebner, and Gabriel Marcel (a group that later came to include Jozef Tischner), who developed the idea of the Other as a unique and unrepeatable entity, in more or less direct opposition to two phenomena that arose in the 20th century: the birth of the masses that abolished the separateness of the individual, and the expansion of destructive **totalitarian ideologies**.

18   These philosophers attempted to salvage what they regarded as the paramount value, the human individual—me, you, the Other, the Others—from being obliterated by the actions of the masses and of totalitarianism (which is why these philosophers promoted the concept of "the Other" to emphasize the differences between one individual and another, the differences of non-interchangeable and irreplaceable characteristics).

19   This was an incredibly important movement that rescued and elevated the human being, a movement that rescued and elevated the Other, with whom, as Levinas suggested, one must not only stand face to face and conduct a dialogue, but for whom one must "take responsibility." In terms of relations with the Other and Others, the philosophers of dialogue rejected war because it led to annihilation; they criticized the attitudes of indifference or building walls; instead, they proclaimed the need—or even the ethical obligation—for closeness, openness, and kindness.

20   In the circle of just such ideas and convictions, a similar type of inquiry and reflection, a similar attitude, arises and develops in the great research work of a man who did his undergraduate work and went on to earn a Ph.D. at Jagiellonian University, and who was a member of the Polish Academy of Sciences—Bronislaw Malinowski.

21   Malinowski's problem was how to approach the Other, not as an exclusively hypothetical and abstract entity, but as a concrete person belonging to a different race, with beliefs and values different from ours, and with his own culture and customs.

22   Let us point out that the concept of the Other is usually defined from the white man's—the European's—point of view. But today, when I walk through a village in the mountains of Ethiopia, a crowd of children runs after me, pointing at me in merriment and calling out: "Ferenchi! Ferenchi!"—which means "foreigner, other." This is an example of the dismantling of the hierarchy of the world and its cultures. Others are indeed Others, but for those Others, I am the one who is Other.

23   In this sense, we're all in the same boat. All of us inhabitants of our planet are Other for Others—Me for Them, and Them for Me.

24   In Malinowski's era and in the preceding centuries, the white man, the European, left his continent almost exclusively for gain—to take over new land, capture slaves, trade, or convert. These expeditions, at times, were incredibly bloody—Columbus conquering America, and then the white settlers, the conquest of Africa, Asia, and Australia.

25   Malinowski set out for the Pacific islands with a different goal—to learn about the Other. To learn about his neighbor's customs and language, and to see how he lived. He wanted to see and experience this for himself, personally—to experience it so that he could later tell about it. It might seem like an obvious undertaking, yet it turned out to be revolutionary, and it stood the world on its ear.

26   It laid bare a weakness or perhaps simply a characteristic that appears to a differing degree in all cultures: the fact that cultures have difficulty understanding other cultures, and that people belonging to a given culture—the participants in and carriers of that culture— have this difficulty. Namely, Malinowski stated after arriving at his research site in the Trobriand Islands that the white people who had lived there for years not only knew nothing about the local people and their culture, but also, in fact, held an entirely erroneous image characterized by contempt and arrogance.

⌄ A village in the Trobriand Islands

27   He himself, as if to spite all colonial customs, pitched his tent in the middle of a local village and lived among the local people. What he experienced turned out to be no easy experience. In his *A Diary in the Strict Sense of the Term*, he continually mentions problems, bad moods, despair, and depression. You pay a high price for breaking free of your culture. That is why it is so important to have your own distinct identity, and a sense of your own strength, worth, and maturity. Only then can you confidently face a different culture. Otherwise, you will withdraw into your own hiding place and timorously cut yourself off from others.

28   All the more so because the Other is a mirror into which you peer, or in which you are observed, a mirror that unmasks and denudes, which we would prefer to avoid. It is interesting that, while the First World War was under way in Malinowski's native Europe, the young anthropologist was concentrating on research into the culture of exchange, contacts, and common rituals among the inhabitants of the Trobriand Islands, to which he devotes his excellent Argonauts of the Western Pacific, and formulating his important thesis, so seldom observed by others, that "to judge something, you have to be there."

29   Malinowski advanced another thesis, incredibly bold for its time: namely that there is no such thing as a higher or a lower culture—there are only different cultures, with varying ways of meeting the needs and expectations of their participants. For him, a different person, of a different race and culture, is nevertheless a person whose behavior, like ours, is characterized by dignity, respect for acknowledged values, and respect for tradition and customs.

30   While Malinowski began his work at the moment of the birth of the masses, we are living today in the period of transition from that mass society to a new, planetary society. Many factors lie behind this—the electronics revolution, the unprecedented development of all forms of communication, the great advances in transport and movement, and also, in connection with this, the transformation at work in the consciousness of the youngest generation and in culture broadly conceived.

31   How will this alter the relations between us, the people of one culture, and the people of some other culture, or of Other cultures? How will this influence the I-Other relationship within my culture and beyond it? It is very difficult to give an unequivocal final answer, since the process is ongoing and we ourselves, with no chance for the distance that fosters reflection, are immersed in it.

32   Levinas considered the I-Other relation within the bounds of a single, racially and historically homogeneous civilization. Malinowski studied the Melanesian tribes at a time when they were still in their primal state, not yet violated by the influence of Western technology, organization and markets.

33   Today, this is ever less frequently possible. Cultures are becoming increasingly hybridized and heterogeneous. I recently saw something astonishing in Dubai. A girl, surely a Muslim, was walking along the

beach. She was dressed in tight jeans and a close-fitting blouse, but her head, and only her head, was covered so hermetically that not even her eyes were visible.

34   Today there are whole schools of philosophy, anthropology, and literary criticism that devote their major attention to hybridization and linking. This cultural process is under way especially in those regions where the borders of states are the boundaries of different cultures, such as the American-Mexican border, and also in the gigantic megalopolises (like São Paolo, New York, or Singapore) that are home to populations representing the most variegated cultures and races. We say today that the world has become multiethnic and multicultural not because there are more of these communities and cultures than before, but rather because they are speaking out more loudly, with increasing self-sufficiency and forcefulness, demanding acceptance, recognition, and a place at the round table of nations.

35   Yet the true challenge of our time, the encounter with the new Other, derives as well from a broader historical context. Namely, the second half of the 20th century was a time when two-thirds of humanity freed themselves of colonial dependency and became citizens of their own states that, at least nominally, were independent. Gradually, these people are beginning to rediscover their own pasts, myths, and legends, their roots, their feelings of identity and, of course, the pride that flows from this. They are beginning to realize that they are the masters in their own house and the captains of their fate, and they look with abhorrence on any attempts to reduce them to things, to extras, to the victims and passive objects of domination.

36   Today, our planet, inhabited for centuries by a narrow group of free people and broad throngs of the enslaved, is filled with an increasing number of nations and societies that have a growing sense of their own separate value and significance. This process is often occurring amidst enormous difficulties, conflicts, dramas, and losses.

37   We may be moving toward a world so entirely new and changed that our previous historical experience will prove to be insufficient to grasp and move around in it. In any case, the world that we are entering is the Planet of Great Opportunities. Yet these are not unconditional opportunities, but rather opportunities open only to those who take their tasks seriously and thus prove that they take themselves seriously. This is a world that potentially has a lot to offer, but that also demands a lot, and in which taking easy shortcuts is often the road to nowhere. '

38   We will constantly be encountering the new Other, who will slowly emerge from the chaos and tumult of the present. It is possible that this new Other will arise from the meeting of two contradictory currents that shape the culture of the contemporary world—the current of the globalization of our reality and the current of the conservation of our diversity, our differences, our uniqueness. The Other may be the offspring and the heir of these two currents.

39   We should seek dialogue and understanding with the new Other. The experience of spending years among remote Others has taught me that kindness toward another being is the only attitude that can strike a chord of humanity in the Other. Who will this new Other be? What will our encounter be like? What will we say? And in what language? Will we be able to listen to each other? To understand each other?

40   Will we both want to appeal, as Joseph Conrad put it, to what "speaks to our capacity for delight and wonder, to the sense of mystery surrounding our lives; to our sense of pity, and beauty, and pain; to the latent feeling of fellowship with all creation—and to the subtle but invincible conviction of solidarity that knits together the loneliness of innumerable hearts: to the solidarity in dreams, in joy, in sorrow, in aspirations, in illusions, in hope, in fear, which binds men to each other, which binds together all humanity—the dead to the living and the living to the unborn." ❧

Comprehension Check

Complete the following items after you finish your first read. Review and clarify details with your group.

1. According to the author, how would an early family-tribe discover that there were other people in the world?

2. What way of treating people began with the idea that any stranger might have been sent by the gods?

3. According to the author, why have Europeans throughout history usually left their own continent to visit others?

4. 📔 **Notebook** Confirm your understanding of the text by writing a summary.

- -

RESEARCH

Research to Clarify Choose at least one unfamiliar detail from the text. Briefly research that detail. In what way does the information you learned shed light on an aspect of the lecture?

Research to Explore Choose something that interested you from the text, and formulate a research question.

ENCOUNTERING THE OTHER:
THE CHALLENGE FOR THE
21ST CENTURY

WORD NETWORK

Add interesting words
related to outsiders from the
text to your Word Network.

STANDARDS

Reading Informational Text
• Determine a central idea of a text
and analyze its development over
the course of the text, including
how it emerges and is shaped and
refined by specific details; provide an
objective summary of the text.
• Analyze in detail how an author's
ideas or claims are developed and
refined by particular sentences,
paragraphs, or larger portions of a
text.

Language
• Identify and correctly use patterns
of word changes that indicate
different meanings or parts of
speech.

Close Read the Text

With your group, revisit sections of the text you marked
during your first read. **Annotate** details that you notice.
What **questions** do you have? What can you **conclude**?

Analyze the Text

CITE TEXTUAL EVIDENCE
to support your answers.

Complete the activities.

1. **Review and Clarify** With your group, reread paragraph 10 of the
   selection. Discuss the three choices people can make in dealing with the
   Other, reminding yourselves of the examples the author gives for each one.

2. **Present and Discuss** Now, share with your group the passages from the
   selection that you found particularly important. Take turns presenting your
   passages. Discuss what you noticed in the text, what questions you asked,
   and what conclusions you reached.

3. **Essential Question:** *Do people need to belong?* What has this lecture
   taught you about being an outsider and confronting others? Discuss.

Concept Vocabulary

doctrine	totalitarian	ideologies

Why These Words? The three concept vocabulary words are related. With
your group, discuss the words, and determine what they have in common.
Write other words that relate to this concept.

Practice

Notebook Confirm your understanding of these words by using them
in sentences. Include context clues that hint at each word's meaning.

Word Study

Greek Root: *-log-* In "Encountering the Other," the author uses the word
ideologies. The word *ideologies* is built from two Greek roots: *-ideo-*, which
means "idea," and *-log-*, which may mean either "to speak" or "study
or theory of." Write the meanings of these words from the selection that
contain the root *-log-*: *archaeologists*, *anthropology*, *dialogue*. Consult a
dictionary as needed.

Analyze Craft and Structure

Literary Nonfiction "Encountering the Other" is a **lecture**—a speech that is given to teach or inform listeners about a topic. The lecturer often uses special techniques to engage listeners and help them understand information. In the **introduction,** or beginning, he or she may use a **rhetorical question.** This is a question that the listener should think about, not answer out loud. In the **discussion,** or body, the lecturer may use **repetition** because hearing information more than once helps listeners remember ideas. In the **conclusion,** or end, the lecturer might summarize ideas or leave the audience with a challenge or lasting thought.

TIP

CLARIFICATION
A lecture often begins and ends with a memorable story, quotation, question, fact, or statement. The intention is to make the listener curious at the beginning and inspired at the end.

Practice

CITE TEXTUAL EVIDENCE
to support your answers.

Work independently to gather your notes in the chart. Then, share and discuss your responses with your group.

INTRODUCTION
Which paragraphs make up the introduction?
What story, surprising fact, or rhetorical question appears in the introduction?
What is the main idea statement?

DISCUSSION
Which paragraphs make up the discussion?
Cite statements that develop or explain the main idea.
Cite examples of repetition.

CONCLUSION
Which paragraphs make up the conclusion?
Is there a challenge to listeners? Is there another technique that creates a memorable ending?

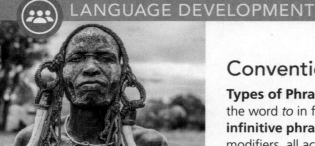

ENCOUNTERING THE OTHER:
THE CHALLENGE FOR THE
21ST CENTURY

Conventions

Types of Phrases An **infinitive** is a verb form that generally appears with the word *to* in front of it and acts as a noun, an adjective, or an adverb. An **infinitive phrase** consists of an infinitive and its objects, complements, or modifiers, all acting together as a single part of speech. Like an infinitive, an infinitive phrase acts as a noun, an adjective, or an adverb.

The examples in the chart show uses of infinitives and infinitive phrases.

INFINITIVE	INFINITIVE PHRASE
Used as a Noun *To succeed* requires dedication. (functions as the subject of the sentence)	**Used as a Noun** We chose *to take the old foot path.* (functions as the direct object of the verb *chose*)
Used as an Adjective I wish I had the ability *to fly.* (tells *what kind* of ability)	**Used as an Adjective** Dana's desire *to do well* made Mama proud (tells *which* desire)
Used as an Adverb When Derrick sat down *to study,* he concentrated. (tells *why* Derrick sat down)	**Used as an Adverb** She called the editor *to voice her opinion.* (tells *why* she called)

Read It

Work individually. Mark the infinitive or infinitive phrase in each sentence from "Encountering the Other," and label it as a noun, an adjective, or an adverb.

1. Had it been smaller, it would have found it harder to defend itself effectively. . . .

2. But it might be the case that . . . this family-tribe that we are watching decides to fence itself off from others. . . .

3. Malinowski set out for the Pacific islands with a different goal—to learn about the Other.

4. This is a world that potentially has a lot to offer, but that also demands a lot. . . .

Write It

Notebook Write three sentences about this lecture. Use an infinitive or infinitive phrase as a noun in one sentence, an adjective in the second sentence, and an adverb in the third sentence.

STANDARDS

Writing
• Use technology, including the Internet, to produce, publish, and update individual or shared writing products, taking advantage of technology's capacity to link to other information and to display information flexibly and dynamically.
• Gather relevant information from multiple authoritative print and digital sources, using advanced searches effectively; assess the usefulness of each source in answering the research question; integrate information into the text selectively to maintain the flow of ideas, avoiding plagiarism and following a standard format for citation.

Language
• Demonstrate command of the conventions of standard English grammar and usage when writing or speaking.

Research

Assignment

Research, write, and deliver a **digital presentation** about one of the cultures Kapuscinski mentions in the lecture. Explain how each culture responded to others through combat, isolation, or cooperation. Choose one of the following topics and projects:

☐ Create an **illustrated timeline** showing how the ancient Chinese perceived people from other cultures and responded to outsiders.

☐ Create a **slide show** about the Inca and their architecture.

☐ Create a **video** about the ancient Greek idea of hospitality.

Project Plan Before you begin, make a list of the tasks you will need to accomplish in order to complete your digital presentation, from finding information to researching images to making final choices about design and layout. Decide ahead of time how you will make those final choices. Then, assign group members to each task.

Finding Visuals Use a variety of reliable sources for your images so that they will accurately illustrate your text. Use this chart to keep track of what you want and what you find. Remember to include appropriate citations.

Text That Image Illustrates	Description of Image	Source Information for Citation

TIP

PROCESS

When researching images online, you may start with a search engine. However, you should always go to the page where the image is located to make sure of its accuracy. Collect information to properly credit the source.

🖉 **EVIDENCE LOG**

Before moving on to a new selection, go to your Evidence Log and record what you learned from "Encountering the Other."

SOURCES

- THE DOLL'S HOUSE
- SONNET, WITH BIRD
- ELLIPTICAL
- FENCES
- REVENGE OF THE GEEKS
- ENCOUNTERING THE OTHER: THE CHALLENGE FOR THE 21ST CENTURY

Deliver a Multimedia Presentation

Assignment

You have read a story, poems, an argument, and a lecture addressing ideas about what it means to belong and what it means to be an outsider. Work with your group to develop a position on the following questions:

Is difference a weakness? Is sameness a strength?

Then, create a **multimedia presentation** in which you use text, audio, and visuals to clearly state and defend your position.

Plan With Your Group

Analyze the Texts With your group, discuss the people—real or fictional—in the selections you have read. For each selection, identify a person or people who are deemed outsiders. Are these people weakened by this label? Are they strengthened by it? Use the chart to gather your ideas and supporting textual evidence. Then, come to a consensus about the questions posed in the prompt.

Title	Ideas About Outsiders	Evidence From Text
The Doll's House		
Sonnet, With Bird		
Elliptical		
Fences		
Revenge of the Geeks		
Encountering the Other: The Challenge for the 21st Century		

Gather Evidence and Media Examples Scan the selections to record specific examples that support your group's position. Then, brainstorm for types of media you can use to illustrate or elaborate on each example. Consider photographs, illustrations, music, charts, graphs, and video clips. Allow each group member to make suggestions.

STANDARDS
Speaking and Listening
Present information, findings, and supporting evidence clearly, concisely, and logically such that listeners can follow the line of reasoning and the organization, development, substance, and style are appropriate to purpose, audience, and task.

Organize Your Ideas Use a graphic organizer like this one to plan the script for your presentation. Decide who will be responsible for each of the various elements. Then, take note of when each section begins, and record what the speaker will say. Also, note where specific media will be used.

MULTIMEDIA PRESENTATION SCRIPT		
	Media Cues	Script
Presenter 1		
Presenter 2		
Presenter 3		

Rehearse With Your Group

Practice With Your Group Use this checklist to evaluate the effectiveness of your group's first run-through. Then, use your evaluation and the instruction here to guide your revision.

CONTENT	USE OF MEDIA	PRESENTATION TECHNIQUES
☐ The presentation presents a clear argument. ☐ Main ideas are supported with evidence from the texts in Small-Group Learning.	☐ The media support the argument. ☐ The media communicate key ideas. ☐ Media are used evenly throughout the presentation. ☐ Equipment functions properly.	☐ Media are visible and audible. ☐ Transitions are smooth. ☐ Each speaker uses eye contact and speaks with adequate volume.

Fine-Tune the Content To make your presentation stronger, you may need to make sure the group has provided adequate evidence to support the argument. Check with your group to identify key points that are not clear to listeners. Find another way to word these ideas.

Improve Your Use of Media Review all visuals, music, and sound effects to make sure they communicate key ideas and help create a cohesive presentation. If a visual or sound cue is not clearly related to the presentation, replace it with a more relevant item.

Brush Up on Your Presentation Techniques Practice your presentation several times before you deliver it. Give one another notes on how to improve speaking skills or how to move smoothly from one segment to another.

Present and Evaluate

When you present as a group, be sure that each member has taken into account each of the checklist items. As you listen to other groups, evaluate how well they meet the checklist.

STANDARDS
Speaking and Listening
• Work with peers to set rules for collegial discussions and decision-making, clear goals and deadlines, and individual roles as needed.
• Make strategic use of digital media in presentations to enhance understanding of findings, reasoning, and evidence and to add interest.

ESSENTIAL QUESTION:

Do people need to belong?

Being an outsider is an experience almost everyone will have at some point in life. In this section, you will complete your study of literature about outsiders by exploring an additional selection related to the topic. You'll then share what you learn with classmates. To choose a text, follow these steps.

Look Back Think about the selections you have already studied. What more do you want to know about the topic of outsiders and outcasts?

Look Ahead Preview the texts by reading the descriptions. Which one seems most interesting and appealing to you?

Look Inside Take a few minutes to scan the text you chose. Choose a different one if this text doesn't meet your needs.

Independent Learning Strategies

Throughout your life, in school, in your community, and in your career, you will need to rely on yourself to learn and work on your own. Review these strategies and the actions you can take to practice them during Independent Learning. Add ideas of your own for each category.

STRATEGY	ACTION PLAN
Create a schedule	• Understand your goals and deadlines. • Make a plan for what to do each day. •
Practice what you've learned	• Use first-read and close-read strategies to deepen your understanding. • After you read, evaluate the usefulness of the evidence to help you understand the topic. • Consider the quality and reliability of the source. •
Take notes	• Record important ideas and information. • Review your notes before preparing to share with a group. • •

CONTENTS

Choose one selection. Selections are available online only.

First-Read Guide

Use this page to record your first-read ideas.

Selection Title: _____

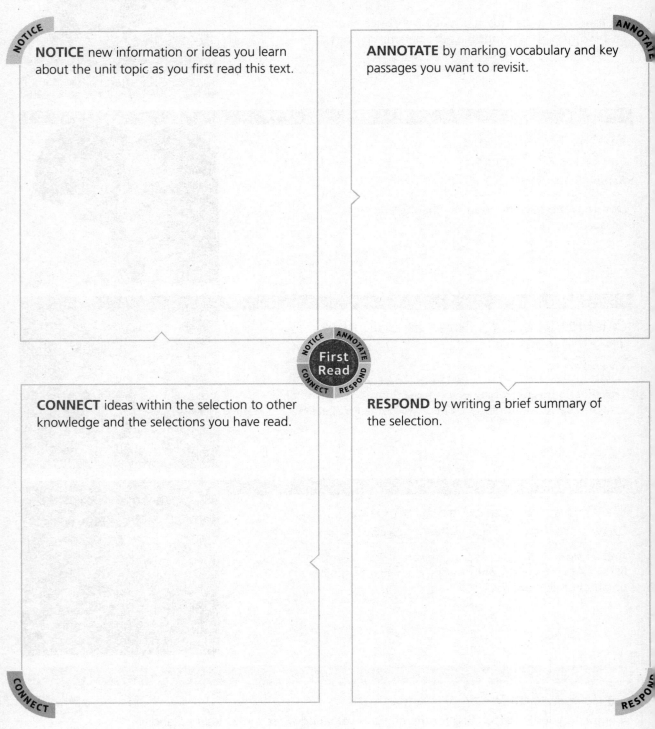

NOTICE new information or ideas you learn about the unit topic as you first read this text.

ANNOTATE by marking vocabulary and key passages you want to revisit.

CONNECT ideas within the selection to other knowledge and the selections you have read.

RESPOND by writing a brief summary of the selection.

First Read

NOTICE   ANNOTATE   CONNECT   RESPOND

≣ STANDARD

Reading Read and comprehend complex literary and informational texts independently and proficiently.

Close-Read Guide

Use this page to record your close-read ideas.

Selection Title: _____

Close Read the Text

Revisit sections of the text you marked during your first read. Read these sections closely and **annotate** what you notice. Ask yourself **questions** about the text. What can you **conclude?** Write down your ideas.

Analyze the Text

Think about the author's choices of patterns, structure, techniques, and ideas included in the text. Select one, and record your thoughts about what this choice conveys.

QuickWrite

Pick a paragraph from the text that grabbed your interest. Explain the power of this passage.

_____
_____
_____
_____
_____
_____
_____
_____

≣ STANDARD

Reading Read and comprehend complex literary and informational texts independently and proficiently.

Share Your Independent Learning

Prepare to Share

Do people need to belong?

Even when you read something independently, your understanding continues to grow when you share what you have learned with others. Reflect on the text you explored independently and write notes about its connection to the unit. In your notes, consider why this text belongs in this unit.

Learn From Your Classmates

💬 **Discuss It** Share your ideas about the text you explored on your own. As you talk with your classmates, jot down ideas that you learn from them.

Reflect

Underline the most important insight you gained from these writing and discussion activities. Explain how this idea adds to your understanding of the topic of being an outsider or outcast.

Review Evidence for Argument

At the beginning of this unit, you took a position on the following question:

> Is the experience of being an outsider universal?

✎ EVIDENCE LOG

Review your Evidence Log and your QuickWrite from the beginning of the unit. Has your position changed?

☐ YES	☐ NO
Identify at last three pieces of evidence that convinced you to change your mind.	Identify at last three new pieces of evidence that reinforced your initial position.
1.	1.
2.	2.
3.	3.

State your position now: _____

_____

_____

Identify a possible counterclaim: _____

_____

_____

Evaluate the Strength of Your Evidence Consider your argument. Do you have enough evidence to support your claim? Do you have enough evidence to refute a counterclaim? If not, make a plan.

☐ Do more research   ☐ Talk with my classmates

☐ **Reread a selection**   ☐ Ask an expert

☐ Other: _____

≣ STANDARDS
Writing
Introduce precise claim(s), distinguish the claim(s) from alternate or opposing claims, and create an organization that establishes clear relationships among claim(s), counterclaims, reasons, and evidence.

SOURCES

- WHOLE-CLASS SELECTIONS
- SMALL-GROUP SELECTIONS
- INDEPENDENT-LEARNING SELECTION

PART 1
Writing to Sources: Argument

In this unit, you read about various characters, both real and fictional, who were considered outsiders or outcasts. Some struggled to belong, while others seemed more comfortable with being outside of a group.

Assignment

Write an **argumentative essay** in which you state and defend a claim about the following question:

Is the experience of being an outsider universal?

Use credible evidence from at least three of the selections you read and researched in this unit to support your claim. Try to address possible objections to your argument by presenting and refuting counterclaims. Ensure that your claims are fully supported; that you use a formal, academic tone; and that your organization is logical and easy to follow.

Reread the Assignment Review the assignment to be sure you fully understand it. The task may reference some of the academic words presented at the beginning of the unit. Be sure you understand each of the words given below in order to complete the assignment correctly.

Academic Vocabulary

contradict	negate	objection
advocate	verify	

🔀 WORD NETWORK

As you write and revise your argument, use your Word Network to help vary your word choices.

Review the Elements of Effective Argument Before you begin writing, read the Argument Rubric. Once you have completed your first draft, check it against the rubric. If one or more of the elements are missing or not as strong as they could be, revise your essay to add or strengthen those components.

▤ STANDARDS
Writing
• Write arguments to support claims in an analysis of substantive topics or texts, using valid reasoning and relevant and sufficient evidence.
• Draw evidence from literary or informational texts to support analysis, reflection, and research.
• Write routinely over extended time frames and shorter time frames for a range of tasks, purposes, and audiences.

Argument Rubric

	Focus and Organization	Evidence and Elaboration	Conventions
4	The introduction engages the reader and establishes a claim in a compelling way. The argument includes valid reasons and evidence that address and support the claim while clearly acknowledging counterclaims. The ideas progress logically, and transitions make connections among ideas clear. The conclusion offers fresh insight into the claim.	The sources of evidence are comprehensive and specific and contain relevant information. The tone of the argument is always formal and objective. The vocabulary is always appropriate for the audience and purpose.	The argument intentionally uses standard English conventions of usage and mechanics.
3	The introduction engages the reader and establishes the claim. The argument includes reasons and evidence that address and support the claim while acknowledging counterclaims. The ideas progress logically, and some transitions are used to help make connections among ideas clear. The conclusion restates the claim and important information.	The sources of evidence contain relevant information. The tone of the argument is mostly formal and objective. The vocabulary is generally appropriate for the audience and purpose.	The argument demonstrates general accuracy in standard English conventions of usage and mechanics.
2	The introduction establishes a claim. The argument includes some reasons and evidence that address and support the claim while briefly acknowledging counterclaims. The ideas progress somewhat logically. A few sentence transitions are used that connect readers to the argument. The conclusion offers some insight into the claim and restates information.	The sources of evidence contain some relevant information. The tone of the argument is occasionally formal and objective. The vocabulary is somewhat appropriate for the audience and purpose.	The argument demonstrates some accuracy in standard English conventions of usage and mechanics.
1	The introduction does not clearly state the claim. The argument does not include reasons or evidence for the claim. No counterclaims are acknowledged. The ideas do not progress logically. Transitions are not included to connect ideas. The conclusion does not restate any information that is important.	Reliable and relevant evidence is not included. The vocabulary used is limited or ineffective. The tone of the argument is not objective or formal.	The argument contains mistakes in standard English conventions of usage and mechanics.

PART 2

Speaking and Listening: Oral Presentation

Assignment

After completing the final draft of your argument, use it as the foundation for a three- to five-minute **oral presentation**.

Do not simply read your essay aloud. Instead, take the following steps to make your presentation lively and engaging.

- Go back to your essay and annotate the most important claims and supporting details from your introduction, body paragraphs, and conclusion.
- Refer to your annotated text to guide your presentation and keep it focused.
- Deliver your argument with conviction, speaking with adequate volume and maintaining eye contact with your audience.

Review the Oral Presentation Rubric The criteria by which your oral presentation will be evaluated appear in the rubric below. Review these criteria before presenting to ensure that you are prepared.

	Content	Organization	Presentation Technique
3	Introduction is engaging and establishes a claim in a compelling way.	The speaker uses time very effectively by spending the right amount of time on each part.	The speaker maintains effective eye contact.
	Presentation has strong valid reasons and evidence that support the claim while clearly acknowledging counterclaims.	Ideas progress logically, supported by a variety of sentence transitions. Listeners can follow presentation.	The speaker presents with strong conviction and energy.
	Conclusion offers fresh insight into the claim.		
2	Introduction establishes a claim.	The speaker uses time effectively by spending the right amount of time on most parts.	The speaker mostly maintains effective eye contact.
	Presentation includes some valid reasons and evidence that support the claim while acknowledging counterclaims.	Ideas progress logically, supported by some sentence transitions. Listeners are mostly able to follow presentation.	The speaker presents with some level of conviction and energy.
	Conclusion offers some insight into claim and restates important information.		
1	Introduction does not clearly state a claim.	The speaker does not use time effectively; the parts of the presentation are too long or too short.	The speaker does not establish eye contact.
	Presentation does not include reasons or evidence to support a claim or acknowledge counterclaims.	Ideas do not progress logically. Listeners have difficulty following presentation.	The speaker presents without conviction or energy.
	Conclusion does not restate important information about a claim.		

Reflect on the Unit

Now that you've completed the unit, take a few moments to reflect on your learning. Use the questions below to think about where you succeeded, what skills and strategies helped you, and where you can continue to grow in the future.

Reflect on the Unit Goals

Look back at the goals at the beginning of the unit. Use a different colored pen to rate yourself again. Think about readings and activities that contributed the most to the growth of your understanding. Record your thoughts.

Reflect on the Learning Strategies

◎ Discuss It Write a reflection on whether you were able to improve your learning based on your Action Plans. Think about what worked, what didn't, and what you might do to keep working on these strategies. Record your ideas before a class discussion.

Reflect on the Text

Choose a selection that you found challenging and explain what made it difficult.

Explain something that surprised you about a text in the unit.

Which activity taught you the most about whether people need to belong? What did you learn?

⋮≡ STANDARDS

Speaking and Listening
Present information, findings, and supporting evidence clearly, concisely, and logically such that listeners can follow the line of reasoning and the organization, development, substance, and style are appropriate to purpose, audience, and task.

Extending Freedom's Reach

What factors determine who is free and who remains oppressed?

We Are All Born Free

Discuss It What are the basic rights and freedoms that belong to everyone, everywhere?

Write your response before sharing your ideas.

UNIT INTRODUCTION

ESSENTIAL QUESTION:

What is the relationship between power and freedom?

LAUNCH TEXT
INFORMATIVE MODEL
Born Free: Children and the Struggle for Human Rights

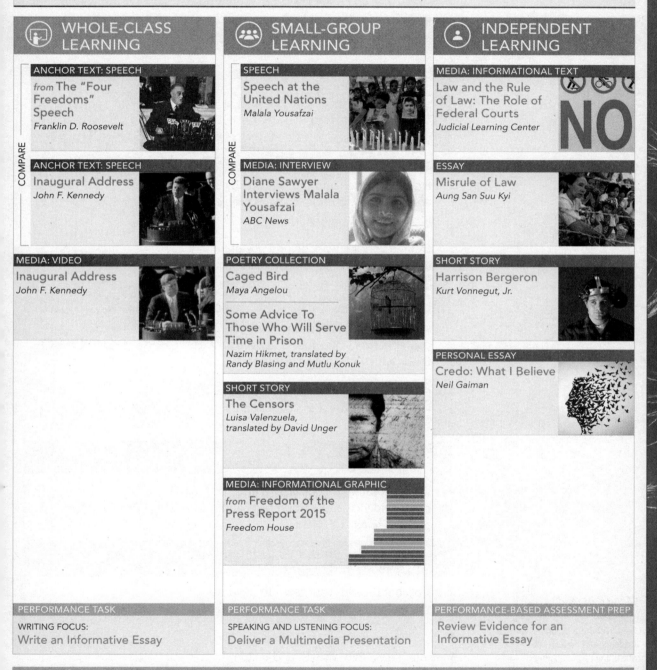

WHOLE-CLASS LEARNING

ANCHOR TEXT: SPEECH
from The "Four Freedoms" Speech
Franklin D. Roosevelt

ANCHOR TEXT: SPEECH
Inaugural Address
John F. Kennedy

COMPARE

MEDIA: VIDEO
Inaugural Address
John F. Kennedy

SMALL-GROUP LEARNING

SPEECH
Speech at the United Nations
Malala Yousafzai

MEDIA: INTERVIEW
Diane Sawyer Interviews Malala Yousafzai
ABC News

COMPARE

POETRY COLLECTION
Caged Bird
Maya Angelou

Some Advice To Those Who Will Serve Time in Prison
Nazim Hikmet, translated by Randy Blasing and Mutlu Konuk

SHORT STORY
The Censors
Luisa Valenzuela, translated by David Unger

MEDIA: INFORMATIONAL GRAPHIC
from Freedom of the Press Report 2015
Freedom House

INDEPENDENT LEARNING

MEDIA: INFORMATIONAL TEXT
Law and the Rule of Law: The Role of Federal Courts
Judicial Learning Center

ESSAY
Misrule of Law
Aung San Suu Kyi

SHORT STORY
Harrison Bergeron
Kurt Vonnegut, Jr.

PERSONAL ESSAY
Credo: What I Believe
Neil Gaiman

PERFORMANCE TASK

WRITING FOCUS:
Write an Informative Essay

PERFORMANCE TASK

SPEAKING AND LISTENING FOCUS:
Deliver a Multimedia Presentation

PERFORMANCE-BASED ASSESSMENT PREP

Review Evidence for an Informative Essay

PERFORMANCE-BASED ASSESSMENT

Informative Text: Essay and Multimedia Presentation

PROMPT:

What does it mean to "be free"?

Unit Goals

Throughout the unit, you will deepen your perspective on the literature of freedom by reading, writing, speaking, presenting, and listening. These goals will help you succeed on the Unit Performance-Based Assessment.

Rate how well you meet these goals right now. You will revisit your ratings later when you reflect on your growth during this unit.

SCALE

1	2	3	4	5
NOT AT ALL WELL	NOT VERY WELL	SOMEWHAT WELL	VERY WELL	EXTREMELY WELL

READING GOALS   1 2 3 4 5

• Evaluate written informative texts by analyzing how authors convey complex ideas, concepts, and information.

• Expand your knowledge and use of academic and concept vocabulary.

WRITING AND RESEARCH GOALS   1 2 3 4 5

• Write an informative essay in which you effectively introduce and develop a thesis with well-chosen evidence.

• Conduct research projects of various lengths to explore a topic and clarify meaning.

LANGUAGE GOALS   1 2 3 4 5

• Correctly integrate quotations and other evidence into written texts and presentations.

SPEAKING AND LISTENING GOALS   1 2 3 4 5

• Collaborate with your team to build on the ideas of others, develop consensus, and communicate.

• Integrate audio, visuals, and text in presentations.

STANDARDS

Language
Acquire and use accurately general academic and domain-specific words and phrases, sufficient for reading, writing, speaking, and listening at the college and career readiness level; demonstrate independence in gathering vocabulary knowledge when considering a word or phrase important to comprehension or expression.

Academic Vocabulary: Informative Text

Academic terms appear in all subjects and can help you read, write, and discuss with more precision. Here are five academic words that will be useful to you in this unit as you analyze and write informative texts.

Complete the chart.

1. Review each word, its root, and the mentor sentences.

2. Use the information and your own knowledge to predict the meaning of each word.

3. For each word, list at least two related words.

4. Refer to a dictionary or other resources if needed.

TIP

FOLLOW THROUGH
Study the words in this chart, and mark them or their forms wherever they appear in the unit.

WORD	MENTOR SENTENCES	PREDICT MEANING	RELATED WORDS
attribute ROOT: **-trib-** "assign"; "give"	1. In the nineteenth century, such an *attribute* was seen as ordinary. 2. They *attribute* their success this season to teamwork and training.		attribution; attributable
hierarchy ROOT: **-hier-** "sacred"; "holy"	1. In high school, freshmen are usually considered to be at the bottom of the social *hierarchy*. 2. Making an outline is a good way to organize a *hierarchy* of ideas.		
demarcate ROOT: **-marc- / -mark-** "separate from"	1. The bold black lines on the map *demarcate* the borders of each country. 2. Our neighbors planted trees to *demarcate* the edge of their property.		
fundamental ROOT: **-fund-** "base"; "bottom"	1. The order of operations is a *fundamental* concept in mathematics. 2. The *fundamental* reason our team lost was because the starting quarterback was injured.		
democracy ROOT: **-demo-** "people"; "populace"	1. In a *democracy*, the people hold the power, and the government represents their interests. 2. When we complained about having a cumulative final exam, our teacher reminded us that her classroom was not a *democracy* and overruled us.		

LAUNCH TEXT | INFORMATIVE MODEL

This selection is an example of an **informative essay**, a type of writing in which the author examines concepts through the careful selection, organization, and analysis of information. This is the type of writing you will develop in the Performance-Based Assessment at the end of the unit.

As you read, notice the way the writer provides information about the topic. How are ideas organized, and how do the details support the main points?

Born Free: Children and the Struggle for Human Rights

NOTES

1   In our national anthem, "The Star-Spangled Banner," we sing of America as "the land of the free and the home of the brave." Throughout much of our history, though, many groups have struggled to share fully in the nation's promise of freedom and justice. Like other groups who have faced unfair or undignified treatment, young people have also realized that in order to be heard, they might have to make some noise.

2   One incident of children raising their voices to advance their rights occurred in New York City during the "newsies" strike of 1899. Newsies were children who sold newspapers on the sidewalks of major cities. In the late 1890s, there were roughly 2,500 newsies in New York City, most between the ages of 6 and 16. The shouts of these children calling, "Extra! Extra! Read all about it!" were part of the soundtrack of urban life. In that long-ago era before computers, smartphones, television, and even radio, newspapers were the main source of news.

3   The newsies suffered a host of problems. While some lived with their families, many others were orphans, homeless, or both. The United States did not institute laws protecting child workers until 1916, and the newsies were victims of unscrupulous business practices. They often worked 10- or 12-hour days. Most gave any money they earned to their families, or used it to pay the costs of food and shelter for a night. Newsies did not go to school.

4   The newsies' circumstances deteriorated even further during the Spanish-American War of 1898. The public's hunger for news of the war led to increased demand for newspapers. Newsies bought the newspapers from publishers and then sold them to the public. During the war, the price newsies paid for a bundle of 100 papers

rose from 50 to 60 cents. Once the war ended, readership declined. Most newspaper owners responded by returning the price of a bundle to 50 cents, but the two biggest publishers—Joseph Pulitzer of the *New York World* and William Randolph Hearst of the *New York Journal*—refused to lower their prices. In addition, both Pulitzer and Hearst discontinued the practice of buying back unsold papers. Instead, they forced the newsies to absorb the losses.

5 On July 20, 1899, the newsies took on Pulitzer and Hearst by launching a strike. They refused to sell either newspaper and warned off anyone who tried. They brought traffic to a halt by marching through the streets and gathering at the Brooklyn Bridge. They made signs asking the public not to buy Pulitzer and Hearst newspapers, and they chased off men who were attempting to deliver bundles of papers for distribution. The public showed its support, raining coins down on the strikers from the windows of offices and apartments. What began as a localized strike by about 300 newsies near Manhattan's Wall Street soon spread—west to New Jersey, south to Brooklyn, north to the Bronx, and east to Queens.

6 The newspapers that covered the strike found ways to show their disrespect for the newsies. "Dere's t'ree t'ousand of us, and we'll win for sure," is how one newspaper mockingly quoted a newsie's reference to the number of strikers. Another newspaper explained that the newsies were striking for their "rights," using quotation marks to imply that the children had no rights and that it was quaint for them to suggest they did.

7 The strike lasted two weeks. Some newsies were arrested for vandalism. Others were arrested for stealing copies of the Pulitzer or Hearst papers. Although some adults reached out to help the newsies, most of the power stayed where it started. Pulitzer and Hearst did not lower the cost of newspaper bundles to the prewar price, but they did agree to buy back unsold copies from the newsies. It may have been a small victory, but it was more than the newsies would have received had they not raised their voices. ❧

NOTES

WORD NETWORK FOR EXTENDING FREEDOM'S REACH

Vocabulary A Word Network is a collection of words related to a topic. As you read the selections in this unit, identify interesting words related to the idea of freedom and add them to your Word Network. For example, you might begin by adding words from the Launch Text, such as *justice, laws,* and *victory.* Continue to add words as you complete the unit.

🔧 **Tool Kit** Word Network Model

justice

laws

victory

FREEDOM

Summary

Write a summary of "Born Free: Children and the Struggle for Human Rights." A **summary** is a concise, complete, and accurate overview of a text. It should not include a statement of your opinion or an analysis.

Launch Activity

Vote Consider this statement: **People who stand up for their rights will always win.**

- Record your position on the statement, and explain your thinking.

  ☐ Strongly Agree ☐ Agree ☐ Disagree ☐ Strongly Disagree

  _____

  _____

- After everyone has recorded their positions, take a poll of the class to find out how each person voted.

- Count the number of votes in each category, and record those numbers on the board or in another place where everyone can see them.

- Contribute to a discussion about why students took the positions they did. Be sure to provide reasons and examples that support your position.

- At the end of the discussion, take another poll. Has anyone changed his or her mind? If so, why? If not, why not?

QuickWrite

Consider class discussions, the video, and the Launch Text as you think about the prompt. Record your first thoughts here.

PROMPT: **What does it mean to "be free"?**

EVIDENCE LOG FOR EXTENDING FREEDOM'S REACH

Review your QuickWrite, and summarize your initial position in one sentence to record in your Evidence Log. Then, record evidence from "Born Free: Children and the Struggle for Human Rights" that supports your initial position.

Prepare for the Performance-Based Assessment at the end of the unit by completing the Evidence Log after each selection.

🔧 **Tool Kit**
Evidence Log Model

Title of Text: _____ Date: _____

CONNECTION TO PROMPT	TEXT EVIDENCE/DETAILS	ADDITIONAL NOTES/IDEAS

How does this text change or add to my thinking?   Date: _____

ESSENTIAL QUESTION:

What is the relationship between power and freedom?

Can you be free if you don't have power, at least over your own life? Can a government guarantee freedom to its citizens if its leaders fear their own loss of power? The selections you are going to read offer insight into the complex relationship between power and freedom for individuals and for nations.

Whole-Class Learning Strategies

Throughout your life, in school, in your community, and in your career, you will continue to learn and work in large-group environments.

Review these strategies and the actions you can take to practice them as you work with your whole class. Add ideas of your own for each step. Get ready to use these strategies during Whole-Class Learning.

STRATEGY	ACTION PLAN
Listen actively	• Eliminate distractions. For example, put your cellphone away. • Keep your eyes on the speaker. •
Clarify by asking questions	• If you're confused, other people probably are, too. Ask a question to help your whole class. • If you see that you are guessing, ask a question instead. •
Monitor understanding	• Notice what information you already know and be ready to build on it. • Ask for help if you are struggling. •
Interact and share ideas	• Share your ideas and answer questions, even if you are unsure. • Build on the ideas of others by adding details or making a connection. •

CONTENTS

PERFORMANCE TASK

WRITING FOCUS
Write an Informative Essay

The Whole-Class selections deal with freedom and its costs. After studying the excerpt from Roosevelt's "Four Freedoms" speech and Kennedy's inaugural address, you will write an informative essay about the ideas these two leaders express.

from THE "FOUR FREEDOMS" SPEECH

Comparing Texts

In this lesson, you will read and compare two famous speeches, Franklin Roosevelt's "Four Freedoms" speech and John F. Kennedy's inaugural address. First, you will complete the first-read and close-read activities for the excerpt from the "Four Freedoms" speech.

INAUGURAL ADDRESS

About the Speaker

Franklin Delano Roosevelt (1882–1945) realized his potential as a leader only after falling victim to polio at age thirty-nine. He was twice elected governor of New York; then, in 1932, he defeated President Herbert Hoover to become the nation's thirty-second president. Roosevelt won an unprecedented four terms as president and led the nation through two great challenges: the Great Depression and World War II.

🛠 **Tool Kit**
First-Read Guide and Model Annotation

STANDARDS
Reading Informational Text
By the end of grade 10, read and comprehend literary nonfiction at the high end of the grades 9–10 text complexity band independently and proficiently.

from The "Four Freedoms" Speech

Concept Vocabulary

You will encounter the following words as you read the excerpt from Roosevelt's "Four Freedoms" speech. Before reading, note how familiar you are with each word. Then, rank the words in order from most familiar (1) to least familiar (6).

WORD	YOUR RANKING
pacification	*diplomacy to negotiate*
tyranny	*opressive ruling*
propaganda	*I know: anything*
disarmament	*limit weapons*
appeasement	*I know: make agreeme... to continue pea...*
treachery	*danger*

After completing the first read, come back to the concept vocabulary and review your rankings. Mark changes to your original rankings as needed.

First Read NONFICTION

Apply these strategies as you conduct your first read. You will have an opportunity to complete the close-read notes after your first read.

NOTICE the general ideas of the text. *What* is it about? *Who* is involved?

ANNOTATE by marking vocabulary and key passages you want to revisit.

CONNECT ideas within the selection to what you already know and what you have already read.

RESPOND by completing the Comprehension Check and by writing a brief summary of the selection.

First Read: NOTICE, ANNOTATE, CONNECT, RESPOND

from
The "Four Freedoms" Speech

Franklin Delano Roosevelt

BACKGROUND

Roosevelt gave this speech as a State of the Union address in 1941, following his 1940 election to a third term as president. At the time, much of the world was in turmoil as Nazi Germany, under the leadership of Adolf Hitler, had already invaded Norway, Belgium, the Netherlands, and France, and attacked Great Britain. A significant number of Americans wanted to remain uninvolved in the war, insisting that problems overseas did not affect the United States. However, others felt that German aggression threatened democracy throughout the world and that Hitler must be stopped.

NOTES

1   *Mr. President, Mr. Speaker, Members of the Seventy-seventh Congress:*

2   I address you, the Members of the Seventy-seventh Congress, at a moment unprecedented in the history of the Union. I use the word "unprecedented," because at no previous time has American security been as seriously threatened from without as it is today.

3   Since the permanent formation of our Government under the Constitution, in 1789, most of the periods of crisis in our history have related to our domestic affairs. Fortunately, only one of these—the four-year War Between the States[1]—ever threatened our national

---

1. **four-year War Between the States** United States Civil War, 1861–1865.

CLOSE READ
ANNOTATE: Mark words and phrases in paragraph 5 that suggest something that is absolute—unchanging and without compromise.

QUESTION: Why has Roosevelt used words that suggest an unbending point of view?

CONCLUDE: What do these word choices suggest about the quality of leadership Roosevelt is trying to convey?

unity. Today, thank God, one hundred thirty million Americans, in forty-eight States, have forgotten points of the compass in our national unity.

4 It is true that prior to 1914 the United States often had been disturbed by events in other continents. We had even engaged in two wars with European nations and in a number of undeclared wars in the West Indies, in the Mediterranean, and in the Pacific for the maintenance of American rights and for the principles of peaceful commerce. But in no case had a serious threat been raised against our national safety or our continued independence.

5 What I seek to convey is the historic truth that the United States as a nation has at all times maintained clear, definite opposition to any attempt to lock us in behind an ancient Chinese wall[2] while the procession of civilization went past. Today, thinking of our children and of their children, we oppose enforced isolation for ourselves or for any other part of the Americas.

6 That determination of ours, extending over all these years, was proved, for example, during the quarter century of wars following the French Revolution.

7 While the Napoleonic struggles did threaten interests of the United States because of the French foothold in the West Indies and in Louisiana, and while we engaged in the War of 1812 to vindicate our right to peaceful trade, it is nevertheless clear that neither France nor Great Britain, nor any other nation, was aiming at domination of the whole world.

8 In like fashion from 1815 to 1914—ninety-nine years—no single war in Europe or in Asia constituted a real threat against our future or against the future of any other American nation.

9 Except in the Maximilian interlude in Mexico,[3] no foreign power sought to establish itself in this hemisphere; and the strength of the British fleet in the Atlantic has been a friendly strength. It is still a friendly strength.

10 Even when the World War broke out in 1914, it seemed to contain only small threat of danger to our own American future. But, as time went on, the American people began to visualize what the downfall of democratic nations might mean to our own democracy.

11 We need not overemphasize imperfections in the Peace of Versailles.[4] We need not harp on failure of the democracies to deal

---

2. **ancient Chinese wall** Great Wall of China, the stone-and-earth wall built as a defense against invaders, starting in the third century B.C.
3. **Maximilian interlude in Mexico** period from 1863 to 1867 during which Maximilian I, Archduke of Austria, ruled as Emperor of Mexico as part of a scheme to remove then-President Benito Juárez.
4. **Peace of Versailles** (vuhr SY) Treaty of Versailles, a treaty signed in 1919 that formally brought an end to World War I (1914–1918).

with problems of world reconstruction. We should remember that the Peace of 1919 was far less unjust than the kind of "pacification" which began even before Munich, and which is being carried on under the new order of tyranny that seeks to spread over every continent today. The American people have unalterably set their faces against that tyranny.

12   Every realist knows that the democratic way of life is at this moment being directly assailed in every part of the world—assailed either by arms or by secret spreading of poisonous propaganda by those who seek to destroy unity and promote discord in nations that are still at peace.

13   During sixteen long months, this assault has blotted out the whole pattern of democratic life in an appalling number of independent nations, great and small. The assailants are still on the march, threatening other nations, great and small.

14   Therefore, as your President, performing my constitutional duty to "give to the Congress information of the state of the Union," I find it, unhappily, necessary to report that the future and the safety of our country and of our democracy are overwhelmingly involved in events far beyond our borders.

15   Armed defense of democratic existence is now being gallantly waged in four continents. If that defense fails, all the population and all the resources of Europe and Asia and Africa and Australasia[5] will be dominated by conquerors. Let us remember that the total of those populations and their resources in those four continents greatly exceeds the sum total of the population and the resources of the whole of the Western Hemisphere—many times over.

16   In times like these it is immature—and, incidentally, untrue—for anybody to brag that an unprepared America, single-handed, and with one hand tied behind its back, can hold off the whole world.

17   No realistic American can expect from a dictator's peace international generosity, or return of true independence, or world disarmament, or freedom of expression, or freedom of religion—or even good business.

18   Such a peace would bring no security for us or for our neighbors. "Those who would give up essential liberty to purchase a little temporary safety deserve neither liberty nor safety."[6]

19   As a nation, we may take pride in the fact that we are softhearted; but we cannot afford to be softheaded.

20   We must always be wary of those who with sounding brass and a tinkling cymbal preach the "ism" of appeasement.

---

5. **Australasia** region consisting of Australia, New Zealand, New Guinea, and the neighboring islands of the Pacific Ocean.
6. **"Those . . . safety"** quotation from a famous letter written by Benjamin Franklin.

NOTES

pacification (pas uh fuh KAY shuhn) n. state of peace put in place through diplomacy, or political negotiation; also, use of force to suppress a hostile or resistant population

tyranny (TEER uh nee) n. harsh rule over a nation or people

propaganda (prop uh GAN duh) n. information, often of a false or misleading nature, used to promote a cause

disarmament (dihs AHR muh muhnt) n. limiting or getting rid of weapons

appeasement (uh PEEZ muhnt) n. giving in to demands in order to keep peace

treachery (TREHCH uhr ee) *n.* act of betrayal

CLOSE READ

ANNOTATE: In paragraphs 27–29, mark the group of words that is repeated.

QUESTION: What does the repetition of this particular group of words emphasize?

CONCLUDE: What is the effect of this repetition?

21   We must especially beware of that small group of selfish men who would clip the wings of the American eagle in order to feather their own nests.

22   I have recently pointed out how quickly the tempo of modern warfare could bring into our very midst the physical attack which we must eventually expect if the dictator nations win this war.

23   There is much loose talk of our immunity from immediate and direct invasion from across the seas. Obviously, as long as the British Navy retains its power, no such danger exists. Even if there were no British Navy, it is not probable that any enemy would be stupid enough to attack us by landing troops in the United States from across thousands of miles of ocean, until it had acquired strategic bases from which to operate.

24   But we learn much from the lessons of the past years in Europe— particularly the lesson of Norway, whose essential seaports were captured by treachery and surprise built up over a series of years.

25   The first phase of the invasion of this hemisphere would not be the landing of regular troops. The necessary strategic points would be occupied by secret agents and by their dupes—and great numbers of them are already here, and in Latin America.

26   As long as the aggressor nations maintain the offensive, they—not we—will choose the time and the place and the method of their attack.

27   That is why the future of all the American republics is today in serious danger.

28   That is why this Annual Message to the Congress is unique in our history.

29   That is why every member of the executive branch of the government and every member of the Congress face great responsibility and great accountability.

30   The need of the moment is that our actions and our policy should be devoted primarily—almost exclusively—to meeting this foreign peril. For all our domestic problems are now a part of the great emergency.

31   Just as our national policy in internal affairs has been based upon a decent respect for the rights and the dignity of all of our fellow men within our gates, so our national policy in foreign affairs has been based on a decent respect for the rights and the dignity of all nations, large and small. And the justice of morality must and will win in the end.

32   Our national policy is this:

33   First, by an impressive expression of the public will and without regard to partisanship, we are committed to all-inclusive national defense.

34   Second, by an impressive expression of the public will and without regard to partisanship, we are committed to full support of all those resolute peoples, everywhere, who are resisting aggression and are

thereby keeping war away from our hemisphere. By this support, we express our determination that the democratic cause shall prevail, and we strengthen the defense and the security of our own nation.

35   Third, by an impressive expression of the public will and without regard to partisanship, we are committed to the proposition that principles of morality and considerations for our own security will never permit us to acquiesce in a peace dictated by aggressors and sponsored by appeasers. We know that enduring peace cannot be bought at the cost of other people's freedom.

36   In the recent national election, there was no substantial difference between the two great parties in respect to that national policy. No issue was fought out on this line before the American electorate. Today, it is abundantly evident that American citizens everywhere are demanding and supporting speedy and complete action in recognition of obvious danger.

37   Therefore, the immediate need is a swift and driving increase in our armament production. . . .

⌄ Four Freedoms Park, Roosevelt Island, New York

IN THE FUTURE DAYS WHICH WE SEEK TO MAKE SECURE, WE LOOK FORWARD TO A WORLD FOUNDED UPON FOUR ESSENTIAL HUMAN FREEDOMS. THE FIRST IS FREEDOM OF SPEECH AND EXPRESSION - EVERYWHERE IN THE WORLD. THE SECOND IS FREEDOM OF EVERY PERSON TO WORSHIP GOD IN HIS OWN WAY - EVERYWHERE IN THE WORLD. THE THIRD IS FREEDOM FROM WANT...EVERYWHERE IN THE WORLD. THE FOURTH IS FREEDOM FROM FEAR...ANYWHERE IN THE WORLD. THAT IS NO VISION OF A DISTANT MILLENNIUM. IT IS A DEFINITE BASIS FOR A KIND OF WORLD ATTAINABLE IN OUR OWN TIME AND GENERATION.   FRANKLIN D. ROOSEVELT JANUARY 6, 1941

38   Let us say to the democracies: "We Americans are vitally concerned in your defense of freedom. We are putting forth our energies, our resources, and our organizing powers to give you the strength to regain and maintain a free world. We shall send you, in ever-increasing numbers, ships, planes, tanks, guns. This is our purpose and our pledge."

39   In fulfillment of this purpose, we will not be intimidated by the threats of dictators that they will regard as a breach of international law or as an act of war our aid to the democracies which dare to resist their aggression. Such aid is not an act of war, even if a dictator should unilaterally proclaim it so to be.

40   When the dictators—if the dictators—are ready to make war upon us, they will not wait for an act of war on our part. They did not wait for Norway or Belgium or the Netherlands to commit an act of war.

41   Their only interest is in a new one-way international law, which lacks mutuality in its observance and, therefore, becomes an instrument of oppression.

42   The happiness of future generations of Americans may well depend upon how effective and how immediate we can make our aid felt. No one can tell the exact character of the emergency situations that we may be called upon to meet. The nation's hands must not be tied when the nation's life is in danger.

43   We must all prepare to make the sacrifices that the emergency— almost as serious as war itself—demands. Whatever stands in the way of speed and efficiency in defense preparations must give way to the national need.

44   A free nation has the right to expect full cooperation from all groups. A free nation has the right to look to the leaders of business, of labor, and of agriculture to take the lead in stimulating effort, not among other groups but within their own groups.

45   The best way of dealing with the few slackers or troublemakers in our midst is, first, to shame them by patriotic example, and, if that fails, to use the sovereignty of government to save government.

46   As men do not live by bread alone, they do not fight by armaments alone. Those who man our defenses, and those behind them who build our defenses, must have the stamina and the courage which come from unshakable belief in the manner of life which they are defending. The mighty action that we are calling for cannot be based on a disregard of all things worth fighting for.

47   The nation takes great satisfaction and much strength from the things which have been done to make its people conscious of their individual stake in the preservation of democratic life in America. Those things have toughened the fiber of our people, have renewed their faith and strengthened their devotion to the institutions we make ready to protect.

48   Certainly this is no time for any of us to stop thinking about the social and economic problems which are the root cause of the social revolution which is today a supreme factor in the world.

49   For there is nothing mysterious about the foundations of a healthy and strong democracy. The basic things expected by our people of their political and economic systems are simple. They are:

>   Equality of opportunity for youth and for others.
>   Jobs for those who can work.
>   Security for those who need it.
>   The ending of special privilege for the few.
>   The preservation of civil liberties for all.
>   The enjoyment of the fruits of scientific progress in a wider and constantly rising standard of living.

50   These are the simple, basic things that must never be lost sight of in the turmoil and unbelievable complexity of our modern world. The inner and abiding strength of our economic and political systems is dependent upon the degree to which they fulfill these expectations.

51   Many subjects connected with our social economy call for immediate improvement. As examples:

52   We should bring more citizens under the coverage of old-age pensions and unemployment insurance.

53   We should widen the opportunities for adequate medical care.

54   We should plan a better system by which persons deserving or needing gainful employment may obtain it.

55   I have called for personal sacrifice. I am assured of the willingness of almost all Americans to respond to that call.

56   A part of the sacrifice means the payment of more money in taxes. In my Budget Message, I shall recommend that a greater portion of this great defense program be paid for from taxation than we are paying today. No person should try, or be allowed, to get rich out of this program and the principle of tax payments in accordance with ability to pay should be constantly before our eyes to guide our legislation.

57   If the Congress maintains these principles, the voters, putting patriotism ahead of pocketbooks, will give you their applause.

58   In the future days, which we seek to make secure, we look forward to a world founded upon four essential human freedoms.

59   The first is freedom of speech and expression—everywhere in the world.

60   The second is freedom of every person to worship God in his own way—everywhere in the world.

61   The third is freedom from want—which, translated into world terms, means economic understandings which will secure to every

CLOSE READ
ANNOTATE: In paragraph 49, mark changes you see in sentence lengths.

QUESTION: How do the short sentences relate to the long ones?

CONCLUDE: How does this structure help clarify the president's meaning?

nation a healthy peacetime life for its inhabitants—everywhere in the world.

62   The fourth is freedom from fear—which, translated into world terms, means a worldwide reduction of armaments to such a point and in such a thorough fashion that no nation will be in a position to commit an act of physical aggression against any neighbor—anywhere in the world.

63   That is no vision of a distant millennium. It is a definite basis for a kind of world attainable in our own time and generation. That kind of world is the very antithesis of the so-called new order of tyranny which the dictators seek to create with the crash of a bomb.

64   To that new order we oppose the greater conception—the moral order. A good society is able to face schemes of world domination and foreign revolutions alike without fear.

65   Since the beginning of our American history, we have been engaged in change—in a perpetual peaceful revolution—a revolution which goes on steadily, quietly adjusting itself to changing conditions—without the concentration camp or the quicklime in the ditch. The world order which we seek is the cooperation of free countries, working together in a friendly, civilized society.

66   This nation has placed its destiny in the hands and heads and hearts of its millions of free men and women, and its faith in freedom under the guidance of God. Freedom means the supremacy of human rights everywhere. Our support goes to those who struggle to gain those rights or keep them. Our strength is our unity of purpose. To that high concept there can be no end save victory. ❧

Comprehension Check

Complete the following items after you finish your first read.

1. According to Roosevelt, with what nations and events is the future of the United States intertwined?

2. What does Roosevelt say about attempts to isolate the United States from the rest of the world?

3. What does Roosevelt say is happening at that present moment to the democratic way of life around the world?

4. According to Roosevelt, what are the four freedoms to which everyone in the world is entitled?

5. ⊟ **Notebook** Write a summary of this excerpt from the "Four Freedoms" speech.

- -

RESEARCH

Research to Clarify Choose at least one unfamiliar detail from the text. Briefly research that detail. In what way does the information you learned shed light on an aspect of the speech?

Research to Explore Choose a topic from the speech that sparked your interest. Then, formulate a research question about that topic.

Close Read the Text

1. This model, from paragraph 36 of the text, shows sample annotations, with questions and conclusions. Close read the passage, and find another detail to annotate. Then, write a question and your conclusion.

ANNOTATE: Roosevelt restates information about election results and American voters.

QUESTION: What is his purpose in restating this information?

CONCLUDE: He wants to convince his listeners that Americans are unified in their views.

ANNOTATE: These strong adjectives and adjective phrases appear close together.

QUESTION: Why does Roosevelt use all these powerful words and phrases in sequence?

CONCLUDE: Roosevelt wants to emphasize the urgency of the moment and his certainty about the best way forward.

> In the recent national election, there was no substantial difference between the two great parties in respect to that national policy. No issue was fought out on this line before the American electorate. Today, it is abundantly evident that American citizens everywhere are demanding and supporting speedy and complete action in recognition of obvious danger.

🔧 Tool Kit

Close-Read Guide and
Model Annotation

2. For more practice, go back into the text, and complete the close-read notes.

3. Revisit a section of the text you found important during your first read. Read this section closely, and **annotate** what you notice. Ask yourself **questions** such as "Why did the author make this choice?" What can you **conclude**?

Analyze the Text

CITE TEXTUAL EVIDENCE
to support your answers.

📓 **Notebook** Respond to these questions.

1 (a) **Connect** How does Roosevelt link his assertion that this speech occurs at an unprecedented moment to his later claim that this speech "is unique in our history"? (b) **Analyze** What language does Roosevelt use to emphasize the unique circumstances surrounding the speech?

2. Evaluate How effectively does Roosevelt's discussion of domestic issues help him build his case for helping other countries? Use examples from the speech to support your evaluation.

3. Essential Question: *What is the relationship between power and freedom?* What has this speech taught you about power and freedom?

Analyze Craft and Structure

Seminal Documents: Persuasive Appeals This speech by President Roosevelt is a seminal document that helped shape history. Knowing that his **central idea**—his main claim or position—will not be popular with all of his listeners, the president uses persuasion to present a convincing case. Roosevelt employs three kinds of **persuasive appeals:**

- **Appeals to logic** ask the audience to follow a line of reasoning. Roosevelt uses verifiable evidence to support his interpretation of the world's crisis and the validity of his plan.

- **Appeals to emotion** evoke listeners' feelings, including sympathy for others. These types of appeals often use words that have strong positive or negative connotations. They may also refer to moral, religious, or patriotic feelings.

- **Appeals to authority** encourage the audience to trust the speaker's credibility. In some cases, such an appeal can be a **logical fallacy,** or an argument that does not have a true foundation. However, by invoking his power and the privileged knowledge he has as president, Roosevelt attempts to strengthen his argument.

Practice

CITE TEXTUAL EVIDENCE to support your answers.

📓 **Notebook** Respond to these questions.

1. **(a)** Review paragraphs 2–10, and identify closely related words and phrases that Roosevelt repeats. **(b)** Does this use of repetition represent an appeal to logic, to emotions, to his own authority, or to a combination of these? Explain.

2. **(a)** Why does Roosevelt refer to a "realist" in paragraph 12 and to a "realistic American" in paragraph 17? **(b)** How do these references relate to paragraph 19? Explain.

3. Use the chart to link Roosevelt's reasoning to his central idea. First, identify the central idea of the speech. Then, give three examples of appeals to logic in the speech, and note how each example shapes or refines the central idea.

Central Idea: _____

EXAMPLE OF APPEAL TO LOGIC	HOW IT SHAPES OR REFINES THE CENTRAL IDEA

4. Read the paragraphs that follow Roosevelt's list of four freedoms (paragraphs 63–66). **(a)** What persuasive appeals does Roosevelt use in these paragraphs? **(b)** What is his purpose for using these particular appeals?

from THE "FOUR FREEDOMS" SPEECH

Concept Vocabulary

pacification	propaganda	appeasement
tyranny	disarmament	treachery

Why These Words? The concept vocabulary words all relate to conflicts between or among nations or other political groups. For example, *pacification* is the attempt to achieve, maintain, or force an end to hostilities. People might try to do this by promoting policies of *appeasement* or *disarmament*.

1. As expressed in this speech, what is Roosevelt's opinion of each concept these words represent?

2. Identify another word in the selection that relates to pacification and another word in the selection that relates to tyranny. Define each word.

WORD NETWORK

Add words related to power and freedom from the text to your Word Network.

Practice

Notebook The concept words appear in the "Four Freedoms" speech.

1. Use pairs of concept words in sentences that demonstrate their meanings. Write three sentences, each with two of the concept words.

2. Rewrite the sentences you just wrote using an antonym for each concept word. Consult a thesaurus as needed. How do your replacements change the impact each sentence would have on a reader?

Word Study

Latin Root: -pac- The word *pacification* contains the Latin root *-pac-*, which comes from the Latin word *pax*, meaning "peace." The words in the chart all share this same root. Using your knowledge of suffixes, write the meaning of each word. Use a college-level dictionary to verify your definitions.

WORD	MEANING
pacifier	
pacific	
pacifist	
pacify	

STANDARDS

Language
• Demonstrate command of the conventions of standard English grammar and usage when writing or speaking.
• Use various types of phrases and clauses to convey specific meanings and add variety and interest to writing or presentations.
• Identify and correctly use patterns of word changes that indicate different meanings or parts of speech.
• Verify the preliminary determination of the meaning of a word or phrase.

Conventions

Types of Phrases Writers and speakers, such as President Roosevelt, use various types of phrases, such as noun phrases, to convey specific meanings. A **noun phrase** consists of a noun, called the head noun, and one or more modifiers that tell *which one* or *what kind*. Modifiers may consist of adjectives, adjective phrases, prepositional phrases, participles, articles, or other grammatical elements. They can appear before the noun, after the noun, or in both locations. This chart shows some examples of noun phrases.

NOUN	NOUN PHRASES
people	those **people**; those **people** in huts; those **people** in huts and villages
threat	the small **threat**; the small, but real, **threat**; the small, but real, **threat** of danger
member	every **member**; every former **member**; every former **member** of Congress

Read It

1. Mark the noun phrases and head nouns in these sentences based on President Roosevelt's "Four Freedoms" speech. Each sentence may contain more than one noun phrase, and one noun phrase may form part of another.

   a. That is why the future of the American Republics is today in serious danger.

   b. The first phase of the invasion would not be the landing of regular troops.

   c. Our national policy in foreign affairs has been based on a decent respect for all nations, large and small.

2. Choose a sentence from paragraph 63 of the "Four Freedoms" speech. Mark the head nouns and modifiers in its noun phrases.

Write It

📓 **Notebook** In the example, the original sentence has been revised to include another noun phrase. Following the example, rewrite each sentence below by adding a noun phrase. Mark the noun phrase you added, as well as its head noun.

> EXAMPLE
>
> **ORIGINAL:** The United States still had not declared war.
>
> **REVISION:** The United States still had not declared war against <u>the other Axis powers.</u>

1. Roosevelt's program calls for jobs.
2. The program increases insurance coverage.

TIP

CLARIFICATION
One noun phrase may form part of another. For example, read this sentence: "He sat in the rocking chair on the porch." The short noun phrase "the porch" forms part of the longer noun phrase "the rocking chair on the porch."

Comparing Texts

You will now read Kennedy's inaugural address. First, complete the first-read and close-read activities. Then, compare the ways in which Roosevelt and Kennedy use persuasive appeals.

INAUGURAL ADDRESS

from THE "FOUR FREEDOMS" SPEECH

About the Speaker

John F. Kennedy
(1917–1963) graduated from Harvard University and served with distinction in the United States Navy during World War II. After his service, Kennedy won election to the House of Representatives in 1946, and was elected Senator from Massachusetts in 1952. In 1960, at the age of forty-three, Kennedy became the youngest person ever to be elected to the office of the presidency. Tragically, Kennedy was assassinated on November 22, 1963, in Dallas, Texas.

🔧 Tool Kit
First-Read Guide and Model Annotation

≡ STANDARDS

Reading Informational Text
By the end of grade 10, read and comprehend literary nonfiction at the high end of the grades 9–10 text complexity band independently and proficiently.

Inaugural Address

Concept Vocabulary

You will encounter the following words as you read John F. Kennedy's inaugural address. Before reading, note how familiar you are with each word. Then, rank the words in order from most familiar (1) to least familiar (6).

WORD	YOUR RANKING
revolution	
asunder	
invective	
belaboring	
invoke	
beachhead	

After completing the first read, come back to the concept vocabulary and review your rankings. Mark changes to your original rankings as needed.

First Read NONFICTION

Apply these strategies as you conduct your first read, You will have an opportunity to complete the close-read notes after your first read.

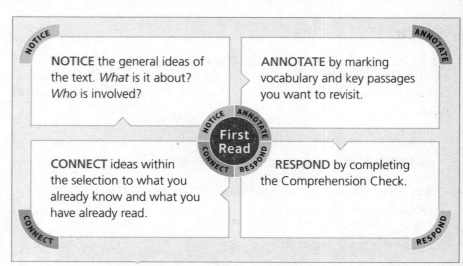

NOTICE the general ideas of the text. *What* is it about? *Who* is involved?

ANNOTATE by marking vocabulary and key passages you want to revisit.

First Read

CONNECT ideas within the selection to what you already know and what you have already read.

RESPOND by completing the Comprehension Check.

Inaugural Address

John F. Kennedy

BACKGROUND

When John F. Kennedy took office in 1961, the United States was locked in a potentially explosive stalemate with the Soviet Union and its allies. Fierce adversaries in the Cold War, the United States and the Soviet Union were stockpiling nuclear weapons, creating the possibility of a disastrous war that could destroy the earth.

1 *Vice President Johnson, Mr. Speaker, Mr. Chief Justice, President Eisenhower, Vice President Nixon, President Truman,[1] Reverend Clergy, fellow citizens:*

NOTES

2   We observe today not a victory of party but a celebration of freedom—symbolizing an end as well as a beginning—signifying renewal as well as change. For I have sworn before you and Almighty God the same solemn oath our forbears prescribed nearly a century and three quarters ago.

3   The world is very different now. For man holds in his mortal hands the power to abolish all forms of human poverty and all forms of

---

1. **Vice President . . . Truman** present at Kennedy's inauguration were Lyndon B. Johnson, Kennedy's vice president; Dwight D. Eisenhower, 34th president; Richard M. Nixon, Eisenhower's vice president; and Harry S. Truman, 33rd president.

NOTES

revolution (rehv uh LOO shuhn) *n.* overthrow of a government that is replaced by a new system

human life. And yet the same revolutionary beliefs for which our forebears fought are still at issue around the globe—the belief that the rights of man come not from the generosity of the state but from the hand of God.

4   We dare not forget today that we are the heirs of that first **revolution**. Let the word go forth from this time and place, to friend and foe alike, that the torch has been passed to a new generation of Americans—born in this century, tempered by war, disciplined by a hard and bitter peace, proud of our ancient heritage—and unwilling to witness or permit the slow undoing of those human rights to which this nation has always been committed, and to which we are committed today at home and around the world.

5   Let every nation know, whether it wishes us well or ill, that we shall pay any price, bear any burden, meet any hardship, support any friend, oppose any foe to assure the survival and the success of liberty.

6   This much we pledge—and more.

7   To those old allies whose cultural and spiritual origins we share, we pledge the loyalty of faithful friends. United there is little we cannot do in a host of cooperative ventures. Divided there is little we can do—for we dare not meet a powerful challenge at odds and split **asunder**.[2]

asunder (uh SUHN duhr) *adv.* divided; torn into separate pieces

8   To those new states whom we welcome to the ranks of the free, we pledge our word that one form of colonial control shall not have passed away merely to be replaced by a far more iron tyranny. We shall not always expect to find them supporting our view. But we shall always hope to find them strongly supporting their own freedom—and to remember that, in the past, those who foolishly sought power by riding the back of the tiger ended up inside.

9   To those people in the huts and villages of half the globe struggling to break the bonds of mass misery, we pledge our best efforts to help them help themselves, for whatever period is required—not because the communists[3] may be doing it, not because we seek their votes, but because it is right. If a free society cannot help the many who are poor, it cannot save the few who are rich.

10   To our sister republics south of our border, we offer a special pledge—to convert our good words into good deeds—in a new alliance for progress—to assist free men and free governments in casting off the chains of poverty. But this peaceful revolution of hope cannot become the prey of hostile powers. Let all our neighbors know that we shall join with them to oppose aggression or subversion anywhere in the Americas. And let every other

CLOSE READ
ANNOTATE: In paragraphs 5–12, mark references to specific nations or groups the president is addressing in this speech.

QUESTION: Why does Kennedy acknowledge all these groups?

CONCLUDE: What is the effect of these references?

to show that the freedom he wants to establish freedom not just in usa, but in all the lands.

---

2. **United . . . Divided . . . split asunder** Kennedy echoes the famous lines from Abraham Lincoln's second inaugural address: "United we stand . . . divided we fall."
3. **communists** *n.* refers to members or allies of the Soviet Union, a state whose government was based on the principles of communism, such as total government ownership of land and factories, laid out by Karl Marx (1818–1883).

power know that this hemisphere intends to remain the master of its own house.

11   To that world assembly of sovereign states, the United Nations, our last best hope in an age where the instruments of war have far outpaced the instruments of peace, we renew our pledge of support—to prevent it from becoming merely a forum for **invective**—to strengthen its shield of the new and the weak—and to enlarge the area in which its writ may run.

12   Finally, to those nations who would make themselves our adversary, we offer not a pledge but a request: that both sides begin anew the quest for peace, before the dark powers of destruction unleashed by science[4] engulf all humanity in planned or accidental self-destruction.

13   We dare not tempt them with weakness. For only when our arms are sufficient beyond doubt can we be certain beyond doubt that they will never be employed.

14   But neither can two great and powerful groups of nations take comfort from our present course—both sides overburdened by the cost of modern weapons, both rightly alarmed by the steady spread of the deadly atom, yet both racing to alter that uncertain balance of terror that stays the hand of mankind's final war.

15   So let us begin anew—remembering on both sides that civility is not a sign of weakness, and sincerity is always subject to proof. Let us never negotiate out of fear. But let us never fear to negotiate.

16   Let both sides explore what problems unite us instead of **belaboring** those problems which divide us.

17   Let both sides, for the first time, formulate serious and precise proposals for the inspection and control of arms—and bring the absolute power to destroy other nations under the absolute control of all nations.

18   Let both sides seek to **invoke** the wonders of science instead of its terrors. Together let us explore the stars, conquer the deserts, eradicate disease, tap the ocean depths, and encourage the arts and commerce.

19   Let both sides unite to heed in all corners of the earth the command of Isaiah—to "undo the heavy burdens . . . [and] let the oppressed go free."[5]

20   And if a **beachhead** of cooperation may push back the jungle of suspicion, let both sides join in creating a new endeavor, not a new balance of power, but a new world of law, where the strong are just and the weak secure and the peace preserved.

21   All this will not be finished in the first one hundred days. Nor will it be finished in the first one thousand days, nor in the life of this administration, nor even perhaps in our lifetime on this planet. But let us begin.

---

4. **dark powers of destruction unleashed by science** nuclear war.
5. **"Isaiah . . . free"** refers to a Biblical passage, Isaiah 58:6.

22   In your hands, my fellow citizens, more than mine, will rest the final success or failure of our course. Since this country was founded, each generation of Americans has been summoned to give testimony to its national loyalty. The graves of young Americans who answered the call to service surround the globe.

23   Now the trumpet summons us again—not as a call to bear arms, though arms we need—not as a call to battle, though embattled we are—but as a call to bear the burden of a long twilight struggle, year in and year out, "rejoicing in hope, patient in tribulation"[6]—a struggle against the common enemies of man: tyranny, poverty, disease, and war itself.

24   Can we forge against these enemies a grand and global alliance, North and South, East and West, that can assure a more fruitful life for all mankind? Will you join in that historic effort?

25   In the long history of the world, only a few generations have been granted the role of defending freedom in its hour of maximum danger. I do not shrink from this responsibility—I welcome it. I do not believe that any of us would exchange places with any other people or any other generation. The energy, the faith, the devotion which we bring to this endeavor will light our country and all who serve it—and the glow from that fire can truly light the world.

26   And so, my fellow Americans: Ask not what your country can do for you—ask what you can do for your country.

27   My fellow citizens of the world: Ask not what America will do for you—but what together we can do for the freedom of man.

28   Finally, whether you are citizens of America or citizens of the world, ask of us here the same high standards of strength and sacrifice which we ask of you. With a good conscience our only sure reward, with history the final judge of our deeds, let us go forth to lead the land we love, asking His blessing and His help, but knowing that here on earth God's work must truly be our own. ❧

---

6. **"rejoicing . . . tribulation"** refers to a Biblical passage, Romans 12:12. In Paul's letter to the Romans, he calls people to work together in love and mutual respect.

Comprehension Check

Complete the following items after you finish your first read.

1. According to Kennedy, inauguration day is not a celebration of the victory of a party. Of what is it a celebration?

It is a celebration of freedom,

2. How far does Kennedy say the United States is willing to go to assure liberty for all nations?

The United States is willing to pay any price, bear any burden, meet any hardship, support any friend, and oppose any foe.

3. Kennedy singles out one group of countries that the United States will defend against any attacker. What countries are they?

The countries are the sister republics south of the borders,

4. At the end of the speech, what does Kennedy urge his fellow Americans to do?

Kennedy urges his fellow Americans to come together for the freedom of man.

RESEARCH

Research to Clarify Choose at least one unfamiliar detail from the text. Briefly research that detail. How does the information you learned shed light on an aspect of the speech?

INAUGURAL ADDRESS

Close Read the Text

This model, from paragraph 25 of the text, shows two sample annotations, along with questions and conclusions. Close read the passage, and find another detail to annotate. Then, write a question and your conclusion.

Close Read
ANNOTATE · QUESTION · CONCLUDE

ANNOTATE: These nouns in sequence are very powerful.

QUESTION: Why does Kennedy use these emotionally charged words?

CONCLUDE: These words emphasize Kennedy's conviction that America is a force for good in the world.

ANNOTATE: Kennedy connects the abstract idea of defending freedom to the concrete idea of fire.

QUESTION: Why does the president use this comparison?

CONCLUDE: Fire represents light, warmth, and safety. Kennedy's comparison creates a vision of a world that is a safe haven for all.

> The energy, the faith, the devotion, which we bring to this endeavor will light our country and all who serve it— and the glow from that fire can truly light the world.

Tool Kit
Close-Read Guide and Model Annotation

2. For more practice, go back into the text, and complete the close-read notes.

3. Revisit a section of the text you found important during your first read. Read this section closely, and **annotate** what you notice. Ask yourself **questions** such as "Why did the author make this choice?" What can you **conclude**?

- -

Analyze the Text

CITE TEXTUAL EVIDENCE to support your answers.

▤ **Notebook** Respond to these questions.

1. (a) **Compare and Contrast** What similarities and differences does Kennedy see between the world now and the world as it was during the American Revolution? (b) **Interpret** How does he think these similarities and differences affect the American commitment to human rights?

2. **Infer** Why does Kennedy repeatedly refer to "both sides" in the middle of the speech? What effect might this repetition have on listeners, including those from the other "side"?

3. **Synthesize** Kennedy chooses language meant to remind people of wartime experiences and quotes religious literature. How do these choices reflect the purpose and occasion of the speech?

4. **Essential Question:** *What is the relationship between power and freedom?* What have you learned about power and freedom from reading this speech?

STANDARDS

Reading Informational Text
• Cite strong and thorough textual evidence to support analysis of what the text says explicitly as well as inferences drawn from the text.

• Determine a central idea of a text and analyze its development over the course of the text, including how it emerges and is shaped and refined by specific details; provide an objective summary of the text.

• Determine an author's point of view or purpose in a text and analyze how an author uses rhetoric to advance that point of view or purpose.

• Analyze seminal U.S. documents of historical and literary significance, including how they address related themes and concepts.

Analyze Craft and Structure

Seminal Documents: Emotional Appeals Kennedy's inaugural address is an example of **persuasion**, a type of writing in which an author or speaker attempts to influence an audience to think a certain way or take a particular action. The rhetorical techniques Kennedy uses in the speech, including charged language and restatement, appeal to listeners' emotions, thus making listeners more receptive to the ideas he expresses.

- **Charged Language:** words and phrases that have strong positive or negative connotations—Charged language encourages listeners to connect with a speaker's message through emotion rather than logic. Kennedy's listeners would have been stirred by his description of Americans as "tempered by war, disciplined by a hard and bitter peace." The words *tempered, disciplined,* and *bitter* are emotionally charged. They suggest toughness and self-control in the face of hardship.

- **Restatement:** the expression of similar ideas in different words— Speakers use restatement to clarify and emphasize ideas and to add urgency. For example, in paragraph 5, Kennedy says, "we shall pay any price, bear any burden, meet any hardship." The restatements emphasize the idea of America's commitment to freedom, while adding a sense of urgency and rhythmic intensity.

Practice

> **CITE TEXTUAL EVIDENCE** to support your answers.

📓 **Notebook** Respond to these questions.

1. Reread paragraphs 9 and 10 of Kennedy's inaugural address. **(a)** Which words and phrases have negative connotations, and what do they describe? **(b)** What do these examples of charged language reveal about Kennedy's purpose in the speech?

2. Reread paragraphs 21 and 22. What idea does Kennedy reinforce through restatement?

3. Use this chart to further analyze Kennedy's speech. Find at least three ways Kennedy uses restatement to emphasize his message of working together. Then, find at least three instances of charged language with which Kennedy describes atomic weapons. Finally, describe how his use of rhetoric supports Kennedy's purpose in this speech.

RESTATEMENT	CHARGED LANGUAGE
How rhetoric supports purpose:	

INAUGURAL ADDRESS

Concept Vocabulary

| revolution | invective | invoke |
| asunder | belaboring | beachhead |

Why These Words? These concept words all relate to instances of physical or verbal confrontation. *Revolution* and *beachhead* call up images of military conflict. *Asunder* emphasizes the division of something that was once united. Speakers *invoke* powerful aid as they appeal for help. An abusive speaker uses *invective,* whereas a *belaboring* speaker deflects attention from significant issues by focusing too much on one topic.

1. Read paragraphs 11 and 16, and consider the context in which Kennedy uses the concept words *invective* and *belaboring*. What do the paragraphs have in common? How does Kennedy's word choice connect the paragraphs?

2. Find other words in the speech that refer to physical confrontation. Which ones does Kennedy use to suggest that people are in danger? Which ones does he use to inspire people to stand up for what they believe?

WORD NETWORK

Add words related to freedom and power from the text to your Word Network.

Practice

📓 **Notebook** The concept words appear in Kennedy's inaugural address.

1. Use each concept word in a sentence about a current event that demonstrates your understanding of the word's meaning.

2. For each sentence you just wrote, write a companion sentence about a historical event that uses the same concept word.

Word Study

Latin Root: *-vol-* In his inaugural address, Kennedy uses the concept vocabulary word *revolution* twice—once when referring to the American Revolutionary War and once when describing a new "peaceful revolution of hope." *Revolution* is formed from the Latin root *-vol-*, meaning "to roll" or "to turn." The words in the chart all share this same root. Use a print or online dictionary to look up each word, and write its meaning.

STANDARDS

Reading Informational Text
Determine an author's point of view or purpose in a text and analyze how an author uses rhetoric to advance that point of view or purpose.

Language
• Use parallel structure.
• Identify and correctly use patterns of word changes that indicate different meanings or parts of speech.
• Consult general and specialized reference materials, both print and digital, to find the pronunciation of a word or determine or clarify its precise meaning, its part of speech, or its etymology.

WORD	MEANING
voluble	
convolution	
involve	
revolve	
evolve	

Author's Style

Author's Choices: Use of Language **Rhetorical devices** are special patterns of words and ideas that create emphasis and stir emotion, especially in speeches or other oratory. In his inaugural address, Kennedy uses three closely related rhetorical devices: repetition, parallelism, and antithesis.

- **Repetition** is the use multiple times of the same word or phrase to emphasize key concepts.

  Example: "Let freedom ring from every hill and molehill of Mississippi. From every mountainside, let freedom ring."—from the "I Have a Dream" speech, Martin Luther King, Jr.

- **Parallelism** is the repetition of related ideas in the same grammatical structure. There are many kinds of parallelism, all of which establish a rhythm that makes ideas memorable. One kind is **anaphora**, in which a word or group of words repeats at the beginnings of phrases, clauses, or sentences that appear in close succession.

  Example: "This blessed plot, this earth, this realm, this England . . ." —from *Richard III*, William Shakespeare

- In **antithesis**, two strongly contrasting ideas, expressed using parallel structure, are placed side-by-side.

  Example: "To err is human; to forgive divine." —from "An Essay on Criticism," Alexander Pope

Read It

1. Identify the rhetorical device in each passage as either simple parallelism or antithesis. Then, explain your choice.

   a. We shall not always expect to find them supporting our view. But we shall always hope to find them strongly supporting their own freedom. . . .

   b. Let every nation know . . . that we shall pay any price, bear any burden, meet any hardship, support any friend, oppose any foe to assure the survival and the success of liberty.

2. Find at least one example each of parallelism, anaphora, and antithesis in paragraphs 16–20 of Kennedy's inaugural address. For each passage you chose, identify the type of rhetorical device being used. Then, explain why the passage is a good example of that device.

Write It

🖉 **Notebook** Rewrite the following sentences to create one sentence that uses parallelism.

> We walked through the forest quietly. Loudly over a stream we splashed. We happily climbed up a mountain.

INAUGURAL ADDRESS

from THE "FOUR FREEDOMS" SPEECH

Writing to Compare

You have studied two seminal American texts—Roosevelt's "Four Freedoms" speech, delivered in 1941, and Kennedy's inaugural address, delivered in 1961. Now, deepen your understanding of the two speeches by comparing and writing about them.

Assignment

Both of these speeches were given at critical moments in American history. They reflect the concerns of the era, and define each president's vision for the country and its role in the world. Write a **comparison-and-contrast essay** in which you explain what each leader means when he talks about "freedom." Include the following elements in your essay:

- a summary of the historical context of each speech—The **historical context** involves the state of the country and the world at these two moments in history.

- an explanation of each speaker's purpose—the call to action each leader issues

- an explanation of the role each president thinks America should play in the world

Prewriting

🗒 **Notebook** Make sure you are clear about the historical context of each speech. Answer these questions to clarify your understanding.

1. **(a)** As Roosevelt delivers his speech, what conflict is growing around the world? **(b)** How does Roosevelt want America to respond to that conflict?
2. **(a)** What concerns about the Cold War does Kennedy express in his speech? **(b)** What does Kennedy want the opposing side in that conflict to consider?

Analyze the Texts Reread each speech, and identify passages related to the concept of freedom, particularly in regard to America's responsibilities in the world.

PASSAGES RELATED TO FREEDOM	
"FOUR FREEDOMS" SPEECH	INAUGURAL ADDRESS

⠿ STANDARDS

Reading Informational Text
Analyze seminal U.S. documents of historical and literary significance, including how they address related themes and concepts.

Writing
• Write informative/explanatory texts to examine and convey complex ideas, concepts, and information clearly and accurately through the effective selection, organization, and analysis of content.
• Apply *grades 9–10 Reading standards* to literary nonfiction.

Drafting

Write a Thesis Statement In a comparison-and-contrast essay about literary nonfiction, the thesis statement should indicate the major similarities and differences between the two works being compared. Draft a thesis statement consisting of two or three sentences. State how the "Four Freedoms" speech and the inaugural address are similar, as well as how they are different. Use comparison-and-contrast key words, such as those underlined in this thesis frame:

> **Thesis Frame:**
> Both Roosevelt's "Four Freedoms" speech and Kennedy's inaugural address _____,
> However, Roosevelt's speech _____,
> whereas Kennedy's speech _____.

Choose a Structure Decide how best to organize your essay. Point-by-point organization and block organization are two commonly used structures for essays of comparison.

- **Block Format:** Discuss the historical context, purpose, and meaning of freedom in one speech. Then, discuss the historical context, purpose, and meaning of freedom in the other speech.

- **Point-by-Point Format:** First, discuss the historical context and purpose of each speech. Next, discuss the meaning of freedom presented in each speech.

Make sure to include a section in which you explain the vision of America and its role in the world that the two presidents put forward.

Use Varied Evidence Include supporting evidence in a variety of ways.

- **Direct Quotations:** use of exact language from the text

  Avoid misrepresenting a speaker's meaning. For example, if one part of a quotation supports your ideas, but another part does not, explain the discrepancy—don't use only the part that fits your analysis.

- **Summaries:** brief retellings of parts of the text

  Summarize complex sequences of events or ideas so that readers have the information they need to understand your analysis. The use of summaries can help you give readers necessary knowledge without unnecessary detail.

- **Paraphrases:** restatements of a text in your own words

  Use paraphrases when the speaker's exact words are not that distinctive, or when you wish to clarify someone else's ideas or demonstrate your knowledge of a text.

Review, Revise, and Edit

When you have finished drafting, reread your essay. Mark ideas that need more support, and then return to your Prewriting notes or the texts themselves to find additional evidence. Check for logical, clear transitions between paragraphs. Edit your work for grammar, sentence structure, and word choice. Finally, proofread your essay to eliminate spelling and punctuation errors.

📝 EVIDENCE LOG

Before moving on to a new selection, go to your Evidence Log and record what you learned from Roosevelt's "Four Freedoms" speech and Kennedy's inaugural address.

About the Speaker

John F. Kennedy (1917–1963) came from a family with extensive political connections and ambitions, but it was Joseph, his older brother, who was expected to run for high office. Joseph, however, died in World War II, and John became the family's political hope. As a United States senator, he advocated for foreign aid to developing nations in Africa and Asia, and for France to grant Algerian independence. A concern with foreign affairs would become a major element of his presidency.

Inaugural Address

Media Vocabulary

The following words or concepts will be useful to you as you analyze, discuss, and write about videos.

tone: sound of a voice with respect to pitch, volume, and overall quality	• Pitch refers to how high or low in frequency a voice sounds. • Overall quality refers to such traits as squeakiness, depth, resonance, or thinness.
inflection: changes to pitch or volume within a single word or between words	• Inflection can go up or down or be loud or soft. • Speakers use inflection to emphasize certain words, to modify rhythm, or to add drama.
gesture: movement of the body that conveys meaning	• Gestures are a form of nonverbal communication that help emphasize meaning. • Some gestures, such as a thumbs-up sign, have meanings that are essentially the same in any situation. Other gestures, such as a wave of the hands, reflect a speaker's emotions and meaning in a specific situation.
enunciation: manner in which a speaker pronounces words	• A speaker with good enunciation speaks clearly and avoids slurring words, omitting syllables, or dropping word endings. • Enunciation is sometimes referred to as "diction."

First Review MEDIA: VIDEO

Apply these strategies as you conduct your first review. You will have an opportunity to complete a close review after your first review.

WATCH *who* speaks, *what* they say, and *how* they say it.

NOTE elements that you find interesting and want to revisit.

CONNECT ideas in the video to other media you've experienced, texts you've read, or images you've seen.

RESPOND by completing the Comprehension Check.

First Review

▤ STANDARDS

Reading Informational Text
By the end of grade 10, read and comprehend literary nonfiction at the high end of the grades 9–10 text complexity band independently and proficiently.

Language
Acquire and use accurately general academic and domain-specific words and phrases, sufficient for reading, writing, speaking, and listening at the college and career readiness level; demonstrate independence in gathering vocabulary knowledge when considering a word or phrase important to comprehension or expression.

Inaugural Address

John F. Kennedy

BACKGROUND

Harry S. Truman was the first United States president to deliver a televised inaugural address. Kennedy, in turn, was the first to deliver a televised inaugural address on color TV. Furthermore, Kennedy used the newly global mass media of television to speak to both the American people and the entire world, addressing the country's allies and adversaries, the United Nations, and other international audiences.

NOTES

Comprehension Check

Complete the following items after you finish your first review.

1. Describe the setting in which Kennedy delivers the speech.

2. What are some phrases Kennedy emphasizes with voice and gestures?

3. Which parts of the speech does the audience respond to most enthusiastically?

RESEARCH

Research to Explore Choose an element of the speech that sparked your interest. Then, formulate a research question about that topic.

MEDIA VOCABULARY

Use these words as you discuss and write about the video.

tone
inflection
gesture
enunciation

🔲 **WORD NETWORK**

Add words related to freedom and power from the text to your Word Network.

Close Review

Watch and listen to the speech again. Write any new observations that seem important. What **questions** do you have? What can you **conclude**?

Analyze the Media

CITE TEXTUAL EVIDENCE
to support your answers.

📓 **Notebook** Respond to these questions.

1. **(a) Interpret** Rewatch the part of the speech that starts at the 8:12 mark—beginning with "we dare not tempt them with weakness"—and ends at 9:19. What international issue is Kennedy addressing?
   (b) Connect What do Kennedy's references to "both sides" suggest about the issue?

2. **(a) Interpret** Listen for the word *pledge* in the speech. For whom is Kennedy speaking when he uses this word? **(b) Evaluate** How credible are the promises he makes in these statements? Explain.

3. **Connect** To date, John F. Kennedy is the youngest elected United States president. Listen for the word *generation* as you review the speech. What connections does Kennedy make between his generation and his vision for the future? Explain.

4. **Essential Question:** *What is the relationship between power and freedom?* What have you learned about power and freedom from listening to this speech?

⚏ **STANDARDS**

Speaking and Listening
• Evaluate a speaker's point of view, reasoning, and use of evidence and rhetoric, identifying any fallacious reasoning or exaggerated or distorted evidence.
• Adapt speech to a variety of contexts and tasks, demonstrating command of formal English when indicated or appropriate.

Writing to Sources

INAUGURAL ADDRESS (video)

Assignment

Imagine you are a television journalist in 1961 covering the Kennedy inauguration. Write the text for a **news report** about the event.

- **Write an introduction.** Find the answers to questions such as these: *What were the major issues in the 1960 election? Against whom did Kennedy run? How close was the election?*

- **Describe the scene.** Answer questions such as these: *What is the weather like? How many people seem to be in attendance? What is the mood of the crowd? Who is assembled on the steps of the Capitol building?*

- **Describe Kennedy's delivery.** Answer questions such as these: *How does Kennedy look? What is the tone of his speech? How do his gestures and body language affect his message? What can you say about his rhetoric?*

- **Review the content of the speech.** State Kennedy's central idea, and describe the crowd's reception of that idea. Report what Kennedy says about the country's rich and poor, its allies and enemies. Also, identify what you consider to be the high points of the address. What challenge does Kennedy issue to the American public?

Speaking and Listening

Assignment

Adapt the text of the news report you wrote, and deliver it as a **newscast**. You may either present it live or record it and share it digitally.

- **Integrate visuals.** Review your news report, and find visuals or audio that will enhance its transition into a newscast. Plan how to integrate the visuals into your presentation.

- **Consider your speaking style.** Choose a speaking style that suits your audience and purpose. Your style might be informal, but still highly informational. Alternatively, you might choose a formal approach in acknowledgment of the importance of the event.

- **Vary your pitch and volume.** Avoid speaking in a monotone. Instead, vary the pitch and volume of your voice. Likewise, find a middle ground between speaking too slowly and too quickly. Make sure you clearly enunciate so that listeners fully understand what you are saying.

- **Rehearse your delivery.** Practice your newscast either in front of a mirror if you plan to perform live, or in an audio recording if you plan to share a digital version. Look for ways in which you can strengthen your delivery through gestures, tone, or enunciation.

✎ EVIDENCE LOG

Before moving on to a new selection, go to your Evidence Log and record what you learned from listening to and watching Kennedy's inaugural address.

WRITING TO SOURCES

- *from* THE "FOUR FREEDOMS" SPEECH
- INAUGURAL ADDRESS
- INAUGURAL ADDRESS (video)

🔧 Tool Kit

Student Model of an Informative Essay

ACADEMIC VOCABULARY

As you craft your informative essay, consider using some of the academic vocabulary you learned in the beginning of the unit.

attribute
hierarchy
demarcate
fundamental
democracy

⣿ STANDARDS

Writing
• Write informative/explanatory texts to examine and convey complex ideas, concepts, and information clearly and accurately through the effective selection, organization, and analysis of content.
• Conduct short as well as more sustained research projects to answer a question or solve a problem; narrow or broaden the inquiry when appropriate; synthesize multiple sources on the subject, demonstrating understanding of the subject under investigation.
• Write routinely over extended time frames and shorter time frames for a range of tasks, purposes, and audiences.

Write an Informative Essay

You have read two speeches that shed light on the relationship between power and freedom. In his "Four Freedoms" speech, Franklin D. Roosevelt speaks of the need for the United States to protect itself during a time of danger, and of universal freedoms that deserve protection throughout the world. In his inaugural address, John F. Kennedy argues that Americans must appreciate their own freedom while understanding the country's importance in the world.

Assignment

Use the knowledge you have gained from reading Roosevelt's "Four Freedoms" speech and from reading and listening to Kennedy's inaugural address to write about the power of the individual. Write a brief **informative essay** in which you focus on answering this question:

> **What can one person do to defend the human rights of all people?**

Elements of an Informative Essay

An **informative essay** develops a thesis, or main idea, about a topic through the effective selection, organization, and analysis of content. An effective informative essay includes these elements:

- an engaging introduction to its topic
- the writer's main idea about the topic, supported by facts, definitions, details, examples, quotations, and other information from credible sources
- an organization that helps readers make connections and distinctions among ideas
- clear transitions that clarify relationships among ideas
- a conclusion that restates the thesis and follows from the information presented
- correct grammar, a formal style, and an objective tone

Model Informative Essay For a model of a well-crafted informative essay, see the Launch Text, "Born Free: Children and the Struggle for Human Rights."

Challenge yourself to find all of the elements of effective informative writing in the text. You will have the opportunity to review these elements as you start to write your own informative essay.

Prewriting / Planning

Develop a Working Thesis Reread the assignment and rephrase it to state your topic. Then, compose an answer to the question. This is your initial thesis, or main idea. You may return to it and change it as you gather more information and work through the writing process.

Topic: _____

Thesis: _____

_____

Review the texts and media that you have studied in this unit so far. Take note of details that support your main idea. Then, decide whether outside research will help you develop your ideas more fully.

Focus Research If a short research project is in order, plan to use several sources. Focus your efforts by developing a research question, such as "Who are three individuals known for their defense of human rights?" or "What opportunities exist in my hometown for a person to defend human rights?" You can find primary and secondary sources in print or online. You can conduct original research as well, through surveys or personal interviews.

Research Question: _____

_____

Possible Sources:

1. _____

2. _____

3. _____

Gather Evidence Be sure that your sources are reliable. Ask your librarian about the best sources to use. This excerpt from the Launch Text shows that the writer used newspapers as a source of information.

> *"Dere's t'ree t'ousand of us, and we'll win for sure," is how one newspaper mockingly quoted a newsie's reference to the number of strikers.*
>
> —from "Born Free: Children and the Struggle for Human Rights"

Take notes as you find and connect relevant information from multiple sources, and keep a reference list of every source you use. Create a notecard that includes each source's author, title, publisher, city, and date of publication, along with the fact or idea you discovered. For Internet sources, record the name and Web address of the site, as well as the date you accessed the information. For print sources, note the page numbers on which you found useful information.

Connect Across Texts As you write your informative essay, you will be combining facts, examples, and details from multiple sources. Remember to identify the source of every exact quotation. Cite President Roosevelt, President Kennedy, and any other authority who helps you formulate and support your main idea. As you compile evidence from various texts, note any information that may help you revise or refine your main idea.

EVIDENCE LOG

Review your Evidence Log and identify key details you may want to cite in your informative essay.

STANDARDS

Writing
- Introduce a topic; organize complex ideas, concepts, and information to make important connections and distinctions; include formatting, graphics, and multimedia when useful to aiding comprehension.
- Develop the topic with well-chosen, relevant, and sufficient facts, extended definitions, concrete details, quotations, or other information and examples appropriate to the audience's knowledge of the topic.

Drafting

Organize Your Essay Consider your topic statement, your main idea, and the supporting information you have gathered, and then choose an organizational structure. Make sure your choice will help you sequence information so that it flows logically from your introduction, through your body paragraphs, to your conclusion. There are a variety of useful structures, including the ones described here. Place a check in the box of the one you plan to use.

☐ **Problem-Solution Order:** Present a problem, such as a specific example of a human rights violation, and offer information about possible solutions. In your conclusion, identify the solution that most strongly supports your main idea.

☐ **Order of Importance:** State your thesis in your introduction. Then, present your supporting reasons and evidence in order of importance, from most important to least.

☐ **Nestorian Order, or Reverse Order of Importance:** State your thesis in your introduction. Then, offer supporting reasons and evidence starting with weaker or less dramatic ideas and building to stronger or more dramatic ones. This can be an effective way to lead readers to a powerful conclusion.

☐ **Cause-Effect Order:** Present a person's actions as a cause that has the effect of defending human rights, or present defending human rights as a cause that has the effect of inspiring individual actions.

☐ **Steps in a Process:** Present the stages through which an individual progresses in his or her defense of human rights. In your conclusion, link this process to your main idea.

Notice how the Launch Text is organized. The first paragraph states, "young people have also realized that in order to be heard, they might have to make some noise." The body paragraphs report causes and effects in chronological order. The concluding paragraph revisits the main idea: "It may have been a small victory, but it was more than the newsies would have received had they not raised their voices."

Write a First Draft Use your chosen organization to write a first draft. As you write, your style should be formal, and your tone should be objective. Avoid revealing your own personal biases, and do not use slang or expressions that sound overly conversational. Instead, choose words that convey your ideas precisely, and define or explain terms that may be unfamiliar to your audience. Make sure to include transitional words and phrases that clarify the relationships among your ideas.

▤ STANDARDS

Writing
• Introduce a topic; organize complex ideas, concepts, and information to make important connections and distinctions; include formatting, graphics, and multimedia when useful to aiding comprehension.
• Develop the topic with well-chosen, relevant, and sufficient facts, extended definitions, concrete details, quotations, or other information and examples appropriate to the audience's knowledge of the topic.
• Use appropriate and varied transitions to link the major sections of the text, create cohesion, and clarify the relationships among complex ideas and concepts.
• Use precise language and domain-specific vocabulary to manage the complexity of the topic.
• Establish and maintain a formal style and objective tone while attending to the norms and conventions of the discipline in which they are writing.
• Provide a concluding statement or section that follows from and supports the information or explanation presented.

Create Cohesion: Integrate Information in Different Ways

As you write your draft, use the following methods to present the ideas, facts, examples, and quotations you use to support your thesis. In each case, you must credit the source.

- **Direct Quotations:** Use the writer's exact words when they provide the strongest support for an idea. Indicate omitted material with ellipses.
- **Paraphrase:** Restate a writer's specific ideas in your own words, accurately reflecting the original meaning.
- **Summary:** To provide background or general information, condense complex material into a briefer statement in your own words.

NOTE: If you find a fact in only one source, include documentation. If you find identical facts in multiple sources, you need not provide documentation.

Read It

These sentences from the Launch Text show different methods of incorporating information.

- *In our national anthem, "The Star-Spangled Banner," we sing of America as "the land of the free and the home of the brave."* (direct quotation)
- *Another newspaper explained that newsies were striking for their "rights," using quotation marks to suggest that the children had no rights and that it was quaint for them to suggest they did.* (direct quotation combined with paraphrase)
- *The newsies' circumstances deteriorated even further during the Spanish-American War of 1898.* (summary)

Write It

As you draft your essay, keep track of your sources, and include appropriate citations to avoid plagiarism, or the presentation of another's work as your own. You may use a chart like this to track your information.

Source title	
Author	
Publisher or site	
Date of publication or update	
Date you accessed (for online sources)	
Website URL (for online sources)	
Direct quotation	
Summary or paraphrase	

TIP

PUNCTUATION
Make sure to enclose direct quotations in quotation marks. Do not use quotation marks for paraphrased remarks.

STANDARDS
Writing
Gather relevant information from multiple authoritative print and digital sources, using advanced searches effectively; assess the usefulness of each source in answering the research question; integrate information into the text selectively to maintain the flow of ideas, avoiding plagiarism and following a standard format for citation.

Revising
Evaluating Your Draft

Use the following checklist to evaluate the effectiveness of your first draft. Then, use your evaluation and the instruction on this page to guide your revision.

FOCUS AND ORGANIZATION	EVIDENCE AND ELABORATION	CONVENTIONS
☐ The introduction clearly states the topic.	☐ Specific reasons, details, facts, and quotations support the main idea.	☐ Attends to the norms and conventions of the discipline, especially regarding the proper crediting of sources.
☐ The introduction presents a specific thesis.	☐ The main idea is developed with relevant information from multiple credible sources.	☐ Uses precise language appropriate for the audience and purpose.
☐ The organization is logical, allowing for effective development of ideas.	☐ Accurate credit is provided to sources of information.	☐ Establishes an objective tone and formal style.
☐ The conclusion clearly connects back to the introduction.		

⬡ WORD NETWORK

Include interesting words from your Word Network in your informative essay.

Revising for Focus and Organization

Internal Logic Reread your essay, making sure the ideas you set up in the introduction are clearly developed in the body and echoed in the conclusion. Rearrange paragraphs or sections that do not build in a logical way. Consider adding or revising transitional words and phrases to clarify the connections you want to emphasize.

Revising for Evidence and Elaboration

Correct Citations Consider how you have used and cited researched information in your essay. Have you accurately identified the sources of all the evidence you use to support your main idea? If not, review your notes to find and add the proper citations.

Language Clear, strong language will help make your ideas memorable. Consider these options:

- **Comparatives and Superlatives:** Comparative adjectives, such as *sharper* and *bolder*, clarify ideas. Avoid overuse of predictable or subjective superlatives, such as *best, strongest,* or *bravest*.

- **Action Verbs:** Whenever possible, replace weaker linking verbs with stronger action verbs.

≣ STANDARDS

Writing
Gather relevant information from multiple authoritative print and digital sources, using advanced searches effectively; assess the usefulness of each source in answering the research question; integrate information into the text selectively to maintain the flow of ideas, avoiding plagiarism and following a standard format for citation.

> EXAMPLE
> **LINKING VERB:** The policy *is* unfair.
>
> **ACTION VERB:** The policy *cheats* us all.

Review your essay, looking for any ineffective uses of language. Replace weaker word choices with stronger alternatives.

PEER REVIEW

Exchange essays with a classmate. Use the checklist to evaluate your classmate's informative essay and provide supportive feedback.

1. Is the thesis, or main idea, clear?

☐ yes   ☐ no   If no, explain what confused you.

2. Is the text organized logically?

☐ yes   ☐ no   If no, what aspect of organization does not work?

3. Does the essay fully address the assignment?

☐ yes   ☐ no   If no, write a brief note explaining what you thought was missing.

4. What is the strongest part of your classmate's essay? Why?

_____

_____

_____

_____

Editing and Proofreading

Edit for Conventions Reread your draft for accuracy and consistency. Correct errors in grammar and word usage. Use a style guide if you need help crediting your sources correctly.

Proofread for Accuracy Read your draft carefully, looking for errors in spelling and punctuation. Double-check that you have used quotation marks correctly and that there is an ending quotation mark for every beginning quotation mark.

Publishing and Presenting

Create a final version of your essay and share it with your classmates. Together, determine what your different essays convey about the values Roosevelt and Kennedy promote in their speeches.

Reflecting

Think about what you learned while writing your essay. What techniques did you learn that you could use when writing another informative essay? How could you improve the process? For example, you might choose to spend more time examining primary sources.

≣ STANDARDS

Writing
Develop and strengthen writing as needed by planning, revising, editing, rewriting, or trying a new approach, focusing on addressing what is most significant for a specific purpose and audience.

Language
• Demonstrate command of the conventions of standard English grammar and usage when writing or speaking.
• Demonstrate command of the conventions of standard English capitalization, punctuation, and spelling when writing.
• Spell correctly.

ESSENTIAL QUESTION:

What is the relationship between power and freedom?

What does it mean to have your freedom to learn, read, or think what you want threatened? Is freedom of thought and expression something we treasure only when we might lose it? The selections you will read present various perspectives on these questions. You will work in a group to continue your exploration of the relationship between power and freedom.

Small-Group Learning Strategies

Throughout your life, in school, in your community, and in your career, you will continue to develop strategies when you work in teams.

Review these strategies and the actions you can take to practice them. Add ideas of your own for each step. Get ready to use these strategies during Small-Group Learning.

STRATEGY	ACTION PLAN
Prepare	• Complete your assignments so that you are prepared for group work. • Organize your thinking so you can contribute to your group's discussions. •
Participate fully	• Make eye contact to signal that you are listening and taking in what is being said. • Use text evidence when making a point. •
Support others	• Build off ideas from others in your group. • Invite others who have not yet spoken to do so. •
Clarify	• Paraphrase the ideas of others to ensure that your understanding is correct. • Ask follow-up questions. •

PERFORMANCE TASK

SPEAKING AND LISTENING FOCUS

Deliver a Multimedia Presentation

The Small-Group readings explore the conflicts that arise when governments try to
control the freedom to create and share knowledge and information. After reading,
your group will create a multimedia presentation about these concepts.

Working as a Team

1. **Take a Position** With your group, discuss the following question:

   In what ways do laws both protect and limit our personal freedom?

   As you take turns sharing your ideas, be sure to provide supporting reasons and examples. After all group members have shared, discuss which aspect of the law you think is more important—the power to protect or the power to restrict.

2. **List Your Rules** As a group, decide on the rules that you will follow as you work together. Samples are provided; add two more of your own. As you work together, you may add or revise rules based on your experience together.

   - Everyone should participate in group discussions.
   - People should not interrupt.

   - _____

     _____

   - _____

     _____

3. **Apply the Rules** Practice working as a group. Share what you have learned about personal freedom and the law. Make sure each person in the group contributes. Take notes on and be prepared to share with the class one thing that you heard from another member of your group.

4. **Name Your Group** Choose a name that reflects the unit topic.

   Our group's name: _____

5. **Create a Communication Plan** Decide how you want to communicate with one another. For example, you might use online collaboration tools, email, or instant messaging.

   Our group's decision: _____

   _____

Making a Schedule

First, find out the due dates for the small-group activities. Then, preview the texts and activities with your group, and make a schedule for completing the tasks.

SELECTION	ACTIVITIES	DUE DATE
Speech at the United Nations		
Diane Sawyer Interviews Malala Yousafzai		
Caged Bird Some Advice To Those Who Will Serve Time in Prison		
The Censors		
from Freedom of the Press Report 2015		

Working on Group Projects

As your group works together, you'll find it more effective if each person has a specific role. Different projects require different roles. Before beginning a project, discuss the necessary roles, and choose one for each group member. Here are some possible roles; add your own ideas.

Project Manager: monitors the schedule and keeps everyone on task

Researcher: organizes research activities

Recorder: takes notes during group meetings

_____

_____

_____

_____

_____

SPEECH AT THE UNITED NATIONS

Comparing Texts

In this lesson, you will compare the speech that Malala Yousafzai delivered at the United Nations with an interview of Yousafzai by journalist Diane Sawyer. First, complete the first-read and close-read activities for Yousafzai's speech.

DIANE SAWYER INTERVIEWS MALALA YOUSAFZAI

About the Speaker

Malala Yousafzai (b. 1997) was born and raised in the Swat Valley of Pakistan. In 2007, the area was invaded by the Taliban, a radical Islamist group. When the Taliban outlawed education for girls, Yousafzai spoke out, becoming a highly visible advocate. For this reason, when she was just 15 years old, a member of the Taliban shot her in the head. Miraculously, she recovered. Since then, she has spoken publicly about universal education and gender equality. In 2014, she became the youngest person ever awarded the Nobel Peace Prize.

Speech at the United Nations

Concept Vocabulary

As you perform your first read, you will encounter these words.

beneficent	envoy	initiative

Familiar Word Parts Separating a word into its parts can often help you identify its meaning. Those parts might include base words, roots, or affixes.

Unfamiliar Word: *unidirectional*

Familiar Base Word: *direction*, meaning "point toward which something faces or moves"

Familiar Affixes: the prefix *uni-*, meaning "one"; the suffix *-al*, which forms adjectives

Conclusion: *Unidirectional* may mean "moving in only one direction, or toward only one point."

Apply your knowledge of familiar word parts and other vocabulary strategies to determine the meanings of unfamiliar words you encounter during your first read.

First Read NONFICTION

Apply these strategies as you conduct your first read. You will have an opportunity to complete a close read after your first read.

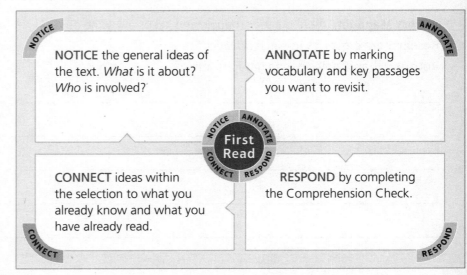

NOTICE the general ideas of the text. *What* is it about? *Who* is involved?

ANNOTATE by marking vocabulary and key passages you want to revisit.

First Read

CONNECT ideas within the selection to what you already know and what you have already read.

RESPOND by completing the Comprehension Check.

☷ STANDARDS

Reading
By the end of grade 10, read and comprehend literary nonfiction at the high end of the grades 9–10 text complexity band independently and proficiently.

Language
Identify and correctly use patterns of word changes that indicate different meanings or parts of speech.

Speech at the United Nations

Malala Yousafzai

BACKGROUND

The Taliban emerged following the defeat and withdrawal of Russian forces from Afghanistan in the early 1990s. The Taliban's mission is to restore its interpretation of strict Sharia, or Islamic, law, which calls for such things as banning music, covering the faces of women, and forbidding school for girls. By the time Malala Yousafzai was growing up in northern Pakistan, the Taliban were a major force in her area.

1   In the name of God, The Most **Beneficent**, The Most Merciful.

2   Honorable UN Secretary-General Mr. Ban Ki-moon,

3   Respected President of the General Assembly Vuk Jeremic,

4   Honorable UN **envoy** for Global education Mr. Gordon Brown,

5   Respected elders and my dear brothers and sisters;

6   Today, it is an honor for me to be speaking again after a long time. Being here with such honorable people is a great moment in my life.

NOTES

Mark familiar word parts or indicate another strategy you used that helped you determine meaning.

beneficent (buh NEHF uh suhnt) *adj.*

MEANING:

envoy (EHN voy) *n.*

MEANING:

NOTES

Mark familiar word parts or indicate another strategy you used that helped you determine meaning.

initiative (ih NIH shuh tihv) *n.*

MEANING:

7   I don't know where to begin my speech. I don't know what people would be expecting me to say. But first of all, thank you to God, for whom we all are equal, and thank you to every person who has prayed for my fast recovery and a new life. I cannot believe how much love people have shown me. I have received thousands of good-wish cards and gifts from all over the world. Thank you to all of them. Thank you to the children, whose innocent words encouraged me. Thank you to my elders, whose prayers strengthened me.

8   I would like to thank my nurses, doctors, and the staff of the hospitals in Pakistan and the UK, and the UAE government, who have helped me get better and recover my strength. I fully support Mr. Ban Ki-moon, the Secretary-General, in his Global Education First Initiative; and the work of the UN Special Envoy, Mr. Gordon Brown. And I thank them both for the leadership they continue to give. They continue to inspire all of us to action.

9   Dear brothers and sisters, do remember one thing: Malala Day is not my day. Today is the day of every woman, every boy, and every girl who have raised their voice for their rights. There are hundreds of human-rights activists and social workers who are not only speaking for their rights, but who are struggling to achieve their goals of peace, education, and equality. Thousands of people have been killed by the terrorists, and millions have been injured. I am just one of them.

10   So here I stand . . . one girl among many.

11   I speak—not for myself, but for all girls and boys.

12   I raise up my voice—not so that I can shout, but so that those without a voice can be heard.

13   Those who have fought for their rights:

   Their right to live in peace.
   Their right to be treated with dignity.
   Their right to equality of opportunity.
   Their right to be educated.

14   Dear friends, on the ninth of October 2012, the Taliban shot me on the left side of my forehead. They shot my friends, too. They thought that the bullets would silence us. But they failed. And then, out of that silence came thousands of voices. The terrorists thought that they would change my aims and stop my ambitions, but nothing changed in my life except this: Weakness, fear, and hopelessness died. Strength, power, and courage were born. I am the same Malala. My ambitions are the same. My hopes are the same. My dreams are the same.

15   Dear sisters and brothers, I am not against anyone. Neither am I here to speak in terms of personal revenge against the Taliban or any other terrorist group. I am here to speak up for the right of education of every child. I want education for the sons and daughters of the Taliban and all terrorists and extremists.

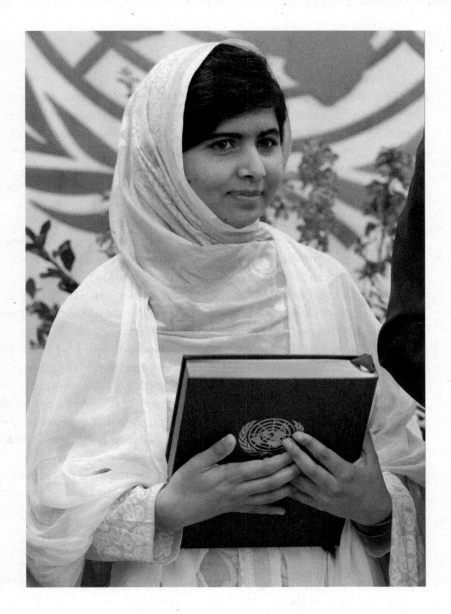

16   I do not even hate the Talib[1] who shot me. Even if there is a gun in my hand and he stands in front of me, I would not shoot him. This is the compassion that I have learned from Muhammad—the prophet of mercy—Jesus Christ, and Lord Buddha. This is the legacy of change that I have inherited from Martin Luther King, Nelson Mandela, and Muhammad Ali Jinnah.[2] This is the philosophy of nonviolence that I have learned from Gandhi Jee,[3] Bacha Khan,[4] and Mother Teresa.[5] And

1. **Talib** member of the Taliban.
2. **Muhammad Ali Jinnah** politician who fought for a Muslim state separate from India during the early twentieth century. He became the founder of this state, now known as Pakistan.
3. **Gandhi Jee** Mohandas "Mahatma" Gandhi, a religious leader who fought for India's independence from Great Britain during the early twentieth century.
4. **Bacha Khan** twentieth century leader of the Pashtuns, an ethnic group in Afghanistan and Pakistan, and a close friend and follower of Gandhi.
5. **Mother Teresa** Catholic nun who received the Nobel Peace Prize in 1979 for her work helping poor and sick people in India.

this is the forgiveness that I have learned from my father and mother. This is what my soul is telling me: Be peaceful, and love everyone.

17   Dear sisters and brothers, we realize the importance of light when we see darkness. We realize the importance of our voice when we are silenced. In the same way, when we were in Swat, the north of Pakistan, we realized the importance of pens and books when we saw the guns.

18   The wise saying "The pen is mightier than the sword" was true. The extremists were, and they are, afraid of books and pens. The power of education frightens them. They are afraid of women. The power of the voice of women frightens them. And that is why they killed 14 innocent students in the recent attack in Quetta.[6] And that is why they killed female teachers and polio workers in Khyber Pukhtoon Khwa[7] and FATA.[8] That is why they are blasting schools every day. Because they were, and they are, afraid of change, afraid of the equality, that we will bring into our society.

19   I remember that there was a boy in our school who was asked by a journalist, "Why are the Taliban against education?" He answered very simply. By pointing to his book, he said, "A Talib doesn't know what is written inside this book." They think that God is a tiny, little conservative being who would send girls to hell just because of going to school. The terrorists are misusing the name of Islam and Pashtun society for their own personal benefits. Pakistan is a peace-loving, democratic country. Pashtuns want education for their daughters and sons. And Islam is a religion of peace, humanity, and brotherhood. Islam says that it is not only each child's right to get education; rather, it is their duty and responsibility.

20   Honorable Secretary-General, peace is necessary for education. In many parts of the world, especially Pakistan and Afghanistan, terrorism, wars, and conflicts stop children to go to their schools. We are really tired of these wars. Women and children are suffering in many ways in many parts of the world. In India, innocent and poor children are victims of child labor. Many schools have been destroyed in Nigeria. People in Afghanistan have been affected by the hurdles of extremism for decades. Young girls have to do domestic child labor and are forced to get married at early age. Poverty, ignorance, injustice, racism, and the deprivation of basic rights are the main problems faced by both men and women.

21   Dear fellows, today I am focusing on women's rights and girls' education because they are suffering the most. There was a time

6. **Quetta** (KWEHT uh) city in Pakistan.
7. **Khyber Pukhtoon Khwa** (KY buhr PUHK toon KWAH) northernmost province in Pakistan.
8. **FATA** *abbr.* Federally Administered Tribal Areas, a semi-independent area of Pakistan.

when women social activists asked men to stand up for their rights. But this time, we will do it by ourselves. I am not telling men to step away from speaking for women's rights; rather, I am focusing on women to be independent to fight for themselves.

22   Dear sisters and brothers, now it's time to speak up.

23   So today, we call upon the world leaders to change their strategic policies in favor of peace and prosperity.

24   We call upon the world leaders that all the peace deals must protect women and children's rights. A deal that goes against the rights of women is unacceptable.

25   We call upon all governments to ensure free compulsory education all over the world for every child.

26   We call upon all governments to fight against terrorism and violence; to protect children from brutality and harm.

27   We call upon the developed nations to support the expansion of educational opportunities for girls in the developing world.

28   We call upon all communities to be tolerant; to reject prejudice based on caste, creed, sect, color, religion, or gender; to ensure freedom and equality for women so that they can flourish. We cannot all succeed when half of us are held back.

29   We call upon our sisters around the world to be brave; to embrace the strength within themselves and realize their full potential.

30   Dear brothers and sisters, we want schools and education for every child's bright future. We will continue our journey to our destination of peace and education. No one can stop us. We will speak up for our rights, and we will bring change through our voice. We believe in the power and the strength of our words. Our words can change the whole world.

31   Because we are all together, united for the cause of education. And if we want to achieve our goal, then let us empower ourselves with the weapon of knowledge, and let us shield ourselves with unity and togetherness.

32   Dear brothers and sisters, we must not forget that millions of people are suffering from poverty, injustice, and ignorance. We must not forget that millions of children are out of schools. We must not forget that our sisters and brothers are waiting for a bright peaceful future.

33   So let us wage a global struggle against illiteracy, poverty, and terrorism. Let us pick up our books and pens. They are our most powerful weapons.

34   One child, one teacher, one book, and one pen can change the world.

35   Education is the only solution. Education First.

36   Thank you. ❧

Comprehension Check

Complete the following items after you finish your first read. Review and clarify details with your group.

1. According to Yousafzai, whom does Malala Day honor?

2. What does Yousafzai believe the terrorists hope to accomplish through violence?

3. Cite three people Yousafzai names as role models.

4. According to Yousafzai, what basic condition is necessary for education?

5. 🗐 **Notebook** Confirm your understanding of the speech by stating at least two actions Yousafzai urges world leaders to take.

- -

RESEARCH

Research to Clarify Choose at least one unfamiliar detail from the text. Briefly research that detail. In what way does the information you learned shed light on an aspect of the speech?

Research to Explore Choose something that interested you from the text, and formulate a research question.

Close Read the Text

With your group, revisit sections of the text you marked during your first read. **Annotate** what you notice. What **questions** do you have? What can you **conclude**?

Analyze the Text

CITE TEXTUAL EVIDENCE to support your answers.

Notebook Complete the activities.

1. **Review and Clarify** With your group, reread paragraph 15 of the speech. Why do you think Yousafzai wants the sons and daughters of extremists to receive an education? Why might their education be particularly important? What does this idea suggest about the importance of education?

2. **Present and Discuss** Now, work with your group to share the passages from the text that you found especially important. Take turns presenting your passages. Discuss what you notice in the text, what questions you asked, and what conclusions you reached.

3. **Essential Question:** *What is the relationship between power and freedom?* What has this speech taught you about power and freedom? Discuss with your group.

LANGUAGE DEVELOPMENT

Concept Vocabulary

beneficent	envoy	initiative

Why These Words? The three concept vocabulary words are related. With your group, determine what the words have in common. Write your ideas, and add another word that fits the category.

WORD NETWORK

Add words related to power and freedom from the text to your Word Network.

Practice

With your group, conduct an informal discussion on an issue of your choice. During the conversation, challenge yourselves to include the concept vocabulary as normally as possible. Be sure you are using the words correctly.

Word Study

Latin Prefix: *bene-* The concept vocabulary word *beneficent* includes the Latin prefix *bene-*, meaning "well." Reread paragraph 19 of Yousafzai's speech. Mark the word that contains the prefix *bene-*, and write the word's meaning. With your group, identify other words that contain this prefix, and discuss their meanings.

STANDARDS
Language
Identify and correctly use patterns of word changes that indicate different meanings or parts of speech.

SPEECH AT THE UNITED NATIONS

☷ STANDARDS

Reading Informational Text
• Determine a central idea of a text and analyze its development over the course of the text, including how it emerges and is shaped and refined by specific details; provide an objective summary of the text.
• Determine an author's point of view or purpose in a text and analyze how an author uses rhetoric to advance that point of view or purpose.

Analyze Craft and Structure

Author's Purpose: Rhetorical Devices An **author's purpose** is his or her reason for speaking or writing. General purposes are *to inform, to entertain,* and *to persuade.* Speakers also have specific purposes that vary with the topic and audience. Most speeches delivered in the public arena, including this one by Yousafzai, are primarily persuasive. They may also provide information or entertain, but the speaker's main agenda is to convince listeners to think or do something specific. In order to advance that purpose, persuasive speakers employ a variety of different types of **evidence,** or supporting content. In this speech, Yousafzai uses anecdotes, proverbs, and examples.

- **Anecdote:** a brief story that illustrates a point
- **Proverb:** a pithy, clever saying that offers wisdom about life or communicates a belief or value
- **Example: a** specific instance of a general issue or idea

Speakers include different types of evidence to achieve particular effects. They may clarify a point, add emotional intensity, or serve another function.

Practice

CITE TEXTUAL EVIDENCE
to support your answers.

Work independently to complete the chart. Identify at least one example from Yousafzai's speech of each type of evidence noted. Explain how each example develops her key ideas, adds emotional intensity, or has another effect. Then, share and discuss your responses with your group.

TYPE OF EVIDENCE	PASSAGE(S) FROM THE SPEECH	EFFECT
Anecdote		
Proverb		
Example		

Conventions

Types of Clauses Writers and speakers, such as Yousafzai, use various types of clauses to clarify the relationships among ideas and to add variety to sentences. An **adverbial clause** is a type of clause that begins with a subordinating conjunction and functions as an adverb in a sentence. It tells *when*, *where*, *why*, *to what extent*, *in what way*, or *under what condition*. This box shows twenty common **subordinating conjunctions** that may begin adverbial clauses.

after	because	so that	when
although	before	than	whenever
as	even though	though	where
as if	if	unless	wherever
as long as	since	until	while

These sentences from Yousafzai's speech at the United Nations show examples of adverbial clauses and their functions.

SENTENCE	FUNCTION
I raise up my voice . . . <u>so that</u> <u>those without a voice can be heard</u>. (paragraph 12)	tells *why* she is raising up her voice
Dear sisters and brothers, we realize the importance of light <u>when we see darkness</u>. (paragraph 17)	tells *when* or *under what condition* we realize the importance of light

Read It

Working individually, read each of these sentences from Yousafzai's speech at the United Nations. Mark the adverbial clause in each sentence, identify the subordinating conjunction, and describe the clause's function in the sentence. Discuss your answers with your group.

1. In the same way, when we were in Swat, the north of Pakistan, we realized the importance of pens and books. . . .

2. Dear fellows, today I am focusing on women's rights and girls' education because they are suffering the most.

3. And if we want to achieve our goal, then let us empower ourselves with the weapon of knowledge. . . .

Write It

📝 **Notebook** Using what you've learned from Yousafzai's speech, write a paragraph that explains when a person should speak up for his or her rights and why doing so is important. Use at least three adverbial clauses in your paragraph.

TIP

CLARIFICATION
Recall that a **subordinate clause** is a group of words that includes a subject and a verb but cannot stand on its own as a complete sentence. Refer to the Grammar Handbook to learn more about this and other terms.

✏️ **EVIDENCE LOG**

Before moving on to a new selection, go to your Evidence Log and record what you learned from "Speech at the United Nations."

STANDARDS
Language
Use various types of phrases and clauses to convey specific meanings and add variety and interest to writing or presentations.

SPEECH AT THE UNITED NATIONS

Comparing Text to Media

In this part of the lesson, you will view Diane Sawyer's interview with Malala Yousafzai. As you watch the interview, think back to Yousafzai's United Nations speech. Consider ways in which the two texts connect with one another.

DIANE SAWYER INTERVIEWS MALALA YOUSAFZAI

About the Journalist

Diane Sawyer (b. 1945) began her career as a TV journalist on a local station in Kentucky. From there, Sawyer went on to the Nixon White House where she worked in the press office. In 1984, she joined CBS News and became the first woman correspondent for the highly acclaimed *60 Minutes*. Since then, Sawyer has assumed lead roles in a number of high-profile newscasts and special reports. Sawyer conducted her interview of Malala Yousafzai as the anchor for *ABC WorldNews*.

Diane Sawyer Interviews Malala Yousafzai

Media Vocabulary

The following words or concepts will be useful to you as you analyze, discuss, and write about newscasts.

Lead-In: in a newscast, the short preliminary section that is used to set up the main story or interview	• The purpose of the lead-in is to spark interest in the story that follows. • The lead-in usually provides important background information.
Close-Up Shot: close-range view of the subject	• Close-ups typically focus on a single face. • Close-ups are often used to show increasing emotion. • Close-ups may also focus on objects, such as the fine print on a sign.
Slant: attitude or opinion that a reporter takes toward a story	• A slant can be positive or negative, objective or subjective, critical or noncritical. • Typical slants a reporter may take: an analytical slant, a humorous slant, a skeptical slant.

First Review MEDIA: VIDEO

Apply these strategies as you conduct your first review. You will have an opportunity to complete a close review after your first review.

WATCH *who* speaks, *what* they say, and *how* they say it.

NOTE elements that you find interesting and want to revisit.

CONNECT ideas in the video to other media you've experienced, texts you've read, or images you've seen.

RESPOND by completing the Comprehension Check and by writing a brief summary of the selection.

First Review

Diane Sawyer Interviews
Malala Yousafzai

ABC News

BACKGROUND

After the United States invaded Afghanistan in 2001, the country of Pakistan allied itself with the United States in the battle against terrorism. The Pakistani government had denounced the Taliban, a terrorist group operating both within Pakistan and elsewhere. However, the Taliban continued to maintain control of a few Pakistani regions and provinces, including Malala Yousafzai's home of Swat Province. There, they imposed a strict interpretation of religious ideology, fought the Pakistani army, and planned attacks against Western nations.

NOTES

Comprehension Check

Complete the following items after you finish your first review. Review and clarify details with your group.

1. What publication coincides with the airing of this interview?

2. As a young child, how did Yousafzai begin to publicize her ideas for a larger audience?

3. According to Yousafzai, what is more powerful than guns?

4. Before her attack, how did Yousafzai imagine she might speak to an attacker?

5. 📓 **Notebook** Confirm your understanding of the interview by writing a summary of it.

- -

RESEARCH

Research to Clarify Choose at least one unfamiliar detail from the interview. Briefly research that detail. In what way does the information you learned shed light on an aspect of Yousafzai's story?

Research to Explore Choose something that interested you from the interview, and formulate a research question.

Close Review

Watch the interview again. Write any new observations that seem important. What **questions** do you have? What can you **conclude**?

DIANE SAWYER INTERVIEWS MALALA YOUSAFZAI

Analyze the Media

Complete the activities.

1. **Present and Discuss** Identify the comment from Yousafzai you found most powerful. Share your choice with your group, and explain why you chose it. Explain why you found the comment powerful, and share any questions it raised for you. Discuss the conclusions you reached about it.

2. **Review and Synthesize** With your group, listen again to the retelling of Yousafzai's shooting. Note details Yousafzai provides, as well as those Diane Sawyer adds. How would you describe Yousafzai's character, based on her actions that day? Discuss.

3. 📓 **Notebook** **Essential Question:** *What is the relationship between power and freedom?* What does Yousafzai's experience suggest about an individual's power to secure freedom for herself and others? Support your response with evidence from the interview.

LANGUAGE DEVELOPMENT

Media Vocabulary

lead-in	close-up	slant

Use the vocabulary words in your responses to the questions.

1. How does the introduction to the interview engage viewers' attention?

2. What camera techniques help viewers understand the mood on the day of Yousafzai's shooting? Explain.

3. How would you describe Sawyer's approach to the interview? Explain.

🔗 **WORD NETWORK**

Add words related to power and freedom from the text to your Word Network.

📑 **STANDARDS**

Reading Informational Text
Cite strong and thorough textual evidence to support analysis of what the text says explicitly as well as inferences drawn from the text.

Language
Acquire and use accurately general academic and domain-specific words and phrases, sufficient for reading, writing, speaking, and listening at the college and career readiness level; demonstrate independence in gathering vocabulary knowledge when considering a word or phrase important to comprehension or expression.

SPEECH AT THE UNITED NATIONS

DIANE SAWYER INTERVIEWS
MALALA YOUSAFZAI

Writing to Compare

You have read Malala Yousafzai's speech at the United Nations and watched her interview with Diane Sawyer. Both texts recount the young woman's experience and convey her undaunted passion for education.

Assignment

Write an **explanatory essay** in which you discuss why Yousafzai has been able to attract supporters from all over the world. What makes her message and her story so compelling? Consider which details are emphasized in the speech and the interview, as well as the effect these details have on your understanding of Yousafzai, her experience, and her activism. Cite evidence from both texts in your essay.

Planning and Prewriting

Analyze the Texts Reread the speech, and—with your group—watch the interview again. Look for mirror details, or those that are very similar in the speech and the interview. Consider how these details are presented in the two texts. Also, look for details that appear in only one text or the other. Collect your observations in the chart.

BOTH TEXTS	JUST THE INTERVIEW	JUST THE SPEECH

Notebook Answer these questions.

1. How do both texts depict Yousafzai's character, the conditions under which she lived in Pakistan, and her development as an activist?

2. **(a)** Which facts or other information appear in both the speech and the interview but are presented differently? **(b)** How do you account for those differences? Consider the medium of each text—one a written text, and one a work of broadcast journalism.

≡ STANDARDS

Reading Informational Text
Analyze various accounts of a subject told in different mediums, determining which details are emphasized in each account.

Writing
• Write informative/explanatory texts to examine and convey complex ideas, concepts, and information clearly and accurately through the effective selection, organization, and analysis of content.
• Apply *grades 9–10 Reading standards* to literary nonfiction.

Drafting

Write a Thesis Work on your own to plan and write your essay. First, review the notes you took with your group. Organize observations into logical categories. For example, you might group one set of details related to facts, another set related to emotional impact, and another set related to the way information can be presented in a written text versus a broadcast. Then, use the sentence starter to write a working thesis.

> **Working Thesis:** As both her speech at the United Nations and her interview with Diane Sawyer demonstrate, Malala Yousafzai is a compelling figure because _____
> _____
> _____.

Provide Varied Details Include supporting evidence for every point you make. Try to use different types of evidence to make your essay more interesting.

- **Exact quotations** can illustrate a speaker's attitude.
- **Examples** can help readers visualize a reporter's actions or an interviewee's responses.
- **Paraphrases,** or restatements using your own words, can help clarify others' ideas.

Establish a Structure Follow this guide to plan the order in which you will present your ideas and evidence.

Introduction	Body	Conclusion
• Grab readers' attention • Briefly summarize Yousafzai's story • State thesis	• Present supporting ideas • Use a new paragraph for each idea • Use supporting details	• End in a strong, memorable way • Restate thesis

Review, Revise, and Edit

Share your writing with your group, and review one another's work. Ask for feedback about the clarity of your organization and the strength of your supporting details. Use the feedback to improve any elements that are unclear or ineffective. Then, check your essay for spelling or grammatical errors, and make any necessary fixes.

📝 EVIDENCE LOG

Before moving on to a new selection, go to the Evidence Log and record what you've learned from Malala Yousafzai's speech at the United Nations and "Diane Sawyer Interviews Malala Yousafzai."

POETRY COLLECTION

Caged Bird
Some Advice to Those Who Will Serve Time in Prison

Concept Vocabulary

As you perform your first read of these poems, you will encounter the following words.

current	trill	flurry

Context Clues If these words are unfamiliar, try using **context clues**— other words and phrases that appear nearby in the text—to help you determine their meanings. There are various types of context clues that you may find useful as you read.

> **Synonyms:** Sadly, Tim concluded that his laptop computer was **obsolete**, rendered outdated by new advances in technology.
>
> **Restatement of Ideas:** Sara's facial expression was **enigmatic**, so no one could tell for sure what she was thinking.
>
> **Contrast of Ideas:** Though usually quite **prudent**, they threw caution to the wind and jumped into the pounding surf.

Apply your knowledge of context clues and other vocabulary strategies to determine the meanings of unfamiliar words you encounter during your first read.

First Read POETRY

Apply these strategies as you conduct your first read. You will have an opportunity to complete a close read after your first read.

NOTICE *who* or *what* is "speaking" the poem and whether the poem tells a story or describes a single moment.

ANNOTATE by marking vocabulary and key passages you want to revisit.

CONNECT ideas within the selection to what you already know and what you have already read.

RESPOND by completing the Comprehension Check.

STANDARDS

Reading Literature
• By the end of grade 10, read and comprehend literature, including stories, dramas, and poems, at the high end of the grades 9–10 text complexity band independently and proficiently.

Language
• Determine or clarify the meaning of unknown and multiple-meaning words and phrases based on *grades 9–10 reading and content*, choosing flexibly from a range of strategies.
• Use context as a clue to the meaning of a word or phrase.

About the Poets

Maya Angelou (1928–2014) was born in St. Louis, Missouri, and raised in a rural, segregated section of Arkansas. Growing up, she faced racial discrimination, but she also learned strong values. As a single mother, she worked a wide array of jobs to support her family before discovering her talent as a writer. Angelou raised her voice during the Civil Rights movement, speaking out for racial and gender equality. She received numerous awards for her work, including more than fifty honorary doctorates and the 2011 Presidential Medal of Freedom.

Nazim Hikmet (1902–1963) was raised in Istanbul, Turkey, but attended university in Moscow, Russia. He returned to Turkey after completing his studies and was jailed by the anti-Communist government, which objected to Hikmet's writing in support of leftist causes. Although Hikmet resisted, the regime's harshness forced him to eventually leave Turkey forever. Hikmet's writing was censored during his lifetime, but his poetry and other writings became widely available after his death. Today, Hikmet is regarded as one of the greatest international poets of the twentieth century.

Backgrounds

Caged Bird

This poem joins a number of others by important African American poets in which a caged or injured bird is a central image. For example, in Paul Laurence Dunbar's poem "Sympathy," the speaker says, "I know what the caged bird feels," and "I know why the caged bird sings." Likewise, in Langston Hughes's poem "Dreams," life becomes a "broken-winged bird / that cannot fly."

Some Advice to Those Who Will Serve Time in Prison

This poem is informed by Nazim Hikmet's personal experiences. Repeatedly arrested for his political beliefs and writings, Hikmet spent most of his life either in prison or in exile from Turkey, his home country.

Caged Bird

Maya Angelou

A free bird leaps
on the back of the wind
and floats downstream
till the current ends
5 and dips his wing
in the orange sun rays
and dares to claim the sky.

But a bird that stalks
down his narrow cage
10 can seldom see through
his bars of rage
his wings are clipped and
his feet are tied
so he opens his throat to sing.

15 The caged bird sings
with a fearful trill
of things unknown
but longed for still
and his tune is heard
20 on the distant hill
for the caged bird
sings of freedom.

The free bird thinks of another breeze
and the trade winds soft through the sighing trees
25 and the fat worms waiting on a dawn bright lawn
and he names the sky his own

But a caged bird stands on the grave of dreams
his shadow shouts on a nightmare scream
his wings are clipped and his feet are tied
30 so he opens his throat to sing.

The caged bird sings
with a fearful trill
of things unknown
but longed for still
35 and his tune is heard
on the distant hill
for the caged bird
sings of freedom.

NOTES

Mark context clues or indicate another strategy you used that helped you determine meaning.

current (KUR uhnt) *n.*
MEANING:

trill (trihl) *n.*
MEANING:

Some Advice
to Those Who Will
Serve Time in Prison

Nazim Hikmet

translated by
Randy Blasing and Mutlu Konuk

NOTES

If instead of being hanged by the neck
    you're thrown inside
    for not giving up hope
in the world, your country, and people,
5   if you do ten or fifteen years
    apart from the time you have left,
you won't say,
    "Better I had swung from the end of a rope
        like a flag"—

10 you'll put your foot down and live.
It may not be a pleasure exactly,
but it's your solemn duty
      to live one more day
            to spite the enemy.
15 Part of you may live alone inside,
            like a stone at the bottom of a well.
But the other part
      must be so caught up
      in the flurry of the world
20   that you shiver there inside
      when outside, at forty days' distance, a leaf moves.
To wait for letters inside,
to sing sad songs,
or to lie awake all night staring at the ceiling
25   is sweet but dangerous.
Look at your face from shave to shave,
forget your age,
watch out for lice
                  and for spring nights,
30   and always remember
            to eat every last piece of bread—
also, don't forget to laugh heartily.
And who knows,
the woman you love may stop loving you.
35 Don't say it's no big thing:
it's like the snapping of a green branch
                              to the man inside.
To think of roses and gardens inside is bad,
to think of seas and mountains is good.
40 Read and write without rest,
and I also advise weaving
and making mirrors.
I mean, it's not that you can't pass
            ten or fifteen years inside
45   and more—
            you can,
            as long as the jewel
            on the left side of your chest doesn't lose its luster!

NOTES

Mark context clues or indicate another strategy you used that helped you determine meaning.

flurry (FLUR ee) *n.*

MEANING:

Comprehension Check

Complete the following items after you finish your first read. Review and clarify details with your group.

CAGED BIRD

1. According to the speaker, what are three things the free bird does?

2. What has been done to the caged bird's wings and feet?

3. What is the subject of the caged bird's song?

4. How does the free bird regard the sky?

5. Where is the caged bird's song heard?

1. According to the speaker, for what reasons might someone be imprisoned, or "thrown inside"?

2. According to the speaker, what is the prisoner's "solemn duty"?

3. How does the speaker say the prisoner should be affected by the movement of a leaf at forty days' distance?

4. According to the speaker, what kinds of scenes are "bad" and what kinds are "good" for prisoners to imagine?

5. According to the speaker, of what must the prisoner make sure in order to "pass ten or fifteen years inside"?

- -

RESEARCH

Research to Clarify Choose at least one unfamiliar detail from one of the poems. Briefly research that detail. In what way does the information you learned shed light on an aspect of the poem?

Research to Explore Locate another poem by one of the poets, or research his or her life in greater detail. Share what you find with your group.

POETRY COLLECTION

GROUP DISCUSSION

There are many different kinds of cages or prisons—physical ones, emotional ones, intellectual ones. As you discuss the poems with your group, consider whether their meanings change when you view them in the context of various types of cages or prisons.

WORD NETWORK

Add words related to power and freedom from the texts to your Word Network.

Close Read the Text

With your group, revisit sections of the poems you marked during your first read. **Annotate** details that you notice. What **questions** do you have? What can you **conclude**?

Analyze the Text

CITE TEXTUAL EVIDENCE
to support your answers.

📓 **Notebook** Complete the activities.

1. **Review and Clarify** Reread the second stanza of "Caged Bird." What feelings does the caged bird experience? What does this suggest about the song the caged bird sings?

2. **Present and Discuss** Now, work with your group to share the passages from the texts that you found especially important. Take turns presenting your passages. Discuss what you noticed in the texts, what questions you asked, and what conclusions you reached.

3. **Essential Question:** *What is the relationship between power and freedom?* What have these poems taught you about the connection between power and freedom? Discuss with your group.

LANGUAGE DEVELOPMENT

Concept Vocabulary

current	trill	flurry

Why These Words? The three concept vocabulary words are related. With your group, determine what the words have in common. Write your ideas, and add another word that fits the category.

Practice

📓 **Notebook** Confirm your understanding of the concept words by using them in sentences. Include context clues that hint at each word's meaning.

Word Study

📓 **Notebook** **Multiple-Meaning Words** Many English words have multiple meanings, or more than one distinct definition. For instance, the concept vocabulary word *current* can be a noun, as it is in "Caged Bird," but it can also be an adjective meaning "up-to-date."

Identify two meanings for each of the following words: *grave, well, weaving, care, chain*. First, determine the word's meaning in either "Caged Bird" or "Some Advice to Those Who Will Serve Time in Prison." Then, determine another meaning of the word, consulting a dictionary as needed. Record both meanings for each word.

Analyze Craft and Structure

Author's Choices: Figurative Language Language that is used imaginatively rather than literally is referred to as **figurative language**. Poets rely on figurative language because it helps them express ideas in vivid ways and invest even small details with meaning. Simile, metaphor, and extended metaphor are three commonly used types of figurative language.

- A **simile** is a direct comparison, using the words *like* or *as,* that shows similarities between two seemingly unlike things: "life is too much like a pathless wood" (from "Birches," by Robert Frost).

- A **metaphor** is a comparison of two seemingly unlike things that does not use an explicit comparison word: "The sun and the moon are eternal voyagers" (from "Narrow Road of the Interior," by Bashō).

- An **extended metaphor** involves a metaphorical comparison that does not end after a single line or image, but continues for several lines or throughout an entire work.

Practice

CITE TEXTUAL EVIDENCE to support your answers.

1. Working individually, use this chart to identify and analyze three similes and one metaphor that appear in Nazim Hikmet's poem. Compare and discuss your responses with your group.

EXAMPLE	THINGS COMPARED	MEANING AND EFFECT
Simile:		
Simile:		
Simile:		
Metaphor:		

2. ⊟ **Notebook** Explain how Maya Angelou's "Caged Bird" can be read as an extended metaphor. What implied comparison is the poet making between the free bird, the caged bird, and people or ideas in the real world?

POETRY COLLECTION

Author's Style

Specific Details An **image** is a word or phrase that appeals to one or more of the senses—sight, hearing, touch, taste, or smell. We often refer to multiple images or patterns of images as **imagery**. Poets use images to create word pictures in readers' minds. Imagery enriches meaning, suggests emotions, and adds vividness to a text.

> **Image appealing to taste and touch:** "sweet, slippery mango slices"
> **Image appealing to sight and hearing:** "glaring lights and wailing sirens"

Read It

Work individually. Use this chart to identify images in each poem. Then, explain how each image helps create meaning. Discuss your responses with your group.

CAGED BIRD	SOME ADVICE TO THOSE WHO WILL SERVE TIME IN PRISON
Images:	Images:
Meaning:	Meaning:

Write It

🔵 **Notebook** Write a paragraph that includes at least three images.

Writing to Sources

Assignment

Working individually, write an original **poem** based on one of the poems in this collection. Choose from the following prompts:

☐ Using "Caged Bird" as a model, write a poem on the theme of freedom/imprisonment that develops a different extended metaphor.

☐ Imagine that the speaker of "Some Advice to Those Who Will Serve Time in Prison" is set free after many years of unjust imprisonment. Using the poem as a model, write another poem of advice from the speaker's point of view about a first day of freedom.

☐ Choose an image in one of the poems that you thought was particularly powerful. Use this image as a starting point for your own poem about freedom, imprisonment, or both.

Project Plan As a group, decide whether you will all work on the same prompt or will each choose the one you prefer. Then, work together to help one another brainstorm for ideas or clarify your thoughts.

Identifying Models As you plan your poem, go back to the poem you chose as inspiration, and identify elements you like or find effective. For example, notice how the poet uses repetition or rhyme, and think about how you can incorporate those elements into your work. Use this chart to record examples of elements you would like to use and how you might do so.

✐ EVIDENCE LOG

Before moving on to a new selection, go to your Evidence Log and record what you learned from "Caged Bird" and "Some Advice to Those Who Will Serve Time in Prison."

ELEMENT TO INCLUDE IN POEM	EXAMPLE FROM TEXT	NOTES

About the Author

Luisa Valenzuela (b. 1938) was born in Buenos Aires, Argentina. She first pursued a career as a painter, but she soon discovered her true calling as a writer. Like many contemporary Latin American writers, Valenzuela takes an experimental approach to literary style and language. She believes that writers derive their power and influence from the way they use and define words. Influenced by the political turmoil in Argentina, Valenzuela examines the repression of speech and identity in much of her fiction.

The Censors

Concept Vocabulary

As you perform your first read of "The Censors," you will encounter the following words.

> sabotage   intercept   subversive

Context Clues If these words are unfamiliar, try using **context clues**—other words and phrases that appear nearby in the text—to help you determine their meanings. There are various types of context clues that you may find useful as you read.

> **Synonyms:** The newspaper editor **incited** the rebellion, stirring up the government's opponents.
>
> **Restatement of Ideas:** Periodically, Sam grew **nostalgic**, as he yearned to see his homeland once more.
>
> **Contrast of Ideas:** Abandoning her customary **nonchalance**, Sofia felt anxious and tense that afternoon.

Apply your knowledge of context clues and other vocabulary strategies to determine the meanings of unfamiliar words you encounter during your first read. Use a resource such as a dictionary or a thesaurus to verify the meanings you identify.

First Read FICTION

Apply these strategies as you conduct your first read. You will have an opportunity to complete a close read after your first read.

NOTICE *whom* the story is about, *what* happens, *where* and *when* it happens, and *why* those involved react as they do.

ANNOTATE by marking vocabulary and key passages you want to revisit.

CONNECT ideas within the selection to what you know and what you have already read.

RESPOND by completing the Comprehension Check and by writing a brief summary of the selection.

▤ STANDARDS

Reading Literature
By the end of grade 10, read and comprehend literature, including stories, dramas, and poems, at the high end of the grades 9–10 text complexity band independently and proficiently.

Language
• Use context as a clue to the meaning of a word or phrase.
• Verify the preliminary determination of the meaning of a word or phrase.

The Censors

Luisa Valenzuela
translated by David Unger

BACKGROUND
Like many other Latin American writers, Luisa Valenzuela often addresses political issues in her fiction. Her native country, Argentina, now a democracy, has had a troubled history of censorship and extreme human-rights violations. In the 1970s, a military regime took power, brutally hunted down suspected political foes, and censored news and mail. In "The Censors," Valenzuela explores the absurd aspects of life under such oppression.

NOTES

1   Poor Juan! One day they caught him with his guard down before he could even realize that what he had taken as a stroke of luck was really one of fate's dirty tricks. These things happen the minute you're careless, as one often is. Juancito let happiness—a feeling you can't trust—get the better of him when he received from a confidential source Mariana's new address in Paris and knew that she hadn't forgotten him. Without thinking twice, he sat down at his table and wrote her a letter. *The* letter that now keeps his mind off his job during the day and won't let him sleep at night (what had he scrawled, what had he put on that sheet of paper he sent to Mariana?).

2   Juan knows there won't be a problem with the letter's contents, that it's irreproachable, harmless. But what about the rest? He knows that they examine, sniff, feel, and read between the lines of each and every letter, and check its tiniest comma and most accidental stain. He knows that all letters pass from hand to hand and go through all sorts of tests in the huge censorship offices and that, in the end, very few continue on their way. Usually it takes months, even years, if there aren't any snags; all this time the freedom, maybe even the life, of both sender and receiver is in jeopardy. And that's why Juan's so troubled: thinking that something might happen to Mariana because of his letters. Of all people, Mariana, who must finally feel safe there where she always dreamt she'd live. But he knows that the *Censor's Secret Command* operates all over the world and cashes in on the discount in airfares; there's nothing to stop them from going as far as

sabotage (SAB uh tozh) *v.*

MEANING:

intercept (ihn tuhr SEHPT) *v.*

MEANING:

that hidden Paris neighborhood, kidnapping Mariana, and returning to their cozy homes, certain of having fulfilled their noble mission.

3   Well, you've got to beat them to the punch, do what everyone tries to do: **sabotage** the machinery, throw sand in its gears, get to the bottom of the problem so as to stop it.

4   This was Juan's sound plan when he, like many others, applied for a censor's job—not because he had a calling or needed a job: no, he applied simply to **intercept** his own letter, a consoling albeit unoriginal idea. He was hired immediately, for each day more and more censors are needed and no one would bother to check on his references.

5   Ulterior motives couldn't be overlooked by the *Censorship Division*, but they needn't be too strict with those who applied. They knew how hard it would be for the poor guys to find the letter they wanted and even if they did, what's a letter or two when the new censor would snap up so many others? That's how Juan managed to join the *Post Office's Censorship Division*, with a certain goal in mind.

6   The building had a festive air on the outside that contrasted with its inner staidness. Little by little, Juan was absorbed by his job, and he felt at peace since he was doing everything he could to get his letter for Mariana. He didn't even worry when, in his first month, he was sent to *Section K* where envelopes are very carefully screened for explosives.

7   It's true that on the third day, a fellow worker had his right hand blown off by a letter, but the division chief claimed it was sheer negligence on the victim's part. Juan and the other employees were allowed to go back to their work, though feeling less secure. After work, one of them tried to organize a strike to demand higher wages for unhealthy work, but Juan didn't join in; after thinking it over, he reported the man to his superiors and thus got promoted.

8   You don't form a habit by doing something once, he told himself as he left his boss's office. And when he was transferred to *Section F*, where letters are carefully checked for poison dust, he felt he had climbed a rung in the ladder.

9   By working hard, he quickly reached *Section E* where the job became more interesting, for he could now read and analyze the letters' contents. Here he could even hope to get hold of his letter, which, judging by the time that had elapsed, had gone through the other sections and was probably floating around in this one.

subversive (suhb VUR sihv) *adj.*

MEANING:

10   Soon his work became so absorbing that his noble mission blurred in his mind. Day after day he crossed out whole paragraphs in red ink, pitilessly chucking many letters into the censored basket. These were horrible days when he was shocked by the subtle and conniving ways employed by people to pass on **subversive** messages; his instincts were so sharp that he found behind a simple "the weather's unsettled" or "prices continue to soar" the wavering hand of someone secretly scheming to overthrow the Government.

11   His zeal brought him swift promotion. We don't know if this made him happy. Very few letters reached him in *Section B*—only a handful passed the other hurdles—so he read them over and over again,

passed them under a magnifying glass, searched for microprint with an electronic microscope, and tuned his sense of smell so that he was beat by the time he made it home. He'd barely manage to warm up his soup, eat some fruit, and fall into bed, satisfied with having done his duty. Only his darling mother worried, but she couldn't get him back on the right track. She'd say, though it wasn't always true: Lola called, she's at the bar with the girls, they miss you, they're waiting for you. Or else she'd leave a bottle of red wine on the table. But Juan wouldn't overdo it: any distraction could make him lose his edge and the perfect censor had to be alert, keen, attentive, and sharp to nab cheats. He had a truly patriotic task, both self-denying and uplifting.

12   His basket for censored letters became the best fed as well as the most cunning basket in the whole *Censorship Division*. He was about to congratulate himself for having finally discovered his true mission, when his letter to Mariana reached his hands. Naturally, he censored it without regret. And just as naturally, he couldn't stop them from executing him the following morning, another victim of his devotion to his work. ❧

Comprehension Check

Complete the following items after you finish your first read. Review and clarify details with your group.

1. Why does Juan take a job as a censor?

2. Why is the Censorship Division not particularly careful about whom it hires?

3. What is the result of Juan's enthusiasm on the job?

4. What does Juan do when he finds his letter to Mariana?

5. 🗐 **Notebook** Confirm your understanding of the story by writing a summary.

- -

RESEARCH

Research to Clarify Choose at least one unfamiliar detail from the text. Briefly research that detail. In what way does the information you learned shed light on an aspect of the story?

THE CENSORS

TIP

GROUP DISCUSSION
Keep in mind that the narrator plays an important role in this short story. Consider how the narration affects your understanding of the story as you analyze and discuss the text.

⊹ WORD NETWORK

Add words related to power and freedom from the text to your Word Network.

⊞ STANDARDS

Reading Literature
• Determine the meaning of words and phrases as they are used in the text, including figurative and connotative meanings; analyze the cumulative impact of specific word choices on meaning and tone.
• Analyze a particular point of view or cultural experience reflected in a work of literature from outside the United States, drawing on a wide reading of world literature.

Language
• Identify and correctly use patterns of word changes that indicate different meanings or parts of speech.
• Verify the preliminary determination of the meaning of a word or phrase.

Close Read the Text

With your group, revisit sections of the text you marked during your first read. **Annotate** what you notice. What **questions** do you have? What can you **conclude**?

Analyze the Text

CITE TEXTUAL EVIDENCE
to support your answers.

📄 **Notebook** Complete the activities.

1. **Review and Clarify** Reread the first two paragraphs of "The Censors" carefully. What emotion leads Juan to write and send Mariana a letter? How does he feel after he has sent the letter? Why do his feelings change? What does this communicate about the society in which he lives?

2. **Present and Discuss** Now, work with your group to share the passages from the text that you found especially important. Take turns presenting your passages. Discuss what you notice in the text, what questions you asked, and what conclusions you reached.

3. **Essential Question:** *What is the relationship between power and freedom?* What has this story taught you about the nature of freedom and power in an oppressive society? Discuss with your group.

LANGUAGE DEVELOPMENT

Concept Vocabulary

| sabotage | intercept | subversive |

Why These Words? The three concept vocabulary words are related. With your group, determine what the words have in common. Write your ideas, and add another word that fits the category.

Practice

📄 **Notebook** Confirm your understanding of these words by using them in sentences. Include context clues that hint at each word's meaning.

Word Study

📄 **Notebook Latin Prefix: *sub-*** The concept vocabulary word *subversive* begins with the Latin prefix *sub-*, meaning "under," "below," or "from beneath."

Use your understanding of the prefix *sub-* to determine the meaning of each of the following words: *submissive, subculture, subterranean*. After you have recorded a meaning for each word, use a dictionary to confirm or correct your definitions.

Analyze Craft and Structure

Author's Choices: Satire A **satire** is a work that ridicules individuals, ideas, institutions, social conventions, or humanity in general. While satire may be funny, its purpose is serious—to improve society by exposing absurdity, corruption, or other social ills. Because of this serious purpose, satire is a vehicle for **social commentary,** or writing that criticizes institutions or behaviors.

Satiric writings vary in **tone,** or attitude toward the subject and reader. Some satire is bitter and cynical, whereas other satire is gentle and funny. A writer establishes tone through word choice, details, and even grammatical structures.

Practice

CITE TEXTUAL EVIDENCE
to support your answers.

Work independently to complete the following items. Then, share your responses with your group, and discuss any differences in your ideas.

1. What tone is created by the narrator's use of expressions such as "beat them to the punch" and "throw sand in its gears"? Explain.

2. Use the chart to identify three other examples of diction (or word choice) that contribute to the narrator's tone. Explain the tone each example helps create.

PASSAGE	TONE IT CREATES

3. Briefly describe the social ills that are the target of the satire in this story.

4. 📓 **Notebook** **(a)** How does the tone of this story contrast with the seriousness of its subject? Explain. **(b)** In what ways does the tone of the story add to the satire? Explain.

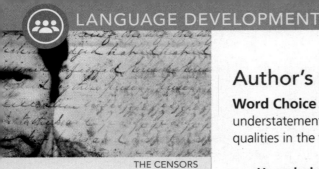

THE CENSORS

Author's Style

Word Choice Many satiric works use the literary devices of hyperbole and understatement to add humor. These devices also help emphasize specific qualities in the target of the satire.

- **Hyperbole** is a deliberate exaggeration or overstatement, often to emphasize emotion or to create a comic effect. For example, calling the discovery of a missing sock a "joyous reunion" is an example of hyperbole.

- **Understatement** is the opposite of hyperbole. It is the deliberate minimizing of the seriousness or gravity of an event or idea. Mark Twain is famous for this understated comment: "The reports of my death are greatly exaggerated."

Read It

Work individually. Use the chart to record examples of hyperbole and understatement in "The Censors." Then, explain how these elements help create humor and add to the satire of the story. Discuss your responses with your group.

HYPERBOLE	UNDERSTATEMENT
Examples:	Examples:
Effects:	Effects:

STANDARDS

Reading Literature
Determine the meaning of words and phrases as they are used in the text, including figurative and connotative meanings; analyze the cumulative impact of specific word choices on meaning and tone.

Speaking and Listening
Initiate and participate effectively in a range of collaborative discussions with diverse partners on *grades 9–10 topics, texts, and issues*, building on others' ideas and expressing their own clearly and persuasively.

Language
Interpret figures of speech in context and analyze their role in the text.

Write It

📓 **Notebook** Write a brief, humorous invitation to an event such as a birthday party or a school dance. Include at least one example of hyperbole and one example of understatement.

Speaking and Listening

Assignment

Conduct a **small-group discussion** about one of the following topics. Then, summarize the main points of the discussion, and share your ideas with the class.

- [ ] How would your life be different if mail and other forms of communication—such as text messages and emails—were censored? Connect your sense of privacy to Juan's experiences in the story.

- [ ] How might various characters in the story describe Juan? Consider what Mariana, Juan's mother, and his coworkers at the Censorship Bureau might say about him.

- [ ] Discuss the evolution of Juan's work ethic and his feelings about his job at the Censorship Bureau. Why does he become so dedicated to his job?

Discussing Juan's Character If your group chooses to discuss how other characters view Juan, use the chart to record your notes.

CHARACTER	VIEW OF JUAN
Mariana	
Juan's Mother	
Juan's Coworkers	

📝 EVIDENCE LOG

Before moving on to a new selection, go to your Evidence Log and record what you learned from "The Censors."

About the Organization

Freedom House is an independent, nonprofit organization dedicated to the expansion of freedom around the world. The organization was established in 1941 in response to the Nazi threat then growing throughout Europe. In the decades following the war, Freedom House has sought to fight oppressive ideologies through the spread of democracy, the strengthening of human rights, and the expansion of civil liberties for all. The organization publishes a number of significant documents each year, including the *Freedom of the Press* report.

from Freedom of the Press Report 2015

Media Vocabulary

The following words or concepts will be useful to you as you analyze, discuss, and write about informational graphics.

Infographic: display that combines text with visual elements and design to represent data	• The word *infographic* is short for *informational graphic*. • An infographic allows the user to see trends and make comparisons at a glance.
Bar Graph: representation of data points using rectangular bars	• Bar graphs can be organized vertically or horizontally. • Bar graphs can compare two or more data points in the same segment by clustering bars of different colors.
Line Graph: representation of data points using a line that connects points	• Line graphs are especially useful for showing how data changes over time. • Line graphs can compare two (or more) sets of data with two (or more) lines.
Pie Chart: representation of data points using a circle cut into segments	• Pie charts are especially useful for showing how the size of each data point compares to the total size of all the data. • Typically, each segment is a different color.

First Read

Apply these strategies as you conduct your first read. You will have an opportunity to complete a close read after your first read.

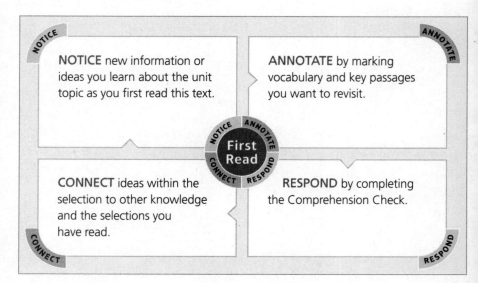

NOTICE new information or ideas you learn about the unit topic as you first read this text.

ANNOTATE by marking vocabulary and key passages you want to revisit.

First Read

CONNECT ideas within the selection to other knowledge and the selections you have read.

RESPOND by completing the Comprehension Check.

STANDARDS

Reading Informational Text
By the end of grade 10, read and comprehend literary nonfiction at the high end of the grades 9–10 text complexity band independently and proficiently.

Language
Acquire and use accurately general academic and domain-specific words and phrases, sufficient for reading, writing, speaking, and listening at the college and career readiness level; demonstrate independence in gathering vocabulary knowledge when considering a word or phrase important to comprehension or expression.

from Freedom of the Press Report 2015

Freedom House

BACKGROUND

From the introduction to the *Freedom of the Press Report* 2015: "Conditions for the media deteriorated sharply in 2014 as journalists around the world faced mounting restrictions on the free flow of news and information—including grave threats to their own lives. Governments employed tactics including arrests and censorship to silence criticism. Terrorists and other nonstate forces kidnapped and murdered journalists attempting to cover armed conflicts and organized crime. . . . The share of the world's population that enjoys a free press stood at 14 percent, meaning only one in seven people live in countries where coverage of political news is robust, the safety of journalists is guaranteed, state intrusion in media affairs is minimal, and the press is not subject to onerous legal or economic pressures."

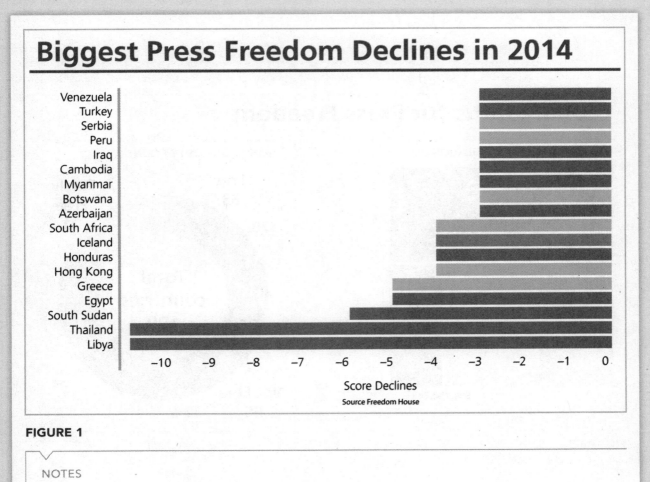

Biggest Press Freedom Declines in 2014

Score Declines

Source Freedom House

FIGURE 1

NOTES

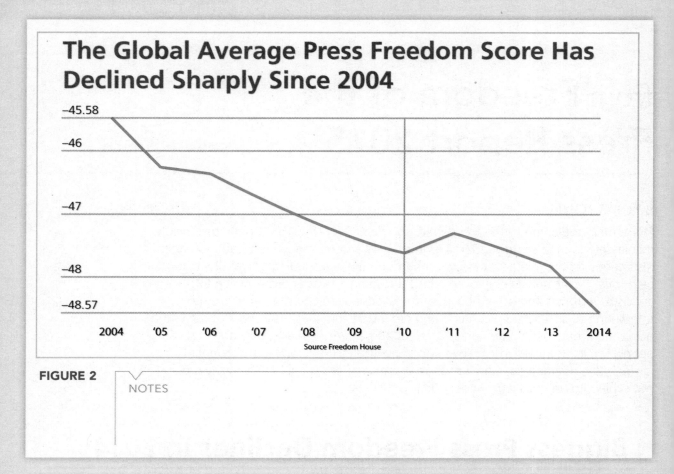

The Global Average Press Freedom Score Has Declined Sharply Since 2004

Source Freedom House

FIGURE 2

NOTES

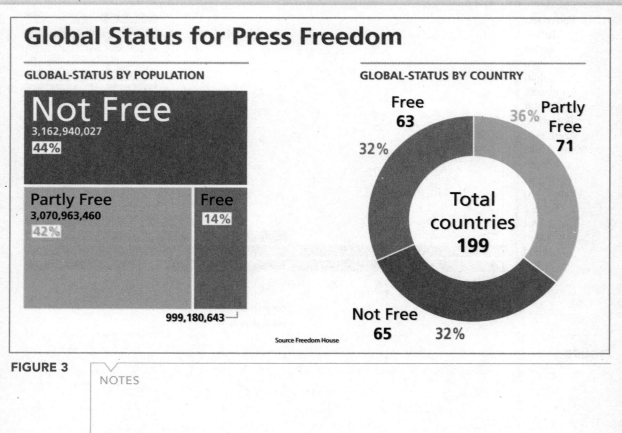

Global Status for Press Freedom

GLOBAL-STATUS BY POPULATION

Not Free
3,162,940,027
44%

Partly Free
3,070,963,460
42%

Free
14%

999,180,643

Source Freedom House

GLOBAL-STATUS BY COUNTRY

Free
63
32%

Partly Free
71
36%

Not Free
65
32%

Total countries
199

FIGURE 3

NOTES

Comprehension Check

Complete the following items after you finish your first read. Review and clarify details with your group.

1. What two countries showed the greatest decline in press freedom in 2014?

2. What has happened to global average press freedom since 2004?

3. In which year between 2004 and 2014 did global average press freedom increase?

4. By what two different measures is press freedom measured in Figure 3?

5. Which category was greater in 2014: the number of nations with free press or the number of nations without free press?

- -

RESEARCH

Research to Clarify Choose at least one unfamiliar detail from the infographics. Briefly research that detail. In what way does the information you learned shed light on an aspect of the infographics?

from FREEDOM OF THE
PRESS REPORT 2015

TIP

GROUP DISCUSSION
Consider what it means for
the press to truly operate
freely and independently.
What conditions would have
to be met? Keep this in mind
as you analyze and discuss
the data in the graphs.

Close Read

With your group, look at the infographic again. **Annotate**
details that you notice. What **questions** do you have? What
can you **conclude**?

Analyze the Media

Complete the activities.

1. **Review and Clarify** With your group, review Figures 2 and 3. How is it
   possible that 32 percent of the countries in the world have a free press,
   but only 14 percent of the world's people have access to a free press?
   Discuss.

2. **Present and Discuss** Now, work with your group to share other
   important data from the infographics. Take turns presenting your data.
   Discuss what you noticed in the data, what questions you asked, and what
   conclusions you reached.

3. **Essential Question:** *What is the relationship between power and
   freedom?* What have the data in this infographic taught you about power
   and freedom? Discuss with your group.

LANGUAGE DEVELOPMENT

Media Vocabulary

| infographic | bar graph | line graph | pie chart |

Use the vocabulary words in your responses to these questions.

1. In Figure 1, how does the presentation of the data enable readers to make
   comparisons?

2. In Figure 2, how does the type of graph help illustrate a trend in the
   change of global average press freedom over time?

3. In what way are the images in Figure 3 similar to pie charts?

STANDARDS

Language
Acquire and use accurately general
academic and domain-specific
words and phrases, sufficient for
reading, writing, speaking, and
listening at the college and career
readiness level; demonstrate
independence in gathering
vocabulary knowledge when
considering a word or phrase
important to comprehension or
expression.

Research

Assignment

Research the issue of freedom of the press in at least two countries, and then create an **infographic** that captures your findings. Your research can begin with the information provided in the informational graphics from *Freedom of the Press Report* 2015.

Use the following questions as a starting point for your research:

- Who owns or controls the major media outlets in each country? The government? Private owners?
- What are the consequences of violating a regulation or publishing unpopular information in each country?
- In each country, how free are journalists to pursue stories?
- Are foreign journalists allowed to report in each country?

Add more questions of your own as you gather information.

Plan Your Research As a group, decide which countries you will research. Then, consider how to collect the kinds of information and data you need. Use the space here to record your decisions. Then, split the work among your team members, and gather information.

Country 1: _____

Country 2: _____

Types of Information and Data: _____

_____

_____

_____

_____

Assess Your Data Meet regularly to evaluate the data you have collected, and to consider any elements that are missing or need more work. Once you have all the information and data you need, consider how best to organize it. Will one infographic be sufficient, or do you need two or more to present information clearly and effectively?

Create and Deliver the Presentation Write an introduction to your findings. Explain which countries you chose and why, as well as how you conducted your research. Also, explain how you chose to organize the data. If possible, share your presentation digitally by posting it online or using a computer and projector to display it. Alternatively, print your presentation and distribute it to the class.

EVIDENCE LOG

Before moving on to a new selection, go to your Evidence Log and record what you learned from *Freedom of the Press Report* 2015.

STANDARDS

Writing
Use technology, including the internet, to produce, publish, and update individual or shared writing products, taking advantage of technology's capacity to link to other information and to display information flexibly and dynamically.

Speaking and Listening
• Work with peers to set rules for collegial discussions and decision-making, clear goals and deadlines, and individual roles as needed.
• Present information, findings, and supporting evidence clearly, concisely, and logically such that listeners can follow the line of reasoning and the organization, development, substance, and style are appropriate to purpose, audience, and task.
• Make strategic use of digital media in presentations to enhance understanding of findings, reasoning, and evidence and to add interest.

SOURCES

- SPEECH AT THE UNITED NATIONS

- DIANE SAWYER INTERVIEWS MALALA YOUSAFZAI

- CAGED BIRD

- SOME ADVICE TO THOSE WHO WILL SERVE TIME IN PRISON

- THE CENSORS

- *from* FREEDOM OF THE PRESS REPORT 2015

Deliver a Multimedia Presentation

Assignment

You have read many selections and watched an interview that deal with issues of power and freedom. Work with your group to develop, refine, and deliver a **multimedia presentation** that addresses this question:

When, if ever, are limits on freedom necessary?

Plan With Your Group

Analyze the Texts With your group, discuss the purposes and messages of the selections you have read and viewed in this section. As you conduct your discussion, consider the idea that freedom offers both privileges and obligations. Talk about what those privileges and obligations might be, and how limits on freedom may or may not be necessary. Use the chart to list your ideas. Then, come to a consensus about which ideas you want to include in your presentation.

TITLE	PRIVILEGES AND OBLIGATIONS OF FREEDOM
Speech at the United Nations	
Diane Sawyer Interviews Malala Yousafzai	
Caged Bird	
Some Advice to Those Who Will Serve Time in Prison	
The Censors	
from Freedom of the Press Report 2015	

Gather Evidence and Media Examples Identify specific details from the selections that support your group's ideas. Number the details in order of relevance to your position—from most to least relevant. Use this analysis to choose the details you will include in your presentation. Then, brainstorm for types of media you can use to elaborate on each detail. Consider photographs, illustrations, charts, graphs, music, and audio and video clips. Allow each group member to make suggestions.

STANDARDS

Speaking and Listening
• Come to discussions prepared, having read and researched material under study; explicitly draw on that preparation by referring to evidence from texts and other research on the topic or issue to stimulate a thoughtful, well-reasoned exchange of ideas.
• Present information, findings, and supporting evidence clearly, concisely, and logically such that listeners can follow the line of reasoning and the organization, development, substance, and style are appropriate to purpose, audience, and task.

Organize Your Ideas Decide who will perform which task in each part of the presentation. Use a chart like the one shown to note when each section begins, and what each speaker will say. Also note where images, music, and audio and video clips will be used.

MULTIMEDIA PRESENTATION SCRIPT		
	Media Cues	Script
Presenter 1		
Presenter 2		
Presenter 3		

Rehearse With Your Group

Practice With Your Group Use this checklist to evaluate the effectiveness of your group's first run-through. Then, use your evaluation and the instruction here to guide your revision.

CONTENT	USE OF MEDIA	PRESENTATION TECHNIQUES
☐ The presentation conveys main ideas clearly.	☐ Appropriate types of media are used to convey main ideas.	☐ Media are visible and audible.
☐ Main ideas are supported with relevant evidence from the texts in Small-Group Learning.	☐ Media are distributed evenly throughout the presentation.	☐ Transitions between media segments are smooth.
	☐ Equipment functions properly.	☐ Each presenter makes eye contact and speaks at an appropriate volume and pace.

Fine-Tune the Content Strengthen your presentation by ensuring that ideas are conveyed clearly. With your group, identify any points of confusion or vagueness. Revise the content to clarify these elements, adding supporting material as needed.

Improve Your Use of Media Review all multimedia elements to ensure that they add interest and help create a cohesive presentation. If an element is not clearly related to the presentation, replace it with a more relevant item or omit it.

Brush Up on Your Presentation Techniques Practice your presentation before you deliver it to the class. During the presentation, speak clearly and with both liveliness and conviction.

Present and Evaluate

When you deliver your presentation, be sure that each member has taken into account all of the checklist items. As you listen to other groups' presentations, evaluate how well they meet the checklist requirements.

≡≡ STANDARDS

Speaking and Listening
• Work with peers to set rules for collegial discussions and decision-making, clear goals and deadlines, and individual roles as needed.
• Make strategic use of digital media in presentations to enhance understanding of findings, reasoning, and evidence and to add interest.
• Adapt speech to a variety of contexts and tasks, demonstrating command of formal English when indicated or appropriate.

ESSENTIAL QUESTION:

What is the relationship between power and freedom?

The struggle for human rights around the world is an ongoing battle. In this section, you will complete your study of the literature of freedom by exploring an additional selection related to the topic. You'll then share what you learn with classmates. To choose a text, follow these steps.

Look Back Think about the selections you have already studied. What more do you want to know about the topic of power and freedom?

Look Ahead Preview the texts by reading the descriptions. Which one seems most interesting and appealing to you?

Look Inside Take a few minutes to scan the text you chose. Choose a different one if this text doesn't meet your needs.

Independent Learning Strategies

Throughout your life, in school, in your community, and in your career, you will need to rely on yourself to learn and work on your own. Review these strategies and the actions you can take to practice them during Independent Learning. Add ideas of your own for each category.

STRATEGY	ACTION PLAN
Create a schedule	• Understand your goals and deadlines. • Make a plan for what to do each day. •
Practice what you've learned	• Use first-read and close-read strategies to deepen your understanding. • After you read, evaluate the usefulness of the evidence to help you understand the topic. • Consider the quality and reliability of the source. •
Take notes	• Record important ideas and information. • Review your notes before preparing to share with a group. • •

Choose one selection. Selections are available online only.

CONTENTS

First-Read Guide

Use this page to record your first-read ideas.

Selection Title: _____

🔧 **Tool Kit**
First-Read Guide and
Model Annotation

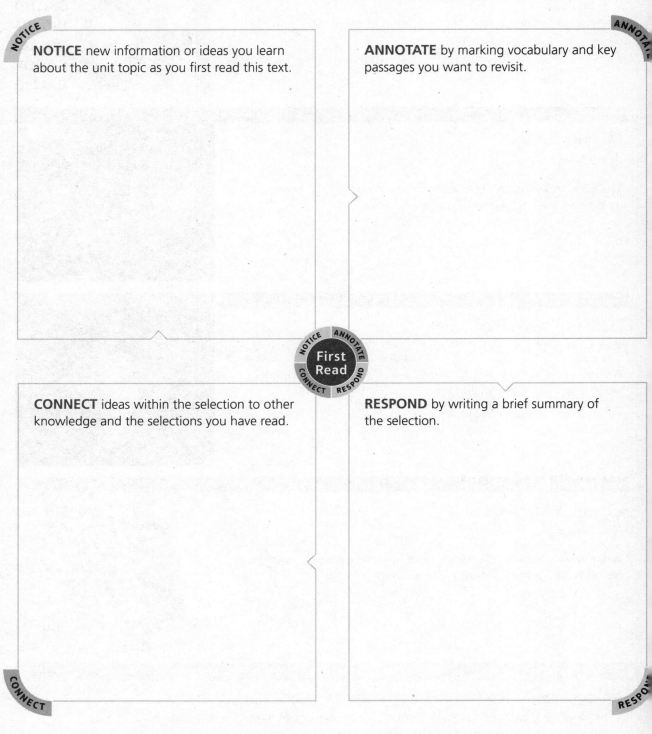

NOTICE new information or ideas you learn about the unit topic as you first read this text.

ANNOTATE by marking vocabulary and key passages you want to revisit.

CONNECT ideas within the selection to other knowledge and the selections you have read.

RESPOND by writing a brief summary of the selection.

First Read

NOTICE • ANNOTATE • CONNECT • RESPOND

⊞ STANDARD

Reading Read and comprehend complex literary and informational texts independently and proficiently.

Close-Read Guide

Use this page to record your close-read ideas.

🔧 Tool Kit
Close-Read Guide and
Model Annotation

Selection Title: _____

Close Read the Text

Revisit sections of the text you marked during your first read. Read these sections closely and **annotate** what you notice. Ask yourself **questions** about the text. What can you **conclude?** Write down your ideas.

Close Read
ANNOTATE · QUESTION · CONCLUDE

Analyze the Text

Think about the author's choices of patterns, structure, techniques, and ideas included in the text. Select one, and record your thoughts about what this choice conveys.

QuickWrite

Pick a paragraph from the text that grabbed your interest. Explain the power of this passage.

☷ STANDARD
Reading Read and comprehend complex literary and informational texts independently and proficiently.

Share Your Independent Learning

Prepare to Share

What is the relationship between power and freedom?

Even when you read or learn something independently, you can continue to
grow by sharing what you have learned with others. Reflect on the text you
explored independently, and write notes about its connection to the unit. In
your notes, consider why this text belongs in this unit.

Learn From Your Classmates

Discuss It Share your ideas about the text you explored on your own.
As you talk with your classmates, jot down ideas that you learn from them.

Reflect

Mark the most important insight you gained from these writing and
discussion activities. Explain how this idea adds to your understanding of the
topics of power and freedom.

STANDARDS

Speaking and Listening
Initiate and participate effectively in
a range of collaborative discussions
with diverse partners on *grades 9–10
topics, texts, and issues,* building on
others' ideas and expressing their
own clearly and persuasively.

Review Evidence for an Informative Essay

At the beginning of the unit, you responded to the following question:

What does it mean to "be free"?

✐ EVIDENCE LOG

Review your Evidence Log and your QuickWrite from the beginning of the unit. Have your ideas changed?

☐ YES	☐ NO
Identify at least three pieces of evidence that influenced your ideas.	Identify at least three pieces of evidence that reinforced your initial ideas.
1.	**1.**
2.	**2.**
3.	**3.**

State your ideas now: _____

_____

_____

Identify a possible addition: _____

_____

_____

Evaluate the Strength of Your Evidence Do you have enough evidence to support your ideas? If not, make a plan.

☐ Do more research   ☐ Talk with my classmates

☐ Reread a selection   ☐ Ask an expert

☐ Other: _____

⦂ STANDARDS
Writing
Introduce a topic; organize complex ideas, concepts, and information to make important connections and distinctions; include formatting, graphics and multimedia when useful to aiding comprehension.

⊞ WORD NETWORK

As you write and revise your informative essay, use your Word Network to help vary your word choices.

PART 1

Writing to Sources: Informative Essay

In this unit, you read about various people, both real and fictional, who have struggled to extend freedom's reach. Their efforts focused on both people in their own countries and their fellows around the world.

Assignment

Write an **informative essay** in which you gather and present information to respond to the following question:

What does it mean to "be free"?

Introduce the topic by defining freedom and explaining what it means to be free. Then, develop the topic with facts, details, quotations, examples, and other evidence from at least three of the selections you read. Select the most relevant ideas about fundamental human freedoms and democracy from the texts, and organize these ideas logically using appropriate and varied transitions. Conclude by clearly restating the main idea. Use a formal style and an objective tone, and follow the conventions of standard English.

Reread the Assignment Review the assignment to be sure you fully understand it. The assignment may reference some of the academic words presented at the beginning of the unit. Be sure you understand each of the words given here in order to complete the assignment correctly.

Academic Vocabulary

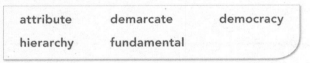

| attribute | demarcate | democracy |
| hierarchy | fundamental | |

Review the Elements of Informative Text Before you begin writing, read the Informative Text Rubric. Once you have completed your first draft, check it against the rubric. If one or more of the elements is missing or not as strong as it could be, revise your essay to add or strengthen that component.

Informative Text Rubric

	Focus and Organization	Evidence and Elaboration	Language Conventions
4	The introduction is very engaging and features a clear and complete explanation of the topic. All ideas are organized logically using appropriate and varied transitions. The conclusion clearly restates the main idea and connects it to the supporting information.	The topic is developed fully with well-chosen evidence from three or more texts. The most relevant text evidence is used to support and elaborate on the topic.	A formal style and an objective tone are maintained throughout the entire essay. The conventions of standard English are maintained throughout the entire essay.
3	The introduction is somewhat engaging and features an adequate explanation of the topic. Most ideas are organized logically using appropriate and varied transitions. The conclusion provides a clear restatement of the main idea but the connection to supporting information is unclear.	The topic is developed adequately with sufficient evidence from at least three texts. Relevant text evidence is used to support and elaborate on the topic.	A formal style and an objective tone are maintained throughout most of the essay. The conventions of standard English are maintained throughout most of the essay.
2	The introduction is unclear or contains only a partial explanation of the topic. Some ideas are organized logically using transitions; some transitions may be incorrect or overused. The conclusion is unclear or provides only a partial restatement of the main idea.	The topic is only partially developed with evidence from three texts or includes evidence from fewer than three texts. Tangential or less relevant text evidence is used to support and elaborate on the topic.	An informal style and a nonobjective tone are sometimes used in the essay. The conventions of standard English are sometimes used in the essay.
1	The introduction is missing or does not contain an adequate explanation of the topic. Ideas are not organized logically using transitions, or transitions are mostly absent or used incorrectly. The conclusion is missing or does not provide an adequate restatement of the main idea.	The topic is not adequately developed with text evidence. Irrelevant text evidence is used to support and elaborate on the topic, or text evidence is mostly or completely absent.	An informal style and a nonobjective tone appear throughout the essay. The conventions of standard English are rarely or never used in the essay.

PART 2
Speaking and Listening: Multimedia Presentation

Assignment
After completing the final draft of your informative essay, use it as the foundation for a five- to ten-minute **multimedia presentation.**

Follow these steps to create an informative, engaging presentation.

- Annotate the most important ideas and supporting details in your essay. Consider which ideas and details could best be enhanced by digital media.
- Choose various digital media (e.g, audio and video clips, images, interactive elements) to include in your presentation.
- Mark your essay to note when to present each multimedia element. Use these annotations to keep your presentation on track.
- As you deliver your presentation, speak clearly and at an adequate volume and rate. Maintain eye contact with your audience.

Review the Multimedia Presentation Rubric The criteria by which your multimedia presentation will be evaluated appear in this rubric. Review these criteria before presenting to ensure that you are prepared.

	Content	Use of Media	Presentation Technique
3	The presentation conveys main ideas clearly and thoroughly.	Well-chosen media are used to support all or most main ideas.	Media are sufficiently visible and audible.
			Transitions between media segments are consistently smooth.
	Main ideas are strongly supported with relevant evidence from texts.	Media are distributed evenly throughout the presentation.	Each presenter maintains appropriate eye contact, volume, and pacing throughout the presentation.
2	The presentation conveys main ideas somewhat clearly and thoroughly.	Somewhat well-chosen media are used to support some main ideas.	Media are somewhat visible and audible.
			Transitions between media segments are somewhat smooth.
	Main ideas are partially supported with evidence from the texts.	Media are distributed somewhat evenly throughout the presentation.	Each presenter uses eye contact and speaks at an appropriate volume and pace at times during the presentation.
1	The presentation does not convey main ideas clearly or thoroughly.	Poorly chosen media are used and do not support main ideas.	Media are insufficiently visible and audible.
			Transitions between media segments are very disjointed or are absent.
	Main ideas are not supported with evidence from the texts.	Media are not used or are distributed very unevenly throughout the presentation.	Each presenter does not use eye contact or speak at an appropriate volume or pace throughout the presentation.

Reflect on the Unit

Now that you've completed the unit, take a few moments to reflect on your learning. Use the questions below to think about where you succeeded, what skills and strategies helped you, and where you can continue to grow in the future.

Reflect on the Unit Goals

Look back at the goals at the beginning of the unit. Use a different colored pen to rate yourself again. Think about readings and activities that contributed the most to the growth of your understanding. Record your thoughts.

Reflect on the Learning Strategies

💬 **Discuss It** Write a reflection on whether you were able to improve your learning based on your Action Plans. Think about what worked, what didn't, and what you might do to keep working on these strategies. Record your ideas before a class discussion.

Reflect on the Text

Choose a selection that you found challenging, and explain what made it difficult.

Explain something that surprised you about a text in the unit.

Which activity taught you the most about the relationship between power and freedom? What did you learn?

▤ STANDARDS

Speaking and Listening
• Initiate and participate effectively in a range of collaborative discussions with diverse partners on *grades 9–10 topics, texts, and issues*, building on others' ideas and expressing their own clearly and persuasively.
• Come to discussions prepared, having read and researched material under study; explicitly draw on that preparation by referring to evidence from texts and other research on the topic or issue to stimulate a thoughtful, well-reasoned exchange of ideas..

RESOURCES

CONTENTS

Marking the Text: Strategies and Tips for Annotation

When you close read a text, you read for comprehension and then reread to unlock layers of meaning and to analyze a writer's style and techniques. Marking a text as you read it enables you to participate more fully in the close-reading process.

Following are some strategies for text mark-ups, along with samples of how the strategies can be applied. These mark-ups are suggestions; you and your teacher may want to use other mark-up strategies.

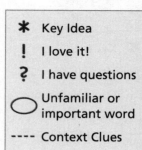

✱ Key Idea

! I love it!

? I have questions

◯ Unfamiliar or important word

---- Context Clues

Suggested Mark-Up Notations

WHAT I NOTICE	HOW TO MARK UP	QUESTIONS TO ASK
Key Ideas and Details	• Highlight key ideas or claims. • Underline supporting details or evidence.	• What does the text say? What does it leave unsaid? • What inferences do you need to make? • What details lead you to make your inferences?
Word Choice	• Circle unfamiliar words. • Put a dotted line under context clues, if any exist. • Put an exclamation point beside especially rich or poetic passages.	• What inferences about word meaning can you make? • What tone and mood are created by word choice? • What alternate word choices might the author have made?
Text Structure	• Highlight passages that show key details supporting the main idea. • Use arrows to indicate how sentences and paragraphs work together to build ideas. • Use a right-facing arrow to indicate foreshadowing. • Use a left-facing arrow to indicate flashback.	• Is the text logically structured? • What emotional impact do the structural choices create?
Author's Craft	• Circle or highlight instances of repetition, either of words, phrases, consonants, or vowel sounds. • Mark rhythmic beats in poetry using checkmarks and slashes. • Underline instances of symbolism or figurative language.	• Does the author's style enrich or detract from the reading experience? • What levels of meaning are created by the author's techniques?

CLOSE READING

* Key Idea
! I love it!
? I have questions
◯ Unfamiliar or important word
---- Context Clues

NOTES

In a first read, work to get a sense of the main idea of a text. Look for key details and ideas that help you understand what the author conveys to you. Mark passages that prompt a strong response from you.

Here is how one reader marked up this text.

MODEL

INFORMATIONAL TEXT

from Classifying the Stars

Cecilia H. Payne

1   Sunlight and starlight are composed of waves of various lengths, *
which the eye, even aided by a telescope, is unable to separate.
We must use more than a telescope. In order to sort out the
? component colors, the light must be dispersed by a prism, or
split up by some other means. For instance, sunbeams passing
through rain drops, are transformed into the myriad tinted
rainbow. The familiar rainbow spanning the sky is Nature's most
! glorious demonstration that light is composed of many colors.

2   The very beginning of our knowledge of the nature of a star *
dates back to 1672, when Isaac Newton gave to the world the
results of his experiments on passing sunlight through a prism.
To describe the beautiful band of rainbow tints, produced when
sunlight was dispersed by his three-cornered piece of glass, he
took from the Latin the word *spectrum*, meaning an appearance.
The rainbow is the spectrum of the Sun. . . .

3   In 1814, more than a century after Newton, the spectrum of the *
Sun was obtained in such purity that an amazing detail was seen
and studied by the German optician, Fraunhofer. He saw that
the multiple spectral tints, ranging from delicate violet to deep
red, were crossed by hundreds of fine dark lines. In other words,
there were narrow gaps in the spectrum where certain shades
were wholly blotted out. We must remember that the word
spectrum is applied not only to sunlight, but also to the light of
any glowing substance when its rays are sorted out by a prism or
a grating.

First-Read Guide

Use this page to record your first-read ideas.

You may want to use a guide like this to organize your thoughts after you read. Here is how a reader completed a First-Read Guide.

Selection Title: _____Classifying the Stars_____

NOTICE

NOTICE new information or ideas you learned about the unit topic as you first read this text.

Light = different waves of colors. (Spectrum)

Newton - the first person to observe these waves using a prism.

Faunhofer saw gaps in the spectrum.

ANNOTATE

ANNOTATE by marking vocabulary and key passages you want to revisit.

Vocabulary
   myriad
   grating
   component colors

Different light types = different lengths

Isaac Newton also worked theories of gravity.

<u>Multiple spectral tints?</u> "colors of various appearance"

Key Passage:
Paragraph 3 shows that Fraunhofer discovered more about the nature of light spectrums: he saw the spaces in between the tints.

First Read

CONNECT

CONNECT ideas within the selection to other knowledge and the selections you have read.

I remember learning about prisms in science class.

Double rainbows! My favorite. How are they made?

RESPOND

RESPOND by writing a brief summary of the selection.

Science allows us to see things not visible to the naked eye. What we see as sunlight is really a spectrum of colors. By using tools, such as prisms, we can see the components of sunlight and other light. They appear as single colors or as multiple colors separated by gaps of no color. White light contains a rainbow of colors.

CLOSE READING

* **Key Idea**
! **I love it!**
? **I have questions**
⬭ **Unfamiliar or important word**
---- **Context Clues**

In a close read, go back into the text to study it in greater detail. Take the time to analyze not only the author's ideas but the way that those ideas are conveyed. Consider the genre of the text, the author's word choice, the writer's unique style, and the message of the text.

Here is how one reader close read this text.

MODEL

INFORMATIONAL TEXT

from **Classifying the Stars**
Cecilia H. Payne

NOTES

explanation of sunlight and starlight

What is light and where do the colors come from?

This paragraph is about Newton and the prism.

What discoveries helped us understand light?

Fraunhofer and gaps in spectrum

*

1 Sunlight and starlight are composed of waves of various lengths, which the eye, even aided by a telescope, is unable to separate. We must use more than a telescope. In order to sort out the component colors, the light must be dispersed by a prism, or split up by some other means. For instance, sunbeams passing through rain drops, are transformed into the myriad-tinted rainbow. The familiar rainbow spanning the sky is Nature's most glorious demonstration that light is composed of many colors.

*

2 The very beginning of our knowledge of the nature of a star dates back to 1672, when Isaac Newton gave to the world the results of his experiments on passing sunlight through a prism. To describe the beautiful band of rainbow tints, produced when sunlight was dispersed by his three-cornered piece of glass, he took from the Latin the word *spectrum*, meaning an appearance. The rainbow is the spectrum of the Sun. . . .

*

3 In 1814, more than a century after Newton, the spectrum of the Sun was obtained in such purity that an amazing detail was seen and studied by the German optician, Fraunhofer. He saw that the multiple spectral tints, ranging from delicate violet to deep red, were crossed by hundreds of fine dark lines. In other words, there were narrow gaps in the spectrum where certain shades were wholly blotted out. We must remember that the word spectrum is applied not only to sunlight, but also to the light of any glowing substance when its rays are sorted out by a prism or a grating.

Close-Read Guide

Use this page to record your close-read ideas.

Selection Title: _Classifying the Stars_

Close Read the Text

Revisit sections of the text you marked during your first read. Read these sections closely and **annotate** what you notice. Ask yourself **questions** about the text. What can you **conclude?** Write down your ideas.

Paragraph 3: Light is composed of waves of various lengths. Prisms let us see different colors in light. This is called the spectrum. Fraunhofer proved that there are gaps in the spectrum, where certain shades are blotted out.

More than one researcher studied this and each built off the ideas that were already discovered.

Analyze the Text

Think about the author's choices of patterns, structure, techniques, and ideas included in the text. Select one, and record your thoughts about what this choice conveys.

The author showed the development of human knowledge of the spectrum chronologically. Helped me see how ideas were built upon earlier understandings. Used dates and "more than a century after Newton" to show time.

QuickWrite

Pick a paragraph from the text that grabbed your interest. Explain the power of this passage.

The first paragraph grabbed my attention, specifically the sentence "The familiar rainbow spanning the sky is Nature's most glorious demonstration that light is composed of many colors." The paragraph began as a straightforward scientific explanation. When I read the word "glorious," I had to stop and deeply consider what was being said. It is a word loaded with personal feelings. With that one word, the author let the reader know what was important to her.

Argument

When you think of the word *argument*, you might think of a disagreement between two people, but an argument is more than that. An argument is a logical way of presenting a belief, conclusion, or stance. A good argument is supported with reasoning and evidence.

Argument writing can be used for many purposes, such as to change a reader's point of view or opinion or to bring about an action or a response from a reader.

Elements of an Argumentative Text

An **argument** is a logical way of presenting a viewpoint, belief, or stand on an issue. A well-written argument may convince the reader, change the reader's mind, or motivate the reader to take a certain action.

An effective argument contains these elements:

- a precise claim
- consideration of counterclaims, or opposing positions, and a discussion of their strengths and weaknesses
- logical organization that makes clear connections among claim, counterclaim, reasons, and evidence
- valid reasoning and evidence
- a concluding statement or section that logically completes the argument
- formal and objective language and tone
- error-free grammar, including accurate use of transitions

ARGUMENT: SCORE 1

Selfies, Photoshop, and You: Superficial Image Culture is Hurtful for Teens

Selfies are kind of cool, also kind of annoying, and some say they might be bad for you if you take too many. Selfies of celebrities and ordinary people are everywhere. People always try to smile and look good, and they take a lot of selfies when they are somewhere special, like at the zoo or at a fair. Some people spend so much time taking selfies they forget to just go ahead and have fun.

> The writer does not clearly state the claim in the introduction.

TV and other media are full of beautiful people. Looking at all those model's and celebrities can make kids feel bad about their one bodies, even when they are actually totally normal and fine and beautiful they way they are. Kids start to think they should look like the folks on TV which is mostly impossible. It's also a cheat because lots of the photos we see of celebrities and model's have been edited so they look even better.

> The argument contains mistakes in standard English conventions of usage and mechanics.

Selfies make people feel even worse about the way they look. They're always comparing themselves and feeling that maybe they aren't as good as they should be. Selfies can make teens feel bad about their faces and bodies, and the stuff they are doing every day.

Regular people edit and change things before they post their pictures. That means, the pictures are kind of fake and it's impossible to compete with something that is fake. It's sad to think that teens can start to hate themselves and feel depressed just because they don't and can't look like a faked photo of a movie star.

> The tone of the argument is informal, and the vocabulary is limited or ineffective.

Kids and teens post selfies to hear what others think about them, to show off, and to see how they compare with others. It can be kind of full of pressure always having to look great and smile. Even if you get positive comments about a selfie that you post, and everyone says you look beautiful, that feeling only lasts for a few minutes. After all, what you look like is just something on the outside. What's more important is what you are on the inside and what you do.

It's great for those few minutes, but then what? If you keep posting, people will not want to keep writing nice comments. Kids and teens should take a break from posting selfies all the time. It's better to go out and have fun rather than always keeping on posting selfies.

> The writer does not address counterclaims.

> The conclusion does not restate any information that is important.

WRITING

ARGUMENT: SCORE 2

Selfies and You: Superficial Image Culture is Hurtful for Teens

Selfies are bad for teens and everyone else. Selfies of celebrities and ordinary people are everywhere. It seems like taking and posting selfies is not such a big deal and not harmful, but that's not really true. Actually, taking too many selfies can be really bad.

TV and other media are full of beautiful people. Looking at all those models and celebrities can make kids feel bad about their own bodies. Kids start to think they should look like the folks on TV which is mostly impossible. It's also a cheat because lots of the photos we see of celebrities and model's have been edited so they look even better.

Regular people use image editing software as well. They edit and change things before they post their pictures. That means, the pictures are kind of fake and it's impossible to compete with something that is fake.

Selfies make people feel even worse about the way they look. They're always comparing themselves and feeling that maybe they aren't as good as they should be. Selfies can make teens feel bad about their faces and bodies.

But maybe selfies are just a fun way to stay in touch, but that's not really how people use selfies, I don't think. Kids and teens post selfies show off. It can be full of pressure always having to look great and smile.

Sometimes posting a selfie can make you feel good if it gets lots of 'likes' and positive comments. But you can never tell. Someone also might say something mean. Also, even if you get positive comments and everyone says you look beautiful, that feeling only lasts for a few minutes. It's great for those few minutes, but then what? If you keep posting and posting, people will not want to keep writing nice comments.

The selfie culture today is just too much. Kids and teens can't be happy when they are always comparing themselves and worrying about what they look like. It's better to go out and have fun rather than always keeping on posting selfies.

The introduction establishes the writer's claim.

The tone of the argument is occasionally formal and objective.

The writer briefly acknowledges one counterclaim.

The conclusion offers some insight into the claim and restates information.

ARGUMENT: SCORE 3

Selfies and You: Superficial Image Culture is Hurtful for Teens

Selfies are everywhere. Check out any social media site and you'll see an endless parade of perfect smiles on both celebrities and ordinary people. It may seem as if this flood of seflies is harmless, but sadly that is not true. Selfies promote a superficial image culture that is harmful and dangerous for teens.

The argument's claim is clearly stated.

The problem starts with the unrealistic: idealized images teens are exposed to in the media. Most models and celebrities are impossibly beautiful and thin. Even young children can feel that there is something wrong with they way they look. According to one research group, more than half of girls and one third of boys ages 6-8 feel their ideal body is thinner than their current body weight. Negative body image can result in serious physical and mental health problems.

The tone of the argument is mostly formal and objective.

The writer includes reasons and evidence that address and support claims.

When teens look at selfies they automatically make comparisons with the idealized images they have in their minds. This can make them feel inadequate and sad about themselves, their bodies, and their lives. And with social media sites accessible 24/7, it's difficult to get a break from the constant comparisons, competition, and judgment.

Image editing software plays a role too. A recent study carried out by the Renfrew Center Foundation said that about 50% of people edit pictures of themselves before posting. They take away blemishes, change skin tone, maybe even make themselves look thinner. And why not? Even the photos of models and celebrities are heavily edited. Teens can start to hate themselves and feel depressed just because they don't and can't look like a faked photo of a movie star.

Some say that posting a selfie is like sending a postcard to your friends and family, but that's not how selfies are used: teens post selfies to get feedback, to compare themselves with others, and to present a false image to the world. There is a lot of pressure to look great and appear happy.

The ideas progress logically, and the writer includes sentence transitions that connect the reader to the argument.

It's true that sometimes a selfie posted on social media gets 'likes' and positive comments that can make a person feel pretty. However, the boost you get from feeling pretty for five minutes doesn't last.

A million selfies are posted every day—and that's way too many. Selfies promote a superficial image culture that is harmful to teens. In the end, the selfie life is not a healthy way to have fun. Let's hope the fad will fade.

The conclusion restates important information.

MODEL

ARGUMENT: SCORE 4

Selfies and You: Superficial Image Culture Is Hurtful for Teens

Smile, Snap, Edit, Post—Repeat! That's the selfie life, and it's everywhere. A million selfies are posted every day. But this **tsunami** of self-portraits is not as harmless as it appears. Selfies promote a superficial image culture that is hurtful and dangerous for teens.

It all starts with the unrealistic: When teens look at selfies they automatically make comparisons with the idealized images they have in their minds. This can cause them to feel inadequate and sad about themselves, their bodies, and their lives. According to Common Sense Media, more than half of girls and one third of boys ages 6-8 feel their ideal body is thinner than their current body weight. Negative body image can result in serious physical and mental health problems such as anorexia and other eating disorders.

To make matter worse, many or even most selfies have been edited. A recent study carried out by the Renfrew Center Foundation concluded that about 50% of people edit their own images before posting. They use image-editing software to take away blemishes, change skin tone, maybe even make themselves look thinner. And why not? Even the photos of models and celebrities are heavily edited.

Some say that selfies are a harmless and enjoyable way to communicate: posting a selfie is like sending a postcard to your friends and family, inviting them to share in your fun. But that is not how selfies are used: teens post selfies to get feedback, to compare themselves with others, and to present an (often false) image to the world.

It's true that posting a selfie on social media can generate 'likes' and positive comments that can make a person feel good.

However, the boost one gets from feeling pretty for five minutes is like junk food: it tastes good but it is not nourishing.

The selfie culture that is the norm today is out of control. The superficial image culture promoted by selfies is probably behind the recent 20 percent increase in plastic surgery—something with its own dangers and drawbacks. Let's hope the fad will fade, and look forward to a future where people are too busy enjoying life to spend so much time taking, editing, and posting pictures of themselves.

The introduction is engaging, and the writer's claim is clearly stated at the end of the paragraph.

The writer has included a variety of sentence transitions such as "To make matters worse…" "Some say…" "Another claim…" "It is true that…"

The sources of evidence are specific and contain relevant information.

The writer clearly acknowledges counterclaims.

The conclusion offers fresh insights into the claim.

Argument Rubric

	Focus and Organization	Evidence and Elaboration	Conventions
4	The introduction engages the reader and establishes a claim in a compelling way. The argument includes valid reasons and evidence that address and support the claim while clearly acknowledging counterclaims. The ideas progress logically, and transitions make connections among ideas clear. The conclusion offers fresh insight into the claim.	The sources of evidence are comprehensive and specific and contain relevant information. The tone of the argument is always formal and objective. The vocabulary is always appropriate for the audience and purpose.	The argument intentionally uses standard English conventions of usage and mechanics.
3	The introduction engages the reader and establishes the claim. The argument includes reasons and evidence that address and support my claim while acknowledging counterclaims. The ideas progress logically, and some transitions are used to help make connections among ideas clear. The conclusion restates the claim and important information.	The sources of evidence contain relevant information. The tone of the argument is mostly formal and objective. The vocabulary is generally appropriate for the audience and purpose.	The argument demonstrates general accuracy in standard English conventions of usage and mechanics.
2	The introduction establishes a claim. The argument includes some reasons and evidence that address and support the claim while briefly acknowledging counterclaims. The ideas progress somewhat logically. A few sentence transitions are used that connect readers to the argument. The conclusion offers some insight into the claim and restates information.	The sources of evidence contain some relevant information. The tone of the argument is occasionally formal and objective. The vocabulary is somewhat appropriate for the audience and purpose.	The argument demonstrates some accuracy in standard English conventions of usage and mechanics.
1	The introduction does not clearly state the claim. The argument does not include reasons or evidence for the claim. No counterclaims are acknowledged. The ideas do not progress logically. Transitions are not included to connect ideas. The conclusion does not restate any information that is important.	Reliable and relevant evidence is not included. The vocabulary used is limited or ineffective. The tone of the argument is not objective or formal.	The argument contains mistakes in standard English conventions of usage and mechanics.

Informative/Explanatory Texts

Informative and explanatory writing should rely on facts to inform or explain. Informative writing can serve several purposes: to increase readers' knowledge of a subject, to help readers better understand a procedure or process, or to provide readers with an enhanced comprehension of a concept. It should also feature a clear introduction, body, and conclusion.

Elements of Informative/Explanatory Texts

Informative/explanatory texts present facts, details, data, and other kinds of evidence to give information about a topic. Readers turn to informational and explanatory texts when they wish to learn about a specific idea, concept, or subject area, or if they want to learn how to do something.

An effective informative/explanatory text contains these elements:

- a topic sentence or thesis statement that introduces the concept or subject
- relevant facts, examples, and details that expand upon a topic
- definitions, quotations, and/or graphics that support the information given
- headings (if desired) to separate sections of the essay
- a structure that presents information in a direct, clear manner
- clear transitions that link sections of the essay
- precise words and technical vocabulary where appropriate
- formal and object language and tone
- a conclusion that supports the information given and provides fresh insights

INFORMATIVE/EXPLANATORY: SCORE 1

Moai: The Giant Statues of Easter Island

Easter Island is a tiny Island. It's far out in the middle of the pacific ocean, 2200 miles off the coast. The closest country is Chile, in south america. The nearest island where people live is called Pitcairn, and that's about 1,300 miles away, and only about 60 people live so their most of the time. Easter island is much bigger than Pitcairn, and lots more people live there now—about 5,000-6,000. Although in the past there were times when only about 111 people lived there.

Even if you don't really know what it is, you've probably seen pictures of the easter island Statues. You'd recognize one if you saw it, with big heads and no smiles. Their lots of them on the island. Almost 900 of them. But some were never finished They're called *moai*. They are all different sizes. All the sizes together average out to about 13 feet tall and 14 tons of heavy.

Scientists know that Polynesians settled Easter Island (it's also called Rapa Nui, and the people are called the Rapanui people). Polynesians were very good at boats. And they went big distances across the Pacific. When these Polynesians arrived was probably 300, but it was probably 900 or 1200.

The island was covered with forests. They can tell by looking at pollin in lakes. The Rapanui people cut trees, to build houses. They didn't know that they wood run out of wood). They also carved *moai*.

The *moai* were made for important chiefs. They were made with only stone tools. They have large heads and narrow bodies. No 2 are the same. Although they look the same as far as their faces are concerned. They are very big and impressive and special.

Over the years, many of the statues were tipped over and broken. But some years ago scientists began to fix some of them and stand them up again. They look more better like that. The ones that have been fixed up are probably the ones you remember seeing in photographs.

The essay does not include a thesis statement.

The writer includes many details that are not relevant to the topic of the essay.

The essay has many errors in grammar, spelling, capitalization, punctuation. The errors detract from the fluency and effectiveness of the essay.

The sentences are often not purposeful, varied, or well controlled.

The essay ends abruptly and lacks a conclusion.

TOOL KIT: WRITING

MODEL

INFORMATIVE/EXPLANATORY: SCORE 2

Moai: The Giant Statues of Easter Island

Easter Island is a tiny Island. It's far out in the middle of the pacific ocean, 2200 miles off the coast. The closest South American country is Chile. The nearest island where people live is called Pitcairn, and that's almost 1,300 miles away. Even if don't know much about it, you've probably seen pictures of the Easter Island statues. You'd recognize one if you saw it. They're almost 900 of them. They're called *moai.* The average one is about 13 feet high (that's tall) and weighs a lot— almost 14 tons.

Scientists know that Polynesians settled Easter Island (it's also called Rapa Nui, and the people are called the Rapanui). Polynesians were very good sailers. And they traveled big distances across the Pacific. Even so, nobody really can say exactly *when* these Polynesians arrived and settled on the Island. Some say 300 A.D., while others say maybe as late as 900 or even 1200 A.D.

Scientists can tell that when the settlers first arrived, the island was covered with forests of palm and hardwood. They can tell by looking at pollin deposits in lakes on the island. The Rapanui people cut trees, built houses, planted crops, and a thriving culture. They didn't know that cutting so many trees would cause problems later on (like running out of wood). They also began to carve *moai.*

The *moai* were built to honor important Rapanui ancestors or chiefs. The statues all have large heads and narrow bodies, but no too are exactly the same. There faces are all similar. Some have places where eyes could be inserted.

Why did the Rapanui stopped making *moai*? Part of it might have been because there were no more trees and no more of the wood needed to transport them. Part of it was maybe because the people were busy fighting each other because food and other necessary things were running out. In any case, they stopped making moai and started tipping over and breaking the ones that were there already. Later on, archeologists began to try to restore some of the statues and set them up again. But even now that some have been set up again, we still don't know a lot about them. I guess some things just have to remain a mystery!

The writer does not include a thesis statement.

Some of the ideas are reasonably well developed.

The essay has many errors in grammar, spelling, capitalization, punctuation. The errors decrease the effectiveness of the essay.

The writer's word choice shows that he is not fully aware of the essay's purpose and tone.

The writer does not include a clear conclusion.

INFORMATIVE/EXPLANATORY: SCORE 3

Moai: The Giant Statues of Easter Island

Easter Island is a tiny place, far out in the middle of the Pacific Ocean, 2200 miles off the coast of South America. Another name for the island is Rapa Nui. Even if you don't know much about it, you would probably recognize the colossal head-and-torso carvings known as *moai*. Even after years of research by scientists, many questions about these extraordinary statues remain unanswered.

Scientists now agree that it was Polynesians who settled Easter Island. Earlier some argued South American voyagers were the first. But the Polynesians were expert sailors and navigators known to have traveled huge distances across the Pacific Ocean. However, scientists do not agree about *when* the settlers arrived. Some say A.D. 300, while others suggest as late as between A.D. 900 and 1200.

Scientists say that when the settlers first arrived on Rapa Nui, the island was covered with forests of palm and hardwood. They can tell by looking at the layers of pollen deposited over the years in the lakes on the island. The Rapa Nui began to carve *moai*. They developed a unique artistic and architectural tradition all of their own.

Archeologists agree that the *moai* were created to honor ancestor's or chief's. Most *moai* are made from a soft rock called *tuff* that's formed from hardened volcanic ash. The statues all have large heads on top of narrow bodies, but no two are exactly the same. Some have indented eye sockets where eyes could be inserted.

At some point, the Rapanui stopped making *moai*. Why? Was it because there were no more trees and no longer enough wood needed to transport them? Was it because the people were too busy fighting each other over resources which had begun to run out? No one can say for sure. Rival groups began toppling their enemys' *moai* and breaking them. By the 19th century, most of the statues were tipped over, and many were destroyed. It wasn't until many years later that archeologists began to restore some of the statues.

The *moai* of Easter Island are one of the most awe-inspiring human achievements ever. Thanks to scientific studies, we know much more about the *moai, ahu,* and Rapanui people than we ever did in the past. But some questions remain unanswered. At least for now, the *moai* are keeping their mouths shut, doing a good job of guarding their secrets.

The thesis statement is clearly stated.

The essay has many interesting details, but some do not relate directly to the topic.

There are very few errors in grammar, usage, and punctuation. These errors do not interrupt the fluency and effectiveness of the essay.

The writer's conclusion sums up the main points of the essay and supports the thesis statement.

`MODEL`

`INFORMATIVE/EXPLANATORY: SCORE 4`

Moai: The Giant Statues of Easter Island

Easter Island, 2200 miles off the coast of South America, is "the most remote inhabited island on the planet." Few have visited this speck in the middle of the vast Pacific Ocean, but we all recognize the colossal statues that bring this tiny island its fame: the head-and-torso carvings known as *moai*. Yet even after years of research by scientists, many questions about the *moai* remain unanswered.

> The thesis statement of is clearly stated in an engaging manner.

Scientists now agree that it was Polynesians, not South Americans, who settled Easter Island (also known as Rapa Nui). Polynesians were expert sailors and navigators known to have traveled huge distances across the Pacific Ocean. Even so, there is little agreement about *when* the settlers arrived. Some say A.D. 300, while others suggest as late as between A.D. 900 and 1200.

> The ideas in the essay relate to the thesis statement and focus on the topic.

Most archeologists agree that the *moai* were created to honor ancestors, chiefs, or other important people. Most *moai* are made from a soft rock called *tuff* that's formed from hardened volcanic ash. The statues have large heads atop narrow torsos, with eyes wide open and lips tightly closed. While the moai share these basic characteristics, no two are exactly the same: while all are huge, some are bigger than others. Some are decorated with carvings. Some have indented eye sockets where white coral eyes could be inserted. It's possible that the eyes were only put in for special occasions.

> The writer includes many specific and well-chosen details that add substance to the essay.

In the late 1600s, the Rapanui stopped carving *moai*. Was it because the forests had been depleted and there was no longer enough wood needed to transport them? Was it because they were too busy fighting each other over dwindling resources? No one can say for sure. What is known is that rival groups began toppling their enemies' *moai* and breaking them. By the 19th century, most of the statues were tipped over, and many were destroyed. It wasn't until many years later that archeologists began restoration efforts.

> The fluency of the writing and effectiveness of the essay are unaffected by errors.

The *moai* of Easter Island are one of humanity's most awe-inspiring cultural and artistic achievements. Part of Rapa Nui was designated as a World Heritage Site in 1995 to recognize and protect these extraordinary creations. Thanks to scientific studies, we know much more about the *moai* than we ever did in the past. But some questions remain unanswered, some mysteries unsolved. Don't bother asking the *moai*: their lips are sealed.

> The conclusion relates to the thesis statement and is creative and memorable.

Informative/Explanatory Rubric

	Focus and Organization	Evidence and Elaboration	Conventions
4	The introduction engages the reader and states a thesis in a compelling way. The essay includes a clear introduction, body, and conclusion. The conclusion summarizes ideas and offers fresh insight into the thesis.	The essay includes specific reasons, details, facts, and quotations from selections and outside resources to support the thesis. The tone of the essay is always formal and objective. The language is always precise and appropriate for the audience and purpose.	The essay uses standard English conventions of usage and mechanics. The essay contains no spelling errors.
3	The introduction engages the reader and sets forth the thesis. The essay includes an introduction, body, and conclusion. The conclusion summarizes ideas and supports the thesis.	The essay includes some specific reasons, details, facts, and quotations from selections and outside resources to support the thesis. The tone of the essay is mostly formal and objective. The language is generally precise and appropriate for the audience and purpose.	The essay demonstrates general accuracy in standard English conventions of usage and mechanics. The essay contains few spelling errors.
2	The introduction sets forth the thesis. The essay includes an introduction, body, and conclusion, but one or more parts are weak. The conclusion partially summarizes ideas but may not provide strong support of the thesis.	The essay includes a few reasons, details, facts, and quotations from selections and outside resources to support the thesis. The tone of the essay is occasionally formal and objective. The language is somewhat precise and appropriate for the audience and purpose.	The essay demonstrates some accuracy in standard English conventions of usage and mechanics. The essay contains some spelling errors.
1	The introduction does not state the thesis clearly. The essay does not include an introduction, body, and conclusion. The conclusion does not summarize ideas and may not relate to the thesis.	Reliable and relevant evidence is not included. The tone of the essay is not objective or formal. The language used is imprecise and not appropriate for the audience and purpose.	The essay contains mistakes in standard English conventions of usage and mechanics. The essay contains many spelling errors.

Narration

Narrative writing conveys experience, either real or imaginary, and uses time to provide structure. It can be used to inform, instruct, persuade, or entertain. Whenever writers tell a story, they are using narrative writing. Most types of narrative writing share certain elements, such as characters, setting, a sequence of events, and, often, a theme.

Elements of a Narrative Text

A **narrative** is any type of writing that tells a story, whether it is fiction, nonfiction, poetry, or drama.

An effective nonfiction narrative usually contains these elements:

- an engaging beginning in which characters and setting are established
- characters who participate in the story events
- a well-structured, logical sequence of events
- details that show time and place
- effective story elements such as dialogue, description, and reflection
- the narrator's thoughts, feelings, or views about the significance of events
- use of language that brings the characters and setting to life

An effective fictional narrative usually contains these elements:

- an engaging beginning in which characters, setting, or a main conflict is introduced
- a main character and supporting characters who participate in the story events
- a narrator who relates the events of the plot from a particular point of view
- details that show time and place
- conflict that is resolved in the course of the narrative
- narrative techniques such as dialogue, description, and suspense
- use of language that vividly brings to life characters and events

NARRATIVE: SCORE 1

The Remark-a-Ball

Eddie decided to invent a Remark-a-Ball. Eddie thought Barnaby should be able to speak to him.

That's when he invited the Remark-a-Ball.

Barnaby had a rubber ball. It could make a bunchs of sounds that made Barnaby bark. It had always seemed that Barnaby was using his squeaky toy to talk, almost.

This was before Barnaby got hit by a car and died. This was a big deal. He took his chemistry set and worked real hard to created a thing that would make the toy ball talk for Barnaby, his dog.

Eddie made a Remark-a-Ball that worked a little too well, tho. Barnaby could say anything he wanted too. And now he said complaints—his bed didn't feel good, he wanted to be walks, he wanted to eat food.

Barnaby became bossy to Eddy to take him on walks or wake up. It was like he became his boss. Like my dad's boss. Eddy didn't like having a mean boss for a dog.

Eddy wished he hadn't invented the Remark-a-Ball.

The story's beginning is choppy and vague.

The sequence of events is unclear and hard to follow.

The narrative lacks descriptive details and sensory language.

The narrative contains many errors in standard English conventions of usage and mechanics.

The conclusion is abrupt and unsatisfying.

TOOL KIT: WRITING

MODEL

NARRATIVE: SCORE 2

The Remark-a-Ball

Eddie couldn't understand what his dog was barking about, so he decided to invent a Remark-a-Ball. Eddie thought Barnaby should be able to speak to him.

That's when he invented the Remark-a-Ball.

Barnaby had a rubber ball the size of an orange. It could make a bunch of sounds that made Barnaby bark. It had always seemed to Eddie that Barnaby was almost talking with his squeaky toy.

This was a big deal. Eddy would be the first human ever to talk to a dog, which was a big deal! He took his chemistry set and worked real hard to created a thing that would make the toy ball talk for Barnaby, his dog.

Eddie made a Remark-a-Ball that worked a little too well, tho. Barnaby could say anything he wanted now. And now he mostly said complaints—his bed didn't feel good, he wanted to be walked all the time, he wanted to eat people food.

Barnaby became bossy to Eddy to take him on walks or wake him up. It was like he became his boss. His really mean boss, like my dad's boss. Eddy didn't like having a mean boss for a dog.

Eddy started to ignore his best friend, which used to be his dog named Barnaby. He started tot think maybe dogs shouldn't be able to talk.

Things were much better when Barnaby went back to barking

The story's beginning provides few details to establish the situation.

Narrative techniques such as dialogue, pacing, and description are used sparingly.

The narrative contains some errors in standard English conventions of usage and mechanics.

The conclusion comes abruptly and provides little insight about the story's meaning.

NARRATIVE: SCORE 3

The Remark-a-Ball

Any bark could mean anything: *I'm hungry*, *Take me outside*, or *There's that dog again*. Eddie thought Barnaby should be able to speak to him.

And that's how the Remark-a-Ball was born.

Barnaby had a rubber ball the size of an orange. It could make a wide range of sounds that made Barnaby howl. It had always seemed to Eddie that Barnaby was almost communicating with his squeaky toy.

This was big. This was epic. He would be the first human ever to bridge the communication gap between species! He dusted off his old chemistry set and, through trial and error, created a liquid bath that would greatly increase the toy's flexibility, resilience, and mouth-feel.

Eddie had a prototype that worked—perhaps too well. Barnaby was ready to speak his mind. This unleashed a torrent of complaints—his bed was lumpy, he couldn't *possibly* exist on just three walks a day, he wanted table food like the poodle next door.

Barnaby made increasingly specific demands to Eddie to take him on walks or wake him up. This kind of conversation did not bring them closer, as Eddie had thought, but instead it drove them apart.

Eddie started to avoid his former best friend, and he came to the realization that there is a good reason different species don't have a common language.

So Eddie quit letting Barnaby use the toy.

"Hey, Barn, want to go outside?" Eddie would say, and the dog, as if a switch was turned on, would shake, wag, pant, run in circles, and bark—just like he used to.

The story's beginning establishes the situation and the narrator's point of view but leaves some details unclear.

The narrative consistently uses standard English conventions of usage and mechanics.

Narrative techniques such as dialogue and description are used occasionally.

The conclusion resolves the situation or problem, but does not clearly convey the significance of the events in the story.

TOOL KIT: WRITING

MODEL

NARRATIVE: SCORE 4

The Remark-a-Ball

Barnaby, for no apparent reason, leapt up and began to bark like a maniac. "Why are you barking?" asked Eddie, holding the leash tight. But Barnaby, being a dog, couldn't say. It could have been anything—a dead bird, a half-eaten sandwich, the Taj Mahal.

This was one of those times Eddie wished that Barnaby could talk. Any bark could mean anything: *I'm hungry, Take me outside,* or *There's that dog again.* Eddie thought, as buddies, they should be able to understand each other.

And that's how the Remark-a-Ball was born.

Barnaby had a squeaky toy—a rubber ball the size of an orange. It could emit a wide range of sounds. It made Barnaby howl even as he was squeaking it. And it had always seemed to Eddie that through this process Barnaby was almost communicating.

This was big. This was epic. He, Edward C. Reyes III, would be the first human ever to bridge the communication gap between species! He dusted off his old chemistry set and, through trial and error, created a liquid bath that would greatly increase the toy's flexibility, resilience, and mouth-feel.

By the end of the week Eddie had a prototype that worked—perhaps too well. Barnaby was ready to speak his mind. This unleashed a torrent of complaints—his bed was lumpy, he couldn't *possibly* exist on just three walks a day, he wanted table food like the poodle next door.

Barnaby made increasingly specific demands, such as "Wake me in ten minutes," and "I want filtered water." This kind of conversation did not bring them closer, as Eddie had thought, but instead it drove them apart.

Eddie started to avoid his former best friend, and he came to the realization that there is a good reason different species don't have a common language. It didn't take long for the invention to be relegated to the very bottom of Barnaby's toy chest, too far down for him to get.

There followed a period of transition, after which Eddie and Barnaby returned to their former mode of communication, which worked out just fine.

"Hey, Barn, want to go outside?" Eddie would say, and the dog, as if a switch was turned on, would shake, wag, pant, run in circles, and bark—just like he used to.

"You're a good boy, Barnaby," Eddie would say, scratching him behind the ears.

The story's beginning is engaging, sets up a point of view, and establishes characters and tone.

The narrative uses standard English conventions of usage and mechanics, except where language is manipulated for effect.

Events are presented in a logical sequence, and the progression from one even to another is smooth.

Narrative techniques are used effectively to develop characters and events.

The conclusion resolves the situation or problem and clearly conveys the significance of the events in the story.

Narrative Rubric

	Focus and Organization	Development of Ideas/Elaboration	Conventions
4	The introduction establishes a clear context and point of view. Events are presented in a clear sequence, building to a climax, then moving toward the conclusion. The conclusion follows from and reflects on the events and experiences in the narrative.	Narrative techniques such as dialogue, pacing, and description are used effectively to develop characters, events, and setting. Descriptive details, sensory language, and precise words and phrases are used to convey the experiences in the narrative and to help the reader imagine the characters and setting. Voice is established through word choice, sentence structure, and tone.	The narrative uses standard English conventions of usage and mechanics. Deviations from standard English are intentional and serve the purpose of the narrative. Rules of spelling and punctuation are followed.
3	The introduction gives the reader some context and sets the point of view. Events are presented logically, though there are some jumps in time. The conclusion logically ends the story, but provides only some reflection on the experiences related in the story.	Narrative techniques such as dialogue, pacing, and description are used occasionally. Descriptive details, sensory language, and precise words and phrases are used occasionally. Voice is established through word choice, sentence structure, and tone occasionally, though not evenly.	The narrative mostly uses standard English conventions of usage and mechanics, though there are some errors. There are few errors in spelling and punctuation.
2	The introduction provides some description of a place. The point of view can be unclear at times. Transitions between events are occasionally unclear. The conclusion comes abruptly and provides only a small amount of reflection on the experiences related in the narrative.	Narrative techniques such as dialogue, pacing, and description are used sparingly. The story contains few examples of descriptive details and sensory language. Voice is not established for characters, so that it becomes difficult to determine who is speaking.	The narrative contains some errors in standard English conventions of usage and mechanics. There are many errors in spelling and punctuation.
1	The introduction fails to set a scene or is omitted altogether. The point of view is not always clear. The events are not in a clear sequence, and events that would clarify the narrative may not appear. The conclusion does not follow from the narrative or is omitted altogether.	Narrative techniques such as dialogue, pacing, and description are not used. Descriptive details are vague or missing. No sensory language is included. Voice has not been developed.	The text contains mistakes in standard English conventions of usage and mechanics. Rules of spelling and punctuation have not been followed.

Conducting Research

We are lucky to live in an age when information is accessible and plentiful. However, not all information is equally useful, or even accurate. Strong research skills will help you locate and evaluate information.

Narrowing or Broadening a Topic

The first step of any research project is determining your topic. Consider the scope of your project and choose a topic that is narrow enough to address completely and effectively. If you can name your topic in just one or two words, it is probably too broad. Topics such as Shakespeare, jazz, or science fiction are too broad to cover in a single report. Narrow a broad topic into smaller subcategories.

When you begin to research a topic, pay attention to the amount of information available. If you feel overwhelmed by the number of relevant sources, you may need to narrow your topic further.

If there isn't enough information available as your research, you might need to broaden your topic. A topic is too narrow when it can be thoroughly presented in less space than the required size of your assignment. It might also be too narrow if you can find little or no information in library and media sources, so consider broadening your topic to include other related ideas.

Generating Research Questions

Use research questions to focus your research. Specific questions can help you avoid time-wasting digressions. For example, instead of simply hunting for information about Mark Twain, you might ask, "What jobs did Mark Twain have, other than being a writer?" or "Which of Twain's books was most popular during his lifetime?"

In a research report, your research question often becomes your thesis statement, or may lead up to it. The question will also help you focus your research into a comprehensive but flexible search plan, as well as prevent you from gathering unnecessary details. As your research teaches you more about your topic, you may find it necessary to refocus your original question.

Consulting Print and Digital Sources

Effective research combines information from several sources, and does not rely too heavily on a single source. The creativity and originality of your research depends on how you combine ideas from multiple sources. Plan to consult a variety of resources, such as the following:

- **Primary and Secondary Sources:** To get a thorough view of your topic, use primary sources (firsthand or original accounts, such as interview transcripts, eyewitness reports, and newspaper articles) and secondary sources (accounts, created after an event occurred, such as encyclopedia entries).

- **Print and Digital Resources:** The Internet allows fast access to data, but print resources are often edited more carefully. Use both print and digital resources in order to guarantee the accuracy of your findings.

- **Media Resources:** You can find valuable information in media resources such as documentaries, television programs, podcasts, and museum exhibitions. Consider attending public lectures given by experts to gain an even more in-depth view of your topic.

- **Original Research:** Depending on your topic, you may wish to conduct original research to include among your sources. For example, you might interview experts or eyewitnesses, or conduct a survey of people in your community.

Evaluating Sources It is important to evaluate the credibility, validity, and accuracy of any information you find, as well as its appropriateness for your purpose and audience. You may find the information you need to answer your research question in specialized and authoritative sources, such as almanacs (for social, cultural, and natural statistics), government publications (for law, government programs, and subjects such as agriculture), and information services. Also, consider consumer, workplace, and public documents.

Ask yourself questions such as these to evaluate these additional sources:

- **Authority:** Is the author well known? What are the author's credentials? Does the source include references to other reliable sources? Does the author's tone win your confidence? Why or why not?

- **Bias:** Does the author have any obvious biases? What is the author's purpose for writing? Who is the target audience?

- **Currency:** When was the work created? Has it been revised? Is there more current information available?

Using Online Encyclopedias

Online encyclopedias are often written by anonymous contributors who are not required to fact-check information. These sites can be very useful as a launching point for research, but should not be considered accurate. Look for footnotes, endnotes, or hyperlinks that support facts with reliable sources that have been carefully checked by editors.

Using Search Terms

Finding information on the Internet can be both easy and challenging. Type a word or phrase into a general search engine and you will probably get hundreds—or thousands—of results. However, those results are not guaranteed to be relevant or accurate.

These strategies can help you find information from the Internet:

- Create a list of keywords that apply to your topic before you begin using a search engine. Consult a thesaurus to expand your list.

- Enter six to eight keywords.

- Choose precise nouns. Most search engines ignore articles and prepositions. Verbs may be used in multiple contexts, leading to sources that are not relevant. Use modifiers, such as adjectives, when necessary to specify a category.

- Use quotation marks to focus a search. Place a phrase in quotation marks to find pages that include exactly that phrase. Add several phrases in quotation marks to narrow your results.

- Spell carefully. Many search engines autocorrect spelling, but they cannot produce accurate results for all spelling errors.

- Scan search results before you click them. The first result isn't always the most relevant. Read the text and consider the domain before make a choice.

- Utilize more than one search engine.

Evaluating Internet Domains

Not everything you read on the Internet is true, so you have to evaluate sources carefully. The last three letters of an Internet URL identify the Website's domain, which can help you evaluate the information of the site.

- **.gov**—Government sites are sponsored by a branch of the United States federal government, such as the Census Bureau, Supreme Court, or Congress. These sites are considered reliable.

- **.edu**—Education domains include schools from kindergartens to universities. Information from an educational research center or department is likely to be carefully checked. However, education domains can also include student pages that are not edited or monitored.

- **.org**—Organizations are nonprofit groups and usually maintain a high level of credibility. Keep in mind that some organizations may express strong biases.

- **.com** and **.net**—Commercial sites exist to make a profit. Information may be biased to show a product or service in a good light. The company may be providing information to encourage sales or promote a positive image.

Taking Notes

Take notes as you locate and connect useful information from multiple sources, and keep a reference list of every source you use. This will help you make distinctions between the relative value and significance of specific data, facts, and ideas.

For long-term research projects, create source cards and notecards to keep track of information gathered from multiple resources.

Source Cards
Create a card that identifies each source.

- For print materials, list the author, title, publisher, date of publication, and relevant page numbers.
- For Internet sources, record the name and Web address of the site, and the date you accessed the information.
- For media sources, list the title, person, or group credited with creating the media, and the year of production.

Notecards
Create a separate notecard for each item of information.

- Include the fact or idea, the letter of the related source card, and the specific page(s) on which the fact or idea appears.
- Use quotation marks around words and phrases taken directly from print or media resources.
- Mark particularly useful or relevant details using your own annotation method, such as stars, underlining, or colored highlighting.

Source Card	[A]

Marsh, Peter. *Eye to Eye: How People Interact.* Salem House Publishers, 1988.

Notecard

Gestures vary from culture to culture. The American "OK" symbol (thumb and forefinger) is considered insulting in Greece and Turkey.

Source Card: A, p. 54.

Quote Accurately Responsible research begins with the first note you take. Be sure to quote and paraphrase your sources accurately so you can identify these sources later. In your notes, circle all quotations and paraphrases to distinguish them from your own comments. When photocopying from a source, include the copyright information. When printing out information from an online source, include the Web address.

Reviewing Research Findings

While conducting research, you will need to review your findings, checking that you have collected enough accurate and appropriate information.

Considering Audience and Purpose

Always keep your audience in mind as you gather information, since different audiences may have very different needs. For example, if you are writing an in-depth analysis of a text that your entire class has read together and you are writing for your audience, you will not need to gather background information that has been thoroughly discussed in class. However, if you are writing the same analysis for a national student magazine, you cannot assume that all of your readers have the same background information. You will need to provide facts from reliable sources to help orient these readers to your subject. When considering whether or not your research will satisfy your audience, ask yourself:

- Who are my readers? For whom am I writing?
- Have I collected enough information to explain my topic to this audience?
- Are there details in my research that I can omit because they are already familiar to my audience?

Your purpose for writing will also influence your review of research. If you are researching a question to satisfy your own curiosity, you can stop researching when you feel you understand the answer completely. If you are writing a research report that will be graded, you need to consider the criteria of the assignment. When considering whether or not you have enough information, ask yourself:

- What is my purpose for writing?
- Will the information I have gathered be enough to achieve my purpose?
- If I need more information, where might I find it?

Synthesizing Sources

Effective research writing does not merely present facts and details; it synthesizes—gathers, orders, and interprets—them. These strategies will help you synthesize information effectively:

- Review your notes and look for connections and patterns among the details you have collected.
- Arrange notes or notecards in different ways to help you decide how to best combine related details and present them in a logical way.
- Pay close attention to details that support one other, emphasizing the same main idea.
- Also look for details that challenge each other, highlighting ideas about which there is no single, or consensus, opinion. You might decide to conduct additional research to help you decide which side of the issue has more support.

Types of Evidence

When reviewing your research, also consider the kinds of evidence you have collected. The strongest writing contains a variety of evidence effectively. This chart describes three of the most common types of evidence: statistical, testimonial, and anecdotal.

TYPE OF EVIDENCE	DESCRIPTION	EXAMPLE
Statistical evidence includes facts and other numerical data used to support a claim or explain a topic.	Examples of statistical evidence include historical dates and information, quantitative analyses, poll results, and quantitative descriptions.	"Although it went on to become a hugely popular novel, the first edition of William Goldman's book sold fewer than 3,000 copies."
Testimonial evidence includes any ideas or opinions presented by others, especially experts in a field.	Firsthand testimonies present ideas from eyewitnesses to events or subjects being discussed.	"The ground rose and fell like an ocean at ebb tide." —Fred J. Hewitt, eyewitness to the 1906 San Francisco earthquake
	Secondary testimonies include commentaries on events by people who were not involved. You might quote a well-known literary critic when discussing a writer's most famous novel, or a prominent historian when discussing the effects of an important event	Gladys Hansen insists that "there was plenty of water in hydrants throughout [San Francisco] . . . The problem was this fire got away."
Anecdotal evidence presents one person's view of the world, often by describing specific events or incidents.	Compelling research should not rely solely on this form of evidence, but it can be very useful for adding personal insights and refuting inaccurate generalizations. An individual's experience can be used with other forms of evidence to present complete and persuasive support.	Although many critics claim the novel is universally beloved, at least one reader "threw the book against a wall because it made me so angry."

Incorporating Research Into Writing

Avoiding Plagiarism

Plagiarism is the unethical presentation of someone else's ideas as your own. You must cite sources for direct quotations, paraphrased information, or facts that are specific to a single source. When you are drafting and revising, circle any words or ideas that are not your own. Follow the instructions on pages R32 and R33 to correctly cite those passages.

Review for Plagiarism Always take time to review your writing for unintentional plagiarism. Read what you have written and take note of any phrases or sentences that do not have your personal writing voice. Compare those passages with your resource materials. You might have copied them without remembering the exact source. Add a correct citation to give credit to the original author. If you cannot find the questionable phrase in your notes, revise it to ensure that your final report reflects your own thinking and not someone else's work.

Quoting and Paraphrasing

When including ideas from research into your writing, you will decide to quote directly or paraphrase.

Direct Quotation Use the author's exact words when they are interesting or persuasive. You might decide to include direct quotations for these reasons:

- to share an especially clear and relevant statement
- to reference a historically significant passage
- to show that an expert agrees with your position
- to present an argument that you will counter in your writing.

Include complete quotations, without deleting or changing words. If you need to omit words for space or clarity, use ellipsis points to indicate the omission. Enclose direct quotations in quotation marks and indicate the author's name.

Paraphrase A paraphrase restates an author's ideas in your own words. Be careful to paraphrase accurately. Beware of making sweeping generalizations in a paraphrase that were not made by the original author. You may use some words from the original source, but a legitimate paraphrase does more than simply rearrange an author's phrases, or replace a few words with synonyms.

Original Text	"*The Tempest* was written as a farewell to art and the artist's life, just before the completion of his forty-ninth year, and everything in the play bespeaks the touch of autumn." Brandes, Georg. "Analogies Between *The Tempest* and *A Midsummer Night's Dream*." *The Tempest*, by William Shakespeare, William Heinemann, 1904, p. 668.
Patchwork Plagiarism phrases from the original are rearranged, but too closely follows the original text.	A farewell to art, Shakespeare's play, *The Tempest*, was finished just before the completion of his forty-ninth year. The artist's life was to end within three years. The touch of autumn is apparent in nearly everything in the play.
Good Paraphrase	Images of autumn occur throughout *The Tempest*, which Shakespeare wrote as a way of saying goodbye to both his craft and his own life.

Maintaining the Flow of Ideas

Effective research writing is much more that just a list of facts. Be sure to maintain the flow of ideas by connecting research information to your own ideas. Instead of simply stating a piece of evidence, use transition words and phrases to explain the connection between information you found from outside resources and your own ideas and purpose for writing. The following transitions can be used to introduce, compare, contrast, and clarify.

Useful Transitions

When providing examples:

for example   for instance   to illustrate   in [name of resource], [author]

When comparing and contrasting ideas or information:

in the same way   similarly   however   on the other hand

When clarifying ideas or opinions:

in other words   that is   to explain   to put it another way

Choosing an effective organizational structure for your writing will help you create a logical flow of ideas. Once you have established a clear organizational structure, insert facts and details from your research in appropriate places to provide evidence and support for your writing.

ORGANIZATIONAL STRUCTURE	USES
Chronological order presents information in the sequence in which it happens.	historical topics; science experiments; analysis of narratives
Part-to-whole order examines how several categories affect a larger subject.	analysis of social issues; historical topics
Order of importance presents information in order of increasing or decreasing importance.	persuasive arguments; supporting a bold or challenging thesis
Comparison-and-contrast organization outlines the similarities and differences of a given topic.	addressing two or more subjects

Formats for Citing Sources

In research writing, cite your sources. In the body of your paper, provide a footnote, an endnote, or a parenthetical citation, identifying the sources of facts, opinions, or quotations. At the end of your paper, provide a bibliography or a Works Cited list, a list of all the sources referred to in your research. Follow an established format, such as Modern Language Association (MLA) style.

Parenthetical Citations (MLA Style)

A parenthetical citation briefly identifies the source from which you have taken a specific quotation, factual claim, or opinion. It refers readers to one of the entries on your Works Cited list. A parenthetical citation has the following features:

- It appears in parentheses.
- It identifies the source by the last name of the author, editor, or translator, or by the title (for a lengthy title, list the first word only).
- It provides a page reference, the page(s) of the source on which the information cited can be found.

A parenthetical citation generally falls outside a closing quotation mark but within the final punctuation of a clause or sentence. For a long quotation set off from the rest of your text, place the citation at the end of the excerpt without any punctuation following.

Works Cited List (MLA Style)

A Works Cited list must contain accurate information to enable a reader to locate each source you cite. The basic components of an entry are as follows:

- name of the author, editor, translator, and/or group responsible for the work
- title of the work
- publisher
- date of publication

For print materials, the information for a citation generally appears on the copyright and title pages. For the format of a Works Cited list, consult the examples on this page and in the MLA Style for Listing Sources chart.

Sample Parenthetical Citations

It makes sense that baleen whales such as the blue whale, the bowhead whale, the humpback whale, and the sei whale (to name just a few) grow to immense sizes (Carwardine et al. 19–21). The blue whale has grooves running from under its chin to partway along the length of its underbelly. As in some other whales, these grooves expand and allow even more food and water to be taken in (Ellis 18–21).

Authors' last names

Page numbers where information can be found

Sample Works Cited List (MLA 8th Edition)

Carwardine, Mark, et al. *The Nature Company Guides: Whales, Dolphins, and Porpoises*. Time-Life, 1998.

"Discovering Whales." *Whales on the Net*. Whales in Danger, 1998, www.whales.org.au/discover/index.html. Accessed 11 Apr. 2017.

Neruda, Pablo. "Ode to Spring." *Odes to Opposites*, translated by Ken Krabbenhoft, edited and illustrated by Ferris Cook, Little, 1995, p. 16.

The Saga of the Volsungs. Translated by Jesse L. Byock, Penguin, 1990.

List an anonymous work by title.

List both the title of the work and the collection in which it is found.

Works Cited List or Bibliography?

A Works Cited list includes only those sources you paraphrased or quoted directly in your research paper. By contrast, a bibliography lists all the sources you consulted during research—even those you did not cite.

MLA (8th Edition) Style for Listing Sources

Book with one author	Pyles, Thomas. *The Origins and Development of the English Language.* 2nd ed., Harcourt Brace Jovanovich, 1971. [Indicate the edition or version number when relevant.]
Book with two authors	Pyles, Thomas, and John Algeo. *The Origins and Development of the English Language.* 5th ed., Cengage Learning, 2004.
Book with three or more authors	Donald, Robert B., et al. *Writing Clear Essays.* Prentice Hall, 1983.
Book with an editor	Truth, Sojourner. *Narrative of Sojourner Truth.* Edited by Margaret Washington, Vintage Books, 1993.
Introduction to a work in a published edition	Washington, Margaret. Introduction. *Narrative of Sojourner Truth,* by Sojourner Truth, edited by Washington, Vintage Books, 1993, pp. v–xi.
Single work in an anthology	Hawthorne, Nathaniel. "Young Goodman Brown." *Literature: An Introduction to Reading and Writing,* edited by Edgar V. Roberts and Henry E. Jacobs, 5th ed., Prentice Hall, 1998, pp. 376–385. [Indicate pages for the entire selection.]
Signed article from an encyclopedia	Askeland, Donald R. "Welding." *World Book Encyclopedia,* vol. 21, World Book, 1991, p. 58.
Signed article in a weekly magazine	Wallace, Charles. "A Vodacious Deal." *Time,* 14 Feb. 2000, p. 63.
Signed article in a monthly magazine	Gustaitis, Joseph. "The Sticky History of Chewing Gum." *American History,* Oct. 1998, pp. 30–38.
Newspaper article	Thurow, Roger. "South Africans Who Fought for Sanctions Now Scrap for Investors." *Wall Street Journal,* 11 Feb. 2000, pp. A1+. [For a multipage article that does not appear on consecutive pages, write only the first page number on which it appears, followed by the plus sign.]
Unsigned editorial or story	"Selective Silence." Editorial. *Wall Street Journal,* 11 Feb. 2000, p. A14. [If the editorial or story is signed, begin with the author's name.]
Signed pamphlet or brochure	[Treat the pamphlet as though it were a book.]
Work from a library subscription service	Ertman, Earl L. "Nefertiti's Eyes." *Archaeology,* Mar.–Apr. 2008, pp. 28–32. *Kids Search,* EBSCO, New York Public Library. Accessed 7 Jan. 2017. [Indicating the date you accessed the information is optional but recommended.]
Filmstrips, slide programs, videocassettes, DVDs, and other audiovisual media	*The Diary of Anne Frank.* 1959. Directed by George Stevens, performances by Millie Perkins, Shelley Winters, Joseph Schildkraut, Lou Jacobi, and Richard Beymer, Twentieth Century Fox, 2004. [Indicating the original release date after the title is optional but recommended.]
CD-ROM (with multiple publishers)	Simms, James, editor. *Romeo and Juliet.* By William Shakespeare, Attica Cybernetics / BBC Education / Harper, 1995.
Radio or television program transcript	"Washington's Crossing of the Delaware." *Weekend Edition Sunday,* National Public Radio, 23 Dec. 2013. Transcript.
Web page	"Fun Facts About Gum." ICGA, 2005–2017, www.gumassociation.org/index.cfm/facts-figures/fun-facts-about-gum. Accessed 19 Feb. 2017. [Indicating the date you accessed the information is optional but recommended.]
Personal interview	Smith, Jane. Personal interview, 10 Feb. 2017.

All examples follow the style given in the MLA Handbook, 8th edition, published in 2016.

MODEL

Evidence Log

Unit Title: _Discovery_

Perfomance-Based Assessment Prompt:
Do all discoveries benefit humanity?

My initial thoughts:
Yes - all knowledge moves us forward.

As you read multiple texts about a topic, your thinking may change. Use an Evidence Log like this one to record your thoughts, to track details you might use in later writing or discussion, and to make further connections.

Here is a sample to show how one reader's ideas deepened as she read two texts.

Title of Text: _Classifying the Stars_   Date: _Sept. 17_

CONNECTION TO THE PROMPT	TEXT EVIDENCE/DETAILS	ADDITIONAL NOTES/IDEAS
Newton shared his discoveries and then other scientists built on his discoveries.	Paragraph 2: "Isaac Newton gave to the world the results of his experiments on passing sunlight through a prism." Paragraph 3: "In 1814 . . . the German optician, Fraunhofer . . . saw that the multiple spectral tints . . . were crossed by hundreds of fine dark lines."	It's not always clear how a discovery might benefit humanity in the future.

How does this text change or add to my thinking?   This confirms what I think.   Date: _Sept. 20_

Title of Text: _Cell Phone Mania_   Date: _Sept. 21_

CONNECTION TO THE PROMPT	TEXT EVIDENCE/DETAILS	ADDITIONAL NOTES/IDEAS
Cell phones have made some forms of communication easier, but people don't talk to each other as much as they did in the past.	Paragraph 7: "Over 80% of young adults state that texting is their primary method of communicating with friends. This contrasts with older adults who state that they prefer a phone call."	Is it good that we don't talk to each other as much? Look for article about social media to learn more about this question.

How does this text change or add to my thinking?   Date: _Sept. 25_
Maybe there are some downsides to discoveries. I still think that knowledge moves us forward, but there are sometimes unintended negative effects.

Word Network

A word network is a collection of words related to a topic. As you read the selections in a unit, identify interesting theme-related words and build your vocabulary by adding them to your Word Network.

Use your Word Network as a resource for your discussions and writings. Here is an example:

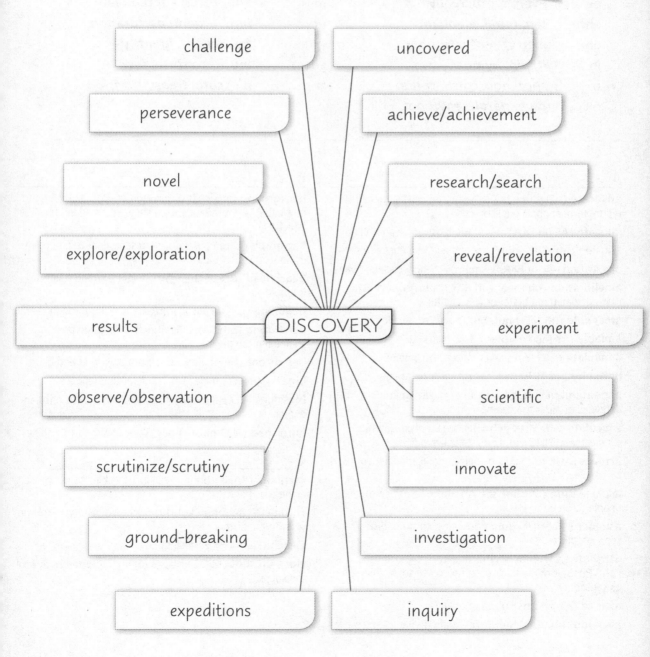

challenge

uncovered

perseverance

achieve/achievement

novel

research/search

explore/exploration

reveal/revelation

results

DISCOVERY

experiment

observe/observation

scientific

scrutinize/scrutiny

innovate

ground-breaking

investigation

expeditions

inquiry

ACADEMIC / CONCEPT VOCABULARY

Academic vocabulary appears in **blue type**.

Pronunciation Key

Symbol	Sample Words	Symbol	Sample Words
a	_at, catapult, Alabama_	oo	_boot, soup, crucial_
ah	_father, charms, argue_	ow	_now, stout, flounder_
ai	_care, various, hair_	oy	_boy, toil, oyster_
aw	_law, maraud, caution_	s	_say, nice, press_
awr	_pour, organism, forewarn_	sh	_she, abolition, motion_
ay	_ape, sails, implication_	u	_full, put, book_
ee	_even, teeth, really_	uh	_ago, focus, contemplation_
eh	_ten, repel, elephant_	ur	_bird, urgent. perforation_
ehr	_merry, verify, terribly_	y	_by, delight, identify_
ih	_it, pin, hymn_	yoo	_music, confuse, few_
o	_shot, hopscotch, condo_	zh	_pleasure, treasure, vision_
oh	_own, parole, rowboat_		

A

advocate (AD vuh kiht) _n._ supporter; (AD vuh kayt) _v._ represent or support publicly

allocate (AL uh kayt) _v._ set aside; assign or portion

allusion (uh LOO zhuhn) _n._ indirect reference

altercation (awl tuhr KAY shuhn) _n._ angry dispute; quarrel

amelioration (uh meel yuh RAY shuhn) _n._ act of making something better or less painful

amenable (uh MEH nuh buhl) _adj._ agreeable

amiably (AY mee uh blee) _adv._ pleasantly

annihilate (uh NY uh layt) _v._ destroy completely

antiquity (an TIHK wuh tee) _n._ very great age

appeasement (uh PEEZ muhnt) _n._ giving in to demands in order to keep peace

articulate (ahr TIHK yuh liht) _adj._ spoken clearly; distinct; (ahr TIHK yuh layt) _v._ clearly express

artifact (AHR tuh fakt) _n._ object made, modified, or used by people

asphyxiation (uhs fihk see AY shuhn) _n._ state of being unable to breathe

asunder (uh SUHN duhr) _adv._ divided; torn into separate pieces

attribute (A truh byoot) _n._ quality or characteristic; (uh TRIHB yoot) _v._ think of as belonging to; to think of as caused by

avarice (AV uh rihs) _n._ great greed

aversion (uh VUR zhuhn) _n._ strong dislike

B

background music (BAK grownd) (MYOO zihk) _n._ music that is not the focus of a show but is added for effect

bar graph (bahr) (graf) _n._ representation of data points using rectangular bars

beachhead (BEECH hehd) _n._ secure starting point; foothold

beguiling (bih GY lihng) _adj._ influencing through charm

belaboring (bih LAY buhr ihng) _v._ focusing on something too much

beneficent (buh NEHF uh suhnt) _adj._ kind and good

bigotry (BIHG uh tree) _n._ intolerance; prejudice

blessings (BLEHS ihngz) _n._ things that benefit or bring happiness

burnished (BUR nihsht) _adj._ shiny; polished to a shine

C

cartilage (KAHR tuh lihj) _n._ firm, flexible tissue almost as hard as bone

chronicle (KRON uh kuhl) _n._ recorded history; narrative _v._ write the history of

clench (klehnch) _v._ close tightly

close-up shot (KLOS uhp) (shot) _n._ close-range view of the subject

cognitive (KOG nuh tihv) *adj.* relating to the process of thinking

commentators (KOM uhn tay tuhrz) *n.* people who discuss or write about events for film, television, radio, or newspapers

communal (kuh MYOON uhl) *adj.* belonging to all in a community or group

composition (kom puh ZIHSH uhn) *n.* arrangement of the parts of a photograph

contentious (kuhn TEHN shuhs) *adj.* fond of arguing; quarrelsome; controversial

context (KON tehkst) *n.* position and immediate surroundings of an artifact or other feature in the location where it is found

contradict (kon truh DIHKT) *v.* do, say, or mean the opposite of; disagree with

current (KUR uhnt) *n.* flow of liquid, air, electricity, etc.

D

decree (dih KREE) *n.* decision made by an authority

deduce (dih DOOS) *v.* reach a conclusion by reasoning

delineate (dih LIHN ee ayt) *v.* trace an outline; draw or sketch out; describe

delusions (dih LOO zhuhnz) *n.* false beliefs

demarcate (DEE mahr kayt) *v.* set the limits of

democracy (dih MOK ruh see) *n.* government that is run by the people

democratic (dehm uh KRAT ihk) *adj.* belonging to a democracy; of, by, and for the people

desperate (DEHS puhr iht) *adj.* extremely bad; reckless; without hope

despoiled (dih SPOYLD) *v.* robbed; stripped of possessions

dimension (duh MEHN shuhn) *n.* measurement of length, width, or depth; quality or part

disarmament (dihs AHR muh muhnt) *n.* limiting or getting rid of weapons

dissolution (dihs uh LOO shuhn) *n.* ending or downfall

dissonance (DIHS uh nuhns) *n.* lack of agreement or harmony

distress (dihs TREHS) *n.* unhappiness or pain

doctrine (DOK truhn) *n.* set of principles or beliefs

dominating (DOM uh nay ting) *adj.* rising high above; towering over

E

edicts (EE dihkts) *n.* commands from a public authority

editing (EHD iht ihng) *v.* taking pieces of film or video and putting them together in a new way.

Egyptology (ee jihp TOL uh jee) *n.* study of the language, culture, and history of ancient Egypt

elemental (ehl uh MEHN tuhl) *adj.* basic; necessary; as found in nature

entitled (ehn TY tuhld) *adj.* having the rights to something; having privileges

entreating (ehn TREET ihng) *adj.* asking; pleading

enunciation (ih nuhn see AY shuhn) *n.* manner in which a speaker pronounces words

envoy (EHN voy) *n.* messenger

ethereal (ih THIHR ee uhl) *adj.* extremely delicate and light in a way that seems too perfect for this world

exquisite (EHKS kwihz iht) *adj.* very beautiful or lovely

F

fissure (FIHSH uhr) *n.* long, narrow crack or opening

flurry (FLUR ee) *n.* sudden burst of activity or excitement

fundamental (fuhn duh MEHN tuhl) *adj.* basic; essential; most important

G

gallantries (GAL uhn treez) *n.* acts of polite attention to the needs of women

gesture (JEHS chuhr) *n.* movement of the body that conveys meaning

gilded (GIHLD ihd) *v.* covered in a thin layer of gold; *adj.* golden

gregarious (gruh GAIR ee uhs) *adj.* sociable

H

heir (air) *n.* person who is legally entitled to inherit

hierarchy (HY uh rahr kee) *n.* people or things organized in higher and lower ranks or classes

homage (OM ihj) *n.* something done to honor someone

hounded (HOWN dihd) *v.* chased; hunted; urged

I

iconography (y kuh NOG ruh fee) *n.* system of symbolic images that conveys a subject, worldview, or concept

ideologies (y dee OL uh jeez) *n.* sets of beliefs of a people, groups, or cultures

implore (ihm PLAWR) *v.* beg or plead

incite (ihn SYT) *v.* strongly encourage

incoherent (ihn koh HIHR uhnt) *adj.* not understandable; confused

indomitable (ihn DOM uh tuh buhl) *adj.* bravely or stubbornly unyielding

industrious (ihn DUHS tree uhs) *adj.* hard-working

inestimable (ihn EHS tuh muh buhl) *adj.* too great to count or measure

inexorable (ihn EHK suhr uh buhl) *adj.* impossible to prevent or stop

inflection (ihn FLEHK shuhn) *n.* changes to pitch or volume within a single word or between words

influence (IHN floo uhns) *n.* dishonest persuasion; bribery

infographic (ihn foh GRAF ihk) *n.* display that combines text with visual elements and design to represent data

initiative (ih NIHSH ee uh tihv) *n.* readiness and abillity to start something; lead

integrate (IHN tuh grayt) *v.* make public facilities availabe to people of all races; bring parts together to make a whole

intemperate (ihn TEHM puhr iht) *adj.* lacking self-control; excessive

interactions (ihn tuhr AK shuhnz) *n.* actions with each other

intercept (ihn tuhr SEHPT) *v.* stop or seize something before it gets to its destination

interdependence (ihn tuhr dih PEHN duhns) *n.* reliance on each other

invective (ihn VEHK tihv) *n.* negative, aggressive language that seeks to harm

invoke (ihn VOHK) *v.* call on

invulnerable (in VUHL nuhr uh buhl) *adj.* incapable of being harmed

L

lead-in (LEED ihn) *n.* in a newscast, the short preliminary section that is used to set up the main story or interview

legacy (LEHG uh see) *n.* something handed down from an ancestor or prior generation

lighting and color (LYT ihng) (KUHL uhr) *n.* use of light, shadow, and color in a photograph

line graph (lyn) (graf) *n.* representation of data points using a line that connects points

listlessly (LIHST lihs lee) *adv.* without energy or interest

location (loh KAY shuhn) *n.* place or scene in which a photograph is taken

luminous (LOO muh nuhs) *adj.* glowing; shining with its own light

lustrous (LUHS truhs) *adj.* shiny; brilliant

M

mail (mayl) *n.* flexible armor

manipulate (muh NIHP yuh layt) *v.* handle or operate; unfairly influence or change

marauding (muh RAW dihng) *adj.* killing and using violence to steal precious items

marginalize (MAHR juh nuh lyz) *v.* treat as unimportant

marvel (MAHR vuhl) *n.* astonishment; used poetically as an adjective meaning "astonished" or "full of wonder"

merciful (MUR sih fuhl) *adj.* showing kindness

motivate (MOH tuh vayt) *v.* provide with an incentive

muffled (MUH fuhld) *adj.* difficult to hear because something is covering and softening the sound

N

navigating (NAV uh gayt ihng) *n.* finding one's way

needy (NEE dee) *adj.* very poor; requiring help

negate (nih GAYT) *v.* make invalid; deny the truth of

O

obdurate (OB duhr iht) *adj.* stubborn; unyielding

objection (uhb JEHK shuhn) *n.* reason or argument against something

obscure (uhb SKYAWR) *adj.* not well-known

opportune (op uhr TOON) *adj.* very favorable

oracles (AWR uh kuhlz) *n.* people who deliver messages from the gods

ore (awr) *n.* any type of mineral, rock, or metal found in the earth

P

pacification (pas uh fuh KAY shuhn) *n.* state of peace put in place through diplomacy, or political negotiation; also, use of force to suppress a hostile or resistent population

paradox (PAR uh doks) *n.* seeming contradiction

pardon (PAHR duhn) *v.* forgive

pariah (puh RY uh) *n.* someone who is despised; social outcast

penitent (PEHN uh tuhnt) *adj.* sorry for one's wrongdoing

perfidious (puhr FIHD ee uhs) *adj.* unfaithful and dishonest

periphery (puh RIHF uhr ee) *n.* outer boundary; edge

perplexity (puhr PLEHK suh tee) *n.* confusion; being in a puzzled state

perspective (puhr SPEHK tihv) *n.* particular way of looking at something; point of view

perspective or angle (puhr SPEHK tihv) (ANG guhl) *n.* vantage point from which a photograph is taken

pie chart (py) (chahrt) *n.* representation of data points using a circle cut into segments

primary (PRY mehr ee) *adj.* first in importance

proclamation (prok luh MAY shuhn) *n.* official announcement

propaganda (prop uh GAN duh) *n.* information, often of a false or misleading nature, used to promote a cause

prophecy (PROF uh see) *n.* prediction about the future

psychological (sy kuh LOJ uh kuhl) *adj.* of the mind

R

recessed (rih SEHST) *adj.* remote; set back

reclusive (rih KLOO sihv) *adj.* solitary; avoiding the company of others

rectify (REHK tuh fy) *v.* correct

refinement (rih FYN muhnt) *n.* politeness; good manners

rending (REHN dihng) *n.* violent or forceful pulling apart of something

resplendent (rih SPLEHN duhnt) *adj.* dazzling; gorgeous

revolution (rehv uh LOO shuhn) *n.* overthrow of a government that is replaced by a new system

S

sabotage (SAB uh tozh) *v.* intentionally ruin or destroy

scarred (skahrd) *adj.* marked by healed wounds

shunned (shuhnd) *v.* rejected; avoided

silhouette (sihl uh WEHT) *n.* dark figure that is seen as a filled-in shape against a light background

sinister (SIHN uh stuhr) *adj.* giving the impression that something harmful or evil is happening or will happen

slant (slant) *n.* attitude or opinion that a reporter takes toward a story

sliver (SLIHV uhr) *n.* small, slender piece of a hard material

sneered (sneerd) *v.* showed dislike with a mean smile

spacious (SPAY shuhs) *adj.* large; roomy

spitefully (SPYT fuhl ee) *adv.* in a way that purposely harms someone or something

stimulus (STIHM yoo luhs) *n.* something that causes a response or reaction

stock footage (stok) (FUT ihj) *n.* film or video that has been shot for one purpose and is available for use in other projects

stoical (STOH ih kuhl) *adj.* keeping strong emotions in check

subject (SUHB jehkt) *n.* primary figure(s), object(s), or other content in a photograph

subversive (suhb VUR sihv) *adj.* causing ruin; destructive

succession (suhk SEHSH uhn) *n.* process by which one is entitled to a privilege, rank or inheritance

supplant (suh PLANT) *v.* replace by unethical means

suppleness (SUHP uhl nihs) *n.* smoothness; fluidity; ability to adapt easily to different situations

surrender (suh REHN duhr) *n.* act of giving up

swollen (SWOH luhn) *adj.* puffed up

T

target (TAHR giht) *n.* object to be hit or shot at

tolerate (TOL uh rayt) *v.* endure; allow to happen without interference

tone (tohn) *n.* sound of a voice with respect to pitch, volume, and overall quality

totalitarian (toh tal uh TAIR ee uhn) *adj.* ruled or governed by a single person or group

transcend (tran SEHND) *v.* go beyond the limits of; be higher or greater than

travail (truh VAYL) *n.* difficult situation or work

traversed (truh VURST) *v.* crossed; traveled across; moved sideways

treacherous (TREHCH uhr uhs) *adj.* not trustworthy

treachery (TREHCH uhr ee) *n.* act of betrayal

trill (trihl) *n.* high-pitched vibrating sound

tumultuous (too MUHL choo uhs) *adj.* loud, excited, and emotional

tyranny (TEER uh nee) *n.* harsh rule over a nation or people

U

unconquerable (uhn KAHNG kuh ruh buhl) *adj.* unable to be defeated

unvoiced (uhn VOYST) *adj.* not spoken out loud or expressed

usurp (yoo ZURP) *v.* take over without having authority

V

valiant (VAL yuhnt) *adj.* brave; courageous

valor (VAL uhr) *n.* personal fortitude or bravery

vehement (VEE uh muhnt) *adj.* showing stong feeling; passionate

verify (VEHR uh fy) *v.* prove to be true

vestibule (VEHS tuh byool) *n.* entrance room

vigilance (VIHJ uh luhns) *n.* watchfulness

vivid (VIHV ihd) *adj.* bright and brilliant; strong and distinct; very intense

volition (voh LIHSH uhn) *n.* act of choosing

vulnerable (VUHL nuhr uh buhl) *adj.* able to be wounded or hurt

W

welt (wehlt) *n.* ridge on the skin caused by a blow

windfall (WIHND fawl) *n.* unexpected good fortune

VOCABULARIO ACADÉMICO/ VOCABULARIO DE CONCEPTOS

El vocabulario académico está en **letra azul**.

A

advocate / abogar *v.* representar o apoyar públicamente

allocate / asignar *v.* apartar; repartir o dividir

allusion / alusión *s.* referencia indirecta

altercation / altercado *s.* disputa; pelea

amelioration / mejoramiento *s.* acto de mejorar algo, o de hacerlo menos doloroso

amenable / dispuesto *adj.* agradable

amiably / amablemente *adv.* cordialmente, afablemente

annihilate / aniquilar *v.* destruir por completo

antiquity / antigüedad *s.* de muchos años; de hace mucho tiempo

appeasement / apaciguamiento *s.* el acto de aceptar exigencias con el fin de mantener la paz

articulate / articular *v.* expresar claramente

articulate / elocuente *adj.* claramente expresado

artifacts / artefactos *s.* objetos de interés histórico hechos por los seres humanos

asphyxiation / asfixia *s.* estado en el que resulta imposible respirar

asunder / dividido *adj.* separado; desarmado en distintas partes

attribute / atribuir *v.* pensar que algo es de la competencia de alguien o algo, o que fue causado por esa persona o hecho

avarice / avaricia *s.* avidez o codicia desmedida

aversion / aversión *s.* fuerte rechazo

B

background music / música de fondo *s.* música que no es el centro de un espectáculo, pero que se incluye para producir un efecto

bar chart / gráfica de barras *s.* representación de datos en la que se usa barras rectangulares

beachhead / cabeza de puente *s.* posición militar; asidero o punto de apoyo

beguiling / encantador *adj.* que influye por medio de su encanto

belaboring / concentrarse *v.* centrarse en algo con mucha intensidad

benificent / bienhechor *adj.* amable, bueno, caritativo

bigotry / intolerancia *s.* prejuicio; fanatismo

blessings / bendiciones *s.* cosas que benefician o que producen felicidad

burnished / bruñido *adj.* brilloso; pulido

C

caption / pie de foto *s.* texto breve que acompaña a una imagen

cartilage / cartílago *s.* tejido fuerte y flexible, casi tan duro como un hueso

chronicle / crónica *s.* relato histórico; narración

clench / apretar *v.* cerrar con fuerza

close-up shot / toma de primer plano *s.* imagen del sujeto tomada muy de cerca

cognitive / cognitivo *adj.* relacionado con el proceso de pensar

commentators / comentaristas *s.* personas que comentan o escriben sobre ciertos eventos para el cine, la televisión, la radio o los periódicos

communal / comunal *adj.* que pertenece a todos los miembros de una comunidad o grupo

composition / composición *s.* distribución o arreglo de las partes de una fotografía

contentious / peleador *adj.* que le gusta discutir o buscar pelea

context / contexto *s.* posición y entorno inmediato de un artefacto u otro elemento en el lugar donde es encontrado

contradict / contradecir *v.* negar que un enunciado sea cierto; discrepar

current / corriente *s.* flujo de líquido, aire, electricidad, etc; *adj.* actual, relativo al tiempo presente

D

decree / decreto *s.* decisión tomada por una autoridad

deduce / deducir *v.* llegar a una conclusión a través del razonamiento

delineate / delinear *v.* trazar un bosquejo; dibujar o esbozar; describir

delusions / delirios *s.* creencias falsas; engaños, ilusiones

demarcate / demarcar *v.* establecer los límites de algo

democracy / democracia *s.* gobierno conducido por el pueblo

democratic / democrático *adj.* que pertenece a una democracia; que es de, por y para el pueblo

desperate / desesperado *adj.* extremadamente mal; sin esperanza

despoiled / depojado *adj.* robado; privado de sus posesiones

dimension / dimensión *s.* medición de la longitud, el ancho o la profundidad; una cualidad o parte

disarmament / desarme *s.* acción de limitar o eliminar las armas

dissolution / disolución *s.* final o ruina

dissonance / disonancia *s.* falta de acuerdo o de armonía

distress / aflicción *s.* infelicidad o dolor

doctrine / doctrina *s.* conjunto de principios o creencias

dominating / dominante *adj.* que se alza por encima; que se destaca de los demás

E

edicts / edictos *s.* mandatos

editing / editar *v.* tomar partes de una película o video y volver a juntarlas de otra manera

Egyptology / egiptología *s.* estudio del lenguaje, la cultura y la historia del Egipto antiguo

elemental / elemental *adj.* básico; necesario; como se encuentra en la naturaleza

entitled / autorizado *adj.* que tiene el derecho a algo; que tiene ciertos privilegios

entreating / suplicante *adj.* que pide o ruega

enunciation / enunciación *s.* la manera en que un hablante expone las palabras

envoy / enviado *s.* mensajero

ethereal / etéreo *adj.* sumamente delicado y ligero

exquisite / exquisito *adj.* muy bello o agradable

F

fissure / fisura *s.* abertura o grieta larga y estrecha

flurry / frenesí *s.* explosión repentina de actividad o entusiasmo

fundamental / fundamental *adj.* que forma el fundamento o base; parte esencial

G

gallantries / galanterías *s.* gestos corteses de atención hacia las mujeres

gesture / gesto *s.* movimiento del cuerpo que transmite un mensaje

gilded / dorado *adj.* cubierto con una ligera capa de oro; de color oro

gregarious / gregario *adj.* sociable

H

heir / heredero *s.* persona que está legalmente autorizada a heredar determinados bienes

hierarchy / jerarquía *s.* personas o cosas organizadas en rangos o clases, del más alto al más bajo

homage / homenaje *s.* algo que se hace para honrar a una persona

hounded / acosado *adj.* perseguido; urgido

I

iconography / iconografía *s.* sistema de imágenes simbólicas que representa a un personaje, tema, visión del mundo o concepto

ideologies / ideologías *s.* conjuntos de creencias de una persona, un grupo o una cultura

implore / implorar *v.* rogar, suplicar

incite / incitar *v.* estimular con firmeza a alguien para que haga algo

incoherent / incoherente *adj.* confuso; difícil de entender

indomitable / indomable *adj.* difícil de dominar, bravío; inflexible

industrious / industrioso *adj.* trabajador

inestimable / inestimable *adj.* tan importante que no se puede estimar o medir

inexorable / inexorable *adj.* imposible de prever o impedir

inflection / inflección *s.* cambios en el tono o volumen dentro de una misma palabra o entre palabras

influence / influencia *s.* persuasión, a veces deshonesta, como cuando se usa de "enchufe" o "palanca", es decir, como contacto para lograr algo

infographic / infografía *s.* representación gráfica de información que incluye símbolos, fotos, mapas, textos y elementos de diseño visuales

initiative / iniciativa *s.* disponibilidad o habilidad para iniciar algo

integrate / integrar *v.* hacer los servicios públicos accesibles a todas las razas; unir las partes de un todo

intemperate / desmedido *adj.* descontrolado; excesivo

interactions / interacciones *s.* acciones de unos con otros

intercept / interceptar *v.* detener o apropiarse de algo antes de que llegue a su destino

interdependence / interdependencia *s.* dependencia o confianza mutua

invective / invectiva *s.* discurso negativo y agresivo que intenta herir

invoke / invocar *v.* llamar, convocar

invulnerable / invulnerable *adj.* que no se puede dañar

L

lead-in / entradilla *s.* introducción a una noticia o entrevista

legacy / legado *s.* algo que se transmite o pasa de un ancestro a sus descendientes, o de una generación a otra

lighting and color / luz y color *s.* modo de usar las luces, las sombras y los colores en una fotografía

line graph / gráfica de líneas *s.* representación de datos mediante una línea para conectar puntos

listlessly / lánguidamente *adv.* sin energía ni interés

location / ubicación *s.* lugar donde se toma una fotografía

luminous / luminoso *adj.* brillante; que brilla con su propia luz

lustrous / lustroso *adj.* brilloso, brillante

M

mail / cota de malla *s.* armadura flexible

manipulate / manipular *v.* manejar u operar; cambiar o influir de manera injusta

marauding / saqueador *adj.* que mata y usa la violencia para robar objetos de valor

marginalize / marginalizar *v.* tratar a alguien como si no fuera importante

marvel / maravilla / maravillarse *s.* algo asombroso; *v.* estar sumamente asombrado

merciful / compasivo *adj.* clemente, misericordioso

motivate / motivar *v.* proporcionar un incentivo para que alguien se interese en algo

muffled / sofocado *adj.* difícil de oír porque algo cubre y suaviza el sonido

N

navigating / navegar *v.* dirigir, guiar

needy / necesitado *adj.* muy pobre; que precisa ayuda

negate / negar *v.* invalidar; negarle razón a algo

O

obdurate / obstinado *adj.* terco; inflexible

objection / objeción *s.* razón o argumento contra algo

obscure / oscuro *adj.* desconocido

opportune / oportuno *adj.* muy conveniente; que sucede en el momento apropiado

oracle / oráculo *s.* persona que da mensajes de los dioses

ore / mineral *s.* cualquier tipo de sustancia inorgánica sólida, piedra o metal que se encuentra en la tierra

P

pacification / pacificación *s.* estado de calma o paz como resultado de la acción de la diplomacia o de la negociación política

paradox / paradoja *s.* enunciado, dato o situación inconsistente con las creencias aceptadas

pardon / perdonar *v.* disculpar

pariah / paria *s.* alguien que es despreciado; un marginado

penitent / penitente *adj.* alguien que se arrepiente de sus malas acciones

perfidious / pérfido *adj.* infiel y deshonesto

periphery / periferia *s.* límite exterior; borde

perplexity / perplejidad *s.* confusión; estado de desconcierto

perspective / perspectiva *s.* punto de vista

perspective / perspectiva *s.* en un cuadro o foto, la ilusión o efecto de profundidad

perspective or angle / perspectiva o ángulo *s.* punto o lugar desde el cual se toma una fotografía

photojournalism / fotoperiodismo *s.* tipo de periodismo en el que las fotos constituyen gran parte del artículo

pie chart / gráfico circular *s.* representación de los datos mediante un círculo dividido en segmentos

portrait / retrato *s.* imagen de una persona o de un grupo de personas

primary / primario / primarias *adj.* primero en importancia; *s.* elección en la que se escoge el candidato de un partido político

proclamation / proclamación *s.* anuncio oficia

propaganda / propaganda *s.* información, por lo general falsa, que se usa para promover una causa

prophecy / profecía *s.* predicción acerca del futuro

psychological / psicológico *adj.* relativo a la mente

R

recessed / retirado *adj.* lejano; oculto

reclusive / aislado *adj.* solitario; que evita la compañía de otros

rectify / rectificar *v.* corregir

refinement / refinamiento *s.* gentileza; buenas maneras

rending / desgarrar *v.* rasgar o romper algo con violencia o por la fuerza

resplendent / resplandeciente *adj.* deslumbrante; espléndido

revolution / revolución *s.* derrocamiento de un gobierno con el fin de reemplazarlo por otro sistema

S

sabotage / sabotear *v.* arruinar; hacer daño

scarred / marcado *adj.* que tiene cicatrices de antiguas heridas

shun / evitar *v.* rechazar; rehuir

silhouette / silueta *s.* figura oscura que se ve como un recorte contra un fondo claro

sinister / siniestro *adj.* malévolo; amenazador

slant / sesgo (ideológico) *s.* actitud u opinión del reportero acerca de una noticia

sliver / astilla *s.* trozo pequeño y fino de un material duro

sneered / se burló *v.* mostró disgusto haciendo una mueca

social documentary / foto documental *s.* género fotográfico que muestra a la gente en su entorno habitual

spacious / espacioso *adj.* grande; amplio

spitefully / maliciosamente *adv.* con el propósito de hacerle daño a alguien o algo

stimulus / estímulo *s.* algo que provoca una respuesta o reacción

stock footage / filmación de archivo *s.* película o video que se ha grabado con un propósito y está disponible para usarse en otros proyectos

stoical / estoico *adj.* de manera que controla las emociones fuertes

subject / sujeto *s.* figura(s), objeto(s) u otro contenido de una fotografía

subversive / subversivo *adj.* que intenta cambiar el orden establecido; destructivo o causante de ruina

succession / sucesión *s.* proceso por el cual una persona adquiere el derecho a un privilegio, rango o herencia

supplant / suplantar *v.* reemplazar a alguien por medios ilegítimos o poco éticos

suppleness / flexibilidad *s.* la habilidad de adaptarse con facilidad a distintas situaciones

surrender / rendirse *s.* darse por vencido

swollen / inflamado *adj.* hinchado

T

target / blanco *s.* objeto al que se debe disparar o tirar

tolerate / tolerar *v.* soportar; permitir que algo suceda, sin interferir

tone / tono *s.* sonido de una voz con respecto a la modulación, volumen y timbre general

totalitarian / totalitario *adj.* dominado o gobernado por un solo grupo o persona

transcend / trascender *v.* traspasar los límites de algo; ser más alto o más grande que algo

travail / esfuerzo *s.* trabajo o situación difícil

traversed / atravesado *adj.* cruzado; recorrido; que se movió de lado

treacherous / traicionero *adj.* que no es digno de confianza

treachery / traición *s.* acción desleal

trill / gorjeo *s.* sonido muy alto y vibrante; *v.* gorjear, producir un sonido muy alto y vibrante

tumultuous / tumultuoso *adj.* fuerte, alterado y emocional

tyranny / tiranía *s.* gobierno cruel de un pueblo o nación

U

unconquerable / inconquistable *adj.* que no puede ser vencido

unvoiced / tácito *adj.* no dicho, implícito

usurp / usurpar *v.* tomar algo por la fuerza, sin tener autoridad para hacerlo

V

valiant / valiente *adj.* bravo; aguerrido

valor / valor *s.* valentía o fortaleza personal

vehement / vehemente *adj.* que demuestra tener sentimientos intensos; apasionado

verify / verificar *v.* comprobar que algo es cierto

vestibule / vestíbulo *s.* entrada o recibidor

vigilance / vigilancia *s.* supervisión, custodia, alerta

vivid / vívido *adj.* luminoso y brillante; fuerte y distinto; muy intenso

volition / volición *s.* acto o capacidad de escoger

vulnerable / vulnerable *adj.* que puede ser herido o dañado

W

welt / verdugón *s.* marca en la piel causada por un golpe

windfall / ganancia inesperada *s.* golpe de suerte; beneficios caídos del cielo

LITERARY TERMS HANDBOOK

GLOSSARY: LITERARY TERMS HANDBOOK

ABSURDISM *Absurdism*, or a*bsurdist literature*, is a form of modernism that includes fantastic or dreamlike elements that blur the boundary between what is real and unreal.

ALLITERATION *Alliteration* is the repetition of initial consonant sounds. Writers use alliteration to give emphasis to words, to imitate sounds, and to create musical effects.

ALLUSION An *allusion* is a reference to a well-known person, place, event, literary work, or work of art.

ANALOGY An *analogy* makes a comparison between two or more things that are similar in some ways but otherwise unalike.

ANAPHORA *Anaphora* is a type of parallel structure in which a word or phrase is repeated at the beginning of successive clauses for emphasis.

ANECDOTE An *anecdote* is a brief story told to entertain or to make a point.

ANTAGONIST An *antagonist* is a character or force in conflict with a main character, or protagonist.

APOSTROPHE An *apostrophe* is a figure of speech in which a speaker directly addresses an absent person or a personified quality, object, or idea.

APPEAL An *appeal* is a rhetorical device used in argumentative writing to persuade an audience.

An appeal to ethics (Ethos) shows that an argument is just or fair.

An appeal to logic (Logos)shows that an argument is well reasoned.

An appeal to authority shows that a higher power supports the ideas.

An appeal to emotion (Pathos) is designed to influence readers.

ARGUMENT An *argument* is writing or speech that attempts to convince a reader to think or act in a particular way. An argument is a logical way of presenting a belief, conclusion, or stance. A good argument is supported with reasoning and evidence.

ASIDE An *aside* is a short speech delivered by a character in a play in order to express his or her thoughts and feelings. Traditionally, the aside is directed to the audience and is presumed not to be heard by the other characters.

AUTOBIOGRAPHY An *autobiography* is a form of nonfiction in which a writer tells his or her own life story. An autobiography may tell about the person's whole life or only a part of it.

BIOGRAPHY A *biography* is a form of nonfiction in which a writer tells the life story of another person.

Biographies have been written about many famous people, historical and contemporary, but they can also be written about "ordinary" people.

BLANK VERSE *Blank verse* is poetry written in unrhymed iambic pentameter lines. This verse form was widely used by William Shakespeare.

CHARACTER A *character* is a person or an animal who takes part in the action of a literary work. The main character, or protagonist, is the most important character in a story. This character often changes in some important way as a result of the story's events.

Characters are sometimes classified as round or flat, dynamic or static. A *round character* shows many different traits—faults as well as virtues. A *flat character* shows only one trait. A *dynamic character* develops and grows during the course of the story; a *static character* does not change.

CHARACTERIZATION *Characterization* is the act of creating and developing a character. In *direct characterization*, the author directly states a character's traits.

In *indirect characterization*, an author gives clues about a character by describing what a character looks like, does, and says, as well as how other characters react to him or her. It is up to the reader to draw conclusions about the character based on this indirect information.

The most effective indirect characterizations usually result from showing characters acting or speaking.

CLIMAX The *climax* of a story, novel, or play is the high point of interest or suspense. The events that make up the rising action lead up to the climax. The events that make up the falling action follow the climax.

COMEDY A *comedy* is a literary work, especially a play, that has a happy ending. Comedies often show ordinary characters in conflict with society. These conflicts are introduced through misunderstandings, deceptions, and concealed identities. When the conflict is resolved, the result is the correction of moral faults or social wrongs. Types of comedy include *romantic comedy*, which involves problems among lovers, and the *comedy of manners*, which satirically challenges the social customs of a sophisticated society. Comedy is often contrasted with tragedy, in which the protagonist meets an unfortunate end.

COMIC RELIEF *Comic relief* is a technique that is used to interrupt a serious part of a literary work by introducing a humorous character or situation.

CONFLICT A *conflict* is a struggle between opposing forces. Characters in conflict form the basis of stories, novels, and plays.

There are two kinds of conflict: **external** and **internal**. In an external conflict, the main character struggles against an outside force. The outside force may be nature itself.

An *internal conflict* involves a character in conflict with himself or herself.

CONNOTATION The *connotation* of a word is the set of ideas associated with it in addition to its explicit meaning.

CONSONANCE *Consonance* is the repetition of final consonant sounds in stressed syllables with different vowel sounds, as in *hat* and *sit*.

COUPLET A *couplet* is a pair of rhyming lines, usually of the same length and meter.

DENOTATION The *denotation* of a word is its dictionary meaning, independent of other associations that the word may have. The denotation of the word *lake*, for example, is "an inland body of water."

DESCRIPTION A *description* is a portrait in words of a person, place, or object. Descriptive writing uses sensory details, those that appeal to the senses: sight, hearing, taste, smell, and touch. Description can be found in all types of writing.

DIALECT *Dialect* is a special form of a language, spoken by people in a particular region or group. It may involve changes to the pronunciation, vocabulary, and sentence structure of the standard form of the language. Rudyard Kipling's "Danny Deever" is a poem written in the Cockney dialect of English, used by working-class Londoners.

DIALOGUE A *dialogue* is a conversation between characters that may reveal their traits and advance the action of a narrative. In fiction or nonfiction, quotation marks indicate a speaker's exact words, and a new paragraph usually indicates a change of speaker.

Quotation marks are not used in *script*, the printed copy of a play. Instead, the dialogue follows the name of the speaker:

DICTION *Diction* refers to an author's choice of words, especially with regard to range of vocabulary, use of slang and colloquial language, and level of formality.

DRAMA A *drama* is a story written to be performed by actors. The script of a drama is made up of **dialogue**—the words the actors say—and **stage directions,** which are descriptions of how and where action happens.

The drama's **setting** is the time and place in which the action occurs. It is indicated by one or more sets, including furniture and backdrops, that suggest interior or exterior scenes. *Props* are objects, such as a sword or a cup of tea, that are used onstage.

At the beginning of most plays, a brief **exposition** gives the audience some background information about the characters and the situation. Just as in a story or novel, the plot of a drama is built around characters in conflict.

Dramas are divided into large units called *acts*, which are divided into smaller units called *scenes*. A long play may include many sets that change with the scenes, or it may indicate a change of scene with lighting.

ESSAY An *essay* is a short nonfiction work about a particular subject. While classification is difficult, five types of essays are sometimes identified.

A *descriptive essay* seeks to convey an impression about a person, place, or object.

An *explanatory essay* describes and summarizes information gathered from a number of sources on a concept.

A *narrative essay* tells a true story. An autobiographical essay is a narrative essay in which the writer tells a story from his or her own life.

A *persuasive essay* tries to convince readers to do something or to accept the writer's point of view.

EXPOSITION *Exposition* is writing or speech that explains a process or presents information. In the plot of a story or drama, the exposition is the part of the work that introduces the characters, the setting, and the basic situation.

EXTENDED METAPHOR In an **extended metaphor,** as in regular metaphor, a writer speaks or writes of a subject as though it were something else. An extended metaphor sustains the comparison for several lines or for an entire poem.

FANTASY A *fantasy* is a work of highly imaginative writing that contains elements not found in real life. Examples of fantasy include stories that involve supernatural elements, such as fairy tales, and stories that deal with imaginary places and creatures.

FICTION *Fiction* is prose writing that tells about imaginary characters and events. The term is usually used for novels and short stories, but it also applies to dramas and narrative poetry. Some writers rely on their imaginations alone to create their works of fiction. Others base their fiction on actual events and people, to which they add invented characters, dialogue, and plot situations.

FIGURATIVE LANGUAGE *Figurative language* is writing or speech not meant to be interpreted literally. It is often used to create vivid impressions by setting up comparisons between dissimilar things.

Some frequently used figures of speech are **metaphor, simile,** and **personification.**

FLASHBACK A *flashback* is a means by which authors present material that occurred earlier than the present time of the narrative. Authors may include this material in the form of a characters' memories, dreams, or accounts of past events, or they may simply shift their narrative back to the earlier time.

FORESHADOWING *Foreshadowing* is the use in a literary work of clues that suggest events that have yet to occur. This technique helps to create suspense, keeping readers wondering about what will happen next.

FREE VERSE *Free verse* is poetry not written in a regular pattern of meter or rhyme.

GENRE A *genre* is a category or form of literature. Literature is commonly divided into three major types of writing: poetry, prose, and drama. For each type, there are several distinct genres, as follows:

1. **Poetry:** Lyric Poetry, Concrete Poetry, Dramatic Poetry, Narrative Poetry, and Epic Poetry
2. **Prose:** Fiction (Novels and Short Stories) and Nonfiction (Biography, Autobiography, Letters, Essays, and Reports)
3. **Drama:** Serious Drama and Tragedy, Comedy, Melodrama, and Farce

GOTHIC LITERATURE A genre that began in England in the late 1700s, *Gothic literature* features bleak or remote settings, characters in psychological torment, plots that include violence or the supernatural, strongly dramatic and intensely descriptive language, and a gloomy, melancholy, or eerie mood.

HYPERBOLE A *hyperbole* is a deliberate exaggeration or overstatement. Hyperboles are often used for comic effect.

IMAGERY *Imagery* is the descriptive or figurative language used in literature to create word pictures for the reader. These pictures, or images, are created by details of sight, sound, taste, touch, smell, or movement.

INFORMATIONAL GRAPHICS *Informational graphics* or *infographics* use images, symbols, graphs, and text to explain and depict the complexities of a topic in a clear and engaging way.

INTERVIEW An *interview* is a structured conversation between two people. In an interview, one person is trying to gain information from another in a question and answer format.

IRONY *Irony* is the general term for literary techniques that portray differences between appearance and reality, or expectation and result. In *verbal irony,* words are used to suggest the opposite of what is meant. In *dramatic irony,* there is a contradiction between what a character thinks and what the reader or audience knows to be true. In *irony of situation,* an event occurs that directly contradicts readers' expectations.

JUXTAPOSITION *Juxtaposition* is setting ideas or details side by side. This effectively helps readers analyze the similarities and differences between two ideas.

LITERARY NONFICTION *Literary nonfiction* is writing that employs many of the same literary devices as fiction while still remaining factual. It may develop a plot, use sensory details, incorporate dialogue, and even use figurative language. Memoirs, autobiographies, speeches, and lectures are often considered literary nonfiction.

LYRIC POEM A *lyric poem* is a poem written in highly musical language that expresses the thoughts, observations, and feelings of a single speaker.

MAGICAL REALISM *Magical realism* incorporates elements of fantasy and myth into otherwise realistic narratives.

METAPHOR A *metaphor* is a figure of speech in which one thing is spoken of as though it were something else. Unlike a simile, which compares two things using *like* or *as,* a metaphor implies a comparison between them.

METER The *meter* of a poem is its rhythmical pattern. This pattern is determined by the number and arrangements of stressed syllables, or beats, in each line. To describe the meter of a poem, you must scan its lines. Scanning involves marking the stressed and unstressed syllables:

Each stressed syllable is marked with a slanted line (´) and each unstressed syllable with a horseshoe symbol (˘). The stressed and unstressed syllables are then divided by vertical lines (|) into groups called *feet.* The following types of feet are common in English poetry:

1. *Iamb:* a foot with one unstressed syllable followed by a stressed syllable, as in the word "again"
2. *Trochee:* a foot with one stressed syllable followed by an unstressed syllable, as in the word "wonder"
3. *Anapest:* a foot with two unstressed syllables followed by one strong stress, as in the phrase "on the beach"
4. *Dactyl:* a foot with one strong stress followed by two unstressed syllables, as in the word "wonderful"
5. *Spondee:* a foot with two strong stresses, as in the word "spacewalk"

Depending on the type of foot that is most common in them, lines of poetry are described as *iambic, trochaic, anapestic,* and so forth.

Lines are also described in terms of the number of feet that occur in them, as follows:

1. *Monometer:* verse written in one-foot lines
2. *Dimeter:* verse written in two-foot lines
3. *Trimeter:* verse written in three-foot lines
4. *Tetrameter:* verse written in four-foot lines
5. *Pentameter:* verse written in five-foot lines
6. *Hexameter:* verse written in six-foot lines
7. *Heptameter:* verse written in seven-foot lines

Blank verse is poetry written in unrhymed iambic pentameter.

Free verse is poetry that does not follow a regular pattern of meter and rhyme.

MODERNISM *Modernism* is a form of creative expression that developed during the early twentieth century. Modernism developed in response to the rapid rise of industry, the shift from rural to urban societies, and the horrors or war. Ambiguity, blurred boundaries between reality and fantasy, and themes of alienation are elements of modernism.

MONOLOGUE A *monologue* in a play is a long speech by one character that, unlike a soliloquy, is addressed to another character or characters.

MOOD *Mood,* or *atmosphere,* is the feeling created in the reader by a literary work or passage. The mood is often suggested by descriptive details. Often the mood can be described in a single word, such as *lighthearted, frightening,* or *despairing*.

NARRATION *Narration* is writing that tells a story. The act of telling a story in speech is also called *narration.* Novels and short stories are fictional narratives. Nonfiction works—such as news stories, biographies, and autobiographies—are also narratives. A narrative poem tells a story in verse.

NARRATIVE A *narrative* is a story told in fiction, nonfiction, poetry, or drama.

NARRATIVE POEM A *narrative poem* is one that tells a story.

NARRATOR A *narrator* is a speaker or character who tells a story. The writer's choice of narrator determines the story's *point of view,* or the perspective from which the story is told. By using a consistent point of view, a writer controls the amount and type of information revealed to the reader.

When a character in the story tells the story, that character is a *first-person narrator.* This narrator may be a major character, a minor character, or just a witness. Readers see only what this character sees, hear only what he or she hears, and so on. Viewing unfolding events from this character's perspective, the reader shares in his discoveries and feels more suspense than another point of view would provide.

When a voice outside the story narrates, the story has a *third-person narrator.* An *omniscient,* or all-knowing, third-person narrator can tell readers what any character thinks and feels. A *limited third-person narrator* sees the world through one character's eyes and reveals only that character's thoughts.

NONFICTION *Nonfiction* is prose writing that presents and explains ideas or that tells about real people, places, ideas, or events. To be classified as nonfiction, a work must be true.

NOVEL A *novel* is a long work of fiction. It has a plot that explores characters in conflict. A novel may also have one or more subplots, or minor stories, and several themes.

ONOMATOPOEIA *Onomatopoeia* is the use of words that imitate sounds. *Whirr, thud, sizzle,* and *hiss* are typical examples. Writers can deliberately choose words that contribute to a desired sound effect.

OXYMORON An *oxymoron* is a combination of words that contradict each other. Examples are "deafening silence," "honest thief," "wise fool," and "bittersweet." This device is effective when the apparent contradiction reveals a deeper truth.

PERSONIFICATION *Personification* is a type of figurative language in which a nonhuman subject is given human characteristics: *The moss embraced the tree.*

PERSUASION *Persuasion* is writing or speech that attempts to convince the reader to adopt a particular opinion or course of action.

An *argument* is a logical way of presenting a belief, conclusion, or stance. A good argument is supported with reasoning and evidence.

PLOT *Plot* is the sequence of events in a literary work. In most novels, dramas, short stories, and narrative poems, the plot involves both characters and a central conflict. The plot usually begins with an *exposition* that introduces the setting, the characters, and the basic situation. This is followed by the *inciting incident,* which introduces the central conflict. The conflict then increases during the *development* until it reaches a high point of interest or suspense, the *climax.* All the events leading up to the climax make up the *rising action.* The climax is followed by the *falling action,* which leads to the *denouement,* or *resolution,* in which the conflict is resolved and in which a general insight may be conveyed.

POETIC STRUCTURE The basic structures of poetry are lines and stanzas. A *line* is a group of words arranged in a row. A line of poetry may break, or end, in different ways. Varied *line lengths* can create unpredictable rhythms.

An *end-stopped line* is one in which both the grammatical structure and sense are complete at the end of the line.

A *run-on,* or *enjambed, line* is one in which both the grammatical structure and sense continue past the end of the line.

POETRY *Poetry* is one of the three major types of literature, the others being prose and drama. Most poems make use of highly concise, musical, and emotionally charged language. Many also make use of imagery, figurative language, and special devices of sound such as rhyme. Poems are often divided into lines and stanzas and often employ regular rhythmical patterns, or meters. Poetry that does not follow a regular metrical pattern is called *free verse.*

POINT OF VIEW *Point of view* is the perspective, or vantage point, from which a story is told. By using a consistent point of view, a writer controls the amount and type of information revealed to the reader. When a character in the story tells the story, that character is a **first-person narrator** and has a **limited point of view.** When a voice outside the story narrates and is all-knowing, the story has an **omniscient point of view.** A narrator that uses the **third-person point of view** sees the world through one character's eyes and reveals only that character's thoughts.

PROSE *Prose* is the ordinary form of written language. Most writing that is not poetry, drama, or song is considered prose. Prose is one of the major categories of literature and occurs in two forms: fiction and nonfiction.

PROSE POEM A **prose poem** is a poetic form that looks like prose, or a non-poetic work, but reads like poetry. Prose poems lack the line breaks most often found in poetry, but they contain other poetic techniques such as repetition or rhyme.

REPETITION *Repetition* is the use of any element of language—a sound, a word, a phrase, a clause, or a sentence—more than once within a passage of text.

Poets use many kinds of repetition. **Alliteration, assonance, consonance, rhyme,** and **rhythm** are repetitions of certain sounds and sound patterns. A *refrain* is a repeated line or group of lines. In both prose and poetry, repetition is used for musical effects and for emphasis.

RHETORICAL DEVICES Rhetorical devices are special patterns of words and ideas that create emphasis and stir emotion, especially in speeches or other oral presentations. *Parallelism,* for example, is the repetition of a grammatical structure in order to create a rhythm and make words more memorable.

Other common rhetorical devices include:
analogy: drawing comparisons between two unlike things
charged language: words that appeal to the emotions
concession: an acknowledgment of the opposition's argument
humor: use of language and details that make characters or situations funny
paradox: statement that seems to contradict but actually presents a truth
restatement: an expression of the same idea in different words
rhetorical questions: questions not meant to be answered because the answers are obvious. For example, *Is freedom a basic human right?* is a rhetorical question.
tone: the author's attitude toward the topic

RHYME *Rhyme* is the repetition of sounds at the end of words. End rhyme occurs when the rhyming words come at the ends of lines.

Internal rhyme occurs when one of the rhyming words appears within a line.

Exact rhyme involves the repetition of the same final vowel and consonant sounds in words like *ball* and *hall. Slant*

rhyme involves the repetition of words that sound alike but do not rhyme exactly, like *grove* and *love.*

RHYME SCHEME A **rhyme scheme** is a regular pattern of rhyming words in a poem. The rhyme scheme of a poem is indicated by using different letters of the alphabet for each new rhyme. In an *aabb* stanza, for example, line 1 rhymes with line 2 and line 3 rhymes with line 4.

Many poems use the same pattern of rhymes, though not the same rhymes, in each stanza.

SATIRE A **satire** is a literary work that ridicules the foolishness and faults of individuals, an institution, society, or even humanity in general.

SENSORY LANGUAGE *Sensory language* is writing or speech that appeals to one or more of the senses.

SEQUENCE OF EVENTS Authors often use **sequence of events,** or the order in which things happened, to structure nonfiction pieces that describe historical events or explain a change over time. Authors frequently describe important events in **chronological order,** or time order.

SETTING The **setting** of a literary work is the time and place of the action. Time can include not only the historical period—past, present, or future—but also a specific year, season, or time of day. Place may involve not only the geographical place—a region, country, state, or town—but also the social, economic, or cultural environment.

In some stories, setting serves merely as a backdrop for action, a context in which the characters move and speak. In others, however, setting is a crucial element.

SHORT STORY A **short story** is a brief work of fiction. In most short stories, one main character faces a conflict that is resolved in the plot of the story. Great craftsmanship must go into the writing of a good story, for it has to accomplish its purpose in relatively few words.

SIMILE A **simile** is a figure of speech in which the words like or as are used to compare two apparently dissimilar items. The comparison, however, surprises the reader into a fresh perception by finding an unexpected likeness.

SOCIAL COMMENTARY In works of **social commentary**, an author seeks to highlight, usually in a critical way, an aspect of society. Social commentary is often the point of **satire**, in which the author points out the absurdity of a practice, custom, or institution.

SOLILOQUY A **soliloquy** is a long speech expressing the thoughts of a character alone on stage.

SONNET A **sonnet** is a fourteen-line lyric poem, usually written in rhymed iambic pentameter. The *English,* or *Shakespearean,* sonnet consists of three quatrains (four-line stanzas) and a couplet (two lines), usually rhyming *abab cdcd efef gg.* The couplet usually comments on the ideas contained in the preceding twelve lines. The sonnet is usually not printed with the stanzas divided, but a reader can see distinct ideas in each.

The *Italian,* or *Petrarchan,* sonnet consists of an octave (eight-line stanza) and a sestet (six-line stanza). Often, the octave rhymes *abbaabba* and the sestet rhymes *cdecde.* The octave states a theme or asks a question. The sestet comments on the theme or answers the question.

SPEAKER The *speaker* is the imaginary voice assumed by the writer of a poem. In many poems, the speaker is not identified by name. When reading a poem, remember that the speaker of a poem may be a person, an animal, a thing, or an abstraction.

STAGE DIRECTIONS *Stage directions* are notes included in a drama to describe how the work is to be performed or staged. These instructions are printed in italics and are not spoken aloud. They are used to describe sets, lighting, sound effects, and the appearance, personalities, and movements of characters.

STANZA A *stanza* is a repeated grouping of two or more lines in a poem that often share a pattern of rhythm and rhyme. Stanzas are sometimes named according to the number of lines they have—for example, a *couplet,* two lines; a *quatrain,* four lines; a *sestet,* six lines; and an *octave,* eight lines.

STYLE *Style* refers to an author's unique way of writing. Elements determining style include diction; tone; characteristic use of figurative language, dialect, or rhythmic devices; and typical grammatical structures and patterns.

SURPRISE ENDING A *surprise ending* is a conclusion that violates the expectations of the reader but in a way that is both logical and believable.

SYMBOL A *symbol* is a character, place, thing or event that stands for something else, often an abstract idea. For example, a flag is a piece of cloth, but it also represents the idea of a country. Writers sometimes use conventional symbols like flags. Frequently, however, they create symbols of their own through emphasis or repetition.

SYNTAX *Syntax* is the structure of sentences.

THEME A *theme* is a central message or insight into life revealed through a literary work.

The theme of a literary work may be stated directly or implied. When the theme of a work is implied, readers infer what the work suggests about people or life.

Archetypal themes are those that occur in folklore and literature across the world and throughout history.

TONE The *tone* of a literary work is the writer's attitude toward his or her audience and subject. The tone can often be described by a single adjective, such as *formal* or *informal, serious* or *playful, bitter* or *ironic.*

TRAGEDY A *tragedy* is a work of literature, especially a play, that tells of a catastrophe, a disaster or great misfortune, for the main character. In ancient Greek drama, the main character was always a significant person—a king or a hero—and the cause of the tragedy was often a tragic flaw, or weakness, in his or her character. In modern drama, the main character can be an ordinary person, and the cause of the tragedy can be some evil in society itself. Tragedy not only arouses fear and pity in the audience, but also, in some cases, conveys a sense of the grandeur and nobility of the human spirit.

VOICE *Voice* is a writer's distinctive "sound" or way of "speaking" on the page. It is related to such elements as word choice, sentence structure, and tone. It is similar to an individual's speech style and can be described in the same way—fast, slow, blunt, meandering, breathless, and so on.

Voice resembles *style,* an author's typical way of writing, but style usually refers to a quality that can be found throughout an author's body of work, while an author's voice may sometimes vary from work to work.

MANUAL DE TÉRMINOS LITERARIOS

ABSURDISM / LITERATURA DEL ABSURDO La *literatura del absurdo* es un tipo de *modernismo* que incluye elementos de fantasía o surreales que borran el límite entre lo real y lo irreal.

ALLITERATION / ALITERACIÓN La *aliteración* es la repetición de los sonidos consonantes iniciales. Los escritores usan la aliteración para dar énfasis a las palabras, para imitar sonidos y para crear efectos de musicalidad.

ALLUSION / ALUSIÓN Una *alusión* es una referencia a una persona, lugar, hecho, obra literaria u obra de arte muy conocida.

ANALOGY / ANALOGÍA Una *analogía* establece una comparación entre dos o más cosas que son parecidas en algunos aspectos pero se diferencian en otros.

ANAPHORA / ANÁFORA La *anáfora* es un tipo de paralelismo en el que una palabra o frase se repite al principio de varias cláusulas para hacer énfasis.

ANECDOTE / ANÉCDOTA Una *anécdota* es un relato breve que se narra con el fin de entretener o decir algo importante.

ANTAGONIST / ANTAGONISTA Un *antagonista* es un personaje o fuerza en conflicto con el personaje principal o protagonista.

APOSTROPHE / APÓSTROFE El *apóstrofe* es una figura retórica en la que el hablante se dirige directamente a una persona ausente o a una idea, objeto o cualidad personificada.

APPEAL / APELACIÓN Una *apelación* es un recurso retórico que se usa en los escritos de argumentación para persuadir al público. Una apelación a la ética (Ethos) muestra que un argumento es justo. Una apelación a la lógica (Logos) muestra que un argumento está bien razonado. Una apelación a la autoridad muestra que las ideas que se presentan están respaldadas por un poder más alto. Una apelación a las emociones (Pathos) se usa con el propósito de influir en los lectores.

ARGUMENT / ARGUMENTO Un *argumento* es un escrito o discurso que trata de convencer al lector para que siga una acción o adopte una opinión en particular. Un argumento es una manera lógica de presentar una creencia, una conclusión, o una postura. Un buen argumento se respalda con razonamientos y pruebas.

ASIDE / APARTE Un *aparte* es un parlamento breve en boca de un personaje en una obra de teatro, en el que expresa sus verdaderos pensamientos y sentimientos. Tradicionalmente, los apartes se dirigen a la audiencia y se suponen inaudibles a los otros personajes.

AUTOBIOGRAPHY / AUTOBIOGRAFÍA Una *autobiografía* es una forma de no-ficción en la que el escritor cuenta su propia vida. Una autobiografía puede contar toda la vida de una persona o solo una parte de ella.

BIOGRAPHY / BIOGRAFÍA Una *biografía* es una forma de no-ficción en la que un escritor cuenta la vida de otra persona. Se han escrito biografías de muchas personas famosas, ya de la historia o del mundo contemporáneo, pero también pueden escribirse biografías de personas comunes.

BLANK VERSE / VERSO BLANCO El *verso blanco* es poesía escrita en líneas de pentámetros yámbicos sin rima. Esta forma de verso fue muy utilizada por William Shakespeare.

CHARACTER / PERSONAJE Un *personaje* es una persona o animal que participa de la acción en una obra literaria. El personaje principal, o protagonista, es el personaje más importante del relato. Este personaje a menudo cambia de una manera importante como resultado de los eventos que se suceden en el cuento.

Los personajes a veces son clasificados como complejos o chatos, dinámicos o estáticos. Un *personaje complejo* muestra muchos rasgos diferentes, tanto faltas como virtudes. *Un personaje chato* muestra solo un rasgo. Un *personaje dinámico* se desarrolla y crece en el curso del relato; mientras que un *personaje estático* no cambia.

CHARACTERIZATION / CARACTERIZACIÓN La *caracterización* es el acto de crear y desarrollar un personaje. En una *caracterización directa,* el autor expresa explícitamente los rasgos de un personaje. En una *caracterización indirecta,* el autor proporciona claves sobre el personaje, describiendo el aspecto del personaje, qué hace, qué dice, así como la manera en que otros personajes lo ven y reaccionan a él. Depende del lector qué conclusiones saque sobre los personajes basándose en información indirecta.

La caracterización indirecta más efectiva resulta por lo general de mostrar cómo hablan y actúan los personajes.

CLIMAX / CLÍMAX El *clímax* de un relato, de una novela o de un drama es el punto de mayor interés o suspenso. Los sucesos que forman el desarrollo de la acción anteceden al clímax. Los sucesos que conducen al desenlace son posteriores al clímax.

COMEDY / COMEDIA Una *comedia* es una obra literaria, por lo general una obra de teatro, que tiene un final feliz. Las comedias a menudo presentan personajes comunes en conflicto con la sociedad. Estos conflictos se producen a partir de malentendidos, engaños y falsas identidades. Cuando el conflicto se resuelve, el resultado es la corrección de fallas morales o de injusticias sociales. Entre los distintos tipos de comedia, se distinguen: *la comedia romántica*, que gira alrededor de problemas entre enamorados o amantes, y *la comedia de costumbres*, que satiriza las costumbres sociales. La comedia suele oponerse a la tragedia, en la cual el protagonista tiene un final desafortunado.

COMIC RELIEF / ALIVIO CÓMICO El *alivio cómico* es una técnica que se usa para interrumpir una parte seria de una obra literaria introduciendo una situación o personaje gracioso.

CONFLICT / CONFLICTO Un *conflicto* es una lucha entre fuerzas opuestas. Los personajes en conflicto forman la base de cuentos, novelas y obras de teatro.

Hay dos tipos de conflicto: *externos* e *internos.* En un *conflicto externo*, el personaje principal lugar contra una fuerza externa.

Un *conflicto interno* atañe a un personaje que entra en conflicto consigo mismo.

CONNOTATION / CONNOTACIÓN La *connotación* de una palabra es el conjunto de ideas que se asocian a ella, además de su significado explícito.

CONSONANCE / CONSONANCIA La *consonancia* es la repetición de los sonidos consonantes finales de sílabas acentuadas con distintos sonidos vocálicos, como en *hat* and *sit*.

COUPLET / PAREADO Un *dístico* o *pareado* es un par de versos rimados, por lo general de la misma extensión y metro.

DENOTATION / DENOTACIÓN La *denotación* de una palabra es su significado en un diccionario, independientemente de otras asociaciones que la palabra suscita. Por ejemplo, la denotación de la palabra "lago" es "masa de agua acumulada en medio de un terreno".

DESCRIPTION / DESCRIPCIÓN Una *descripción* es un retrato en palabras de una persona, un lugar o un objeto. La escritura descriptiva utiliza detalles sensoriales, es decir, aquellos que apelan a los sentidos: la vista, el oído, el gusto, el olfato y el tacto. La descripción puede encontrarse en todo tipo de escritos.

DIALECT / DIALECTO El *dialecto* es la forma de un lenguaje hablado por la gente en una región o grupo particular. Puede incluir diferencias en la pronunciación, el vocabulario y la estructura de la oración, con respecto a la forma estandarizada de esa lengua. "Danny Deever", de Rudyard Kipling, es un poema escrito en el dialecto *cockney* del inglés, usado por las clases trabajadoras de Londres.

DIALOGUE / DIÁLOGO Un *diálogo* es una conversación entre personajes que puede revelar sus rasgos y hacer progresar la acción de un relato. Ya sea en un género de ficción o de no ficción —en inglés— las comillas reproducen las palabras exactas de un personaje, y un nuevo párrafo indica un cambio de personaje. En un guión, es decir, en la versión impresa de una obra de teatro, no se usan comillas, sino que cada parlamento va introducido por el nombre del personaje que debe pronunciarlo.

DICTION / DICCIÓN La *dicción* comprende la elección de palabras que hace el autor, especialmente en relación al vocabulario, al uso de un lenguaje coloquial o jerga y al nivel de formalidad.

DRAMA / DRAMA Un *drama* es una historia escrita para ser representada por actores. El guión de un drama está consituido por *diálogo* —las palabras que dicen los actores— y por *acotaciones*, que son los comentarios acerca de cómo y dónde se sitúa la acción.

La *ambientación* es la época y el lugar donde sucede la acción. Se indica a través de una o varias escenografías, que incluyen el mobiliario y el fondo, o telón de fondo, que sugieren si las escenas son interiores o exteriores. La *tramoya* o *utilería* son los objetos, tales como una espada o una taza de té, que se usan en escena.

Al principio de la mayoría de los dramas, una breve *exposición* le da a la audiencia cierta información de contexto sobre los personajes y la situación. Al igual que en un cuento o una novela, el argumento o trama de una obra dramática se construye a partir de personajes en conflicto.

Los dramas se dividen a grandes unidades llamadas *actos*, que a su vez se dividen en unidades más breves llamadas *escenas*. Un drama de cierta extensión puede incluir muchas escenografías que cambian con las escenas, o pueden indicar un cambio de escena por medio de la iluminación.

ESSAY / ENSAYO Un *ensayo* es una obra breve de no-ficción sobre un tema en particular. Si bien es difícil llegar a una clasificación, suelen diferenciarse cinco tipos de ensayos.

El *ensayo descriptivo* se propone transmitir una impresión acerca de una persona, un lugar o un objeto.

El *ensayo explicativo* describe y resume información sobre un determinado concepto recogida de cierto número de fuentes.

El *ensayo narrativo* narra una historia real.

El *ensayo persuasivo* intenta convencer a los lectores de que hagan algo o que acepten el punto de vista del escritor.

EXPOSITION / EXPOSICIÓN Una *exposición* es un escrito o un discurso que explica un proceso o presenta información. En un cuento o un drama, la exposición es la parte donde se presenta a los personajes, la ambientación y la situación básica.

EXTENDED METAPHOR / METÁFORA EXTENDIDA En una *metáfora extendida*, al igual que en una metáfora habitual, el escritor escribe o habla de algo como si fuera otra cosa. Una metáfora extendida prolonga la comparación a lo largo de varias líneas o de un poema entero.

FANTASY / RELATO FANTÁSTICO Un *relato fantástico* es una obra altamente imaginativa que contiene elementos que no se encuentran en la vida real. Ejemplos de relatos fantásticos son los cuentos que incluyen elementos sobrenaturales, tales como los cuentos de hadas, y cuentos que tratan sobre lugares y criaturas imaginarias.

FICTION / FICCIÓN Una obra de *ficción* es un escrito en prosa que cuenta algo sobre personajes y hechos imaginarios. El término se usa por lo general para referirse a novelas y cuentos, pero también se aplica a dramas y poemas narrativos. Algunos escritores se basan solamente en su imaginación para crear sus obras de ficción. Otros basan su ficción en hechos y personas reales, a las que agregan personajes, diálogos y situaciones de su propia invención.

FIGURATIVE LANGUAGE / LENGUAJE FIGURADO El *lenguaje figurado* es un escrito o discurso que no se debe interpretar literalmente. A menudo se usa para crear impresiones vívidas, estableciendo comparaciones entre cosas disímiles.

Algunas de las formas más usadas del lenguaje figurado son la *metáfora*, el *símil* y la *personificación*.

FLASHBACK / FLASHBACK Un *flashback* o *escena retrospectiva* es una de las maneras a través de las que los autores presentan materiales, que ocurrieron antes del tiempo presente del relato. Los autores pueden incluir estos materiales, como los recuerdos o sueños de un personaje, o narrar directamente hechos anteriores al momento en que empezó el relato.

FORESHADOWING / PREFIGURACIÓN La *prefiguración* es el uso, en una obra literaria, de claves que sugieren hechos que van a suceder. Esta técnica ayuda a crear suspenso, manteniendo a los lectores interesados preguntándose qué sucederá.

FREE VERSE / VERSO LIBRE El *verso libre* es una forma poética en la que no se sigue un patrón regular o metro o de rima.

GENRE / GÉNERO Un *género* es una categoría o tipo de literatura. La literatura se divide por lo general en tres géneros principales: poesía, prosa y drama. Cada uno de estos géneros principales se divide a su vez en géneros más pequeños. Por ejemplo:

1. **Poesía:** Poesía lírica, Poesía concreta, Poesía dramática, Poesía narrativa y Poesía épica.

2. **Prosa:** Ficción (Novelas y Cuentos) y No-ficción (Biografía, Autobiografía, Cartas, Ensayos, Artículos).

3. **Drama:** Drama serio y Tragedia, Comedia, Melodrama y Farsa.

GOTHIC LITERATURE / LITERATURA GÓTICA La *literatura gótica* es un género que comenzó en Inglaterra a finales del siglo XVIII. Algunas de las características de esta literatura son: ambientaciones en lugares sombríos y remotos, personajes atormentados psicológicamente, trama que incluye violencia o lo supernatural, lenguaje altamente descriptivo e intenso y una atmósfera pesimista, melancólica o fantasmal.

HYPERBOLE / HIPÉRBOLE Una *hipérbole* es una exageración o magnificación deliberada. Las hipérboles se usan a menudo para lograr efectos cómicos.

IMAGERY / IMÁGENES Las *imágenes* son el lenguaje figurado o descriptivo que se usa en la literatura para crear una descripción verbal para los lectores. Estas descripciones verbales, o imágenes, se crean mediante el uso de detalles visuales, auditivos, gustativos, táctiles, olfativos o de movimiento.

INFORMATIONAL GRAPHICS / INFOGRAFÍAS Las *infografías* usan imágenes, símbolos, gráficas y texto para explicar y presentar las partes más complejas de un tema de manera clara y atractiva.

INTERVIEW / ENTREVISTA Una *entrevista* es una conversación entre dos personas estructurada en forma de preguntas y respuestas, en la cual una persona trata de obtener información de la otra persona.

IRONY / IRONÍA *Ironía* es un término general para distintas técnicas literarias que subrayan las diferencias entre apariencia y realidad, o entre expectativas y resultado. En una *ironía verbal*, las palabras se usan para sugerir lo opuesto a lo que se dice. En la *ironía dramática* hay una contradicción entre lo que el personaje piensa y lo que el lector o la audiencia sabe que es verdad. En una *ironía situacional*, ocurre un suceso que contradice directamente las expectativas de los personajes, o del lector o la audiencia.

JUXTAPOSITION / YUXTAPOSICIÓN La *yuxtaposición* es una manera de exponer ideas o detalles uno al lado del otro, lo que ayuda a que los lectores puedan analizar las semejanzas y las diferencias entre dos ideas.

LITERARY NONFICTION / LITERATURA DE NO-FICCIÓN La *literatura de no-ficción* es un texto que emplea muchos de los recursos literarios de la ficción, pero presenta hechos y datos reales. Puede tener una trama, usar detalles sensoriales, incorporar diálogo e, incluso, lenguaje figurado. Las memorias, las autobiografías, los discursos y las conferencias se suelen considerar literatura de no-ficción.

LYRIC POEM / POEMA LÍRICO Un *poema lírico* es una sucesión de versos de mucha musicalidad que expresan los pensamientos, observaciones y sentimientos de un único hablante.

MAGICAL REALISM / REALISMO MÁGICO El *realismo mágico* incorpora elementos de fantasía y mito en una narrativa que es, por lo demás, realista.

METAPHOR / METÁFORA Una *metáfora* es una figura literaria en la que algo se describe como si fuera otra cosa. A diferencia del símil, que compara dos cosas usando el conector *como*, la metáfora establece la comparación entre ellas de modo implícito.

METER / METRO El *metro* de un poema es el patrón rítmico que sigue. Este patrón está determinado por el número y disposición de las sílabas acentuadas en cada verso. Para describir el metro de un poema hay que escandir los versos. Escandir significa marcar las sílabas acentuadas y no acentuadas.

Cada sílaba acentuada se marca con un ('), y cada sílaba no acentuada se marca con un ('). Las sílabas acentuadas y no acentuadas se dividen luego con líneas verticales (|) en grupos llamados *pies*. En la poesía en inglés algunos de los pies más frecuentes son:

1. el *yambo*: un pie con una sílaba no acentuada seguida por una sílaba acentuada, como en la palabra "again"

2. el *troqueo*: un pie con una sílaba acentuada seguida por una sílaba no acentuada, como en la palabra "wonder"

3. el *anapesto*: un pie con dos sílabas no acentuadas seguidas por un acento fuerte, como en la frase "on the beach"

4. el *dáctilo*: un pie con un acento fuerte seguido por dos sílabas no acentuadas, como en la palabra "wonderful"

5. el *espondeo*: un pie con dos acentos fuertes, como en la palabra "spacewalk"

Según el tipo de pie más frecuente en ellos, los versos de un poema se describen como *yámbicos, trocaicos, anapésticos,* etc.

Los versos también se describen según el número de pies que los formen. Por ejemplo:

1. *monómetro:* verso de un solo pie

2. *dímetro:* verso de dos pies

3. *trímetro:* verso de tres pies

4. *tetrámetro:* verso de cuatro pies

5. *pentámetro:* verso de cinco pies

6. *hexámetro:* verso de seis pies

7. *heptámetro:* verso de siete pies

Verso blanco: se dice de la poesía escrita en pentámetros yámbicos sin rima.

Verso libre: se dice de la poesía que no sigue un patrón métrico ni rímico regular.

MODERNISM / MODERNISMO NORTEAMERICANO
El **modernismo norteamericano** es una forma de expresión creativa que se desarrolló a principios del siglo XX en respuesta al rápido crecimiento de la industria, el paso de las sociedades rurales a las urbanas y los horrores de la guerra. La ambigüedad, la desaparición de límites claros entre realidad y fantasía, y los temas de la enajenación del ser humano moderno son algunos de los elementos típicos de este movimiento.

MONOLOGUE / MONÓLOGO
Un **monólogo** en una obra de teatro es un parlamento por parte de un personaje que, a diferencia del *soliloquio*, se dirige a otro u otros personajes.

MOOD / ATMÓSFERA
La **atmósfera** es la sensación que un pasaje u obra literaria crea en el lector. Por lo general, la atmósfera se crea a través de detalles descriptivos. A menudo puede ser descrita con una sola palabra, tal como *desenfadado, aterrador* o *desesperante.*

NARRATION / NARRACIÓN
Una **narración** es un escrito que cuenta una historia. El acto de contar una historia de forma oral también se llama narración. Las novelas y los cuentos son obras narrativas de ficción. Las obras de no-ficción, como las noticias, las biografías y las autobiografías, también son narrativas. Un poema narrativo cuenta una historia en verso.

NARRATIVE / RELATO
Se llama **relato** a la historia que se narra en una obra de ficción, obra de de no-ficción, en un poema o en un drama.

NARRATIVE POEM / POEMA NARRATIVO
Un **poema narrativo** es un poema que cuenta una historia.

NARRATOR / NARRADOR
Un **narrador** es el hablante o el personaje que cuenta una historia. La elección del narrador por parte del autor determina el *punto de vista* desde el que se va a narrar la historia, lo que determina el tipo y la cantidad de información que se revelará.

Cuando el que cuenta la historia es uno de los personajes, a ese personaje se lo llama *narrador en primera persona*. Este narrador puede ser uno de los personajes principales, un personaje menor, o solo un testigo. Los lectores ven solo lo que este personaje ve, oyen solo lo que este personaje oye, etc. Al ver cómo se desarrollan los sucesos desde la perspectiva de este personaje, el lector comparte sus descubrimientos y experimenta mayor suspenso que el que producen narraciones desde otros puntos de vista.

Cuando la que cuenta la historia es una voz exterior a la historia, hablamos de un *narrador en tercera persona*. Un narrador en tercera persona, *omnisciente* —es decir, que todo lo sabe— puede decirles a los lectores lo que cualquier personaje piensa o siente. Un narrador en tercera persona *limitado* ve el mundo a través de los ojos de un solo personaje y revela solo los pensamientos de ese personaje.

NONFICTION / NO-FICCIÓN
La **no-ficción** es un escrito en prosa que presenta y explica ideas o cuenta algo acerca de personas, lugares, ideas o hechos reales. Para ser clasificado como no-ficción un escrito debe ser verdadero.

NOVEL / NOVELA
Una **novela** es una obra extensa de ficción. Tiene una trama que explora los personajes en conflicto. Una novela también puede tener una o más tramas secundarias —es decir, historias de menor importancia—, así como tocar varios temas.

ONOMATOPOEIA / ONOMATOPEYA
La **onomatopeya** es el uso de palabras que imitan sonidos, tales como *pío-pío, tic-tac* o *susurro*. Los escritores pueden escoger palabras deliberadamente con el fin de producir el efecto sonoro deseado.

OXYMORON / OXÍMORON
Un **oxímoron** es una combinación de palabras que se contradicen mutuamente. Por ejemplo, "un silencio ensordecedor", "un ladrón honesto", "la música callada". Este recurso es especialmente efectivo cuando la aparente contradicción revela una verdad más profunda.

PERSONIFICATION / PERSONIFICACIÓN
La **personificación** es un tipo de figura retórica en la que se dota a

una instancia no humana de rasgos y actitudes humanas: *El musgo se abrazaba al árbol.*

PERSUASION / PERSUASIÓN La **persuasión** es un recurso escrito u oral por el que se intenta convencer al lector de que adopte una opinión o actúe de determinada manera. Un *argumento* es una manera lógica de presentar una creencia, una conclusión o una postura. Un buen argumento se respalda con razones y evidencias.

PLOT / TRAMA o ARGUMENTO La **trama** o **argumento** es la secuencia de los hechos que se suceden en una obra literaria. En la mayoría de las novelas, dramas, cuentos y poemas narrativos, la trama implica tanto a los personajes como al conflicto central. La trama por lo general empieza con una **exposición** que introduce la ambientación, los personajes y la situación básica. A ello le sigue el **suceso desencadenante**, que introduce el conflicto central. Este conflicto aumenta durante el **desarrollo** hasta que alcanza el punto más alto de interés o suspenso, llamado **clímax**. Todos los sucesos que conducen al clímax contribuyen a la **acción dramática creciente**. Al clímax le sigue la **acción dramática decreciente** que conduce al **desenlace,** o **resolución,** en el que se resuelve el conflicto y en el que puede darse a entender cierta idea o percepción más amplia acerca de la situación tratada.

POETIC STRUCTURE / ESTRUCTURA POÉTICA Las **estructuras poéticas** básicas son los versos y las estrofas. Un **verso** es un grupo de palabras ordenadas en un mismo renglón. Un verso puede terminar, o cortarse, de distintas maneras. Versos de distinta extensión pueden crear ritmos imprevistos.
En un **verso no encabalgado** la estructura gramatical y el sentido se completan al final de esa línea.
En un **verso encabalgado** tanto la estructura gramatical como el sentido de un verso continúan en el verso que sigue.

POETRY / POESÍA La **poesía** es uno de los tres géneros literarios más importantes. Los otros dos son la prosa y el drama. La mayoría de los poemas están escritos en un lenguaje altamente conciso, musical y emocionalmente rico. Muchos también hacen uso de imágenes, de figuras retóricas y de recursos sonoros especiales, tales como la rima. Los poemas a menudo se dividen en versos y estrofas, y emplean patrones rítmicos regulares, llamados metros. Los poemas que no siguen un metro regular están escritos en **verso libre**.

POINT OF VIEW / PUNTO DE VISTA El **punto de vista** es la perspectiva desde la cual se narran o describen los hechos. Al usar un punto de vista constante, el escritor controla la cantidad y tipo de información que quiere revelarle al lector. Cuando quien cuenta la historia es uno de los personajes, ese personaje es el **narrador en primera persona** y tiene un **punto de vista limitado**. Cuando quien narra la historia es una voz exterior al relato que sabe y ve todo lo que ocurre, el relato está escrito desde un **punto de vista omnisciente**. El **relato en tercera persona** presenta el mundo desde la perspectiva de un solo personaje y revela solo lo que piensa ese personaje.

PROSE / PROSA La **prosa** es la forma más común del lenguaje escrito. La mayoría de los escritos que no son poesía, ni drama, ni canciones, se consideran prosa. La prosa es uno de los géneros literarios más importantes y puede ser de dos formas: de ficción y de no-ficción.

PROSE POEM / POEMA EN PROSA Un **poema en prosa** es una forma poética que se ve como si fuera prosa, pero que tiene las características propias de la poesía. Los poemas en prosa no tienen los cortes de verso que suelen encontrarse en la poesía, pero tienen otros elementos de la poesía tales como la repetición y el ritmo.

REPETITION / REPETICIÓN La **repetición** es el uso de cualquier elemento del lenguaje —un sonido, una palabra, una frase, una cláusula, o una oración— más de una vez en un mismo pasaje del texto.

Los poetas usan muchos tipos de repeticiones. La **aliteración**, la **asonancia**, la **consonancia**, la **rima** y el **ritmo** son repeticiones de ciertos sonidos o patrones sonoros. Un *estribillo* es un verso o grupo de versos que se repiten. Tanto en prosa como en poesía, la repetición se usa tanto para lograr efectos de musicalidad como para enfatizar algo.

RHETORICAL DEVICES / FIGURAS RETÓRICAS Las **figuras retóricas** son patrones especiales de palabras e ideas que dan énfasis y producen emoción, especialmente en discursos y otras presentaciones orales. El **paralelismo**, por ejemplo, es la repetición de una estructura gramatical con el propósito de crear un ritmo y hacer que las palabras resulten más memorables.

Otras figuras retóricas muy frecuentes son:

la **analogía**: establece una comparación entre dos cosas diferentes

el **lenguaje emocionalmente cargado**: las palabras apelan a las emociones

la **concesión**: un reconocimiento del argumento del contrario

el **humor**: uso del lenguaje y detalles que hacen que los personajes y las situaciones resulten graciosos

la **paradoja**: un enunciado que parece contradecirse, pero que en realidad presenta una verdad

la **reafirmación**: expresa la misma idea con distintas palabras

las **preguntas retóricas**: preguntas que no se hacen para contestarse porque las respuestas son obvias. Por ejemplo, *¿Es la libertad un derecho esencial del ser humano?* es una pregunta retórica.

el **tono**: la actitud del autor hacia el tema

RHYME / RIMA La **rima** es la repetición de los sonidos finales de las palabras. Se llama *rima de final de verso* a la rima entre las palabras finales de dos o más versos. La *rima interna* se produce cuando una de las palabras que riman está situada en el interior de un verso. En la *rima perfecta (o consonante)* todas las vocales y las consonantes que siguen a la vocal acentuada son iguales, como en *ball* y *hall*. Se llama *rima falsa* a la que se da entre palabras que suenan de modo parecido pero que en realidad no riman, como *grove* y *love*.

RHYME SCHEME / ESQUEMA DE RIMA Un
esquema de rima es el patrón de las palabras que riman en un poema. El esquema de rima de un poema se indica con distintas letras del alfabeto para cada tipo de rima. En una estrofa aabb, por ejemplo, el verso 1 rima con el verso 2 y el verso 3 rima con el verso 4. Muchos poemas siguen el mismo patrón de rimas, aunque no las mismas rimas, en cada estrofa.

SATIRE / SÁTIRA Una *sátira* es una obra literaria que ridiculiza las tonterías y fallas de ciertos individuos o instituciones, de la sociedad o incluso de la humanidad.

SENSORY LANGUAGE / LENGUAJE SENSORIAL El
lenguaje sensorial es un escrito o discurso que incluye detalles que apelan a uno o más de los sentidos.

SEQUENCE OF EVENTS / SECUENCIA DE
SUCESOS Los autores usan a menudo la *secuencia de sucesos*, es decir, el orden en que suceden los hechos, para estructurar textos de no-ficción que tratan sobre hechos históricos o que explican un cambio que se produjo a lo largo del tiempo. Con frecuencia los escritores presentan los hechos en *orden cronológico*, es decir, en el orden en que se sucedieron.

SETTING / AMBIENTACIÓN La *ambientación* de
una obra literaria es la época y el lugar en el que se desarrolla la acción. La época incluye no solo el período histórico —pasado, presente o futuro —, sino también el año específico, la estación, la hora del día. El lugar puede incluir no solo el espacio geográfico —una región, un país, un estado, un pueblo— sino también el entorno social, económico o cultural.

En algunos cuentos, la ambientación sirve solo como un telón de fondo para la acción, un contexto en el que los personajes se mueven y hablan. En otros casos, en cambio, la ambientación es un elemento crucial.

SHORT STORY / CUENTO Un *cuento* es una obra breve
de ficción. En la mayoría de los cuentos, un personaje principal se enfrenta a un conflicto que se resuelve a lo largo de la trama. Para escribir un buen cuento se necesita mucho dominio técnico, porque el cuento debe cumplir su cometido en relativamente pocas palabras.

SIMILE / SÍMIL Un *símil* es una figura retórica en la que
se usa la palabra *como* para establecer una comparación entre dos cosas aparentemente disímiles. La comparación sorprende al lector ofreciéndole una nueva percepción que se deriva de descubrir una semejanza inesperada.

SOCIAL COMMENTARY / COMENTARIO SOCIAL En
las obras de *comentario social* el autor tiene como objetivo resaltar, generalmente de forma crítica, un aspecto de la sociedad. El comentario social suele ser el objetivo de la *sátira*, en la que el autor señala lo absurdo de una práctica, costumbre o institución.

SOLILOQUY / SOLILOQUIO Un *soliloquio* es un largo
parlamento en el que un personaje, solo en escena, expresa sus sentimientos.

SONNET / SONETO Un *soneto* es un poema lírico de
catorce versos, por lo general escritos en pentámetros yámbicos rimados. El *soneto inglés o shakesperiano* consiste en tres cuartetas (estrofas de cuatro versos) y un pareado (estrofa de dos versos), por lo general con rima *abab cdcd efef gg*. El pareado suele consistir en un comentario sobre las ideas expuestas en los doce versos que lo preceden. El soneto inglés no se suele imprimir con la división interestrófica, pero el lector puede identificar las distintas ideas que se presentan en cada estrofa.

El *soneto italiano o petrarquista* consiste en una octava (una estrofa de ocho versos) y una sextina (una estrofa de seis versos). A menudo, las octavas riman *abbaabba* y las sextinas riman *cdecde*. La octava expone el tema y propone una pregunta. La sextina comenta el tema o responde la pregunta que se planteó en las estrofas anteriores.

SPEAKER / HABLANTE El *hablante* es la voz imagi-
naria que asume el escritor en un poema. En muchos poemas, el hablante no se identifica con un nombre. Al leer un poema, recuerda que el hablante puede ser una persona, un animal un objeto o una abstracción.

STAGE DIRECTIONS / ACOTACIONES Las *acota-*
ciones son notas que se incluyen en una obra de teatro para describir cómo debe ser actuada o puesta en escena. Estas instrucciones aparecen en itálicas y no se pronuncian durante la representación. Se usan para describir decorados, la iluminación, los efectos sonoros y el aspecto, la personalidad y los movimientos de los personajes.

STANZA / ESTROFA Una *estrofa* es un grupo de dos o
más versos cuya estructura se repite. Las distintas estrofas de un poema suelen seguir un mismo patrón de ritmo y de rima. Las estrofas a menudo reciben su nombre del número de versos que las componen. Por ejemplo, un *dístico* o *pareado* (dos versos), una *cuarteta* (cuatro versos), una *sextina* (seis versos), y una *octavilla* (ocho versos).

STYLE / ESTILO El *estilo* es la manera particular en que
escribe un autor. Los elementos que determinan el estilo son: la dicción, el tono; el uso característico de ciertas figuras retóricas, del dialecto, o de los recursos rítmicos; y la sintaxis, es decir, los patrones y estructuras gramaticales que usa con más frecuencia.

SURPRISE ENDING / FINAL SORPRESIVO Un *final*
sorpresivo es una conclusión que no responde a las

expectativas del lector, pero que de todos modos resulta lógica y verosímil.

SYMBOL / SÍMBOLO Un *símbolo* es algo que representa otra cosa. Además de tener su propio significado y realidad, un símbolo también representa ideas abstractas. Por ejemplo, una bandera es un trozo de tela, pero también representa la idea de un país. Los escritores a veces usan símbolos convencionales como las banderas. Con frecuencia, sin embargo, crean sus propios símbolos, a veces a través del énfasis o la repetición.

SYNTAX / SINTAXIS La *sintaxis* es la estructura de las oraciones.

THEME / TEMA Un *tema* es el mensaje central o la concepción de la vida que revela una obra literaria.

El tema de una obra literaria puede estar implícito o bien puede expresarse directamente. Cuando el tema de una obra está implícito, los lectores hacen inferencias sobre lo que sugiere la obra acerca de la vida o la gente.

Los *temas arquetípicos* son aquellos que aparecen en el folklore y en la literatura de todo el mundo y a lo largo de toda la historia.

TONE / TONO El *tono* de una obra literaria es la actitud del escritor hacia su tema y su audiencia. A menudo puede describirse con un solo adjetivo, tal como *formal* o *informal*, *serio* o *jocoso*, *amargo* o *irónico*.

TRAGEDY / TRAGEDIA Una *tragedia* es una obra literaria, por lo general una obra de teatro, que termina en una catástrofe, un desastre o un gran infortunio para el personaje principal. En el drama de la antigua Grecia, el personaje principal siempre era una persona importante —un rey o un héroe— y la causa de la tragedia era un *error trágico*, una debilidad de su carácter. En el drama moderno, el personaje principal puede ser una persona común, y la causa de la tragedia puede ser algún problema de la sociedad misma. La tragedia no solo despierta miedo y compasión en la audiencia, sino también, en algunos casos, le hace tomar conciencia de la majestuosidad y la nobleza del espíritu humano.

VOICE / VOZ La *voz* es el "sonido" distintivo de un escritor, o la manera en que "habla" en la página. Se relaciona a elementos tales como la elección del vocabulario, la estructura de las oraciones y el tono. Es similar al estilo en que habla un individuo y puede describirse de la misma manera: rápida, lenta, directa, dispersa, jadeante, etc.

La voz se parece al *estilo*, es decir, a la manera típica en que escribe un autor, pero el estilo por lo general se refiere a una cualidad que puede encontrarse a lo largo de toda la obra de un autor, mientras que la voz de un autor puede variar de una obra a otra.

PARTS OF SPEECH

Every English word, depending on its meaning and its use in a sentence, can be identified as one of the eight parts of speech. These are nouns, pronouns, verbs, adjectives, adverbs, prepositions, conjunctions, and interjections. Understanding the parts of speech will help you learn the rules of English grammar and usage.

Nouns A **noun** names a person, place, or thing. A **common noun** names any one of a class of persons, places, or things. A **proper noun** names a specific person, place, or thing.

Common Noun	Proper Noun
writer, country, novel	Charles Dickens, Great Britain, *Hard Times*

Pronouns A **pronoun** is a word that stands for one or more nouns. The word to which a pronoun refers (whose place it takes) is the **antecedent** of the pronoun.

A **personal pronoun** refers to the person speaking (first person); the person spoken to (second person); or the person, place, or thing spoken about (third person).

	Singular	Plural
First Person	I, me, my, mine	we, us, our, ours
Second Person	you, your, yours	you, your, yours
Third Person	he, him, his, she, her, hers, it, its	they, them, their, theirs

A **reflexive pronoun** reflects the action of a verb back on its subject. It indicates that the person or thing performing the action also is receiving the action.

I keep *myself* fit by taking a walk every day.

An **intensive pronoun** adds emphasis to a noun or pronoun.

It took the work of the president *himself* to pass the law.

A **demonstrative** pronoun points out a specific person(s), place(s), or thing(s).

this, that, these, those

A **relative pronoun** begins a subordinate clause and connects it to another idea in the sentence.

that, which, who, whom, whose

An **interrogative pronoun** begins a question.

what, which, who, whom, whose

An **indefinite pronoun** refers to a person, place, or thing that may or may not be specifically named.

all, another, any, both, each, everyone, few, most, none, no one, somebody

Verbs A **verb** expresses action or the existence of a state or condition.

An **action verb** tells what action someone or something is performing.

gather, read, work, jump, imagine, analyze, conclude

A **linking verb** connects the subject with another word that identifies or describes the subject. The most common linking verb is *be*.

appear, be, become, feel, look, remain, seem, smell, sound, stay, taste

A **helping verb,** or **auxiliary verb,** is added to a main verb to make a verb phrase.

be, do, have, should, can, could, may, might, must, will, would

Adjectives An **adjective** modifies a noun or pronoun by describing it or giving it a more specific meaning. An adjective answers the questions:

What kind?	*purple* hat, *happy* face, *loud* sound
Which one?	*this* bowl
How many?	*three* cars
How much?	*enough* food

The articles *the, a,* and *an* are adjectives.

A **proper adjective** is an adjective derived from a proper noun.

French, Shakespearean

Adverbs An **adverb** modifies a verb, an adjective, or another adverb by telling *where, when, how,* or *to what extent*.

will answer *soon, extremely* sad, calls *more* often

Prepositions A **preposition** relates a noun or pronoun that appears with it to another word in the sentence.

Dad made a meal *for* us. We talked *till* dusk. Bo missed school *because of* his illness.

Conjunctions A **conjunction** connects words or groups of words. A **coordinating conjunction** joins words or groups of words of equal rank.

bread *and* cheese, brief *but* powerful

Correlative conjunctions are used in pairs to connect words or groups of words of equal importance.

both Luis *and* Rosa, *neither* you *nor* I

Subordinating conjunctions indicate the connection between two ideas by placing one below the other in rank or importance. A subordinating conjunction introduces a subordinate, or dependent, clause.

> We will miss her *if* she leaves. Hank shrieked *when* he slipped on the ice.

Interjections An **interjection** expresses feeling or emotion. It is not related to other words in the sentence.

> ah, hey, ouch, well, yippee

PHRASES AND CLAUSES

Phrases A **phrase** is a group of words that does not have both a subject and a verb and that functions as one part of speech. A phrase expresses an idea but cannot stand alone.

Prepositional Phrases A **prepositional phrase** is a group of words that begins with a preposition and ends with a noun or pronoun that is the **object of the preposition.**

> before dawn   as a result of the rain

An **adjective phrase** is a prepositional phrase that modifies a noun or pronoun.

> Eliza appreciates the beauty **of a well-crafted poem.**

An **adverb phrase** is a prepositional phrase that modifies a verb, an adjective, or an adverb.

> She reads Spenser's sonnets **with great pleasure.**

Appositive Phrases An **appositive** is a noun or pronoun placed next to another noun or pronoun to add information about it. An **appositive phrase** consists of an appositive and its modifiers.

> Mr. Roth, **my music teacher,** is sick.

Verbal Phrases A **verbal** is a verb form that functions as a different part of speech (not as a verb) in a sentence. **Participles, gerunds,** and **infinitives** are verbals.

A **verbal phrase** includes a verbal and any modifiers or complements it may have. Verbal phrases may function as nouns, as adjectives, or as adverbs.

A **participle** is a verb form that can act as an adjective. Present participles end in *-ing;* past participles of regular verbs end in *-ed.*

A **participial phrase** consists of a participle and its modifiers or complements. The entire phrase acts as an adjective.

> Jenna's backpack, **loaded with equipment,** was heavy.
> **Barking incessantly,** the dogs chased the squirrels out of sight.

A **gerund** is a verb form that ends in *-ing* and is used as a noun.

A **gerund phrase** consists of a gerund with any modifiers or complements, all acting together as a noun.

> **Taking photographs of wildlife** is her main hobby. [acts as subject]
> We always enjoy **listening to live music.** [acts as object]

An **infinitive** is a verb form, usually preceded by *to,* that can act as a noun, an adjective, or an adverb.

An **infinitive phrase** consists of an infinitive and its modifiers or complements, and sometimes its subject, all acting together as a single part of speech.

> She tries **to get out into the wilderness often.** [acts as a noun; direct object of *tries*]
> The Tigers are the team **to beat.** [acts as an adjective; describes *team*]
> I drove twenty miles **to witness the event.** [acts as an adverb; tells why I drove]

Clauses A **clause** is a group of words with its own subject and verb.

Independent Clauses An independent clause can stand by itself as a complete sentence.

> George Orwell wrote with extraordinary insight.

Subordinate Clauses A subordinate clause, also called a dependent clause, cannot stand by itself as a complete sentence. Subordinate clauses always appear connected in some way with one or more independent clauses.

> George Orwell, **who wrote with extraordinary insight,** produced many politically relevant works.

An **adjective clause** is a subordinate clause that acts as an adjective. It modifies a noun or a pronoun by telling *what kind* or *which one.* Also called relative clauses, adjective clauses usually begin with a **relative pronoun:** *who, which, that, whom, or whose.*

> "The Lamb" is the poem **that I memorized for class.**

An **adverb clause** is a subordinate clause that, like an adverb, modifies a verb, an adjective, or an adverb. An adverb clause tells *where, when, in what way, to what extent, under what condition,* or *why.*

The students will read another poetry collection **if their schedule allows.**

When I recited the poem, Mr. Lopez was impressed.

A **noun clause** is a subordinate clause that acts as a noun.

William Blake survived on **whatever he made as an engraver.**

SENTENCE STRUCTURE

Subject and Predicate A **sentence** is a group of words that expresses a complete thought. A sentence has two main parts: a *subject* and a *predicate*.

A **fragment** is a group of words that does not express a complete thought. It lacks an independent clause.

The **subject** tells *whom* or *what* the sentence is about. The **predicate** tells what the subject of the sentence does or is.

A subject or a predicate can consist of a single word or of many words. All the words in the subject make up the **complete subject.** All the words in the predicate make up the **complete predicate.**

| Complete Subject | Complete Predicate |
Both of those girls | have already read *Macbeth*.

The **simple subject** is the essential noun, pronoun, or group of words acting as a noun that cannot be left out of the complete subject. The **simple predicate** is the essential verb or verb phrase that cannot be left out of the complete predicate.

Both of those girls | **have** already **read** *Macbeth*.
[Simple subject: *Both*; simple predicate: *have read*]

A **compound subject** is two or more subjects that have the same verb and are joined by a conjunction.

Neither the horse nor the driver looked tired.

A **compound predicate** is two or more verbs that have the same subject and are joined by a conjunction.

She **sneezed and coughed** throughout the trip.

Complements A **complement** is a word or word group that completes the meaning of the subject or verb in a sentence. There are four kinds of complements: *direct objects, indirect objects, objective complements,* and *subject complements.*

A **direct object** is a noun, a pronoun, or a group of words acting as a noun that receives the action of a transitive verb.

We watched the **liftoff.**

She drove **Zach** to the launch site.

An **indirect object** is a noun or pronoun that appears with a direct object and names the person or thing to which or for which something is done.

He sold the **family** a mirror. [The direct object is *mirror.*]

An **objective complement** is an adjective or noun that appears with a direct object and describes or renames it.

The decision made her **unhappy.**
[The direct object is *her.*]

Many consider Shakespeare the greatest **playwright.** [The direct object is *Shakespeare.*]

A **subject complement** follows a linking verb and tells something about the subject. There are two kinds: *predicate nominatives* and *predicate adjectives.*

A **predicate nominative** is a noun or pronoun that follows a linking verb and identifies or renames the subject.

"A Modest Proposal" is a **pamphlet.**

A **predicate adjective** is an adjective that follows a linking verb and describes the subject of the sentence.

"A Modest Proposal" is **satirical.**

Classifying Sentences by Structure

Sentences can be classified according to the kind and number of clauses they contain. The four basic sentence structures are *simple, compound, complex,* and *compound-complex.*

A **simple sentence** consists of one independent clause.

Terrence enjoys modern British literature.

A **compound sentence** consists of two or more independent clauses. The clauses are joined by a conjunction or a semicolon.

Terrence enjoys modern British literature, but his brother prefers the classics.

A **complex sentence** consists of one independent clause and one or more subordinate clauses.

Terrence, who reads voraciously, enjoys modern British literature.

A **compound-complex sentence** consists of two or more independent clauses and one or more subordinate clauses.

Terrence, who reads voraciously, enjoys modern British literature, but his brother prefers the classics.

Classifying Sentences by Function

Sentences can be classified according to their function or purpose. The four types are *declarative, interrogative, imperative,* and *exclamatory.*

A **declarative sentence** states an idea and ends with a period.

An **interrogative sentence** asks a question and ends with a question mark.

An **imperative sentence** gives an order or a direction and ends with either a period or an exclamation mark.

An **exclamatory sentence** conveys a strong emotion and ends with an exclamation mark.

PARAGRAPH STRUCTURE

An effective paragraph is organized around one **main idea,** which is often stated in a **topic sentence.** The other sentences support the main idea. To give the paragraph **unity,** make sure the connection between each sentence and the main idea is clear.

> **Max** went to the bakery, but **he** can't buy mints there. [consistent]

Unnecessary Shift in Voice

Do not change needlessly from active voice to passive voice in your use of verbs.

> Elena and I **searched** the trail for evidence, but no clues **were found.** [shift from active voice to passive voice]
> Elena and I **searched** the trail for evidence, but we **found** no clues. [consistent]

Unnecessary Shift in Person

Do not change needlessly from one grammatical person to another. Keep the person consistent in your sentences.

> **Max** went to the bakery, but **you** can't buy mints there. [shift from third person to second person]

AGREEMENT

Subject and Verb Agreement

A singular subject must have a singular verb. A plural subject must have a plural verb.

> **Dr. Boone uses** a telescope to view the night sky.
> The **students use** a telescope to view the night sky.

A verb always agrees with its subject, not its object.

> *Incorrect:* The best part of the show were the jugglers.
> *Correct:* The best part of the show was the jugglers.

A phrase or clause that comes between a subject and verb does not affect subject-verb agreement.

> His **theory**, as well as his claims, **lacks** support.

Two subjects joined by *and* usually take a plural verb.

> The **dog** and the **cat are** healthy.

Two singular subjects joined by *or* or *nor* take a singular verb.

> The **dog** or the **cat is** hiding.

Two plural subjects joined by *or* or *nor* take a plural verb.

> The **dogs** or the **cats are** coming home with us.

When a singular and a plural subject are joined by *or* or *nor*, the verb agrees with the closer subject.

> Either the **dogs** or the **cat is** behind the door.
> Either the **cat** or the **dogs are** behind the door.

Pronoun and Antecedent Agreement

Pronouns must agree with their antecedents in number and gender. Use singular pronouns with singular antecedents and plural pronouns with plural antecedents.

> **Doris Lessing** uses **her** writing to challenge ideas about women's roles.
> **Writers** often use **their** skills to promote social change.

Use a singular pronoun when the antecedent is a singular indefinite pronoun such as *anybody, each, either, everybody, neither, no one, one,* or *someone.*

> Judge **each** of the articles on **its** merits.

Use a plural pronoun when the antecedent is a plural indefinite pronoun such as *both, few, many,* or *several.*

> **Both** of the articles have **their** flaws.

The indefinite pronouns *all, any, more, most, none,* and *some* can be singular or plural depending on the number of the word to which they refer.

> **Most** of the *books* are in **their** proper places.
> **Most** of the *book* has been torn from **its** binding.

Principal Parts of Regular and Irregular Verbs

A verb has four principal parts:

Present	Present Participle	Past	Past Participle
learn	learning	learned	learned
discuss	discussing	discussed	discussed
stand	standing	stood	stood
begin	beginning	began	begun

Regular verbs such as *learn* and *discuss* form the past and past participle by adding *-ed* to the present form. **Irregular verbs** such as *stand* and *begin* form the past and past participle in other ways. If you are in doubt about the principal parts of an irregular verb, check a dictionary.

The Tenses of Verbs

The different tenses of verbs indicate the time an action or condition occurs.

The **present tense** expresses an action that happens regularly or states a current condition or a general truth.

> Tourists **flock** to the site yearly.

Daily exercise **is** good for your heallth.

The **past tense** expresses a completed action or a condition that is no longer true.

> The squirrel **dropped** the nut and **ran** up the tree.
> I **was** very tired last night by 9:00.

The **future tense** indicates an action that will happen in the future or a condition that will be true.

> The Glazers **will visit** us tomorrow.
> They **will be** glad to arrive from their long journey.

The **present perfect tense** expresses an action that happened at an indefinite time in the past or an action that began in the past and continues into the present.

> Someone **has cleaned** the trash from the park.
> The puppy **has been** under the bed all day.

The **past perfect tense** shows an action that was completed before another action in the past.

> Gerard **had revised** his essay before he turned it in.

The **future perfect tense** indicates an action that will have been completed before another action takes place.

> Mimi **will have painted** the kitchen by the time we finish the shutters.

Degrees of Comparison

Adjectives and adverbs take different forms to show the three degrees of comparison: the *positive*, the *comparative*, and the *superlative*.

Positive	Comparative	Superlative
fast	faster	fastest
crafty	craftier	craftiest
abruptly	more abruptly	most abruptly
badly	worse	worst

Using Comparative and Superlative Adjectives and Adverbs

Use comparative adjectives and adverbs to compare two things. Use superlative adjectives and adverbs to compare three or more things.

> This season's weather was **drier** than last year's.
> This season has been one of the **driest** on record.
> Jake practices **more often** than Jamal.
> Of everyone in the band, Jake practices **most often.**

Pronoun Case

The **case** of a pronoun is the form it takes to show its function in a sentence. There are three pronoun cases: *nominative*, *objective*, and *possessive*.

Nominative	Objective	Possessive
I, you, he, she, it, we, you, they	me, you, him, her, it, us, you, them	my, your, yours, his, her, hers, its, our, ours, their, theirs

Use the **nominative case** when a pronoun functions as a *subject* or as a *predicate nominative*.

> **They** are going to the movies. [subject]
> The biggest movie fan is **she.** [predicate nominative]

Use the **objective case** for a pronoun acting as a *direct object*, an *indirect object*, or the *object of a preposition*.

> The ending of the play surprised **me.** [direct object]
> Mary gave **us** two tickets to the play. [indirect object]
> The audience cheered for **him.** [object of preposition]

Use the **possessive case** to show ownership.

> The red suitcase is **hers.**

Diction The words you choose contribute to the overall effectiveness of your writing. **Diction** refers to word choice and to the clearness and correctness of those words. You can improve one aspect of your diction by choosing carefully between commonly confused words, such as the pairs listed below.

accept, except

Accept is a verb that means "to receive" or "to agree to." *Except* is a preposition that means "other than" or "leaving out."

>   Please **accept** my offer to buy you lunch this weekend.

>   He is busy every day **except** the weekends.

affect, effect

Affect is normally a verb meaning "to influence" or "to bring about a change in." *Effect* is usually a noun meaning "result."

>   The distractions outside **affect** Steven's ability to concentrate.

>   The teacher's remedies had a positive **effect** on Steven's ability to concentrate.

among, between

Among is usually used with three or more items, and it emphasizes collective relationships or indicates distribution. *Between* is generally used with only two items, but it can be used with more than two if the emphasis is on individual (one-to-one) relationships within the group.

>   I had to choose a snack **among** the various vegetables.

>   He handed out the booklets **among** the conference participants.

>   Our school is **between** a park and an old barn.

>   The tournament included matches **between** France, Spain, Mexico, and the United States.

amount, number

Amount refers to overall quantity and is mainly used with mass nouns (those that can't be counted). *Number* refers to individual items that can be counted.

>   The **amount** of attention that great writers have paid to Shakespeare is remarkable.

>   A **number** of important English writers have been fascinated by the legend of King Arthur.

assure, ensure, insure

Assure means "to convince [someone of something]; to guarantee." *Ensure* means "to make certain [that something happens]." *Insure* means "to arrange for payment in case of loss."

>   The attorney **assured** us we'd win the case.

>   The rules **ensure** that no one gets treated unfairly.

>   Many professional musicians **insure** their valuable instruments.

bad, badly

Use the adjective *bad* before a noun or after linking verbs such as *feel, look,* and *seem*. Use *badly* whenever an adverb is required.

>   The situation may seem **bad**, but it will improve over time.

>   Though our team played **badly** today, we will focus on practicing for the next match.

beside, besides

Beside means "at the side of" or "close to." *Besides* means "in addition to."

>   The stapler sits **beside** the pencil sharpener in our classroom.

>   **Besides** being very clean, the classroom is also very organized.

can, may

The helping verb *can* generally refers to the ability to do something. The helping verb *may* generally refers to permission to do something.

>   I **can** run one mile in six minutes.

>   **May** we have a race during recess?

complement, compliment

The verb *complement* means "to enhance"; the verb *compliment* means "to praise."

>   Online exercises **complement** the textbook lessons.

>   Ms. Lewis **complimented** our team on our excellent debate.

compose, comprise

Compose means "to make up; constitute." *Comprise* means "to include or contain." Remember that the whole comprises its parts or is composed of its parts, and the parts compose the whole.

>   The assignment **comprises** three different tasks.

>   The assignment is **composed** of three different tasks.

>   Three different tasks **compose** the assignment.

different from, different than

Different from is generally preferred over *different than*, but *different than* can be used before a clause. Always use *different from* before a noun or pronoun.

>   Your point of view is so **different from** mine.

>   His idea was so **different from** [or **different than**] what we had expected.

farther, further

Use *farther* to refer to distance. Use *further* to mean "to a greater degree or extent" or "additional."

>   Chiang has traveled **farther** than anybody else in the class.

>   If I want **further** details about his travels, I can read his blog.

fewer, less

Use *fewer* for things that can be counted. Use *less* for amounts or quantities that cannot be counted. *Fewer* must be followed by a plural noun.

Fewer students drive to school since the weather improved.

There is **less** noise outside in the mornings.

good, well

Use the adjective *good* before a noun or after a linking verb. Use *well* whenever an adverb is required, such as when modifying a verb.

I feel **good** after sleeping for eight hours.

I did **well** on my test, and my soccer team played **well** in that afternoon's game. It was a **good** day!

its, it's

The word *its* with no apostrophe is a possessive pronoun. The word *it's* is a contraction of "it is."

Angelica will try to fix the computer and **its** keyboard.

It's a difficult job, but she can do it.

lay, lie

Lay is a transitive verb meaning "to set or put something down." Its principal parts are *lay, laying, laid, laid*. *Lie* is an intransitive verb meaning "to recline" or "to exist in a certain place." Its principal parts are *lie, lying, lay, lain*.

Please **lay** that box down and help me with the sofa.

When we are done moving, I am going to **lie** down.

My hometown **lies** sixty miles north of here.

like, as

Like is a preposition that usually means "similar to" and precedes a noun or pronoun. The conjunction *as* means "in the way that" and usually precedes a clause.

Like the other students, I was prepared for a quiz.

As I said yesterday, we expect to finish before noon.

Use **such as,** not **like,** before a series of examples.

Foods **such as** apples, nuts, and pretzels make good snacks.

of, have

Do not use *of* in place of *have* after auxiliary verbs such as *would, could, should, may, might,* or *must*. The contraction of *have* is formed by adding *-ve* after these verbs.

I **would have** stayed after school today, but I had to help cook at home.

Mom **must've** called while I was still in the gym.

principal, principle

Principal can be an adjective meaning "main; most important." It can also be a noun meaning "chief officer of a school." *Principle* is a noun meaning "moral rule" or "fundamental truth."

His strange behavior was the **principal** reason for our concern.

Democratic **principles** form the basis of our country's laws.

raise, rise

Raise is a transitive verb that usually takes a direct object. *Rise* is intransitive and never takes a direct object.

Iliana and Josef **raise** the flag every morning.

They **rise** from their seats and volunteer immediately whenever help is needed.

than, then

The conjunction *than* is used to connect the two parts of a comparison. The adverb *then* usually refers to time.

My backpack is heavier **than** hers.

I will finish my homework and **then** meet my friends at the park.

that, which, who

Use the relative pronoun *that* to refer to things or people. Use *which* only for things and *who* only for people.

That introduces a restrictive phrase or clause, that is, one that is essential to the meaning of the sentence. *Which* introduces a nonrestrictive phrase or clause—one that adds information but could be deleted from the sentence—and is preceded by a comma.

Ben ran to the park **that** just reopened.

The park, **which** just reopened, has many attractions.

The man **who** built the park loves to see people smiling.

when, where, why

Do not use *when, where,* or *why* directly after a linking verb, such as *is*. Reword the sentence.

Incorrect: The morning is when he left for the beach.

Correct: He left for the beach in the morning.

who, whom

In formal writing, use *who* only as a subject in clauses and sentences. Use *whom* only as the object of a verb or of a preposition.

Who paid for the tickets?

Whom should I pay for the tickets?

I can't recall to **whom** I gave the money for the tickets.

your, you're

Your is a possessive pronoun expressing ownership. *You're* is the contraction of "you are."

Have you finished writing **your** informative essay?

You're supposed to turn it in tomorrow. If **you're** late, **your** grade will be affected.

Capitalization

First Words

Capitalize the first word of a sentence.

Stories about knights and their deeds interest me.

Capitalize the first word of direct speech.

Sharon asked, "**D**o you like stories about knights?"

Capitalize the first word of a quotation that is a complete sentence.

Einstein said, "**A**nyone who has never made a mistake has never tried anything new."

Proper Nouns and Proper Adjectives

Capitalize all proper nouns, including geographical names, historical events and periods, and names of organizations.

Thames **R**iver   **J**ohn **K**eats   the **R**enaissance

United **N**ations   **W**orld **W**ar II   **S**ierra **N**evada

Capitalize all proper adjectives.

Shakespearean play   **B**ritish invaision

American citizen   **L**atin **A**merican literature

Academic Course Names

Capitalize course names only if they are language courses, are followed by a number, or are preceded by a proper noun or adjective.

Spanish **H**onors **C**hemistry   **H**istory 101

geology **a**lgebra   **s**ocial **s**tudies

Titles

Capitalize personal titles when followed by the person's name.

Ms. Hughes **D**r. Perez **K**ing George

Capitalize titles showing family relationships when they are followed by a specific person's name, unless they are preceded by a possessive noun or pronoun.

Uncle Oscar   Mangan's **s**ister   his **a**unt Tessa

Capitalize the first word and all other key words in the titles of books, stories, songs, and other works of art.

Frankenstein   "**S**hooting an **E**lephant"

Punctuation

End Marks

Use a **period** to end a declarative sentence or an imperative sentence.

We are studying the structure of sonnets.
Read the biography of Mary Shelley.

Use periods with initials and abbreviations.

D. H. Lawrence   Mrs. Browning
Mt. Everest   Maple St.

Use a **question mark** to end an interrogative sentence.

What is Macbeth's fatal flaw?

Use an **exclamation mark** after an exclamatory sentence or a forceful imperative sentence.

That's a beautiful painting!   Let me go now!

Commas

Use a **comma** before a coordinating conjunction to separate two independent clauses in a compound sentence.

The game was very close, but we were victorious.

Use commas to separate three or more words, phrases, or clauses in a series.

William Blake was a writer, artist, and printer.

Use commas to separate coordinate adjectives.

It was a witty, amusing novel.

Use a comma after an introductory word, phrase, or clause.

When the novelist finished his book, he celebrated with his family.

Use commas to set off nonessential expressions.

Old English, of course, requires translation.

Use commas with places and dates.

Coventry, England   September 1, 1939

Semicolons

Use a **semicolon** to join closely related independent clauses that are not already joined by a conjunction.

Tanya likes to write poetry; Heather prefers prose.

Use semicolons to avoid confusion when items in a series contain commas.

They traveled to London, England; Madrid, Spain; and Rome, Italy.

Colons

Use a **colon** before a list of items following an independent clause.

Notable Victorian poets include the following: Tennyson, Arnold, Housman, and Hopkins.

Use a colon to introduce information that summarizes or explains the independent clause before it.

She just wanted to do one thing: rest.
Malcolm loves volunteering: He reads to sick children every Saturday afternoon.

Quotation Marks

Use **quotation marks** to enclose a direct quotation.

"Short stories," Ms. Hildebrand said, "should have rich, well-developed characters."

An **indirect quotation** does not require quotation marks.

Ms. Hildebrand said that short stories should have well-developed characters.

Use quotation marks around the titles of short written works, episodes in a series, songs, and works mentioned as parts of collections.

"The Lagoon"   "Boswell Meets Johnson"

Italics

Italicize the titles of long written works, movies, television and radio shows, lengthy works of music, paintings, and sculptures.

Howards End   *60 Minutes*   *Guernica*

For handwritten material, you can use underlining instead of italics.

<u>The Princess Bride</u>   <u>Mona Lisa</u>

Dashes

Use **dashes** to indicate an abrupt change of thought, a dramatic interrupting idea, or a summary statement.

I read the entire first act of *Macbeth*—you won't believe what happens next.
The director—what's her name again?—attended the movie premiere.

Hyphens

Use a **hyphen** with certain numbers, after certain prefixes, with two or more words used as one word, and with a compound modifier that comes before a noun.

seventy-two
self-esteem
president-elect
five-year contract

Parentheses

Use **parentheses** to set off asides and explanations when the material is not essential or when it consists of one or more sentences. When the sentence in parentheses interrupts the larger sentence, it does not have a capital letter or a period.

He listened intently (it was too dark to see who was speaking) to try to identify the voices.

When a sentence in parentheses falls between two other complete sentences, it should start with a capital letter and end with a period.

The quarterback threw three touchdown passes. (We knew he could do it.) Our team won the game by two points.

Apostrophes

Add an **apostrophe** and an *s* to show the possessive case of most singular nouns and of plural nouns that do not end in -*s* or -*es*.

Blake's poems   the mice's whiskers

Names ending in *s* form their possessives in the same way, except for classical and biblical names, which add only an apostrophe to form the possessive.

Dickens's   Hercules'

Add an apostrophe to show the possessive case of plural nouns ending in -*s* and -*es*.

the girls' songs   the Ortizes' car

Use an apostrophe in a contraction to indicate the position of the missing letter or letters.

She's never read a Coleridge poem she didn't like.

Brackets

Use **brackets** to enclose clarifying information inserted within a quotation.

Columbus's journal entry from October 21, 1492, begins as follows: "At 10 o'clock, we arrived at a cape of the island [San Salvador], and anchored, the other vessels in company."

Ellipses

Use three ellipsis points, also known as an **ellipsis,** to indicate where you have omitted words from quoted material.

Wollestonecraft wrote, "The education of women has of late been more attended to than formerly; yet they are still . . . ridiculed or pitied. . . ."

In the example above, the four dots at the end of the sentence are the three ellipsis points plus the period from the original sentence.

Use an ellipsis to indicate a pause or interruption in speech.

"When he told me the news," said the coach, "I was . . . I was shocked . . . completely shocked."

Spelling

Spelling Rules

Learning the rules of English spelling will help you make **generalizations** about how to spell words.

Word Parts

The three word parts that can combine to form a word are roots, prefixes, and suffixes. Many of these word parts come from the Greek, Latin, and Anglo-Saxon languages.

The **root word** carries a word's basic meaning.

Root and Origin	Meaning	Examples
-leg- (-log-) [Gr.]	to say, speak	*legal, logic*
-pon- (-pos-) [L.]	to put, place	*postpone, deposit*

A **prefix** is one or more syllables added to the beginning of a word that alter the meaning of the root.

Prefix and Origin	Meaning	Example
anti- [Gr.]	against	*antipathy*
inter- [L.]	between	*international*
mis- [A.S.]	wrong	*misplace*

A **suffix** is a letter or group of letters added to the end of a root word that changes the word's meaning or part of speech.

Suffix and Origin	Meaning and Example	Part of Speech
-ful [A.S.]	full of: *scornful*	adjective
-ity [L.]	state of being: *adversity*	noun
-ize (-ise) [Gr.]	to make: *idolize*	verb
-ly [A.S.]	in a manner: *calmly*	adverb

Rules for Adding Suffixes to Root Words

When adding a suffix to a root word ending in *y* preceded by a consonant, change *y* to *i* unless the suffix begins with *i*.

ply + -able = pliable   happy + -ness = happiness
defy + -ing = defying   cry + -ing = crying

For a root word ending in *e*, drop the *e* when adding a suffix beginning with a vowel.

drive + -ing = driving   move + -able = movable
SOME EXCEPTIONS: traceable, seeing, dyeing

For root words ending with a consonant + vowel + consonant in a stressed syllable, double the final consonant when adding a suffix that begins with a vowel.

mud + -y = muddy   submit + -ed = submitted
SOME EXCEPTIONS: mixing, fixed

Rules for Adding Prefixes to Root Words

When a prefix is added to a root word, the spelling of the root remains the same.

un- + certain = uncertain   mis- + spell = misspell

With some prefixes, the spelling of the prefix changes when joined to the root to make the pronunciation easier.

in- + mortal = immortal   ad- + vert = avert

Orthographic Patterns

Certain letter combinations in English make certain sounds. For instance, *ph* sounds like *f*, *eigh* usually makes a long *a* sound, and the *k* before an *n* is often silent.

pharmacy   n**eigh**bor   **k**nowledge

Understanding **orthographic patterns** such as these can help you improve your spelling.

Forming Plurals

The plural form of most nouns is formed by adding -*s* to the singular.

computer**s**   gadget**s**   Washington**s**

For words ending in *s, ss, x, z, sh,* or *ch,* add -*es*.

circus**es**   tax**es**   wish**es**   bench**es**

For words ending in *y* or *o* preceded by a vowel, add -*s*.

key**s**   patio**s**

For words ending in *y* preceded by a consonant, change the *y* to an *i* and add -*es*.

citi**es**   enemi**es**   trophi**es**

For most words ending in *o* preceded by a consonant, add -*es*.

echo**es**   tomato**es**

Some words form the plural in irregular ways.

women   oxen   children   teeth   deer

Foreign Words Used in English

Some words used in English are actually foreign words that have been adopted. Learning to spell these words requires memorization. When in doubt, check a dictionary.

sushi   enchilada   au pair   fiancé
laissez faire   croissant

INDEX OF SKILLS

Speaking and Listening

Argument
  plan with your group, 246, 644
  present and evaluate, 247, 645
  rehearse with your group, 247, 645
Critique
  analyze the performances, 727
  share and discuss, 727
  write your critique, 727
Debate
  anticipate counterarguments, 185
  debate plan, 479
  organize ideas and evidence, 185
  take a position, 185
  write and opening statement, 185
Discussion, 189
Dramatic reading
  analyze the scene, 571
  choose your scene, 571
  develop your characters, 571
  evaluate readings, 571
  rehearse, 571
Explanatory presentation
  plan with your group, 114
  present and evaluate, 115
  rehearse with your group, 115
Group presentation
  project plan, 113
Informal talk, 124
Informational graphic
  evaluate presentations, 57
  organize your content, 57
  prepare your presentation, 57
Informative text
  plan with your group, 480
  present and evaluate, 481
  rehearse with your group, 481
Monologue
  choose an emotional tone, 387
  evaluate, 387
  plan your interpretation, 387
  prepare your delivery, 387
Multimedia presentation, 360
  develop your argument, 231
  plan with your group, 350
  present and evaluate, 351
  project plan, 231
  rehearse with your group, 351
Multimedia project
  plan it, 407
  present it, 407
News report, 297
Oral interpretation
  connect to the theme, 401

evaluate oral interpretations, 401
  identify the excerpt, 401
  practice your reading, 401
Oral presentation, 256, 490
  anticipate counterarguments, 603
  classroom discussion, 757
  deliver and evaluate presentations, 603
  draft and practice, 603
  outline your argument, 603
  presentation plan, 801
  project plan, 757
Oral retelling
  plan with your group, 802
  present and evaluate, 803
  rehearse with your group, 803
Photojournalism, 407
Poetry reading
  present and discuss, 223
  project plan, 223
Small-group discussion, 343
Small group learning
  making a schedule, 67, 199, 307, 417,
    623, 737
  strategies for
    clarify, 64, 196, 304, 414, 620,
      734
    participate fully, 64, 196, 304, 414,
      620, 734
    prepare, 64, 196, 304, 414, 620,
      734
    support others, 64, 196, 304, 414,
      620, 734
  working as a team
    apply your rules, 66, 198, 306,
      416, 622, 736
    choose a topic, 66, 198, 416
    create a communication plan, 66,
      198, 306, 416, 622, 736
    list your rules, 66, 198, 306, 416,
      622, 736
    name your group, 66, 198, 306,
      416, 622, 736
    roles for group projects, 67, 199,
      307, 417, 623, 737
    take a position, 306, 622, 736
Speech, 654
Storytelling, 812
Visual presentation
  coordinate text and images, 89
  project plan, 89
Whole-class learning strategies
  clarify by asking questions, 10, 134,
    266, 370, 500, 664
  interact and share ideas, 10, 134,
    266, 370, 500, 664
  listen actively, 10, 134, 266, 370,
    500, 664

monitor understanding, 10, 134, 266,
    370, 500, 664

Vocabulary

Academic vocabulary
  advocate, 129, 190, 254
  allocate, 365, 408, 488
  allusion, 495, 614, 652
  altercation, 659, 728, 810
  articulate, 495, 614, 652
  attribute, 261, 298, 358
  chronicle, 365, 408, 488
  contentious, 495, 614, 652
  contradict, 129, 190, 254
  deduce, 365, 408, 488
  delineate, 659, 728, 810
  demarcate, 261, 298, 358
  democracy, 261, 298, 358
  dimension, 5, 58, 122
  fundamental, 261, 298, 358
  hierarchy, 261, 298, 358
  integrate, 659, 728, 810
  manipulate, 5, 58, 122
  motivate, 5, 58, 122
  negate, 129, 190, 254
  objection, 129, 190, 254
  paradox, 365, 408, 488
  perspective, 5, 58, 122
  primary, 365, 408, 488
  psychological, 5, 58, 122
  tolerate, 495, 614, 652
  vehement, 495, 614, 652
  verify, 129, 190, 254
  vivid, 659, 728, 810
  volition, 659, 728, 810
Concept vocabulary
  amelioration, 136, 149, 182, 184
  amenable, 388, 390, 398, 400
  amiably, 68, 69, 78
  annihilate, 12, 14, 34
  antiquity, 12, 15, 34
  appeasement, 268, 271, 280
  artifacts, 470, 471, 476
  asphyxiation, 136, 154, 182, 184
  asunder, 282, 284, 290
  avarice, 430, 433, 438
  aversion, 136, 152, 182, 184
  beachhead, 282, 285, 290
  beguiling, 100, 105, 110
  belaboring, 282, 285, 290
  beneficent, 308, 309, 315
  bigotry, 224, 226, 228
  blessings, 388, 389, 398, 400
  burnished, 442, 444, 457

INDEX OF SKILLS

Writing

INDEX OF AUTHORS AND TITLES

The following authors and titles appear in the print and online versions of *my*Perspectives.

ADDITIONAL SELECTIONS: AUTHOR AND TITLE INDEX

The following authors and titles appear in the Interactive Student Edition only.

INDEX OF AUTHORS AND TITLES

Acknowledgments

The following selections appear in Grade 10 of *my*Perspectives. Some selections appear online only.

ABC News - Permissions Dept. Spooky Business: American Economy ©ABC News; Diane Sawyer Sits Down With the Inspirational Malala Yousafzai ©ABC News; 14-Year-Old Teaches Family the 'Power of Half' ©ABC News; Dr. Geoffrey Tabin Helps Blind Ethiopians Gain Sight ©ABC News.

American Folklore. "What We Plant, We Will Eat" by S. E. Schlosser; Used with permission from S.E. Schlosser and American Folklore. Copyright 2015. All rights reserved.

American Foundation for the Blind. "The Empire State Building" by Helen Keller, originally appeared in *New York Times,* January 17, 1932. Courtesy of the American Foundation for the Blind, Helen Keller Archives.

Amnesty International UK. Everybody—we are all born free ©Amnesty International UK.

Anchor Books. "The Sun Parlor" from *The Richer, The Poorer* by Dorothy West, copyright ©1995 by Dorothy West. Used by permission of Doubleday, an imprint of the Knopf Doubleday Publishing Group, a division of Penguin Random House LLC. All rights reserved. Any third party use of this material, outside of this publication, is prohibited. Interested parties must apply directly to Penguin Random House LLC for permission.

Arte Publico Press. "Fences" is reprinted with permission from the publisher of *Communion,* by Pat Mora ©1991 Arte Publico Press—University of Houston.

Atlantic Monthly. "Why Do Some Dreams Enjoy Fear?" ©2013 The Atlantic Media Co., as first published in *The Atlantic Magazine.* All rights reserved. Distributed by Tribune Content Agency, LLC.

BBC News Online. "How Your Eyes Trick Your Mind," from BBC; Used with permission.

BBC Worldwide Americas, Inc. *Franz Kafka and Metamorphosis* ©BBC Worldwide Learning; Socrates ©BBC Worldwide Learning; Episode 1: Rock the Ship ©BBC Worldwide Learning; Blind Teen ©BBC Worldwide Learning; How Your Eyes Trick Your Mind ©BBC Worldwide Learning.

Black Moon Theatre Company. Kafka's *The Metamorphosis* ©Black Moon Theatre Company.

Bowers, Jai. "By Any Other Name" from *Gifts of Passage* by Santha Rama Rau. Copyright ©Santha Rama Rau. Reprinted by permission of the author's estate.

Cambridge University Press - US – Journals. "A Dose of What the Doctor Never Orders," from *The Japanese Family Storehouse* by Ihara Saikaku, translated by G. W. Sargent. Copyright ©1959 Cambridge University Press. Reprinted with the permission of Cambridge University Press.

Carmen Balcells Agencia Literaria. Julio Cortazar, "House Taken Over," *Blow-Up and Other Stories* ©The Estate of Julio Cortazar, 1967.

Curtis Brown, Ltd. (UK). "They are hostile nations" from *Power Politics* by Margaret Atwood. Copyright ©1976 by Margaret Atwood. Used with permission.

Dancing Bear, J. P. "Caliban," Copyright ©J. P. Dancing Bear. Used with permission of the author.

Farrar, Straus and Giroux. "Avarice" from *Talking Dirty to the Gods* by Yusef Komunyakaa. Copyright ©2000 by Yusef Komunyakaa. Reprinted by permission of Farrar, Straus and Giroux, LLC. CAUTION: Users are warned that this work is protected under copyright laws and downloading is strictly prohibited. The right to reproduce or transfer the work via any medium must be secured with Farrar, Straus and Giroux, LLC.

Forgiveness Project. "The Forgiveness Project: Eric Lomax," ©The Forgiveness Project.

Freedom House. "Harsh Laws and Violence Drive Global Decline," Freedom of the Press 2015. By permission of Freedom House.

Frost, Adam. Adapted from "How to tell you're reading a gothic novel—in pictures" by Adam Frost and Zhenia Vasiliev, from *The Guardian,* May 9, 2014.

Getty Images. JFK Inaugural Address ©MediaRecall Holdings/Archive ED/Getty Images.

Gibbons, Reginald. "Money" copyright by Reginald Gibbons. Reprinted by permission of the author.

Goldsmith, Margie. "The Thrill of the Chase" by Margie Goldsmith, from *Hemispheres Magazine,* January 2013. Copyright ©2013 by Margie Goldsmith. Used with permission of the author.

Graywolf Press. Tracy K. Smith, "The Good Life" from *Life on Mars.* Copyright ©2011 by Tracy K. Smith. Reprinted with the permission of The Permissions Company, Inc., on behalf of Graywolf Press, Minneapolis, Minnesota.

Guardian News and Media Limited. "Stone Age man's terrors still stalk modern nightmares," Copyright Guardian News & Media Ltd 2015; "A Dish Best Served Cold," Copyright Guardian News & Media Ltd 2015; "Experience: I first saw my wife 10 years after we married," Copyright Guardian News & Media Ltd 2015.

Hanging Loose Press. "Sonnet With Bird," reprinted from *What I've Stolen, What I've Earned* ©2014 by Sherman Alexie, by permission of Hanging Loose Press.

HarperCollins Publishers. "Harrison Bergeron" from *Welcome to the Monkey House* (audio) by Kurt Vonnegut. Copyright © 1950, 1951, 1953, 1954, 1955, 1956, 1958, 1960, 1961, 1962, 1964, 1966, 1968 by Kurt Vonnegut Jr. (p) & © 2006 HarperCollins Publishers. Used by permission of HarperCollins Publishers.

HarperCollins Publishers Ltd. (UK). "Windigo" from Jacklight by Louise Erdrich. Reprinted by permission of HarperCollins Publishers Ltd ©1984 Louise Erdrich

Houghton Mifflin Harcourt. "They are Hostile Nations" from *Selected Poems I:* 1965–1975 by Margaret Atwood. Copyright ©1976 by Margaret Atwood. Reprinted with permission of Houghton Mifflin Harcourt Publishing Company. All rights reserved.

Houghton Mifflin Harcourt Publishing Co. Excerpt from *Blindness* by Jose Saramago, translated from the Portuguese by Giovanni Pontiero. Copyright ©1995 by Jose Saramago and Editorial Caminho, SA. English translation copyright ©1997 by Juan Sager. Reprinted by permission of Houghton Mifflin Harcourt Publishing Company. All rights reserved.

Ivan R. Dee, Publisher. *Oedipus the King.* Copyright ©2000 by Ivan R. Dee, Inc. Translation copyright ©2000 by Nicholas Rudall. All rights reserved.

ACKNOWLEDGMENTS AND CREDITS

Credits

ACKNOWLEDGMENTS AND CREDITS

A Peoples Education Skillbook for
AP*/Honors

Advanced Composition Skills
20 Lessons for AP* Success

Peoples Education™
Your partner in student success™
www.PeoplesEducation.com

Steven Fox

About The Author

Steven Fox taught for more than 30 years at Shaker Heights (Ohio) High School. After many years of teaching AP English Literature, he proposed and then designed and taught his high school's AP English Language and Composition program. He has been a reader and table leader at both the English Literature and English Language AP exam readings for many years. Steven has been an essay reader for several other national examination programs and a test item writer for the ACT. He is currently an assistant examiner for the International Baccalaureate Program.

As an endorsed consultant and National Leader for the College Board, Steven Fox provides workshops and summer institutes for both AP English courses and many pre-AP programs as well. He also works as a writer and staff developer for the AVID Center of San Diego. For the College Board he wrote *The Official SAT Study Guide* in preparation for the revised SAT, and the accompanying *Teachers' Guide*.

In 1988 Steven was chosen by the Ohio Council of Teachers of English Language Arts as Ohio's Outstanding English Language Arts Instructor of the year. In that same year he was awarded a Fulbright Teachers' Exchange, and spent the 1988–1989 school year teaching at the Charles Read Secondary Modern School in Corby Glen, Lincolnshire, England.

Executive Editor: Doug Falk

Supervising Copy Editor: Lee Laddy

Editorial Services: DWJ Books, LLC

Senior Production Manager: Jason Grasso

Assistant Production Manager: Steven Genzano

Marketing Manager: Brian Moore

Permissions Manager: Kristine Liebman

*AP is a registered trademark of the College Board, which was not involved in the production of, and does not endorse, this book.

Your partner in student success™

ISBN 978-1-4138-4880-9

CONTENTS Reading and Composition Skills by Lesson

Here is a guide to reading and composition skills that you will need to succeed in English Language and Composition. You will practice these skills as you work through Lessons 1–20.

	Reading Skill	**Composition Skill**
Lesson 11 page 69	Reading with an awareness of the author's attitude toward the subject	**Analysis** of tone
Lesson 12 page 79	Understanding the organization of a reading selection	**Argument** in favor of or against the author's view; **Analysis** of diction and arrangement of material
Lesson 13 page 88	Observing repeated imagery and patterns	**Analysis** of how rhetorical strategies reveal attitudes
Lesson 14 page 92	Recognizing abstract and concrete language; Reading nineteenth and seventeenth century prose	**Synthesizing** from several details
Lesson 15 page 102	Understanding how the author creates atmosphere	**Analysis** of rhetorical strategies; observing details
Lesson 16 page 107	Responding to the author's pathos and ethos	**Analysis** of the author's emotional appeal; **Synthesizing** opinions from several sources
Lesson 17 page 117	Observing the author's style	**Analysis** of how an author creates a style; **Argument** in response to a person's beliefs
Lesson 18 page 123	Determining the author's purpose	**Analysis** of the purpose and how it is achieved; **Analysis** of the relationship between purpose and theme
Lesson 19 page 133	Recognizing the character of the speaker	**Analysis** of the personality behind the author's voice
Lesson 20 page 139	Reading holistically; appreciating the overall effect of a writer's achievement	**Analysis** of how rhetorical strategies contribute to a writing's overall effect; **Argument** with reference to a writer's assertions; **Synthesizing** a solution to a complex problem

CONTENTS Lesson Topics and Reading Selections

INTRODUCTION To The Student

The purpose of this Skillbook is to help you succeed in the **Advanced Placement English Language and Composition** course and on the examination. An important feature of the AP* English Language program is that it emphasizes and rewards developed skills more than accumulated knowledge.

The English Language program's focus on skills does not imply that the test expects no knowledge; on the contrary, some terminology and some awareness of rhetorical strategies will be useful. The skills that this program emphasizes are close and accurate reading, logical thinking, and clear writing. If you can demonstrate that you can do those things successfully, you will get a good score on the AP English Language test.

The test contains two major sections, each with several parts. The first section, for which one hour is allowed, is a series of readings—passages the test developers assume you have not studied—and multiple-choice questions based on those readings. The readings will illustrate a variety of literary periods and styles and may represent both nonfiction and fiction from the Renaissance to the present day, although in recent years nonfiction has appeared more frequently than fiction.

Accurate, Thorough Reading

The multiple-choice questions in the first section of the exam test the accuracy and thoroughness of your reading. They are difficult because they are not about the obvious facts of the passages; rather, they ask about matters such as the purpose of a particular sentence in the overall passage or a change in the writer's attitude between the beginning and the end of the material. Because some of the readings in this book are accompanied by sample multiple-choice questions, you will have a chance to practice this activity in the following pages.

Three Kinds of Essays

The second section of the examination, the part that seems to occupy most teachers' and students' preparation time, is the free-response section. Here you will be asked to write three essays in two hours and fifteen minutes. Typically, there will be one **analytical** essay, one **argumentative** essay, and one **synthesis** essay. Each type will be explained and illustrated in the different lessons in this book. As with any other skill, the best way to improve is to practice, so each lesson will give you an opportunity to write one or more of the three types of essays. If you work your way through the lessons, you will have plenty of practice writing the kinds of essays the test requires.

This Skillbook, therefore, addresses the three kinds of writing—**analysis, argument, and synthesis**—found on the AP English Language and Composition test, and not imaginative writing such as poetry and fiction. The AP English Language program is not a program of imaginative writing; as a result, you will not be asked to demonstrate those skills on the test.

Lessons in This Book

The lessons in this book are designed in response to questions that reflect the skills required for AP tests. If you look at past examinations, you can see the kinds of understandings and skills the test developers expected students to demonstrate. Those skills that appeared most often, collected and arranged in a progression from most basic to most advanced, helped determine the organizing principle of this Skillbook.

The skills you learn in these lessons will serve you well in any field of study. Unlike detailed knowledge, which we are likely to forget as we acquire new information, the reading, thinking, and writing skills we learn remain with us forever. Learning to read accurately, to think logically, and to express yourself clearly will prepare you not only for success on the AP exam but also for success in your further education and in your adult life.

Here is how lessons are organized:

Introduction   This section presents the lesson's main objective, the skills to be practiced, and the purpose of the readings. In a few lessons, a detailed introduction explains one or more important language concepts.

Focus on the Reading   This feature calls attention to the reading skill emphasized in the reading that follows. In a few lessons, 2–3 readings are grouped under one Focus on the Reading prompt.

Readings   Each reading—identified by author and title—will have line numbers on the left border. **Sidebar comments** on the right border guide you where you might need assistance or clarification. Sidebar comments with numbers in parentheses guide you to the relevant line number in the reading.

Commentary on the Reading   This section guides you to find meaning and connect the reading to the skill. You will find commentary in all but four lessons.

Focus on Writing   This feature in all lessons directs you to write an analytic essay, argumentative essay, synthesis essay, or other original composition, based upon your reading.

Guidance on Your Writing   This section guides you in effective planning and writing in response to a Focus on Writing prompt. Most guidance is in lessons 1–10, after which you will become more confident in writing with less support.

Exam Practice — Reading Comprehension   There are AP-style multiple-choice questions for practice in close reading and comprehension in three of the lessons.

About the English Language and Composition Examination   This guidance is needed only in lessons 1-2, where it addresses the specific format of the AP exam.

AP Exam Advice   This brief support tells how to apply what you are practicing to the English Language and Composition exam. This advice, in 14 lessons, emphasizes successful essay writing and comprehension of challenging texts.

Now, look at pages ix–xv to see examples of the lesson features described above.

Lesson Title

All lesson titles ask a question that focuses on what you will do.

Introduction

This section presents the lesson's main objective, the skills to be practiced, and the purpose of the readings.

Lesson 2 — In what ways does the passage require especially careful reading?

Introduction

Traditionally, the Advanced Placement English Language and Composition course and examination include readings from the seventeenth century to the modern day. Students who have not been exposed to language of past literary periods are frequently frustrated with these passages. The sentences are often long and complicated, the vocabulary is elevated and unfamiliar, and the relationships between elements of the passage, such as sentences within a paragraph, are often unclear.

It is vital, therefore, that you practice reading passages from past times and pay careful attention to the vocabulary and sentence structure of those passages. The vocabulary may be challenging if the passage includes unfamiliar words or if the writer uses words in unfamiliar ways, and the sentences may seem long and complex, but if you develop the habit of reading carefully to discover the relationship between parts of a long sentence, the meaning will become apparent.

Paine and Jefferson: Two Influential Writers

Thomas Paine and Thomas Jefferson were two very important writers of eighteenth-century America. Their writings had a profound influence on the formation of our nation.

Paine's pamphlet *The Crisis* was read aloud to Washington's soldiers during a difficult winter encampment. This essay is believed to have provided the men with the motivation to continue their fight for independence against the British. Here you will be reading only a few paragraphs, but the essay is worth reading in its entirety.

Jefferson, the author of the Declaration of Independence (a classic example of an argumentative essay), wrote several other worthy pieces, including his *Notes on the State of Virginia*, from which the excerpt on page 10 is taken.

In both pieces, you will find the author making a case for a particular **point of view**, paying careful attention to **word choices** and **sentence structures**. As you read each piece, note unfamiliar words and then see what context clues help you understand what the words mean. If you need to reread a paragraph or sentence because it is long and complicated, make note of that passage so that you can **analyze** it for its meaning. Comments in the margins of these passages should help you.

> **Focus on the Reading: Close Reading with Attention to Diction**
> Look for the author's particular point of view, and pay careful attention to word choices and sentence structures.

Focus on the Reading

This feature tells you the skills emphasized in the reading selection that follows.

Thomas Paine
from *The Crisis*

THESE are the times that try men's souls. The summer soldier and the sunshine patriot will, in this crisis, shrink from the service of their country; but he that stands it now, deserves the love and thanks of man and woman. Tyranny, like hell, is not easily conquered; yet we have this

5 consolation with us, that the harder the conflict, the more glorious the triumph. What we obtain too cheap, we esteem too lightly: it is dearness only that gives every thing its value. Heaven knows how to put a proper price upon its goods; and it would be strange indeed if so celestial an article as **freedom** should not be highly rated. Britain, with an army to

10 enforce her tyranny, has declared that she has a right (not only to **tax**) but "to **bind** us in **all cases whatsoever**," and if being bound in that manner is not slavery, then is there not such a thing as slavery upon earth. Even the expression is impious; for so unlimited a power can belong only to God.

…

15 I have as little superstition in me as any man living, but my secret opinion has ever been, and still is, that God Almighty will not give up a people to military destruction, or leave them unsupportedly to perish, who have so earnestly and so repeatedly sought to avoid the calamities of war, by every decent method which wisdom could invent. Neither

20 have I so much of the infidel in me, as to suppose that He has relinquished the government of the world, and given us up to the care of devils; and as I do not, I cannot see on what grounds the king of Britain can look up to heaven for help against us: a common murderer, a highwayman, or a house-breaker, has as good a pretence as he.

25 'Tis surprising to see how rapidly a panic will sometimes run through a country. All nations and ages have been subject to them. Britain has trembled like an ague at the report of a French fleet of flat-bottomed boats; and in the fourteenth [fifteenth] century the whole English army, after ravaging the kingdom of France, was driven back

30 like men petrified with fear; and this brave exploit was performed by a few broken forces collected and headed by a woman, Joan of Arc. Would that heaven might inspire some Jersey maid to spirit up her countrymen, and save her fair fellow sufferers from ravage and ravishment! Yet panics, in some cases, have their uses; they produce as much good as hurt.

35 Their duration is always short; the mind soon grows through them, and acquires a firmer habit than before. But their peculiar advantage is, that they are the touchstones of sincerity and hypocrisy, and bring things and men to light, which might otherwise have lain forever undiscovered. In fact, they have the same effect on secret traitors, which an imaginary

40 apparition would have upon a private murderer. They sift out the hidden thoughts of man, and hold them up in public to the world. Many a disguised Tory has lately shown his head, that shall penitentially solemnize with curses the day on which Howe arrived upon the Delaware.

…

I shall conclude this paper with some miscellaneous remarks on

45 the state of our affairs; and shall begin with asking the following ques-

Lesson 2 • In what ways does the passage require especially careful reading?   **7**

(6) Here is an unusual application of the word "dearness." Are you familiar with "dear" as a synonym for "expensive"? When you think of how we apply the word to a person we care about, the connection might be clear.

(15) The first sentence of this paragraph has many clauses. To what word does the pronoun "who" refer? If you understood that connection when you first read it, the meaning of the sentence was probably clear. If you need to stop and determine that connection, you will better understand what Paine is saying once you do.

(27) Do you know what an ague is? Do you have to know in order to understand this sentence?

(37) A touchstone is a quality or characteristic that allows us to measure the excellence of another. Be sure you understand exactly what Paine identifies as these touchstones. In other words, to what noun do "they" and "their" refer in these sentences?

Readings
Each reading—identified by author and title—will have line numbers on the left border.

Sidebar Comments
These guide you where you might need assistance or clarification. Comments with numbers in parentheses guide you to the relevant line number in the reading.

35
ceeding from him. With the morals of the people, their industry also is destroyed. For in a warm climate, no man will labour for himself who can make another labour for him. This is so true, that of the proprietors of slaves a very small proportion indeed are ever seen to labour. And can the liberties of a nation be thought secure when we have removed their only firm basis, a conviction in the minds of the people that these liberties are of the gift of God? That they are not to be violated but with his wrath? Indeed I tremble for my country when I reflect that God
40
is just: that his justice cannot sleep for ever: that considering numbers, nature and natural means only, a revolution of the wheel of fortune, an exchange of situation, is among possible events: that it may become probable by supernatural interference! The Almighty has no attribute which can take side with us in such a contest.—But it is impossible to be
45
temperate and to pursue this subject through the various considerations of policy, of morals, of history natural and civil. We must be contented to hope they will force their way into every one's mind. I think a change already perceptible, since the origin of the present revolution. The spirit of the master is abating, that of the slave rising from the dust, his condi-
50
tion mollifying, the way I hope preparing, under the auspices of heaven, for a total emancipation, and that this is disposed, in the order of events, to be with the consent of the masters, rather than by their extirpation.

Do you see Jefferson and Paine as similar or different in their reference to the role of religion in their arguments?

Commentary on the Reading

This paragraph is a good candidate for paraphrasing, which is simply putting the ideas of the original into your own language. For example, in the third sentence, where Jefferson wrote, "There must doubtless be an unhappy influence on the manners of our people produced by the existence of slavery among us," you, as a contemporary reader, might say, "Slavery is a bad influence on our lives." Because the purpose of paraphrasing is to be sure we understand what the author is saying, it is important to remain faithful to the original ideas rather than to interpret them or comment on them. Your teacher might suggest that you paraphrase this reading to be certain you are aware of what Jefferson's main point is and how he develops his argument in support of it.

There are basically four main points in this argument, and a discussion of the piece ought to consider all four:

- what effect slavery has on our children;
- how slavery creates discord between two portions of our population;
- how slavery affects our work habits; and
- God's view of slavery.

If you were asked to explain Jefferson's position on slavery, you would want to say more than that he thought it was bad. You would give a much better answer if you explained why he felt as he did.

It is very tempting in a situation like this one, where you know that Jefferson was himself a slave owner, to offer an opinion on his sincerity or morality. The reading may certainly lead to conversations on those topics. However, if the essay prompt asks you to analyze the argument, that is all you should do. On the other hand, some prompts might ask you to comment on the argument, and if that is your instruction, that is what you should address in your essay. In short, be sure to follow directions and to answer the question that is asked.

Lesson 2 • In what ways does the passage require especially careful reading? **11**

Commentary on the Reading

This section guides you to find meaning and connect the reading to the skill.

describing Parks's house and religious behavior to display an almost reverential attitude toward his subject." By no means is that the only acceptable response to the essay prompt, but whatever you write, you need to address the two-part task as presented in the question: explain Brinkley's attitude and show how his choice of detail communicates that attitude. This opening statement would then be followed with references to the text that further illustrate what details he uses and how they contribute to the meaning of the passage.

After you have written your essay, you should ask your teacher for a quick evaluation of your work. AP essays are graded according to a scoring guide that instructs the reader to judge the writing according to the reasonableness of the writer's response to the prompt, the appropriateness and thoroughness of the essay's development, and the writer's general command of the conventions of the English language.

The passage from Frederick Douglass's autobiography also suggests an analytical response. Try this sample question. Approach it in a manner similar to the question on the Brinkley excerpt: what did the author do, and how did the author do it?

AP Exam Advice

Focus on Writing: Analysis
Frederick Douglass's autobiography begins with a description of his early years as a slave. Read the passage carefully, and then write an essay in which you explain the writer's purpose in recounting the details of his early childhood. Support your observations with details from the narrative. Do not merely summarize the passage.

Guidance on Your Writing

First, you will want to be sure you are addressing both parts of the task: what did the author do, and how did the author do it? What is the purpose of the passage, and how do the details support that purpose? Your response to this essay question will also need to begin with a statement showing that you understand the author's direct language in the passage you read. While there are many ways you can express that understanding, you will need a sentence like "Frederick Douglass tells about his mother's life and death to make the reader understand the brutality of life on the plantation." Then, after deciding which details of the narrative support that observation, you will have to provide them in your essay.

Lesson 1 • What does the passage mean?   **5**

AP Exam Advice

This brief support tells how to apply what you are practicing to the English Language and Composition exam. This advice emphasizes successful essay writing and comprehension of challenging texts.

Focus on Writing

This feature directs you to write an analytic essay, argumentative essay, or synthesis essay, based upon your reading.

Guidance on Your Writing

This section helps you plan and write an essay in response to a Focus on Writing prompt. Most guidance is in lessons 1–10, after which you will become more confident in writing with less support.

You might find a question like the following on the AP English Language and Composition test. In writing an argument, you must take a position and provide reasons that support it.

AP Exam Advice

Focus on Writing —
This prompt directs you to compose an argument.

Focus on Writing: Argumentation
Read the excerpt from Thomas Jefferson's *Notes on the State of Virginia*, in which he presents several criticisms of slavery. Think of a practice or behavior with which you are familiar from your own experience, and write an argument showing it to be justified or unjustified. For example, you might want to write about your school's dress code (or lack of one), or your community's curfew, or a policy concerning athletic eligibility. While you may be tempted to treat the subject satirically, you will write a better argument if you handle it seriously.

Guidance on Your Writing

The most successful responses to this question will clearly identify the topic and offer three or four solid reasons for defending or challenging the status quo. A common weakness is to offer one idea and then rephrase it rather than to go on to express new ideas. For example, if you were arguing that your town should not have a curfew for teenagers, you might say that a curfew suggests that people think teenagers out at night would cause trouble. If you then say that a curfew shows that adults just don't trust teenagers, you haven't offered a new argument; you've only restated the previous idea. If instead you go on to say that sometimes teenagers have legitimate reasons for being out late, such as traveling to and from school activities, you are offering something new, thereby providing a better response.

Exam Practice — Reading Comprehension

As a practice exercise, try these questions. See if you can find the answer in the passage before reading the choices provided. You might work with a friend to see if you can explain why you chose the answer you did. Can you indicate the place where the text supports your choice?

1. In the second sentence, Paine draws a distinction between

   (A) patriots and traitors.
   (B) soldiers and civilians.
   (C) convenience and hardship.
   (D) obligation and gratitude.
   (E) the Tories and the revolutionaries.

2. Upon what basis do we determine the value of freedom?

   (A) the opportunities it offers us
   (B) the cost of obtaining it
   (C) how much the King does not want us to have it
   (D) the amount of tax we have to pay because we are not free
   (E) the threat of slavery if we fail

3. Why does Paine believe that God is on the side of the revolutionaries?

   (A) They have tried to avoid war.
   (B) The British king is evil.
   (C) He has had a vision like Joan of Arc.
   (D) He has heard sermons to that effect.
   (E) Freedom is celestial.

4. Which of the following is not a reason for Paine telling about Joan of Arc?

   (A) He is trying to humiliate the English army.
   (B) He hopes some colonial girl will imitate Joan's actions.
   (C) He is trying to illustrate the power of panic.
   (D He is hoping to get the French to come to the aid of the revolutionaries.
   (E) He is trying to boost the spirits of the colonial soldiers.

5. Which of the following is characteristic of a panic?

   I.   It is over quickly.
   II. It allows us to see good qualities in others.
   III. It reveals the truth of a person's private thinking.
   (A) I alone
   (B) I and II
   (C) I and III
   (D) II and III
   (E) I, II, and III

6. In the next to last paragraph, what does Paine imply about Tories?

   (A) There are fewer Tories in New England than in the middle colonies.
   (B) Tories are weaker than Whigs.
   (C) Tories are cowards.
   (D) Tories are like rats or vermin.
   (E) Tories are interested in their own well-being.

7. The purpose of the illustration in the final paragraph, in which Paine tells about the tavern keeper, is to

   (A) show the Tories as selfish.
   (B) evoke pity for children during wartime.
   (C) suggest that the Tories were more interested in peace than the revolutionaries were.
   (D) demonstrate the cruelty of the Tories.
   (E) prophesy that more wars will follow this one.

The Crisis is such a rich piece of writing that we cannot make full use of it in one lesson. We will refer to it again in later lessons, where it will serve to illustrate other reading and writing skills.

Lesson 2 • In what ways does the passage require especially careful reading?   **9**

Exam Practice — Reading Comprehension

There are AP-style multiple-choice questions for practice in close reading and comprehension in three of the lessons.

tion, Why is it that the enemy have left the New England provinces, and made these middle ones the seat of war? The answer is easy: New England is not infested with Tories, and we are. I have been tender in raising the cry against these men, and used numberless arguments to show them their danger, but it will not do to sacrifice a world either to their folly or their baseness. The period is now arrived, in which either they or we must change our sentiments, or one or both must fall. And what is a Tory? Good God! what is he? I should not be afraid to go with a hundred Whigs against a thousand Tories, were they to attempt to get into arms. Every Tory is a coward; for servile, slavish, self-interested fear is the foundation of Toryism; and a man under such influence, though he may be cruel, never can be brave.

…

I once felt all that kind of anger, which a man ought to feel, against the mean principles that are held by the Tories: a noted one, who kept a tavern at Amboy, was standing at his door, with as pretty a child in his hand, about eight or nine years old, as I ever saw, and after speaking his mind as freely as he thought was prudent, finished with this unfatherly expression, "Well! give me peace in my day." Not a man lives on the continent but fully believes that a separation must some time or other finally take place, and a generous parent should have said, "If there must be trouble, let it be in my day, that my child may have peace;" and this single reflection, well applied, is sufficient to awaken every man might be so happy as America. Her situation is remote from all the wrangling world, and she has nothing to do but to trade with them. A man can distinguish himself between temper and principle, and I am as confident, as I am that God governs the world, that America will never be happy till she gets clear of foreign dominion. Wars, without ceasing, will break out till that period arrives, and the continent must in the end be conqueror; for though the flame of liberty may sometimes cease to shine, the coal can never expire.

*(marginal line numbers: 50, 55, 60, 65, 70, 75)*

(48) Why do you suppose Paine used the word "infested" here? What other words would also provide the same general meaning, that there aren't a lot of Tories in New England? What associations does the word "infested" suggest?

(58) "Mean" is a word that has several meanings. If you know it only as a synonym for "unkind" or "somewhat cruel," you might be surprised, when looking it up in a dictionary, at how many meanings it has. Which of them seems most appropriate here?

(68) "Happy" is another word whose meaning has changed over time. In the eighteenth century, "happy" meant not only glad or cheerful but also fortunate. It was this meaning that Jefferson had in mind when he wrote of the rights of "life, liberty, and the pursuit of happiness." Paine means the same here.

About the English Language and Composition Exam

This guidance is needed only in lessons 1–2, where it addresses the specific format of the AP exam.

About the English Language and Composition Exam

The first hour of the AP examination consists of readings like this one and multiple-choice questions based upon them. These questions—designed to make sure you have read and understood the passage accurately—can be quite difficult, but they may actually increase your comprehension by focusing on important details or matters you may not have understood on your own.

Each question stem will be followed by five possible answers, and the test directions will instruct you to choose the best of the five offered. Such direction suggests that more than one answer might be defensible or that an even better answer exists that is not among the five offered. You have to work with the choices given and choose the best answer.

Lesson 1   What does the passage mean?

Introduction

In this lesson, you will read the opening paragraphs of two American books, one from the twentieth century and one from the nineteenth. Both are life stories, one written about an important historical figure and the other written by the man himself. Both writers use specific information to illustrate generalities about the larger world their subjects lived in, and both use language rather straightforwardly. If you read these pieces literally—that is, if you read without looking for any "hidden meaning" or figurative interpretation—you should still feel as though the pieces provide a satisfying meaning. Readers sometimes make their jobs harder than they need to be because they assume that everything they read needs to be interpreted. If they don't "read between the lines," they think they are falling short of their responsibilities. That is not always the case, and one way to prevent yourself from misreading a passage is to be sure that you understand its literal meaning.

Read the following excerpts by Douglas Brinkley and Frederick Douglass, and pay attention to the sidebar comments that accompany them. These comments are designed to guide your observations while you read and will be useful in later lessons as well.

> **Focus on the Reading: Literal Comprehension**
> Read for literal meaning, and consider figurative or interpretive language afterward.

Douglas Brinkley
from *Rosa Parks*

Nobody knows exactly where in Tuskegee, Alabama, Rosa McCauley was born on February 4, 1913. The town newspaper reported that the skies were clear and it was unseasonably warm that day, but beyond that, and the fact that she was named after her maternal grandmother, Rose, virtually no reliable documentation exists on the early years of Rosa Louise Parks. It wouldn't matter so much were not some entrepreneurial Tuskegeeans anxious to attract tourists by opening a multicultural human and civil rights center boasting her name, and others, less commerce-minded, eager to post a bronze plaque somewhere in town marking her inclusion in Tuskegee's extraordinary roster of African-American heroes, from Booker T. Washington to George Washington Carver to Ralph Ellison.

A photograph does exist of Rosa Parks's Tuskegee birthplace, but it raises more questions than it answers. The faded photo shows a plywood shanty fronted by six wobbly steps leading up to a porch seemingly on the verge of collapse. A portion of the front picture window has

(11) Booker T. Washington (1856–1915) was a pioneering African American educator. George Washington Carver (1864–1943) was a scientist who did much of his work at the Tuskegee Institute. Ralph Ellison (1913–1994) was the author of the novel *Invisible Man.*

been shattered as though from a rock thrown into the living room, and the picket fence that marks the property is severely splintered. But for a sturdy brick chimney, the edifice would appear no better than the share-croppers' shacks photographed so hauntingly by Walker Evans in *Let Us Now Praise Famous Men*. But it's another disparity that dominates the picture: Carved into the roof's rough wood is a large star in the style of the distelfinks Amish farmers hang on their barns in Pennsylvania's Dutch country. Just as nobody knows where the house was, nobody knows when or why the star was carved on Parks's birthplace—or what, if anything, it signifies. This has not kept some of Alabama's Christian mystics from insisting it was a sign, like the Star of Bethlehem, that God had a special interest in bringing Rosa Parks into the world.

Indeed even as a dreamy, mild-mannered young girl, Rosa McCau-ley had found the black pulpit intoxicating in the openness it accorded preachers to weave the joyous exaltations and heartrending laments that were legacies of the West African culture passed down from genera-tions of slaves to the sharecroppers of 1920s Alabama. "The Church, with its musical rhythms and echoes of Africa, thrilled me when I was young," Parks recalled. For a long time Southern whites hadn't wanted blacks to become Christian, preferring to pretend that slaves had no souls. From 1619, when the first human captives landed in Virginia, until 1773 there were no black churches anywhere in America, and the only blacks in white churches were relegated to the galleries. But from the Revolutionary War era onward, African Americans took not only the Bible but organized religious gatherings and rituals as passionately to heart as their ancestors had those of their native African faiths, such as the Yoruba religion, whose adherents memorized thousand of proverbs and allegories. Some Yoruba priests brought over on slave ships could recite a King James Bible's worth of African religious teachings, a prac-tice that lived on in African-American Christianity. Thus it was that at an early age the inquisitive Rosa McCauley began memorizing Bible verses, routinely quoting Scripture with Sunday school pride. Naturally demure, she was reserved in church, but just hearing her family and friends shouting "Amen!" and "Hallelujah!" filled Parks with a certitude in her deep Christian faith. "God is everything to me," she explained.

(20) Let Us Now Praise Famous Men, with text by James Agee and photographs by Walker Evans, was a Depression-era book about three poor Alabama families.

(26–51) Think about the connection between this paragraph that you have just finished reading and the comment Brinkley makes at the end of the paragraph before it. What does this passage tell us about the role traditional religion played in the lives of the people among whom Rosa Parks grew up?

Frederick Douglass
from *Narrative of the Life of Frederick Douglass, An American Slave*

I was born in Tuckahoe, near Hillsborough, and about twelve miles from Easton, in Talbot County, Maryland. I have no accurate knowl-edge of my age, never having seen any authentic record containing it. By far the larger part of the slaves know as little of their ages as horses know of theirs, and it is the wish of most masters within my knowledge to keep their slaves thus ignorant. I do not remember to have ever met a slave who could tell of his birthday. They seldom come nearer to it than planting-time, harvest-time, cherry-time, spring-time, or fall-time.

A want of information concerning my own was a source of unhappiness to me even during childhood. The white children could tell their ages. I could not tell why I ought to be deprived of the same privilege. I was not allowed to make any inquiries of my master concerning it. He deemed all such inquiries on the part of a slave improper and impertinent, and evidence of a restless spirit. The nearest estimate I can give makes me now between twenty-seven and twenty-eight years of age. I come to this, from hearing my master say, some time during 1835, I was about seventeen years old.

My mother was named Harriet Bailey. She was the daughter of Isaac and Betsey Bailey, both colored, and quite dark. My mother was of a darker complexion than either my grandmother or grandfather.

My father was a white man. He was admitted to be such by all I ever heard speak of my parentage. The opinion was also whispered that my master was my father; but of the correctness of this opinion, I know nothing; the means of knowing was withheld from me. My mother and I were separated when I was but an infant—before I knew her as my mother. It is a common custom, in the part of Maryland from which I ran away, to part children from their mothers at a very early age. Frequently, before the child has reached its twelfth month, its mother is taken from it, and hired out on some farm a considerable distance off, and the child is placed under the care of an old woman, too old for field labor. For what this separation is done, I do not know, unless it be to hinder the development of the child's affection toward its mother, and to blunt and destroy the natural affection of the mother for the child. This is the inevitable result.

I never saw my mother, to know her as such, more than four or five times in my life; and each of these times was very short in duration, and at night. She was hired by a Mr. Stewart, who lived about twelve miles from my home. She made her journeys to see me in the night, travelling the whole distance on foot, after the performance of her day's work. She was a field hand, and a whipping is the penalty of not being in the field at sunrise, unless a slave has special permission from his or her master to the contrary—a permission which they seldom get, and one that gives to him that gives it the proud name of being a kind master. I do not recollect of ever seeing my mother by the light of day. She was with me in the night. She would lie down with me, and get me to sleep, but long before I waked she was gone. Very little communication ever took place between us. Death soon ended what little we could have while she lived, and with it her hardships and suffering. She died when I was about seven years old, on one of my master's farms, near Lee's Mill. I was not allowed to be present during her illness, at her death, or burial. She was gone long before I knew any thing about it. Never having enjoyed, to any considerable extent, her soothing presence, her tender and watchful care, I received the tidings of her death with much the same emotions I should have probably felt at the death of a stranger.

Called thus suddenly away, she left me without the slightest intimation of who my father was. The whisper that my master was my father, may or may not be true; and, true or false, it is of but little consequence to my purpose whilst the fact remains, in all its glaring odiousness, that slaveholders have ordained, and by law established,

The passage begins with Douglass saying he was not allowed to know when his birthday was. It goes on to speak of other things he was not allowed to know. What are they? If you go on to read more of this autobiography, you will see that the theme of Douglass's quest for knowledge continues throughout the entire narrative.

(31) Can you think of other reasons for separating the slave child from its mother?

(47–54) Does Douglass's reaction to his mother's death suggest that the separation had the intended result?

(56) Put this last long sentence into your own words to be sure you understand what Douglass is saying that the slaveholders "have ordained, and … established."

that the children of slave women shall in all cases follow the condition of their mothers; and this is done too obviously to administer to their own lusts, and make a gratification of their wicked desires profitable as well as pleasurable; for by this cunning arrangement, the slaveholder, in cases not a few, sustains to his slaves the double relation of master

and father.

About the English Language and Composition Exam

One of the essay questions on the Advanced Placement test will ask you to analyze a passage that you have read. To **analyze** is to break a complicated item into its component parts, examine those parts individually, and explain how they work together to create the larger, more complex entity you are studying. No matter how the question is worded, the task remains the same: observe what the author has done and explain how he or she did it.

Obviously there isn't time to discuss everything the passage contains. You will want to choose those items that best allow you to show that you understand the effects of the author's choices of the following:

diction (the words the author chose)

syntax (the arrangements of words and phrases into sentences and paragraphs)

tone (the author's attitude toward the subject or audience)

purpose (the reasons the author had for writing the piece)

choice of details, or any other feature of the language the question prompts you to consider.

Here is a sample question based on the readings in this lesson. At exam time, you will have forty minutes to read the passage and write your essay. If you have never written a practice AP essay before, your teacher might allow you a little more time, but as you become more familiar with writing practice essays, you should limit yourself so that on the day of the test you don't have problems managing your time.

AP Exam Advice

Focus on Writing: Analysis

The excerpt from Douglas Brinkley's biography of Rosa Parks begins with a description of the house in which his subject was born and the religious background in which she grew up. Read the passage carefully, paying attention to the details the author chose to include in both those sections. Then write a well-organized essay in which you show how the author's choice of details communicates his attitude toward his subject. Do not summarize the passage.

Guidance on Your Writing

Remember that in all analysis questions, you must respond to the double task of explaining what the author did and how he or she did it. This question asks you to explain what Brinkley's attitude toward Rosa Parks is and to show how the details in his writing communicate that attitude toward the reader. You might begin with a statement such as "In *Rosa Parks*, Douglas Brinkley uses details describing Parks's house and religious behavior to display an almost reverential attitude toward his subject." By no means is that the only acceptable response to the essay prompt, but whatever you write, you need to address the two-part task as presented in the question: explain Brinkley's attitude and show how his choice of detail communicates that attitude. This opening statement would then be followed with references to the text that further illustrate what details he uses and how they contribute to the meaning of the passage.

After you have written your essay, you should ask your teacher for a quick evaluation of your work. AP essays are graded according to a scoring guide that instructs the reader to judge the writing according to the reasonableness of the writer's response to the prompt, the appropriateness and thoroughness of the essay's development, and the writer's general command of the conventions of the English language.

AP Exam Advice

The passage from Frederick Douglass's autobiography also suggests an analytical response. Try this sample question. Approach it in a manner similar to the question on the Brinkley excerpt: what did the author do, and how did the author do it?

Focus on Writing: Analysis

Frederick Douglass's autobiography begins with a description of his early years as a slave. Read the passage carefully, and then write an essay in which you explain the writer's purpose in recounting the details of his early childhood. Support your observations with details from the narrative. Do not merely summarize the passage.

Guidance on Your Writing

First, you will want to be sure you are addressing both parts of the task: what did the author do, and how did the author do it? What is the purpose of the passage, and how do the details support that purpose? Your response to this essay question will also need to begin with a statement showing that you understand the author's direct language in the passage you read. While there are many ways you can express that understanding, you will need a sentence like "Frederick Douglass tells about his mother's life and death to make the reader understand the brutality of life on the plantation." Then, after deciding which details of the narrative support that observation, you will have to provide them in your essay.

Lesson 2

In what ways does the passage require especially careful reading?

Introduction

Traditionally, the Advanced Placement English Language and Composition course and examination include readings from the seventeenth century to the modern day. Students who have not been exposed to language of past literary periods are frequently frustrated with these passages. The sentences are often long and complicated, the vocabulary is elevated and unfamiliar, and the relationships between elements of the passage, such as sentences within a paragraph, are often unclear.

It is vital, therefore, that you practice reading passages from past times and pay careful attention to the vocabulary and sentence structure of those passages. The vocabulary may be challenging if the passage includes unfamiliar words or if the writer uses words in unfamiliar ways, and the sentences may seem long and complex, but if you develop the habit of reading carefully to discover the relationship between parts of a long sentence, the meaning will become apparent.

Paine and Jefferson: Two Influential Writers

Thomas Paine and Thomas Jefferson were two very important writers of eighteenth-century America. Their writings had a profound influence on the formation of our nation.

Paine's pamphlet *The Crisis* was read aloud to Washington's soldiers during a difficult winter encampment. This essay is believed to have provided the men with the motivation to continue their fight for independence against the British. Here you will be reading only a few paragraphs, but the essay is worth reading in its entirety.

Jefferson, the author of the Declaration of Independence (a classic example of an argumentative essay), wrote several other worthy pieces, including his *Notes on the State of Virginia,* from which the excerpt on page 10 is taken.

In both pieces, you will find the author making a case for a particular **point of view**, paying careful attention to **word choices** and **sentence structures**. As you read each piece, note unfamiliar words and then see what context clues help you understand what the words mean. If you need to reread a paragraph or sentence because it is long and complicated, make note of that passage so that you can **analyze** it for its meaning. Comments in the margins of these passages should help you.

> **Focus on the Reading: Close Reading with Attention to Diction**
> Look for the author's particular point of view, and pay careful attention to word choices and sentence structures.

Thomas Paine
from *The Crisis*

THESE are the times that try men's souls. The summer soldier and the sunshine patriot will, in this crisis, shrink from the service of their country; but he that stands it now, deserves the love and thanks of man and woman. Tyranny, like hell, is not easily conquered; yet we have this consolation with us, that the harder the conflict, the more glorious the triumph. What we obtain too cheap, we esteem too lightly: it is dearness only that gives every thing its value. Heaven knows how to put a proper price upon its goods; and it would be strange indeed if so celestial an article as **freedom** should not be highly rated. Britain, with an army to enforce her tyranny, has declared that she has a right (not only to **tax**) but "to **bind** us in **all cases whatsoever**," and if being bound in that manner is not slavery, then is there not such a thing as slavery upon earth. Even the expression is impious; for so unlimited a power can belong only to God.

…

I have as little superstition in me as any man living, but my secret opinion has ever been, and still is, that God Almighty will not give up a people to military destruction, or leave them unsupportedly to perish, who have so earnestly and so repeatedly sought to avoid the calamities of war, by every decent method which wisdom could invent. Neither have I so much of the infidel in me, as to suppose that He has relinquished the government of the world, and given us up to the care of devils; and as I do not, I cannot see on what grounds the king of Britain can look up to heaven for help against us: a common murderer, a highwayman, or a house-breaker, has as good a pretence as he.

'Tis surprising to see how rapidly a panic will sometimes run through a country. All nations and ages have been subject to them. Britain has trembled like an ague at the report of a French fleet of flat-bottomed boats; and in the fourteenth [fifteenth] century the whole English army, after ravaging the kingdom of France, was driven back like men petrified with fear; and this brave exploit was performed by a few broken forces collected and headed by a woman, Joan of Arc. Would that heaven might inspire some Jersey maid to spirit up her countrymen, and save her fair fellow sufferers from ravage and ravishment! Yet panics, in some cases, have their uses; they produce as much good as hurt. Their duration is always short; the mind soon grows through them, and acquires a firmer habit than before. But their peculiar advantage is, that they are the touchstones of sincerity and hypocrisy, and bring things and men to light, which might otherwise have lain forever undiscovered. In fact, they have the same effect on secret traitors, which an imaginary apparition would have upon a private murderer. They sift out the hidden thoughts of man, and hold them up in public to the world. Many a disguised Tory has lately shown his head, that shall penitentially solemnize with curses the day on which Howe arrived upon the Delaware.

…

I shall conclude this paper with some miscellaneous remarks on the state of our affairs; and shall begin with asking the following ques-

(6) Here is an unusual application of the word "dearness." Are you familiar with "dear" as a synonym for "expensive"? When you think of how we apply the word to a person we care about, the connection might be clear.

(15) The first sentence of this paragraph has many clauses. To what word does the pronoun "who" refer? If you understood that connection when you first read it, the meaning of the sentence was probably clear. If you need to stop and determine that connection, you will better understand what Paine is saying once you do.

(27) Do you know what an ague is? Do you have to know in order to understand this sentence?

(37) A touchstone is a quality or characteristic that allows us to measure the excellence of another. Be sure you understand exactly what Paine identifies as these touchstones. In other words, to what noun do "they" and "their" refer in these sentences?

tion, Why is it that the enemy have left the New England provinces, and made these middle ones the seat of war? The answer is easy: New England is not infested with Tories, and we are. I have been tender in raising the cry against these men, and used numberless arguments to show them their danger, but it will not do to sacrifice a world either to their folly or their baseness. The period is now arrived, in which either they or we must change our sentiments, or one or both must fall. And what is a Tory? Good God! what is he? I should not be afraid to go with a hundred Whigs against a thousand Tories, were they to attempt to get into arms. Every Tory is a coward; for servile, slavish, self-interested fear is the foundation of Toryism; and a man under such influence, though he may be cruel, never can be brave.
…

I once felt all that kind of anger, which a man ought to feel, against the mean principles that are held by the Tories: a noted one, who kept a tavern at Amboy, was standing at his door, with as pretty a child in his hand, about eight or nine years old, as I ever saw, and after speaking his mind as freely as he thought was prudent, finished with this unfatherly expression, "Well! give me peace in my day." Not a man lives on the continent but fully believes that a separation must some time or other finally take place, and a generous parent should have said, "If there must be trouble, let it be in my day, that my child may have peace;" and this single reflection, well applied, is sufficient to awaken every man to duty. Not a place upon earth might be so happy as America. Her situation is remote from all the wrangling world, and she has nothing to do but to trade with them. A man can distinguish himself between temper and principle, and I am as confident, as I am that God governs the world, that America will never be happy till she gets clear of foreign dominion. Wars, without ceasing, will break out till that period arrives, and the continent must in the end be conqueror; for though the flame of liberty may sometimes cease to shine, the coal can never expire.

(48) Why do you suppose Paine used the word "infested" here? What other words would also provide the same general meaning, that there aren't a lot of Tories in New England? What associations does the word "infested" suggest?

(58) "Mean" is a word that has several meanings. If you know it only as a synonym for "unkind" or "somewhat cruel," you might be surprised, when looking it up in a dictionary, at how many meanings it has. Which of them seems most appropriate here?

(68) "Happy" is another word whose meaning has changed over time. In the eighteenth century, "happy" meant not only glad or cheerful but also fortunate. It was this meaning that Jefferson had in mind when he wrote of the rights of "life, liberty, and the pursuit of happiness." Paine means the same here.

About the English Language and Composition Exam

The first hour of the AP examination consists of readings like this one and multiple-choice questions based upon them. These questions—designed to make sure you have read and understood the passage accurately—can be quite difficult, but they may actually increase your comprehension by focusing on important details or matters you may not have understood on your own.

Each question stem will be followed by five possible answers, and the test directions will instruct you to choose the best of the five offered. Such direction suggests that more than one answer might be defensible or that an even better answer exists that is not among the five offered. You have to work with the choices given and choose the best answer.

Exam Practice — Reading Comprehension

As a practice exercise, try these questions. See if you can find the answer in the passage before reading the choices provided. You might work with a friend to see if you can explain why you chose the answer you did. Can you indicate the place where the text supports your choice?

1. In the second sentence, Paine draws a distinction between

    (A) patriots and traitors.
    (B) soldiers and civilians.
    (C) convenience and hardship.
    (D) obligation and gratitude.
    (E) the Tories and the revolutionaries.

2. Upon what basis do we determine the value of freedom?

    (A) the opportunities it offers us
    (B) the cost of obtaining it
    (C) how much the King does not want us to have it
    (D) the amount of tax we have to pay because we are not free
    (E) the threat of slavery if we fail

3. Why does Paine believe that God is on the side of the revolutionaries?

    (A) They have tried to avoid war.
    (B) The British king is evil.
    (C) He has had a vision like Joan of Arc.
    (D) He has heard sermons to that effect.
    (E) Freedom is celestial.

4. Which of the following is not a reason for Paine telling about Joan of Arc?

    (A) He is trying to humiliate the English army.
    (B) He hopes some colonial girl will imitate Joan's actions.
    (C) He is trying to illustrate the power of panic.
    (D He is hoping to get the French to come to the aid of the revolutionaries.
    (E) He is trying to boost the spirits of the colonial soldiers.

5. Which of the following is characteristic of a panic?

    I.   It is over quickly.
    II. It allows us to see good qualities in others.
    III. It reveals the truth of a person's private thinking.
    (A) I alone
    (B) I and II
    (C) I and III
    (D) II and III
    (E) I, II, and III

6. In the next to last paragraph, what does Paine imply about Tories?

    (A) There are fewer Tories in New England than in the middle colonies.
    (B) Tories are weaker than Whigs.
    (C) Tories are cowards.
    (D) Tories are like rats or vermin.
    (E) Tories are interested in their own well-being.

7. The purpose of the illustration in the final paragraph, in which Paine tells about the tavern keeper, is to

    (A) show the Tories as selfish.
    (B) evoke pity for children during wartime.
    (C) suggest that the Tories were more interested in peace than the revolutionaries were.
    (D) demonstrate the cruelty of the Tories.
    (E) prophesy that more wars will follow this one.

The Crisis is such a rich piece of writing that we cannot make full use of it in one lesson. We will refer to it again in later lessons, where it will serve to illustrate other reading and writing skills.

Reading Selection by Thomas Jefferson

Here is another passage from the eighteenth century. While Jefferson is more famous for writing the Declaration of Independence, he was actually a prolific author of documents that help us to understand colonial life in Virginia. *Notes on the State of Virginia* covers many different topics. This one, addressing the problem of slavery, is perhaps all the more interesting because Jefferson himself owned slaves. As you read, think about the purpose of each sentence and its contribution to the total effect of the **argument**.

> ## Focus on the Reading: Close Reading with Attention to Diction
> Think about the purpose of each sentence and its contribution to the total effect of the argument.

Thomas Jefferson
Notes on the State of Virginia

Query 18: "Manners"
The particular customs and manners that may happen to be received in that state?

It is difficult to determine on the standard by which the manners of a
5   nation may be tried, whether *catholic*, or *particular*. It is more difficult for a native to bring to that standard the manners of his own nation, familiarized to him by habit. There must doubtless be an unhappy influence on the manners of our people produced by the existence of slavery among us. The whole commerce between master and slave is a per-
10   petual exercise of the most boisterous passions, the most unremitting despotism on the one part, and degrading submissions on the other. Our children see this, and learn to imitate it; for man is an imitative animal. This quality is the germ of all education in him. From his cradle to his grave he is learning to do what he sees others do. If a parent could find
15   no motive either in his philanthropy or his self-love, for restraining the intemperance of passion towards his slave, it should always be a sufficient one that his child is present. But generally it is not sufficient. The parent storms, the child looks on, catches the lineaments of wrath, puts on the same airs in the circle of smaller slaves, gives a loose to his worst
20   of passions, and thus nursed, educated, and daily exercised in tyranny, cannot but be stamped by it with odious peculiarities. The man must be a prodigy who can retain his manners and morals undepraved by such circumstances. And with what execration should the statesman be loaded, who permitting one half the citizens thus to trample on the rights
25   of the other, transforms those into despots, and these into enemies, destroys the morals of the one part, and the amor patriae of the other. For if a slave can have a country in this world, it must be any other in preference to that in which he is born to live and labour for another: in which he must lock up the faculties of his nature, contribute as far as depends
30   on his individual endeavours to the evanishment of the human race, or entail his own miserable condition on the endless generations pro-

(5) The word "catholic" here obviously does not refer to the Roman Catholic Church. If you don't know the word's meaning, how can you determine it from the context?

(7) Note the word "unhappy," and remember the comment made in the Paine reading.

(26) "Amor patriae" is Latin for "love of country."

ceeding from him. With the morals of the people, their industry also is destroyed. For in a warm climate, no man will labour for himself who can make another labour for him. This is so true, that of the proprietors of slaves a very small proportion indeed are ever seen to labour. And can the liberties of a nation be thought secure when we have removed their only firm basis, a conviction in the minds of the people that these liberties are of the gift of God? That they are not to be violated but with his wrath? Indeed I tremble for my country when I reflect that God is just: that his justice cannot sleep for ever: that considering numbers, nature and natural means only, a revolution of the wheel of fortune, an exchange of situation, is among possible events: that it may become probable by supernatural interference! The Almighty has no attribute which can take side with us in such a contest.—But it is impossible to be temperate and to pursue this subject through the various considerations of policy, of morals, of history natural and civil. We must be contented to hope they will force their way into every one's mind. I think a change already perceptible, since the origin of the present revolution. The spirit of the master is abating, that of the slave rising from the dust, his condition mollifying, the way I hope preparing, under the auspices of heaven, for a total emancipation, and that this is disposed, in the order of events, to be with the consent of the masters, rather than by their extirpation.

Do you see Jefferson and Paine as similar or different in their reference to the role of religion in their arguments?

Commentary on the Reading

This paragraph is a good candidate for paraphrasing, which is simply putting the ideas of the original into your own language. For example, in the third sentence, where Jefferson wrote, "There must doubtless be an unhappy influence on the manners of our people produced by the existence of slavery among us," you, as a contemporary reader, might say, "Slavery is a bad influence on our lives." Because the purpose of paraphrasing is to be sure we understand what the author is saying, it is important to remain faithful to the original ideas rather than to interpret them or comment on them. Your teacher might suggest that you paraphrase this reading to be certain you are aware of what Jefferson's main point is and how he develops his argument in support of it.

There are basically four main points in this argument, and a discussion of the piece ought to consider all four:

- what effect slavery has on our children;
- how slavery creates discord between two portions of our population;
- how slavery affects our work habits; and
- God's view of slavery.

If you were asked to explain Jefferson's position on slavery, you would want to say more than that he thought it was bad. You would give a much better answer if you explained why he felt as he did.

It is very tempting in a situation like this one, where you know that Jefferson was himself a slave owner, to offer an opinion on his sincerity or morality. The reading may certainly lead to conversations on those topics. However, if the essay prompt asks you to analyze the argument, that is all you should do. On the other hand, some prompts might ask you to comment on the argument, and if that is your instruction, that is what you should address in your essay. In short, be sure to follow directions and to answer the question that is asked.

You might find a question like the following on the AP English Language and Composition test. In writing an argument, you must take a position and provide reasons that support it.

> **Focus on Writing: Argumentation**
> Read the excerpt from Thomas Jefferson's *Notes on the State of Virginia*, in which he presents several criticisms of slavery. Think of a practice or behavior with which you are familiar from your own experience, and write an argument showing it to be justified or unjustified. For example, you might want to write about your school's dress code (or lack of one), or your community's curfew, or a policy concerning athletic eligibility. While you may be tempted to treat the subject satirically, you will write a better argument if you handle it seriously.

Guidance on Your Writing

The most successful responses to this question will clearly identify the topic and offer three or four solid reasons for defending or challenging the status quo. A common weakness is to offer one idea and then rephrase it rather than to go on to express new ideas. For example, if you were arguing that your town should not have a curfew for teenagers, you might say that a curfew suggests that people think teenagers out at night would cause trouble. If you then say that a curfew shows that adults just don't trust teenagers, you haven't offered a new argument; you've only restated the previous idea. If instead you go on to say that sometimes teenagers have legitimate reasons for being out late, such as traveling to and from school activities, you are offering something new, thereby providing a better response.

Lesson 3   What are the author's assertions?

Introduction

When you are speaking with someone about a topic that you really care about, you might check to see that your listener is following your argument by asking a question. Your listener's answer will tell you how much of what you are saying he or she understands. When you are writing, however, you cannot stop and check whether your reader understands or agrees; you have no way of knowing what he or she is thinking.

Fortunately, you do have the technique of the **rhetorical question**, one to which you expect no answer either because the answer is self-evident ("Do I have to explain why I am disappointed in your grades?") or because there is no answer ("How many times do I have to tell you that I'm sorry?"). Writers use rhetorical questions to emphasize their ideas to be sure that their readers are following their lines of thought.

Using Rhetorical Questions

It sometimes sounds as if a rhetorical question is an argument-winner. When you ask, "What other explanation is there?" and no one answers you, you may think you've proved your point and that the discussion is over. However, you must realize that as powerful as a rhetorical question might be, it is not proof of anything. It is only an emphatic way of making an assertion. Because you don't know what a reader might say in reply to your question, you can't be sure that there are no meaningful responses. Therefore, use rhetorical questions sparingly—only when you are sure there is no answer available or when it wouldn't matter what the answer is. Sometimes you will want to follow a rhetorical question with your own answer, hoping that the reader will see the value of your reasoning.

In the following reading, a speech by the Nobel Peace Prize winner Elie Wiesel, you will find many rhetorical questions. You may wonder whether Wiesel took unnecessary risks in asking so many questions, but he was sure that no one would interrupt him while he was speaking and that he wouldn't have to respond to any challenges his listeners, certainly a friendly and supportive audience, might make.

Wiesel's personal history is very important as the background of this speech. As a young Holocaust survivor, he witnessed many of the horrors he refers to in the speech, and, in a life spent working for justice around the world, he has seen that inhumane treatment is widespread and deserving of our attention. In the speech, Wiesel alludes to both historical and contemporary figures. Even if you don't recognize all of them, you will find that the accumulated mention of their names creates a powerful effect.

The speech was delivered in the White House at the invitation of First Lady Hillary Clinton in 1999.

Elie Wiesel
The Perils of Indifference
April 12, 1999, The White House

Mr. President, Mrs. Clinton, members of Congress, Ambassador Holbrooke, Excellencies, friends: Fifty-four years ago to the day, a young Jewish boy from a small town in the Carpathian Mountains woke up, not far from Goethe's beloved Weimar, in a place of eternal infamy called Buchenwald. He was finally free, but there was no joy in his heart. He thought there never would be again.

Liberated a day earlier by American soldiers, he remembers their rage at what they saw. And even if he lives to be a very old man, he will always be grateful to them for that rage, and also for their compassion. Though he did not understand their language, their eyes told him what he needed to know—that they, too, would remember, and bear witness.

And now, I stand before you, Mr. President—Commander-in-Chief of the army that freed me, and tens of thousands of others—and I am filled with a profound and abiding gratitude to the American people.

Gratitude is a word that I cherish. Gratitude is what defines the humanity of the human being. And I am grateful to you, Hillary—or Mrs. Clinton—for what you said, and for what you are doing for children in the world, for the homeless, for the victims of injustice, the victims of destiny and society. And I thank all of you for being here.

We are on the threshold of a new century, a new millennium. What will the legacy of this vanishing century be? How will it be remembered in the new millennium? Surely it will be judged, and judged severely, in both moral and metaphysical terms. These failures have cast a dark shadow over humanity: two World Wars, countless civil wars, the senseless chain of assassinations—Gandhi, the Kennedys, Martin Luther King, Sadat, Rabin—bloodbaths in Cambodia and Nigeria, India and Pakistan, Ireland and Rwanda, Eritrea and Ethiopia, Sarajevo and Kosovo; the inhumanity in the gulag and the tragedy of Hiroshima. And, on a different level, of course, Auschwitz and Treblinka. So much violence, so much indifference.

What is indifference? Etymologically, the word means "no difference." A strange and unnatural state in which the lines blur between light and darkness, dusk and dawn, crime and punishment, cruelty and compassion, good and evil.

What are its courses and inescapable consequences? Is it a philosophy? Is a philosophy of indifference conceivable? Can one possibly view indifference as a virtue? Is it necessary at times to practice it simply to keep one's sanity, live normally, enjoy a fine meal and a glass of wine, as the world around us experiences harrowing upheavals?

(5) Buchenwald was the site of one of Nazi Germany's concentration camps.

(21) Here is a case where Wiesel asks rhetorical questions and then provides answers for them.

(35) You may be tempted to answer "yes" to these questions. Wiesel is probably counting on that response so that he can argue the opposite.

Of course, indifference can be tempting—more than that, seductive. It is so much easier to look away from victims. It is so much easier to avoid such rude interruptions to our work, our dreams, our hopes. It is, after all, awkward, troublesome, to be involved in another person's pain and despair. Yet, for the person who is indifferent, his or her neighbors are of no consequence. And, therefore, their lives are meaningless. Their hidden or even visible anguish is of no interest. Indifference reduces the other to an abstraction.

Over there, behind the black gates of Auschwitz, the most tragic of all prisoners were the "Muselmänner," as they were called. Wrapped in their torn blankets, they would sit or lie on the ground, staring vacantly into space, unaware of who or where they were, strangers to their surroundings. They no longer felt pain, hunger, thirst. They feared nothing. They felt nothing. They were dead and did not know it.

Rooted in our tradition, some of us felt that to be abandoned by humanity then was not the ultimate. We felt that to be abandoned by God was worse than to be punished by Him. Better an unjust God than an indifferent one. For us to be ignored by God was a harsher punishment than to be a victim of His anger. Man can live far from God—not outside God. God is wherever we are. Even in suffering? Even in suffering.

In a way, to be indifferent to that suffering is what makes the human being inhuman. Indifference, after all, is more dangerous than anger and hatred. Anger can at times be creative. One writes a great poem, a great symphony, one does something special for the sake of humanity because one is angry at the injustice that one witnesses. But indifference is never creative. Even hatred at times may elicit a response. You fight it. You denounce it. You disarm it. Indifference elicits no response. Indifference is not a response.

Indifference is not a beginning, it is an end. And, therefore, indifference is always the friend of the enemy, for it benefits the aggressor—never his victim, whose pain is magnified when he or she feels forgotten. The political prisoner in his cell, the hungry children, the homeless refugees—not to respond to their plight, not to relieve their solitude by offering them a spark of hope is to exile them from human memory. And in denying their humanity we betray our own.

Indifference, then, is not only a sin, it is a punishment. And this is one of the most important lessons of this outgoing century's wide-ranging experiments in good and evil.

In the place that I come from, society was composed of three simple categories: the killers, the victims, and the bystanders. During the darkest of times, inside the ghettoes and death camps—and I'm glad that Mrs. Clinton mentioned that we are now commemorating that event, that period, that we are now in the Days of Remembrance—but then, we felt abandoned, forgotten. All of us did.

And our only miserable consolation was that we believed that Auschwitz and Treblinka were closely guarded secrets; that the leaders of the free world did not know what was going on behind those black gates and barbed wire; that they had no knowledge of the war against the Jews that Hitler's armies and their accomplices waged as part of the war against the Allies.

If they knew, we thought, surely those leaders would have moved heaven and earth to intervene. They would have spoken out with great

(85) Auschwitz, Treblinka, and Birkenau (in the next paragraph) were among the largest of the German concentration camps.

outrage and conviction. They would have bombed the railways leading to Birkenau, just the railways, just once.

And now we knew, we learned, we discovered that the Pentagon knew, the State Department knew. And the illustrious occupant of the White House then, who was a great leader—and I say it with some anguish and pain, because, today is exactly 54 years marking his death—Franklin Delano Roosevelt died on April the 12th, 1945, so he is very much present to me and to us.

No doubt, he was a great leader. He mobilized the American people and the world, going into battle, bringing hundreds and thousands of valiant and brave soldiers in America to fight fascism, to fight dictatorship, to fight Hitler. And so many of the young people fell in battle. And, nevertheless, his image in Jewish history—I must say it—his image in Jewish history is flawed.

The depressing tale of the *St. Louis* is a case in point. Sixty years ago, its human cargo—maybe 1,000 Jews—was turned back to Nazi Germany. And that happened after the *Kristallnacht*, after the first state sponsored pogrom, with hundreds of Jewish shops destroyed, synagogues burned, thousands of people put in concentration camps. And that ship, which was already on the shores of the United States, was sent back.

I don't understand. Roosevelt was a good man, with a heart. He understood those who needed help. Why didn't he allow these refugees to disembark? A thousand people—in America, a great country, the greatest democracy, the most generous of all new nations in modern history. What happened? I don't understand. Why the indifference, on the highest level, to the suffering of the victims?

But then, there were human beings who were sensitive to our tragedy. Those non-Jews, those Christians, that we called the "Righteous Gentiles," whose selfless acts of heroism saved the honor of their faith. Why were they so few? Why was there a greater effort to save SS murderers after the war than to save their victims during the war?

Why did some of America's largest corporations continue to do business with Hitler's Germany until 1942? It has been suggested, and it was documented, that the *Wehrmacht* could not have conducted its invasion of France without oil obtained from American sources. How is one to explain their indifference?

And yet, my friends, good things have also happened in this traumatic century: the defeat of Nazism, the collapse of communism, the rebirth of Israel on its ancestral soil, the demise of apartheid, Israel's peace treaty with Egypt, the peace accord in Ireland. And let us remember the meeting, filled with drama and emotion, between Rabin and Arafat that you, Mr. President, convened in this very place. I was here and I will never forget it.

And then, of course, the joint decision of the United States and NATO to intervene in Kosovo and save those victims, those refugees, those who were uprooted by a man whom I believe that because of his crimes, should be charged with crimes against humanity. But this time, the world was not silent. This time, we do respond. This time, we intervene.

Does it mean that we have learned from the past? Does it mean that society has changed? Has the human being become less indifferent and more human? Have we really learned from our experiences? Are

(110) The *St. Louis* was a humanitarian ship that carried many wartime refugees from Europe to the United States, where it was refused permission to berth and sent back to Europe. Some of its passengers found asylum in safe places, but many of them died after returning to the countries they were trying to escape from.

(125) The *Wehrmacht* were the German armed forces under Hitler.

(137) Wiesel is speaking here of Slobodon Milošević, at the time the president of Serbia, believed by many to be responsible for atrocities committed against the people of several Balkan nations. He was indicted for crimes against humanity but died in 2006 before his trial was completed.

145

we less insensitive to the plight of victims of ethnic cleansing and other forms of injustices in places near and far? Is today's justified intervention in Kosovo, led by you, Mr. President, a lasting warning that never again will the deportation, the terrorization of children and their parents be allowed anywhere in the world? Will it discourage other dictators in other lands to do the same?

150

What about the children? Oh, we see them on television, we read about them in the papers, and we do so with a broken heart. Their fate is always the most tragic, inevitably. When adults wage war, children perish. We see their faces, their eyes. Do we hear their pleas? Do we feel their pain, their agony? Every minute one of them dies of disease, violence, famine. Some of them—so many of them— could be saved.

155

160

And so, once again, I think of the young Jewish boy from the Carpathian Mountains. He has accompanied the old man I have become throughout these years of quest and struggle. And together we walk towards the new millennium, carried by profound fear and extraordinary hope.

Commentary on the Reading

Even though Wiesel wrote and delivered this speech with no intention of eliciting answers to his questions, you might want to reply to one or more of them. He expresses a strong attitude toward his subject, and he hopes not only to communicate that attitude but also to encourage others to adopt his opinions. Do you find the technique of the rhetorical question likely to sway you to his point of view, or do you feel you want to reply and perhaps express another view?

Focus on Writing: Argumentation

In Elie Wiesel's speech "The Perils of Indifference," he expresses fervently held opinions about human suffering and tragedy, and he attempts to convince his audience to share his point of view. Choose a general topic on which you have a strong opinion and can form an argument. It does not need to be of global significance, as Wiesel's is. You might feel very strongly about a local matter, such as the availability of recreational facilities in your community. Then write an argument on this topic and explain how you want others to think about it.

Guidance on Your Writing

For the practice writing in this lesson, try to include a rhetorical question in the body of your essay. Don't make the mistake of assuming that because you asked the question, you needn't explain your reasoning. Use the question to emphasize your idea, not to excuse yourself from developing it.

Try to write this essay in about thirty-five minutes so that you have a few minutes to read over your work and make any quick revisions that seem appropriate. The people who read the AP exam understand that you are writing under pressure and do not have time to make extensive corrections, but you can probably make a noticeable difference in your essay if you go over it once. This is a good habit to develop, so you may as well start it now.

AP Exam Advice

Lesson 4   What is the author implying?

Introduction

The first lesson in this book presented two readings that were very straightforward and recommended that when you read such material, you first make sure you understand what the writer is saying literally. "Hidden meanings" do not lurk beneath the surface of every text. Then again, sometimes they do, and while it is certainly important for a reader to recognize when an author is to be read literally or interpretively, it is also true that a writer needs to recognize when his or her words can have some unintended meaning.

Ted Diadiun, an ombudsman for the Cleveland *Plain Dealer*, addresses that problem in the article below. Although his conclusion—that in their quest for clarity, journalists need to avoid language that defeats their purpose—is not a profound one, it is instead a point that needs to be made again and again to be sure that people remain vigilant.

Remember how Thomas Paine said that New England was not "infested" with Tories. Supporters of the king probably did not like that word and its associations with rats, vermin, and disease. Yet that is precisely why Paine chose the word and why we react to it more than two and a quarter centuries later. If you pay attention to political figures making public speeches, you will no doubt hear complaints about insensitive or ill-chosen remarks, and these complaints will be followed by apologies assuring the offended parties that no slight was intended. We must be aware that people are often very sensitive to the implications of particular words, and as writers, we must avoid creating meanings we do not intend.

Focus on the Reading: Awareness of Implications
Try to recognize when an author is to be read literally or interpretively.

Ted Diadiun

Words Sometimes Convey More Than Literal Meaning
September 11, 2005

The word "refugee," used in recent days to describe people who fled or were displaced by Hurricane Katrina and its aftermath, has caused some chagrin.

5   This strikes some people as a trivial matter, not worth draining off any of our attention while so many more important issues need to be addressed. To be sure, the debate is indeed trivial, and perhaps ill-timed, when compared with the tragedies and future challenges left in Katrina's wake.

10   But speaking as one who has spent a lifetime selecting words, observing their impact and dealing with their consequences, I would

Do you think the word "refugee" is offensive in this context? If you do, can you suggest language that would not offend?

never agree that words and their meanings are trivialities. Choosing our words with precision is one of the most important things we do in the newspaper business, and readers have every right to expect our most serious effort in that part of our job.

This is never more important than when we are using a word to describe a group of people. In addition to the literal meaning, what we choose can get bound up in the history of the word, people's prejudices about it and, like it or not in a world of instant communication, the television images it conjures. Mix in a little politics and the fact that everyone thinks he or she should get a vote, and you can wind up with controversy where you never expected to find it.

Actually, people do get a vote where possible. Most of the time, if there is no good linguistic argument to the contrary, the newspaper will try to call people what they wish to be called.

Take the abortion debate. You would never believe the amount of time and energy that was spent in newsrooms across the country debating the issue of what we should call the two sides. Attempting to be as accurate and considerate as possible about what the sides wished to be called, we finally settled on the uneasy truce of calling people who support a woman's right to choose "abortion rights supporter," and people who oppose abortion "anti-abortion." That solution was reached only after a long, bumpy haul across the terms pro-choice, anti-choice, pro-life, pro-abortion and as many others as you can imagine.

Other socially incendiary issues have included homosexuality (we refer to "sexual orientation" rather than "sexual preference," for what I think are perfectly defensible reasons) and physical impairment ("crippled" has given way to "disabled" but fortunately not yet to "differently abled.")

On issues of race, newspapers have chased a moving target that is more indicative of an increasingly enlightened outlook than on linguistic purity. We have proceeded from "colored" to "Negro" to "black" and "African-American," and from "Oriental" to "Asian-American." In Spanish-speaking cultures there is disagreement between "Hispanic" and "Latino," so when in doubt we ask and use the person's preferred term.

Consistent re-examination is a good thing, however, because unexamined habit can undercut our best efforts at precision. Not long ago I got a letter from a reader who objected to the paper's routine description of the "militant" Palestinian Hamas and the "extremist" Israeli Gaza Strip settlers.

His argument—and it is a good one— was that we should simply describe what each side was doing, and let the reader decide which side was extremist, militant or anything else. As I wrote him back, words that fall too easily together are a danger sign.

When a newspaper reporter finds himself automatically typing out phrases and word pairings without thinking, it is always a good idea to stop and think about what the words mean. At best, the writer will find himself in the middle of a cliché; at worst, in a characterization of uncertain accuracy.

All of that brings us back to "refugee."

Before Katrina, "refugee" is a word I—and I suspect most others—used often without a second thought. I considered it to mean "one seeking refuge" and employed it that way without distinction.

(34) All of these examples address topics that many people prefer not to discuss—the abortion question, sexual identity, ethnicity—for the very reasons the writer brings them up. Do these topics arise in your conversations? Do you have difficulty finding language that does not cause discomfort?

As the hurricane horror continued, *The Plain Dealer* and many other newspapers routinely referred to people escaping from the floods as "refugees," and we were stunned when we began getting emotional objections from readers who argued that the word marginalized the flood victims and treated them like foreigners. Most of the objections I heard came from black readers, fueled by comments from the Congressional Black Caucus, from the Rev. Jesse Jackson and from the pulpits of their churches.

Look in your dictionary, as I looked in mine, and you will find an argument for either side. Clearly, it is a word that describes someone who is fleeing home or country from some calamity. Just as clearly, the calamity is usually specified as being of a political or religious nature.

Many journalists initially reacted with stubbornness or anger to pleas that we refrain. "It's a perfectly good word," we argued, "and we'll decide whether we use it."

However, after some reflection, more than a few newspapers decided that this was a case where by winning they would lose. What would be the point in continuing to use a word that was becoming more politically charged by the day, if it made no difference to most of our readers but saddened or annoyed the rest?

The Plain Dealer was one newspaper that decided to find another word to describe the hurricane survivors.

"Words have literal and suggestive meaning," said Editor Doug Clifton, who made the decision. "This was one that was neutral and correct on the literal level, but neither neutral nor correct on the suggestive level."

Some people will see this debate as simply the forces of political correctness taking over the language. But one of the primary jobs of a newspaper is to be clear and understandable.

As someone who doesn't like to be pushed around either physically or linguistically, I have to admit that when word choice threatens to get in the way of clarity, the best choice is to find another word.

What is your reaction to this solution? If you do not like it, do you have another?

Commentary on the Reading

Diadiun argues that it is the writer's obligation to choose words carefully so that they do not communicate unintended ideas. The writer may or may not mean to say any more than the fact that some people were forced to relocate as a result of the hurricane. However, because people may object to the word "refugee," it is the writer's obligation to find a word to which they do not object.

On the other hand, writers have been known to use language that deliberately ridicules or insults their subjects. When we write, we must be careful not to use language that will be misinterpreted in this way, and when we read, we must take such language into account as we interpret and evaluate the pieces we are reading. In some cases such language seems appropriate, but in others it comes off as unnecessarily nasty and even counterproductive. In a review of *Everybody's Autobiography* by Gertrude Stein, Katherine Anne Porter says that as a young girl Gertrude was "upholstered in good clothes." Because upholstery is generally associated with furniture, it is hard not to see the remark as unflattering toward its subject. That may be the point Porter wants to make (the description goes on to say other unflattering things about Gertrude Stein), and certainly other available words—like "dressed," "arrayed," or even "decked out"—communicate altogether different messages.

Writers also choose their words carefully when they want to make an unpleasant topic less objectionable (we call that **euphemism**) or make an ordinary subject seem better than it really is. Whether reading or writing, it is important to pay attention to the possible meanings that each word carries.

Reading Selection by Peter Salgo

Physician Peter Salgo, in the article that follows, responds to a growing use of language that describes the medical world in terms we associate more readily with the business world. As you read the article, consider what alternative choices are available for these business-oriented words and what differences would result if those choices had been used instead.

> **Focus on the Reading: Awareness of Implications**
> Pay attention to the possible meanings that each word carries.

Peter Salgo
The Doctor Will See You For Exactly Seven Minutes

WHEN politicians speak of America's health care needs, they often miss an important point: the doctor-patient relationship has become frayed. Patients aren't unhappy just because health care costs too much (though they would certainly like it to be more affordable). Rather, peo-

5   ple sense a malaise within the system that has eroded the respect they feel patients deserve.

There has been a shift in attitude within the profession. I see examples of it every day. I was making rounds in my intensive care unit recently when one of the interns presented a case. "This is the first

10   admission for this 55-year-old male," he said.

"Stop," I said. "He is a man."

"That's what I said," the intern replied.

"Not exactly," I answered. Clearly, the intern didn't get it. Neither do a lot of other health care professionals anymore.

15   The problem has been sneaking up on us for almost two decades. As health-care dollars became scarce in the 1980's and 90's, hospitals asked their business people to attend clinical meetings. The object was to see what doctors were doing that cost a lot of money, then to try and do things more efficiently. Almost immediately, I noticed that business

20   jargon was becoming commonplace. "Patients" began to disappear. They were replaced by "consumers." They eventually became "customers."

This may seem a trivial matter, but it is not. You treat "patients" as if they were members of your family. You talk to them. You comfort them. You take time to explain to them what the future may hold in

25   store. Sometimes, that future will be bleak. But you assure them you will be there to help them face it.

(13) Do you "get it"? What difference does it make whether you refer to someone as "a male" or as "a man"?

You treat "customers" quite differently. Customers are in your place of business to purchase health care. You complete the transaction such a relationship suggests: health care for money. And then they aren't your customers any more. Taken a step further, you can make the case that the less time you spend with your customers, the better your bottom line will be. This gets everyone's attention.

"Length of stay" became a buzz phrase in hospitals in the 1990's. So did "throughput," an awful neologism for the number of patients per hospital bed per week. One of my colleagues joked that a hospital stay was a lot like a taxi ride. The institution collected a big fee when a patient got admitted, just as a cab driver saw most of his fare when he first turned the meter on.

The additional money collected over time wasn't nearly as impressive as that initial charge. The economics of the situation favored short trips, or lengths of stay, and lots of new riders, or throughput. The arithmetic worked, but I didn't notice a lot of people laughing.

Doctors in hospitals all over the country began hearing the same business language and facing the same pressures to "keep things moving." I used to be asked how well my patients were doing. Suddenly administrators were asking how long I was planning on keeping sick people in the intensive care unit. Each day a patient spent in my unit was a day some other paying patient would have to wait for a bed. Eventually, I was warned, some of those patients "in orbit" would go elsewhere, and we would not only "lose their business," but we risked losing future referrals from other centers.

It wasn't just hospitalized patients who were taking up space other "customers" could use. Outpatients "consumed" health care "resources," too. Publicly traded H.M.O.'s, for example, began restricting doctors to an average seven-minute "encounter" with each customer. This apparently kept shareholders happy. But it reduced the doctor-patient relationship to a financial concept in a business school term paper.

Doctors know you cannot provide compassion in seven-minute aliquots. But we have felt powerless to change things. The medical establishment has, many of us feel, simply rolled over and gone along to get along. It has sacrificed patients' best interests on the altar of financial return.

This leaves the solution to the problem in the hands of our patients. You, the patient, are the system's best hope. In the age of seven-minute health care, you need to realize that you employ doctors. That is, your doctor works for you. Although doctors shouldn't think of patients as customers, you can, and should, adopt a business mind-set when shopping for health care.

Evaluate what it is you expect from your doctor, then ask for it. If you are unhappy with your doctor, fire him. If you cannot get more than a seven-minute face-to-face encounter with your doctor, he needs fewer patients. The true power in the health care economy rests not with the doctors and certainly not with the backroom business staff. It rests with you. If you insist on being treated with care and respect, you will be. And the system will improve as a result.

A pediatrician I know put it quite succinctly. "There are a lot of doctors in town," she said. "There's no need to settle for one that doesn't treat you well."

(27) Do you share the writer's view about the differences between "patients" and "customers"?

(53) The writer puts certain words inside quotation marks to emphasize that they are the business words that have infiltrated the medical community. Can you think of others?

In one respect the business people are right. Restoring the doctor-patient relationship will not save anyone any money. But I submit that it doesn't have to. There are other ways to curtail health care costs. Some involve high technology; others do not. None of them requires patients to sacrifice their self-respect.

We can and must reduce health care expenses. But we cannot do it at the expense of patients' well-being. The doctor-patient relationship is critical to the integrity of the health care system. It is not disposable. Turning doctors into shopkeepers who regard patients as customers is unacceptable.

How will the M.B.A.'s and the politicians respond to what can only be termed a "patient-driven revolution"? They will have to cope. I suspect doctors will be thrilled.

Commentary on the Reading

This essay seeks to persuade us to believe what the writer believes, that patients are unhappy with what they consider disrespectful treatment brought on by a business-oriented medical administration. Among the many techniques the persuasive writer has available, this author depends heavily on illustration, specifically illustrating which words communicate that business attitude and explaining how that attitude is contrary to good medical practice as he sees it.

You will notice in your other readings, especially in newspapers and magazines, a similar phenomenon of language—that a writer will employ the words of one profession or activity to describe another and in that way communicate an attitude or a message about the subject that a more straightforward exposition might not make as effectively. Perhaps you can find a piece of writing that displays this technique, and then share it with your class.

> ### Focus on Writing: Argumentation
> Some people feel that our society needs to be more vigilant about the potentially negative effects of some speakers' and writers' language, and others feel as though pressure to avoid offending anyone inhibits the expression of passionately held ideas. On which side of this debate do you find yourself? Write an essay in which you explain your position on this topic and why you feel as you do.

Guidance on Your Writing

Now that you have read what two authors have written about the effects of certain word choices, consider your own experience with that problem. In this essay, it is important for you to think about how your views have been influenced by the spoken or written words of others. The essay prompt above resembles some English Language and Composition argumentative essays in that it asks you to take a position on a topic and defend it. When you write essays like these on the actual exam, you are not judged according to what position you take but according to how well you develop the arguments that support your chosen position.

AP Exam Advice

Lesson 5   What is the author's point of view?

Introduction

When you read a work of fiction—a short story or a novel—you pay attention to the point of view the author has chosen. When you realize through whose eyes you are seeing the story's events or meeting its characters, you assess those events and characters accordingly. For example, Harper Lee's *To Kill a Mockingbird* derives a good deal of its effect from the fact that the story is told through the eyes of a young girl. It would be quite a different story if Atticus Finch had told it, or Boo Radley, or Mayella Ewell.

When we read nonfiction, we also pay attention to the character of the speaker. You frequently hear people say that you should consider the source of a comment. Certainly a description of a presidential candidate's visit to your community will be affected by whether or not the writer supports that candidate.

Upton Sinclair's novel *The Jungle* was, in its time, a sensational piece of propaganda. It told the stories of several Lithuanian immigrants at the beginning of the twentieth century. They came to Chicago and worked in the meatpacking industry, and the novel details many shocking elements of their poverty and work experience. The author is clearly not objective in his presentation of the material. As you read these paragraphs from the opening of a chapter in the middle of the book, see what clues you find as to the attitude of the speaker. How do the author's choices influence the way you feel about the main character, Jurgis, and the police he deals with in this scene?

> **Focus on the Reading: Understanding the Writer's Character**
> See what clues you find as to the attitude of the speaker.

Upton Sinclair
from *The Jungle*

When Jurgis got up again he went quietly enough. He was exhausted and half-dazed, and besides he saw the blue uniforms of the policemen. He drove in a patrol wagon with half a dozen of them watching him; keeping as far away as possible, however, on account of the fertilizer.
5 Then he stood before the sergeant's desk and gave his name and address, and saw a charge of assault and battery entered against him. On his way to his cell a burly policeman cursed him because he started down the wrong corridor, and then added a kick when he was not quick enough; nevertheless, Jurgis did not even lift his eyes—he had lived
10 two years and a half in Packingtown, and he knew what the police were. It was as much as a man's very life was worth to anger them, here in their inmost lair; like as not a dozen would pile on to him at once, and pound his face into a pulp. It would be nothing unusual if he got his

(4) The police keep their distance from Jurgis because he works with fertilizer and smells bad.

skull cracked in the melee—in which case they would report that he had been drunk and had fallen down, and there would be no one to know the difference or to care.

So a barred door clanged upon Jurgis and he sat down upon a bench and buried his face in his hands. He was alone; he had the afternoon and all of the night to himself.

At first he was like a wild beast that has glutted itself; he was in a dull stupor of satisfaction. He had done up the scoundrel pretty well—not as well as he would have if they had given him a minute more, but pretty well, all the same; the ends of his fingers were still tingling from their contact with the fellow's throat. But then, little by little, as his strength came back and his senses cleared, he began to see beyond his momentary gratification; that he had nearly killed the boss would not help Ona—not the horrors that she had borne, nor the memory that would haunt her all her days. It would not help to feed her and her child; she would certainly lose her place, while he—what was to happen to him God only knew.

Half the night he paced the floor, wrestling with this nightmare; and when he was exhausted he lay down, trying to sleep, but finding instead, for the first time in his life, that his brain was too much for him. In the cell next to him was a drunken wife-beater and in the one beyond a yelling maniac. At midnight they opened the station house to the homeless wanderers who were crowded about the door, shivering in the winter blast, and they thronged into the corridor outside of the cells. Some of them stretched themselves out on the bare stone floor and fell to snoring, others sat up, laughing and talking, cursing and quarreling. The air was fetid with their breath, yet in spite of this some of them smelled Jurgis and called down the torments of hell upon him, while he lay in a far corner of his cell, counting the throbbings of the blood in his forehead.

They had brought him his supper, which was "duffers and dope"—being hunks of dry bread on a tin plate, and coffee, called "dope" because it was drugged to keep the prisoners quiet. Jurgis had not known this, or he would have swallowed the stuff in desperation; as it was, every nerve of him was aquiver with shame and rage. Toward morning the place fell silent, and he got up and began to pace his cell; and then within the soul of him there rose up a fiend, red-eyed and cruel, and tore out the strings of his heart.

The author said that Jurgis was "like a wild beast." Observe the details that develop this comparison. Some are stated and some are implied.

Commentary on the Reading

This quick glimpse into the jail cell where Jurgis is held is enough to make us realize that the writer wants us to adopt a particular attitude toward him. What details has Sinclair included that guide us toward his opinion? Which words appear to be chosen specifically for the emotional reactions they will elicit from the reader? In this case, it seems that Sinclair's **diction**—the words the author has chosen—is intended to make us sympathize with Jurgis and dislike the police.

Imagine that this scene is told from the point of view of one of the other characters—that burly police officer, for example, or a fellow prisoner, or one of the homeless men allowed inside after midnight. What details would they emphasize? What conclusions would they want the reader to reach? What alterations in language would be necessary to bring about that change in point of view? How would your choice of subject influence your diction?

Guidance on Your Writing

When you are writing about diction, you need to be as specific as possible. In the first paragraph, for example, the policeman is described as "burly." That word communicates strength in a way that other words do not. If the policeman had been described as "husky," he perhaps would be large but not necessarily strong. If he had been "sturdy," he would be strong but not necessarily big. "Robust" suggests health as well as strength. "Muscular" is a bit more complimentary than "burly." "Burly" has just the right combination of size, strength, and lack of grace to make the policeman seem somewhat threatening—a message aided by the cursing and kicking that go on in that same sentence.

A reading of this length is typical for an AP analytical question. Plan to take about five minutes to read the prompt and the text, and use another thirty-five minutes to write your response. Try to write this essay in thirty-five minutes. Leave some time to reread your work in case you see some feature you would like to improve.

AP Exam Advice

Reading Selection by James Gorman

Even though the title of this next reading is similar to the one in the previous lesson, the two articles are not about the same thing. In this case, you are reading the opinion of a doctor addressing one of the very serious health issues of our day, the AIDS epidemic. As you read his essay, be sure you know what position he is taking. Let his word choices—his diction—guide you toward this understanding.

James Gorman
The Doctor Won't See You Now

In the confusion, hypocrisy, and animosity generated by the AIDS epidemic, finally we hear a voice of *sanity*—and from the medical profession at that. Thirty percent of doctors surveyed by the American Medical Association in November [1991] said they felt no ethical responsibility to treat AIDS patients.

5

How do you react to the writer's initial premise, that the AIDS crisis has led to "confusion, hypocrisy, and animosity"?

And why should they? For too long, this country has faced rising medical costs and malpractice mania caused in large part by the mistaken notion that doctors are supposed to treat any slob who comes to them. This involves dealing with old people who are on the way out anyway, with all sorts of nasty sores and tumors, and now with AIDS patients, most of whom got sick because of some sort of disgusting behavior. Except, of course, hemophiliacs, the *good* AIDS patients.

No other profession faces such obligations. Does a stockbroker have to take on poor clients wanting to invest pathetically small amounts of money earned during years of wage slavery? No way. Do architects have to design your house if you are stupid and have no taste? Only if you are filthy rich. Do real estate developers have to build apartments for the homeless? Enough said.

Part of the medical profession is finally beginning to see that patients have a responsibility for their own health and that doctoring is no different from any other small business. When you run a convenience store, you want to keep the riffraff out. If doctors would only build on this insight and expand their notion of what constitutes riffraff, we'd be getting somewhere. We could cut down medical costs and stop a lot of disgusting habits as well.

Here are a few of the illnesses they should refuse to treat: coronary artery disease—caused by the willful, piglike consumption of steak, butter, cream, and blintzes; skin cancer—the result of taking off your clothes and lying around, offending those of us with common sense, while soaking up ultraviolet radiation; lung cancer and cancer of the lip and throat and larynx and tongue, all fostered by smoking and alcohol. Also, carpal tunnel syndrome in people who write a lot of trash about ethics and responsibility.

(32) Why does the writer include this last example?

In fact, I don't think doctors need to specify diseases. A number of respondents to the AIDS survey said they didn't like treating drug addicts or homosexuals, period. Smart thinking. Let's also exclude smokers, drinkers, meat eaters, and anyone who has sex more often than I do.

I hope no one counters with the tired argument that doctors, because of the place they occupy in society, not to mention their incomes, should treat anybody who is sick. This plea is based on the long-discredited idea that doctoring is a profession, a calling, requiring commitment and integrity on the part of those who practice it. Really. How dumb can you get?

Commentary on the Reading

You may have agreed or disagreed with Upton Sinclair and his depiction of Jurgis's treatment at the hands of the Chicago police. You may also agree or disagree with Dr. James Gorman's opinion of the work doctors should and should not have to do. No doubt your reaction to Gorman's article will depend on how you respond to his diction.

In preparation for writing on this piece, go back to the beginning and note any word that strikes you as having an effect beyond its literal meaning. We call those meanings **connotations**. That is what Ted Diadiun addressed when he wrote about "refugees," what Peter Salgo was referring to when he tried to distinguish between patients and customers, and what Upton Sinclair took advantage of when he wrote of the "drunken wife-beater" and the "yelling maniac" in the cells next to Jurgis's cell.

When you have identified the words with strong connotations, consider what effects they have on your reaction to the piece. Are they irritating? Funny? Poignant? Confusing? Your response to these connotative words will significantly affect your understanding of the author's overall meaning.

A question often arises about how literally we are intended to take a piece of writing. Indeed, that is one of the reading skills a mature reader and writer must develop. If the writer wants to be taken literally—that is, if the words are to mean nothing other than what they say—we go wrong when we ascribe meanings the author never intended. We end up with some far-fetched, even ludicrous, interpretations of what we read. However, if the writer wants us to put literal meaning aside in favor of figurative meaning—using words to communicate something other than or more than their literal sense—we are equally mistaken to insist on being literal.

The problem is knowing when to read literally and when to read figuratively. The lessons in this book so far have guided you to ways of addressing that problem. As you continue through your AP English course, you will find that you are hardly ever able to ignore that question. If you took the Gorman piece literally, you probably had a reaction quite different from that of a classmate who thought Gorman was not saying exactly what he meant. If your classmates had different interpretations, you can have a very instructive conversation about how each of you arrived at your understanding.

Focus on Writing: Analysis

What is the overall effect of James Gorman's presentation in "The Doctor Won't See You Now"? How does his diction communicate his attitude toward his fellow physicians and the demands our society makes on them? Write an essay that provides specific answers to these questions.

Guidance on Your Writing

You will need to identify specific words that have particular effects. You will also need to explain how Gorman uses these words to achieve those effects.

How does syntax contribute to the passage's meaning?

See what you make of the opening of this favorite short story by Edgar Allan Poe.

Edgar Allan Poe
from *The Tell-tale Heart*

TRUE!—nervous—very, very dreadfully nervous I had been and am; but why will you say that I am mad? The disease had sharpened my senses—not destroyed—not dulled them. Above all was the sense of hearing acute. I heard all things in the heaven and in the earth. I heard many things in hell. How, then, am I mad? Hearken! And observe how healthily—how calmly I can tell you the whole story.

It is impossible to say how first the idea entered my brain; but once conceived, it haunted me day and night. Object there was none. Passion there was none. I loved the old man. He had never wronged me. He had never given me insult. For his gold I had no desire. I think it was his eye! Yes, it was this! He had the eye of a vulture—a pale blue eye, with a film over it. Whenever it fell upon me, my blood ran cold; and so by degrees—very gradually—I made up my mind to take the life of the old man, and thus rid myself of the eye forever.

Now this is the point. You fancy me mad. Madmen know nothing. But you should have seen me. You should have seen how wisely I proceeded—with what caution—with what foresight—with what dissimulation I went to work! I was never kinder to the old man than during the whole week before I killed him. And every night, about midnight, I turned the latch of his door and opened it—oh so gently!

(2) "Mad" in Poe's day meant "insane." There was very little, if any, sense of anger in the word.

(17) "Dissimulation" is the act of disguising. The word suggests dishonesty. Which trait do the qualities mentioned here illustrate— "how wisely I proceeded" or "I was never kinder"?

Commentary on the Reading

You probably reacted to the style from the very beginning of the passage. The speaker in the story, protesting that he is completely sane, appears to be quite mad.

If you were asked to explain why you think the voice behind this writing is a madman's voice, you might comment on the author's **diction** (word choice), but more likely you would point to the **syntax** (sentence construction). The sentences are short and choppy. In the following sequence of eight sentences Poe uses unusual word order, relying on repetitions and juxtapositions that suggest a mind somewhat out of control:

> Object there was none. Passion there was none. I loved the old man. He had never wronged me. He had never given me insult. For his gold I had no desire. I think it was his eye! Yes, it was this!

The same qualities appear in the excerpt's final paragraph, much to the same effect. There is a disturbed mind behind this narrative.

Syntax

The term *syntax* refers not only to the structure of sentences, their types, their uses, their connection, and the variations authors choose but also to smaller structures within sentences. Phrases (any group of words) and clauses (groups of words that contain a subject and a verb) are also syntactic elements that deserve our attention.

The typical and most common English sentence <u>pattern</u> <u>is</u> S-V-C, <u>which</u> <u>indicates</u> subject-verb-complement. In every sentence in this paragraph, as well as in every clause within those sentences, the <u>subject</u> (underlined once) <u>comes</u> before the verb (underlined twice). Most of the time <u>we</u> <u>want</u> to tell the reader what <u>we</u> <u>are</u> <u>talking about</u> (the subject) before <u>we</u> <u>tell</u> what <u>that subject</u> <u>is doing</u>. So usually the <u>subject</u> <u>precedes</u> the verb. Any additional <u>information</u>, such as the direct object of the verb, or prepositional phrases telling where or when <u>something</u> <u>happened</u>, usually <u>follows</u> the verb.

When writers want to emphasize a certain point, they sometimes depart from normal syntax. Here are two common ways that writers cue the reader to notice something out of the ordinary:

1. Inverted sentences — sentences in which the verb precedes the subject

2. Periodic sentences — sentences in which the important information is delayed until near the end of the sentence

A sudden change in sentence length can have the same effect.

The best approach to syntactic analysis is to note the kinds of sentences the author is using and to determine why the author chose those structures. Sometimes it will seem that there was no other choice, or that the author "just wrote what came to mind." More often the writer makes a conscious choice, and that choice will be evident when there is an unusual structure or departure from the norm. There are no formulas to learn, and occasionally the author's effect can be very subtle. Sometimes the syntax makes a significant contribution to the meaning, and a careful reader does not want to miss what the syntax can reveal.

As a writer, you want to pay attention to the sentences you use. The scoring guides for essays on many standardized tests require syntactic variety before a paper can earn a high score. Unrelieved simple sentences lead to monotony or a sense that the writer is working on a very simple intellectual level. Just as you do not want to be spoken to as a child, your reader does not want to be addressed as a child either. The best writing demonstrates careful choices in both diction and syntax.

AP Exam Advice

Reading Selection by Nathaniel Hawthorne

The prose of earlier centuries tends to be syntactically more complicated than that of our own day, and you will want to practice reading and writing examples of these less accessible styles. The following reading, from Nathaniel Hawthorne's *The Scarlet Letter,* illustrates the nineteenth century's typical style—ornate description, elevated language, and sentences in which several parts combine to describe the subject or to clarify the major action of the verb.

The following passage, from Chapter 2, describes the appearance of Hester Prynne, the heroine of the novel, who has been imprisoned in Puritan Boston, Massachusetts, for committing adultery. Her punishment is to stand on a scaffold in the town square wearing a letter *A* on her blouse to signify to the entire community that she is an adulteress.

The first sentence of Hawthorne's passage employs an inverted sentence structure. The subject is "the grim and grisly presence of the town-beadle," and the verb "appeared" precedes it. The word "there," which seems like the grammatical subject, is actually only a place holder, since it doesn't tell us what has appeared.

Compare what Hawthorne wrote to a more conventional alternative:

> The door of the jail being flung open from within, the grim and grisly presence of the town-beadle appeared in the first place like a black shadow emerging into sunshine, with a sword by his side, and his staff of office in his hand.

There is as much information here as there is in Hawthorne's sentence, but the connection between the presence of the beadle (a town official) and the details describing him (his sword and staff) is weakened by intervening material. Read the following passage slowly. You will find that Hawthorne arranged his material carefully.

Focus on the Reading: Understanding Syntax
Note the kinds of sentences the author is using and determine why the author chose those structures.

Nathaniel Hawthorne
from *The Scarlet Letter*

The door of the jail being flung open from within there appeared, in the first place, like a black shadow emerging into sunshine, the grim and grisly presence of the town-beadle, with a sword by his side, and his staff of office in his hand. This personage prefigured and represented in

5   his aspect the whole dismal severity of the Puritanic code of law, which it was his business to administer in its final and closest application to the offender. Stretching forth the official staff in his left hand, he laid his right upon the shoulder of a young woman, whom he thus drew forward, until, on the threshold of the prison-door, she repelled him, by an

10   action marked with natural dignity and force of character, and stepped into the open air as if by her own free will. She bore in her arms a child, a baby of some three months old, who winked and turned aside its little face from the too vivid light of day; because its existence, heretofore, had brought it acquaintance only with the grey twilight of a dungeon, or

15   other darksome apartment of the prison.

    When the young woman—the mother of this child—stood fully revealed before the crowd, it seemed to be her first impulse to clasp the infant closely to her bosom; not so much by an impulse of motherly affection, as that she might thereby conceal a certain token, which was

20   wrought or fastened into her dress. In a moment, however, wisely judging that one token of her shame would but poorly serve to hide another, she took the baby on her arm, and with a burning blush, and yet a haughty smile, and a glance that would not be abashed, looked around at her

(8) Hester Prynne has been imprisoned for adultery in seventeenth century Boston, and in this scene she makes her first public appearance since going into the jail.

townspeople and neighbours. On the breast of her gown, in fine red cloth, surrounded with an elaborate embroidery and fantastic flourishes of gold thread, appeared the letter A. It was so artistically done, and with so much fertility and gorgeous luxuriance of fancy, that it had all the effect of a last and fitting decoration to the apparel which she wore, and which was of a splendour in accordance with the taste of the age, but greatly beyond what was allowed by the sumptuary regulations of the colony.

The young woman was tall, with a figure of perfect elegance on a large scale. She had dark and abundant hair, so glossy that it threw off the sunshine with a gleam; and a face which, besides being beautiful from regularity of feature and richness of complexion, had the impressiveness belonging to a marked brow and deep black eyes. She was ladylike, too, after the manner of the feminine gentility of those days; characterised by a certain state and dignity, rather than by the delicate, evanescent, and indescribable grace which is now recognised as its indication. And never had Hester Prynne appeared more ladylike, in the antique interpretation of the term, than as she issued from the prison. Those who had before known her, and had expected to behold her dimmed and obscured by a disastrous cloud, were astonished, and even startled, to perceive how her beauty shone out, and made a halo of the misfortune and ignominy in which she was enveloped. It may be true that, to a sensitive observer, there was some thing exquisitely painful in it. Her attire, which indeed, she had wrought for the occasion in prison, and had modelled much after her own fancy, seemed to express the attitude of her spirit, the desperate recklessness of her mood, by its wild and picturesque peculiarity. But the point which drew all eyes, and, as it were, transfigured the wearer—so that both men and women who had been familiarly acquainted with Hester Prynne were now impressed as if they beheld her for the first time—was that **SCARLET LETTER**, so fantastically embroidered and illuminated upon her bosom. It had the effect of a spell, taking her out of the ordinary relations with humanity, and enclosing her in a sphere by herself.

(30) "Sumptuary" refers to those laws that concern personal behavior, especially of a moral nature.

Commentary on the Reading

In order to produce a good syntactic analysis of a passage like this one, you should develop a system for untangling the language. Get into the habit of noting where the subjects and verbs are. Sometimes it will be quite obvious and will reveal nothing out of the ordinary. On the other hand, in a passage such as this one, it is easy to lose track of what the author is saying. A good technique to adopt is to underline the subject with a single line and the verb with a double line. You might also note unusual arrangements, such as inversions. You will be surprised at how much information this simple note-taking technique can provide. While it may seem cumbersome at first, you will find it becoming almost automatic with practice, and you will notice your reading comprehension improving dramatically.

Here is what the second paragraph of the above passage would look like in such a system.

When <u>the young woman</u>—the mother of this child—<u>stood</u> fully revealed before the crowd, it <u>seemed</u> to be <u>her first impulse</u> to clasp the infant closely to her bosom; not so much by an impulse of motherly affection, as that <u>she might thereby conceal</u> a certain token, <u>which was wrought</u> or <u>fastened</u> into her dress. In a moment, however, wisely judging that <u>one token of her shame</u> <u>would but poorly serve</u> to hide another, <u>she took</u> the baby on her arm, and with a burning blush, and yet a haughty smile, and a glance that would not be abashed, <u>looked</u> around at her townspeople and neighbours. On the breast of her gown, in fine red cloth, surrounded with an elaborate embroidery and fantastic flourishes of gold thread, <u>appeared the letter A</u>. <u>It was</u> so artistically <u>done</u>, and with so much fertility and gorgeous luxuriance of fancy, that <u>it had</u> all the effect of a last and fitting decoration to the apparel which <u>she wore</u>, and <u>which was</u> of a splendour in accordance with the taste of the age, but greatly beyond <u>what was allowed</u> by the sumptuary regulations of the colony.

5

10

15

"It seemed to be her first impulse = her first impulse seemed to be"

"appeared the letter A = the letter A appeared"

You should do the same with the first and third paragraphs. When you are actually taking the examination, you should read with pencil in hand to make any notations in the text you might find helpful.

Reading Selection by Edgar Allen Poe

Below is a bit more of the opening of Poe's "The Tell-tale Heart." You may have read the entire story in a literature class, but don't be concerned if you have not. For this task, consider only the excerpt you see here.

> **Focus on the Reading: Understanding Syntax**
> Note the kinds of sentences the author is using and determine why the author chose those structures.

TRUE!—nervous—very, very dreadfully nervous I had been and am; but why will you say that I am mad? The disease had sharpened my senses—not destroyed—not dulled them. Above all was the sense of hearing acute. I heard all things in the heaven and in the earth. I heard many things in hell. How, then, am I mad? Hearken! And observe how healthily—how calmly I can tell you the whole story.

It is impossible to say how first the idea entered my brain; but once conceived, it haunted me day and night. Object there was none. Passion there was none. I loved the old man. He had never wronged me. He had never given me insult. For his gold I had no desire. I think it was his eye! Yes, it was this! He had the eye of a vulture—a pale blue eye, with a film over it. Whenever it fell upon me, my blood ran cold; and so by degrees—very gradually—I made up my mind to take the life of the old man, and thus rid myself of the eye forever.

5

10

15   Now this is the point. You fancy me mad. Madmen know nothing. But you should have seen me. You should have seen how wisely I proceeded—with what caution—with what foresight—with what dissimulation I went to work! I was never kinder to the old man than during the whole week before I killed him. And every night, about
20 midnight, I turned the latch of his door and opened it—oh so gently! And then, when I had made an opening sufficient for my head, I put in a dark lantern, all closed, closed, that no light shone out, and then I thrust in my head. Oh, you would have laughed to see how cunningly I thrust it in! I moved it slowly—very, very slowly, so that I might not disturb the old man's sleep. It took me an hour to place my whole
25 head within the opening so far that I could see him as he lay upon his bed. Ha! would a madman have been so wise as this? And then, when my head was well in the room, I undid the lantern cautiously—oh, so cautiously—cautiously (for the hinges creaked)—I undid it just so much that a single thin ray fell upon the vulture eye. And this I did
30 for seven long nights—every night just at midnight—but I found the eye always closed; and so it was impossible to do the work; for it was not the old man who vexed me, but his Evil Eye. And every morning, when the day broke, I went boldly into the chamber, and spoke courageously to him, calling him by name in a hearty tone, and inquiring
35 how he has passed the night. So you see he would have been a very profound old man, indeed, to suspect that every night, just at twelve, I looked in upon him while he slept.

Focus on Writing: Analysis

The writer's sentence structure can reveal a great deal about the mentality of the character in the story. Study the passage and then write an essay in which you explain how the writer's syntax indicates the mental state of the speaker. Do not summarize the passage.

Guidance on Your Writing

It is unlikely that you will be asked to write an analysis that addresses only syntax, but this practice essay focuses on that one feature so that you can give it your full attention. You may see other features of the writing that you'll want to include in your analysis, but be sure to spend most of your time considering the contribution the author's syntax makes to the overall effect of the passage.

Lesson 7 Where has the author used figurative language?

Introduction

Hyperbole, **metaphor**, **irony**, and **analogy** are all literary techniques writers might choose when deciding how best to make a particular point. While some readings are meant to be taken literally, others require some interpretation, and it takes practice and experience to develop the ability to recognize figurative or ironic language. The readings in this lesson will give you the opportunity to discover and interpret such nonliteral language.

Analogy

Of the four techniques, perhaps the comparative technique known as **analogy** requires the most explanation. The excerpt from Benjamin Franklin's *Autobiography* makes especially good use of analogy. You may have seen analogies on standardized tests, in which you are asked to complete a statement such as "lemon is to yellow as lime is to ____," and from the choices that are offered ("sour," "tropical," "green," "nutritious," "juicy") you would choose "green" because the relationship between "lime" and "green" (one of color) is the same as the relationship between "lemon" and "yellow." Notice that all five choices offer words that are true of limes, but only "green" expresses the same relationship to "lime" as "yellow" does to "lemon."

When writers use analogies, they are expecting the reader to recognize a relationship. They hope to explain an unfamiliar item or situation in terms of a familiar one. To do this, they emphasize points of comparison and ignore possible differences the two might also share. For that reason, analogies are very good for explanation and clarification, but they are not at all good for proving an argument. You might assume that a woman who has been a teacher will be a good mother because she has had experience with children. But the similarities of the two situations ignore the differences: the professional relationship the teacher shares with her pupils is quite different from the emotional relationship she has with her own children; what she teaches her pupils is not at all the same as what she must teach her children; her legal relationship to the schoolchildren is not the same as her legal relationship to her children; and so on. The analogy may illustrate that she knows about children, but it doesn't guarantee that she will be a good mother.

Hyperbole, Metaphor, and Irony

The other techniques emphasized in this lesson are probably more familiar and require less explanation. **Hyperbole** is overstatement or exaggeration, but exaggeration in the service of truth. It is not the same as lying. If you were very hungry, you might say "I'm so hungry I could eat that whole extra-large four-topping pizza myself," because just saying "I'm very hungry" might not communicate the point as effectively.

Metaphor is comparison, and while you have learned to distinguish metaphor (the implied comparison—"my love is a red, red rose") from simile (the expressed comparison—"my love is like a red, red rose"), here we use the term *metaphor* to mean comparison in general, of which simile, personification, and even analogy are specific types.

Irony is the general term for any use of language in which there is a discrepancy between what is said and what is meant, what is expected and what actually happens, or what you think is so and what actually is so. Hyperbole is a kind of irony, because there is a difference between what you say (you could eat a whole pizza) and what you mean (you could eat more than you normally would).

As you read the excerpt from Franklin below, note where he uses any of these four techniques. Consider how much less effective his narrative would be if he wrote only straightforward, literal prose.

Focus on the Reading: Understanding Figurative Language
Practice developing your ability to recognize and comprehend figurative or ironic language.

Benjamin Franklin
from *The Autobiography*

It was about this time I conceiv'd the bold and arduous project of arriving at moral perfection. I wish'd to live without committing any fault at any time; I would conquer all that either natural inclination, custom, or company might lead me into. As I knew, or thought I knew, what was right and wrong, I did not see why I might not always do the one and avoid the other. But I soon found I had undertaken a task of more difficulty than I had imagined. While my care was employ'd in guarding against one fault, I was often surprised by another; habit took the advantage of inattention; inclination was sometimes too strong for reason. I concluded, at length, that the mere speculative conviction that it was our interest to be completely virtuous, was not sufficient to prevent our slipping; and that the contrary habits must be broken, and good ones acquired and established, before we can have any dependence on a steady, uniform rectitude of conduct. For this purpose I therefore contrived the following method.

In the various enumerations of the moral virtues I had met with in my reading, I found the catalogue more or less numerous, as different writers included more or fewer ideas under the same name. Temperance, for example, was by some confined to eating and drinking, while by others it was extended to mean the moderating of every other pleasure, appetite, inclination, or passion, bodily or mental, even to our avarice and ambition. I propos'd to myself, for the sake of clearness, to use rather more names, with fewer ideas annex'd to each, than a few names with more ideas; and I included under thirteen names of virtues all that at that time occurr'd to me as necessary or desirable, and annexed to each a short precept, which fully express'd the extent I gave to its meaning.

These names of virtues, with their precepts, were:

1. **Temperance:** Eat not to dullness; drink not to elevation.

2. **Silence:** Speak not but what may benefit others or yourself; avoid trifling conversation.

3. **Order:** Let all your things have their places; let each part of your business have its time.

Recall the word "sumptuary" from the passage from *The Scarlet Letter*. Franklin expresses a view quite opposite to what a Puritan would believe. Franklin believed that a person could attain perfect behavior. The Puritans of Hester Prynne's time believed that humans were essentially sinful and moral perfection was not the human condition.

4. **Resolution:** Resolve to perform what you ought; perform without fail what you resolve.

5. **Frugality:** Make no expense but to do good to others or yourself; *i.e.*, waste nothing.

6. **Industry:** Lose no time; be always employ'd in something useful; cut off all unnecessary actions.

7. **Sincerity:** Use no hurtful deceit; think innocently and justly, and, if you speak, speak accordingly.

8. **Justice:** Wrong none by doing injuries, or omitting the benefits that are your duty.

9. **Moderation:** Avoid extremes; forbear resenting injuries so much as you think they deserve

10. **Cleanliness:** Tolerate no uncleanliness in body, cloaths, or habitation.

11. **Tranquillity:** Be not disturbed at trifles, or at accidents common or unavoidable.

12. **Chastity:** Rarely use venery but for health or offspring, never to dullness, weakness, or the injury of your own or another's peace or reputation.

13. **Humility:** Imitate Jesus and Socrates.

My intention being to acquire the *habitude* of all these virtues, I judg'd it would be well not to distract my attention by attempting the whole at once, but to fix it on one of them at a time; and, when I should be master of that, then to proceed to another, and so on, till I should have gone thro' the thirteen; and, as the previous acquisition of some might facilitate the acquisition of certain others, I arrang'd them with that view, as they stand above. *Temperance* first, as it tends to procure that coolness and clearness of head, which is so necessary where constant vigilance was to be kept up, and guard maintained against the unremitting attraction of ancient habits, and the force of perpetual temptations. This being acquir'd and establish'd, *Silence* would be more easy; and my desire being to gain knowledge at the same time that I improv'd in virtue, and considering that in conversation it was obtain'd rather by the use of the ears than of the tongue, and therefore wishing to break a habit I was getting into of prattling, punning, and joking, which only made me acceptable to trifling company, I gave *Silence* the second place. This and the next, *Order*, I expected would allow me more time for attending to my project and my studies. *Resolution*, once become habitual, would keep me firm in my endeavors to obtain all the subsequent virtues; *Frugality* and *Industry* freeing me from my remaining debt, and producing affluence and independence, would make more easy the practice of *Sincerity* and *Justice*, etc., etc. Conceiving then, that, agreeably to the advice of

Are these the virtues that would lead to a successful life in the twenty-first century?

Pythagoras in his Golden Verses, daily examination would be necessary, I contrived the following method for conducting that examination.

  I made a little book, in which I allotted a page for each of the virtues. I rul'd each page with red ink, so as to have seven columns, one for each day of the week, marking each column with a letter for the day. I cross'd these columns with thirteen red lines, marking the beginning of each line with the first letter of one of the virtues, on which line, and in its proper column, I might mark, by a little black spot, every fault I found upon examination to have been committed respecting that virtue upon that day.

Form of the pages:

TEMPERANCE							
Eat not to dullness; Drink not to elevation							
	Sun.	M.	T.	W.	Th.	F.	S.
Tem.							
Sil.	x	x		x		x	
Ord.	x	x	x		x	x	x
Res.		x	x			x	
Fru.		x				x	
Ind.			x				
Sinc.							
Jus.							
Mod.							
Clea.							
Tran.							
Chas.							
Hum.							

  I determined to give a week's strict attention to each of the virtues successively. Thus, in the first week, my great guard was to avoid every the least offence against Temperance, leaving the other virtues to their ordinary chance, only marking every evening the faults of the day. Thus, if in the first week I could keep my first line, marked T, clear of spots, I suppos'd the habit of that virtue so much strengthen'd and its opposite weaken'd, that I might venture extending my attention to include the next, and for the following week keep both lines clear of spots. Proceeding thus to the last, I could go thro' a course compleat in thirteen weeks, and four courses in a year. And like him who, having a garden to weed, does not attempt to eradicate all the bad herbs at once, which would exceed his reach and his strength, but works on one of the beds at a time, and, having accomplish'd the first, proceeds to a second, so I should have, I hoped, the encouraging pleasure of seeing on my pages the progress I made in virtue, by clearing successively my lines of their spots, till in the end, by a number of courses, I should he happy in viewing a clean book, after a thirteen weeks' daily examination.

Here is a good example of an analogy. What is the familiar item in this analogy? What is unfamiliar?

And conceiving God to be the fountain of wisdom, I thought it right and necessary to solicit his assistance for obtaining it; to this end I formed the following little prayer, which was prefix'd to my tables of examination, for daily use.

> O powerful Goodness! bountiful Father! merciful Guide!
> Increase in me that wisdom which discovers my truest interest.
> Strengthen my resolutions to perform what that wisdom dictates.
> Accept my kind offices to thy other children as the only return
> in my power for thy continual favors to me.

I used also sometimes a little prayer which I took from Thomson's *Poems*, viz.:

> Father of light and life, thou Good Supreme!
> O teach me what is good; teach me Thyself!
> Save me from folly, vanity, and vice,
> From every low pursuit; and fill my soul
> With knowledge, conscious peace, and virtue pure;
> Sacred, substantial, never-fading bliss!

The precept of Order requiring that *every part of my business should have its allotted time*, one page in my little book contain'd the following scheme of employment for the twenty-four hours of a natural day:

The morning question, What good shall I do this day?	5 6 7	Rise, wash, and address *Powerful Goodness*; Contrive day's business, and take the resolution of the day; prosecute the present study, and breakfast.
	8 9 10 11	Work
	12 1	Read or overlook my accounts and dine
	2 3 4 5	Work
The evening question, What good have I done to-day?	6 7 8 9	Put things in their places. Supper. Music or diversion, or conversation. Examination of the day.
	10 11 12 1 2 3 4	Sleep

The orderliness of Franklin's typical day is characteristic of the eighteenth century. It shows in the architecture, music, painting, sculpture, and prose of the period.

I enter'd upon the execution of this plan for self-examination, and continu'd it with occasional intermissions for some time. I was surpris'd to find myself so much fuller of faults than I had imagined; but I had the satisfaction of seeing them diminish. To avoid the trouble of renewing now and then my little book, which, by scraping out the marks on the paper of old faults to make room for new ones in a new course, became full of holes, I transferr'd my tables and precepts to the ivory leaves of a memorandum book, on which the lines were drawn with red ink, that made a durable stain, and on those lines I mark'd my faults with a black-lead pencil, which marks I could easily wipe out with a wet sponge. After a while I went thro' one course only in a year, and afterward only one in several years, till at length I omitted them entirely, being employ'd in voyages and business abroad, with a multiplicity of affairs that interfered; but I always carried my little book with me.

My scheme of *Order* gave me the most trouble; and I found that, tho' it might be practicable where a man's business was such as to leave him the disposition of his time, that of a journeyman printer, for instance, it was not possible to be exactly observed by a master, who must mix with the world, and often receive people of business at their own hours. Order, too, with regard to places for things, papers, etc., I found extreamly difficult to acquire. I had not been early accustomed to it, and, having an exceeding good memory, I was not so sensible of the inconvenience attending want of method. This article, therefore, cost me so much painful attention, and my faults in it vexed me so much, and I made so little progress in amendment, and had such frequent relapses, that I was almost ready to give up the attempt, and content myself with a faulty character in that respect, like the man who, in buying an ax of a smith, my neighbour, desired to have the whole of its surface as bright as the edge. The smith consented to grind it bright for him if he would turn the wheel; he turn'd, while the smith press'd the broad face of the ax hard and heavily on the stone, which made the turning of it very fatiguing. The man came every now and then from the wheel to see how the work went on, and at length would take his ax as it was, without farther grinding. "No," said the smith, "turn on, turn on; we shall have it bright by-and-by; as yet, it is only speckled." "Yes," said the man, *"but I think I like a speckled ax best."* And I believe this may have been the case with many, who, having, for want of some such means as I employ'd, found the difficulty of obtaining good and breaking bad habits in other points of vice and virtue, have given up the struggle, and concluded that "a speckled ax was best"; for something, that pretended to be reason, was every now and then suggesting to me that such extream nicety as I exacted of myself might be a kind of foppery in morals, which, if it were known, would make me ridiculous; that a perfect character might be attended with the inconvenience of being envied and hated; and that a benevolent man should allow a few faults in himself, to keep his friends in countenance.

In truth, I found myself incorrigible with respect to *Order*; and now I am grown old, and my memory bad, I feel very sensibly the want of it. But, on the whole, tho' I never arrived at the perfection I had been so ambitious of obtaining, but fell far short of it, yet I was, by the endeavor, a better and a happier man than I otherwise should have been if

What does the ax have to do with Franklin's attempts to become more orderly?

I had not attempted it; as those who aim at perfect writing by imitating the engraved copies, tho' they never reach the wish'd-for excellence of those copies, their hand is mended by the endeavor, and is tolerable while it continues fair and legible.

It may be well my posterity should be informed that to this little artifice, with the blessing of God, their ancestor ow'd the constant felicity of his life, down to his 79th year, in which this is written. What reverses may attend the remainder is in the hand of Providence; but, if they arrive, the reflection on past happiness enjoy'd ought to help his bearing them with more resignation. To *Temperance* he ascribes his long-continued health, and what is still left to him of a good constitution; to *Industry* and *Frugality*, the early easiness of his circumstances and acquisition of his fortune, with all that knowledge that enabled him to be a useful citizen, and obtained for him some degree of reputation among the learned; to *Sincerity* and *Justice*, the confidence of his country, and the honorable employs it conferred upon him; and to the joint influence of the whole mass of the virtues, even in the imperfect state he was able to acquire them, all that evenness of temper, and that cheerfulness in conversation, which makes his company still sought for, and agreeable even to his younger acquaintance. I hope, therefore, that some of my descendants may follow the example and reap the benefit.

The title of the next short essay by Franklin is a clue that he has something in mind other than the little insect of the title. Does the analogy work for you?

Benjamin Franklin
The Ephemera: An Emblem of Human Life
1778

You may remember, my dear friend, that when we lately spent that happy day in the delightful garden and sweet society of the Moulin Joly, I stopped a little in one of our walks, and stayed some time behind the company. We had been shown numberless skeletons of a kind of little fly, called an ephemera, whose successive generations, we were told, were bred and expired within the day. I happened to see a living company of them on a leaf, who appeared to be engaged in conversation. You know I understand all the inferior animal tongues. My too great application to the study of them is the best excuse I can give for the little progress I have made in your charming language. I listened through curiosity to the discourse of these little creatures; but as they, in their national vivacity, spoke three or four together, I could make but little of their conversation. I found, however, by some broken expressions that I heard now and then, they were disputing warmly on the merit of two foreign musicians, one a cousin, the other a moscheto; in which dispute they spent their time, seemingly as regardless of the shortness of life as if they had been sure of living a month. Happy people! thought I; you are certainly, under a wise, just and mild government, since you have

(1) Who do you suppose is speaking? To whom is that person speaking?

(8, 10) How should we interpret the word "inferior" here? What is the "charming language" of the person being spoken to?

(15) a mosquito

no public grievances to complain of, nor any subject of contention but
the perfections and imperfections of foreign music. I turned my head
from them to an old gray-headed one, who was single on another leaf,
and talking to himself. Being amused with his soliloquy, I put it down in
writing, in hopes it will likewise amuse her to whom I am so much indebted for the most pleasing of all amusements, her delicious company
and heavenly harmony.

(23) He writes the monologue of the elderly ephemera, he says, to amuse his companion.

"It was," said he, "the opinion of learned philosophers of our race,
who lived and flourished long before my time, that this vast world, the
Moulin Joly, could not itself subsist more than eighteen hours; and I
think there was some foundation for that opinion, since, by the apparent
motion of the great luminary that gives life to all nature, and which in
my time has evidently declined considerably toward the ocean at the end
of our earth, it must then finish its course, be extinguished in the waters
that surround us, and leave the world in cold and darkness, necessarily
producing universal death and destruction. I have lived seven of those
hours, a great age, being no less than four hundred and twenty minutes
of time. How very few of us continue so long! I have seen generations
born, flourish and expire. My present friends are the children and grand-
children of the friends of my youth, who are now, alas, no more! And
I must soon follow them; for, by the course of nature, though still in
health, I cannot expect to live above seven or eight minutes longer. What
now avails all my toil and labor, in amassing honey-dew on this leaf
which I cannot live to enjoy! What the political struggles I have been engaged in, for the good of my compatriot inhabitants of this bush, or my
philosophical studies for the benefit of our race in general! for, in politics, what can laws do without morals? Our present race of ephemerae
will in a course of minutes become corrupt, like those of other and older
bushes, and consequently as wretched. And in philosophy how small our
progress! Alas! art is long, and life is short! My friends would comfort
me with the idea of a name, they say, I shall leave behind me; and they
tell me I have lived long enough to nature and to glory. But what will
fame be to an ephemera who no longer exists? And what will become of
all history in the eighteenth hour, when the world itself, even the whole
Moulin Joly, shall come to its end, and be buried in universal ruin?"

(30) What is this "great luminary"?

To me, after all my eager pursuits, no solid pleasures now remain,
but the reflection of a long life spent in meaning well, the sensible conversation of a few good lady ephemerae, and now and then a kind smile
and a tune from the ever amiable Brillante.

(57) A brillante is a sparkling, happy piece of music.

Reading Selection by John Donne

John Donne's famous sermon, from which the following excerpt is taken,
provides us with one of the most celebrated extended metaphors in literature.
While the immediate situation he describes is real (in his day, a bell was rung
when a hearse passed by), we come to realize that his concern is not with bells
but with something else. At what point will you recognize the analogy in Donne's
writing? What points of similarity do you accept? How important are the
differences?

John Donne
from *Meditation XVII*

Perchance, he for whom this bell tolls may be so ill, as that he knows not it tolls for him; and perchance I may think myself so much better than I am, as that they who are about me, and see my state, may have caused it to toll for me, and I know not that. The church is Catholic, universal, so are all her actions; all that she does belongs to all. When she baptizes a child, that action concerns me; for that child is thereby connected to that body which is my head too, and ingrafted into that body whereof I am a member. And when she buries a man, that action concerns me: all mankind is of one author, and is one volume; when one man dies, one chapter is not torn out of the book, but translated into a better language; and every chapter must be so translated; God employs several translators; some pieces are translated by age, some by sickness, some by war, some by justice; but God's hand is in every translation, and his hand shall bind up all our scattered leaves again for that library where every book shall lie open to one another. As therefore the bell that rings to a sermon calls not upon the preacher only, but upon the congregation to come, so this bell calls us all; but how much more me, who am brought so near the door by this sickness.

There was a contention as far as a suit (in which both piety and dignity, religion and estimation, were mingled), which of the religious orders should ring to prayers first in the morning; and it was determined, that they should ring first that rose earliest. If we understand aright the dignity of this bell that tolls for our evening prayer, we would be glad to make it ours by rising early, in that application, that it might be ours as well as his, whose indeed it is.

The bell doth toll for him that thinks it doth; and though it intermit again, yet from that minute that this occasion wrought upon him, he is united to God. Who casts not up his eye to the sun when it rises? but who takes off his eye from a comet when that breaks out? Who bends not his ear to any bell which upon any occasion rings? but who can remove it from that bell which is passing a piece of himself out of this world?

No man is an island, entire of itself; every man is a piece of the continent, a part of the main. If a clod be washed away by the sea, Europe is the less, as well as if a promontory were, as well as if a manor of thy friend's or of thine own were: any man's death diminishes me, because I am involved in mankind, and therefore never send to know for whom the bell tolls; it tolls for thee.

Neither can we call this a begging of misery, or a borrowing of misery, as though we were not miserable enough of ourselves, but must fetch in more from the next house, in taking upon us the misery

In this paragraph we saw images of gardening and publishing. How do they pertain to the general subject of the sermon?

of our neighbours. Truly it were an excusable covetousness if we did, for affliction is a treasure, and scarce any man hath enough of it. No man hath affliction enough that is not matured and ripened by it, and made fit for God by that affliction. If a man carry treasure in bullion, or in a wedge of gold, and have none coined into current money, his treasure will not defray him as he travels. Tribulation is treasure in the nature of it, but it is not current money in the use of it, except we get nearer and nearer our home, heaven, by it. Another man may be sick too, and sick to death, and this affliction may lie in his bowels, as gold in a mine, and be of no use to him; but this bell, that tells me of his affliction, digs out and applies that gold to me: if by this consideration of another's danger I take mine own into contemplation, and so secure myself, by making my recourse to my God, who is our only security.

45

50

Donne employs images from many fields of human endeavor in this piece, yet he always returns to the ringing of the bell. This use of seemingly unrelated imagery is characteristic of seventeenth-century writing.

Commentary on the Readings

You have just been reading passages written in the eighteenth and seventeenth centuries, and you may have found them challenging. That is intentional. The AP English Language and Composition examination can use literature from the Renaissance forward, and you would be at a disadvantage if you had no practice in reading the language of centuries past. You probably encountered in these readings more unfamiliar words than you usually do, and you likely found the sentences to be longer and more complex than those in contemporary writing. (In other words, both the diction and the syntax presented challenges.) You should not shy away from these authors, however. Not only do they present ideas and experiences worth encountering even today, but they also help you to become more adept at handling rigorous material that you will encounter again in college. Your teacher can recommend additional selections that will help you become more comfortable with these writers.

AP Exam
Advice

Focus on Writing: Argumentation
In his explanation of how he tried to achieve moral perfection, Benjamin Franklin lists and organizes thirteen virtues he believes necessary to help him reach his goal. Suppose you wanted to embark on a course of self-improvement. Write an essay in which you choose two virtues that you believe are essential for your purpose, define them, and explain how you would set about to achieve them or at least to make progress toward improving yourself with regard to them.

Guidance on Your Writing

The virtues you choose can come from Benjamin Franklin's list in the reading from *The Autobiography*. Or, they might be other virtues you think of yourself. Try to employ some use of analogy, hyperbole, metaphor, or irony in your explanation. This work will help you better recognize these kinds of figurative language when you encounter them in the writings of other authors.

Introduction

Why is it more effective to say, "Ask not what your country can do for you; ask what you can do for your country" than "Do what you can do for your country instead of asking what your country can do for you"? Both sentences mean the same thing, but if John F. Kennedy had spoken the second during his inaugural address, he would not have been quoted so widely.

Why does nearly everyone who has ever read *A Tale of Two Cities* remember the opening sentence , "It was the best of times, it was the worst of times"?

When asked how much homework you have, you could say, "I have to do math, English, French, physics, and government." Why would it sound like so much more if you said, "I have to do math and English and French and physics and government"?

Last, why do people thrill at Lincoln's closing words, "government of the people, by the people, for the people," when he could have said "the people's government" and spared us the extra words?

Why? Because these are examples of **rhetoric**. The word *rhetoric*, which is sometimes used quite loosely, refers to skillful, effective use of language, often employing certain specific patterns and structures called, as a group, **rhetorical devices**. To some, rhetoric implies the artificial; to others, it suggests the artful. We will use the term in the second way. Writers use rhetorical devices to express themselves more effectively and memorably.

Language for Maximum Effect

Rhetoric does not mean **figures of speech,** like metaphor, simile, personification, and symbol. It does not mean **sound devices,** like alliteration, internal rhyme, or onomatopoeia, though these devices often accompany rhetorical devices. We are also not speaking of most of the ironies—hyperbole, **metonymy**, **synecdoche**, and so on. Rhetoric is *language carefully arranged for maximum effect,* and that effect usually is emotional. This is a bit tricky, because most rhetorical devices are the product of a planned intellectual approach to writing rather than a spontaneous emotional one.

However, like all good writing techniques, they work best when the writer, not the reader, is in control.

Rhetoric began when public discourse was oral more often than written. Therefore, many of these rhetorical devices are especially effective in speech. Since ancient times, people have been aware that certain arrangements of words can produce desired effects. We still find those arrangements useful, and we usually still refer to them by their ancient Greek names.

In this lesson you will learn a few of these rhetorical devices and observe them in use. You might try your hand at composing some yourself. You want to be able to recognize them when you encounter them, to understand what effects they create and why they do, and to employ them appropriately in your own writing.

A complete list of classical rhetorical devices would be too long for our purposes, so we will content ourselves with just a few. We will use the following familiar text, Lincoln's Gettysburg Address, to get started.

Focus on the Reading: Recognizing Rhetorical Devices
Study how Lincoln uses rhetorical devices to express himself effectively and memorably.

Abraham Lincoln
Gettysburg Address

Four score and seven years ago, our fathers brought forth upon this continent a new nation: conceived in liberty, and dedicated to the proposition that all men are created equal.

5 Now we are engaged in a great civil war, testing whether that nation, or any nation so conceived and so dedicated, can long endure. We are met on a great battlefield of that war.

We have come to dedicate a portion of that field, as a final resting place for those who here gave their lives that that nation might live. It is altogether fitting and proper that we should do this.

10 But, in a larger sense, we cannot dedicate, we cannot consecrate, we cannot hallow this ground. The brave men, living and dead, who struggled here, have consecrated it, far above our poor power to add or detract. The world will little note, nor long remember what we say here, but it can never forget what they did here.

15 It is for us the living, rather, to be dedicated here to the unfinished work which they who fought here have thus far so nobly advanced. It is rather for us to be here dedicated to the great task remaining before us, that from these honored dead we take increased devotion to that cause for which they gave the last full measure of devotion, that we 20 here highly resolve that these dead shall not have died in vain, that this nation, under God, shall have a new birth of freedom, and that government of the people, by the people, for the people, shall not perish from the earth.

Commentary on the Reading

Tricolon

Study the first sentence of the fourth paragraph, "But in a larger sense, we cannot dedicate, we cannot consecrate, we cannot hallow this ground." This provides opportunity to observe several rhetorical devices. There are three successive clauses, each beginning with the same words, "we cannot." Any series of three coordinate items is called a **tricolon.** Ancient peoples had a lot of respect for the number three. In some cases it was magical, and in some cases it was feared. They believed the number three had a lot of power, and here we see one instance of it. There is an emotionally satisfying completeness about a series of three that a simple pair of items does not produce. You often encounter series of three items in your everyday reading.

Anaphora

Lincoln emphasizes the tricolon by beginning each item with the same words, a technique known as **anaphora,** a Greek word that means literally "to bring forth again." An anaphora is a repetition at the beginning of successive phrases or clauses. Anaphora is to the phrase or clause what alliteration is to the word. Our ear hears the repetition, and our mind makes a connection because of the repeated sounds. Anaphora and tricolon are natural companions, because the effect of anaphora is not usually apparent until the third item in the series.

Asyntedon

Lincoln completes the effect by omitting the conjunction we expect at the end of the series. Usually when we have three items in a row, we expect the word "and" between the second and the third items. Deliberate omission of a conjunction is known as **asyntedon,** Greek for "no glue." The effect of asyndeton depends on the situation in which it is used. Often it gives a sense of haste, and in this case it seems that Lincoln is connecting three words with very similar connotations—consecrate, dedicate, hallow. It is as if he is speaking of one action three times, not as three different actions; thus the conjunction "and," which normally indicates addition or accumulation, would be out of place here.

One sentence with so much craft: was this intentional on Lincoln's part? In spite of the legends that claim he wrote the speech on the back of an envelope while on the train to the battlefield, it seems likely that he was aware of the emotional appeal this arrangement of words would have. This level of artistic effect does not happen by accident. If you want to achieve maximum results from your own reading and writing efforts, you will make more progress working toward the desired effects than by expecting them to happen spontaneously.

Epistrophe

Another reason to believe that Lincoln crafted that sentence deliberately is that we see the same techniques displayed in the closing words of the final sentence: "government of the people, by the people, for the people, shall not perish from the earth." These famous words end a very long and complex sentence that is full of rhetorical devices, but this final segment alone contains a tricolon, asyndeton, and a repetition of words in each of the three phrases of the tricolon. This time, however, the words appear at the end, not at the beginning, so we call the device **epistrophe,** an after-stroke. Anaphora appears at the beginning of a phrase, and epistrophe appears at the end.

The entire final sentence is a masterpiece of careful arrangement.

> It is rather for us to be here dedicated to the great task remaining before us, that from these honored dead we take increased devotion to that cause for which they gave the last full measure of devotion, that we here highly resolve that these dead shall not have died in vain, that this nation, under God, shall have a new birth of freedom, and that government of the people, by the people, for the people, shall not perish from the earth.

Tetracolon

Lincoln speaks near the beginning of the sentence of "the great task remaining before us." He defines that task in a series of clauses beginning with the word "that": that we take devotion, that we resolve, that this nation shall have a new birth, that government shall not perish. In this instance there are four, not three, items in the series, and the Greeks had a name for that, too: **tetracolon.** While three in a row produced a powerful effect, four in a row was also seen as very effective. Beyond that, we don't distinguish how many items there are in a series. If you can't make your point with four examples, you might need to rework the expression.

Lincoln's tetracolon here employs an anaphora beginning with the word "that." The repetition of that relative pronoun causes parallelism—each of the items in the series is a noun clause making the generality of "the great task remaining before us" specific:

> that from these honored dead <u>we take</u> increased devotion to that
> cause for which they gave the last full measure of devotion,
>
> that <u>we</u> here highly <u>resolve</u> that these dead shall not have died
> in vain,
>
> that <u>this nation</u>, under God, <u>shall have</u> a new birth of freedom, and
>
> that <u>government</u> of the people, by the people, for the people, <u>shall
> not perish</u> from the earth.

In such a complex sentence, it is a good idea to pay attention to subjects and verbs: we take, we resolve, this nation shall have, and government shall not perish. These four components of the "great task" are treated coordinately through parallelism and the use of the conjunction "and" before the last item in the series. There is no asyndeton in this last tetracolon, because Lincoln is speaking of four different things, each one added to the list. That represents a change from the sentence at the beginning of the fourth paragraph, where asyndeton allowed him to express one idea in three different ways.

Thus far you have learned five rhetorical devices and their definitions:

anaphora—the repetition of a word or words at the beginning of successive phrases or sentences

asyndeton—the absence of expected conjunctions

epistrophe—the repetition of a word or words at the end of successive phrases or sentences

tetracolon—a succession of four coordinate items

tricolon—a succession of three coordinate items

We aren't quite finished with Mr. Lincoln and his use of rhetorical devices in his speech.

Tautology

In dedicating the battlefield to the soldiers who fell there, he says that "it is altogether fitting and proper that we should do this." You might ask what is the difference between "fitting" and "proper," and the answer is "not much." These two words mean roughly the same thing, and Lincoln is here employing a technique known as **tautology,** the deliberate repetition of an idea for emphasis. You will encounter the word when you study logic, but in logic, tautology is a pejorative term for an argument that is empty or self-evident. In rhetoric, however, it can provide very effective emphasis, and that's how Lincoln uses it here. The words "dedicate," "consecrate," and "hallow" might strike you as tautological, too.

Synchises

In the first paragraph, Lincoln describes the "new nation" with a pair of adjective phrases in parallel structure:

"conceived in liberty and dedicated to the proposition…"

In each phrase we have an adjective followed by a prepositional phrase, connected with a coordinating conjunction. This device can be expressed with the pattern AB and AB, in which A is the adjective and B is the prepositional phrase. This balanced pairing of items in similar and coordinate fashion is called **synchises.** Its force comes from the combination of repetition and balance, and in addition to being very powerful, it is also very common.

Lincoln repeats the structure in the next sentence when he says,

"... any nation so conceived and so dedicated," —AB and AB.

In the third paragraph he says,

"The world will little note nor long remember …." —AB nor AB.

That phrase actually extends into another synchises when Lincoln says,

"The world will little note nor long remember what we say here, but it can never forget what they did here."

Do you sense the repetition in "what we say" and "what they did"? Do you get the sense of balance? Do you see how coordination is achieved with the conjunction "but"?

Antithesis

The preceding example might serve to illustrate another rhetorical device that Lincoln does not use here. If you see "nor long remember" as the opposite of "never forget" and "what we say" as a contrast to "what they did," you might think of that expression as an **antithesis,** the balanced pairing of opposites, again usually on either side of a coordinating conjunction. If synchises is AB and AB, antithesis would be A and not A. The most famous example of antithesis is the one quoted in the opening paragraph of this chapter: "It was the best of times, it was the worst of times," or perhaps Hamlet's "To be, or not to be." You might think Lincoln has an antithesis in the expression "our poor power to add or detract," but it is better not to think that every contrast is an antithesis. Rhetoric suggests the deliberate arrangement of words and structures for some particular effect, and if we think that everything is a deliberately manipulative device on the author's part, we might mistrust the author's sincerity.

The Gettysburg Address, a little speech of 271 words, has already yielded more than its share of illustrations of rhetorical devices. However, we could analyze it even further. The third paragraph has an interesting progression in the phrases "who struggled here," "what we say here," "what they did here," and "who fought here." Throughout the speech, there is an interplay between death and life and between death and birth: "a final resting place" and "that nation might live," and later "these dead shall not have died in vain.… this nation… shall have a new birth." There is even an allusion to Thomas Jefferson's Declaration of Independence at the end of the first sentence. Lincoln packed a great deal of rhetorical artistry into this short speech.

More Rhetorical Devices

You should be introduced to a few more rhetorical devices that are not illustrated in Lincoln's Gettysburg Address.

Chiasmus

If you understand synchises to be the pattern AB and AB, you will not confuse it with **chiasmus,** which has the pattern AB and BA. A chiasmus takes a pair of elements on one side of the coordinator and reverses it on the other. The coordinator can be a conjunction, a semicolon, a conjunctive adverb ("therefore," "however," "nevertheless," etc.), or even a period. Alexandre Dumas rallied his three musketeers with the chiasmus "All for one and one for all!" The environmentalist motto "Not blind opposition to all progress but opposition to all blind progress" is a modern-day example.

Polysyndeton

Asyndeton, the absence of expected conjunctions, has its counterpart in **polysyndeton,** the presence of more conjunctions than normal. "Tomorrow and tomorrow and tomorrow creeps in this petty pace from day to day" is a familiar line from Shakespeare's *Macbeth,* and most listeners to the speech sense the stretching out of time. The example on page 45 about how much homework you have shows that adding conjunctions can make a list of items seem longer or greater. Where asyndeton gives a sense of urgency and speed, polysyndeton suggests instead a slowing down. If asyndeton is A B C D E, polysyndeton is A and B and C and D and E.

Oxymoron

A writer who places two words that are normally contradictory side by side has used an **oxymoron,** a word that is itself an oxymoron, since "oxy" means "bright" and "moron" means "dull." The sophomore is a "wise fool," so that single word was coined with oxymoronic intent. The oxymoron is a special type of paradox. Phrases like "honest thief," "cruel kindness," and "light burden" are oxymorons. They are not absolute impossibilities, because at the heart of any paradox there is often truth.

Pun

A word that is used in more than one sense simultaneously, one of them literal and one of them figurative, is a **pun,** the rhetorical term for which is **paronomasia.** Puns can be funny, and occasionally someone makes an unintentional one and causes unexpected, and perhaps unwanted, laughter. Whoever said, "I was wondering why the baseball was getting bigger, and then it hit me," made a good pun.

Zeugma

The last rhetorical device we will address in this chapter is the most difficult to find and to construct, the **zeugma.** A zeugma, whose name comes from the Greek word for "yoke," occurs when one word in a sentence relates to at least two other words in the sentence, but in different ways. The classic example of zeugma comes from Alexander Pope's *Rape of the Lock:* "or stain her honour or her new brocade." The stain on the woman's brocade (an expensive fabric) would be a literal one, and to a lady of high society probably of minor consequence. The stain on her honor would be figurative, but much more serious. The irony results from the coordination of these two phrases, because coordination suggests equality of importance. A woman who considers a stain on her reputation to be equal to a stain on her dress might deserve Pope's ridicule.

Here, then, are the eight terms that have been presented in the second part of our discussion:

antithesis—a balanced pairing of opposites

chiasmus—a balanced pair of phrases or clauses in which the order of the elements in the first pair is reversed in the second pair

oxymoron—the juxtaposition of two normally incompatible words; in essence, a two-word paradox

polysyndeton—the use of more conjunctions than is normal

pun—a word used in two senses simultaneously, usually one literal and one figurative

synchises—a balanced pair of phrases or clauses in which the order of the first pair is repeated in the second pair

tautology—the repetition of an idea in two words that are nearly synonymous

zeugma—the use of a single word to refer to or to describe two different words in a sentence resulting in two different meanings

No rhetorical device is an end in itself. The goal is not simply to notice them but to try to understand what role they play in the overall effect of a piece of writing. In Lincoln's case, it is fair to say that the amount of rhetoric was appropriate to the occasion. He was speaking at a solemn gathering of serious people, and he wanted to say something that would be heartfelt and memorable. The highly emotional impact of the tricolons and anaphoras he used helped him to achieve his goal. No good writer employs a rhetorical device just because he or she thought of it. The device appears in the final draft of the writing because it is right for the moment. Because he expressed himself so effectively, Lincoln's "moment" has lasted for nearly a century and a half.

Before we leave our discussion of the Gettysburg Address, it is important to understand that what you have read in this commentary is not a good analysis of the role rhetorical devices play in the speech. What you have been reading is a catalogue of rhetorical devices and examples in order to introduce you to the patterns and devices that make the speech effective. A true analysis needs a thesis—for example, "Lincoln's careful arrangement of words and phrases into classical rhetorical structures helps to make his otherwise simple language emotional and memorable." The statement "Lincoln uses a lot of rhetorical devices in the Gettysburg Address" would be a poor thesis statement for an analytical essay on the AP exam.

AP Exam Advice

Reading Selection by John F. Kennedy

As you read John F. Kennedy's inaugural address, note the carefully crafted expressions—repetitions (like anaphora, epistrophe, and tricolon), contrasts (like antithesis and chiasmus), and other arrangements (like synchises and polysyndeton). You should find many of the devices illustrated above. A few of them will be indicated in marginal comments.

Focus on the Reading: Recognizing Rhetorical Devices
Study how the speaker uses rhetorical devices to express himself effectively and memorably.

John Fitzgerald Kennedy
Inaugural Address
Friday, January 20, 1961

Vice President Johnson, Mr. Speaker, Mr. Chief Justice, President Eisenhower, Vice President Nixon, President Truman, reverend clergy, fellow citizens, we observe today not a victory of party, but a celebration of freedom—symbolizing an end, as well as a beginning—signifying renewal, as well as change. For I have sworn before you and Almighty God the same solemn oath our forebears prescribed nearly a century and three quarters ago.

The world is very different now. For man holds in his mortal hands the power to abolish all forms of human poverty and all forms of human life. And yet the same revolutionary beliefs for which our forebears fought are still at issue around the globe—the belief that the rights of man come not from the generosity of the state, but from the hand of God.

We dare not forget today that we are the heirs of that first revolution. Let the word go forth from this time and place, to friend and foe alike, that the torch has been passed to a new generation of Americans—born in this century, tempered by war, disciplined by a hard and bitter peace, proud of our ancient heritage—and unwilling to witness or permit the slow undoing of those human rights to which this Nation has always been committed, and to which we are committed today at home and around the world.

Let every nation know, whether it wishes us well or ill, that we shall pay any price, bear any burden, meet any hardship, support any friend, oppose any foe, in order to assure the survival and the success of liberty.

This much we pledge—and more.

To those old allies whose cultural and spiritual origins we share, we pledge the loyalty of faithful friends. United, there is little we cannot do in a host of cooperative ventures. Divided, there is little we can do—for we dare not meet a powerful challenge at odds and split asunder.

To those new States whom we welcome to the ranks of the free, we pledge our word that one form of colonial control shall not have passed away merely to be replaced by a far more iron tyranny. We shall not always expect to find them supporting our view. But we shall always hope to find them strongly supporting their own freedom—and to remember that, in the past, those who foolishly sought power by riding the back of the tiger ended up inside.

To those peoples in the huts and villages across the globe struggling to break the bonds of mass misery, we pledge our best efforts to help them help themselves, for whatever period is required—not because the Communists may be doing it, not because we seek their votes, but because it is right. If a free society cannot help the many who are poor, it cannot save the few who are rich.

To our sister republics south of our border, we offer a special pledge—to convert our good words into good deeds—in a new alliance for progress—to assist free men and free governments in casting off the chains of poverty. But this peaceful revolution of hope cannot become the prey of hostile powers. Let all our neighbors know that we shall join

(16–17) The phrase between the dashes is a good example of tetracolon combined with asyndeton— four coordinate adjective phrases and no conjunction connecting them.

(26) Here is an antithesis— united/divided; little we cannot do/little we can do.

(38) What has Kennedy written here: "not because ..., not because ..., but because ..."? What do we find in the last sentence of the paragraph: "the many who are poor/the few who are rich"?

with them to oppose aggression or subversion anywhere in the Americas. And let every other power know that this Hemisphere intends to remain the master of its own house.

To that world assembly of sovereign states, the United Nations, our last best hope in an age where the instruments of war have far outpaced the instruments of peace, we renew our pledge of support—to prevent it from becoming merely a forum for invective—to strengthen its shield of the new and the weak—and to enlarge the area in which its writ may run.

Finally, to those nations who would make themselves our adversary, we offer not a pledge but a request: that both sides begin anew the quest for peace, before the dark powers of destruction unleashed by science engulf all humanity in planned or accidental self-destruction.

We dare not tempt them with weakness. For only when our arms are sufficient beyond doubt can we be certain beyond doubt that they will never be employed.

But neither can two great and powerful groups of nations take comfort from our present course—both sides overburdened by the cost of modern weapons, both rightly alarmed by the steady spread of the deadly atom, yet both racing to alter that uncertain balance of terror that stays the hand of mankind's final war.

So let us begin anew—remembering on both sides that civility is not a sign of weakness, and sincerity is always subject to proof. Let us never negotiate out of fear. But let us never fear to negotiate.

(70) Here is a chiasmus: negotiate—fear/fear—negotiate.

Let both sides explore what problems unite us instead of belaboring those problems which divide us.

Let both sides, for the first time, formulate serious and precise proposals for the inspection and control of arms—and bring the absolute power to destroy other nations under the absolute control of all nations.

Let both sides seek to invoke the wonders of science instead of its terrors. Together let us explore the stars, conquer the deserts, eradicate disease, tap the ocean depths, and encourage the arts and commerce.

Let both sides unite to heed in all corners of the earth the command of Isaiah—to "undo the heavy burdens…and to let the oppressed go free."

And if a beachhead of cooperation may push back the jungle of suspicion, let both sides join in creating a new endeavor, not a new balance of power, but a new world of law, where the strong are just and the weak secure and the peace preserved.

(84) Here is a polysyndeton. And while Kennedy is adding the additional conjunctions, he is omitting the repeated verb ("are"), a technique known as **ellipsis**.

All this will not be finished in the first 100 days. Nor will it be finished in the first 1,000 days, nor in the life of this Administration, nor even perhaps in our lifetime on this planet. But let us begin.

In your hands, my fellow citizens, more than in mine, will rest the final success or failure of our course. Since this country was founded, each generation of Americans has been summoned to give testimony to its national loyalty. The graves of young Americans who answered the call to service surround the globe.

Now the trumpet summons us again—not as a call to bear arms, though arms we need; not as a call to battle, though embattled we are—but a call to bear the burden of a long twilight struggle, year in and year out, "rejoicing in hope, patient in tribulation"—a struggle against the common enemies of man: tyranny, poverty, disease, and war itself.

100 Can we forge against these enemies a grand and global alliance, North and South, East and West, that can assure a more fruitful life for all mankind? Will you join in that historic effort?

In the long history of the world, only a few generations have been granted the role of defending freedom in its hour of maximum danger.
105 I do not shrink from this responsibility—I welcome it. I do not believe that any of us would exchange places with any other people or any other generation. The energy, the faith, the devotion which we bring to this endeavor will light our country and all who serve it—and the glow from that fire can truly light the world.

And so, my fellow Americans: ask not what your country can do
110 for you—ask what you can do for your country.

My fellow citizens of the world: ask not what America will do for you, but what together we can do for the freedom of man.

Finally, whether you are citizens of America or citizens of the world, ask of us the same high standards of strength and sacrifice which we ask of you. With a good conscience our only sure reward, with his-
115 tory the final judge of our deeds, let us go forth to lead the land we love, asking His blessing and His help, but knowing that here on earth God's work must truly be our own.

(109–110) Perhaps the words most often quoted from all of Kennedy's speeches, this sentence has become a textbook illustration of chiasmus.

Commentary on the Reading

The few marginal comments alongside Kennedy's speech touch on only a small sampling of the many classical rhetorical devices in the speech. You should find anaphoras and antitheses throughout, and examples of several of the other devices you learned in this lesson. But simply finding and identifying them is not a sufficient response to the speechwriter's skill. That would be like standing before Monet's *Water Lilies* and saying, "Here is blue and here is green and here is purple." Once you have recognized what the writer has done, your job must be to determine why the writer has done it. This sample exam question will give you a chance to do that.

Focus on Writing: Analysis
Choose one or two rhetorical devices that you see used significantly in Kennedy's Inaugural Address. Write an essay in which you determine the purpose of Kennedy's speech, and explain how these devices help him to achieve his purpose. Avoid a mere listing of examples.

Reading Selection by Martin Luther King, Jr.

One of the most widely admired speeches in American history was delivered by Martin Luther King, Jr., on the steps of the Lincoln Memorial (a location to which he alludes in the speech) to commemorate the hundredth anniversary of the Emancipation Proclamation. The speech is rich with rhetorical devices, which certainly contributed to the assembled audience's overall experience on hearing it. We should not focus on these devices to the exclusion of the speech's content, but it is hard not to be aware of how artfully King organized the language. If you have a chance to hear a recording of him delivering the speech, you will want to read along as you listen. As you read the speech, try to absorb as much of the effect of the rhetoric as you can. After you read it, think about the contribution of the language to the overall experience.

Focus on the Reading: Recognizing Rhetorical Devices

Pay attention to how King skillfully organized the language of his speech.

Martin Luther King, Jr.
I Have A Dream

Washington, DC, August 28, 1963

I am happy to join with you today in what will go down in history as the greatest demonstration for freedom in the history of our nation.

Five score years ago, a great American, in whose symbolic shadow we stand today, signed the Emancipation Proclamation. This momentous decree came as a great beacon light of hope to millions of Negro slaves who had been seared in the flames of withering injustice. It came as a joyous daybreak to end the long night of their captivity.

But one hundred years later, the Negro still is not free. One hundred years later, the life of the Negro is still sadly crippled by the manacles of segregation and the chains of discrimination. One hundred years later, the Negro lives on a lonely island of poverty in the midst of a vast ocean of material prosperity. One hundred years later, the Negro is still languishing in the corners of American society and finds himself an exile in his own land. So we have come here today to dramatize a shameful condition.

In a sense we have come to our nation's capital to cash a check. When the architects of our republic wrote the magnificent words of the Constitution and the Declaration of Independence, they were signing a promissory note to which every American was to fall heir. This note was a promise that all men, yes, black men as well as white men, would be guaranteed the unalienable rights of life, liberty, and the pursuit of happiness.

It is obvious today that America has defaulted on this promissory note insofar as her citizens of color are concerned. Instead of honoring this sacred obligation, America has given the Negro people a bad check, a check which has come back marked "insufficient funds." But we refuse to believe that the bank of justice is bankrupt. We refuse to believe that there are insufficient funds in the great vaults of opportunity of this nation. So we have come to cash this check — a check that will give us upon demand the riches of freedom and the security of justice. We have also come to this hallowed spot to remind America of the fierce urgency of now. This is no time to engage in the luxury of cooling off or to take the tranquilizing drug of gradualism. Now is the time to make real the promises of democracy. Now is the time to rise from the dark and desolate valley of segregation to the sunlit path of racial justice. Now is the time to lift our nation from the quick sands of racial injustice to the solid rock of brotherhood. Now is the time to make justice a reality for all of God's children.

It would be fatal for the nation to overlook the urgency of the moment. This sweltering summer of the Negro's legitimate discontent

As we saw in the reading by John Donne, we see here the same technique in Martin Luther King, Jr. He uses images and metaphors from a wide range of human activity, but he tends to focus on one—at this point on the idea of banking and economics.

will not pass until there is an invigorating autumn of freedom and equality. Nineteen sixty-three is not an end, but a beginning. Those who hope that the Negro needed to blow off steam and will now be content will have a rude awakening if the nation returns to business as usual. There will be neither rest nor tranquility in America until the Negro is granted his citizenship rights. The whirlwinds of revolt will continue to shake the foundations of our nation until the bright day of justice emerges.

But there is something that I must say to my people who stand on the warm threshold which leads into the palace of justice. In the process of gaining our rightful place we must not be guilty of wrongful deeds. Let us not seek to satisfy our thirst for freedom by drinking from the cup of bitterness and hatred.

We must forever conduct our struggle on the high plane of dignity and discipline. We must not allow our creative protest to degenerate into physical violence. Again and again we must rise to the majestic heights of meeting physical force with soul force. The marvelous new militancy which has engulfed the Negro community must not lead us to distrust all white people, for many of our white brothers, as evidenced by their presence here today, have come to realize that their destiny is tied up with our destiny and their freedom is inextricably bound to our freedom. We cannot walk alone.

As we walk, we must make the pledge that we shall march ahead. We cannot turn back. There are those who are asking the devotees of civil rights, "When will you be satisfied?" We can never be satisfied as long as the Negro is the victim of the unspeakable horrors of police brutality. We can never be satisfied, as long as our bodies, heavy with the fatigue of travel, cannot gain lodging in the motels of the highways and the hotels of the cities. We can never be satisfied as long as a Negro in Mississippi cannot vote and a Negro in New York believes he has nothing for which to vote. No, no, we are not satisfied, and we will not be satisfied until justice rolls down like waters and righteousness like a mighty stream.

I am not unmindful that some of you have come here out of great trials and tribulations. Some of you have come fresh from narrow jail cells. Some of you have come from areas where your quest for freedom left you battered by the storms of persecution and staggered by the winds of police brutality. You have been the veterans of creative suffering. Continue to work with the faith that unearned suffering is redemptive.

Go back to Mississippi, go back to Alabama, go back to South Carolina, go back to Georgia, go back to Louisiana, go back to the slums and ghettos of our northern cities, knowing that somehow this situation can and will be changed. Let us not wallow in the valley of despair.

I say to you today, my friends, so even though we face the difficulties of today and tomorrow, I still have a dream. It is a dream deeply rooted in the American dream.

I have a dream that one day this nation will rise up and live out the true meaning of its creed: "We hold these truths to be self-evident: that all men are created equal."

I have a dream that one day on the red hills of Georgia the sons of former slaves and the sons of former slave owners will be able to sit down together at the table of brotherhood.

King is acknowledging that not everyone wanted to address the nation's racial problems in this non-violent way. Without mentioning their names, he counters their arguments in favor of more militant action.

I have a dream that one day even the state of Mississippi, a state sweltering with the heat of injustice, sweltering with the heat of oppression, will be transformed into an oasis of freedom and justice.

I have a dream that my four little children will one day live in a nation where they will not be judged by the color of their skin but by the content of their character.

I have a dream today.

I have a dream that one day, down in Alabama, with its vicious racists, with its governor having his lips dripping with the words of interposition and nullification; one day right there in Alabama, little black boys and black girls will be able to join hands with little white boys and white girls as sisters and brothers.

I have a dream today.

I have a dream that one day every valley shall be exalted, every hill and mountain shall be made low, the rough places will be made plain, and the crooked places will be made straight, and the glory of the Lord shall be revealed, and all flesh shall see it together.

This is our hope. This is the faith that I go back to the South with. With this faith we will be able to hew out of the mountain of despair a stone of hope. With this faith we will be able to transform the jangling discords of our nation into a beautiful symphony of brotherhood. With this faith we will be able to work together, to pray together, to struggle together, to go to jail together, to stand up for freedom together, knowing that we will be free one day.

This will be the day when all of God's children will be able to sing with a new meaning, "My country, 'tis of thee, sweet land of liberty, of thee I sing. Land where my fathers died, land of the pilgrim's pride, from every mountainside, let freedom ring."

And if America is to be a great nation this must become true. So let freedom ring from the prodigious hilltops of New Hampshire. Let freedom ring from the mighty mountains of New York. Let freedom ring from the heightening Alleghenies of Pennsylvania!

Let freedom ring from the snowcapped Rockies of Colorado!

Let freedom ring from the curvaceous slopes of California!

But not only that; let freedom ring from Stone Mountain of Georgia!

Let freedom ring from Lookout Mountain of Tennessee!

Let freedom ring from every hill and molehill of Mississippi. From every mountainside, let freedom ring.

And when this happens, When we allow freedom to ring, when we let it ring from every village and every hamlet, from every state and every city, we will be able to speed up that day when all of God's children, black men and white men, Jews and Gentiles, Protestants and Catholics, will be able to join hands and sing in the words of the old Negro spiritual, "Free at last! free at last! thank God Almighty, we are free at last!"

Guidance on Your Writing

A speech of this length requires more time and space than you are generally allotted during an AP exam for a meaningful analysis, since you would need time to read the speech as well as write about it. This writing opportunity, then, will not replicate an exam condition, but it will give you a chance to analyze the full text instead.

As you analyze the Kennedy and King speeches, remember that your goal is to link rhetorical strategies to the purposes and overall effects of the speeches. In other words, you should link "how the speaker said it" to "the meaning of what he said." Do not merely list examples, but be sure to show the relationship between the language of the speech and the purpose of the speaker.

What are the purposes of particular words, phrases, and sentences in the passage?

Introduction

When we're learning to write, we often think that inspiration travels from the brain through the hand and onto the paper. It is hard for some people to believe that writers toil over individual words and phrases, yet they do. Richard Brinsley Sheridan, the eighteenth-century playwright, said, "Easy writing's vile hard reading," and many writers before and since have commented on the great difficulty of finding the best expression of an idea. Mark Twain wrote that "the difference between the right word and the almost right word is the difference between lightning and a lightning bug." As both reader and writer, we should learn to appreciate the efforts of writers who succeed in finding just the right word, phrase, and arrangement of elements to make their writing a pleasure to read.

When we read, we usually do not know what alternatives the writer considered before making the final choice. Nonetheless, we can be impressed with a well-chosen word or phrase. Remember the Paine excerpt in Lesson 2. The word "infested" seemed especially well chosen. We do not know if the word came to Paine in his first draft or during a period of revision, but we do know that the word has a powerful effect on the reader. When you read, it is a good habit to note especially well-chosen words; this will add to both your understanding and your enjoyment. As a writer, you will find yourself more satisfied with the results of your work, and more of your own readers will be impressed with your clarity, accuracy, and command of language. Among the characteristics of memorable writing, carefully chosen diction ranks as among the most impressive.

When we have determined that a particular word or phrase is well chosen, we want to be sure we understand its purpose. The passages from two American writers separated by 100 years give us opportunities to explore this feature of writing. As you read the Emerson passage, see if particular words strike you. Later you will be asked to explain what they contribute to the overall effect of the piece. The passage is followed by 12 questions, including six multiple-choice questions that can help you make more sense of the passage.

> **Focus on the Reading: Purposes of Words and Phrases**
> Look for the writer's use of just the right word, phrase, and arrangement of elements to make their writing a pleasure to read.

Ralph Waldo Emerson
from *Self-Reliance*

I read the other day some verses written by an eminent painter which were original and not conventional. The soul always hears an admonition in such lines, let the subject be what it may. The sentiment they instill is of more value than any thought they may contain. To believe your own thought, to believe that what is true for you in your private heart is true for all men, — that is genius. Speak your latent conviction, and it shall be the universal sense; for the inmost in due time becomes the outmost, — and our first thought is rendered back to us by the trumpets of the Last Judgment. Familiar as the voice of the mind is to each, the highest merit we ascribe to Moses, Plato, and Milton is, that they set at naught books and traditions, and spoke not what men but what they thought. A man should learn to detect and watch that gleam of light which flashes across his mind from within, more than the lustre of the firmament of bards and sages. Yet he dismisses without notice his thought, because it is his. In every work of genius we recognize our own rejected thoughts: they come back to us with a certain alienated majesty. Great works of art have no more affecting lesson for us than this. They teach us to abide by our spontaneous impression with good-humored inflexibility then most when the whole cry of voices is on the other side. Else, to-morrow a stranger will say with masterly good sense precisely what we have thought and felt all the time, and we shall be forced to take with shame our own opinion from another.

There is a time in every man's education when he arrives at the conviction that envy is ignorance; that imitation is suicide; that he must take himself for better, for worse, as his portion; that though the wide universe is full of good, no kernel of nourishing corn can come to him but through his toil bestowed on that plot of ground which is given to him to till. The power which resides in him is new in nature, and none but he knows what that is which he can do, nor does he know until he has tried. Not for nothing one face, one character, one fact, makes much impression on him, and another none. This sculpture in the memory is not without preestablished harmony. The eye was placed where one ray should fall, that it might testify of that particular ray. We but half express ourselves, and are ashamed of that divine idea which each of us represents. It may be safely trusted as proportionate and of good issues, so it be faithfully imparted, but God will not have his work made manifest by cowards. A man is relieved and gay when he has put his heart into his work and done his best; but what he has said or done otherwise, shall give him no peace. It is a deliverance which does not deliver. In the attempt his genius deserts him; no muse befriends; no invention, no hope.

Do you follow the line of Emerson's thinking in this paragraph? Which idea is the main idea? How does he illustrate it?

If you found this reading obscure, perhaps the questions that follow will clarify the meaning for you.

Reading Comprehension Exercise

First, consider the following questions as though they were a sentence-completion exercise. How would you finish each statement so that it reflected accurately what Emerson is saying in this excerpt? After you have written your completions, look at the choices offered for each one. You should have an easier time picking the correct choice from those available. This strategy might help you on the day of the AP exam.

AP Exam
Advice

1. Emerson's definition of genius in paragraph 1 is _____.

2. We should be most certain to stick to our own "spontaneous impression" when

_____.

3. If we don't stick to our spontaneous impressions, one result will be _____.

4. When Emerson says that "envy is ignorance," he means that envious people are ignorant of

_____.

5. We know the limits of our own abilities when _____.

6. Overall, Emerson's attitude seems to be one of _____.

Exam Practice — Reading Comprehension

Now, using your own sentence completions, find the best answers among the choices in the set below.

1. Emerson's definition of genius in paragraph 1 is

    (A) the ability to paint and write verse.
    (B) the sentiment instilled by lines of thought.
    (C) believing that what is true for you is true for everyone.
    (D) the highest merit of Moses, Plato, and Milton.
    (E) rejected thoughts that come back to us with majesty.

2. When should we be most certain to stick to our own "spontaneous impression"?

    (A) when other people disagree with us
    (B) when others agree with our opinions
    (C) when young people are listening to us
    (D) at the Last Judgment
    (E) when there is a flicker of light from within our spirits

3. If we don't stick to our spontaneous impressions, what will happen?

    (A) We'll make foolish errors.
    (B) We will find ourselves taking up ideas put forth by others.
    (C) The firmament will lose its luster.
    (D) We will fail to recognize our own rejected thoughts.
    (E) Bards and sages will dismiss us.

4. Emerson says that "envy is ignorance." Of what does he think envious people are ignorant?

    (A) the major ideas of their culture
    (B) the value of their own thoughts
    (C) the contributions of great thinkers like Moses, Plato, and Milton
    (D) education and conviction
    (E) the arts (specifically, sculpture and harmony)

5. When do we know the limits of our own abilities?

    (A) when our teachers tell us
    (B) when we compare ourselves to the great thinkers of past times
    (C) when we have cultivated our talents as we cultivate a crop of corn
    (D) when genius deserts us
    (E) when we have tried to exercise our powers

6. Overall, the author's attitude seems to be one of

    (A) daring.
    (B) resignation.
    (C) ambivalence.
    (D) confidence.
    (E) dismay.

Commentary on the Reading

Now that you have read and considered the passage (it is not an easy one), think about any words or phrases that you sense carry especially significant meaning. Which did you choose? What effects do they have on your overall understanding? Compare your choices with those of a classmate, and try to explain to your friend why you singled out the ones you did.

For example, you might have been struck by the word "suicide" in the second paragraph. It is not a word we use lightly, and we must be aware, if we choose to use it, how powerfully emotional the word is likely to be for many of our readers. So when we encounter it, we should contemplate all that it might accomplish in its place in the essay. "Suicide" is not a hard word to define—it is the act of killing oneself, of depriving oneself of life and existence. In what way, then, is Emerson saying that imitation is the equivalent of killing oneself? Does the answer lie in a particular sense of the word "self," a word we use with reference to our own identities? Clearly, when we imitate someone, we do not cease to be; we do not fall lifeless to the floor; we continue to breathe and function as we did before that "fatal" act of imitation. So we must pause and reassess Emerson's use of the word "suicide," and probably of the word "imitation" as well.

Do other words in the passage guide your understanding in a significant way?

We also have here an example of how our language lives and changes over time. Near the end of the passage, Emerson writes, "A man is relieved and gay when he has put his heart into his work and done his best." In the nineteenth century and well into the twentieth, "gay" was a synonym for "carefree" and "easygoing" and in general use did not refer to a person's sexual orientation. As with "happy" in the Jefferson and Franklin readings, we must know something about what words meant when the authors chose them and not ascribe meanings to the passages that the writers never intended.

Reading Selection by Lillian Hellman

On a different specific subject, Lillian Hellman, in her series of autobiographical sketches, considers a similar mystical attitude toward the subject of memory. She is about to tell the story of a girlhood friend who became socially and politically active during the period of World War II. This passage is from the chapter of *Pentimento* called "Julia," and it is certainly worth reading in its entirety. Here she gives a glimpse of her concern over the accuracy of her memory and her writing about a subject so important to her. The passage should be a lot easier to understand than Emerson's was, but you will again find examples of powerful words that no careful reader should overlook.

Focus on the Reading: Purposes of Words and Phrases
Find examples of powerful words that no careful reader should overlook.

Lillian Hellman
from *Pentimento*

Childhood is less clear to me than to many people: when it ended I turned my face away from it for no reason that I know about, certainly without the usual reason of unhappy memories. For many years that worried me, but then I discovered that the tales of former children are seldom to be trusted. Some people supply too many past victories or pleasures with which to comfort themselves, and other people cling to pains, real and imagined, to excuse what they have become.

I think I have always known about my memory: I know when it is to be trusted and when some dream or fantasy entered on the life, and the dream, the need of dream, led to distortion of what happened. And so I knew early that the rampage angers of an only child were distorted night-mares of reality. But I trust absolutely what I remember about Julia.

Now, so many years later, I could climb the steps without a light, move in the night through the crowded rooms of her grandparents' great Fifth Avenue house with the endless chic-shabby rooms, their walls covered with pictures, their tables crowded with objects whose value I didn't know. True, I cannot remember anything said or done in that house except for the first night I was allowed to sleep there. Julia and I were both twelve years old that New Year's Eve night, sitting at a late dinner, with courses of fish and meats, and sherbets in between to change the tastes, "clear the palate" is what her grandmother said, with watered wine for us, and red and white wine and champagne for the two old people. (Were they old? I don't know: they were her grandparents.) I cannot remember any talk at the table, but after dinner we were allowed to go with them to the music room. A servant had already set the pho-nograph for "So Sheep May Safely Graze," and all four of us listened until Julia rose, kissed the hand of her grandmother, the brow of her grandfather, and left the room, motioning for me to follow. It was an odd ritual, the whole thing, I thought, the life of the very rich, and beyond my understanding.

(26) "So Sheep May Safely Graze" is a popular hymn from a cantata by Johann Sebastian Bach.

Commentary on the Reading

In the first paragraph, consider such seemingly simple words as "tales" and "cling." What other words were available to the author in their places? Would the passage have a different meaning if she had written "the stories of former children are seldom to be trusted," and "other people hold on to pains, real and imagined, to excuse what they have become"? Can you find other words that appear to be careful choices for some desired effect?

> **Focus on Writing: Analysis**
> Reread the Hellman excerpt and choose several words whose synonyms, had they been used (such as "stories" for "tales" and "hold on" for "cling"), would have created a noticeably different overall effect in the piece.
> Then write an essay that explains what effect you believe Lillian Hellman achieved in her description, how the words you chose contribute to that effect, and how the synonyms you imagine for them would have changed the passage's impact. Do not merely summarize the passage.

Guidance on Your Writing

Though you cannot know for certain all the particular words Hellman considered, you must address how different her writing might have been if a few of her words had been different. Therefore you must identify the effect that Hellman achieves in this passage, and show how her word choices contribute to that effect.

Lesson 10 Who is the author's intended audience?

Introduction

When you write a paper for a school assignment, you probably write as though your teacher is your audience. You are probably right, because other than your friends and parents who might give you feedback during your creative process, it is unlikely that anyone besides your teacher is going to read that piece of writing. However, the matter of audience is a huge consideration for the mature writer. An awareness of who is likely to be reading the finished piece influences many decisions the writer makes along the way. The following questions indicate examples of these decisions.

What level of vocabulary is right for the intended audience?

How much background explanation does this audience require?

Does this audience probably agree with my assumptions, or do I need to persuade them?

Will this audience relate to my material in an intellectual way, or will they be highly emotional?

Is the audience likely to be a group of similar-minded people, or am I writing for a group characterized by a diversity of background, opinion, education, and experience?

What attitude, if any, does my audience bring to this topic?

How can I get my audience to trust and believe me?

All of these questions, and others too, require the writer's attention.

Audiences for King's "I Have a Dream"

The reader, then, must consider the intended audience among the factors that give a text meaning. In Lesson 8, where you read Martin Luther King's "I Have a Dream," you probably knew that the speech was delivered to a large and diverse audience gathered in front of the Lincoln Memorial in Washington, D.C. The speech was also broadcast to millions of listeners on radio and television stations around the nation and the world. Dr. King knew that his audience would include many people with a variety of opinions and very different backgrounds, both academic and spiritual, and that his speech was likely to be rebroadcast and reread in years to come. He faced the enormous problem of how to speak in a way that would make each person listening feel that he or she was the intended audience.

He accomplished that huge task in several ways, one of which was by choosing his language very carefully. In the first moments of the speech, he alludes to Lincoln's Gettysburg Address by saying "five score years ago." He could have said "100 years ago," but by reminding the audience of Lincoln, he draws in a group of people who identify with American history and the principles Lincoln stood for.

A few moments later, King says that "the Negro…finds himself an exile in his own land," words that will echo in the minds of people familiar with the Old Testament and the story of Moses (Exodus 2:21–22), in which Moses says of himself that he has been "a stranger in a strange land." Many of Dr. King's listeners knew him as a Baptist preacher, and they expected his speech to have some biblical references. King had to believe that those in his audience who expected a biblical allusion would recognize and understand the applicability of this one.

To reach out to another segment of the audience, those listeners who were highly educated and perhaps skeptical about this young preacher, King offers one more allusion in an early paragraph of the speech. He says, "This sweltering summer of the Negro's legitimate discontent will not pass until there is an invigorating autumn of freedom and equality." Many in the audience would recognize the words "summer of…discontent" and recall that Shakespeare, in the opening lines of *Richard III*, has the title character express his frustration and envy of his brother's success in lines that begin, "Now is the winter of our discontent made glorious summer." Again, King knew his audience, and he knew that those who recognized the allusion would understand its relevance. With these three allusions, the speaker was able to acknowledge his audience and welcome them as participants in his speech.

There is no question that King put a lot of energy into determining not only who his audience would be and what their characteristics would be but also how he would use that information in crafting his speech. It is important that readers, or in this case listeners, have some idea of whom the speaker was addressing so that they can most thoroughly understand and evaluate what he said.

Reading Selection by Franklin Roosevelt

In the following reading, a speech delivered by President Franklin D. Roosevelt, the immediate audience is the 1940 graduating class of the University of Virginia and their guests. Before you read the speech, think about who probably comprised that audience and what their expectations might have been.

Focus on the Reading: Awareness of Audience
Try to determine the audience or audiences that this speaker addresses.

Franklin Delano Roosevelt
Graduation Address
University of Virginia, Charlottesville, 10 June 1940

President Newcomb, my friends of the University of Virginia:

I notice by the program that I am asked to address the class of 1940. I avail myself of that privilege. But I also take this very apt occasion to speak to many other classes that have graduated through
5 all the years, classes that are still in the period of study, not alone in the schools of learning of the Nation, but classes that have come up through the great schools of experience; in other words a cross section of the country, just as you who graduate today are a cross section of the Nation as a whole.

10 Every generation of young men and women in America has questions to ask the world. Most of the time they are the simple but nevertheless difficult questions, questions of work to do, opportunities to find, ambitions to satisfy.

But every now and again in the history of the Republic a differ-
15 ent kind of question presents itself—a question that asks, not about the

(12) Notice the tricolon asyndeton here. What effect does it have on Roosevelt's speech?

future of an individual or even of a generation, but about the future of the country, the future of the American people.

There was such a time at the beginning of our history as a Nation. Young people asked themselves in those days what lay ahead, not for themselves, but for the new United States.

There was such a time again in the seemingly endless years of the War Between the States. Young men and young women on both sides of the line asked themselves, not what trades or professions they would enter, what lives they would make, but what was to become of the country they had known.

There is such a time again today. Again today the young men and the young women of America ask themselves with earnestness and with deep concern this same question: "What is to become of the country we know?"

Now they ask it with even greater anxiety than before. They ask, not only what the future holds for this Republic, but what the future holds for all peoples and all nations that have been living under democratic forms of Government—under the free institutions of a free people.

It is understandable to all of us that they should ask this question. They read the words of those who are telling them that the ideal of individual liberty, the ideal of free franchise, the ideal of peace through justice, are decadent ideals. They read the word and hear the boast of those who say that a belief in force—force directed by self-chosen leaders—is the new and vigorous system which will overrun the earth. They have seen the ascendancy of this philosophy of force in nation after nation where free institutions and individual liberties were once maintained.

It is natural and understandable that the younger generation should first ask itself what the extension of the philosophy of force to all the world would lead to ultimately. We see today in stark reality some of the consequences of what we call the machine age.

Where control of machines has been retained in the hands of mankind as a whole, untold benefits have accrued to mankind. For mankind was then the master; and the machine was the servant.

But in this new system of force the mastery of the machine is not in the hands of mankind. It is in the control of infinitely small groups of individuals who rule without a single one of the democratic sanctions that we have known. The machine in hands of irresponsible conquerors becomes the master; mankind is not only the servant; it is the victim, too. Such mastery abandons with deliberate contempt all the moral values to which even this young country for more than three hundred years has been accustomed and dedicated.

Surely the new philosophy proves from month to month that it could have no possible conception of the way of life or the way of thought of a nation whose origins go back to Jamestown and Plymouth Rock.

Conversely, neither those who spring from that ancient stock nor those who have come hither in later years can be indifferent to the destruction of freedom in their ancestral lands across the sea.

Perception of danger to our institutions may come slowly or it may come with a rush and a shock as it has to the people of the United States in the past few months. This perception of danger has come to us clearly and overwhelmingly; and we perceive the peril in a world-wide

(26) Roosevelt is speaking shortly before the United States entered World War II. Already certain events in Europe were pulling nations there into conflict with each other, and most Americans believed that American involvement was inevitable.

Roosevelt is not speaking of a specific machine here. Of what could he be speaking? How might we describe this machine in our own time?

arena—an arena that may become so narrowed that only the Americas will retain the ancient faiths.

Some indeed still hold to the now somewhat obvious delusion that we of the United States can safely permit the United States to become a lone island, a lone island in a world dominated by the philosophy of force.

Such an island may be the dream of those who still talk and vote as isolationists. Such an island represents to me and to the overwhelming majority of Americans today a helpless nightmare of a people without freedom—the nightmare of a people lodged in prison, handcuffed, hungry, and fed through the bars from day to day by the contemptuous, unpitying masters of other continents.

It is natural also that we should ask ourselves how now we can prevent the building of that prison and the placing of ourselves in the midst of it.

Let us not hesitate—all of us—to proclaim certain truths. Overwhelmingly we, as a nation—and this applies to all the other American nations—are convinced that military and naval victory for the gods of force and hate would endanger the institutions of democracy in the western world, and that equally, therefore, the whole of our sympathies lie with those nations that are giving their life blood in combat against these forces.

[*Here follow several paragraphs in which President Roosevelt explains recent diplomatic efforts to negotiate with the Italian government, which was about to enter an alliance with Germany. The president expresses regret that these diplomatic efforts were unsuccessful.*]

On this tenth day of June, 1940, the hand that held the dagger has struck it into the back of its neighbor.

On this tenth day of June, 1940, in this University founded by the first great American teacher of democracy, we send forth our prayers and our hopes to those beyond the seas who are maintaining with magnificent valor their battle for freedom.

(92) To whom is Roosevelt alluding here?

In our American unity, we will pursue two obvious and simultaneous courses; we will extend to the opponents of force the material resources of this nation; and, at the same time, we will harness and speed up the use of those resources in order that we ourselves in the Americas may have equipment and training equal to the task of any emergency and every defense.

All roads leading to the accomplishment of these objectives must be kept clear of obstructions. We will not slow down or detour. Signs and signals call for speed—full speed ahead.

(101) The United States did not enter World War II until eighteen months after this speech, but by the time Roosevelt gave this speech, many people believed that American involvement was inevitable.

It is right that each new generation should ask questions. But in recent months the principal question has been somewhat simplified. Once more the future of the nation and of the American people is at stake.

We need not and we will not, in any way, abandon our continuing effort to make democracy work within our borders. We still insist on the need for vast improvements in our own social and economic life. But that is a component part of national defense itself.

The program unfolds swiftly and into that program will fit the responsibility and the opportunity of every man and woman in the land to preserve his and her heritage in days of peril.

I call for effort, courage, sacrifice, devotion. Granting the love of freedom, all of these are possible.

And the love of freedom is still fierce and steady in the nation today.

Commentary on the Reading

As you review this graduation speech, keep in mind that President Roosevelt was addressing a college graduating class and their families before America's entry into World War II. On May 10, 1940, one month before Roosevelt made this speech, Germany attacked France, Belgium, Holland, and Luxembourg. On the day of this speech, Italy—an ally of Germany—declared war on France and England. Imagine that you are sitting in that audience—one of the young people whose future will be shaped by the coming war. How do those thoughts affect your understanding of the speech?

Focus on Writing: Analysis

President Franklin Roosevelt delivered this speech at the commencement ceremony of a major American university. Write an essay in which you analyze the relationship between the speech's audience and its content. Do not merely summarize the speech. Be sure to explain how it was affected by its intended audience.

Guidance on Your Writing

Try to imagine the audience for this speech. Who would have been graduating from that university in 1940? What can you say about their families? What components of the speech—diction, examples, allusions, underlying assumptions—reflect Roosevelt's awareness of this audience?

Lesson 11

What is the author's attitude toward the subject and the audience?

Introduction

One element of careful writing is **tone**, the term used to describe the author's attitude toward the subject or the audience. All writing has tone, just as all physical matter has temperature. If you can't sense the temperature of the book in your hand or the arm of the chair you are sitting in, you would say that they are at room temperature; you would not say that they had none. Likewise, in every piece of writing, the author is expressing an attitude, even if that attitude is objective or neutral.

How will you describe the tone of a text? Any word that can describe an attitude might describe an author's tone. Here are some examples:

cautious

irritated

skeptical

welcoming

enthusiastic

impatient

angry

bored

Few students lack such a vocabulary. The challenge for you is realizing how many words you already know that can be used to discuss a writer's tone.

The choice of tone is a major decision for the writer, because it will determine how the reader will react and what opinion the reader will form of the author. If you are writing a piece about an apartment house fire that resulted in the deaths of several people, you would express a serious and respectful attitude toward the victims; perhaps you would employ a tone that expresses outrage at the building inspectors or that communicates some fear that other buildings in similar condition could also catch fire. A reader of such a piece would probably take you and your message seriously, which in this case is the desired response. However, if in this situation you employ a flippant tone, make jokes about the subject, and use the occasion to show off your wit, most readers will find your approach distasteful and will reject what you have to say, even if some of it is thoughtful and intelligent. Tone is often a deal-maker or breaker in the relationship between the author and the reader.

Tone and Diction

We determine an author's tone in several ways. The foremost indicator of a writer's attitude is the diction of the piece. You have already observed that good writers choose their words carefully to communicate exactly the meaning they intend, either directly or through connotation. These connotations can frequently express an attitude. Once again, we can turn to Lesson 2, and our example from Thomas Paine: "New England is not infested with Tories, and we are." "Infested," with its dictionary meaning of inhabited or occupied with something unpleasant to a dangerous degree, as well as its suggestions of vermin and disease, certainly communicates an attitude of disgust toward its subject, the Tories. Not all word choices are so blatant; sometimes a writer's subtlety is itself an ingredient in the tone of the piece.

AP Exam Advice

Diction, while the most obvious indicator of tone, is by no means the only indicator. Another is the kind and source of examples used. In the Paine piece, shortly after implying that the Tories are vermin, Paine writes,

> I once felt all that kind of anger, which a man ought to feel, against the mean principles that are held by the Tories: a noted one, who kept a tavern at Amboy, was standing at his door, with as pretty a child in his hand, about eight or nine years old, as I ever saw, and after speaking his mind as freely as he thought was prudent, finished with this unfatherly expression, "Well! give me peace in my day."

We are meant to feel special disgust, even loathing, for this "unfatherly" man, who selfishly, as Paine goes on to explain, wants peace for himself, even if it means his pretty child will have to face the inevitable war in the future. That example helps Paine establish how he feels about this particular Tory.

If you consider the portrait of Julia's grandparents in the excerpt from *Pentimento* in Lesson 9, you might think about the attitude Lillian Hellman is expressing toward those people. What do the details of the New Year's Eve dinner suggest about her feelings for Julia and her family?

Formal and Informal Language

The level of formality a writer uses to communicate tone to an audience is also significant. A writer who uses excessively simple words, or "talks down" to the reader, is telegraphing that he or she does not think much of the reader's intelligence or maturity. We all recognize condescension when we hear it, and we can recognize it in writing, too.

Conversely, writers who use language that is inappropriately complicated for a simple subject might be indicating an attitude of intellectual superiority to their readers. This technique might intimidate a reader who doesn't feel as smart as the writer. It may or may not be what the author intended, but it may certainly be what the reader senses. If you are reading an article in a professional journal, you expect the writer to use the vocabulary known to people in that field. Such language communicates professional respect.

On the other hand, slang, colloquialisms, and regional dialect can limit an audience to those who understand those language subsets, and they communicate a familiarity and casualness that is generally not appropriate in formal writing situations. Profanity suggests a level of familiarity with the reader that most writers cannot risk taking. The risk, of course, is that the reader will simply close the book when the language seems disrespectful or repellant.

The pieces that follow all use tone as part of their authors' overall messages. As you read them, try to notice what cues you in to these authors' attitudes, and decide what words most accurately describe what those attitudes are.

Reading Selection by Henry Fielding

The following passage, an introduction to Sophia Western, the heroine of Henry Fielding's novel *Tom Jones*, can serve as a warm-up for the readings and exercises that follow it. The tone should be evident in Fielding's word choice and imagery. The setting is eighteenth century England.

Henry Fielding
from *Tom Jones*

A short hint of what we can do in the sublime, and a description of Miss Sophia Western.

Hushed be every ruder breath. May the heathen ruler of the winds confine in iron chains the boisterous limbs of noisy Boreas, and the sharp-pointed nose of bitter-biting Eurus. Do thou, sweet Zephyrus, rising from thy fragrant bed, mount the western sky, and lead on those delicious gales, the charms of which call forth the lovely Flora from her chamber, perfumed with pearly dews, when on the 1st of June, her birthday, the blooming maid, in loose attire, gently trips it over the verdant mead, where every flower rises to do her homage, till the whole field becomes enamelled, and colours contend with sweets which shall ravish her most.

So charming may she now appear! and you the feathered choristers of nature, whose sweetest notes not even Handel can excel, tune your melodious throats to celebrate her appearance. From love proceeds your music, and to love it returns. Awaken, therefore that gentle passion in every swain: for, lo! adorned with all the charms in which nature can array her; bedecked with beauty, youth, sprightliness, innocence, modesty, and tenderness, breathing sweetness from her rosy lips, and darting brightness from her sparkling eyes, the lovely Sophia comes!

Reader, perhaps thou hast seen the statue of the *Venus de Medicis*. Perhaps, too, thou hast seen the gallery of beauties at Hampton Court. Thou mayest remember each bright Churchill of the galaxy, and all the toasts of the Kit-cat. Or, if their reign was before thy times, at least thou hast seen their daughters, the no less dazzling beauties of the present age; whose names, should we here insert, we apprehend they would fill the whole volume.

Now if thou hast seen all these, be not afraid of the rude answer which Lord Rochester once gave to a man who had seen many things. No. If thou hast seen all these things without knowing what beauty is, thou hast no eyes; if without feeling its power, thou hast no heart.

(4) Fielding is referring to the winds by their Greek mythological names: Boreas (north), Eurus (east), and Zephyrus (west). There is also a south wind, Notus, which he does not invoke here. Flora is the goddess of flowers.

(14) George Friederich Handel was the foremost composer of Fielding's day. He is best known for his oratorio *Messiah* and for his *Water Music*.

(21) Venus, as the goddess of love, was the subject of many works of art, and here Fielding compares other beautiful women of his time to that ideal of beauty.

Commentary on the Reading

In this brief excerpt, one tone—one attitude—dominates. We discover the speaker's overwhelming adoration of Sophia. The intensity of his feeling is evident in the allusions to mythological figures, the instructions to the winds and the birds to prepare the way for her entrance, and the comparisons to the great beauties of his day. Even if we don't know who they are, we feel the impact of words like "gallery of beauties," "bright," "galaxy," and "dazzling." We cannot fail to see how abundantly he admires her beauty.

Reading Selection by Zora Neale Hurston

Zora Neale Hurston, in the essay that follows, presents a more complicated view. She speaks of her own experience, but she communicates attitudes toward several subjects. Taken together, however, they add up to an overarching statement of how she feels about herself.

> **Focus on the Reading: Awareness of Author Attitude**
> Try to notice the author's attitudes, and decide what words most accurately describe what those attitudes are.

Zora Neale Hurston
How It Feels to Be Colored Me

I am colored but I offer nothing in the way of extenuating circumstances except that I am the only Negro in the United States whose grandfather on the mother's side was not an Indian chief.

5　I remember the very day that I became colored. Up to my thirteenth year I lived in the little Negro town of Eatonville, Florida. It is exclusively a colored town. The only white people I knew passed through the town going to or coming from Orlando. The native whites rode dusty horses, the Northern tourists chugged down the sandy village road in automobiles. The town knew the Southerners and never stopped

10　cane chewing when they passed. But the Northerners were something else again. They were peered at cautiously from behind curtains by the timid. The more venturesome would come out on the porch to watch them go past and got just as much pleasure out of the tourists as the tourists got out of the village.

15　The front porch might seem a daring place for the rest of the town, but it was a gallery seat for me. My favorite place was atop the gatepost. Proscenium box for a born first-nighter. Not only did I enjoy the show, but I didn't mind the actors knowing that I liked it. I usually spoke to them in passing. I'd wave at them and when they returned my salute, I

20　would say something like this: "Howdy-do-well-I-thank-you-where-you goin'?" Usually the automobile or the horse paused at this, and after a queer exchange of compliments, I would probably go "a piece of the way" with them, as we say in the farthest Florida. If one of my family happened to come to the front in time to see me, of course negotiations

25　would be rudely broken off. But even so, it is clear that I was the first "welcome-to-our-state" Floridian, and I hope the Miami Chamber of Commerce will please take notice.

During this period, white people differed from colored to me only in that they rode through town and never lived there. They liked to hear

30　me "speak pieces" and sing and wanted to see me dance the parse-me-la, and gave me generously of their small silver for doing these things,

(15) How would you describe the personality of the speaker in this paragraph? How is that personality created?

(30) The parse-me-la is a type of Southern African-American folk dancing.

which seemed strange to me for I wanted to do them so much that I needed bribing to stop. Only they didn't know it. The colored people gave no dimes. They deplored any joyful tendencies in me, but I was their Zora nevertheless. I belonged to them, to nearby hotels, to the county—everybody's Zora.

But changes came in the family when I was thirteen, and I was sent to school in Jacksonville. I left Eatonville, the town of the oleanders, as Zora. When I disembarked from the river-boat at Jacksonville, she was no more. It seemed that I had suffered a sea change. I was not Zora of Orange County anymore, I was now a little colored girl, I found it out in certain ways. In my heart as well as in the mirror, I became fast brown—warranted not to rub nor run.

But I am not tragically colored. There is no great sorrow dammed up in my soul, nor lurking behind my eyes. I do not mind at all. I do not belong to the sobbing school of Negrohood who hold that nature somehow has given them a lowdown dirty deal and whose feelings are all hurt about it. Even in the helter-skelter skirmish that is my life, I have seen that the world is to the strong regardless of a little pigmentation more or less. No, I do not weep at the world—I am too busy sharpening my own oyster knife.

Someone is always at my elbow reminding me that I am the grand-daughter of slaves. It fails to register depression with me. Slavery is sixty years in the past. The operation was successful and the patient is doing well, thank you. The terrible struggle that made me an American out of a potential slave said "On the line!" The Reconstruction said "Get Set!"; and the generation before said "Go!" I am off to a flying start and I must not halt in the stretch to look behind and weep. Slavery is the price I paid for civilization, and the choice was not with me. It is a bully adventure and worth all that I have paid through my ancestors for it. No one on earth ever had a greater chance for glory. The world to be won and nothing to be lost. It is thrilling to think—to know that for any act of mine, I shall get twice as much praise or twice as much as blame. It is quite exciting to hold the center of the national stage, with the spectators not knowing whether to laugh or to weep.

The position of my white neighbor is much more difficult. No brown specter pulls up a chair beside me when I sat down to eat. No dark ghost thrusts its leg against mine in bed. The game of keeping what one has is never so exciting as the game of getting.

I do not always feel colored. Even now I often achieve the unconscious Zora of Eatonville before the Hegira. I feel most colored when I am thrown against a sharp white background.

For instance at Barnard, "Beside the waters of the Hudson" I feel my race. Among the thousand white persons, I am a dark rock surged upon, and overswept, but through it all, I remain myself. When covered by the waters, I am; and the ebb but reveals me again.

(73) Hurston received a scholarship to Barnard College in New York and completed a bachelor's degree in anthropology there in 1927.

Sometimes it is the other way around. A white person is set down in our midst, the contrast is just as sharp for me. For instance, when I sit in the drafty basement that is The New World Cabaret with a white person, my color comes. We enter chatting about any little nothing that we have in common and are seated by the jazz waiters. In the abrupt way that jazz orchestras have, this one plunges into a number. It loses no time in circumlocutions, but gets right down to business. It constricts the thorax and splits the heart with its tempo and narcotic harmonies. This orchestra grows rambunctious, rears on its hind legs and attacks the tonal veil with primitive fury, tending it, clawing it until it breaks through to the jungle beyond. I follow those heathen—follow them exultantly. I dance wildly inside myself; I yell within, I whoop; I shake my assegai above my head, I hurl it true to the mark yeeeeooww! I am in the jungle and living in the jungle way. My face is painted red and yellow and my body is painted blue. My pulse is throbbing like a war drum. I want to slaughter something—give pain, give death to what, I do not know. But the piece ends. The men of the orchestra wipe their lips and rest their fingers. I creep back slowly to the veneer we call civilization with the last tone and find the white friend sitting motionless in his seat, smoking calmly.

(88) An assegai is a spear.

"Good music they have here," he remarks, drumming the table with his fingertips.

Music. The great blobs of purple and red emotion have not touched him. He has only heard what I felt. He is far away and I see him but dimly across the ocean and the continent that have fallen between us. He is so pale with his whiteness then and I am so colored.

At certain times, I have no race, I am *me*. When I set my hat a certain angle and saunter down Seventh Avenue, Harlem City, feeling as snooty as the lions in front of the Forty-Second Street Library, for instance. So far as my feelings are concerned, Peggy Hopkins Joyce on the Boule Mich with her gorgeous raiment, stately carriage, knees knocking together in a most aristocratic manner, has nothing on me. The cosmic Zora emerges. I belong to no race nor time. I am the eternal feminine with its string of beads.

I have no separate feeling about being an American citizen and colored. I am merely a fragment of the Great Soul that surges within the boundaries. My country, right or wrong.

Sometimes I feel discriminated against, but it does not make me angry. It merely astonishes me. How can any deny themselves the pleasure of my company? It's beyond me.

(113) Is the speaker's personality here the same as on page 72? How do these expressions of personality reflect the author's attitude toward her subject and toward her audience?

But in the main, I feel like a brown bag of miscellany propped against a wall. Against a wall in company with other bags, white, red, and yellow. Pour out the contents, and there is discovered a jumble of small things priceless and worthless. A first-water diamond, an empty spool, bits of broken glass, lengths of string, a key to a door long since crumbled away, a rusty knife-blade, old shoes saved for a road that never was and never will be, a nail bent under the weight of things too heavy for any nail, a dried flower or two still a little fragrant. In your hand is the brown bag. On the ground before you is the jumble it held—so much like the jumble in the bags, could they be emptied, that all might be dumped in a single heap and the bags refilled without altering the content of any greatly. A bit of colored glass more or less would not matter. Perhaps that is how the Great Stuffer of Bags filled them in the first place—who knows?

Commentary on the Reading

You may have noticed that in this essay Zora Neale Hurston begins quite personally and matter-of-factly, but ends with a paragraph based on an imaginative simile. Can you identify it? Do you see how it relates to the discussion that precedes it?

Reading Selection by William Bradford

One of America's earliest writers, William Bradford, kept a journal of the founding of the Pilgrims' Plymouth Colony. The following is a brief passage about the first winter. As you read, be sure you understand what the subject of the passage is. Then determine what Bradford's diction and choice of illustrations tell us about his attitudes toward his subject.

William Bradford
Of Plymouth Plantation, 1620–1647

But that which was most sad and lamentable was, that in two or three months' time half of the company died, especially in January and February, being the depth of winter, and wanting houses and other comforts; being infected with the scurvy and other diseases which this long
5   voyage and their inaccommodate condition had brought upon them. So as there died some times two or three of a day in the foresaid time, that of 100 and odd persons, scarce fifty remained. And of these, in the time of most distress, there was but six or seven sound persons who to their great commendations, be it spoken, spared no pains night nor day, but
10   with abundance of toil and hazard of their own health, fetched them wood, made them fires, dressed them meat, made their beds, washed their loathsome clothes, clothed and unclothed them. In a word, did all the homely and necessary offices for them which dainty and queasy stomachs cannot endure to hear named; and all this willingly and cheer-
15   fully, without any grudging in the least, showing herein their true love unto their friends and brethren; a rare example and worthy to be remembered. Two of these seven were Mr. William Brewster, their reverend Elder, and Myles Standish, their Captain and military commander, unto whom myself and many others were much beholden in our low and sick
20   condition. And yet the Lord so upheld these persons as in this general calamity they were not at all infected either with sickness or lameness. And what I have said of these I may say of many others who died in this general visitation, and others yet living; that whilst they had health, yea,

This first paragraph turns out to be about the six or seven people who remained healthy. How do we know what Bradford feels about them?

or any strength continuing, they were not wanting to any that had need
of them. And I doubt not but their recompense is with the Lord.

But I may not here pass by another remarkable passage not to be
forgotten. As this calamity fell among the passengers that were to be
left here to plant, and were hasted ashore and made to drink water that
the seamen might have the more beer, and one in his sickness desiring
but a small can of beer, it was answered that if he were their own father
he should have none. The diseases began to fall amongst them also, so
as almost half of their company died before they went away, and many
of their officers and lustiest men, as the boatswain, gunner, three quar-
termasters, the cook and others. At which the Master was something
strucken and sent to the sick ashore and told the Governor he should
send for beer for them that had need of it, though he drunk water home-
ward bound.

But now amongst his company there was far another kind of carriage in this misery than amongst the passengers. For they that before
had been boon companions in drinking and jollity in the time of their
health and welfare, began now to desert one another in this calamity,
saying they would not hazard their lives for them, they should be infected by coming to help them in their cabins; and so, after they came
to lie by it, would do little or nothing for them but, "if they died, let
them die." But such of the passengers as were yet aboard showed them
what mercy they could, which made some of their hearts relent, as the
boatswain (and some others) who was a proud young man and would
often curse and scoff at the passengers. But when he grew weak, they
had compassion on him and helped him; then he confessed he did not
deserve it at their hands, he had abused them in word and deed. "Oh!"
(saith he) "you, I now see, show your love like Christians indeed one
to another, but we let one another lie and die like dogs." Another lay
cursing his wife, saying if it had not been for her he had never come this
unlucky voyage, and anon cursing his fellows, saying he had done this
and that for some of them; he had spent so much and so much amongst
them, and they were now weary of him and did not help him, having
need. Another gave his companion all he had, if he died, to help him
in his weakness; he went and got a little spice and made him a mess of
meat once or twice, and because he died not so soon as he expected, he
went amongst his fellows, and swore the rogue would cozen him, he
would see him choked before he made him any more meat; and yet the
poor fellow died before morning.

(29) That "one in his
sickness" was Bradford
himself. The Pilgrims did
not drink beer to get drunk.
Why might a person in this
situation want beer instead
of water? What attitude
(toward what subject) is
Bradford communicating by
relating this example?

Commentary on the Reading

What effect did the words "inaccommodate conditions," "loathsome clothes," and
"dainty and queasy stomachs" have on you as you formulated your picture of the
scene Bradford is describing? In other words, what attitude is Bradford asking the
reader to adopt about the plight of the Pilgrims of the Plymouth Colony? What
other diction and examples in the passage affect the reader in the same way?

Reading Selection by Tom and Ray Magliozzi

The reading that follows is an installment from an advice column that appears in many American newspapers. Usually the authors are asked to give advice about mechanical matters, but here they are asked a question of a different kind. If you have ever listened to their radio program, you will have a hard time not hearing their actual voices in their response. Try to put that aside as you read, and let the language of the column do its job.

> **Focus on the Reading: Awareness of Author Attitude**
> Try to notice the columnists' attitude toward their questioner.

Tom and Ray Magliozzi (Click & Clack)
Checks And Balances

Q: Dear Tom and Ray:

5

10

15

20

Am I a jerk or a genius? When my son was 15, I wrote him a check for $1,500, postdated three years. I told him that if he managed to reach the date of the check without (1) receiving any tickets, (2) being involved in any accidents or (3) breaking any of our house driving rules, I'd cash the check for him. My goal was to provide an incentive for him to play by the rules long enough to form some good driving habits. Anyway, my son very nearly made it. A few months shy of his 18th birthday, he was cruising along the highway, singing. And he suddenly realized that the light show accompanying his karaoke act was being provided by the flashing lights on top of a cruiser. He fessed up about the ticket promptly, and was bemoaning the fine of $126. I gently reminded him that the ticket had actually cost him $1,626, as he had failed to fulfill our bargain. My question: Am I a genius for coming up with the carrot that made him a good driver during his crucial first years behind the wheel, or am I a jerk for piling on a $1,500 fine? Please note that his younger sister is watching carefully to see how this is resolved. She's 14, and whether I fold on this will go a long way in setting her expectations. My son took the news well, but I have friends who are treating me as though I smashed the kid's piggy bank and took his inheritance.—Ted

Are you responding to this father's depiction of his children? What language gives you your impression?

> **Focus on Writing: Argumentation**
> Take a position. Write an argument in favor of withdrawing the check, of forgiving the speeding ticket, or some other decision relevant to the situation. Support your position with appropriate reasons. After you have written your argument, read what Click & Clack had to say on the subject. (This is not an exercise in tone but in argument. The exercise in tone will follow at the end of the reading.)

A: TOM: Are you a jerk or a genius? Well, it's possible to be both, Ted. I'd say you're definitely a genius. I think this is a brilliant way to encourage a kid to drive responsibly, and I'm all for anything that accomplishes that.

25 RAY: For nearly three years, the kid was careful, he avoided getting tickets, he avoided accidents and he lived by the rules of the household. Do you know how many insanely jealous parents are reading about this kid today?

TOM: So you definitely get points for parenting. Now, are you also a 30 jerk? The fact that you're asking means you're not one. Clearly, you sense, somewhere in that hard little dried-up stone of a heart you have, you're being a little rough on the kid.

RAY: I understand the desire to teach your kids that "a deal is a deal." But it's also worth teaching them about fairness, flexibility and that 35 there's value in trying hard, even if you don't always succeed. After all, your mission is essentially accomplished. After driving responsibly for his first three years, your son is unlikely to turn around now and go out and drive like a moron.

TOM: So I would extend your offer. Make it clear to him—and to his 40 younger sister—that since he dutifully fulfilled the contract for most of the three years, you appreciate his effort and you want to offer him a chance to redeem himself.

RAY: Right. Tell him that if he maintains a clean record for an additional six months after the original deadline, you'll still cash the check 45 for him. Or you'll cash a slightly smaller check—say $1,400—for him. And you can make it clear to both kids that were it not for his excellent performance up until the speeding ticket, you wouldn't be offering him a second chance.

TOM: You can also make it clear that this is a one-time offer. That if he 50 fails again, you intend to cash the check yourself and spend the money on that vibrating recliner you've had your eye on.

RAY: But you both deserve a lot of credit. You came up with a great idea, and your son has had the good sense to buy into the deal.

(39) Do you think Tom and Ray understand the situation well? Do you approve of their compromise? Do you think the son will be satisfied? The daughter?

Focus on Writing: Analysis

After reading the columnists' response to the question, determine what you see as their attitude toward the father and toward the son. Write an essay in which you explain how Ray and Tom Magliozzi use the writer's resources regarding tone to communicate not only the information they want to share but also how they feel about their subject (the son and his driving record) and their audience (the father who wrote the letter). Refer to specific portions of the column that support your view.

Lesson 12 How does the author arrange details?

Introduction

As writers, we have an obligation to help our readers understand the important elements of what we have to say. We may make choices about the organization of information based on several factors, but ultimately we have to think of how we can best communicate with our readers. These choices can make our writing either clearer or more obscure. Three common organizing principles are time, location, and order of importance.

Time

Sometimes the order of items in a series is determined by time. We call that **chronological order**, and it is a very normal order to use when providing narration. In fact, when telling a story, not using chronological order tends to be confusing to the listener or reader. If you were giving instructions for how to do something, for example, you would want to put the information in chronological order. You would want to use time-related words like "then," "after," "before," and "during" to clue your reader in to the order in which you expect him or her to perform certain actions.

Location

Sometimes we choose to organize information by location. We call that **spatial** order, and we are likely to use that when we are describing something. Often a writer will have a starting point for a description, and then provide further details by taking the reader's eye either upward or downward from that point, or to the left or to the right, or clockwise or counterclockwise. It is unlikely that the reader would see the scene as clearly if the details were provided in random order. When describing people, it is common to proceed from head to foot, beginning at the top of the head and continuing as far down the body as the description needs to go. A landscape description usually begins at some eye-catching point and travels from there in one direction or another. Some descriptions are circular and end by returning to their starting points, and others are linear, ending some distance from their origins. Recall Hawthorne's description of Hester Prynne that you read in Lesson 6:

> The young woman was tall, with a figure of perfect elegance on a large scale. She had dark and abundant hair…and a face which… had…a marked brow and deep black eyes…. Her attire…seemed to express the attitude of her spirit…. But the point which drew all eyes…was that SCARLET LETTER, so fantastically embroidered and illuminated upon her bosom.

The reader's eye is drawn from Hester's head to her brow and eyes, and then to her clothing, and is brought to rest at last on the letter she wears on her chest. This description is organized spatially.

Order of Importance

A third common organizing principle is to put information in the order of importance. We call that **climactic** order, and it is very effective for showing what you consider to be the most important among the different pieces of information you are providing. Since your writing in this course will be more expository than narrative or descriptive, you are likely to use this method of organizing more often than chronological or spatial order.

Because the end of a sentence is the most emphatic position, placing an item at the end of a series, and putting that series at the end of the sentence, will have the effect of stressing that information even though you don't use words like "most important," or "significantly." The sentence "I moved into the country so that I would have some land to plant a garden, some distance between my neighbors' houses and mine, and some peace and quiet so that I wouldn't have another nervous breakdown" offers three reasons for the move. We know that the peace and quiet are more important than the garden and the privacy because of the order in which the reasons are given. Consider this example from the closing sentence of the Declaration of Independence:

> And for the support of this declaration, with a firm reliance on the protection of Divine Providence, we mutually pledge to each other our lives, our fortunes and our sacred honor.

Thomas Jefferson informs us, through his choice of climactic order, that of the three pledges made, their lives and fortunes are less important than their honor. It is not that they are unimportant, but honor is greater than either of them. Climactic order is a very powerful tool.

Reading Selection by Jacob A. Riis

The reading that follows is a chapter from a social worker's account of poverty in New York at the end of the nineteenth century. Jacob Riis, a Dane, was well-known as one of the early social reformers in American urban history. He was writing at a time of increased immigration and industrialization. His writing employs all three of the organizing principles described in this lesson, and sometimes combines them. Be on the lookout for examples of each of them. By the end of the reading, you should have a clear picture of what he is describing and a good idea of what he thinks his readers should do about it. Multiple-choice questions and an essay follow the reading.

> ### Focus on the Reading: Understanding Organization
> Notice the use of three common organizing principles: time, location, and order of importance.

Jacob A. Riis
from *How the Other Half Lives* (1890)

XV. The Problem of the Children

THE problem of the children becomes, in these swarms, to the last degree perplexing. Their very number makes one stand aghast. I have already given instances of the packing of the child population in East Side tenements. They might be continued indefinitely until the array would be enough to startle any community. For, be it remembered, these children with the training they receive—or do not receive—with the instincts they inherit and absorb in their growing up, are to be our future rulers, if our theory of government is worth anything. More than a working majority of our voters now register from the tenements. I counted the other day the little ones, up to ten years or so, in a Bayard Street tenement that for a yard has a triangular space in the centre with sides fourteen or fifteen feet long, just room enough for a row of ill-smelling closets at the base of the triangle and a hydrant at the apex. There was about as much light in this "yard" as in the average cellar. I gave up my self-imposed task in despair when I had counted one hundred and twenty-eight in forty families. Thirteen I had missed, or not found in. Applying the average for the forty to the whole fifty-three, the house contained one hundred and seventy children. It is not the only time I have had to give up such census work. I have in mind an alley—an inlet rather to a row of rear tenements—that is either two or four feet wide according as the wall of the crazy old building that gives on it bulges out or in. I tried to count the children that swarmed there, but could not. Sometimes I have doubted that anybody knows just how many there are about. Bodies of drowned children turn up in the rivers right along in summer whom no one seems to know anything about. When last spring some workmen, while moving a pile of lumber on a North River pier, found under the last plank the body of a little lad crushed to death, no one had missed a boy, though his parents afterward turned up. The truant officer assuredly does not know, though he spends his life trying to find out, somewhat illogically, perhaps, since the department that employs him admits that thousands of poor children are crowded out of the schools year by year for want of room. There was a big tenement in the Sixth Ward, now happily appropriated by the beneficent spirit of business that blots out so many foul spots in New York—it figured not long ago in the official reports as "an out-and-out hogpen"—that had a record of one hundred and two arrests in four years among its four hundred and seventy-eight tenants, fifty-seven of them for drunken and disorderly conduct. I do not know how many children there were in it, but the inspector reported that he found only seven in the whole house who owned that they went to school. The rest gathered all the instruction they received running for beer for their elders. Some of them claimed the "flat" as their home as a mere matter of form. They slept in the streets at night. The official came upon a little party of four drinking beer out of the cover of a milk-can in the hallway. They were of the seven good boys and proved their claim to the title by offering him some.

Consider the details Riis provides in this paragraph about the children. Try to imagine how the impact of this information would be different if the final details—how few children go to school and how they are drinking beer—had been given early in the paragraph instead of late.

The old question, what to do with the boy, assumes a new and serious phase in the tenements. Under the best conditions found there, it is not easily answered. In nine cases out of ten he would make an excellent mechanic, if trained early to work at a trade, for he is neither dull nor slow, but the short-sighted despotism of the trades unions has practically closed that avenue to him. Trade-schools, however excellent, cannot supply the opportunity thus denied him, and at the outset the boy stands condemned by his own to low and ill-paid drudgery, held down by the hand that of all should labor to raise him. Home, the greatest factor of all in the training of the young, means nothing to him but a pigeon-hole in a coop along with so many other human animals. Its influence is scarcely of the elevating kind, if it have any. The very games at which he takes a band in the street become polluting in its atmosphere. With no steady hand to guide him, the boy takes naturally to idle ways. Caught in the street by the truant officer, or by the agents of the Children's Societies, peddling, perhaps, or begging, to help out the family resources, he runs the risk of being sent to a reformatory, where contact with vicious boys older than himself soon develop the latent possibilities for evil that lie hidden in him. The city has no Truant Home in which to keep him, and all efforts of the children's friends to enforce school attendance are paralyzed by this want. The risk of the reformatory is too great. What is done in the end is to let him take chances—with the chances all against him. The result is the rough young savage, familiar from the street. Rough as he is, if any one doubt that this child of common clay have in him the instinct of beauty, of love for the ideal of which his life has no embodiment, let him put the matter to the test. Let him take into a tenement block a handful of flowers from the fields and watch the brightened faces, the sudden abandonment of play and fight that go ever hand in hand where there is no elbow-room, the wild entreaty for "posies," the eager love with which the little messengers of peace are shielded, once possessed; then let him change his mind. I have seen an armful of daisies keep the peace of a block better than a policeman and his club, seen instincts awaken under their gentle appeal, whose very existence the soil in which they grew made seem a mockery. I have not forgotten the deputation of ragamuffins from a Mulberry Street alley that knocked at my office door one morning on a mysterious expedition for flowers, not for themselves, but for "a lady," and having obtained what they wanted, trooped off to bestow them, a ragged and dirty little band, with a solemnity that was quite unusual. It was not until an old man called the next day to thank me for the flowers that I found out they had decked the bier of a pauper, in the dark rear room where she lay waiting in her pine-board coffin for the city's hearse. Yet, as I knew, that dismal alley with its bare brick walls, between which no sun ever rose or set, was the world of those children. It filled their young lives. Probably not one of them had ever been out of the sight of it. They were too dirty, too ragged, and too generally disreputable, too well hidden in their slum besides, to come into line with the Fresh Air summer boarders.

With such human instincts and cravings, forever unsatisfied, turned into a haunting curse; with appetite ground to keenest edge by a hunger that is never fed, the children of the poor grow up in joyless homes to lives of wearisome toil that claims them at an age when the play of

Riis develops this paragraph by using a combination of spatial and climactic order.

their happier fellows has but just begun. Has a yard of turf been laid and a vine been coaxed to grow within their reach, they are banished and barred out from it as from a heaven that is not for such as they. I came upon a couple of youngsters in a Mulberry Street yard a while ago that were chalking on the fence their first lesson in "writin'." And this is what they wrote: "Keeb of te Grass." They had it by heart, for there was not, I verily believe, a green sod within a quarter of a mile. Home to them is an empty name. Pleasure? A gentleman once catechized a ragged class in a down-town public school on this point, and recorded the result: Out of forty-eight boys twenty had never seen the Brooklyn Bridge that was scarcely five minutes' walk away, three only had been in Central Park, fifteen had known the joy of a ride in a horse-car. The street, with its ash-barrels and its dirt, the river that runs foul with mud, are their domain. What training they receive is picked up there. And they are apt pupils. If the mud and the dirt are easily reflected in their lives, what wonder? Scarce half-grown, such lads as these confront the world with the challenge to give them their due, too long withheld, or—. Our jails supply the answer to the alternative.

A little fellow who seemed clad in but a single rag was among the flotsam and jetsam stranded at Police Headquarters one day last summer. No one knew where he came from or where he belonged. The boy himself knew as little about it as anybody, and was the least anxious to have light shed on the subject after he had spent a night in the matron's nursery. The discovery that beds were provided for boys to sleep in there, and that he could have "a whole egg" and three slices of bread for breakfast put him on the best of terms with the world in general, and he decided that Headquarters was "a bully place." He sang "McGinty" all through, with Tenth Avenue variations, for the police, and then settled down to the serious business of giving an account of himself. The examination went on after this fashion:

"Where do you go to church, my boy?"

"We don't have no clothes to go to church." And indeed his appearance, as he was, in the door of any New York church would have caused a sensation.

"Well, where do you go to school, then?"

"I don't go to school," with a snort of contempt.

"Where do you buy your bread?"

"We don't buy no bread; we buy beer," said the boy, and it was eventually the saloon that led the police as a landmark to his "home." It was worthy of the boy. As he had said, his only bed was a heap of dirty straw on the floor, his daily diet a crust in the morning, nothing else.

Into the rooms of the Children's Aid Society were led two little girls whose father had "busted up the house" and put them on the street after their mother died. Another, who was turned out by her step-mother "because she had five of her own and could not afford to keep her," could not remember ever having been in church or Sunday-school, and only knew the name of Jesus through hearing people swear by it. She had no idea what they meant. These were specimens of the overflow from the tenements of our home-heathen that are growing up in New York's streets to-day, while tender-hearted men and women are busying themselves with the socks and the hereafter of well-fed little Hottentots thousands of miles away. According to Canon Taylor, of York, one hundred

Here Riis has told a little story, and therefore used chronological order.

and nine missionaries in the four fields of Persia, Palestine, Arabia, and Egypt spent one year and sixty thousand dollars in converting one little heathen girl. If there is nothing the matter with those missionaries, they might come to New York with a good deal better prospect of success.

By those who lay flattering unction to their souls in the knowledge that to-day New York has, at all events, no brood of the gutters of tender years that can be homeless long unheeded, let it be remembered well through what effort this judgment has been averted. In thirty-seven years the Children's Aid Society, that came into existence as an emphatic protest against the tenement corruption of the young, has sheltered quite three hundred thousand outcast, homeless, and orphaned children in its lodging-houses, and has found homes in the West for seventy thousand that had none. Doubtless, as a mere stroke of finance, the five millions and a half thus spent were a wiser investment than to have let them grow up thieves and thugs. In the last fifteen years of this tireless battle for the safety of the State the intervention of the Society for the Prevention of Cruelty to Children has been invoked for 138,891 little ones; it has thrown its protection around more than twenty-five thousand helpless children, and has convicted nearly sixteen thousand wretches of child-beating and abuse. Add to this the standing army of fifteen thousand dependent children in New York's asylums and institutions, and some idea is gained of the crop that is garnered day by day in the tenements, of the enormous force employed to check their inroads on our social life, and of the cause for apprehension that would exist did their efforts flag for ever so brief a time.

Nothing is now better understood than that the rescue of the children is the key to the problem of city poverty, as presented for our solution to-day; that character may be formed where to reform it would be a hopeless task. The concurrent testimony of all who have to undertake it at a later stage: that the young are naturally neither vicious nor hardened, simply weak and undeveloped, except by the bad influences of the street, makes this duty all the more urgent as well as hopeful. Helping hands are held out on every side. To private charity the municipality leaves the entire care of its proletariat of tender years, lulling its conscience to sleep with liberal appropriations of money to foot the bills. Indeed, it is held by those whose opinions are entitled to weight that it is far too liberal a paymaster for its own best interests and those of its wards. It deals with the evil in the seed to a limited extent in gathering in the outcast babies from the streets. To the ripe fruit the gates of its prisons, its reformatories, and its workhouses are opened wide the year round. What the showing would be at this end of the line were it not for the barriers wise charity has thrown across the broad highway to ruin—is building day by day—may be measured by such results as those quoted above in the span of a single life.

Commentary on the Reading

Sometimes we are surprised to find that social conditions characteristic of our own time existed and were actually important in previous centuries. This essay illustrates that phenomenon well. The plight of poor children has concerned thinking people for a long time, not only Jacob Riis in the nineteenth century, but also Jonathan Swift in the eighteenth, whose famous essay *A Modest Proposal* appears in lesson 20.

Exam Practice — Reading Comprehension

These questions will help you focus on the author's purpose and intended audience.

1. Within the context of the first paragraph, lines 1–46, which of these is the purpose of the sentence "More than a working majority...tenements"?

    (A) to show that these children will have to work hard for a living
    (B) to predict that these children will never be able to move out of the slums
    (C) to demonstrate the basic inequality of the election laws
    (D) to suggest that the children of the tenements will likely be the future officeholders in their neighborhood's government
    (E) to illustrate the close-knit relationships of people in this neighborhood

2. Why, in paragraph 1, is the author trying to count the children?

    (A) to get a complete census for the government
    (B) to demonstrate that many children have "slipped between the cracks"
    (C) to assist the truant officer in getting the children to school
    (D) to protest child labor practices
    (E) to suggest a relationship between overpopulation and alcoholism

3. Which of the following assumptions does the author not make in the second paragraph, lines 47–94?

    (A) Most children can be educated.
    (B) The greatest influence on a child's development is the school.
    (C) People are often more corrupt after being in prison than they were before going in.
    (D) Poor children seek beauty in their lives.
    (E) Most tenement children spend little time out of the slums.

4. What is ironic about the sign chalked on the fence by the youngsters (described in paragraph 3, lines 95–116)?

    (A) Three of the four words are misspelled.
    (B) The boys stole the chalk from school.
    (C) There was no grass nearby.
    (D) They didn't know what the sign meant.
    (E) They thought it was funny.

5. The episode of the boy stranded at the police station (lines 117–139) serves what purpose?

    (A) It shows that the boy normally lives in appalling conditions.
    (B) It shows how brutally the police treat the poor.
    (C) It shows how the poor children are trained to be defiant of authority.
    (D) It exposes the inability of the church to take care of its parishioners.
    (E) It criticizes the saloon owners who sell beer to the children.

6. The author's purpose in paragraph 11, lines 140–154, where he tells of the missionaries, is to

    (A) compliment them on their good work.
    (B) point out how the police in New York can be more effective.
    (C) criticize foreign governments for allowing poverty to affect their citizens' lives.
    (D) demonstrate that the problems of New York's poor deserve their attention.
    (E) compare poverty levels of America and the Middle East.

7. Why, according to paragraphs 12–13, lines 155–194, does the author focus on the plight of children?

    (A) He knows that readers will be more sympathetic to the needs of children than they would be to the needs of adults.
    (B) He believes that most problems can be avoided if children are given a decent upbringing.
    (C) He wants the efforts of the Children's Aid Society to be more widely publicized.
    (D) He thinks he can convince the voters to elect a more responsive government.
    (E) He is advocating a reform in child labor and education laws.

Reading Selection by Sojourner Truth

Sojourner Truth was the adopted name of Isabella Baumfree, born a slave in the 1790s. Becoming free when New York State abolished slavery in the 1820s, she worked throughout her adult life as an abolitionist and suffragist. Although she spoke at perhaps hundreds of events, the speech that follows is her most famous public address. She was not formally educated (and in fact, as a child, she spoke only Dutch), but you will find in this short speech several illustrations of effective uses of language.

Sojourner Truth
Speech at the Women's Convention
Akron, Ohio, 1851

Well, children, where there is so much racket there must be something out of kilter. I think that 'twixt the negroes of the South and the women at the North, all talking about rights, the white men will be in a fix pretty soon. But what's all this here talking about?

5   That man over there says that women need to be helped into carriages, and lifted over ditches, and to have the best place everywhere. Nobody ever helps me into carriages, or over mud-puddles, or gives me any best place! And ain't I a woman? Look at me! Look at my arm! I have ploughed and planted, and gathered into barns, and no man could head me! And ain't I a woman? I could work as much and eat as much 10 as a man—when I could get it—and bear the lash as well! And ain't I a woman? I have borne thirteen children, and seen most all sold off to slavery, and when I cried out with my mother's grief, none but Jesus heard me! And ain't I a woman?

15   Then they talk about this thing in the head; what's this they call it? [member of audience whispers, "intellect"] That's it, honey. What's that got to do with women's rights or negroes' rights? If my cup won't hold

Examine the four situations Sojourner Truth describes in this paragraph. Which does she save for last? Why?

but a pint, and yours holds a quart, wouldn't you be mean not to let me have my little half measure full?

Then that little man in black there, he says women can't have as much rights as men, 'cause Christ wasn't a woman! Where did your Christ come from? Where did your Christ come from? From God and a woman! Man had nothing to do with Him.

If the first woman God ever made was strong enough to turn the world upside down all alone, these women together ought to be able to turn it back, and get it right side up again! And now they is asking to do it, the men better let them.

Obliged to you for hearing me, and now old Sojourner ain't got nothing more to say.

Focus on Writing: Analysis

Reread Sojourner Truth's speech and pay particular attention to her diction and arrangement of material. Then write an essay in which you explain how she uses those elements of writing to establish the tone of her speech.

Introduction

Repeating images can be a very powerful way for a writer to create atmosphere. Atmosphere is important because it helps the writer establish an attitude toward the subject.

In the case of Charles Dickens, whose novel *Bleak House* has a celebrated opening passage, the oppressive atmosphere of the fog—familiar to Londoners of Dickens's time—begins as a routine annual feature of the climate, much as winter snow in the American North or summer heat and humidity in the South. If you read with purpose, you will experience the fog vicariously, and you will be prepared for the more significant description that follows it, the description of the court system. That subject will turn out to be the real focus of the novel. In the beginning, however, we can appreciate how effectively Dickens uses detail and repeated images to create the desired effect of gloom and defeat.

Dickens's Syntax

The syntax of the first paragraph is interesting because it is so different from what most writers were writing at the time. It is a series of impressionistic statements, not grammatical sentences, which toss bits of experience the reader's way. Many of Dickens's readers lived in London and would have immediately recognized locations like Lincoln's Inn and Holborn Hill. Descriptions of chimney pots and umbrellas would have been very familiar to them as well. This paragraph reads like a slide show, with one image following another almost automatically.

The second paragraph, by contrast, takes one image and explores it relentlessly. We see the fog from what appears to be every conceivable angle. The repeated word at the beginning of each sentence—an extended anaphora—has the effect of reminding us of the inescapability of this fog. We still don't get complete sentences, but that doesn't matter. The missing verbs seem unnecessary. There is no movement or action in this fog anyway.

Even the third paragraph lacks standard, traditional syntactic grammar. It isn't until the fourth paragraph that Dickens begins to write in sentences, and that is where he begins to describe the courts of law, the Temple Bar, about which he has nothing good to say.

Focus on the Reading: Observing Imagery

See how effectively Dickens uses detail and repeated images to create the desired effect.

Charles Dickens
from *Bleak House*

London. Michaelmas Term lately over, and the Lord Chancellor sitting in Lincoln's Inn Hall. Implacable November weather. As much mud in the streets, as if the waters had but newly retired from the face of the earth, and it would not be wonderful to meet a Megalosaurus, forty feet long or so, waddling like an elephantine lizard up Holborn Hill. Smoke lowering down from chimney-pots, making a soft black drizzle, with flakes of soot in it as big as full-grown snowflakes—gone into mourning, one might imagine, for the death of the sun. Dogs, undistinguishable in mire. Horses, scarcely better; splashed to their very blinkers. Foot passengers, jostling one another's umbrellas in a general infection of ill temper, and losing their foot-hold at street-corners, where tens of thousands of other foot passengers have been slipping and sliding since the day broke (if this day ever broke), adding new deposits to the crust upon crust of mud, sticking at those points tenaciously to the pavement, and accumulating at compound interest.

Fog everywhere. Fog up the river, where it flows among green aits and meadows; fog down the river, where it rolls defiled among the tiers of shipping, and the waterside pollutions of a great (and dirty) city. Fog on the Essex marshes, fog on the Kentish heights. Fog creeping into the cabooses of collier-brigs; fog lying out on the yards, and hovering in the rigging of great ships; fog drooping on the gunwales of barges and small boats. Fog in the eyes and throats of ancient Greenwich pensioners, wheezing by the firesides of their wards; fog in the stem and bowl of the afternoon pipe of the wrathful skipper, down in his close cabin; fog cruelly pinching the toes and fingers of his shivering little 'prentice boy on deck. Chance people on the bridges peeping over the parapets into a nether sky of fog, with fog all round them, as if they were up in a balloon and hanging in the misty clouds.

Gas looming through the fog in divers places in the streets, much as the sun may, from the spongey fields, be seen to loom by husbandman and ploughboy. Most of the shops lighted two hours before their time—as the gas seems to know, for it has a haggard and unwilling look.

The raw afternoon is rawest, and the dense fog is densest, and the muddy streets are muddiest near that leaden-headed old obstruction, appropriate ornament for the threshold of a leaden-headed old corporation; Temple Bar. And hard by Temple Bar, in Lincoln's Inn Hall, at the very heart of the fog, sits the Lord High Chancellor in his High Court of Chancery.

Never can there come fog too thick, never can there come mud and mire too deep, to assort with the groping and floundering condition which this High Court of Chancery, most pestilent of hoary sinners, holds this day in the sight of heaven and earth.

On such an afternoon, if ever, the Lord High Chancellor ought to be sitting here—as here he is—with a foggy glory round his head, softly fenced in with crimson cloth and curtains, addressed by a large advocate with great whiskers, a little voice, and an interminable brief, and out-

Dickens uses spatial organization here very effectively.

(40) Up until now the fog and mud have been literal images, providing an unpleasant description of London at this time. Here they take on the suggestion of symbolism, indicating the obscure and filthy atmosphere of the court.

wardly directing his contemplation to the lantern in the roof, where he
can see nothing but fog. On such an afternoon some score of members
of the High Court of Chancery bar ought to be—as here they are—mist-
ily engaged in one of the ten thousand stages of an endless cause, tripping one another up on slippery precedents, groping knee-deep in tech-
nicalities, running their goat-hair and horsehair warded heads against
walls of words and making a pretence of equity with serious faces, as
players might. On such an afternoon, the various solicitors in the cause,
some two or three of whom have inherited it from their fathers, who
made a fortune by it, ought to be—as are they not?—ranged in a line, in
a long matted well (but you might look in vain for truth at the bottom of
it) between the registrar's red table and the silk gowns, with bills, cross-
bills, answers, rejoinders, injunctions, affidavits, issues, references to
masters, masters' reports, mountains of costly nonsense, piled before
them. Well may the court be dim, with wasting candles here and there;
well may the fog hang heavy in it, as if it would never get out; well
may the stained-glass windows lose their colour and admit no light of
day into the place; well may the uninitiated from the streets, who peep
in through the glass panes in the door, be deterred from entrance by
its owlish aspect and by the drawl, languidly echoing to the roof from
the padded dais where the Lord High Chancellor looks into the lantern
that has no light in it and where the attendant wigs are all stuck in a
fog-bank! This is the Court of Chancery; which has its decaying houses
and its blighted lands in every shire, which has its worn-out lunatic in
every madhouse and its dead in every churchyard, which has its ruined
suitor with his slipshod heels and threadbare dress borrowing and begging through the round of every man's acquaintance, which gives to
monied might the means abundantly of wearing out the right, which so
exhausts finances, patience, courage, hope, so overthrows the brain and
breaks the heart, that there is not an honourable man among its prac-
titioners who would not give—who does not often give—the warning,
"Suffer any wrong that can be done you rather than come here!"

Focus on Writing: Analysis
The preceding passage opens Charles Dickens's novel *Bleak House*. Read
the passage carefully, and then write an essay in which you analyze how
Dickens's rhetorical strategies reveal his attitude toward the legal system of
his day.

Guidance on Your Writing

The Dickens passage is typical of the kind used in the free-response section of
the English Language and Composition exam, with an instruction that looks
like the writing prompt above. In order to answer such a question, you have to
solve two problems.

First, you must explain what Dickens's attitude toward the legal system is.

Second, you have to decide which rhetorical strategies to discuss to show how
he reveals that attitude.

In fact, all analytical questions on the AP test fall into that pattern: you have to explain both what the author does and how the author does it. Failure to do both tasks earns you a score in the lower half of the scoring range, even if you do a brilliant job with the one task you do undertake. To earn a high score, you have to respond successfully to both parts of the question.

Most of the time the wording of the question will present the "how" first and the "what" second, but you will probably want to answer the "what" first and follow that with the "how." A straightforward statement of what you see as Dickens's attitude is a good place to start: for example,

"In the opening of *Bleak House,* Dickens expresses an attitude of _____ toward the legal system of his day, an attitude revealed by the rhetorical strategies of _____, _____, and _____."

This kind of opening statement is not clever, splashy, or original, but it gets the job done, and it is the kind of opening that will make your reader think that you are going to follow up with something worthwhile.

If you have had difficulty with some of the analytical essay questions in earlier lessons, you might go back now and see if you can approach them in this manner. It is not necessary to rewrite the essays, but you will probably benefit from determining how the question asks for a "what" and a "how," and then framing an opening statement that you can successfully support.

Introduction

In order for writers to share their ideas, they must express those ideas in terms of actual, specific things. They have to find the best balance between two kinds of words, the **abstract** and the **concrete.** Nouns that name intangible, conceptual things are abstract, while nouns that name examples of those abstract ideas are concrete. We perceive concrete nouns through our five senses; we perceive abstract nouns through our imaginations. The more concrete a noun is, the more likely it is that we will all understand it the same way. The more abstract it is, the more likely it is that our understandings will differ.

The words that communicate ideas are, by their nature, difficult to define precisely. The word "courage," for example, represents an idea that requires that the writer and the reader share a common understanding of what constitutes courage. To one person, courage might be volunteering to join the military and fight a war. To another, it might be getting up on the stage of a high school auditorium and singing a solo in front of one's classmates. To another, it might be defying an authoritarian ruling that seems unjust. To another, it might mean crossing a high ravine on a rickety footbridge. A further complication is that any of these specific actions could easily call up other abstract ideas in a reader's mind. A story about someone defying authority might make the reader think about rebelliousness, recklessness, disrespect, or a host of other interpretations. Trusting that footbridge might seem courageous to some, but to others it might appear to be sheer folly.

We cannot illustrate one abstract noun with equally abstract synonyms. Courage can be illustrated with any of the examples given above or others that are meaningful to you. It is not clarified by using words such as "valor," "bravery," or "guts."

In your own writing, abstract words tend to occupy topic sentences and, therefore, often appear early in a paragraph. In the work of a professional writer, abstractions may come up anywhere, and the careful reader is on the lookout not only for the ideas the writer is expressing but also for the concrete illustrations that help one envision those abstract ideas.

Abstract nouns in English often end in recognizable suffixes: *-age, -ance, -ment, -ness, -ity* (or just *-ty*), *-tion*, and variations on the spellings of those suffixes, such as *-ence* and *-sion*.

It is natural to think of abstract as the opposite of concrete, but it is actually more useful to see them as the end points of a long continuum on which many word choices can be placed, each word more or less concrete than its neighbor. "Dog" is a fairly specific word (more specific than "animal," for example), but less specific than "collie." A continuum that stretches from most concrete to most abstract might look like this:

| **Concrete** ←————————————————→ **Abstract** |
| Fido   collie   dog   canine   mammal   animal   living being |

A good way to recognize abstract and concrete language is to note the abstract idea that is supported by each concrete detail, and to note the details that make the abstract ideas meaningful. Because it is easier to see this process at work in fiction, the first reading comes from the opening of a popular nineteenth-century short story. In these paragraphs, the author Washington Irving establishes the setting and introduces the main character. You probably know that later on in the story, Rip will fall asleep in the woods and wake up twenty years later, confused by the changes that took place while he slept. In the beginning of the story, we focus on where he lived and what his home life was like. Read these paragraphs with attention to the abstract language Irving uses and the specific details that accompany the abstract ideas.

Focus on the Reading: Abstract and Concrete Language
Read with attention to the abstract language Irving uses and the specific details that accompany the abstract ideas.

Washington Irving
from *Rip Van Winkle*

Whoever has made a voyage up the Hudson must remember the Kaatskill mountains. They are a dismembered branch of the great Appalachian family, and are seen away to the west of the river, swelling up to a noble height, and lording it over the surrounding country. Every
5   change of season, every change of weather, indeed, every hour of the day produces some change in the magical hues and shapes of these mountains; and they are regarded by all the good wives, far and near, as perfect barometers. When the weather is fair and settled, they are clothed in blue and purple, and print their bold outlines on the clear evening sky; but
10   sometimes, when the rest of the landscape is cloudless, they will gather a hood of gray vapors about their summits, which, in the last rays of the setting sun, will glow and light up like a crown of glory.

At the foot of these fairy mountains, the voyager may have descried the light smoke curling up from a Village, whose shingle roofs
15   gleam among the trees, just where the blue tints of the upland melt away into the fresh green of the nearer landscape. It is a little village of great antiquity, having been founded by some of the Dutch colonists, in the early times of the province, just about the beginning of the government of the good Peter Stuyvesant (may he rest in peace!), and there were
20   some of the houses of the original settlers standing within a few years, built of small yellow bricks, brought from Holland, having latticed windows and gable fronts, surmounted with weathercocks.

In that same village, and in one of these very houses (which, to tell the precise truth, was sadly time-worn and weather-beaten), there
25   lived, many years since, while the country was yet a province of Great Britain, a simple, good-natured fellow, of the name of Rip Van Winkle. He was a descendant of the Van Winkles who figured so gallantly in the chivalrous days of Peter Stuyvesant, and accompanied him to the

> Notice the spatial arrangement of this description. Irving begins with the mountains in general, shows us their peaks, then brings us to their feet, takes us into the village, and finally to one house in that village. This is a very cinematic opening, as though he were first shooting the scene with a wide lens and then focusing narrower and narrower.

siege of Fort Christina. He inherited, however, but little of the martial character of his ancestors. I have observed that he was a simple, good-natured man; he was, moreover, a kind neighbor, and an obedient henpecked husband. Indeed, to the latter circumstance might be owing that meekness of spirit which gained him such universal popularity; for those men are apt to be obsequious and conciliating abroad, who are under the discipline of shrews at home. Their tempers, doubtless, are rendered pliant and malleable in the fiery furnace of domestic tribulation, and a curtain-lecture is worth all the sermons in the world for teaching the virtues of patience and long-suffering. A termagant wife may, therefore, in some respects, be considered a tolerable blessing, and if so, Rip Van Winkle was thrice blessed.

Certain it is, that he was a great favorite among all the good wives of the village, who, as usual with the amiable sex, took his part in all family squabbles, and never failed, whenever they talked those matters over in their evening gossipings, to lay all the blame on Dame Van Winkle. The children of the village, too, would shout with joy whenever he approached. He assisted at their sports, made their playthings, taught them to fly kites and shoot marbles, and told them long stories of ghosts, witches, and Indians. Whenever he went dodging about the village, he was surrounded by a troop of them hanging on his skirts, clambering on his back, and playing a thousand tricks on him with impunity; and not a dog would bark at him throughout the neighborhood.

The great error in Rip's composition was an insuperable aversion to all kinds of profitable labor. It could not be for want of assiduity or perseverance; for he would sit on a wet rock, with a rod as long and heavy as a Tartar's lance, and fish all day without a murmur, even though he should not be encouraged by a single nibble. He would carry a fowling-piece on his shoulder, for hours together, trudging through woods and swamps, and up hill and down dale, to shoot a few squirrels or wild pigeons. He would never refuse to assist a neighbor even in the roughest toil, and was a foremost man in all country frolics for husking Indian corn, or building stone fences; the women of the village, too, used to employ him to run their errands, and to do such little odd jobs as their less obliging husbands would not do for them. In a word, Rip was ready to attend to anybody's business but his own; but as to doing family duty, and keeping his farm in order, he found it impossible.

In fact, he declared it was of no use to work on his farm; it was the most pestilent little piece of ground in the whole country; everything about it went wrong, in spite of him. His fences were continually falling to pieces; his cow would either go astray, or get among the cabbages; weeds were sure to grow quicker in his fields than anywhere else; the rain always made a point of setting in just as he had some out-door work to do; so that though his patrimonial estate had dwindled away under his management, acre by acre, until there was little more left than a mere patch of Indian corn and potatoes, yet it was the worst-conditioned farm in the neighborhood.

His children, too, were as ragged and wild as if they belonged to nobody. His son Rip, an urchin begotten in his own likeness, promised to inherit the habits, with the old clothes, of his father. He was generally seen trooping like a colt at his mother's heels, equipped in a pair of his

(31) What does it mean to be "a kind neighbor" or "a hen-pecked husband"? How does Irving illustrate those characteristics?

When you consider the details of this paragraph, what abstract quality in Rip's character do you come up with?

father's cast-off galligaskins, which he had much ado to hold up with one hand, as a fine lady does her train in bad weather.

Rip Van Winkle, however, was one of those happy mortals, of foolish, well-oiled dispositions, who take the world easy, eat white bread or brown, whichever can be got with least thought or trouble, and would rather starve on a penny than work for a pound. If left to himself, he would have whistled life away, in perfect contentment; but his wife kept continually dinning in his ears about his idleness, his carelessness, and the ruin he was bringing on his family. Morning, noon, and night, her tongue was incessantly going, and every thing he said or did was sure to produce a torrent of household eloquence. Rip had but one way of replying to all lectures of the kind, and that, by frequent use, had grown into a habit. He shrugged his shoulders, shook his head, cast up his eyes, but said nothing. This, however, always provoked a fresh volley from his wife, so that he was fain to draw off his forces, and take to the outside of the house—the only side which, in truth, belongs to a henpecked husband.

(82) How do you understand the word "happy" here? Is it as Jefferson used it, with a sense of good fortune? Is it as we use it today, suggesting gladness? Is it some combination of the two, indicating that the meaning of the word is in the process of change?

Commentary on the Reading

The language of Washington Irving's story deserves some comment. Students of the twenty-first century can find nineteenth-century language challenging in terms of vocabulary and sentence structure. It is a good idea to practice reading such material, however, because you are likely to encounter it on the AP test. In fact, you may find readings and essay prompts that use materials from as far back as the seventeenth century. The further back in time the readings go, the more carefully and slowly you will have to consider the diction and syntax. It would be a mistake to reject such readings just because they are difficult. Also, because you may encounter them on the AP test, you should have some practice with the language.

AP Exam Advice

Synthesis

From the amount of Washington Irving's story that you just read, you have a good idea about the kind of man Rip Van Winkle is. You developed that idea by combining individual details into a larger, overriding idea, probably most easily expressed as an abstraction. What you have done is actually a simple exercise in **synthesis.**

Synthesis is the third major skill tested in the essay portion of the AP examination. You have already seen many examples of the first two skills, analysis and argument. Synthesis might be understood as the opposite of analysis. When you analyze, you break something complex into its component parts and examine those parts individually to get a clearer understanding of the original entity. When you synthesize, you begin with the component parts and combine them into something greater than the original. In fact, you create something that has not been understood or seen before.

Building furniture might be seen as a synthesizing activity. You have certain raw materials—lumber, nails, screws, glue, knobs, drawer runners, and so on. You have tools with which to shape these materials—saws, planes, hammers, screwdrivers, clamps. You begin with all these component parts, but you end up with a bookcase or a table. In fact, different people starting with the same component parts might end up with very different pieces of furniture, depending on which parts they use and what they do with them.

It is the same when synthesizing ideas. You are presented with an array of information, and from all that is available, you choose what works best together. You combine the individual pieces into something that makes sense as a whole. Your final product will probably not resemble anyone else's, because you might have chosen differently, organized differently, or emphasized different details.

Think back to Rip's life and personality, and try a short synthesis essay according to the following instructions:

Focus on Writing: Synthesis
Washington Irving provides several details and illustrations to make the reader see what kind of person Rip Van Winkle is. Read the excerpt from the story and synthesize in writing a character description of Rip. Use only the information provided, and refer to specific language in the story when writing your essay.

Reading Selection by Cotton Mather

The following reading provides another opportunity for synthesis. It comes from the late seventeenth century and deals with a topic of current events—the witch trials at Salem Village, Massachusetts. It is a long reading, but you will find it manageable if you read it as a series of individual testimonies concerning Bridget Bishop's trial. The reader is intended, of course, to synthesize the information and arrive at the conclusion suggested by the author.

Focus on the Reading: Abstract and Concrete Language
Read slowly and carefully in order to study the author's diction and syntax, especially in writings from previous centuries.

Cotton Mather
Wonders of the Invisible World

The Tryal of Bridget Bishop, alias Oliver, At the Court of Oyer and Terminer Held at Salem, June 2, 1692.

I. She was Indicted for Bewitching of several persons in the Neighbourhood, the Indictment being drawn up, according to the Form in
5 such Cases usual. And pleading, Not Guilty, there were brought in several persons, who had long undergone many kinds of Miseries, which were preternaturally Inflicted, and generally ascribed unto an horrible Witchcraft. There was little Occasion to prove the Witchcraft, it being Evident and Notorious to all Beholders. Now to fix the Witchcraft on
10 the Prisoner at the Bar, the first thing used, was the Testimony of the Bewitched; whereof several Testify'd, That the Shape of the Prisoner did oftentimes very grievously pinch them, choak them, Bite them, and Afflict them; urging them to write their Names in a Book, which the

This seventeenth-century prose is challenging partly because its spelling and punctuation do not conform to the standards we are familiar with today. It probably requires an adjustment in your reading technique.

said Spectre called, Ours. One of them did further Testify, that it was
the Shape of this Prisoner, with another, which one Day took her from
her Wheel, and carrying her to the River side, threatned there to Drown
her, if she did not Sign to the Book mentioned: which yet she refused.

Others of them did also Testify, that the said Shape did in her
Threats brag to them that she had been the Death of sundry persons,
then by her Named; that she had Ridden a man then likewise Named.
Another Testify'd the Apparition of Ghosts unto the Spectre of Bishop,
crying out, You Murdered us! About the Truth whereof, there was in the
matter of Fact but too much Suspicion.

II.   It was Testify'd, That at the Examination of the Prisoner before
the Magistrates, the Bewitched were extreamly Tortured. If she did but
cast her Eyes on them, they were presently struck down; and this in
such a manner as there could be no Collusion in the Business. But upon
the Touch of her Hand upon them, when they lay in their Swoons, they
would immediately Revive; and not upon the Touch of any ones else.
Moreover, upon some Special Actions of her Body, as the shaking of
her Head, or the Turning of her Eyes, they presently and painfully fell
into the like postures. And many of the like Accidents now fell out,
while she was at the Bar. One at the same time testifying, That she said,
She could not be Troubled to see the Afflicted thus Tormented.

III.   There was Testimony likewise brought in, that a man striking once
at the place, where a Bewitched person said, the Shape of this Bishop
stood, the Bewitched cried out, that he had Tore her Coat, in the place
then particularly specify'd; and the Womans Coat was found to be Torn
in that very place.

IV.   One Deliverance Hobbs, who had Confessed her being a Witch,
was now Tormented by the Spectres, for her Confession. And she now
Testify'd, That this Bishop tempted her to Sign the Book again, and to
Deny what she had Confess'd. She affirmed, that it was the Shape of
this Prisoner, which whipped her with Iron Rods, to compel her there-
unto. And she affirmed, that this Bishop was at a General Meeting of the
Witches, in a Field at Salem-Village, and there partook of a Diabolical
Sacrament in Bread and Wine then Administred!

V.   To render it further Unquestionable, that the prisoner at the Bar
was the Person truly charged in *this* Witchcraft, there were produced
many Evidences of *other* Witchcrafts, by her perpetrated. For Instance,
John Cook testify'd, that about five or six years ago, One morning,
about Sun-Rise, he was in his Chamber assaulted by the Shape of this
prisoner: which Look'd on him, grin'd at him, and very much hurt him
with a Blow on the side of the Head: and that on the same day, about
Noon, the same Shape walked in the Room where he was, and an Apple
strangely flew out of his Hand, into the Lap of his Mother, six or eight
foot from him.

VI.   Samuel Gray testify'd, That about fourteen years ago, he wak'd
on a Night, and saw the Room where he lay full of Light; and that he
then saw plainly a Woman between the Cradle and the Bed-side, which
look'd upon him. He Rose, and it vanished; tho' he found the Doors all
fast. Looking out at the Entry-Door, he saw the same Woman, in the
same Garb again; and said, In Gods Name, what do you come for? He
went to Bed, and had the same Woman again assaulting him. The Child

Mather now provides a
succession of witnesses,
each of whom testifies to the
accused woman's guilt.

65 in the Cradle gave a great schreech, and the Woman Disappeared. It was long before the Child could be quieted; and tho' it were a very likely thriving Child, yet from this time it pined away, and after divers months dy'd in a sad Condition. He knew not Bishop, nor her Name; but when he saw her after this, he knew by her Countenance, and Apparrel, and 70 all Circumstances, that it was the Apparition of this Bishop which had thus troubled him.

VII.   John Bly and his Wife testify'd, that he bought a sow of Edward Bishop, the Husband of the prisoner; and was to pay the price agreed, unto another person. This Prisoner being Angry that she was thus hin-75 dred from fingring the money, Quarrell'd with Bly. Soon after which, the Sow was taken with strange Fits, Jumping, Leaping, and knocking her head against the Fence; she seem'd Blind and Deaf, and would nei-ther eat nor be suck'd. Whereupon a neighbour said, she believed the Creature was Over-Looked; and sundry other circumstances concurred, 80 which made the Deponents Belive that Bishop had Bewitched it.

VIII.   Richard Coman testify'd, that eight years ago, as he lay Awake in his Bed, with a Light Burning in the Room, he was annoy'd with the Apparition of this Bishop, and of two more that were strangers to him, who came and oppressed him so, that he could neither stir himself, nor 85 wake any one else, and that he was the night after molested again in the like manner; the said Bishop taking him by the Throat, and pulling him almost out of the Bed. His kinsman offered for this cause to lodge with him; and that Night, as they were Awake, Discoursing together, this Co-man was once more visited by the Guests which had formerly been so 90 troublesome; his kinsman being at the same time strook speechless and unable to move Hand or Foot. He had laid his sword by him, which these unhappy spectres did strive much to wrest from him; only he held too fast for them. He then grew able to call the People of his house; but altho' they heard him, yet they had not power to speak or stirr; until at last, one 95 of the people crying out, what's the matter? the spectres all vanished.

IX.   Samuel Shattock testify'd, That in the Year 1680, this Bridget Bishop often came to his house upon such frivolous and foolish er-rands, that they suspected she came indeed with a purpose of mischief. Presently whereupon his eldest child, which was of as promising Health 100 and Sense as any child of its Age, began to droop exceedingly; and the oftener that Bishop came to the House, the worse grew the Child. As the Child would be standing at the Door, he would be thrown and bruised against the Stones, by an Invisible Hand, and in like sort knock his Face against the sides of the House, and bruise it after a miserable manner. 105 Afterwards this Bishop would bring him things to Dy, whereof he could not Imagine any use; and when she paid him a piece of Money, the Purse and Money were unaccountably conveyed out of a Lock'd box, and never seen more. The Child was immediately hereupon taken with terrible fits, whereof his Friends thought he would have dyed: indeed he 110 did almost nothing but cry and Sleep for several Months together; and at length his understanding was utterly taken away. Among other Symp-toms of an Inchantment upon him, one was, that there was a Board in the Garden, whereon he would walk; and all the invitations in the world could never fetch him off. About Seventeen or Eighteen years after, 115 there came a Stranger to Shattocks House, who seeing the Child, said,

"This poor Child is Bewitched; and you have a Neighbour living not far off, who is a Witch." He added, "Your Neighbour has had a falling out with your Wife; and she said in her Heart, your Wife is a proud Woman, and she would bring down her Pride in this Child." He then Remembred, that Bishop had parted from his Wife in muttering and menacing Terms, a little before the Child was taken Ill. The abovesaid Stranger would needs carry the Bewitched Boy with him to Bishops House, on pretence of buying a pot of Cyder. The Woman Entertained him in furious manner; and flew also upon the Boy, scratching his Face till the Blood came; and saying, "Thou Rogue, what, dost thou bring this Fellow here to plague me?" Now it seems the Man had said, before he went, that he would fetch Blood of *her*. Ever after the Boy was follow'd with grievous Fits, which the Doctors themselves generally ascribed unto Witchcraft; and wherein he would be thrown still into the Fire or the Water, if he were not constantly look'd after; and it was verily believed that Bishop was the cause of it.

X.   John Louder testify'd, that upon some little controversy with Bishop about her fowles, going well to Bed, he did awake in the Night by moonlight, and did see clearly the likeness of this woman grievously oppressing him; in which miserable condition she held him, unable to help him self, till near Day. He told Bishop of this; but she deny'd it, and threatned him very much. Quickly after this, being at home on a Lords day, with the doors shutt about him, he saw a Black Pig approach him; at which he going to kick, it vanished away. Immediately after, sitting down, he saw a Black thing Jump in at the Window, and come and stand before him. The Body was like that of a Monkey, the Feet like a Cocks, but the Face much like a mans. He being so extreemly affrighted, that he could not speak, this Monster spoke to him, and said, "I am a Messenger sent unto you, for I understand that you are in some Trouble of Mind, and if you will be ruled by me, you shall want for nothing in this world." Whereupon he endeavoured to clap his hands upon it; but he could feel no substance, and it jumped out of the window again; but immediately came in by the Porch, though the Doors were shut, and said, "You had better take my Counsel!" He then struck at it with a stick, but struck only the Groundsel, and broke the Stick. The Arm with which he struck was presently Disenabled, and it vanished away. He presently went out at the Back-Door, and spyed this Bishop, in her Orchard, going toward her House; but he had not power to set one foot forward unto her. Whereupon returning into the House, he was immediately accosted by the Monster he had seen before; which Goblin was now going to Fly at him; whereat he cry'd out, "The whole Armour of God be between me and you!" So it sprang back, and flew over the Apple Tree, shaking many Apples off the Tree, in its flying over. At its Leap, it flung Dirt with its Feet against the Stomach of the Man; whereon he was then struck Dumb, and so continued for three Days together. Upon the producing of this Testimony, Bishop deny'd that she knew this Deponent: yet their two Orchards joined, and they had often had their Little Quarrels for some years together.

XI.   William Stacy Testifyed, That receiving Money of this Bishop, for work done by him, he was gone but a matter of Three Rods from her, and looking for his money, found it unaccountably gone from him.

Some time after, Bishop asked him, whether his Father would grind her grist for her? He demanded why? she Reply'd, "Because Folks count me a Witch." He answered, "No Question, but he will grind it for you." Being then gone about six Rods from her, with a small Load in his Cart, suddenly the Off-wheel slump't and sunk down into an Hole upon plain ground, so that the Deponent was forced to get help for the Recovering of the wheel. But stepping Back to look for the Hole which might give him this disaster, there was none at all to be found. Some time after, he was waked in the Night; but it seem'd as Light as Day, and he perfectly saw the shape of this Bishop in the Room, Troubling of him; but upon her going out, all was Dark again. He charg'd Bishop afterwards with it, and she deny'd it not; but was very angry. Quickly after, this Deponent having been threatned by Bishop, as he was in a dark Night going to the Barn, he was very suddenly taken or lifted from the ground, and thrown against a stone wall; After that, he was again hoisted up and thrown down a Bank, at the end of his House. After this again, passing by this Bishop, his Horse with a small load, striving to Draw, all his Gears flew to pieces, and the Cart fell down; and this deponent going then to lift a Bag of corn, of about two Bushels, could not budge it with all his might.

Many other pranks of this Bishops this Deponent was Ready to testify. He also testify'd, that he verily Believed, the said Bishop was the Instrument of his Daughter Priscilla's Death; of which suspicion, pregnant Reasons were assigned.

XII.   To Crown all, John Bly and William Bly Testify'd, That being Employ'd by Bridget Bishop, to help take down the Cellar-wall of the old House, wherein she formerly Lived, they did in Holes of the said old Wall find several Poppets, made up of Rags and Hogs Brussels, with Headless Pins in them, the Points being outward. Whereof she could give no Account unto the Court, that was Reasonable or Tolerable.

XIII.   One thing that made against the Prisoner was, her being evidently convicted of Gross Lying in the Court, several Times, while she was making her Plea. But besides this, a Jury of Women found a preternatural Teat upon her Body, but upon a second search, within Three or four hours, there was no such thing to be seen. There was also an account of other people whom this woman had afflicted. And there might have been many more, if they had been enquired for. But there was no need of them.

XIV.   There was one very strange thing more, with which the Court was newly Entertained. As this Woman was, under a Guard, passing by the Great and Spacious Meeting-House of Salem, she gave a Look towards the House. And immediately a Dæmon Invisibly Entring the Meeting-house, Tore down a part of it; so that tho' there were no person to be seen there, yet the people at the Noise running in, found a Board, which was strongly fastned with several Nails, transported unto another quarter of the House.

That's quite a bit of information, all of it intended to establish the community's judgment of Bridget Bishop. What do you conclude from the information given?

Focus on Writing: Synthesis

Consider the facts presented in the trial, and determine what conclusions can be drawn from them. You do not have to conclude that Bridget Bishop was a practicing witch. You might read all of this and arrive at some very different conclusion. Once you have thought the matter through, write an essay in which you synthesize your response from the sources provided in Cotton Mather's report. Explain your position, and support it with direct reference to the text.

How does the author's language create the atmosphere of the writing?

Introduction

The passage below—a short excerpt from a sermon that is said to have taken three hours to deliver—was written in 1741, approximately a half century after Cotton Mather's report on the trial of Bridget Bishop. It is perhaps the most famous piece of writing to emerge from a period of American history called the First Great Awakening. The author was a Calvinist minister in Connecticut, a man intent on restoring the previous generation's beliefs in the essential wickedness of humanity and the certainty of divine retribution.

Metaphor and Analogy

In it you will find examples of several different kinds of rhetorical devices, but what might strike you as most notable (aside from the intensity of the message) is the abundant use of comparative language. Jonathan Edwards employs metaphor and analogy very freely, and it is through this figurative language that he expects his listeners to understand the gravity of their moral situation.

Analogy, you will remember from Lesson 7, is the process by which a writer explains the unfamiliar by showing its similarity to something familiar. It is a particular kind of metaphor, which is the general term we use for all comparative language. Edwards's skillful use of analogy and metaphor here makes the setting, the specific date, and the location of its delivery almost irrelevant. We are likely to replace the concrete details of the sermon, which made it so effective in its time, with reference to our own times and beliefs. A modern reader has to decide whether the ideas Edwards expresses are universal and therefore still relevant to us in our time.

You will probably find this piece a little easier to follow than the Mather reading. For one thing, the spelling is modern and consistent. Another common feature of eighteenth-century writing is parallelism, a technique that makes it easy to see which ideas are meant to be grouped together, usually for comparison or for contrast. Again, it is important to have experience with literature from this period so that if you encounter it on the AP exam, you will not be at a disadvantage.

> **Focus on the Reading: Understanding How the Author Creates Atmosphere**
> See how parallelism helps the reader to group ideas together for comparison.

Jonathan Edwards
from *Sinners in the Hands of an Angry God*

Your wickedness makes you as it were heavy as lead, and to tend downwards with great weight and pressure towards hell; and if God should let you go, you would immediately sink and swiftly descend and plunge into the bottomless gulf, and your healthy constitution, and your own care and prudence, and best contrivance, and all your righteousness,

5

Notice how the argument proceeds from a clearly stated assumption, and the author develops it by means of several vivid illustrations.

would have no more influence to uphold you and keep you out of hell, than a spider's web would have to stop a falling rock. Were it not for the sovereign pleasure of God, the earth would not bear you one moment; for you are a burden to it; the creation groans with you; the creature is made subject to the bondage of your corruption, not willingly; the sun does not willingly shine upon you to give you light to serve sin and Satan; the earth does not willingly yield her increase to satisfy your lusts; nor is it willingly a stage for your wickedness to be acted upon; the air does not willingly serve you for breath to maintain the flame of life in your vitals, while you spend your life in the service of God's enemies. God's creatures are good, and were made for men to serve God with, and do not willingly subserve to any other purpose, and groan when they are abused to purposes so directly contrary to their nature and end. And the world would spew you out, were it not for the sovereign hand of him who hath subjected it in hope. There are black clouds of God's wrath now hanging directly over your heads, full of the dreadful storm, and big with thunder; and were it not for the restraining hand of God, it would immediately burst forth upon you. The sovereign pleasure of God, for the present, stays his rough wind; otherwise it would come with fury, and your destruction would come like a whirlwind, and you would be like the chaff of the summer threshing floor.

The wrath of God is like great waters that are dammed for the present; they increase more and more, and rise higher and higher, till an outlet is given; and the longer the stream is stopped, the more rapid and mighty is its course, when once it is let loose. It is true, that judgment against your evil works has not been executed hitherto; the floods of God's vengeance have been withheld; but your guilt in the mean time is constantly increasing, and you are every day treasuring up more wrath; the waters are constantly rising, and waxing more and more mighty; and there is nothing but the mere pleasure of God, that holds the waters back, that are unwilling to be stopped, and press hard to go forward. If God should only withdraw his hand from the flood-gate, it would immediately fly open, and the fiery floods of the fierceness and wrath of God, would rush forth with inconceivable fury, and would come upon you with omnipotent power; and if your strength were ten thousand times greater than it is, yea, ten thousand times greater than the strength of the stoutest, sturdiest devil in hell, it would be nothing to withstand or endure it.

The bow of God's wrath is bent, and the arrow made ready on the string, and justice bends the arrow at your heart, and strains the bow, and it is nothing but the mere pleasure of God, and that of an angry God, without any promise or obligation at all, that keeps the arrow one moment from being made drunk with your blood. Thus all you that never passed under a great change of heart, by the mighty power of the Spirit of God upon your souls; all you that were never born again, and made new creatures, and raised from being dead in sin, to a state of new, and before altogether unexperienced light and life, are in the hands of an angry God. However you may have reformed your life in many things, and may have had religious affections, and may keep up a form of religion in your families and closets, and in the house of God, it is nothing but his mere pleasure that keeps you from being this moment swallowed up in everlasting destruction. However uncon-

(27) Can you see what metaphor controls this paragraph? Do you find it effective with regard to the author's purpose?

(44) What metaphor is the author using now?

vinced you may now be of the truth of what you hear, by and by you will be fully convinced of it. Those that are gone from being in the like circumstances with you, see that it was so with them; for destruction came suddenly upon most of them; when they expected nothing of it, and while they were saying, Peace and safety: now they see, that those things on which they depended for peace and safety, were nothing but thin air and empty shadows.

The God that holds you over the pit of hell, much as one holds a spider, or some loathsome insect over the fire, abhors you, and is dreadfully provoked: his wrath towards you burns like fire; he looks upon you as worthy of nothing else, but to be cast into the fire; he is of purer eyes than to bear to have you in his sight; you are ten thousand times more abominable in his eyes, than the most hateful venomous serpent is in ours. You have offended him infinitely more than ever a stubborn rebel did his prince; and yet it is nothing but his hand that holds you from falling into the fire every moment. It is to be ascribed to nothing else, that you did not go to hell the last night; that you was suffered to awake again in this world, after you closed your eyes to sleep. And there is no other reason to be given, why you have not dropped into hell since you arose in the morning, but that God's hand has held you up. There is no other reason to be given why you have not gone to hell, since you have sat here in the house of God, provoking his pure eyes by your sinful wicked manner of attending his solemn worship. Yea, there is nothing else that is to be given as a reason why you do not this very moment drop down into hell.

O sinner! Consider the fearful danger you are in: it is a great furnace of wrath, a wide and bottomless pit, full of the fire of wrath, that you are held over in the hand of that God, whose wrath is provoked and incensed as much against you, as against many of the damned in hell. You hang by a slender thread, with the flames of divine wrath flashing about it, and ready every moment to singe it, and burn it asunder; and you have no interest in any Mediator, and nothing to lay hold of to save yourself, nothing to keep off the flames of wrath, nothing of your own, nothing that you ever have done, nothing that you can do, to induce God to spare you one moment.

Here is Edwards's most famous comparison. Consider the succession of metaphors that Edwards employed. Do you see climactic organization within this section of the sermon?

Focus on Writing: Analysis
Jonathan Edwards presents his listeners with an intense vision of their relationship with their God. Read this excerpt carefully, and then write an essay in which you analyze how Edwards uses rhetorical strategies to communicate his vision.

Reading Selection by Walt Whitman

Quite different is the quiet, contemplative portrait of Abraham Lincoln provided by Walt Whitman in his diary. The governing idea of this little passage is found almost exactly in the middle of the piece, as quiet and as unobtrusive as its subject. After you have read it, think about the contribution of the rest of the description, and then try your hand at synthesizing in the activity that follows.

Walt Whitman
Diary, 12 August 1863

August 12th.—I SEE the President almost every day, as I happen to live where he passes to or from his lodgings out of town. He never sleeps at the White House during the hot season, but has quarters at a healthy location some three miles north of the city, the Soldiers' home, a United States military establishment. I saw him this morning about 8 1/2 coming in to business, riding on Vermont avenue, near L street. He always has a company of twenty-five or thirty cavalry, with sabres drawn and held upright over their shoulders. They say this guard was against his personal wish, but he let his counselors have their way. The party makes no great show in uniform or horses. Mr. Lincoln on the saddle generally rides a good-sized, easy-going gray horse, is dress'd in plain black, somewhat rusty and dusty, wears a black stiff hat, and looks about as ordinary in attire, &c., as the commonest man. A lieutenant, with yellow straps, rides at his left, and following behind, two by two, come the cavalry men, in their yellow-striped jackets. They are generally going at a slow trot, as that is the pace set them by the one they wait upon. The sabres and accoutrements clank, and the entirely unornamental *cortège* as it trots towards Lafayette square arouses no sensation, only some curious stranger stops and gazes. I see very plainly ABRAHAM LINCOLN'S dark brown face, with the deep-cut lines, the eyes, always to me with a deep latent sadness in the expression. We have got so that we exchange bows, and very cordial ones. Sometimes the President goes and comes in an open barouche. The cavalry always accompany him, with drawn sabres. Often I notice as he goes out evenings—and sometimes in the morning, when he returns early—he turns off and halts at the large and handsome residence of the Secretary of War, on K street, and holds conference there. If in his barouche, I can see from my window he does not alight, but sits in his vehicle, and Mr. Stanton comes out to attend him. Sometimes one of his sons, a boy of ten or twelve, accompanies him, riding at his right on a pony. Earlier in the summer I occasionally saw the President and his wife, toward the latter part of the afternoon, out in a barouche, on a pleasure ride through the city. Mrs. Lincoln was dress'd in complete black, with a long crape veil. The equipage is of the plainest kind, only two horses, and they nothing extra. They pass'd me once very close, and I saw the President in the face fully, as they were moving slowly, and his look, though abstracted, happen'd to be directed steadily in my eye. He bow'd and smiled, but far beneath his smile I noticed well the expression I have alluded to. None of the artists or pictures has caught the deep, though subtle and indirect expression of this man's face. There is something else there. One of the great portrait painters of two or three centuries ago is needed.

It is very difficult for us to imagine Abraham Lincoln without thinking of the assassination and the figure depicted in the Lincoln Memorial. Yet for this reading, which describes Lincoln while he was alive, you should try to clear your mind of all later associations and try to see him as the author did.

Focus on Writing

Whitman's purpose is to communicate the deep feeling he sees in Lincoln's face, but he spends a great deal of time describing the larger picture of the neighborhood in which he sees the president, the carriage the president rides in, the officers who accompany the president, and the president's wife. All of these form a backdrop to the central image of the president's face.

For this writing task, spend some time observing the people with whom you come into contact on a fairly regular basis. Concentrate on one whom you do not know personally very well—a student at your school, or a teacher; someone you see at your after-school job; someone who waits for a bus where you do; a neighbor whom you do not know well; a clerk at a store where you shop. Write a description, as Whitman did, of the times when you see that person, and what you believe that person's appearance—face, posture, demeanor—tells about his or her true self. Respect the person's privacy and do not write anything that your subject would be embarrassed or angry to read. The purpose of this exercise is for you to notice details and to use them to arrive at an insight about the person.

Guidance on Your Writing

The writing task above is neither an analysis, an argument, nor a synthesis, and therefore you will not find a question like it on the AP exam. However, the skill of observing and reporting that it requires is one that you will need when you do write your examination essays. In its most basic sense, it is a synthesizing skill. You are taking information gathered at different times and putting it together in support of an overall conclusion. You use this skill when analyzing as well, when you notice the general features of a writer's style or the individual characteristics of a subject. Of course, when you argue, you need to support your arguments with whatever information you have collected from a variety of sources. So even though a task such as this will not appear per se on the AP test, you will employ this skill in all the essay questions.

AP Exam Advice

How does the author appeal to the reader's feelings and sense of character?

Introduction

In the field of rhetoric, it was the Greek writer and philosopher Aristotle who made one of the most enduring observations about the relationship between the writer and the reader. In *The Art of Rhetoric*, Aristotle speaks of three "appeals" the writer or speaker may make in order to persuade the audience to agree. These three appeals are typically called by their Greek names: *logos, pathos,* and *ethos.* They are the appeals to logic, emotion, and character.

So far our concern has been largely with logos, or logic. We have focused on the content of the readings and the essays you are writing in response to them. In this lesson, we will look at pathos and ethos. Pathos, the appeal to emotion, is a very powerful force in good writing. Some people have great skill in pulling on our heartstrings and getting what they want. As a reader, you must be aware of when a writer is playing on your emotions. As a writer, you must develop the skill to use this technique to your advantage. Emotional appeals can be contrived or sincere.

Pathos

The greatest impact of the speech below, given by **Chief Joseph** of the Nez Perce tribe in 1877, is emotional. The facts—that many of the chiefs are dead and that the Nez Perce people are freezing and starving—are presented as an emotional acknowledgment of defeat rather than as logical reasons for ending the struggle with the United States Army.

> Tell General Howard I know his heart. What he told me before, I have it in my heart. I am tired of fighting. Our Chiefs are killed; Looking Glass is dead, Ta Hool Hool Shute is dead. The old men are all dead. It is the young men who say yes or no. He who led on the young men is dead. It is cold, and we have no blankets; the little children are freezing to death. My people, some of them, have run away to the hills, and have no blankets, no food. No one knows where they are—perhaps freezing to death. I want to have time to look for my children, and see how many of them I can find. Maybe I shall find them among the dead. Hear me, my Chiefs! I am tired; my heart is sick and sad. From where the sun now stands I will fight no more forever.

Commentary on the Reading

The appeal to emotion is a very powerful one, but also important is ethos, the appeal to character or credibility. Sometimes a writer has a good argument backed up by solid information but comes across as someone the reader just cannot trust. Perhaps the writer's language is inappropriate, the credentials are questionable, the motives may seem too self-serving, the writer is arrogant or disrespectful—there are many ways a writer can lose the reader's trust. When you write, you must be careful not to alienate the reader, and when you read, you should be aware of the author's character as a significant component of the entire experience.

Ethos

To observe how a writer creates a positive persona, we can turn back to the father's letter to Click and Clack, which you read in Lesson 11. Here is the letter again:

> Am I a jerk or a genius? When my son was 15, I wrote him a check for $1,500, postdated three years. I told him that if he managed to reach the date of the check without (1) receiving any tickets, (2) being involved in any accidents or (3) breaking any of our house driving rules, I'd cash the check for him. My goal was to provide an incentive for him to play by the rules long enough to form some good driving habits. Anyway, my son very nearly made it. A few months shy of his 18th birthday, he was cruising along the highway, singing. And he suddenly realized that the light show accompanying his karaoke act was being provided by the flashing lights on top of a cruiser. He fessed up about the ticket promptly, and was bemoaning the fine of $126. I gently reminded him that the ticket had actually cost him $1,626, as he had failed to fulfill our bargain. My question: Am I a genius for coming up with the carrot that made him a good driver during his crucial first years behind the wheel, or am I a jerk for piling on a $1,500 fine? Please note that his younger sister is watching carefully to see how this is resolved. She's 14, and whether I fold on this will go a long way in setting her expectations. My son took the news well, but I have friends who are treating me as though I smashed the kid's piggy bank and took his inheritance.—Ted

Commentary on the Reading

This father indicates from the very beginning that his reason for challenging his son was "to provide an incentive for him to play by the rules long enough to form some good driving habits," which is certainly a worthy goal. Even though he dealt with his son "gently," however, he wonders if he wasn't too harsh. He doesn't rejoice in his son's loss (and his own monetary gain); rather, he feels bad for his son, whom he portrays as a good kid who "took the news well." His feelings of doubt speak well for him. He does not fall back on his position of power, but continues to seek the best behavior—perhaps motivated by an awareness that he has a daughter to deal with as well, but even here we get a sense that he is trying to treat his children equally and fairly. In several ways this writer has demonstrated that he is a man of good character. We would probably react differently if we saw him gloating over his son's misfortune instead of reacting with fatherly affection. He has established a very positive ethos.

Ethos and Trust

People sometimes have reputations and already-established characters that we recognize even before we read what they have written. If you were to read an essay on homelessness and charity written by Mother Teresa, you would probably accept that her experiences make her a trustworthy expert on the subject.

Some publications have a reputation for honest and accurate reporting. Even though some people detect bias in a national newspaper like *The New York Times*, it has a reputation for accuracy that the tabloids cannot claim.

Ethos eventually comes down to a matter of credibility and trust. It is probably true that readers want to trust the writers they are reading, but a good writer knows that the trust must be earned. In the pieces that follow, you will observe how the writers establish themselves as people the readers ought to trust on their subjects.

Reading Selection by Marc Gellman

This next reading gives you an opportunity to see both pathos and ethos at work. As you read, observe how the author establishes himself as trustworthy, and be alert when he is counting on you to react more emotionally than logically.

Rabbi Marc Gellman originally published this letter in *Newsweek*.

Focus on the Reading: Pathos and Ethos
You must be aware of when a writer is playing on your emotions.

Marc Gellman
The Death of Miles

March 15, 2006—*A letter to Dr. Alan Coren, chief veterinarian of West Hills Animal Hospital, Huntington, N.Y., who is my friend and who was the veterinarian for my dog Miles who just died....*

Dear Alan,

5   I could not write to you until now to thank you properly and personally for your compassion and care for Miles through his life and up to his last moments, when Miles died on the blanket you had spread out for us in room No. 2. Miles's debilitating renal failure was a death sentence, and thankfully his suffering is now over. As Miles turned cold in
10 my arms and entered a breathless eternal sleep, I was utterly unprepared for the flood of tears and grief I felt at his death. Now I can only begin to sort out my feelings and the first feeling I need to express is a deep thankfulness for your care and love.

   You have cared for all the guide dogs we have raised up from pup-
15 piehood to faithful service. One of them, Topper, who flunked out of Guide Dog School because he was an inveterate cat chaser, now pads around the house looking for his pal. I still find myself instinctively moving my feet under my desk expecting to slip them under Miles's head. Topper is some consolation, but Miles was less like a dog and
20 more like a person in a dog suit. As you know, Miles came to us from my son Max, whose move to New York City could not accommodate Miles's need to chase rabbits and FedEx delivery guys.

   I bury people, and I know that grief at the death of a pet is not the same as grief at the death of a person, but it is still grief. It is still deep
25 and raw and shattering to our admittedly irrational expectations that we will never be separated from those we love. I tell people I counsel through their grief to try to give thanks for the pain they feel, because the pain is a measure of their love. Buddhists teach that the first Noble Truth is that suffering *(dukkah)* arises from our attachments to the
30 beings of the world. Unlike Buddhists, I do not seek the removal of

(15) What is the effect of expressions like "puppiehood" and "flunked out"? What relationship between the writer and his dogs do these words create?

(28) The rabbi, a Jewish clergyman, is referring to Buddhist teachings. How does that affect his ethos?

attachment *(tanhakaya)*. I am happy to be a mess of tears now because I was, and my family was, loved by Miles unconditionally, and I savor this grief as the way the gift of unconditional love is painfully but properly repaid.

35   I also understand the bewilderment and impatience of those who have never loved an animal. Many of them openly or privately harbor condescending thoughts about pet lovers who often seem to them so willing to lavish love and attention on animals that they cannot seem to summon up for the souls for other human beings. My message to them
40 is, "Shut up! Get a pet. Then you will understand."

    I attended a rally to stop the killing in Darfur yesterday, and I was moved and deeply saddened and angered by the inability of the so-called civilized world to stop yet another genocide in the Sudan (and also in the Congo). However, I admit that I could not cry for the dead of Darfur
45 the way I cried for Miles. At first I was embarrassed and ashamed at the constrictions of my grief for human beings, and the lavishness of my grief for a dog. Then I slowly came to understand that the reason for the difference was the distance and the invisibility of Darfur compared with the immediate and devastating absence of Miles's head on my feet.
50 I remember what Aleksandr Solzhenitsyn wrote, "What seems to us more important, more painful, and more unendurable is really not what is more important, more painful and more unendurable, but merely that which is closer to home. Everything distant which for all its moans and muffled cries, its ruined lives and millions of victims, that does not
55 threaten to come rolling up to our threshold today, we consider endurable and of tolerable dimensions."

    So I hope that the cries from Sudan and Congo are not just distant but present and compelling, but I cannot and will not feel embarrassed at feeling bereft because of the death of my dog. I know. I know that
60 they are not on the same moral level, but I remain convinced that the ability to cry for one tutors the tears for the other.

    Alan, I know that you help families move through the grief of the death of a pet as often as I help families move through the grief of the death of a person. I know they need my steady soul to make it through
65 the valley of the shadow. I just wanted you to know how much I needed you and how much I love you and thank you. You were a rabbi to a rabbi, and you were the steady soul of caring for a very good dog whom I loved more than I ever understood until this sad but healing moment.

God bless you,
Marc

(50) Aleksandr Solzhenitsyn was a Nobel Prize-winning Russian novelist who often wrote about life under oppressed conditions.

(66) "Rabbi" actually means "my teacher," so here the writer is saying "you were a teacher to a teacher."

Focus on Writing: Analysis
Marc Gellman expresses himself emotionally when speaking of his dog's death. Read the letter carefully, and then write an essay in which you analyze how the emotional appeals of Gellman's letter helped him achieve his purposes.

Reading Selections by Eugene Robinson, Jeff Jacoby, and E. J. Dionne, Jr.

The following three readings address a broad topic, free speech, from three perspectives. The problem, of course, comes when one person's freedom of expression infringes upon another person's rights.

As you read, note how the three authors handle all of Aristotle's appeals—

- the logos, or the logical content;
- the pathos, or the emotional material; and
- the ethos, or the credibility and trustworthiness of the speaker.

Focus on the Reading: Logos, Pathos, and Ethos
Pay close attention to this author's handling of logical content, emotional material, and credibility or trustworthiness of the speaker.

Eugene Robinson
When Life Makes You Cry Uncle

I am Bus Uncle, potentially, and so are you. Each of us has a tiny, raging Bus Uncle buried deep within, just waiting to burst free. One tap on the shoulder is all it takes.

For knowledgeable habitues of the Internet, this is old news. But for weeks "Bus Uncle" has been a must-see attraction on YouTube.com, one of the Web sites where users can post their homemade short videos. "Bus Uncle" is cinéma vérité, captured surreptitiously with a cellphone camera, and it consists wholly of a six-minute encounter between two passengers who shared a bus in Hong Kong on the evening of April 29.

Here's the back story: A middle-aged man has been barking into his cellphone loudly enough to disturb the young man sitting directly behind him. The young man has just tapped the older man on the shoulder to ask him to lower his voice, and the older man has turned to lean over the back of his seat and confront the young guy. That's the point at which the grainy video begins. The young man uses a Cantonese word that can mean "uncle" to address his elder, hence the video's title.

Bus Uncle goes off.

For five minutes and 59 seconds, Bus Uncle rants, rages, berates, upbraids, taunts, curses and threatens. "Why did you pat on my shoulder?" he demands. "Why should you do that? Hey, everybody has pressure. Did I touch you?"

(By now there are dozens of versions of the video on various Web sites, with subtitles in English; some translations have the young man calling his tormentor "boss," but all are titled "Bus Uncle.") The young man quickly decides forbearance is the way to play this scene, but his patience does him no good. When Bus Uncle demands he apologize, the

(7) Cinéma vérité, which means "cinema of truth," often employs techniques of confrontation.

(17) Young Chinese people often address older men as "uncle." It is a term of respect.

young man says, "Sorry." But Bus Uncle is unmollified: "Why? I didn't disturb you, am I correct?"

The younger guy apologizes again, shakes hands, does everything he can think of to get Bus Uncle to chill, but to no avail. The older man's harangue becomes more and more profane, escalating into "yo' mama" territory. Throughout, Bus Uncle keeps circling back to two main themes—"This is not solved!" and "I face pressure. You face pressure. Why do you provoke me?" According to the South China Morning Post, both have become catchphrases in Hong Kong, where "Bus Uncle" became an immediate sensation.

Like all great films, this one has a perfect conclusion. Just when you start to think there's no way the encounter can end without an actual fight, Bus Uncle's cellphone rings. "Damn," he mutters, as he abruptly turns away to answer it.

Soon after the video was posted, reporters tracked down the two stars: Elvis Ho, a 23-year-old real estate agent, and, in the title role, 51-year-old Chan Yuet-tung, also known as Roger Chan, a gadfly who ran for the office of Hong Kong chief executive three times despite lacking a discernible political constituency. Chan is now basking in his new celebrity. Ho just wishes the whole "Bus Uncle" thing would go away.

And of course it will. Internet sensations have a brief shelf life, and "Bus Uncle" doesn't stand up to repeated viewings. It does make a couple of extremely valuable observations about modern urban life, though.

For one thing, Bus Uncle speaks an unassailable truth: "I face pressure. You face pressure." We all face pressures at work and at home. We all have deadlines to meet and bills to pay. We handle our pressures because that's what being an adult is largely about, managing pressures so they don't end up managing us. But we all have those days, don't we, when it feels like a losing battle.

And then all it takes is an innocent tap on the shoulder at just the wrong moment. I'm not talking about "intermittent explosive disorder," which is the clinical term that encompasses road rage. That's an actual condition that can be treated with therapy and medication. I'm talking about that rare instant when someone inadvertently touches your very last nerve, and Bus Uncle escapes his restraints.

The other lesson from "Bus Uncle" is taught by its very existence. A student sitting across the aisle happened to see the confrontation and decided to record it with the camera in his cellphone, which was able to take still pictures or video. It's amazing that in nanoseconds, a slice of Hong Kong life can be experienced in Washington, Johannesburg or Moscow.

The ubiquity of feature-packed mobile phones and stationary security cameras means that everybody's always potentially on Candid Camera. So don't forget to smile.

Focus on the Reading: Logos, Pathos, and Ethos
Observe how the author establishes himself as trustworthy, and be alert when he is counting on you to react more emotionally than logically.

Jeff Jacoby
Freedom of Hate Speech

FUNNY PEOPLE, the Austrians. If you're Kurt Waldheim—a former Nazi military officer linked to a genocidal massacre during World War II—they elect you president. But if you're David Irving—a British author who claimed that there never was a Nazi genocide during World War II—they throw you in the slammer.

On second thought, not funny at all. Austria disgraced itself when it elected Waldheim president in 1986, apparently unconcerned by the revelation that he had served in a German military unit responsible for mass murder in the Balkans and been listed after the war as a wanted criminal by the UN War Crimes Commission. In a very different way it disgraced itself again last week, when a Vienna court sentenced Irving, a racist and an anti-Semite, to three years in prison for denying that the Nazis annihilated 6 million European Jews.

Irving is a man of great intellectual gifts who devoted his life to a grotesque and evil project: rehabilitating the reputation of Hitler and the Third Reich. Necessarily, that meant denying the Holocaust and ridiculing those who suffered in it, and Irving has long done so with relish. "I don't see any reason to be tasteful about Auschwitz. It's baloney, it's a legend," he told a Canadian audience in September 1991. "There are so many Auschwitz survivors going around—in fact the number increases as the years go past, which is biologically very odd to say the least— I'm going to form an association of Auschwitz Survivors, Survivors of the Holocaust, and Other Liars, or A-S-S-H-O-L-S."

Presumably Irving had in mind people like my father, whose arm bears to this day the number A-10502, tattooed there in blue ink on May 28, 1944, the day he and his family were transported to Auschwitz. My father's parents, David and Leah Jakubovic, and his youngest brother and sister, Alice, 8, and Yrvin, 10, were not tattooed; Jews deemed too old or too young to work were sent immediately to the gas chambers. His teenage siblings, Zoltan and Franceska, were tattooed and, like him, put to work as slave laborers. Zoltan was killed within days; Franceska lasted a few months longer. Of the seven members of the Jakubovic family sent to Auschwitz in the spring of 1944, only my father was alive in the spring of 1945.

So on a personal level, the prospect of David Irving spending his next three years in a prison cell is something over which I will lose no sleep. He is a repugnant, hate-filled liar, who even as a child was enamored of the Nazis and had a pronounced cruel streak.

But as a matter of law and public policy, Irving's sentence is deplorable. The opinions he expressed are vile, and his arguments about the Holocaust are ludicrous. But governments have no business criminalizing opinions and arguments, not even those that are vile or ludicrous. To be sure, freedom of speech is not absolute; laws against libel, death threats, and falsely shouting fire in a crowded theater are both reasonable and necessary. But free societies do not throw people in prison for giving offensive speeches or spouting historical lies.

How does the author's separating his family's experience from Irving's affect your assessment of his character?

Austria, the nation that produced Hitler and cheered the Anschluss, may well believe that its poisoned history requires a strong antidote. Punishing anyone who "denies, grossly trivializes, approves, or seeks to justify" the Holocaust or other Nazi crimes may seem a small price to pay to keep would-be totalitarians and hatemongers at bay. But a government that can make the expression of Holocaust denial a crime today can make the expression of other offensive opinions a crime tomorrow.

Americans, for whom the First Amendment is a birthright, should understand this instinctively. "If there is any principle of the Constitution that more imperatively calls for attachment than any other it is the principle of free thought," wrote Supreme Court Justice Oliver Wendell Holmes, Jr., in 1928. "Not free thought for those who agree with us, but freedom for the thought that we hate."

It is popular in some circles to argue that the United States should do certain things—adopt single-payer health insurance, abolish capital punishment, etc.—to conform to the practice in other democracies. Those who find that a persuasive argument might consider that Irving is behind bars today because Austria doesn't have a First Amendment. Neither do Belgium, Canada, the Czech Republic, France, Germany, Israel, Lithuania, Poland, Romania, Slovakia, or Switzerland—all of which have made Holocaust denial a crime.

"Freedom for the thought we hate" is never an easy sell, but without it there can be no true liberty. David Irving is a scurrilous creep, but he doesn't belong in prison. Austria should let him go free—not for his sake, but for Austria's.

> Do Jacoby's arguments satisfy you? Would you agree if the topic were racist speech?

Focus on the Reading: Logos, Pathos, and Ethos
Note how the author handles the logical content, the emotional material, and the credibility and trustworthiness of the speaker.

E. J. Dionne, Jr.
Divisive in Any Language

Yes, let's talk about the English language and how important it is that immigrants and their children learn it.

And please permit me to be personal about an issue that is equally personal to the tens of millions of Americans who remember their immigrant roots.

My late father was born in the United States, and grew up in French Canadian neighborhoods in and around New Bedford, Mass. When he started school, he spoke English with a heavy accent. A first-grade teacher mercilessly made fun of his command of the language.

My dad would have none of this and proceeded to relearn English, with some help from a generous friend named James Radcliffe who, in turn, asked my dad to teach him French. My dad came to speak flaw-

> (10) How is your opinion of the writer affected by his choice of "my dad" instead of "my father," "my mom" instead of "my mother," and "our nation" instead of "America"?

less, accent-free English. He and my mom insisted that their children speak our nation's language clearly, and without grammatical errors.

None of this caused my parents to turn against their French heritage. On the contrary, my sister and I were taught French before we were taught English because my parents took pride in the language of our forebears and knew that speaking more than one language would be a useful skill.

My mom would give free French lessons at our Catholic parochial school to any kid who wanted to take them. When we were young, we'd visit our cousins on a farm in Quebec during the summer, partly to improve our French. (And Parisian French elitists take note: I still love the much-derided accent of the Quebec countryside, which many have compared to the English of the Tennessee mountains.) I tell you all this by way of explaining why I can't stand the demagoguery directed against immigrants who speak languages other than English. Raging against them shows little understanding of how new immigrants struggle to become loyal Americans who love their country—and come to love the English language.

As it considered the immigration bill last week, the Senate passed an utterly useless amendment sponsored by Sen. James Inhofe (R-Okla.) declaring English to be our "national language" and calling for a government role in "preserving and enhancing" the place of English.

There is no point to this amendment except to say to members of our currently large Spanish-speaking population that they will be legally and formally disrespected in a way that earlier generations of immigrants from—this is just a partial list—Germany, Italy, Poland, Russia, Norway, Sweden, France, Hungary, Greece, China, Japan, Finland, Lithuania, Lebanon, Syria, Bohemia, Slovakia, Serbia, Croatia and Slovenia were not.

Immigrants from all these places honored their origins, built an ethnic press and usually worshiped in the languages of their ancestors. But they also learned English because they knew that advancement in our country required them to do so.

True, we now have English-as-a-Second-Language programs that have created some resentments and, in the eyes of their critics, can slow the transition from Spanish to English. Still, the evidence is overwhelming that Spanish speakers and their kids are as aware as anyone of the importance of learning English. That's why we have an attorney general named Gonzales, senators named Salazar, Martinez and Menendez, and a mayor of Los Angeles named Villaraigosa.

Ken Salazar, a Colorado Democrat, introduced an alternative amendment to Inhofe's that also passed the Senate. It declared English the "common and unifying language of the United States" while also insisting on the existing rights of non-English speakers "to services or materials provided by the government" in languages other than English. As Salazar understands, the best way to make English our unifying language is to avoid making language a divisive national issue.

I make my living writing and speaking in English, and I would preach to anyone the joys of mastering this Anglo-Saxon gift to our nation. My wife and I encourage our kids to speak the language with precision and to show respect for its grammar, as did the nuns who taught

To what extent are the author's comments aimed at logic? Emotion? Character?

me as a kid—even if some of them spoke French better than English. Politicians who care about the language might usefully think about how it can be taught well, to the native-born as well as to immigrants.

When I put my children to bed, I recite the same prayer that my late mother said for my sister and me. The prayer is in French. I certainly hope that it doesn't make my children any less American to hear a few spiritual thoughts in a language other than English before they fall asleep.

Focus on Writing: Synthesis

Read the three essays above, and then synthesize from them a position on the limits of free speech. Then, with specific and direct reference to at least two of the three readings, write an essay that supports, challenges, or modifies the statement: "Entirely free speech is no longer in the national interest." Cite your sources by referring in parentheses to the author's name—Robinson, Jacoby, or Dionne.

Guidance on Your Writing

Be careful, when you write a synthesis essay, not to fall into a common trap. Many students unfamiliar with the process of synthesis write essays that are really summaries of the sources they think they are synthesizing. A synthesis combines information from its sources into a new presentation. It is not merely a summary of the material the writer has chosen to use. To achieve the effect of synthesis, you probably want to blend information from the three sources into each paragraph of the body of your own essay. If each paragraph in your essay treats a source separately, you are probably writing a summary instead of a synthesis.

AP Exam Advice

What questions should the reader ask in order to analyze the author's style?

Introduction

Because every analytical free-response question on the AP English Language test asks you to explore what the author did and how the author did it, you should ask yourself those questions as you read. Even when the passage is essentially persuasive rather than expository, you still need to know what the author intended to accomplish. Once you have determined this, noting how the authors have accomplished their goals will enable you to write meaningful responses. The two passages that follow are narrative rather than argumentative, and they lend themselves well to analysis.

The first is an excerpt from *The Samurai's Garden*, a novel by an American author, Gail Tsukiyama. The story, set in the early years of World War II, is narrated by Stephen, a young Chinese man recovering from tuberculosis. He is recovering in the small Japanese village where his family has a summer home and where Matsu, his family's caretaker, still lives. On the day that this scene takes place, Matsu has announced that he is going to visit a friend in Yamaguchi, a neighboring village, and wonders if Stephen would like to accompany him. Stephen accepts the invitation gladly.

Focus on the Reading: Observing Style
Ask yourself what the author did and how the author did it.

Gail Tsukiyama
The Samurai's Garden

Yamaguchi was a small village in the mountains, Matsu said. He often visited to deliver supplies to a friend. We walked the two miles or so up a narrow, rocky, brush-lined dirt road. Ahead of us I could see the hilly slopes and large pine trees, which could easily cover up any signs of life.

5 "Yamaguchi is also called the Village of Lepers," Matsu said, as we walked slowly up the road. "When some of those who had the disease were no longer wanted by the others in town, they took what few belongings they had and went up into the mountains, hoping to die 10 peacefully. Away from the cruelties of the healthy."

"Aren't you afraid to go there?" I asked hesitantly.

Matsu walked straight ahead. I thought he wasn't going to answer, when he suddenly looked right at me and said, "The first time I went, I wasn't sure what to expect. After all, lepers from all over Japan found 15 their way to Yamaguchi, simply hoping to be accepted, to be swallowed up by the mountain." Matsu looked down at the path again and then walked on. "I began to visit a friend there—someone from my youth.

No one knew. I was young and healthy. And I remember being told long ago by a visiting doctor that there was nothing to fear. Leprosy wasn't a disease that could be spread by simple contact."

When Matsu's voice stopped, I realized he was several steps ahead of me and had turned to wait for me to catch up. I felt a shortness of breath as I drew in more air and let out several long sighs. "I'm fine," I said, increasing my pace and moving past Matsu up the hill.

"Maybe we should visit another day," Matsu said, raising his voice to make sure I heard.

I stopped and turned back to him. "I'm really fine!" I said, with such conviction that Matsu caught up, then continued up the path alongside of me.

The village of Yamaguchi stood in a clearing on the gradual slope of the mountain, hidden away by tall pine trees. Small wooden houses sat in a cluster like any other village. I stopped at the outskirts and let my eyes wander over the tranquil sight. From the distance, the villagers appeared just like Matsu and me. Men were gathered in small groups sipping tea and talking, while others worked in small gardens, and women sat mending clothes. Only with closer scrutiny did I begin to see that the houses were painstakingly pieced together with mismatched scraps of wood. And while some villagers had their heads and hands bandaged, others freely displayed their raw scabs and open wounds. I felt a strange curiosity, rather than fear. In China, lepers had always been feared and shunned. I had heard stories of how they were forced to live on the streets, left to beg or eat rats, while they simply rotted away.

I stood a long time taking it all in. When I finally came out of my trance, Matsu was studying my face with an unusual intensity. He continued to watch me and finally said, "You don't have to be afraid. I wouldn't have brought you here if there were any danger."

I smiled at his concern. "I'm afraid for them," I said, quick to cover my cough.

Matsu laughed, then pointed toward the far end of the village. "My friend's house is that way," he said.

We walked slowly through the village. There was a distinct smell of eucalyptus and something else medicinal. For the first time in my life I saw what it meant to be a leper, a disgraced one. They seemed to watch me with just as much curiosity. I tried not to stare, but I couldn't take my eyes off their wounds; the missing fingers and toes, the large, gaping holes in the sides of their faces, the mangled features that had once been noses and ears. It looked as they were all wearing monstrous masks that I kept waiting for them to remove.

Matsu must have understood my thoughts. He suddenly stopped, turned to me, and said, "Most of them came to this village as young men and women. Now they are too old and set in their ways to move. Even though the Japanese government has acknowledged their situation and would gladly move them to better facilities. Good or bad, Yamaguchi has been their home."

I watched as Matsu then nodded and exchanged pleasantries with several of the villagers.

From some doorways I could also smell the strong, sweet aroma of tea which filled me and my parched throat with longing.

Stephen's description of the houses mirrors the condition of the people he sees.

"Who is the handsome young man, Matsu?" one man asked, taking a few steps closer. His right arm was a gnarled raw stump which looked like it had been eaten away.

"The son of my *Danasama,* my master," Matsu answered, walking on without a pause.

I smiled at all of them self-consciously, then followed Matsu as if he were the master.

We walked to the far end of the village, where there were few houses and the pine trees thickened. Matsu slowed down as we approached a small, sturdier-looking house almost hidden among the trees.

"Who lives here?" I asked, catching my breath.

"A friend," Matsu answered. As he led me toward the house, I noticed how his steps lightened, his body relaxed, and he seemed almost young again.

I stood behind Matsu as he tapped three times on the door and waited, blowing air through his teeth to create a small whistling sound. I'd never seen Matsu so exuberant and was curious to see who lived there. Within moments the door opened just enough for a head, veiled in black, to peek out.

"Sachi-*san,* it's me," Matsu said, gently.

The woman stepped back and opened the door wider, allowing the sunlight to brighten the clean, spare, white room behind her. She looked away from Matsu toward me and held her place behind the door. "Matsu?" she said softly, watching me closely.

Matsu glanced back at me, then said, "This is Stephen-*san,* he's a friend."

"*Konnichiwa,*" I said, smiling and bowing, trying to put her at ease.

The woman stepped back and bowed humbly. Matsu entered the small house, and with a slight wave of his hand urged me to follow. I did, anxious to know more about the timid woman who lived within it. The room smelled of pine branches which sat in a vase on a low table in one corner. Next to the vase were two small, shiny black stones. Other than the table and a few cushions neatly stacked to the side, the room was bare.

"I didn't know you would come today, Matsu," the woman said, keeping her head bowed so low I couldn't see her face under the black scarf. Her voice was soft and hesitant.

"It was a nice day to take a walk. Anyway, since when do I need an invitation to visit you, Sachi?" Matsu said, teasingly.

Sachi laughed, looking down and away from Matsu.

"I will bring some tea," she then said shyly. She adjusted the black scarf so that it covered her face as she turned to leave the room.

Commentary on the Reading

You might have different responses to different features of this passage, but you should be able to identify what causes you to feel as you do. Consider the following questions.

Are you responding to the voice of the narrator? What do you know about him as a person? What do his actions tell you about him? How do the other characters in the scene respond to him, and how do their reactions help shape your impression of him?

Are you reacting to the setting—first the path up the mountain, then the village, and finally Sachi's house? Do you visualize yourself in any of those places?

Are you imagining yourself in the company of Matsu or Sachi and thinking of how you might react to them?

What details of the surroundings seem important to you? Do you sense that the pine branches in the vase have any significance, or the two black stones on Sachi's table?

What is the overall atmosphere of the village, and what in the narration communicates that feeling to you?

These questions do not exhaust the possibilities, but they can get you started on an overall analysis of the piece. You can try responding to these or to other questions that you devise yourself, that your teacher provides, or that your classmates pose. Once you have determined what you think the author has achieved in this piece, you should be able to identify what features of the writing led you to that conclusion.

Focus on Writing: Analysis
Read the excerpt from *The Samurai's Garden* carefully. Then, in a well-developed essay, show how the author used various techniques of language to create the overall effect of the passage. Do not merely summarize the plot.

You can adapt the same questions to apply to whatever passage you are asked to analyze. Basically, you are sorting out several features of the writing for individual consideration. Remember that analysis is the process of separating a complex item into its component parts and examining them separately for greater understanding. The essay you write should consider those separate parts and put them back together into an explanation of the whole.

Reading Selection by Clarence Day, Jr.

The passage that follows—a short excerpt from *God and My Father* by Clarence Day, Jr.—requires some analysis, but it's actually more likely to lead to an argumentative essay. Clarence Day, Sr., was a wealthy New Yorker of the mid–nineteenth century, and the book from which this excerpt comes is his son's reminiscence of the senior Day's eccentric character.

Focus on the Reading: Observing Style
Try to separate complex ideas into their component parts for close examination and greater understanding.

Clarence Day, Jr.
God and My Father

My father's ideas of religion seemed straightforward and simple. He had noticed when he was a boy that there were buildings called churches; he had accepted them as a natural part of the surroundings in which he had been born. He would never have invented such things himself. Nevertheless they were here. As he grew up he regarded them as unquestioningly as he did banks. They were substantial old structures; they were respectable, decent, and venerable. They were frequented by the right sort of people. Well, that was enough.

On the other hand he never allowed churches—or banks—to dictate to him. He gave each the respect that was due to it from his point of view; but he also expected from each of them the respect he felt due to him.

As to creeds, he knew nothing about them, and cared nothing either; yet he seemed to know which sect he belonged with. It had to be a sect with the minimum of nonsense about it; no total immersion, no exhorters, no holy confession. He would have been a Unitarian, naturally, if he'd lived in Boston. Since he was a respectable New Yorker, he belonged in the Episcopal Church.

As to living a spiritual life, he never tackled that problem. Some men who accept spiritual beliefs try to live up to them daily; other men who reject such beliefs, try sometimes to smash them. My father would have disagreed with both kinds entirely. He took a more distant attitude. It disgusted him where atheists attacked religion: he thought they were vulgar. But he also objected to having religion make demands upon him—he felt that religion was too vulgar, when it tried to stir up men's feelings. It had its own proper field of activity, and it was all right there, of course; but there was one place religion should leave alone, and that was a man's soul. He especially loathed any talk of walking hand in hand with his Savior. And if he had ever found the Holy Ghost trying to soften his heart, he would have regarded its behavior as distinctly uncalled for; even ungentlemanly.

How does the syntax contribute to your sense of the father's character?

Commentary on the Reading

It is likely that this short description of Clarence Day, Sr., has provoked a response in you. You might feel that you have quite a bit to say about the kind of man he was. That is fine. However, in academic or professional discourse, you must explain *why* you have the reaction you have. That reaction might be related to your own religious leanings. It might be influenced by your relationship with one of your parents or some other important adult in your life. You may have had conversations on the subject of religion with your friends or class discussions that considered religion and personal belief. Whatever the reason for your reaction, you must work with the material in the passage to analyze it. What has the author told us about his father's attitude and behavior? Do not ignore what the author has said and substitute your own beliefs or opinions for what the passage itself tells you.

What questions can you ask yourself, like the ones that accompany *The Samurai's Garden*, to help you consider the various elements of this description? You might tackle this problem on your own or consult with a friend. To write a good analysis of this passage, you might first make a list of questions to ask and component parts to examine (for example, the father's opinion of churches, his assessments of various religious groups, his view of himself).

This passage will probably elicit a response that's more argumentative than analytical. In other words, when you finish reading it, you will basically tend to agree with Mr. Day, Sr., disagree with him, or feel something in between. Of course, you will not be able to write an effective argument if you don't first understand the content of the original. Thus, you will have to do some analysis before you can argue—but the goal of this writing exercise is to identify the man's opinion and to take a stand on it.

Focus on Writing: Argumentation
Read Clarence Day, Jr.'s account of his father's attitude toward organized religion. Then write a well-developed essay in which you show what the father's position is and explain whether you would defend, challenge, or qualify his beliefs. Do not summarize the passage.

Lesson 18 What is the author's purpose?

Introduction

When we speak of a writer's purpose, we are usually considering one or more of five general possibilities. The purpose can be to **inform,** to **entertain,** to **persuade,** to **inspire,** and to **motivate.** The purpose is intimately associated with the audience. In some situations, the audience will require a good deal of information about a particular subject. In others, because the audience and the speaker share the same opinions, there may be little need for persuasion but a lot of opportunity for motivation. The events or situation that occasioned the writing will also determine the purpose. In some situations, humor is welcome, but in others it is out of place. Some occasions suggest the need for inspiration, while others call for persuasion.

You will see that few pieces of writing can sustain a single purpose throughout. In order to persuade, it is often necessary to provide some information. A reader often retains information better if it is presented in an entertaining way. Motivation almost requires persuasion; in fact, the difference between the two is mostly a matter of result. When you are motivated, you change your course of action. When you are persuaded, you change your way of thinking.

The Crisis, which we read in Lesson 2, is a good example of writing intended principally to motivate. "I Have a Dream," which you read in Lesson 8, is commonly seen as highly inspirational. "How the Other Half Lives," in Lesson 12, is mostly informational, but that information is intended to cause a change in people's thinking about their charitable and social actions.

A review of a few more of the pieces you have already read will show you that you have been exposed to the various purposes of writing all along. What do you think is the main purpose of each of these readings?

> Upton Sinclair, *The Jungle* (Lesson 5)
>
> Benjamin Franklin, *Autobiography* (Lesson 7)
>
> John F. Kennedy, Inaugural Address (Lesson 8)
>
> William Bradford, *Of Plimouth Plantation* (Lesson 11)
>
> Washington Irving, "Rip Van Winkle" (Lesson 14)
>
> Jonathan Edwards, "Sinners in the Hands of an Angry God" (Lesson 15)
>
> Marc Gellman, "The Death of Miles" (Lesson 16)
>
> Jeff Jacoby, "Freedom of Hate Speech" (Lesson 16)

Once you have determined the main purpose of a piece of writing, consider how the writer achieves that purpose. Ask yourself the following: What decisions about the use of language did the writer make?

If the writing is meant to be informational, what choices did the writer make about diction and syntax? If there are a lot of unfamiliar words or complicated sentence structures, the reader might either stop reading altogether or have difficulty understanding and retaining the content.

If the purpose is to entertain, how did the writer try to amuse us? Is there laugh-out-loud humor? Would that have been appropriate? Does the humor take the form of pleasant personal associations rather than outright jokes?

If we are being persuaded, has the writer used logic or emotion, or some combination of the two? Are the arguments effective or weak? If the writer is seeking to rouse you to action, what will it take to get you to do what the writer wants?

These are questions not only for the reader but also, and perhaps more significantly, for the writer. When you have a writing task, it is important that you understand why you are writing. Much of your academic writing has been either informational or persuasive. You must sufficiently inform your reader, usually your teacher, about a topic to prove that you know what you are talking about. In other words, you must prove that you have learned the material. This might also be an act of persuasion if you are hoping to win over a skeptical teacher. How are you going to prove that you are not uninformed on the topic, but actually quite well informed?

The reading that follows comes from a satiric publication and, as such, seeks to entertain. Note that satire also leans in the direction of motivation, because in pointing out human weakness, it hopes to change people's behavior. As you read this article, think about what purposes the writer had in mind and observe the means used to achieve them.

Focus on the Reading: Determining the Author's Purpose
Once you have determined the main purpose of this selection, consider how the writer achieves that purpose.

The Onion

Child in Corner to Exact Revenge As Soon As He Gets Out

Repeat Offender Serving Seven-to-10-Minute Sentence

SEATTLE—Daniel Barriault is serving a time-out for a crime the 5-year-old claims he didn't commit. Charged with possession of three Oreo cookies only a half-hour before supper and sentenced to a bare 8-by-12-inch bedroom corner for eight minutes, Barriault has had just one thing on his mind while waiting for his release. One thing and three people.

"Just a little while longer now," said Barriault, who slowly counted down his corner term to 20 before becoming confused and having to start all over again. "I've learned my lesson, but what they don't realize is that their lesson has not even yet begun."

After four failed getaway attempts into the basement, Barriault was apprehended early Monday evening by household penal authorities Mommy and Daddy, likely operating on an anonymous tip from the "queen of all snitches," Barriault's older sister, Ashley, 7.

"I may have been innocent when they put me in here, but I'm sure as heck not innocent now," said Barriault, who has served time-outs for a wide range of offenses over the years, including public misconduct, second-degree assault of a sibling, and vandalism misdemeanors when only 17 months old. "They took eight minutes of my life away, eight minutes of playtime I'll never get back, eight minutes of cartoons I'll never get the chance to experience—and for that, they will pay."

Monday's capture of the young repeat offender was followed by a lengthy and disorderly trial, in which Barriault, who chose to represent himself, deliberately disrupted the proceedings by screaming and running around in circles until he had to be forcibly detained. Barriault alleges that he was then escorted with unnecessary force to his bedroom, made to empty out his pockets of three Yu-Gi-Oh! trading cards before being "worked over good by Mom" and receiving his sentence.

It remains unclear whether Barriault was ever offered a deal for apologizing for his behavior.

"In this corner, you have plenty of time to think," said Barriault, who claimed to have "tons of friends on the outside," including Jimmy, Josh, and Nana and Papa. "I know exactly what I'm going to do when my time is up. Who I'm going to visit. Plans? Yeah, you could say I've got some plans."

According to Barriault, being in the corner "is unlike anything else in the world." It can break the spirit of even the toughest of 5-year-olds, crush their confidence, and reduce them to nothing more than a "stupid little baby."

"This place, it can make a preschooler forget who they are, why it is they don't like to share their Matchbox cars with other kids, what exactly about the taste of cauliflower makes it so yucky," added Barriault, who admitted that he can no longer remember what the touch of a good crayon feels like. "I wouldn't wish this place on my worst enemies. No. I've got something entirely different in store for them."

Fidgeting either in anticipation of his release or from a growing urge to use the bathroom, Barriault told reporters Monday that despite not even being in the first grade, he never forgets a face.

"I've done my time. I've been a good little boy who's seen the error of his ways," said Barriault with a smile. "And as soon as I get out, I'll make things right. I'll make sure everything gets made right. Cross my heart and hope to die."

"Stick a needle in my eye," he added.

What elements of the writer's craft are creating your response to Daniel and his plight?

Focus on Writing: Analysis
Read "Child in Corner to Exact Revenge as Soon as He Gets Out," and determine what you see as either the primary purpose of the piece or the combination of purposes the author was after. Then, in a well-developed essay, explain how the author used various resources of language to achieve that purpose or combination of purposes. Do not summarize the article, and be sure that your essay provides specific reference to the original text for support.

Reading Selection by Alice Walker

The principles concerning author's purpose apply to fiction as much as to nonfiction. You have no doubt read novels, stories, poems, and plays that have been inspirational, entertaining, and informative. *The Jungle,* from which you read an excerpt in Lesson 5, was written to expose intolerable working conditions in the meatpacking industry and was influential in leading to the passage of the Pure Food and Drug Act of 1906. That book is not especially entertaining, but it is certainly informative and proved to be motivational as well.

Alice Walker's short story "Everyday Use" will provide a certain amount of entertainment, but as you read it, be receptive to the other purposes Walker may have had in mind when she wrote it.

Focus on the Reading: Determining the Author's Purpose
Be receptive to other purposes the author may have had in mind.

Alice Walker
Everyday Use

I will wait for her in the yard that Maggie and I made so clean and wavy yesterday afternoon. A yard like this is more comfortable than most people know. It is not just a yard. It is like an extended living room. When the hard clay is swept clean as a floor and the fine sand around the edges lined with tiny, irregular grooves, anyone can come and sit and look up into the elm tree and wait for the breezes that never come inside the house.

Maggie will be nervous until after her sister goes: she will stand hopelessly in corners, homely and ashamed of the burn scars down her arms and legs, eying her sister with a mixture of envy and awe. She thinks her sister has held life always in the palm of one hand, that "no" is a word the world never learned to say to her.

You've no doubt seen those TV shows where the child who has "made it" is confronted, as a surprise, by her own mother and father, tottering in weakly from backstage. (A pleasant surprise, of course: What would they do if parent and child came on the show only to curse out and insult each other?) On TV mother and child embrace and smile into each other's faces. Sometimes the mother and father weep, the child wraps them in her arms and leans across the table to tell how she would not have made it without their help. I have seen these programs.

Sometimes I dream a dream in which Dee and I are suddenly brought together on a TV program of this sort. Out of a dark and soft-seated limousine I am ushered into a bright room filled with many people. There I meet a smiling, gray, sporty man like Johnny Carson who shakes my hand and tells me what a fine girl I have. Then we are on the stage and Dee is embracing me with tears in her eyes. She pins on my dress a large orchid, even though she has told me once that she thinks orchids are tacky flowers.

(24) Johnny Carson was a very successful late-night talk show host.

In real life I am a large, big-boned woman with rough, man-working hands. In the winter I wear flannel nightgowns to bed and overalls during the day. I can kill and clean a hog as mercilessly as a man. My fat keeps me hot in zero weather. I can work outside all day, breaking ice to get water for washing; I can eat pork liver cooked over the open fire minutes after it comes steaming from the hog. One winter I knocked a bull calf straight in the brain between the eyes with a sledge hammer and had the meat hung up to chill before nightfall. But of course all this does not show on television. I am the way my daughter would want me to be: a hundred pounds lighter, my skin like an uncooked barley pancake. My hair glistens in the hot bright lights. Johnny Carson has much to do to keep up with my quick and witty tongue.

But that is a mistake. I know even before I wake up. Who ever knew a Johnson with a quick tongue? Who can even imagine me looking a strange white man in the eye? It seems to me I have talked to them always with one foot raised in flight, with my head fumed in whichever way is farthest from them. Dee, though. She would always look anyone in the eye. Hesitation was no part of her nature.

"How do I look, Mama?" Maggie says, showing just enough of her thin body enveloped in pink skirt and red blouse for me to know she's there, almost hidden by the door.

"Come out into the yard," I say.

Have you ever seen a lame animal, perhaps a dog run over by some careless person rich enough to own a car, sidle up to someone who is ignorant enough to be kind to him? That is the way my Maggie walks. She has been like this, chin on chest, eyes on ground, feet in shuffle, ever since the fire that burned the other house to the ground.

Dee is lighter than Maggie, with nicer hair and a fuller figure. She's a woman now, though sometimes I forget. How long ago was it that the other house burned? Ten, twelve years? Sometimes I can still hear the flames and feel Maggie's arms sticking to me, her hair smoking and her dress falling off her in little black papery flakes. Her eyes seemed stretched open, blazed open by the flames reflected in them. And Dee. I see her standing off under the sweet gum tree she used to dig gum out of; a look of concentration on her face as she watched the last dingy gray board of the house fall in toward the red-hot brick chimney. Why don't you do a dance around the ashes? I'd wanted to ask her. She had hated the house that much.

I used to think she hated Maggie, too. But that was before we raised money, the church and me, to send her to Augusta to school. She used to read to us without pity; forcing words, lies, other folks' habits, whole lives upon us two, sitting trapped and ignorant underneath her voice. She washed us in a river of make-believe, burned us with a lot of knowledge we didn't necessarily need to know. Pressed us to her with the serious way she read, to shove us away at just the moment, like dimwits, we seemed about to understand.

Dee wanted nice things. A yellow organdy dress to wear to her graduation from high school; black pumps to match a green suit she'd made from an old suit somebody gave me. She was determined to stare down any disaster in her efforts. Her eyelids would not flicker for minutes at a time. Often I fought off the temptation to shake her. At sixteen she had a style of her own: and knew what style was.

I never had an education myself. After second grade the school was closed down. Don't ask my why: in 1927 colored asked fewer questions than they do now. Sometimes Maggie reads to me. She stumbles along good-naturedly but can't see well. She knows she is not bright. Like good looks and money, quickness passes her by. She will marry John Thomas (who has mossy teeth in an earnest face) and then I'll be free to sit here and I guess just sing church songs to myself. Although I never was a good singer. Never could carry a tune. I was always better at a man's job. I used to love to milk till I was hooked in the side in '49. Cows are soothing and slow and don't bother you, unless you try to milk them the wrong way.

I have deliberately turned my back on the house. It is three rooms, just like the one that burned, except the roof is tin; they don't make shingle roofs any more. There are no real windows, just some holes cut in the sides, like the portholes in a ship, but not round and not square, with rawhide holding the shutters up on the outside. This house is in a pasture, too, like the other one. No doubt when Dee sees it she will want to tear it down. She wrote me once that no matter where we "choose" to live, she will manage to come see us. But she will never bring her friends. Maggie and I thought about this and Maggie asked me, "Mama, when did Dee ever have any friends?"

She had a few. Furtive boys in pink shirts hanging about on washday after school. Nervous girls who never laughed. Impressed with her they worshiped the well-turned phrase, the cute shape, the scalding humor that erupted like bubbles in lye. She read to them.

When she was courting Jimmy T she didn't have much time to pay to us, but turned all her faultfinding power on him. He flew to marry a cheap city girl from a family of ignorant flashy people. She hardly had time to recompose herself.

When she comes I will meet—but there they are!

Maggie attempts to make a dash for the house, in her shuffling way, but I stay her with my hand. "Come back here," I say. And she stops and tries to dig a well in the sand with her toe.

It is hard to see them clearly through the strong sun. But even the first glimpse of leg out of the car tells me it is Dee. Her feet were always neat-looking, as if God himself had shaped them with a certain style. From the other side of the car comes a short, stocky man. Hair is all over his head a foot long and hanging from his chin like a kinky mule tail. I hear Maggie suck in her breath. "Uhnnnh," is what it sounds like. Like when you see the wriggling end of a snake just in front of your foot on the road. "Uhnnnh."

Dee next. A dress down to the ground, in this hot weather. A dress so loud it hurts my eyes. There are yellows and oranges enough to throw back the light of the sun. I feel my whole face warming from the heat waves it throws out. Earrings gold, too, and hanging down to her shoulders. Bracelets dangling and making noises when she moves her arm up to shake the folds of the dress out of her armpits. The dress is loose and flows, and as she walks closer, I like it. I hear Maggie go "Uhnnnh" again. It is her sister's hair. It stands straight up like the wool on a sheep. It is black as night and around the edges are two long pigtails that rope about like small lizards disappearing behind her ears.

"Wa-su-zo. Tean-o!" she says, coming on in that gliding way the dress makes her move. The short stocky fellow with the hair to his navel is all grinning and he follows up with "Asalamalakim, my mother and sister!" He moves to hug Maggie but she falls back, right up against the back of my chair. I feel her trembling there and when I look up I see the perspiration falling off her chin.

"Don't get up," says Dee. Since I am stout it takes something of a push. You can see me trying to move a second or two before I make it. She turns, showing white heels through her sandals, and goes back to the car. Out she peeks next with a Polaroid. She stoops down quickly and lines up picture after picture of me sitting there in front of the house with Maggie cowering behind me. She never takes a shot without making sure the house is included. When a cow comes nibbling around the edge of the yard she snaps it and me and Maggie and the house. Then she puts the Polaroid in the back seat of the car, and comes up and kisses me on the forehead.

Meanwhile Asalamalakim is going through motions with Maggie's hand. Maggie's hand is as limp as a fish, and probably as cold, despite the sweat, and she keeps trying to pull it back. It looks like Asalamalakim wants to shake hands but wants to do it fancy. Or maybe he don't know how people shake hands. Anyhow, he soon gives up on Maggie.

"Well," I say. "Dee."

"No, Mama," she says. "Not 'Dee,' Wangero Leewanika Kemanjo!"

"What happened to 'Dee'?" I wanted to know.

"She's dead," Wangero said. "I couldn't bear it any longer, being named after the people who oppress me."

"You know as well as me you was named after your aunt Dicie," I said. Dicie is my sister. She named Dee. We called her "Big Dee" after Dee was born.

"But who was she named after?" asked Wangero.

"I guess after Grandma Dee," I said.

"And who was she named after?" asked Wangero.

"Her mother," I said, and saw Wangero was getting tired. "That's about as far back as I can trace it," I said. Though, in fact, I probably could have carried it back beyond the Civil War through the branches.

"Well," said Asalamalakim, "there you are."

"Uhnnnh," I heard Maggie say.

"There I was not," I said, "before 'Dicie' cropped up in our family, so why should I try to trace it that far back?"

He just stood there grinning, looking down on me like somebody inspecting a Model A car. Every once in a while he and Wangero sent eye signals over my head.

"How do you pronounce this name?" I asked.

"You don't have to call me by it if you don't want to," said Wangero.

"Why shouldn't I?" I asked. "If that's what you want us to call you, we'll call you."

"I know it might sound awkward at first," said Wangero.

"I'll get used to it," I said. "Ream it out again."

Well, soon we got the name out of the way. Asalamalakim had a name twice as long and three times as hard. After I tripped over it two or

(134) *Salaam aleikum* is Arabic for "peace unto thee," a greeting often used by Muslims.

three times he told me to just call him Hakim-a-barber. I wanted to ask him was he a barber, but I didn't really think he was, so I didn't ask.

"You must belong to those beef-cattle peoples down the road," I said. They said "Asalamalakim" when they met you, too, but they didn't shake hands. Always too busy: feeding the cattle, fixing the fences, putting up salt-lick shelters, throwing down hay. When the white folks poisoned some of the herd the men stayed up all night with rifles in their hands. I walked a mile and a half just to see the sight.

Hakim-a-barber said, "I accept some of their doctrines, but farming and raising cattle is not my style." (They didn't tell me, and I didn't ask, whether Wangero (Dee) had really gone and married him.)

We sat down to eat and right away he said he didn't eat collards and pork was unclean. Wangero, though, went on through the chitlins and corn bread, the greens and everything else. She talked a blue streak over the sweet potatoes. Everything delighted her. Even the fact that we still used the benches her daddy made for the table when we couldn't afford to buy chairs.

"Oh, Mama!" she cried. Then turned to Hakim-a-barber. "I never knew how lovely these benches are. You can feel the rump prints," she said, running her hands underneath her and along the bench. Then she gave a sigh and her hand closed over Grandma Dee's butter dish. "That's it!" she said. "I knew there was something I wanted to ask you if I could have." She jumped up from the table and went over in the corner where the churn stood, the milk in it clabber by now. She looked at the churn and looked at it.

"This churn top is what I need," she said. "Didn't Uncle Buddy whittle it out of a tree you all used to have?"

"Yes," I said.

"Un huh," she said happily. "And I want the dasher, too."

"Uncle Buddy whittle that, too?" asked the barber.

Dee (Wangero) looked up at me.

"Aunt Dee's first husband whittled the dash," said Maggie so low you almost couldn't hear her. "His name was Henry, but they called him Stash."

"Maggie's brain is like an elephant's," Wangero said, laughing. "I can use the chute top as a centerpiece for the alcove table," she said, sliding a plate over the chute, "and I'll think of something artistic to do with the dasher."

When she finished wrapping the dasher the handle stuck out. I took it for a moment in my hands. You didn't even have to look close to see where hands pushing the dasher up and down to make butter had left a kind of sink in the wood. In fact, there were a lot of small sinks; you could see where thumbs and fingers had sunk into the wood. It was beautiful light yellow wood, from a tree that grew in the yard where Big Dee and Stash had lived.

After dinner Dee (Wangero) went to the trunk at the foot of my bed and started rifling through it. Maggie hung back in the kitchen over the dishpan. Out came Wangero with two quilts. They had been pieced by Grandma Dee and then Big Dee and me had hung them on the quilt frames on the front porch and quilted them. One was in the Lone Star pattern. The other was Walk Around the Mountain. In both of them were

(206) "Clabber" is milk that has soured and curdled.

scraps of dresses Grandma Dee had worn fifty and more years ago. Bits and pieces of Grandpa Jattell's Paisley shirts. And one teeny faded blue piece, about the size of a penny matchbox, that was from Great Grandpa Ezra's uniform that he wore in the Civil War.

"Mama," Wangero said sweet as a bird. "Can I have these old quilts?"

I heard something fall in the kitchen, and a minute later the kitchen door slammed.

"Why don't you take one or two of the others?" I asked. "These old things was just done by me and Big Dee from some tops your grandma pieced before she died."

"No," said Wangero. "I don't want those. They are stitched around the borders by machine."

"That'll make them last better," I said.

"That's not the point," said Wangero. "These are all pieces of dresses Grandma used to wear. She did all this stitching by hand. Imagine!" She held the quilts securely in her arms, stroking them.

"Some of the pieces, like those lavender ones, come from old clothes her mother handed down to her," I said, moving up to touch the quilts. Dee (Wangero) moved back just enough so that I couldn't reach the quilts. They already belonged to her.

"Imagine!" she breathed again, clutching them closely to her bosom.

"The truth is," I said, "I promised to give them quilts to Maggie, for when she marries John Thomas."

She gasped like a bee had stung her.

"Maggie can't appreciate these quilts!" she said. "She'd probably be backward enough to put them to everyday use."

"I reckon she would," I said. "God knows I been saving 'em for long enough with nobody using 'em. I hope she will!" I didn't want to bring up how I had offered Dee (Wangero) a quilt when she went away to college. Then she had told they were old-fashioned, out of style.

"But they're priceless!" she was saying now, furiously; for she has a temper. "Maggie would put them on the bed and in five years they'd be in rags. Less than that!"

"She can always make some more," I said. "Maggie knows how to quilt."

Dee (Wangero) looked at me with hatred. "You just will not understand. The point is these quilts, these quilts!"

"Well," I said, stumped. "What would you do with them?"

"Hang them," she said. As if that was the only thing you could do with quilts.

Maggie by now was standing in the door. I could almost hear the sound her feet made as they scraped over each other.

"She can have them, Mama," she said, like somebody used to never winning anything, or having anything reserved for her. "I can 'member Grandma Dee without the quilts."

I looked at her hard. She had filled her bottom lip with checkerberry snuff and gave her face a kind of dopey, hangdog look. It was Grandma Dee and Big Dee who taught her how to quilt herself. She stood there with her scarred hands hidden in the folds of her skirt. She

285 looked at her sister with something like fear but she wasn't mad at her. This was Maggie's portion. This was the way she knew God to work.

When I looked at her like that something hit me in the top of my head and ran down to the soles of my feet. Just like when I'm in church and the spirit of God touches me and I get happy and shout. I did some-

290 thing I never done before: hugged Maggie to me, then dragged her on into the room, snatched the quilts out of Miss Wangero's hands and dumped them into Maggie's lap. Maggie just sat there on my bed with her mouth open.

"Take one or two of the others," I said to Dee.

295 But she turned without a word and went out to Hakim-a-barber.

"You just don't understand," she said, as Maggie and I came out to the car.

"What don't I understand?" I wanted to know.

"Your heritage," she said, And then she turned to Maggie, kissed

300 her, and said, "You ought to try to make something of yourself, too, Maggie. It's really a new day for us. But from the way you and Mama still live you'd never know it."

She put on some sunglasses that hid everything above the tip of her nose and chin.

305 Maggie smiled; maybe at the sunglasses. But a real smile, not scared. After we watched the car dust settle I asked Maggie to bring me a dip of snuff. And then the two of us sat there just enjoying, until it was time to go in the house and go to bed.

Focus on Writing: Analysis

At the climax of the story Mama, Dee (Wangero), and Maggie have to make a decision about two old quilts. Understanding what attitude each one takes toward these quilts will help you clarify your sense of the story's purpose. Write an essay in which you consider how each of these characters feels about the quilts and what, ultimately, the author is seeking to accomplish by telling us the story of Mama, her daughters, and these quilts. Support your opinion with references to the story and to the author's use of language. Consider such elements as diction, syntax, figurative language, rhetorical devices, and tone.

Lesson 19 What is the character of the speaker?

Introduction

Lesson 16 introduced the idea of Aristotle's three appeals, *logos*, *pathos*, and *ethos*. Here we will concentrate on the ethos, or the character, of the speaker. Fiction presents us with characters to evaluate. It is easy to forget that nonfiction also presents a persona to the reader, and the character of that persona is a key element in the reader's experience with the writing.

When a nonfiction piece is written in the first person, we usually assume the persona to be the author. The decisions the author makes regarding tone, diction, subject matter, choice of illustrations, figurative language, irony, rhetorical devices, statement of purpose—in short, all the elements you have been studying in your Advanced Placement English Language course—contribute to your sense of who stands behind the words on the page.

In this lesson, you will read three first-person statements by three people from different periods of history and in very different circumstances. The logos, or content, of each piece should be almost self-explanatory. The pathos, or the emotional appeal, will vary from piece to piece. The ethos may require a little more work. In each case, you will recognize it after careful reading and thinking about what you have read.

The first of these pieces is a letter written by John Winthrop, a Puritan settler and colonial governor in seventeenth-century Massachusetts. He is about to leave England for America, and he writes to his wife just before the boat leaves Southampton harbor.

> **Focus on the Reading: Character of the Speaker**
> Consider the character of the writer's persona as you read each of the next three texts.

John Winthrop
A Letter to His Wife

From aboard the *Arbella*, riding at the Cowes, March 28, 1630

My Faithful and Dear Wife,

    It pleaseth God, that thou shouldst once again hear from me before our departure, and I hope this shall come safe to thy hands. I know it
5   will be a great refreshing to thee. And blessed be his mercy, that I can write thee so good news, that we are all in very good health, and, having tried our ship's entertainment now more than a week, we find it agree very well with us. Our boys are well and cheerful, and have no mind of home. They lie both with me, and sleep as soundly in a rug (for we use

no sheets here) as ever they did at Groton; and so I do myself (I praise God). The wind hath been against us this week and more; but this day it has come fair to the north, so as we are preparing (by God's assistance) to set sail in the morning. We have only four ships ready, and some two or three Hollanders go along with us. The rest of our fleet (being seven ships) will not be ready this sennight. We have spent now two Sabbaths on shipboard very comfortably, (God be praised), and are daily more and more encouraged to look for the Lord's presence to go along with us. Henry Kingbury hat a child or two in the Talbot sick of the measles, but like to do well. One of my men had them at Hampton, but he was soon well again. We are, in all our eleven ships, about seven hundred persons, passengers, and two hundred and forty cows, and about sixty horses. The ship, which went from Plimouth, carried about one hundred and forty persons, and the ship, which goes from Bristowe, carrieth about eighty persons. And now (my sweet soul) I must once again take my last farewell of thee in Old England. It goeth very near to my heart to leave thee; but I know to whom I have committed thee, even to him who loves thee much better than any husband can, who hath taken account of the hairs of thy head, and puts all thy tears in his bottle; who can, and (if it be for his glory) will bring us together again with peace and comfort. Oh, how it refresheth my heart, to think, that I shall yet again see thy sweet face in the land of the living!—that lovely countenance that I have so much delighted in and beheld with so great content! I have hitherto been so taken up with business, as I could seldom look back to my former happiness, but now when I shall be at some leisure, I shall not avoid the remembrance of thee, nor the grief for thy absence. Thou hast thy share with me, but I hope the course we have agreed upon will be some ease to us both. Mondays and Fridays, at five of the clock at night, we shall meet in spirit till we meet in person. Yet if all these hopes should fail, blessed be our God, that we are assured we shall meet one day, if not as husband and wife, yet in a better condition. Let that stay and comfort thy heart. Neither can the sea drown thy husband, nor enemies destroy, nor any adversary deprive thee of thy husband or children. Therefore I will only take thee now and my sweet children in mine arms, and kiss and embrace you all, and so leave you with my God. Farewell, farewell. I bless you all in the name of the Lord Jesus. I salute my daughter Winth., Matt. Nan, and the rest, and all my good neighbors and friends. Pray all for us. Farewell. Commend my blessing to my son John. I cannot now write to him, but tell him I have committed thee and thine to him. Labor to draw him yet nearer to God, and he will be the surer staff of comfort to thee. I cannot name the rest of my good friends, but thou canst supply it. I wrote a week since to thee and Mr. Leigh and divers other.

Thine wheresoever,
Jo. Winthrop

(15) "sennight" is seven nights, a week

(24) Note the change in language and style when Winthrop stops writing about the weather and the ship and begins to write about his feelings for his wife.

Commentary on the Reading

Even if you knew nothing about Winthrop's role in settling and governing the Puritan community in Massachusetts, you would know a great deal about him from this letter. When determining his character, you may want to separate his public business from his private business. An analysis of Winthrop's ethos should be possible even from this short sample.

Reading Selection by Susan B. Anthony

In fact, John Winthrop was not a great champion of democracy, so it is unlikely that he would have sympathized with the sentiments expressed by Susan B. Anthony, who was arrested in 1872 for trying to vote in the presidential election of that year. The right to vote was only one of the rights that Anthony and her followers sought to attain. This issue, like Winthrop's journey away from his home and family, could have been handled very emotionally.

Study the following reading. Does Anthony exploit the pathos of her situation, or is her argument more logical? How do her choices create the character behind the speaker?

Susan B. Anthony
On Women's Right to Vote
1873

Friends and fellow citizens: I stand before you tonight under in-dictment for the alleged crime of having voted at the last presidential election, without having a lawful right to vote. It shall be my work this evening to prove to you that in thus doing, I not only committed no
5 crime, but instead simply exercised my citizen's rights, guaranteed to me and all United States citizens by the National Constitution, beyond the power of any state to deny.

The preamble of the Federal Constitution says:

"We, the people of the United States, in order to form a more per-
10 fect union, establish justice, insure domestic tranquillity, provide for the common defense, promote the general welfare, and secure the blessings of liberty to ourselves and our posterity, do ordain and establish this Constitution for the United States of America."

It was we, the people, not we, the white male citizens, nor we, the
15 male citizens; but we, the whole people, who formed this Union. We formed it, not to give the blessings of liberty but to secure them; not to the half of ourselves and the half of our posterity, but to the whole peo-ple—women as well as men. It is downright mockery to talk to women of their enjoyment of the blessings of liberty while they are denied the
20 use of the only means of securing them provided by this democratic-republican government—the ballot.

For any State to make sex a qualification, which must ever result in the disfranchisement of one entire half of the people, is to pass a bill of attainder, or, an ex post facto law, and is therefore a violation of the
25 supreme law of the land. By it the blessings of liberty are forever with-held from women and their female posterity. For them, this government has no just powers derived from the consent of the governed. For them this government is not a democracy; it is not a republic. It is the most odious aristocracy ever established on the face of the globe. An oligar-
30 chy of wealth, where the rich govern the poor; an oligarchy of learning,

where the educated govern the ignorant; or even an oligarchy of race, where the Saxon rules the African, might be endured; but this oligarchy of sex, which makes father, brothers, husband, sons, the oligarchs over the mother and sisters, the wife and daughters of every household; which ordains all men sovereigns, all women subjects—carries discord and rebellion into every home of the nation.

Webster, Worcester, and Bouvier all define a citizen to be a person in the United States, entitled to vote and hold office.

The only question left to be settled now is: Are women persons? And I hardly believe any of our opponents will have the hardihood to say they are not. Being persons, then, women are citizens; and no state has a right to make any law, or to enforce any old law, that shall abridge their privileges or immunities. Hence, every discrimination against women in the constitutions and laws of the several states is today null and void, precisely as is every one against Negroes.

(37) Noah Webster is the most widely known American lexicographer. Joseph Emerson Worcester was for a time his chief rival. He is not well-known today. John Bouvier compiled a dictionary of law in the nineteenth century.

Reading Selection by John Patrick Shanley

John Patrick Shanley's play *Doubt* won the Pulitzer Prize for drama in 2005 and the Tony award for the best play of that year. The play, set in a Catholic school in 1964, concerns one nun's doubts about the relationship between a priest and one of the students, and how various people in the church community are affected by her, by him, and by her doubts.

Shanley's preface to the printed edition of the play seems to be a comment on the times we live in, but from that comment we can deduce a great deal about him as a person.

John Patrick Shanley
Doubt
Preface

What's under a play? What holds it up? You might as well ask what's under me? On what am I built? There's something silent under every person and under every play. There is something unsaid under any given society as well.

There's a symptom apparent in America right now. It's evident in political talk shows, in entertainment coverage, in artistic criticism of every kind, in religious discussion. We are living in a courtroom culture. We *were* living in a celebrity culture, but that's dead. Now we're only interested in celebrities if they're in court. We are living in a culture of extreme advocacy, of confrontation, of judgment, and of verdict. Discussion has given way to debate. Communication has become a contest of wills. Public talking has become obnoxious and insincere. Why? Maybe it's because deep down under the chatter we have come to a place where we know that we don't know…anything. But nobody's willing to say that.

Let me ask you. Have you ever held a position in an argument past the point of comfort? Have you ever defended a way of life you were

(7) Can you think of cases that illustrate Shanley's assertion here?

on the verge of exhausting? Have you ever given service to a creed you no longer believed? Have you ever told a girl you loved her and felt the faint nausea of eroding conviction? I have. That's an interesting moment. For a playwright, it's the beginning of an idea. I saw a piece of real estate on which I might build a play, a play that sat on something silent in my life and in my time. I started with a title: *Doubt*.

What is Doubt? Each of us is like a planet. There's the crust, which seems eternal. We are confident about who we are. If you ask, we can readily describe our current state. I know my answers to so many questions, as do you. What was your father like? Do you believe in God? Who's your best friend? What do you want? Your answers are your current topography, seemingly permanent, but deceptively so. Because under that face of easy response, there is another You. And this wordless Being moves just as the instant moves; it presses upward without explanation, fluid and wordless, until the resisting consciousness has no choice but to give way.

It is Doubt (so often experienced initially as weakness) that changes things. When a man feels unsteady, when he falters, when hard-won knowledge evaporates before his eyes, he's on the verge of growth. The subtle or violent reconciliation of the outer person and the inner core often seems at first like a mistake, like you've gone the wrong way and you're lost. But this is just emotion longing for the familiar. Life happens when the tectonic power of your speechless soul breaks through the dead habits of the mind. Doubt is nothing less than an opportunity to reenter the Present.

The play. I've set my story in 1964, when not just me, but the whole world seemed to be going through some kind of vast puberty. The old ways were still dominant in behavior, dress, morality, world view, but what had been organic expression had become a dead mask. I was in a Catholic church school in the Bronx, run by the Sisters of Charity. These women dressed in black, believed in Hell, obeyed their male counterparts, and educated us. The faith, which held us together, went beyond the precincts of religion. It was a shared dream we agreed to call Reality. We didn't know it, but we had a deal, a social contract. We would all believe the same thing. We would all believe.

Looking back, it seems to me, in those schools at that time, we were an ageless unity. We were all adults and we were all children. We had, like many animals, flocked together for warmth and safety. As a result, we were terribly vulnerable to anyone who chose to hunt us. When trust is the order of the day, predators are free to plunder. And plunder they did. As the ever widening Church scandals reveal, the hunters had a field day. And the shepherds, so invested in the surface, sacrificed actual good for perceived virtue.

I have never forgotten the lessons of that era, nor learned them well enough. I still long for a shared certainty, an assumption of safety, the reassurance of believing that others know better than me what's for the best. But I have been led by the bitter necessities of an interesting life to value that age-old practice of the wise: Doubt.

There is an uneasy time when belief has begun to slip, but hypocrisy has yet to take hold, when consciousness is disturbed but not yet altered. It is the most dangerous, important, and ongoing experience of life. The beginning of change is the moment of Doubt. It is that crucial moment when I renew my humanity or become a lie.

What features of Shanley's explanation of Doubt help you develop a sense of the person behind the essay?

Doubt requires more courage than conviction does, and more energy; because conviction is a resting place and doubt is infinite—it is a passionate exercise. You may come out of my play uncertain. You may want to be sure. Look down on that feeling. We've got to learn to live with a full measure of uncertainty. There is no last word. That's the silence under the chatter of our time.

John Patrick Shanley
Brooklyn, New York
March 2005

Focus on Writing: Analysis

You have just read three pieces by two men and a woman who speak to us from the seventeenth, nineteenth, and twenty-first centuries. Their topics are unrelated, their audiences are different, and their purposes have little in common. We might feel that each is, in his or her own way, something of a troublemaker, yet all three won respect and honor for their achievements. What do these pieces tell us about the character of the person behind the writing? Choose one of the three and compose an essay in which you analyze the writer's ethos, paying special attention to the actual text that provides that information for you. Do not concern yourself with what else you might know about your subject. Rely only on the text you have just read.

Lesson 20   What is the overall effect of the piece?

Introduction

The lessons in this book have dealt with many topics, which are contained in passages written in a variety of styles. You have been asked to write about the passages analytically, persuasively, and synthetically. In all cases, you are encouraged to approach both reading and writing tasks with an inquiring mind. You should ask questions about the following:

- the topic under discussion,
- the person speaking in the piece,
- the reasons for writing it,
- the assumptions the writer makes,
- the intended audience, and
- the author's attitude toward the subject and the audience.

You should pay attention to the choices the author makes in **diction**, **syntax**, **organization**, **figurative language**, **irony**, and **rhetorical devices** and what effects these choices have on the overall experience of reading the literature. Beyond all this, you should consider these same factors when you yourself are the author.

If you can do that, you will achieve great success as a reader and a writer, not only on the Advanced Placement English Language and Composition examination but also in all the reading and writing tasks you will ever face.

Four Essays

In this lesson, you will find four very fine essays that you will enjoy reading. They are good examples of the practices that have been described in these lessons, and they are summary examples of the kind of reading and writing you have been doing throughout this course. Do enjoy them. You will find three writing opportunities as well.

The first essay expresses its author's attitude toward the family gathering at Thanksgiving. You should notice fairly early what that attitude is, and be able to see how he develops that tone as the essay progresses.

The second essay offers an opportunity to engage in conversation with the writer and ask questions about his assertions. The third essay discusses social problems and how society succeeds or fails to address them. The fourth essay can lead you to think about your own family relationships and experiences.

Focus on the Readings: Reading Holistically
Approach the next four reading selections with an inquiring mind. Keep a journal as you read, and note the choices that the writers make in language and style.

Michael Arlen
Ode to Thanksgiving

It is time, at last, to speak the truth about Thanksgiving, and the truth is this. Thanksgiving is really not such a terrific holiday. Consider the traditional symbols of the event: Dried corn husks hanging on the door! Terrible wine! Cranberry jelly in little bowls of extremely doubtful provenance which everyone is required to handle with the greatest of care! Consider the participants, the merrymakers: men and women (also children) who have survived passably well throughout the years, mainly as a result of living at considerable distances from their dear parents and beloved siblings, who on this feast of feasts must apparently forgather (as if beckoned by an aberrant fairy godmother), usually by circuitous routes, through heavy traffic, at a common meeting place, where the very moods, distempers, and obtrusive personal habits that have kept them all happily apart since adulthood are then and there encouraged to slowly ferment beneath the corn husks, and gradually rise with the aid of the terrible wine, and finally burst forth out of control under the stimulus of the cranberry jelly! No, it is a mockery of a holiday. For instance: *Thank you, O Lord, for what we are about to receive*. This is surely not a gala concept. There are no presents, unless one counts Aunt Bertha's sweet rolls a present, which no one does. There is precious little in the way of costumery: miniature plastic turkeys and those witless Pilgrim hats. There is no sex. Indeed, Thanksgiving is the one day of the year (a fact known to everybody) when all thoughts of sex completely vanish, evaporating from apartments, houses, condominiums, and mobile homes like steam from a bathroom mirror.

Consider also the nowhereness of the time of year: the last week or so in November. It is obviously not yet winter: winter, with its death-dealing blizzards and its girls in tiny skirts pirouetting on the ice. On the other hand, it is certainly not much use to anyone as fall: no golden leaves or Oktoberfests, and so forth. Instead, it is a no-man's land between the seasons. In the cold and sobersides northern half of the country, it is a vaguely unsettling interregnum of long, mournful walks beneath leafless trees: the long, mournful walks following the midday repast with the dread inevitability of pie following turkey, and the leafless trees looming or standing about like eyesores, and the ground either as hard as iron or slightly mushy, and the light snow always beginning to fall when one is halfway to the old green gate—flecks of cold, watery stuff plopping between neck and collar, for the reason that, it being not yet winter, one has forgotten or not chosen to bring along a muffler. It is a corollary to the long, mournful Thanksgiving walk that the absence of this muffler is quickly noticed and that four weeks or so later, at Christmastime, instead of the Sony Betamax one had secretly hoped the children might have chipped in to purchase, one receives another muffler: by then the thirty-third. Thirty-three mufflers! Some walk! Of course, things are more fun in the warm and loony southern part of the country. No snow there of any kind. No need of mufflers. Also, no long, mournful walks, because in the warm and loony southern part of the country everybody drives. So everybody drives over to Uncle Jasper's

This may be a surprise to readers who think Thanksgiving *is* a terrific holiday, so don't miss the author's tone as he explains.

(41) The Betamax was one of the original videotape recorders, marketed as a highly desired Christmas present.

house to watch the Cougars play the Gators, a not entirely unimportant conflict which will determine whether the Gators get a Bowl bid or must take another postseason exhibition tour of North Korea. But no sooner do the Cougars kick off (an astonishing end-over-end squiggly thing that floats lazily above the arena before plummeting down toward K. C. McCoy and catching him on the helmet) than Auntie Em starts hustling turkey. Soon Cousin May is slamming around the bowls and platters, and Cousin Bernice is oohing and ahing about "all the fixin's," and Uncle Bob is making low, insincere sounds of appreciation: "Yummy, yummy—Auntie Em, I'll have me some more of these delicious yams!" Delicious yams? Uncle Bob's eyes roll wildly in his head, Billy Joe Quaglino throws his long bomb in the middle of Grandpa Morris saying grace, Grandpa Morris speaking so low nobody can hear him, which is just as well, since he is reciting what he can remember of his last union contract. And then, just as J. B. (Speedy) Snood begins his ninety-two-yard punt return, Auntie Em starts dealing everyone second helpings of her famous stuffing, as if she were pushing a controlled substance, which it well might be, since there are no easily recognizable ingredients visible to the naked eye.

Consider for a moment the Thanksgiving meal itself. It has become a sort of refuge for endangered species of starch: cauliflower, turnips, pumpkin, mince (whatever "mince" is), those blessed yams. Bowls of luridly colored yams, with no taste at all, lying torpid under a lava flow of marshmallow! And then the sacred turkey. One might as well try to construct a holiday repast around a fish—say, a nice piece of haddock. After all, turkey tastes very similar to haddock; same consistency, same quite remarkable absence of flavor. But then, if the Thanksgiving pièce de résistance were a nice piece of boiled haddock instead of turkey, there wouldn't be all that fun for Dad when Mom hands him the sterling-silver, bone-handled carving set (a wedding present from her parents and not sharpened since) and then everyone sits around pretending not to watch while he saws and tears away at the bird as if he were trying to burrow his way into or out of some grotesque, fowllike prison.

What of the good side to Thanksgiving, you ask. There is always a good side to everything. Not to Thanksgiving. There is only a bad side and then a worse side. For instance, Grandmother's best linen tablecloth is a bad side: the fact that it is produced each year, in the manner of a red flag being produced before a bull, and then is always spilled upon by whichever child is doing poorest at school that term and so is in need of greatest reassurance. Thus, "Oh, my God, *Veronica,* you just spilled grape juice [or plum wine or tar] on Grandmother's best linen tablecloth!" But now comes worse. For at this point Cousin Bill, the one who lost all Cousin Edwina's money on the car dealership three years ago and has apparently been drinking steadily since Halloween, bizarrely chooses to say: "Seems to me those old glasses are always falling over." To which Auntie Meg is heard to add: "Somehow I don't remember receivin' any of those old glasses." To which Uncle Fred replies: "That's because you and George decided to go on vacation to Hawaii the summer Grandpa Sam was dying." Now Grandmother is sobbing, though not so uncontrollably that she can refrain from murmuring: "I think that volcano painting I threw away by mistake got sent me from Hawaii, heaven knows why." But the gods are merciful, even the Pilgrim-hatted god of corn husks and soggy stuffing, and there is an end to everything, even to Thanksgiving. Indeed, there is a grandeur to the feelings of finality and doom which usually settle on a house after the Thanksgiving celebration is over, for with the completion of Thanksgiving Day the year itself has been properly terminated: shot through the cranium with a high-velocity candied yam. At this calendrical nadir, all energy on the planet has gone, all fun has fled, all the terrible wine has been drunk.

But then, overnight, life once again begins to stir, emerging, even by the next morning, in the form of Japanese window displays and Taiwanese Christmas lighting, from the primeval ooze of the nation's department stores. Thus, a new year dawns, bringing with it immediate and cheering possibilities of extended consumer debt, office-party flirtations, good—or, at least, mediocre—wine, and visions of Supersaver excursion fares to Montego Bay. It is worth noting, perhaps, that this true new year always starts with the same mute, powerful mythic ceremony: the surreptitious tossing out, in the early morning, of all those horrid aluminum-foil packages of yams and cauliflowers and stuffing and red, gummy cranberry substance which have been squeezed into the refrigerator as if a reenactment of the siege of Paris were shortly expected. Soon afterward, the phoenix of Christmas can be observed as it slowly rises, beating its drumsticks, once again goggle-eyed with hope and unrealistic expectations.

Has the author convinced you that Thanksgiving is not such a terrific holiday?

Focus on Writing: Analysis
In Arlen's essay, the author chooses a familiar subject and treats it in an unfamiliar way. What is the author hoping to accomplish? Write an essay in which you demonstrate how the author uses particular rhetorical strategies to achieve his purpose regarding his description of his family's Thanksgiving dinner.

James Baldwin
Autobiographical Notes

I was born in Harlem thirty-one years ago. I began plotting novels at about the time I learned to read. The story of my childhood is the usual bleak fantasy, and we can dismiss it with the restrained observation that I certainly would not consider living it again. In those days my mother was given to the exasperating and mysterious habit of having babies. As they were born, I took them over with one hand and held a book with the other. The children probably suffered, though they have since been kind enough to deny it, and in this way I read *Uncle Tom's Cabin* and *A Tale of Two Cities* over and over and over again; in this way, in fact, I read just about everything I could get my hands on—except the Bible, probably because it was the only book I was encouraged to read. I must also confess that I wrote—a great deal—and my first professional triumph, in any case, the first effort of mine to be seen in print, occurred at the age of twelve or thereabouts, when a short story I had written about the Span-

Baldwin was born in 1924. This essay was published originally in *Notes of a Native Son* in 1955.

ish revolution won some sort of prize in an extremely short-lived church newspaper. I remember the story was censored by the lady editor, though I don't remember why, and I was outraged.

Also wrote plays, and songs, for one of which I received a letter of congratulations from Mayor La Guardia, and poetry, about which the less said, the better. My mother was delighted by all these goings-on, but my father wasn't; he wanted me to be a preacher. When I was fourteen I became a preacher, and when I was seventeen I stopped. Very shortly thereafter I left home. For God knows how long I struggled with the world of commerce and industry—I guess they would say they struggled with me—and when I was about twenty-one I had enough done of a novel to get a Saxton Fellowship. When I was twenty-two the fellowship was over, the novel turned out to be unsalable, and I started waiting on tables in a Village restaurant and writing book reviews—mostly, as it turned out, about the Negro problem, concerning which the color of my skin made me automatically an expert. Did another book, in company with photographer Theodore Pelatowski, about the store-front churches in Harlem. This book met exactly the same fate as my first—fellowship, but no sale. (It was a Rosenwald Fellowship.) By the time I was twenty-four I had decided to stop reviewing books about the Negro problem—which, by this time, was only slightly less horrible in print than it was in life—and I packed my bags and went to France, where I finished, God knows how, *Go Tell It on the Mountain*.

Any writer, I suppose, feels that the world into which he was born is nothing less than a conspiracy against the cultivation of his talent—which attitude certainly has a great deal to support it. On the other hand, it is only because the world looks on his talent with such a frightening indifference that the artist is compelled to make his talent important. So that any writer, looking back over even so short a span of time as I am here forced to assess, finds that the things which hurt him and the things which helped him cannot be divorced from each other; he could be helped in a certain way only because he was hurt in a certain way; and his help is simply to be enabled to move from one conundrum to the next—one is tempted to say that he moves from one disaster to the next. When one begins looking for influences one finds them by the score. I haven't thought much about my own, not enough anyway; I hazard that the King James Bible, the rhetoric of the store-front church, something ironic and violent and perpetually understated in Negro speech—and something of Dickens' love for bravura—have something to do with me today; but I wouldn't stake my life on it. Likewise, innumerable people have helped me in many ways; but finally, I suppose, the most difficult (and most rewarding) thing in my life has been the fact that I was born a Negro and was forced, therefore, to effect some kind of truce with this reality. (Truce, by the way, is the best one can hope for.)

One of the difficulties about being a Negro writer (and this is not special pleading, since I don't mean to suggest that he has it worse than anybody else) is that the Negro problem is written about so widely. The bookshelves groan under the weight of information, and everyone therefore considers himself informed. And this information, furthermore, operates usually (generally, popularly) to reinforce traditional attitudes. Of traditional attitudes there are only two—For or Against—and I, personally, find it difficult to say which attitude has caused me the most pain. I am speaking as a writer; from a social point of view I am perfectly aware that the change from ill-will to good-will, however motivated, however imperfect, however expressed, is better than no change at all.

But it is part of the business of the writer—as I see it—to examine attitudes, to go beneath the surface, to tap the source. From this point of view the Negro problem is nearly inaccessible. It is not only written about so widely; it is written about so badly. It is quite possible to say that the price a Negro pays for becoming articulate is to find himself, at length, with nothing to be articulate about. ("You taught me language," says Caliban to Prospero, "and my profit on't is I know how to curse.") Consider: the tremendous social activity that this problem generates imposes on whites and Negroes alike the necessity of looking forward, of working to bring about a better day. This is fine, it keeps the waters troubled; it is all, indeed, that has made possible the Negro's progress. Nevertheless, social affairs are not generally speaking the writer's prime concern, whether they ought to be or not; it is absolutely necessary that he establish between himself and these affairs a distance which will allow, at least, for clarity, so that before he can look forward in any meaningful sense, he must first be allowed to take a long look back. In the context of the Negro problem neither whites nor blacks, for excellent reasons of their own, have the faintest desire to look back; but I think that the past is all that makes the present coherent, and further, that the past will remain horrible for exactly as long as we refuse to assess it honestly.

I know, in any case, that the most crucial time in my own development came when I was forced to recognize that I was a kind of bastard of the West; when I followed the line of my past I did not find myself in Europe but in Africa. And this meant that in some subtle way, in a really profound way, I brought to Shakespeare, Bach, Rembrandt, to the stones of Paris, to the cathedral at Chartres, and to the Empire State Building, a special attitude. These were not really my creations, they did not contain my history; I might search in them in vain forever for any reflection of myself. I was an interloper; this was not my heritage. At the same time I had no other heritage which I could possibly hope to use—I had certainly been unfitted for the jungle or the tribe. I would have to appropriate these white centuries, I would have to make them mine—I would have to accept my special attitude, my special place in this scheme—otherwise I would have no place in any scheme. What was the most difficult was the fact that I was forced to admit something I had always hidden from myself, which the American Negro has had to hide from himself as the price of his public progress; that I hated and feared white people. This did not mean that I loved black people; on the contrary, I despised them, possibly because they failed to produce Rembrandt. In effect, I hated and feared the world. And this meant, not only that I thus gave the world an altogether murderous power over me, but also that in such a self-destroying limbo I could never hope to write.

One writes out of one thing only—one's own experience. Everything depends on how relentlessly one forces from this experience the last drop, sweet or bitter, it can possibly give. This is the only real concern of the artist, to recreate out of the disorder of life that order which is art. The difficulty then, for me, of being a Negro writer was the fact that I was, in effect, prohibited from examining my own experience too closely by the tremendous demands and the very real dangers of my social situation.

(75) Baldwin is referring here to Shakespeare's *The Tempest.*

I don't think the dilemma outlined above is uncommon. I do think, since writers work in the disastrously explicit medium of language, that it goes a little way towards explaining why, out of the enormous resources of Negro speech and life, and despite the example of Negro music, prose written by Negroes has been generally speaking so pallid and so harsh. I have not written about being a Negro at such length because I expect that to be my only subject, but only because it was the gate I had to unlock before I could hope to write about anything else. I don't think that the Negro problem in America can be even discussed coherently without bearing in mind its context; its context being the history, traditions, customs, the moral assumptions and preoccupations of the country; in short, the general social fabric. Appearances to the contrary, no one in America escapes its effects and everyone in America bears some responsibility for it. I believe this the more firmly because it is the overwhelming tendency to speak of this problem as though it were a thing apart. But in the work of Faulkner, in the general attitude and certain specific passages in Robert Penn Warren, and, most significantly, in the advent of Ralph Ellison, one sees the beginnings—at least—of a more genuinely penetrating search. Mr. Ellison, by the way, is the first Negro novelist I have ever read to utilize in language, and brilliantly, some of the ambiguity and irony of Negro life.

About my interests: I don't know if I have any, unless the morbid desire to own a sixteen-millimeter camera and make experimental movies can be so classified. Otherwise, I love to eat and drink—it's my melancholy conviction that I've scarcely ever had enough to eat (this is because it's *impossible* to eat enough if you're worried about the next meal)—and I love to argue with people who do not disagree with me too profoundly, and I love to laugh. I do *not* like bohemia, or bohemians, I do not like people whose principal aim is pleasure, and I do not like people who are *earnest* about anything. I don't like people who like me because I'm a Negro; neither do I like people who find in the same accident grounds for contempt. I love America more than any other country in the world, and, exactly for this reason, I insist on the right to criticize her perpetually. I think all theories are suspect, that the finest principles may have to be modified, or may even be pulverized by the demands of life, and that one must find, therefore, one's own moral center and move through the world hoping that this center will guide one aright. I consider that I have many responsibilities, but none greater than this: to last, as Hemingway says, and get my work done.

I want to be an honest man and a good writer.

(133) William Faulkner is the great novelist of the American South. Robert Penn Warren is another Southern novelist, most famous for *All the King's Men*. Ralph Ellison wrote *Invisible Man*. All three are widely admired for the insightfulness of their writing about life in the American South.

Focus on Writing: Argumentation

At the beginning of the third paragraph, line 38, Baldwin writes, "Any writer, I suppose, feels that the world into which he was born is nothing less than a conspiracy against the cultivation of his talent—which attitude certainly has a great deal to support it."

Consider the writers and other artists with whose work you are familiar and write an essay in which you defend, challenge, or qualify Baldwin's assertion. Develop your argument with reference to your reading, your experience, and your conversations with other people.

Jonathan Swift
A Modest Proposal

for Preventing the Children of Poor People in Ireland From Being a Burden
to Their Parents or Country, and for Making Them Beneficial to the Public

It is a melancholy object to those who walk through this great town or travel in the country, when they see the streets, the roads, and cabin doors, crowded with beggars of the female sex, followed by three, four, or six children, all in rags and importuning every passenger for an alms. These mothers, instead of being able to work for their honest livelihood, are forced to employ all their time in strolling to beg sustenance for their helpless infants: who as they grow up either turn thieves for want of work, or leave their dear native country to fight for the Pretender in Spain, or sell themselves to the Barbadoes.

I think it is agreed by all parties that this prodigious number of children in the arms, or on the backs, or at the heels of their mothers, and frequently of their fathers, is in the present deplorable state of the kingdom a very great additional grievance; and, therefore, whoever could find out a fair, cheap, and easy method of making these children sound, useful members of the commonwealth, would deserve so well of the public as to have his statue set up for a preserver of the nation.

But my intention is very far from being confined to provide only for the children of professed beggars; it is of a much greater extent, and shall take in the whole number of infants at a certain age who are born of parents in effect as little able to support them as those who demand our charity in the streets.

As to my own part, having turned my thoughts for many years upon this important subject, and maturely weighed the several schemes of other projectors, I have always found them grossly mistaken in the computation. It is true, a child just dropped from its dam may be supported by her milk for a solar year, with little other nourishment; at most not above the value of 2s., which the mother may certainly get, or the value in scraps, by her lawful occupation of begging; and it is exactly at one year old that I propose to provide for them in such a manner as instead of being a charge upon their parents or the parish, or wanting food and raiment for the rest of their lives, they shall on the contrary contribute to the feeding, and partly to the clothing, of many thousands.

There is likewise another great advantage in my scheme, that it will prevent those voluntary abortions, and that horrid practice of women murdering their bastard children, alas! too frequent among us! sacrificing the poor innocent babes I doubt more to avoid the expense than the shame, which would move tears and pity in the most savage and inhuman breast.

The number of souls in this kingdom being usually reckoned one million and a half, of these I calculate there may be about two hundred thousand couple whose wives are breeders; from which number I subtract thirty thousand couples who are able to maintain their own children, although I apprehend there cannot be so many, under the present distresses of the kingdom; but this being granted, there will remain an hundred and seventy thousand breeders. I again subtract fifty thousand

"This great town" is Dublin, Ireland, in the eighteenth century.

(25) A "dam" is the mother of an animal. "Dropped from its dam" equates these children with livestock. Two shillings, even in Swift's time, is not very much money.

for those women who miscarry, or whose children die by accident or disease within the year. There only remains one hundred and twenty thousand children of poor parents annually born. The question therefore is, how this number shall be reared and provided for, which, as I have already said, under the present situation of affairs, is utterly impossible by all the methods hitherto proposed. For we can neither employ them in handicraft or agriculture; we neither build houses (I mean in the country) nor cultivate land: they can very seldom pick up a livelihood by stealing, till they arrive at six years old, except where they are of towardly parts, although I confess they learn the rudiments much earlier, during which time, they can however be properly looked upon only as probationers, as I have been informed by a principal gentleman in the county of Cavan, who protested to me that he never knew above one or two instances under the age of six, even in a part of the kingdom so renowned for the quickest proficiency in that art.

I am assured by our merchants, that a boy or a girl before twelve years old is no salable commodity; and even when they come to this age they will not yield above three pounds, or three pounds and half-a-crown at most on the exchange; which cannot turn to account either to the parents or kingdom, the charge of nutriment and rags having been at least four times that value.

I shall now therefore humbly propose my own thoughts, which I hope will not be liable to the least objection.

I have been assured by a very knowing American of my acquaintance in London, that a young healthy child well nursed is at a year old a most delicious, nourishing, and wholesome food, whether stewed, roasted, baked, or boiled; and I make no doubt that it will equally serve in a fricassee or a ragout.

(73) Fricassee and ragout are types of stew.

I do therefore humbly offer it to public consideration that of the hundred and twenty thousand children already computed, twenty thousand may be reserved for breed, whereof only one-fourth part to be males; which is more than we allow to sheep, black cattle or swine; and my reason is, that these children are seldom the fruits of marriage, a circumstance not much regarded by our savages, therefore one male will be sufficient to serve four females. That the remaining hundred thousand may, at a year old, be offered in the sale to the persons of quality and fortune through the kingdom; always advising the mother to let them suck plentifully in the last month, so as to render them plump and fat for a good table. A child will make two dishes at an entertainment for friends; and when the family dines alone, the fore or hind quarter will make a reasonable dish, and seasoned with a little pepper or salt will be very good boiled on the fourth day, especially in winter.

I have reckoned upon a medium that a child just born will weigh 12 pounds, and in a solar year, if tolerably nursed, increaseth to 28 pounds.

I grant this food will be somewhat dear, and therefore very proper for landlords, who, as they have already devoured most of the parents, seem to have the best title to the children.

Infant's flesh will be in season throughout the year, but more plentiful in March, and a little before and after; for we are told by a grave author, an eminent French physician, that fish being a prolific diet, there are more children born in Roman Catholic countries about nine months after Lent than at any other season; therefore, reckoning a year after

Swift, as a Catholic living in Protestant England, frequently complained of how the English treated the Irish.

Lent, the markets will be more glutted than usual, because the number of popish infants is at least three to one in this kingdom: and therefore it will have one other collateral advantage, by lessening the number of papists among us.

I have already computed the charge of nursing a beggar's child (in which list I reckon all cottagers, laborers, and four-fifths of the farmers) to be about two shillings per annum, rags included; and I believe no gentleman would repine to give ten shillings for the carcass of a good fat child, which, as I have said, will make four dishes of excellent nutritive meat, when he hath only some particular friend or his own family to dine with him. Thus the squire will learn to be a good landlord, and grow popular among his tenants; the mother will have eight shillings net profit, and be fit for work till she produces another child.

Those who are more thrifty (as I must confess the times require) may flay the carcass; the skin of which artificially dressed will make admirable gloves for ladies, and summer boots for fine gentlemen.

As to our city of Dublin, shambles may be appointed for this purpose in the most convenient parts of it, and butchers we may be assured will not be wanting; although I rather recommend buying the children alive, and dressing them hot from the knife, as we do roasting pigs.

A very worthy person, a true lover of his country, and whose virtues I highly esteem, was lately pleased in discoursing on this matter to offer a refinement upon my scheme. He said that many gentlemen of this kingdom, having of late destroyed their deer, he conceived that the want of venison might be well supplied by the bodies of young lads and maidens, not exceeding fourteen years of age nor under twelve; so great a number of both sexes in every country being now ready to starve for want of work and service; and these to be disposed of by their parents, if alive, or otherwise by their nearest relations. But with due deference to so excellent a friend and so deserving a patriot, I cannot be altogether in his sentiments; for as to the males, my American acquaintance assured me, from frequent experience, that their flesh was generally tough and lean, like that of our schoolboys by continual exercise, and their taste disagreeable; and to fatten them would not answer the charge. Then as to the females, it would, I think, with humble submission be a loss to the public, because they soon would become breeders themselves; and besides, it is not improbable that some scrupulous people might be apt to censure such a practice (although indeed very unjustly), as a little bordering upon cruelty; which, I confess, hath always been with me the strongest objection against any project, however so well intended.

But in order to justify my friend, he confessed that this expedient was put into his head by the famous Psalmanazar, a native of the island Formosa, who came from thence to London above twenty years ago, and in conversation told my friend, that in his country when any young person happened to be put to death, the executioner sold the carcass to persons of quality as a prime dainty; and that in his time the body of a plump girl of fifteen, who was crucified for an attempt to poison the emperor, was sold to his imperial majesty's prime minister of state, and other great mandarins of the court, in joints from the gibbet, at four hundred crowns. Neither indeed can I deny, that if the same use were

(114) Shambles were open-air meatmarkets. The word has come in our time to mean any place that has become run down and filthy.

(140) George Psalmanazar claimed to be the first visitor to Britain from Formosa, but was eventually discredited as a hoax.

made of several plump young girls in this town, who without one single
groat to their fortunes cannot stir abroad without a chair, and appear at
playhouse and assemblies in foreign fineries which they never will pay
for, the kingdom would not be the worse.

Some persons of a desponding spirit are in great concern about
that vast number of poor people, who are aged, diseased, or maimed,
and I have been desired to employ my thoughts what course may be
taken to ease the nation of so grievous an encumbrance. But I am not
in the least pain upon that matter, because it is very well known that
they are every day dying and rotting by cold and famine, and filth and
vermin, as fast as can be reasonably expected. And as to the young
laborers, they are now in as hopeful a condition; they cannot get work,
and consequently pine away for want of nourishment, to a degree that if
at any time they are accidentally hired to common labor, they have not
strength to perform it; and thus the country and themselves are happily
delivered from the evils to come.

I have too long digressed, and therefore shall return to my subject.
I think the advantages by the proposal which I have made are obvious
and many, as well as of the highest importance.

For first, as I have already observed, it would greatly lessen the
number of papists, with whom we are yearly overrun, being the principal
breeders of the nation as well as our most dangerous enemies; and who
stay at home on purpose with a design to deliver the kingdom to the Pretender, hoping to take their advantage by the absence of so many good
protestants, who have chosen rather to leave their country than stay at
home and pay tithes against their conscience to an episcopal curate.

Secondly, The poorer tenants will have something valuable of their
own, which by law may be made liable to distress and help to pay their
landlord's rent, their corn and cattle being already seized, and money a
thing unknown.

Thirdly, Whereas the maintenance of an hundred thousand children, from two years old and upward, cannot be computed at less than
ten shillings a-piece per annum, the nation's stock will be thereby increased fifty thousand pounds per annum, beside the profit of a new dish
introduced to the tables of all gentlemen of fortune in the kingdom who
have any refinement in taste. And the money will circulate among ourselves, the goods being entirely of our own growth and manufacture.

Fourthly, The constant breeders, beside the gain of eight shillings
sterling per annum by the sale of their children, will be rid of the charge
of maintaining them after the first year.

Fifthly, This food would likewise bring great custom to taverns;
where the vintners will certainly be so prudent as to procure the best
receipts for dressing it to perfection, and consequently have their houses
frequented by all the fine gentlemen, who justly value themselves upon
their knowledge in good eating: and a skilful cook, who understands how
to oblige his guests, will contrive to make it as expensive as they please.

Sixthly, This would be a great inducement to marriage, which all
wise nations have either encouraged by rewards or enforced by laws
and penalties. It would increase the care and tenderness of mothers toward their children, when they were sure of a settlement for life to the
poor babes, provided in some sort by the public, to their annual profit

instead of expense. We should see an honest emulation among the married women, which of them could bring the fattest child to the market. Men would become as fond of their wives during the time of their pregnancy as they are now of their mares in foal, their cows in calf, their sows when they are ready to farrow; nor offer to beat or kick them (as is too frequent a practice) for fear of a miscarriage.

Many other advantages might be enumerated. For instance, the addition of some thousand carcasses in our exportation of barreled beef, the propagation of swine's flesh, and improvement in the art of making good bacon, so much wanted among us by the great destruction of pigs, too frequent at our tables; which are no way comparable in taste or magnificence to a well-grown, fat, yearling child, which roasted whole will make a considerable figure at a lord mayor's feast or any other public entertainment. But this and many others I omit, being studious of brevity.

Supposing that one thousand families in this city, would be constant customers for infants flesh, besides others who might have it at merry meetings, particularly at weddings and christenings, I compute that Dublin would take off annually about twenty thousand carcasses; and the rest of the kingdom (where probably they will be sold somewhat cheaper) the remaining eighty thousand.

I can think of no one objection, that will possibly be raised against this proposal, unless it should be urged, that the number of people will be thereby much lessened in the kingdom. This I freely own, and 'twas indeed one principal design in offering it to the world. I desire the reader will observe, that I calculate my remedy for this one individual Kingdom of Ireland, and for no other that ever was, is, or, I think, ever can be upon Earth. Therefore let no man talk to me of other expedients: Of taxing our absentees at five shillings a pound: Of using neither cloaths, nor houshold furniture, except what is of our own growth and manufacture: Of utterly rejecting the materials and instruments that promote foreign luxury: Of curing the expensiveness of pride, vanity, idleness, and gaming in our women: Of introducing a vein of parsimony, prudence and temperance: Of learning to love our country, wherein we differ even from Laplanders, and the inhabitants of Topinamboo: Of quitting our animosities and factions, nor acting any longer like the Jews, who were murdering one another at the very moment their city was taken: Of being a little cautious not to sell our country and consciences for nothing: Of teaching landlords to have at least one degree of mercy towards their tenants. Lastly, of putting a spirit of honesty, industry, and skill into our shop-keepers, who, if a resolution could now be taken to buy only our native goods, would immediately unite to cheat and exact upon us in the price, the measure, and the goodness, nor could ever yet be brought to make one fair proposal of just dealing, though often and earnestly invited to it.

Therefore I repeat, let no man talk to me of these and the like expedients, 'till he hath at least some glympse of hope, that there will ever be some hearty and sincere attempt to put them into practice.

But, as to my self, having been wearied out for many years with offering vain, idle, visionary thoughts, and at length utterly despairing of success, I fortunately fell upon this proposal, which, as it is wholly new, so it hath something solid and real, of no expence and little trouble,

(166–205) Consider how from these advantages Swift has synthesized his solution to the problem.

full in our own power, and whereby we can incur no danger in disobliging England. For this kind of commodity will not bear exportation, and flesh being of too tender a consistence, to admit a long continuance in salt, although perhaps I could name a country, which would be glad to eat up our whole nation without it.

After all, I am not so violently bent upon my own opinion as to reject any offer proposed by wise men, which shall be found equally innocent, cheap, easy, and effectual. But before something of that kind shall be advanced in contradiction to my scheme, and offering a better, I desire the author or authors will be pleased maturely to consider two points. First, as things now stand, how they will be able to find food and raiment for an hundred thousand useless mouths and backs. And secondly, there being a round million of creatures in human figure throughout this kingdom, whose whole subsistence put into a common stock would leave them in debt two millions of pounds sterling, adding those who are beggars by profession to the bulk of farmers, cottagers, and laborers, with their wives and children who are beggars in effect: I desire those politicians who dislike my overture, and may perhaps be so bold as to attempt an answer, that they will first ask the parents of these mortals, whether they would not at this day think it a great happiness to have been sold for food, at a year old in the manner I prescribe, and thereby have avoided such a perpetual scene of misfortunes as they have since gone through by the oppression of landlords, the impossibility of paying rent without money or trade, the want of common sustenance, with neither house nor clothes to cover them from the inclemencies of the weather, and the most inevitable prospect of entailing the like or greater miseries upon their breed for ever.

I profess, in the sincerity of my heart, that I have not the least personal interest in endeavoring to promote this necessary work, having no other motive than the public good of my country, by advancing our trade, providing for infants, relieving the poor, and giving some pleasure to the rich. I have no children by which I can propose to get a single penny; the youngest being nine years old, and my wife past child-bearing.

The End

Commentary on the Reading

This is one of the classic essays of our language, as shocking today as it was when Swift first published it in 1729. As in Swift's day, many readers today do not realize that Swift is being satirical, and take him at his word. Probably no other work so thoroughly demonstrates the dangers of being too literal-minded.

You might think back to Lesson 5, where you read James Gorman's article "The Doctor Won't See You Now." Now that you have read Swift, you might enjoy returning to that piece and rereading it. You might be surprised by the similarities between the two writers' purposes and methods. You might try writing a satire of your own on a suitable topic, such as what to do about too many people in the cafeteria line at your school.

Reading Selection by E. B. White

E. B. White's "Once More to the Lake" is a well-known and well-loved piece from one of the best essay writers America ever produced. White is admired for the elegant simplicity of his style, but that simplicity is deceptive; he exemplifies Richard Brinsley Sheridan's remark that "easy writing's vile hard reading." Here we see the opposite in practice: hard writing (that is, writing that took hard work to do) makes for easy reading. White's easy style gives us more opportunity to pay attention to what he is saying—and that, after all, is the highest compliment we can pay a writer.

This essay is not followed by a writing prompt. After you finish reading it, just sit back for a few moments and reflect on what you have read. Consider the qualities that have caused people to admire this essay so much since it was originally published in 1941.

E. B. White
Once More to the Lake

One summer, along about 1904, my father rented a camp on a lake in Maine and took us all there for the month of August. We all got ringworm from some kittens and had to rub Pond's Extract on our arms and legs night and morning, and my father rolled over in a canoe with all his clothes on; but outside of that the vacation was a success and from then on none of us ever thought there was any place in the world like that lake in Maine. We returned summer after summer—always on August 1st for one month. I have since become a salt-water man, but sometimes in summer there are days when the restlessness of the tides and the fearful cold of the sea water and the incessant wind which blows across the afternoon and into the evening make me wish for the placidity of a lake in the woods. A few weeks ago this feeling got so strong I bought myself a couple of bass hooks and a spinner and returned to the lake where we used to go, for a week's fishing and to revisit old haunts.

I took along my son, who had never had any fresh water up his nose and who had seen lily pads only from train windows. On the journey over to the lake I began to wonder what it would be like. I wondered how time would have marred this unique, this holy spot—the coves and streams, the hills that the sun set behind, the camps and the paths behind the camps. I was sure that the tarred road would have found it out and I wondered in what other ways it would be desolated.

Note the details in White's writing, and how immediately they draw the reader into his narrative.

It is strange how much you can remember about places like that once you allow your mind to return into the grooves which lead back. You remember one thing, and that suddenly reminds you of another thing. I guess I remembered clearest of all the early mornings, when the lake was cool and motionless, remembered how the bedroom smelled of the lumber it was made of and of the wet woods whose scent entered through the screen. The partitions in the camp were thin and did not extend clear to the top of the rooms, and as I was always the first up I would dress softly so as not to wake the others, and sneak out into the sweet outdoors and start out in the canoe, keeping close along the shore in the long shadows of the pines. I remembered being very careful never to rub my paddle against the gunwale for fear of disturbing the stillness of the cathedral.

The lake had never been what you would call a wild lake. There were cottages sprinkled around the shores, and it was in farming although the shores of the lake were quite heavily wooded. Some of the cottages were owned by nearby farmers, and you would live at the shore and eat your meals at the farmhouse. That's what our family did. But although it wasn't wild, it was a fairly large and undisturbed lake and there were places in it which, to a child at least, seemed infinitely remote and primeval.

I was right about the tar: it led to within half a mile of the shore. But when I got back there, with my boy, and we settled into a camp near a farmhouse and into the kind of summertime I had known, I could tell that it was going to be pretty much the same as it had been before—I knew it, lying in bed the first morning, smelling the bedroom, and hearing the boy sneak quietly out and go off along the shore in a boat. I began to sustain the illusion that he was I, and therefore, by simple transposition, that I was my father. This sensation persisted, kept cropping up all the time we were there. It was not an entirely new feeling, but in this setting it grew much stronger. I seemed to be living a dual existence. I would be in the middle of some simple act, I would be picking up a bait box or laying down a table fork, or I would be saying something, and suddenly it would be not I but my father who was saying the words or making the gesture. It gave me a creepy sensation.

We went fishing the first morning. I felt the same damp moss covering the worms in the bait can, and saw the dragonfly alight on the tip of my rod as it hovered a few inches from the surface of the water. It was the arrival of this fly that convinced me beyond any doubt that everything was as it always had been, that the years were a mirage and there had been no years. The small waves were the same, chucking the rowboat under the chin as we fished at anchor, and the boat was the same boat, the same color green and the ribs broken in the same places, and under the floor-boards the same freshwater leavings and debris—the dead hellgrammite, the wisps of moss, the rusty discarded fishhook, the dried blood from yesterday's catch. We stared silently at the tips of our rods, at the dragonflies that came and went. I lowered the tip of mine into the water, tentatively, pensively dislodging the fly, which darted two feet away, poised, darted two feet back, and came to rest again a little farther up the rod. There had been no years between the ducking of this dragonfly and the other one—the one that was part of memory. I looked at the boy, who was silently watching his fly, and it was my hands that held his rod, my eyes watching. I felt dizzy and didn't know which rod I was at the end of.

We caught two bass, hauling them in briskly as though they were mackerel, pulling them over the side of the boat in a businesslike manner without any landing net, and stunning them with a blow on the back of the head. When we got back for a swim before lunch, the lake was exactly where we had left it, the same number of inches from the dock, and there was only the merest suggestion of a breeze. This seemed an utterly enchanted sea, this lake you could leave to its own devices for a few hours and come back to, and find that it had not stirred, this constant and trustworthy body of water. In the shallows, the dark, water-soaked sticks and twigs, smooth and old, were undulating in clusters on the bottom against the clean ribbed sand, and the track of the mussel was plain. A school of minnows swam by, each minnow with its small, individual shadow, doubling the attendance, so clear and sharp in the sunlight. Some of the other campers were in swimming, along the shore, one of them with a cake of soap, and the water felt thin and clear and insubstantial. Over the years there had been this person with the cake of soap, this cultist, and here he was. There had been no years.

Up to the farmhouse to dinner through the teeming, dusty field, the road under our sneakers was only a two-track road. The middle track was missing, the one with the marks of the hooves and the splotches of dried, flaky manure. There had always been three tracks to choose from in choosing which track to walk in; now the choice was narrowed down to two. For a moment I missed terribly the middle alternative. But the way led past the tennis court, and something about the way it lay there in the sun reassured me; the tape had loosened along the backline, the alleys were green with plantains and other weeds, and the net (installed in June and removed in September) sagged in the dry noon, and the whole place steamed with midday heat and hunger and emptiness. There was a choice of pie for dessert, and one was blueberry and one was apple, and the waitresses were the same country girls, there having been no passage of time, only the illusion of it as in a dropped curtain—the waitresses were still fifteen; their hair had been washed, that was the only difference—they had been to the movies and seen the pretty girls with the clean hair.

Summertime, oh summertime, pattern of life indelible, the fade proof lake, the woods unshatterable, the pasture with the sweet fern and the juniper forever and ever, summer without end; this was the background, and the life along the shore was the design, the cottages with their innocent and tranquil design, their tiny docks with the flagpole and the American flag floating against the white clouds in the blue sky, the little paths over the roots of the trees leading from camp to camp and the paths leading back to the outhouses and the can of lime for sprinkling, and at the souvenir counters at the store the miniature birch-bark canoes and the post cards that showed things looking a little better than they looked. This was the American family at play, escaping the city heat, wondering whether the newcomers at the camp at the head of the cove were "common" or "nice," wondering whether it was true that the people who drove up for Sunday dinner at the farmhouse were turned away because there wasn't enough chicken.

Pay attention to the number two in White's narrative. After so many references to things in pairs, what is the effect of the third track in the road? Why does he miss "terribly the middle alternative"?

It seemed to me, as I kept remembering all this, that those times and those summers had been infinitely precious and worth saving. There had been jollity and peace and goodness. The arriving (at the beginning of August) had been so big a business in itself, at the railway station the farm wagon drawn up, the first smell of the pine-laden air, the first glimpse of the smiling farmer, and the great importance of the trunks and your father's enormous authority in such matters, and the feel of the wagon under you for the long ten-mile haul, and at the top of the last long hill catching the first view of the lake after eleven months of not seeing this cherished body of water. The shouts and cries of the other campers when they saw you, and the trunks to be unpacked, to give up their rich burden. (Arriving was less exciting nowadays, when you sneaked up in your car and parked it under a tree near the camp and took out the bags and in five minutes it was all over, no fuss, no loud wonderful fuss about trunks.)

Peace and goodness and jollity. The only thing that was wrong now, really, was the sound of the place, an unfamiliar nervous sound of the outboard motors. This was the note that jarred, the one thing that would sometimes break the illusion and set the years moving. In those other summertimes, all motors were inboard; and when they were at a little distance, the noise they made was a sedative, an ingredient of summer sleep. They were one-cylinder and two-cylinder engines, and some were make-and-break and some were jump-spark, but they all made a sleepy sound across the lake. The one-lungers throbbed and fluttered, and the twin-cylinder ones purred and purred, and that was a quiet sound too. But now the campers all had outboards. In the daytime, in the hot mornings, these motors made a petulant, irritable sound; at night, in the still evening when the afterglow lit the water, they whined about one's ears like mosquitoes. My boy loved our rented outboard, and his great desire was to achieve single-handed mastery over it, and authority, and he soon learned the trick of choking it a little (but not too much), and the adjustment of the needle valve. Watching him I would remember the things you could do with the old one-cylinder engine with the heavy flywheel, how you could have it eating out of your hand if you got really close to it spiritually. Motor boats in those days didn't have clutches, and you would make a landing by shutting off the motor at the proper time and coasting in with a dead rudder. But there was a way of reversing them, if you learned the trick, by cutting the switch and putting it on again exactly on the final dying revolution of the fly-wheel, so that it would kick back against compression and begin reversing. Approaching a dock in a strong following breeze, it was difficult to slow up sufficiently by the ordinary coasting method, and if a boy felt he had complete mastery over his motor, he was tempted to keep it running beyond its time and then reverse it a few feet from the dock. It took a cool nerve, because if you threw the switch a twentieth of a second too soon you would catch the flywheel when it still had speed enough to go up past center, and the boat would leap ahead, charging bull-fashion at the dock.

We had a good week at the camp. The bass were biting well and the sun shone endlessly, day after day. We would be tired at night and lie down in the accumulated heat of the little bedrooms after the long hot day and the breeze would stir almost imperceptibly outside and the smell of the swamp drift in through the rusty screens. Sleep would come easily and in the morning the red squirrel would be on the roof, tapping out his gay routine. I kept remembering everything, lying in bed in the mornings—the small steamboat that had a long rounded stern like the lip of a Ubangi, and how quietly she ran on the moonlight sails, when the older boys played their mandolins and the girls sang and we ate doughnuts dipped in sugar, and how sweet the music was on the water in the shining night, and what it had felt like to think about girls then. After breakfast we would go up to the store and the things were in the same place—the minnows in a bottle, the plugs and spinners disarranged and pawed over by the youngsters from the boys' camp, the fig newtons and the Beeman's gum. Outside, the road was tarred and cars stood in front of the store. Inside, all was just as it had always been, except there was more Coca Cola and not so much Moxie and root beer and birch beer and sarsaparilla. We would walk out with a bottle of pop apiece and sometimes the pop would backfire up our noses and hurt. We explored the streams, quietly, where the turtles slid off the sunny logs and dug their way into the soft bottom; and we lay on the town wharf and fed worms to the tame bass. Everywhere we went I had trouble making out which was I, the one walking at my side, the one walking in my pants.

One afternoon while we were there at that lake a thunderstorm came up. It was like the revival of an old melodrama that I had seen long ago with childish awe. The second-act climax of the drama of the electrical disturbance over a lake in America had not changed in any important respect. This was the big scene, still the big scene. The whole thing was so familiar, the first feeling of oppression and heat and a general air around camp of not wanting to go very far away. In mid-afternoon (it was all the same) a curious darkening of the sky, and a lull in everything that had made life tick; and then the way the boats suddenly swung the other way at their moorings with the coming of a breeze out of the new quarter, and the premonitory rumble. Then the kettle drum, then the snare, then the bass drum and cymbals, then crackling light against the dark, and the gods grinning and licking their chops in the hills. Afterward the calm, the rain steadily rustling in the calm lake, the return of light and hope and spirits, and the campers running out in joy and relief to go swimming in the rain, their bright cries perpetuating the deathless joke about how they were getting simply drenched, and the children screaming with delight at the new sensation of bathing in the rain, and the joke about getting drenched linking the generations in a strong indestructible chain. And the comedian who waded in carrying an umbrella.

When the others went swimming my son said he was going in too. He pulled his dripping trunks from the line where they had hung all through the shower, and wrung them out. Languidly, and with no thought of going in, I watched him, his hard little body, skinny and bare, saw him wince slightly as he pulled up around his vitals the small, soggy, icy garment. As he buckled the swollen belt suddenly my groin felt the chill of death.

A Final Word

For the past several months, you have been reading high-quality writings and responding to them with contemplations, conversations, and writing activities of your own. As a result, you should be much more adept at critical thinking, reading, and writing than you were when your Advanced Placement course began. You will have a chance to demonstrate these skills on the Advanced Placement test. The multiple-choice questions will be challenging, but if you read carefully, you should do well. The free-response questions will resemble the essay prompts you saw in this book. Even though the examination is a demanding exercise, you are ready to face it and do well on it. Good luck to you.

GLOSSARY

abstract language	Language that deals with concepts and intangibles, as distinguished from **concrete language**, which names physical objects (lesson 14)
analogy	A comparison between two situations, usually one familiar and the other less so, so that some features of the more familiar situation help to explain the less familiar one (lesson 7)
analysis	The process of breaking a complex item into its component parts for the purpose of understanding the relationship between each part and the entire item. Compare this to **synthesis**, which is the process by which individual parts are combined into an entirety. (lesson 1)
anaphora	A rhetorical device in which a word or phrase is repeated at the beginnings of successive phrases or sentences. Compare this to **epistrophe**, where such repetitions occur at the ends. (lesson 8)
antithesis	A rhetorical device which employs a balanced pair of opposites (lesson 8)
argument	The process by which a writer tries to persuade a reader to adopt a particular view (lesson 2)
asyndeton	A rhetorical device in which expected conjunctions are omitted. Compare this to **polysyndeton**, where there are more conjunctions than usual. (lesson 8)
chiasmus	A rhetorical device in which words or phrases in the first part are reversed in the second part. Structurally, the chiasmus can be represented AB//BA. Compare this to the **synchises**, in which the elements of the first part are maintained in the second part, in the structure AB//AB. (lesson 8)
chronological order	The order of time, most often employed in narration (lesson 12)
climactic order	The order in which items are arranged in sequence according to their importance, with the most important one last (lesson 12)
concrete language	Language that deals with specific and physical objects, as distinguished from **abstract language**, which deals with concepts and intangibles, such as ideas (lesson 14)
connotation	A suggested association a word communicates along with its dictionary definition, or denotation (lesson 5)
diction	The author or speaker's choice of words (lesson 5)
ellipsis	A rhetorical device in which words are consciously omitted, perhaps because their meaning can be inferred (lesson 8)
epistrophe	A rhetorical device in which a word or words are repeated at the end of successive phrases or sentences. Compare this to **anaphora**, in which the repetitions occur at the beginning. (lesson 8)
ethos	The appeal through the writer's character, or the moral sense (lesson 16)
euphemism	A figure of speech in which a word or phrase is substituted for another that would be unpleasant for the reader or listener to encounter (lesson 4)
figure of speech	Language that is not literal, but which requires some amount of interpretation to be understood as intended (lesson 8)
hyperbole	A figure of speech in which exaggeration or overstatement is used in the service of truth (lesson 7)
inverted sentence	A sentence in which the subject follows the verb (lesson 6)
irony	Language that relies on some kind of discrepancy, usually between what is said and what is meant, between what appears to be true and what is actually true, or between what the reader expects will happen and what does actually happen (lesson 7)

logos	The appeal through logic, or the rational sense (lesson 16)
metaphor	Language that is comparative in nature. Metaphor is the term for both comparative language in general and a specific kind of comparison, one in which a comparison between two unlike objects is implied. (lesson 7)
metonymy	A figure of speech in which a word is used to represent something with which it is closely associated (lesson 8)
oxymoron	A compact apparent contradiction that, nonetheless, expresses a reasonable idea (lesson 8)
pathos	The appeal to feeling, or the emotional sense (lesson 16)
periodic sentence	A sentence in which the important material is delayed until the end or near the end (lesson 6)
polysyndeton	A rhetorical device in which there are more conjunctions than is normal. Compare this to **asyndeton**, in which there are fewer. (lesson 8)
pun (paronomasia)	A rhetorical device in which a word is used in two senses simultaneously, usually one literal and one figurative (lesson 8)
rhetoric	The art or skill of using language for some particular effect (lesson 8)
rhetorical devices	Those structures in which a writer manipulates language, usually with emotional impact, to emphasize a particular phrase or to create a desired effect. There are dozens of such structures. Among the most notable are **anaphora, chiasmus, epistrophe, asyndeton, antithesis,** and **synchises.** (lesson 8)
rhetorical question	A question to which the writer expects no direct verbal response, usually because it is asked to make a point rather than to elicit information (lesson 3)
sound devices	The general term for devices like alliteration, onomatopoeia, assonance, consonance, and rhyme, in which the writer uses the particular sounds of words to achieve a desired effect (lesson 8)
spatial order	The order in which items are arranged according to location, usually used in writing physical description (lesson 12)
synchises	A rhetorical device that contains a repetition in the structure AB//AB, where the order of the elements in the first expression is maintained in the second expression. Compare this to the **chiasmus**, where the order is reversed. (lesson 8)
synecdoche	A figure of speech in which a part of something represents the whole of that thing (lesson 8)
syntax	The arrangement of the structures of language, such as phrases, clauses, and sentences (lesson 6)
synthesis	The process by which component parts are combined into a new entirety. Compare this to **analysis**, in which the entirety is broken into its parts for further examination. (lesson 14)
tautology	A rhetorical device in which an idea is repeated in two words, or phrases, that are nearly synonymous (lesson 8)
tetracolon	A rhetorical device containing a succession of four coordinate items (lesson 8)
tone	The writer's or speaker's attitude toward the subject or audience (lesson 11)
tricolon	A rhetorical device containing a succession of three coordinate items (lesson 8)
zeugma	A rhetorical device in which a single word refers to or describes two different words in the sentence, with two different resulting meanings (lesson 8)

ACKNOWLEDGEMENTS

Peoples Education, Inc. has made every effort to obtain permission for the reprinting of all selections contained herein. If any owner of copyrighted material is not acknowledged herein, please contact the publisher for proper acknowledgement in all future editions or reprintings of this book.

p. 1, "Up From Pine Level", from ROSA PARKS by Douglas Brinkley, copyright © 2000 by Douglas Brinkley. Used by permission of Viking Penguin, a division of Penguin Group (USA) Inc.; p. 2, excerpt from "Narrative of the Life of Frederick Douglass, an American Slave" by Frederick Douglass from FREDERICK DOUGLASS – AUTOBIOGRAPHIES. Published by The Library of America, copyright © 1994 The Literary Classics of the United States, Inc.; p. 7, excerpts from "The Crisis" by Thomas Paine; p. 10, excerpt from Notes On Virginia, "Manners" by Thomas Jefferson; p. 14, "The Perils of Indifference" by Elie Wiesel, April 12, 1999. Reprinted by permission; p. 18, "Words Sometimes Convey More Than Literal Meaning" by Ted Diadiun, from *The Plain Dealer*, September 11, 2005. © The Plain Dealer. All rights reserved. Reprinted with permission; p. 21, "The Doctor Will See You for Exactly Seven Minutes" by Peter Salgo, *The New York Times*, March 22, 2006. Copyright © 2006, The New York Times. Reprinted by permission; p. 24, excerpt from "The Jungle" by Upton Sinclair; p. 26, "The Doctor Won't See You Now" by James Gorman, *The New York Times*, January 12, 1992. Copyright © 1992, The New York Times. Reprinted by permission; p. 29, excerpt from "The Tell-tale Heart" by Edgar Allan Poe; p. 31, excerpt from "The Scarlet Letter" by Nathaniel Hawthorne; p. 36, excerpt from "The Autobiography of Benjamin Franklin" by Benjamin Franklin; p. 41, "The Ephemera: An Emblem of Human Life" by Benjamin Franklin; p. 43, "Meditation XVII" by John Donne; p. 46, "Gettysburg Address" Abraham Lincoln; p. 52, John F. Kennedy: Inaugural Address, January 20, 1961; p. 55, "I Have a Dream" by Martin Luther King, Jr., Washington, DC, August 28, 1963. Reprinted by arrangement with The Heirs to the Estate of Martin Luther King, Jr., c/o Writers House as agent for the proprietor New York, NY. Copyright 1963 Martin Luther King, Jr., copyright renewed 1991 Coretta Scott King; p. 59, excerpt from "Self-Reliance" by Ralph Waldo Emerson; p. 62, excerpt from PENTIMENTO by Lillian Hellman. Copyright © 1973 by Lillian Hellman. By permission of Little, Brown and Co.; p. 65, "Graduation Address at the University of Virginia" by Franklin D. Roosevelt, June 10, 1940; p. 71, excerpt from "Tom Jones" by Henry Fielding; p. 72, excerpt from "How It Feels To Be Colored Me" by Zora Neale Hurston. Used with the permission of the Estate of Zora Neale Hurston; p. 75, excerpt from OF PLYMOUTH PLANTATION 1620-1647 by William Bradford, edited by Samuel Eliot Morison, copyright 1952 by Samuel Eliot Morison and renewed 1980 by Emily M. Beck. Used by permission of Alfred A Knopf, a division of Random House, Inc.; p. 77, "Checks and Balances" by Click and Clack, *The Washington Post*, August 27, 2006. Copyright © 2007 by Tom and Ray Magliozzi and Doug Berman; p. 81, excerpt from "How the Other Half Lives", by Jacob A. Riis, 1890; p. 86, "Speech at the Women's Convention" by Sojourner Truth in Akron, Ohio, 1851; p. 89, excerpt from "Bleak House" by Charles Dickens; p. 93, excerpt from "Rip Van Winkle" by Washington Irving; p. 96, "The Tryal of Bridget Bishop" by Cotton Mather, from THE WONDERS OF THE INVISIBLE WORLD, 1692; p. 102, excerpt from "Sinners in the Hands of an Angry God" by Jonathan Edwards, 1741; p. 105, excerpt from the Diary of Walt Whitman, August 12, 1863; p. 109, "The Death of Miles" by Marc Gellman, Web Exclusive, Special to Newsweek, March 15, 2006. Reprinted by permission of the author; p. 111, "When Life Makes You Cry Uncle" by Eugene Robinson, The Washington Post, June 9, 2006, © 2006, The Washington Post Writer's Group, Reprinted with permission; p. 113, "Freedom of Hate Speech" by Jeff Jacoby, Boston Globe, March 15, 2006 © 2006, The Boston Globe. Reprinted by permission; p. 114, "Divisive In Any Language" by E. J. Dionne Jr., The Washington Post, May 23, 2006. Reprinted with permission from The Washington Post, Copyright © 2006; p. 117, excerpt from "The Samurai's Garden" from THE SAMURAI'S GARDEN by Gail Tsukiyama. Copyright © 1994 by Gail Tsukiyama, Published by St. Martin's Press; p. 121, excerpt from "Life with Father & Mother" by Clarence Day from LIFE WITH FATHER by Clarence Day, copyright 1935 by Clarence Day and renewed 1963 by Mrs. Katherine B. Day. Used by permission of Alfred A. Knopf, a division of Random House, Inc.; p. 124, "Child In Corner To Exact Revenge As Soon As He Gets Out", THE ONION, Vol. 42, No. 34. Reprinted with permission of THE ONION. Copyright 2006, by ONION, INC. www.theonion.com; p. 126, "Everyday Use" from IN LOVE & TROUBLE: STORIES OF BLACK WOMEN, copyright © 1973 by Alice Walker, reprinted by permission of Harcourt, Inc.; p. 133, "A Letter To His Wife" from *aboard the Arbella*, March 1630, by John Winthrop; p. 135, "On Women's Right To Vote" by Susan B. Anthony, 1873; p. 136, "Preface to Doubt" by John Patrick Shanley. Doubt, a parable is copyright © 2005 by John Patrick Shanley. Published by and used by permission of Theatre Communications Group; p. 140, "Ode to Thanksgiving" from CAMERA AGE: ESSAYS ON TELEVISION by Michael J. Arlen. Copyright © 1981 by Michael S. Arlen. Reprinted by permission of Farrar, Straus and Giroux, LLC.; p. 142, excerpt from *Notes of a Native Son* by James Baldwin. Copyright © 1955, renewed 1983, by James Baldwin. Reprinted by permission of Beacon Press, Boston; p. 146, "A Modest Proposal" by Jonathan Swift, 1729; p. 152, "Once More to the Lake" from *One Man's Meat*, text copyright © 1941 by E. B. White. Copyright renewed. Reprinted by permission of Tilbury House, Publishers, Gardiner, Maine